Introducing
the
Pseudepigrapha
of Second Temple
Judaism

Introducing

the

Pseudepigrapha of Second Temple Judaism

MESSAGE, CONTEXT, AND SIGNIFICANCE

Daniel M. Gurtner

Foreword by LOREN T. STUCKENBRUCK

B
Baker Academic
a division of Baker Publishing Group
Grand Rapids, Michigan

© 2020 by Daniel M. Gurtner

Published by Baker Academic
a division of Baker Publishing Group
PO Box 6287, Grand Rapids, MI 49516-6287
www.bakeracademic.com

Paperback edition published 2022
ISBN 978-1-5409-6541-7

Printed in the United States of America

The Library of Congress has cataloged the hardcover edition as follows:
Names: Gurtner, Daniel M., author.
Title: Introducing the Pseudepigrapha of Second Temple Judaism : message, context, and
    significance / Daniel M. Gurtner ; foreword by Loren T. Stuckenbruck.
Description: Grand Rapids, Michigan : Baker Academic, a division of Baker Publishing Group,
    2020. | Includes bibliographical references and index.
Identifiers: LCCN 2020011319 | ISBN 9780801049873 (cloth)
Subjects: LCSH: Apocryphal books (Old Testament)—Criticism, interpretation, etc.
Classification: LCC BS1700 .G87 2020 | DDC 229/.9106—dc23
LC record available at https://lccn.loc.gov/2020011319

Unless otherwise indicated, Scripture translations are the author's own.

Unless otherwise indicated, quotations from pseudepigraphic works are from James H. Charlesworth, ed., *Old Testament Pseudepigrapha*, 2 vols. (New York: Doubleday, 1983, 1985).

Baker Publishing Group publications use paper produced from sustainable forestry practices and post-consumer waste whenever possible.

To Loren T. Stuckenbruck

Contents

Foreword

During the period between the conquests of Alexander the Great (332–323 BCE) and the end of the second Jewish War against Rome (132–135 CE), the production of literature by Jewish authors reached an unparalleled height of creativity and diversity. As Jews throughout the Mediterranean world and in the Levant interfaced with growing Hellenistic and Roman influences while receiving and reworking traditions from the East and from earlier times, a number of learned Jews were striving to make sense, both for themselves and others, of a diverse and rapidly changing world. One of the literary media through which sacred traditions related to the Hebrew Bible or Old Testament (the latter in Christian circles) were transmitted is often referred to as *pseudepigrapha* (meaning, "writings falsely ascribed")—from the perspective of those who generated such literature, perhaps unjustly so (see the Greek text to 1 En. 104:10). This widely attested means of communication during the Second Temple period, one that extended beyond Jewish and Christian circles and that, as a phenomenon, knew no canonical boundaries, is sensitively and constructively covered by Daniel Gurtner in the present volume.

Gurtner's lucid treatment of pseudepigrapha offers an invitation into a world replete with historical and religious-cultural "hybridity." The still impressive collection of these texts drawn together by James H. Charlesworth in the two-volume *The Old Testament Pseudepigrapha*[1] and the published and forthcoming sequel with additional literature in the two-volume *More Old-Testament Pseudepigrapha*[2] introduce and offer translations of texts

1. Published 1983–85 by Doubleday (Garden City, NY), reprinted by Hendrickson Publishers (Peabody, MA) in 2010.
2. Richard Bauckham, James R. Davila, and Alex Panayotov, eds., vol. 1 (Grand Rapids: Eerdmans, 2013). Volume 2 is forthcoming.

dating all the way from the third century BCE up to the late-medieval and premodern periods. Thus, the question of date confronts those interested in Judaism during the Second Temple period with a conundrum: though most of these texts are Jewish or Christian in their current form, those that date to the second century of the Common Era or later leave readers wondering how much access to earlier times they can provide. The success of any bona fide quest to reconstruct Second Temple tradition, of course, varies from work to work and for all its inherent difficulty remains an important task if one wishes to recover aspects of Jewish life and thought that shaped the world of emerging Christianity (before, during, and after the latter self-identified in various times as distinct networks of communities).

In addition to the problem of attributing writings or parts thereof to the Second Temple period, there is the question of situating them within the larger embrace of Judaism and of imagining, on the basis of sometimes minute clues, the socioreligious locations in and for which they initially emerged, as well as their performative functions. To what extent were any of the communities behind a given Jewish pseudepigraphon, scribal or otherwise, socially interactive or in conversation with those behind the traditions that would be collected in the Mishnah, Tosefta, and Talmuds that followed? To what extent were the same cross-fertilizing with Christ-communities? And which traditions played a role in shaping early Christian thought? Do any of the pseudepigrapha covered by Gurtner provide a window into the ways that Jews and early Christians continued to interface, despite a momentum that would lead to the fracturing and splitting of their respective religious identities?

Although the problems just mentioned may never receive definitive answers, the search for answers—or better, insights—carries a significance all its own. Challenges that come out of and lead back into the unknown also go hand in hand with opportunity. Without overlooking the painful processes that led to clear-cut distinctions between Jews and Christians in late antiquity, with many harrowing consequences that persist into the present, Jewish pseude-pigrapha present the possibility of the *joint study* and *meaningful reading* of sources by the women and men to whom they hold the power to speak. Some boundaries between Judaism and Christianity, often thought to be impen-etrable, emerge as mutually illuminating, furnishing insight into what distinc-tive identity between these religious traditions could mean or *not* mean. For example, pseudepigraphic and related traditions have acquired a particular significance in scholarly discourse around the positions, functions, and natures of intermediary beings in Second Temple Judaism and Christianity. More profoundly, however, they attest to continuing attempts by a wide variety of scribal communities, and by extension the groups to which they belonged, to frame and anchor their worldviews within the sacred tradition they reworked to meet the needs and problems of different times. The literature presents us with a smorgasbord of models for scripture interpretation, cosmologies, reflections on life before and after death, ways of understanding time, and perspectives on how spheres of the human and the divine could be thought to share social space.

Transmitted, translated, copied, and edited over centuries and even millennia, many pseudepigraphic traditions were often subject to a "change of religious hands." Study of the pseudepigrapha thus provides opportunities to explore the receiving communities as much as the more ancient ones, not least because in many instances the manuscript witnesses furnish more immediate access to the religious communities that deemed them significant. This ongoing reengagement with sacred traditions attached to ideal figures is not a throwback to recover something important from ancient times because God no longer speaks in the present. Instead, the writings covered in this volume reach back to ancient traditions in order to actualize discourse about the divine for a new time. They point to what Hindy Najman has rightly described as a self-authorizing "vitality"[3] that invites ever widening circles of readers to rediscover themselves within timeworn Jewish narratives. Here a vibrant and creative religiosity was capable of being replicated; Jews and Christians could find meaning as they inscribed themselves anew within paradigmatic story lines and traditions relating to patriarchal and ideal figures known through "the Law and the Prophets and the other (writings) that followed them" (Prologue to Sirach).

In this book, Gurtner has selected for discussion some of the most influential Jewish pseudepigrapha. By offering fresh overviews and mature introductions to each, he draws on recent research and makes them accessible to contemporary readers. This book holds the door open to anyone interested in scripture interpretation and seeks to let the claims of pseudepigrapha speak for themselves. After all, today, as in the past, they invite theological as well as historical and literary engagement.

November 9, 2019
Loren T. Stuckenbruck
Professor of New Testament and Second Temple Judaism
Ludwig-Maximilians-Universität München (Germany)

---

3. For this use of the term, see especially Hindy Najman, "The Vitality of Scripture within and beyond the 'Canon,'" *JSJ* 43 (2012): 497–518.

Preface

The Jewish Pseudepigrapha is perhaps the least-known collection of writings that stem, in part, from the Second Temple period. Ironically, they are really not a collection at all. Outside the study of Second Temple Judaism itself, the writings often categorized as "Old Testament Pseudepigrapha" can be obscure, inaccessible, and confusing. Even within the field of early Judaism it was not until the 1980s that the works of H. F. D. Sparks and James H. Charlesworth "brought the Old Testament pseudepigrapha into popular consciousness and generated and influenced an enormous amount of scholarly study."[1] Despite this and subsequent developments there remains a need for enhanced familiarity with and appreciation for these writings in their own rights and contexts. For many people these works are encountered initially as "background" to the literature of early Christianity or the emergence of rabbinic Judaism. In such instances it can be tempting to delve into the primary sources and secondary scholarship only as far as is needed to make use of these pseudepigrapha for other purposes. Yet to do so necessarily fails to appreciate the complexities and richness these books have to offer while simultaneously running the risk of misunderstanding and so misusing them for the very purpose that was originally intended. The intent of the present volume is to provide readers with a single resource for facilitating their own advancement in this material. It is by no means comprehensive, but it does aim to provide sufficient dialogue on critical issues in scholarly discourse as well as adequate canvassing of the most important primary source material so as to equip the reader whose specializations may lie outside the field of Second Temple Judaism with sufficient material to judiciously handle these ancient

1. Bauckham and Davila, "Introduction," xxvi.

writings. As Charlesworth aptly states, "There has never been an excuse for scholars or historians to ignore, let alone denigrate, the pseudepigrapha, in a historical and theological study of Early Judaism and Early Christianity."[2] This book endeavors to furnish readers with a tool to respond to this charge more effectively. In a sense this book is deliberately complementary to David A. deSilva's excellent *Introducing the Apocrypha: Message, Context, and Significance*. With the exception of a single item (Ps. 151), the present volume deliberately avoids the literature covered by deSilva. It is similar to Susan Docherty's *The Jewish Pseudepigrapha: An Introduction to the Literature of the Second Temple Period*, which is an excellent introduction to much of the literature covered here for beginning students. Readers will find some things in common between the present work and Docherty's, but also differences in scope and arrangement.

The majority of this book was undertaken during a sabbatical leave from the Southern Baptist Theological Seminary, for which I extend my sincere gratitude to the board of trustees; the dean of the School of Theology, Dr. Hershael W. York; the provost and senior vice president of Academic Administration, Dr. Matthew J. Hall; and my colleagues in the faculty of New Testament Studies. I am also grateful to Jim Kinney of Baker Academic for his continued interest in my academic pursuits and Bryan Dyer, also of Baker Academic, for his patience and ongoing support. Thanks also to David Wyman for his tireless efforts in research support. I finished this book while simultaneously completing a more comprehensive, coedited work on Second Temple Judaism.[3] Readers will encounter again and again how much I have gleaned from the contributors to those volumes, both implicitly and explicitly. Throughout that project and while working on this one, I have had the privilege to work alongside and learn from one of the premier scholars in the field of Second Temple Judaism in general and Jewish pseudepigrapha in particular. Professor Loren T. Stuckenbruck has never hesitated to answer questions or lend his expertise to help me sort out difficult problems. His scholarship and character both have influenced me to be a better person and a better student of these ancient texts. It is with gratitude, then, that this volume is dedicated to him.

Daniel M. Gurtner
Louisville, Kentucky (USA)
July 2019

2. Charlesworth, foreword to Bauckham, Davila, and Panayotov, *Old Testament Pseudepigrapha*, xi.

3. Gurtner and Stuckenbruck, *T&T Clark Encyclopedia of Second Temple Judaism*.

Abbreviations

General

§(§)	section(s)	Gr.	Greek
ar	Aramaic	lect.	lectionary
BCE	Before the Common Era	LXX	Septuagint
ca.	*circa*	MS(S)	manuscript(s)
CE	Common Era	MT	Masoretic Text
chap(s).	chapter(s)	NT	New Testament
col(s).	column(s)	OT	Old Testament
d.	died	par(r).	parallel(s)
DSS	Dead Sea Scrolls	pl(s).	plate(s)
esp.	especially	r.	reigned
ESV	English Standard Version	Rec.	Recension
fl.	*floruit*, flourished	sing.	singular
frag(s).	fragment(s)		

Hebrew Bible / Old Testament

Gen.	Genesis	Ezra	Ezra
Exod.	Exodus	Neh.	Nehemiah
Lev.	Leviticus	Esther	Esther
Num.	Numbers	Job	Job
Deut.	Deuteronomy	Ps(s).	Psalm(s)
Josh.	Joshua	Prov.	Proverbs
Judg.	Judges	Eccles.	Ecclesiastes
Ruth	Ruth	Song	Song of Songs
1 Sam.	1 Samuel	Isa.	Isaiah
2 Sam.	2 Samuel	Jer.	Jeremiah
1 Kings	1 Kings	Lam.	Lamentations
2 Kings	2 Kings	Ezek.	Ezekiel
1 Chron.	1 Chronicles	Dan.	Daniel
2 Chron.	2 Chronicles	Hosea	Hosea

Joel	Joel		Hab.	Habakkuk
Amos	Amos		Zeph.	Zephaniah
Obad.	Obadiah		Hag.	Haggai
Jon.	Jonah		Zech.	Zechariah
Mic.	Micah		Mal.	Malachi
Nah.	Nahum			

New Testament

Matt.	Matthew		1 Tim.	1 Timothy
Mark	Mark		2 Tim.	2 Timothy
Luke	Luke		Titus	Titus
John	John		Philem.	Philemon
Acts	Acts		Heb.	Hebrews
Rom.	Romans		James	James
1 Cor.	1 Corinthians		1 Pet.	1 Peter
2 Cor.	2 Corinthians		2 Pet.	2 Peter
Gal.	Galatians		1 John	1 John
Eph.	Ephesians		2 John	2 John
Phil.	Philippians		3 John	3 John
Col.	Colossians		Jude	Jude
1 Thess.	1 Thessalonians		Rev.	Revelation
2 Thess.	2 Thessalonians			

Old Testament Apocrypha

1 Bar.	1 Baruch		Sir.	Sirach (Ecclesiasticus)
1–2 Esd.	1–2 Esdras		Tob.	Tobit
Jdt.	Judith		Wis.	Wisdom (of Solomon)
1–2 Macc.	1–2 Maccabees			

Pseudepigrapha

ALD	Aramaic Levi Document		3 En.	3 Enoch (Hebrew
Apoc. Ab.	Apocalypse of Abraham			Apocalypse)
Apoc. Zeph.	Apocalypse of Zephaniah		Ezek. Trag.	Ezekiel the Tragedian
2 Bar.	2 Baruch (Syriac		Hel. Syn. Pr.	Hellenistic Synagogal
	Apocalypse)			Prayers
3 Bar.	3 Baruch (Greek		Jos. Asen.	Joseph and Aseneth
	Apocalypse)		Jub.	Jubilees
4 Bar.	4 Baruch (*Paraleipomena*		LAB	Biblical Antiquities (*Liber*
	Jeremiou)			*antiquitatum biblicarum*)
1 En.	1 Enoch (Ethiopic			of Pseudo-Philo
	Apocalypse)		LAE	Life of Adam and Eve
2 En.	2 Enoch (Slavonic		Let. Aris.	Letter of Aristeas
	Apocalypse)		Liv. Pro.	Lives of the Prophets
			3 Macc.	3 Maccabees

4 Macc.	4 Maccabees	T. Iss.	Testament of Issachar
Odes	Odes of Solomon	T. Job	Testament of Job
Ps.-Phoc.	The Sentences of	T. Jos.	Testament of Joseph
	Pseudo-Phocylides	T. Jud.	Testament of Judah
Pss. Sol.	Psalms of Solomon	T. Levi	Testament of Levi
Sib. Or.	Sibylline Oracles	T. Mos.	Testament of Moses
T. Ab.	Testament of Abraham	T. Naph.	Testament of Naphtali
T. Ash.	Testament of Asher	T. Reu.	Testament of Reuben
T. Benj.	Testament of Benjamin	T. Sim.	Testament of Simeon
T. Dan	Testament of Dan	T. Sol.	Testament of Solomon
T. Gad	Testament of Gad	T. Zeb.	Testament of Zebulon

Dead Sea Scrolls and Related Texts

CD	Damascus Document	1QSb	Rule of Blessings
1QapGen	Genesis Apocryphon	4Q215	Testament of Naphtali
1QH^{a-b}	Thanksgiving Hymns	4Q242	Prayer of Nabonidus
	(Hodayot^{a-b})	4Q542	Testament of Qahat
1QM	War Scroll	11QMelch	Melchizedek
1QS	Rule of the Community	11QPs^a	Psalms Scroll^a

Philo

Abraham	On the Life of Abraham	Moses	On the Life of Moses
Alleg. Interp.	Allegorical Interpretation	QG	Questions and Answers on
Contempl. Life	On the Contemplative		Genesis
	Life	Spec. Laws	On the Special Laws
Giants	On Giants		
Hypoth.	Hypothetica (Apology for		
	the Jews)		

Josephus

Ag. Ap.	Against Apion	J.W.	Jewish War
Ant.	Jewish Antiquities		

Rabbinic Works

b.	Babylonian Talmud	m.	Mishnah
Exod. Rab.	Exodus Rabbah	t.	Tosefta
Gen. Rab.	Genesis Rabbah	y.	Jerusalem Talmud
Num. Rab.	Numbers Rabbah		

Mishnaic Tractates

Ketub.	Ketubbot	Ta'an.	Ta'anit
Meg.	Megillah		

Apostolic Fathers

Barn.   Barnabas

New Testament Apocrypha and Pseudepigrapha

Apos. Con.   Apostolic Constitutions and Canons

Classical Authors

Caesar

Bell. civ.   Bellum civile (Civil War)

Dio Cassius

Hist. rom.   Historiae romanae (Roman History)

Diogenes Laertius

Vit. phil.   Vitae philosophorum (Lives of Eminent Philosophers)

Livy

Ab urbe cond.   Ab urbe condita

Pausanias

Descr.   Graeciae descriptio (Description of Greece)

Plutarch

Pomp.   Pompeius (Pompey)

Strabo

Geogr.   Geographica (Geography)

Patristic Writings

Augustine

Civ.   De civitate Dei (The City of God)

Clement of Alexandria

Strom.   Stromateis (Miscellanies)

Eusebius

Hist. eccl.   Historia ecclesiastica (Ecclesiastical History)

Praep. ev.   Praeparatio evangelica (Preparation for the Gospel)

Irenaeus

Haer.   Adversus haereses (Elenchos) (Against Heresies)

Justin Martyr

1 Apol.   Apologia i (First Apology)

Origen

Comm. Jo.   Commentarii in evangelium Joannis

Princ.   De principiis / Peri archōn (First Principles)

Tertullian

Apol.   Apologeticus (Apology)

Cult. fem.   De cultu feminarum (The Apparel of Women)

Secondary Sources

ABD   *Anchor Bible Dictionary.* Edited by David Noel Freedman. 6 vols. New York: Doubleday, 1992.

ANRW   *Aufstieg und Niedergang der römischen Welt: Geschichte und Kultur Roms im Spiegel der neueren Forschung.* Part 2, *Principat.* Edited by Hildegard Temporini and Wolfgang Haase. Berlin: de Gruyter, 1972–.

APOT   *The Apocrypha and Pseudepigrapha of the Old Testament.* Edited by R. H. Charles. 2 vols. Oxford: Clarendon, 1913.

AYBD	*The Anchor Yale Bible Dictionary*. Edited by David Noel Freedman. 6 vols. New Haven: Yale University Press, 1992.
BETL	Bibliotheca Ephemeridum Theologicarum Lovaniensium
CBQ	*Catholic Biblical Quarterly*
CBQMS	Catholic Biblical Quarterly Monograph Series
CEJL	Commentaries on Early Jewish Literature
DJD	Discoveries in the Judaean Desert
DSD	*Dead Sea Discoveries*
ECDSS	Eerdmans Commentaries on the Dead Sea Scrolls
EDEJ	*The Eerdmans Dictionary of Early Judaism*. Edited by John J. Collins and Daniel C. Harlow. Grand Rapids: Eerdmans, 2010.
EDSS	*Encyclopedia of the Dead Sea Scrolls*. Edited by Lawrence H. Schiffman and James C. VanderKam. 2 vols. Oxford: Oxford University Press, 2000.
EJL	Early Judaism and Its Literature
ESTJ	*The T&T Clark Encyclopedia of Second Temple Judaism*. Edited by Daniel M. Gurtner and Loren T. Stuckenbruck. 2 vols. London: T&T Clark, 2020.
FAT	Forschungen zum Alten Testament
GAP	Guides to Apocrypha and Pseudepigrapha
Hen	*Henoch*
HTR	*Harvard Theological Review*
HUCA	*Hebrew Union College Annual*
JBL	*Journal of Biblical Literature*
JCT	Jewish and Christian Texts
JJS	*Journal of Jewish Studies*
JQR	*Jewish Quarterly Review*
JSHRZ	Jüdische Schriften aus hellenistisch-römischer Zeit
JSJ	*Journal for the Study of Judaism in the Persian, Hellenistic, and Roman Periods*
JSJSup	Journal for the Study of Judaism Supplement Series
JSP	*Journal for the Study of the Pseudepigrapha*
JSPSup	Journal for the Study of the Pseudepigrapha Supplement Series
JSS	*Journal of Semitic Studies*
JTS	*Journal of Theological Studies*
LSTS	Library of Second Temple Studies
MGWJ	*Monatschrift für Geschichte und Wissenschaft des Judentums*
NovT	*Novum Testamentum*
NTS	*New Testament Studies*
OTB	*Outside the Bible: Ancient Jewish Writings Related to Scripture*. Edited by Louis H. Feldman, James L. Kugel, and Lawrence H. Schiffman. Lincoln: University of Nebraska, 2013.
OTP	*Old Testament Pseudepigrapha*. Edited by James H. Charlesworth. 2 vols. New York: Doubleday, 1983, 1985.
PVTG	Pseudepigrapha Veteris Testamenti Graece
RB	*Revue biblique*
RevQ	*Revue de Qumran*

SBLDS	Society of Biblical Literature Dissertation Series
SBLSP	*Society of Biblical Literature Seminar Papers*
SC	Sources chrétiennes
SCS	Septuagint and Cognate Studies
SNTSMS	Society for New Testament Studies Monograph Series
STDJ	Studies on the Texts of the Desert of Judah
StPB	Studia Post-biblica
SVTP	Studia in Veteris Testamenti Pseudepigraphica
TSAJ	Texte und Studien zum antiken Judentum
VT	*Vetus Testamentum*
VTSup	Vetus Testamentum Supplement Series
WGRW	Writings from the Greco-Roman World
WUNT	Wissenschaftliche Untersuchungen zum Neuen Testament

Introduction

The English word "pseudepigrapha" (sing. "pseudepigraphon") is the transliteration of a Greek term that refers to "falsely attributed writing," from *pseudēs* (false) and *epigraphē* (inscription, superscription). It occurs nowhere in biblical or Second Temple sources but is attributed to Serapion (ca. 191–211 CE) with respect to writings falsely attributed to Christ's apostles and therefore rejected by the church.[1] More generally, it is used to designate works falsely attributed to, or in some way related to, prominent individuals. In the case of the so-called Old Testament Pseudepigrapha, the individuals in view are featured in the body of literature contained in the Hebrew Bible. Yet the category can be misleading. First, the very notion of falsehood with respect to authorship conjures up negative prejudices that can do injustice to the documents in their respective contexts (see below). Second, some works within this category are associated not with an esteemed figure from antiquity but with their real authors.[2] Third, the category of pseudepigrapha can be taken as implying a degree of coherence among its constituent parts. For instance, the Apocrypha are usually identified as works present in the Septuagint but not in the Hebrew Bible. Yet the texts typically identified as pseudepigrapha, even those originating from the Second Temple period, are not attested as collections in any single manuscript. Also unlike the Apocrypha, which are preserved in Greek and many of which stem from a Semitic original, a variety of documents designated as pseudepigrapha are extant also, and sometimes exclusively, in Latin, Syriac, Coptic, Ethiopic, and a number of other languages. Moreover, nearly all the documents in question

---

1. Eusebius, *Hist. eccl.* 6.12.3.
2. Stuckenbruck ("Apocrypha and Pseudepigrapha," 152) cites Aristeas the Exegete, Aristobulus, Artapanus, Cleodemus Malchus, Demetrius the Chronographer, Eupolemus, Ezekiel the Tragedian, and Theodotus as examples.

1

are preserved exclusively in Christian traditions. Finally, unlike the works of the Apocrypha, which date prior to the Bar Kokhba revolt (132–135 CE), the date of composition of some of these pseudepigraphic documents, or even one's ability to ascribe a date, is less clear.

The category "pseudepigrapha" was first used in biblical scholarship by Johann Albert Fabricius (1713).[3] Since then it has been largely adopted by subsequent collections of documents,[4] such as the first English collection by R. H. Charles. Published in 1913, Charles's two-volume *The Apocrypha and Pseudepigrapha of the Old Testament* remained the only English-language collection for seventy years. The term was retained in the anthologies of James H. Charlesworth and, more recently, Richard J. Bauckham, James R. Davila, and Alexander Panayotov.[5] Yet from its inception, the nomenclature has been largely negative. Whereas the designation "Old Testament Apocrypha" has been used since Jerome with reference to collections of books found in Greek codices of the Scriptures (and sometimes the Latin Vulgate) not found in the Hebrew Bible or the Greek New Testament, the Pseudepigrapha enjoys no such ancient grouping. Pseudepigrapha is a classification of omission—a designation not for what type of literature they *are* but for what they are *not*. As Annette Yoshiko Reed observes, they are "not modern, not 'classical,' not preserved with the names of their authors, not found in the Jewish Tanakh, Catholic Bible, or Protestant 'Old Testament apocrypha,' not concerned with figures in the New Testament, and not generally known in the Latin West during the Middle Ages."[6] And so typically the texts listed among the Pseudepigrapha are grouped together simply because they do not fit in any of the other defined collections.

Despite its problems, the term remains "the most familiar and identifiable label for a shifting group of ancient writings deemed *somehow* related to 'the Bible' but also *somehow* distinct."[7] The impasse of nomenclature serves to illustrate the complexity of the documents under consideration.[8] That a work

---

3. See the analysis by Reed, "Modern Invention." For a thorough summary of developments in scholarly research, see DiTommaso, "Pseudepigrapha Research."

4. In 1900, E. Kautzsch edited the first German collection of the Pseudepigrapha, titled *Die Apokryphen und Pseudepigraphen des Alten Testaments*.

5. Charlesworth, *Old Testament Pseudepigrapha*; Bauckham, Davila, and Panayotov, *Old Testament Pseudepigrapha*.

6. Reed, "Modern Invention," 435. Similarly VanderKam, *Introduction to Early Judaism*, 58.

7. Reed, "Modern Invention," 405.

8. Though she calls for new "modes of categorization," Reed offers none herself ("Modern Invention," 436). VanderKam suggests the abandonment of such categories as Apocrypha and Pseudepigrapha in favor of delineating texts in terms of their chronology within the Second Temple period, despite the difficulties that necessarily entails (*Introduction to Early Judaism*, 58). For their volume *Old Testament Pseudepigrapha*, Bauckham, Davila, and Panayotov retain

is classified as a pseudepigraphon should not be taken as a designation, necessarily, of any degree of coherence or uniformity with other texts so classified. It is a diverse collection of texts depicting views and perspectives as disparate as the communities that composed and preserved them. Charlesworth wisely cautions, "Too many critics incorrectly assumed . . . that there was a canon of pseudepigrapha."[9] One may find, however, some very general similarities within the nature and form of these writings. These are ancient documents whose historical authors' identities are (deliberately?) obscure. In this respect, the Pseudepigrapha can be placed within the subset of anonymous writings in which what can be known about the authors is ascertained only from the texts themselves. Furthermore, they tend to communicate either in the first person by assuming the identity of an ancient figure (as in 1 Enoch, 2 Baruch, and the Testament of Job) or in a third-person narration of experiences of a revered figure (as in Jubilees [for Moses], the Life of Adam and Eve, and the Testament of Abraham).[10] This fact provides an intriguing analytical perspective whereby one can examine the development of historical and hagiographic traditions surrounding various Old Testament figures. If one limits the scope of pseudepigrapha to the Second Temple period, some additional characteristics common among them can be adduced:[11] they were written in Hebrew, Aramaic, and Greek, and typically originate from a form of Judaism for whom the Mosaic Torah was central. These generalizations are, of course, fluid, but they illustrate the complexity created by the diversity of genre, setting, outlook, and ideology attested among them on the one hand, and the commonality in the shared matrix of Second Temple Judaism on the other.

Pseudepigraphy in Antiquity

Among the challenges in the study of this literature is its infamous association with falsehood associated with the literary characteristic in which a document is attributed to an individual who did not, in reality, write it.[12] For modern readers this is a distasteful moral matter that casts a dim shadow on the

the term "despite its unsatisfactory associations, because none of the proposed replacement terms ('parabiblical literature,' 'parascriptural literature,' 'scripturesque remnants,' etc.) yet commands general acceptance or is as widely recognized by the public" (xxvii).

9. Charlesworth, foreword to Bauckham, Davila, and Panayotov, *Old Testament Pseudepigrapha*, xiii.

10. Stuckenbruck, "Apocrypha and Pseudepigrapha," 152.

11. Davila, "Pseudepigrapha," 1112–13.

12. Clarke ("Problem of Pseudonymity," 441) carefully observes a distinction between pseudepigraphy and pseudonymity. The former refers to literature, whereas the latter addresses the author. Both, however, employ false titles.

document itself. Recent discussion of ancient pseudonymity in the context of Second Temple Judaism has addressed this matter and shown that careful attention to the practice in antiquity can enhance the modern reader's appreciation for the cultural phenomena at play.

Types of Ancient Pseudepigraphy

As we build on works found among the Dead Sea Scrolls, three general categories of the practice of Jewish pseudepigraphy are evident.[13] First, there are writings attributed to a figure by their title or superscription alone. This is called "decorative" pseudepigraphy in that such documents do not indicate within themselves the identities of the authors responsible. Works such as the Prayer of Manasseh and the Psalms of Solomon would suit this category. Second, scholars identify the use of "convenient" pseudepigraphy,[14] or what others call "pseudepigraphic voices."[15] In these texts one finds traces of a revered figure in editorial interventions or compositional allusions, which serve as a convenient way "to inculcate morals and values in a society which needs chastisement."[16] To this category one may ascribe works such as the Wisdom of Solomon, 1 Baruch, and the Testaments of the Twelve Patriarchs, as well as the respective testaments of Job, Abraham, and Moses. The final category of pseudepigraphy is perhaps the one that more likely comes to mind in this literature. This includes documents in which the primary speaker of a work is the main figure within it and is understood to be a revered ancient figure. This category presses the named figure into service to strengthen the work's authority. This is called "authoritative pseudepigraphy," which is best suited to legal material and prophetic/apocalyptic utterances.[17] Works that fall into this category are autobiographical in nature and would include 1 Enoch, 3 Enoch, Jubilees, 2 Baruch, 3 Baruch, 4 Ezra, the Apocalypse of Abraham, the Apocalypse of Zephaniah, and the Apocalypse of Elijah among the more common pseudepigrapha. From Qumran one could include the Genesis Apocryphon, the Testament of Naphtali, the Aramaic Levi Document, the Temple Scroll, and Psalm 151. As these lists indicate and as we will see below, apocalyptic writings are a common genre in which pseudepigraphy occurs.[18] A subcategory of authoritative pseudepigraphy encompasses the few instances where texts are

---

13. Bernstein, "Pseudepigraphy in the Qumran Scrolls."
14. Bernstein, "Pseudepigraphy in the Qumran Scrolls," 6.
15. Wyrick, "Pseudepigraphy," 1115.
16. Bernstein, "Pseudepigraphy in the Qumran Scrolls," 6.
17. Bernstein, "Pseudepigraphy in the Qumran Scrolls," 6.
18. See esp. Stone, "Pseudepigraphy Reconsidered," 8.

falsely ascribed (pseudonymity) to a figure—fictional or historical—who lacks the authoritative recognition enjoyed by others. These may include works such as Tobit or the Letter of Aristeas.[19] Other works, such as the Biblical Antiquities, are mistakenly attributed to Philo of Alexandria. Still others—Jewish and Christian—may attribute authorship to a figure not from the Hebrew Bible but from pagan contexts (Sibylline Oracles and Pseudo-Orphic Hymns) or to gentile figures (Pseudo-Phocylides, Syriac Menander, Pseudo-Hecataeus, etc.).[20]

Rationale for Pseudepigraphy

Several reasons can be posited for the practice of pseudepigraphy.[21] Some libraries, such as the famous Alexandrian library, collected works of well-known writers. Therefore, one might write in another's name to gain a place among well-known writers. This could be done to get a hearing for one's own views, whether to counter a false claim by an opponent or opponents or to draw the circumstances of the ancient figure into the context of the real author's setting. So, for example, the author of 4 Ezra draws from the biblical Ezra. The book of Ezra is set in a context of the return from exile and reconstitution of the temple. Fourth Ezra, drawing from Ezra's narrative setting, is written after the destruction of the Herodian temple in 70 CE, and "the affinities between biblical context and the time of writing were overwhelmed by the real author's pressing interests."[22] In some instances the genre of a work may influence the figure to whom it is attributed. Sapiential material would be attributed to Solomon, hymnic writings to David, legal matters to Moses, and so on.

Reception of Pseudepigraphy

Although the practice of writing in the name of another was sometimes criticized, particularly in early Christianity, ancient responses to the books

19. Bernstein, "Pseudepigraphy in the Qumran Scrolls," 7.
20. Wyrick, "Pseudepigraphy," 1115–16.
21. Stuckenbruck, "Apocrypha and Pseudepigrapha," 154–55. Clarke ("Problem of Pseudonymity," 448–49) has compiled a list of twelve possible motivations: (1) financial gain; (2) to malign, discredit, or defame opponents or enemies; (3) to guard or preserve traditions or doctrines; (4) to express admiration for an attributed author; (5) to express an author's belief that he is extending teachings of the ascribed author; (6) to express an author's belief that he has received visionary sanction or been filled with the Holy Spirit; (7) out of personal modesty; (8) as an aspect of artistic or dramatic composition; (9) as an educational, literary, or rhetorical exercise; (10) to invoke the reputation of an important figure of antiquity for various reasons, including the desire to secure greater prestige and credence for teaching or doctrine; (11) to create distance from or hide true authorship for various reasons including fear and the need to maintain anonymity; (12) to provide earlier attestation for contemporary requirements.
22. Stuckenbruck, "Apocrypha and Pseudepigrapha," 154.

themselves were not uniform. Perhaps it is this diversity of opinions that led to, from the third century BCE, means to discern the authenticity of the attribution of a text.[23] For instance, in some circles writing in one's own name may have been perceived as unethical, whereas writing in the name of another would have been perceived as a more modest way of expressing one's indebtedness to a tradition. But it is also the case that many ancient readers were unaware that what they were reading was written by someone other than the one to whom it is attributed, since many pseudonymous works were not recognized as such until more recently.[24] A survey of a wide swath of Greco-Roman, Jewish, and Christian contexts in which the practice was employed illustrates this mixed reception.[25] Among Greco-Roman literature, numerous examples can be adduced, including Pythagoras (ca. 582–507 BCE), to whom a large corpus of literature is attributed despite his leaving behind none of his own writings.[26] Yet in some instances the practice was negatively received. Livy (59 BCE–17 CE) expresses disdain for the practice, and in other instances pseudonymity was used to defame the name under which one wrote.[27] Galen describes remuneration for those providing works of respected authors to the libraries of Alexandria and Pergamum, which surely provided some impetus for pseudepigraphy.[28]

In Second Temple Jewish contexts, writings from the Hebrew Bible were often authoritative if derived, in some capacity, from a "succession of prophets" from Moses to Ezra.[29] In the Apocrypha one finds ascriptions of authorship in the books of 2 Esdras (1:1–3), Tobit (1:1–2), Sirach (50:27), and 1 Baruch (1:1–2). Works such as the Wisdom of Solomon, the Letter of Jeremiah, and the Prayer of Manasseh bear less obvious ascriptions, whereas 1 Esdras, Judith, and 1–2 Maccabees are anonymous.[30] Prominent among Jewish writings from the Second Temple period is the pseudepigraphon 1 Enoch, a compilation of works associated with the figure Enoch from the Hebrew Bible (Gen. 5:24). It may be that works written in the name of an esteemed figure were intended to elaborate on that figure and were thus attributed to him.[31] In this rubric, texts expand on traditions associated with the figure on which they are founded.

23. Wyrick, "Pseudepigraphy," 1115; Wyrick, *Ascension of Authorship*, 220–23, 282–90.

24. Clarke, "Problem of Pseudonymity," 458; Grant, *Heresy and Criticism*.

25. Clarke, "Problem of Pseudonymity," 449–58.

26. Cf. Olympiodorus, *Prolegomena to Aristotelian Logic* 11.33–38; Iamblichus, *De vita Pythagorica*, 158, 198.

27. Livy, *Ab urbe cond.* 40.29; Diogenes Laertius, *Vit. phil.* 2.521; Pausanias, *Descr.* 6.18.2–5.

28. Galen, *In Hippocratis de natura hominis librum commentarii* 1.42.

29. Wyrick, *Ascension of Authorship*, 159–85.

30. Metzger, *Introduction to the Apocrypha*, 3–4.

31. Najman, *Seconding Sinai*, 1–40.

Thus, the ancient figure serves to lend credence to the views espoused in his name, and ensuing research examines the evolution of discourse associated with him.[32]

The practice of pseudepigraphy is well attested in early Christianity, where the issue is often one of pseudo-apostolicity.[33] Scholars have long contended that, among early Christians at least, texts known to be pseudepigraphic in nature were rejected as authoritative.[34] Zeal for determining the historical origins of a text with respect to its authorship finds some attention in early Christianity, where the reception of texts as sacred—or not—was often tied to apostolic origin.[35] Tertullian's (ca. 160–220 CE) criticism of a presbyter writing (falsely) in the name of Paul is frequently cited, as is the account of Serapion (d. 211 CE), cited in Eusebius, regarding the pseudonymous Gospel of Peter.[36] At times early Christians received pseudonymous works, mistaking them for authentic works. A letter allegedly from Pilate to Tiberius concerning Christ was thought authentic,[37] as was the Correspondence of Paul and Seneca.[38] Some held Enoch to be the actual author of 1 Enoch and so regarded it as scripture.[39] Others held 1 Enoch in high esteem, regardless of its origin.[40]

Recent scholarly assessment focuses on the canonization of Christian literature,[41] which figures only tangentially into the present purposes. Yet the views expressed in that discussion may exert an influence on views of pseudepigraphy in Second Temple Judaism and so merit some consideration. In the discussion of the canonization of Christian literature, two general modern views on the phenomenon in antiquity are maintained: the first sees the practice as a literary convention without tarnish to the integrity of the pseudepigrapher or the document; the second is quite the opposite, asserting the practice was viewed with disdain. Those with a favorable view of the practice could look to the influence of F. C. Baur (1792–1860), who, in the

32. Such as the work of Stone and Bergen, *Biblical Figures outside the Bible*.

33. Clarke, "Problem of Pseudonymity," 454.

34. Candlish, "Moral Character."

35. Cf. 2 Thess. 2:1–2; 3:17; Origen, *Princ.* Preface 8; *Contra Celsum* 5.54; Rufinus, *Epilogue to Pamphilus*; Eusebius, *Hist. eccl.* 4.23.12, 9.5.1; Jerome, *Adversus Rufinum* 3.25; Augustine, *Civ.* 18.38.

36. Tertullian, *De baptismo* 17; *Adversus Marcionem* 4.5; *Cult. fem.* 3; Eusebius, *Hist. eccl.* 6.12.3–6.

37. Eusebius, *Hist. eccl.* 2.2.1–2; Tertullian, *Apol.* 5; Justin, *1 Apol.* 35 and 48.

38. Jerome, *De viris illustribus* 12; Augustine, *Epistula* 153; Clarke, "Problem of Pseudonymity," 456n71.

39. Barn. 4:3; 16:5–6; Tertullian, *Cult. fem.* 3; *De idololatria* 4.

40. Irenaeus, *Haer.* 4.16; Clement of Alexandria, *Eclogae propheticae* 2.53; Anatolius of Alexandria, *Paschal Canon* 5; Ethiopic Orthodox tradition.

41. See esp. Clarke, "Problem of Pseudonymity," and the literature cited there.

context of critical scholarly inquiry into the origins of New Testament books, was a strong advocate for the presence and acceptability of pseudonymity in the New Testament documents. Others along this trajectory—A. Jülicher, M. Kiley, B. S. Childs, D. G. Meade—collectively point to the notion of intellectual property as a modern construct foreign to ancient contexts where the theological *content* of a work bore greater weight than its historical authorship.[42] Modern criticism of the practice fails to account for the cultural factors of antiquity, particularly in the context of Second Temple Judaism.[43] In Jed Wyrick's view, more culturally aware approaches recognize the practice of pseudepigraphy as an attempt by an ancient author (or authors) to re-create the discourse of esteemed figures of the past,[44] or as a practice of appropriate self-effacement.[45] Regardless of one's assessment of the practice of pseudepigraphy, it is nonetheless a practice used in antiquity and sometimes—though not always—employed in the documents here under discussion. This suggests that negative connotations regarding the nature of a Second Temple Jewish work because of its classification as pseudepigraphic should be held in check.

Study of the Old Testament Pseudepigrapha

Pseudepigrapha in Their Judaic Context

Though the present work analyzes a small cross section of Jewish literature from the Second Temple period, appreciation for the Pseudepigrapha would be lacking without recognition of other contemporary literature. Pseudepigrapha, along with other literature, "need to be read together for a more comprehensive understanding of the diversities of Judaism that flourished during the centuries leading up to and after the turn of the Common Era."[46] Typically, Jewish literature prior to 135 CE is divided into five categories:[47] in addition to the Old Testament Pseudepigrapha, these categories include some of the Old Testament Apocrypha, the writings of Philo, the writings of Josephus, and the Dead Sea Scrolls. In more recent scholarship the writings of the New Testament are factored into the matrix of literature from Second Temple Judaism. Long ago Charles insisted that without the Apocrypha and Pseudepigrapha,

---

42. Clarke, "Problem of Pseudonymity," 445, 458–59.
43. Wyrick, "Pseudepigraphy."
44. Wyrick, "Pseudepigraphy," 1114. This point is contended at length by Najman, *Seconding Sinai*.
45. Wyrick, *Ascension of Authorship*, 80–110, 282–315.
46. Stuckenbruck, "Apocrypha and Pseudepigrapha," 159.
47. Bauckham and Davila, "Introduction," xxx.

and one could add these additional texts as well, "it is absolutely impossible to explain the course of religious development between 200 BC and AD 100."[48]

Since Jerome the term "apocrypha" has been applied to collections of books found in Greek codices of the Scriptures (and sometimes the Latin Vulgate) but not found in the Hebrew Bible or the (Greek) New Testament.[49] The term derives from the Greek adjective *apokryphos*, meaning "hidden," perhaps stemming from apocalyptic traditions that view certain divine disclosures as lying hidden or sealed (cf. Dan. 8:26; 12:4, 9–11; 2 Bar. 20:3–4; 87:1; etc.). However, the decision about which books to include in this category is not uniform, even among the major Greek codices. Works they hold in common are Greek Esther, Judith, Tobit, the Wisdom of Solomon, the Letter of Jeremiah, and Sirach. Additional works include 1 Baruch, Susanna, Bel and the Dragon, 1–4 Maccabees, the Psalms of Solomon, the Prayer of Manasseh, and Psalms 151–155. Modern collections typically also include 1 Esdras, 2 Esdras (a portion of which, chaps. 3–14, is the same as 4 Ezra), and the Prayer of Manasseh, while omitting 3 and 4 Maccabees and the Psalms of Solomon. Some of these works (e.g., Sirach, Tobit, Letter of Jeremiah, Psalm 151) are attested at Qumran. To these lists one could add documents from Qumran previously unknown, such as the Genesis Apocryphon (1Q20 or 1QapGen), Apocryphon of Moses (1Q22, 1Q29, 2Q21, 4Q375, 4Q376, 4Q408), and 11QApocryphal Psalms (11Q11), to name but a few.

These writings are important for our purposes for several reasons. First, they are all Jewish texts from the Second Temple period.[50] Second, like many of the Pseudepigrapha, they are often related to some figure or issue of interest deriving from the Hebrew Bible. Third, like the Pseudepigrapha, the collection as a whole exhibits a diversity of genres, including historical narratives (1 and 2 Maccabees, 1 Esdras), "tales" (Tobit, Judith, 3 Maccabees, Additions to Esther, and Additions to Daniel), Wisdom literature (Wisdom of Solomon and Sirach [or Wisdom of Ben Sira]), prophetic literature (1 Baruch and the Letter of Jeremiah), liturgical or hymnic texts (Psalm 151, Prayer of Manasseh, Prayer of Azariah, and the Song of the Three Young Men), an apocalypse (2 Esdras), and a philosophical treatise (4 Maccabees).[51] Fourth, the Apocrypha illuminate the rich historical, social, and religious contexts of the period. For instance, the narratives of 1 and 2 Maccabees in particular provide historical accounts of events shaping the late Second Temple period.

48. *APOT* 1:x.
49. Gurtner, "Noncanonical Jewish Writings."
50. Most are thought to date from the third century BCE through the first century CE. Some were written in Greek, others in Hebrew or Aramaic.
51. Gurtner, "Introduction," 1.

These include the Hellenization of Palestine under the high priests Jason and
Menelaus (175–164 BCE), the rise of the Hasmoneans and political revolu-
tionary movements (later Zealots), and the shaping of major Jewish sects
and doctrinal distinctives among them. Ben Sira (ca. 180 BCE) affirms Torah
as the means to wisdom, while the Wisdom of Solomon chides the folly of
gentile religions (similarly, 4 Maccabees).

The works of Philo and Josephus are likewise important for the study of
the Pseudepigrapha. Philo (ca. 20 BCE–50 CE) was a Jewish historian and
philosopher from Alexandria, Egypt, whose more than seventy-five treatises
address a variety of issues. His *Allegorical Interpretation* is the work for which
he is perhaps best known and consists of a running biblical commentary in
the Alexandrian allegorical tradition. This method surely drives what seems
to be his chief concern: to articulate the superiority of Judaism to other
philosophical schools. Scholars debate the place of Philo's work in early Judaism and in Hellenistic Judaism in particular. Perhaps more important than
Philo is Flavius Josephus (ca. 37–100 CE), who provides some of the most
significant historical documentation of the events in Palestine from antiquity
available. He is responsible for four works: *Jewish War*, *Jewish Antiquities*,
his *Life*, and *Against Apion*. In his *Jewish War*, Josephus describes, in part,
his own role in the revolt against the Romans and his subsequent surrender to
them, assistance in their intelligence against the Jews, and ultimate liberation
and move to Rome. Throughout this seven-volume work, the author goes to
great pains to show that the revolt was contrary to typical Jewish piety and
instigated by a small group of misguided fanatics, on the one hand, and by
corrupt and incompetent Roman governors on the other. Josephus's *Jewish
Antiquities* and *Life* illustrate the uniqueness of Judaism as a philosophical
school of thought, more ancient, pure, and effective in the promotion of virtue
and punishment of vice than any other. Moreover, the works argue for the
superiority of Israel's theocracy over all other forms of political constitution
(a long-standing debate among Greeks and Romans). Similarly, in *Against
Apion* Josephus provides a concise articulation of the tenets, antiquity, and
virtues of Judaism.

The discovery of ancient Jewish documents, the Dead Sea Scrolls, in the
Judean desert from 1947 to 1956 marks a watershed in the study of the Pseudepigrapha.[52] Among these documents is found some of the earliest manuscript
evidence of previously known, in addition to some previously unknown,
pseudepigrapha. The particulars of these attestations will be addressed in the
following discussions of the respective books. Yet here it is worth noting that

52. See esp. Bernstein, "Pseudepigraphy in the Qumran Scrolls"; Stone, "Dead Sea Scrolls."

among the Qumran documents one finds evidence from 1 Enoch, Jubilees, the Testament of Judah, the Testament of Naphtali, the Aramaic Levi Document, and Psalms 151, 154, and 155. Two general categories of pseudepigrapha are found among the Qumran documents previously unknown: traditions related to the book of Daniel and testamentary material.[53] There is also a curious absence from Qumran of certain texts believed to be circulated in Palestine prior to 70 CE, such as the Psalms of Solomon, the Testament of Moses, and the Similitudes of Enoch.[54] While the pseudepigrapha found at Qumran did not likely originate with the Qumran sectarians, their presence among the Scrolls does provide manuscript evidence from the third century BCE to just prior to the destruction of Jerusalem in 70 CE in an incontrovertibly Jewish context. The significance of their preservation in *Jewish* contexts will become evident in our discussion of their respective provenances. Furthermore, their presence among the Scrolls suggests their acceptance, in some manner, among the Qumran sectarians. The numerous scrolls outside the category of pseudepigrapha are likewise crucial. All of these are Jewish and date from the Second Temple period. These, like the other Jewish texts from antiquity, serve to provide material for a more comprehensive understanding of the diversities of Judaism from the period.

Provenance of the Pseudepigrapha

Among the most challenging topics in recent discussion of the Pseudepigrapha is determining their provenance.[55] That is, are the documents in question Jewish or Christian, and can or should such a distinction be made, and if so, how? Even the categories of "Jewish" and "Christian" may be more fluid than one might expect. Such texts could be associated with Jews, Jewish Christians, gentile Christians, Samaritans, gentile Godfearers, gentiles sympathetic to Judaism, and pagans with some interest in Jewish traditions. Any one of these groups, perhaps more, could lay claim to the interests contained in these documents.

Some texts, such as 1 Enoch and Jubilees, are clearly Jewish, as their presence among the Dead Sea Scrolls attests. But many are not found among the Qumran documents, and most texts of the so-called Old Testament Pseudepigrapha were preserved not by Jews but by Christians. In the course of their transmission, documents could be, and sometimes were, adapted to the communities that preserved them. A document may have been Jewish, even

---

53. Stuckenbruck, "Apocrypha and Pseudepigrapha," 157–58.
54. J. Collins, "Apocrypha and Pseudepigrapha," 1:38–39.
55. The complexities are addressed succinctly by Davila, "Pseudepigrapha, Old Testament."

pre-Christian, yet in the course of its transmission by Christians its Jewish original was lost (e.g., Testaments of the Twelve Patriarchs, 3 Baruch, 4 Baruch). Only in some instances are the interpolations by Christians evident. Still other documents may revere an Old Testament figure and evince no distinctly Christian material, yet originate entirely within Christian contexts. In other words, they are Christian documents making use of Jewish traditions (Lives of the Prophets, History of the Rechabites), or even Christian documents with little evidence of other influences at all (Sibylline Oracles 6–8, Vision of Ezra, Greek Apocalypse of Elijah). Conversely, some Jewish literature could seem just as at home in Jewish or Christian contexts. For example, the Qumran Thanksgiving Hymns (1QH^a) is a Hebrew composition of incontrovertibly Jewish origin. Yet if it had been found among medieval Syriac manuscripts, for example, it could easily be identified as a Christian document of Syriac-speaking origin. Jewish materials can become embedded in Christian literature, such as the writings of Basil of Caesarea, John Chrysostom, and Augustine of Hippo. Lastly, some documents in this corpus give little indication of either Jewish or Christian influences (Sentences of the Syriac Menander).

A final challenge concerning the provenance of the Old Testament Pseudepigrapha is linguistic in nature. Many texts existed at some point in Greek, whether originally in that language or as a translation from Hebrew (e.g., Pseudo-Philo's Biblical Antiquities), even if some or all of a Greek translation is now lost. Some texts are extant today in secondary, even tertiary translations. Moreover, often the Christian manuscript traditions are preserved in a variety of ancient church languages, such as Arabic, Armenian, Coptic, Ethiopic, Georgian, Greek, Latin, Old Church Slavonic, and Syriac. This compounds the difficulties in determining a text's provenance.[56]

The present work examines *Jewish* pseudepigrapha composed *before* or *around* the time of the Bar Kokhba revolt (132–135 CE). How the date of a document is determined will be addressed with individual texts. The concern here is how to determine whether a document is "Jewish" or not. In the past some scholars presumed that if a document that revered an Old Testament figure was void of explicitly Christian content, it must necessarily be a Jewish document. Others held a default position that, for some documents, presumed a Christian provenance influenced by Jewish scriptures and traditions, such as the Testaments of the Twelve Patriarchs, the Ascension of Isaiah, the Lives

---

56. Davila, "Pseudepigrapha, Old Testament," 1110–14. Here Davila distills some key tenets to his *Provenance of the Pseudepigrapha.*

of the Prophets, 3 Baruch, and Joseph and Aseneth.[57] Some have employed a technique of removing Christian interpolations from documents. Yet such a method presumes that Christian elements distinct from the Jewish original can be identified with clarity. One may think, for example, of the New Testament epistles of James or Jude, which, if excised of a few Christian distinctives, would look very "Jewish" indeed. The similarities between what may be Jewish and what may be Christian, coupled with the inevitable complexities involved in the transmission of texts that wove the traditions together, render the method ineffective. More recent scholarship is shifting from the assumption that a text with both Jewish and Christian elements is Jewish and then reworked as Christian to the assumption that it is a Christian document influenced by Jewish traditions.[58]

Robert Kraft advocates understanding these documents in the Christian contexts in which they are preserved, at least initially.[59] More recently, James R. Davila calls for a seemingly more objective set of criteria for discerning the origins of a pseudepigraphon.[60] This he does by isolating what he perceives to be "signature features"—that is, common characteristics among indisputably Jewish texts. These include monotheism; acceptance of certain sacred books and a historical narrative drawn from them; adherence to Jewish customs, laws, and rituals; support of the temple cult; self-identification as Jewish; usage, value, and reading within a specific Jewish community; and recognition of Palestine as the Holy Land. A text need not have all these characteristics, and of course the identification of a text as Jewish depends at least to some extent on what description of Judaism one adopts—that is, what one means by "Jewish." Richard Bauckham challenges this notion of documents exhibiting a sort of "boundary maintenance," for it a priori marginalizes texts congenial to Christianity, some of which are preserved in Christian contexts.[61] Moreover, he suggests, one must be clear about why such documents were preserved in Christian contexts and recognize that a document predates the manuscript in which it is preserved. In this view, a "default" position may be unwarranted. But the question does raise awareness of the difficulties in determining, let alone presuming, a "Jewish" provenance to a pseudepigraphon.

57. Testaments of the Twelve Patriarchs: Jonge, *Pseudepigrapha of the Old Testament*; Ascension of Isaiah: Norelli, *Ascensio Isaiae*; Lives of the Prophets: Satran, *Biblical Prophets*; 3 Baruch: Harlow, *Greek Apocalypse of Baruch*; Joseph and Aseneth: Kraemer, *When Aseneth Met Joseph*.

58. Stuckenbruck, "Apocrypha and Pseudepigrapha," 158.

59. Kraft, "Pseudepigrapha in Christianity"; Kraft, "Pseudepigrapha and Christianity Revisited."

60. Davila, *Provenance of the Pseudepigrapha*.

61. Bauckham, "Continuing Quest."

For the present purposes, the provenance of respective writings will be assessed on an individual basis. Yet the ongoing debate on the matter illustrates the complexities involved in determining the date and religious provenance of these texts, with the stark differences between Jewish and Christian texts on the one hand and the similarities of Jewish, Jewish Christian, and non-Jewish Christian traditions on the other. Again, the collection is rich and diverse and often defies simple categorization with respect to provenance.

The Books of the Pseudepigrapha

Overview

Which books are included among the so-called Old Testament Pseudepigrapha is by no means uniform, even among published collections. The first such collection was that of Albert Fabricius, whose *Codex pseudepigraphus Veteris Testamenti* (1713) included a number of Greek and Latin texts from this category (published in a second edition in 1722 and a second volume in 1723). Works from other languages, such as Ethiopic, were made available for the Ascension of Isaiah (1819) and 1 Enoch (1821). The latter half of the nineteenth century saw the publication of still more books, such as Jubilees, 2 Baruch, 3 Baruch, 2 Enoch, the Apocalypse of Abraham, and the Testament of Abraham. They were eventually published as collections of thirteen (Kautzsch), seventeen (Charles), twenty-five (Sparks), sixty-one (Riessler), sixty-five (Charlesworth), and nearly eighty (Bauckham, Davila, and Panayotov). The first volume of Bauckham, Davila, and Panayotov's collection contains fifty documents and nearly thirty fragments or quotations from other sources. In some instances, writings that properly belong to the Old Testament Pseudepigrapha (e.g., Prayer of Manasseh and 4 Ezra) are contained in the writings of the Old Testament Apocrypha. Similarly, some apocryphal works (e.g., 3 Maccabees, 4 Maccabees, and Ps. 151) are found in collections of pseudepigraphic writings.

One could add to this collection a dizzying array of texts from the Dead Sea Scrolls that fall within this broad category. A selection of these includes documents known about before the discovery of the Dead Sea Scrolls but attested among the Scrolls also, such as the Book of Watchers (1 En. 1–36; 4Q201–202, 4Q204–206), the Animal Apocalypse (1 En. 85–90; 4Q204–207), and the Epistle of Enoch (1 En. 92:1–5; 93:11–105:2; 4Q204, 4Q212). Also found were Hebrew texts from Jubilees (e.g., 1Q17, 1Q18, 2Q19, 2Q20) and Psalms 151, 154, and 155 (11Q5). Some documents attested at Qumran and classified broadly as pseudepigrapha were previously unknown, such as the

Aramaic Prayer of Nabonidus (4Q242), Four Kingdoms (4Q552, 4Q553), and the Testament of Jacob (4Q537), to name but a few. Other works are attributed to the archangel Michael (4Q529), to Obadiah (4Q380), to Manasseh (4Q381), and perhaps to Moses (1Q22, 2Q21, 4Q385a, 4Q387a, 4Q388a, 4Q389, 4Q390).

Scope of the Present Work

Published collections employ their own criteria for inclusion into respective lists of pseudepigrapha. For Charlesworth, a date of origin between 200 BCE and 200 CE is generally in view.[62] H. F. D. Sparks does not employ a cutoff date, and the volume *Old Testament Pseudepigrapha: More Noncanonical Scriptures* (Bauckham, Davila, and Panayotov) includes documents generally composed up to the rise of Islam in the early seventh century CE. Both Charlesworth and Sparks include Jewish and Christian documents, yet the *More Noncanonical Scriptures* volume also includes works of pagan origin. Sparks omits works of pagan origin or works featuring pagan figures. Where there is general agreement pertains to the affiliation of the text. For example, Sparks bases his inclusion on "whether or not any particular item is attributed to (or is primarily concerned with the history or activities of) an Old Testament character (or characters)."[63] Charlesworth considers the category more broadly as works that are typically attributed to ideal figures of Israel's past, lay claim to God's message, and exhibit some continuity with ideas or narratives of the Hebrew Bible.[64] Yet as noted before, these are merely descriptive rather than prescriptive distinctions.

It is important to observe here that the present and likely the future state of Pseudepigrapha scholarship are largely removed from some of the above constraints. It is true that the works of Sparks and Charlesworth alone have "brought the Old Testament pseudepigrapha into popular consciousness and generated and influenced an enormous amount of scholarly study."[65] Bauckham and Davila note the burgeoning of the field in the founding of scholarly journals, monographs, commentaries, bibliographies, and modern-language editions that have been produced since the early 1980s.[66] The study of the Pseudepigrapha has come out of the shadow of Christianity as well as Judaism and taken a place as a field of study in its own right. As Lorenzo

---

62. *OTP* 1:xxv.
63. Sparks, *Apocryphal Old Testament*, xv.
64. *OTP* 1:xxv.
65. Bauckham and Davila, "Introduction," xxvi.
66. Bauckham and Davila, "Introduction," xxvi.

DiTommaso puts it, "As a category, the Pseudepigrapha of Kautzsch and Charles is extinct."[67] If the *More Noncanonical Scriptures* collection is any indication of recent trends, the parameters of provenance and dating will be much more inclusive. DiTommaso observes the evolution of "an inclusive corpus of potentially hundreds of texts—ancient and medieval, Jewish and Christian, attributive and associative, even (according to some) drawn from the Old Testament and the New—plus hundreds of other traditions."[68]

While the field of Pseudepigrapha research as a whole has expanded, there remains a place for the analysis of a subset of these texts within the context of Second Temple Judaism. That is, while acknowledging the important progress the field makes beyond the traditional boundaries of Second Temple Judaism, there remains a place for analysis within. It is within these parameters of provenance and dating that the present study aims to survey Jewish pseudepigrapha composed before or around the time of the Bar Kokhba revolt. This is so despite the fact that these parameters are notoriously difficult, and Bauckham, Davila, and Panayotov rightly caution against optimism in determining the provenance and date of a pseudepigraphon.[69]

The selection of works for inclusion—and exclusion—are waters that must be navigated carefully. As we have seen, the scope of what has been called "pseudepigrapha" is impossibly vast, and lists inevitably vary. The present work includes writings for which little doubt remains pertaining to their place in the above parameters, so primary attention here is devoted to works whose Jewish provenance in the Second Temple period is largely established. However, it is important to note that the works included are by no means intended to be comprehensive but rather representative of either the most important or a particular type of pseudepigraphon. Only cursory attention will be given to those works whose provenance remains generally unresolved. Here too the list of texts addressed is selective.

How to best arrange these texts is also a challenge, and any system of ordering creates problems. A chronological listing is impractical both because of the uncertainty about the date of a number of texts and because their composition occurred over an expanded period of time. An alphabetical listing is inhibited by the fact that some texts are known by more than one title. Charlesworth, as well as Kautzsch and Charles, arranges texts first by genre and secondarily by the name of the character in biblical order. Others, such as Fabricius, Sparks, and Bauckham, Davila, and Panayotov, list texts

67. DiTommaso, "Pseudepigrapha Research," 46.
68. DiTommaso, "Pseudepigrapha Research," 46.
69. Bauckham and Davila, "Introduction," xxxii.

by the name of the Old Testament character with which it is affiliated in its biblical order. Bauckham, Davila, and Panayotov prefer the latter in that it avoids the necessity of categorizing a text by its genre. A further appeal of this arrangement is that it lends itself more readily to comparing traditions relating to the same individual. Nevertheless, it seems expedient here to adopt the system of arrangement based broadly on genre, similar to that employed by Charlesworth. This facilitates the provision of an overview of the nature of that particular genre in general prior to examination of specific writings within it. At the close of each genre segment is a summary of "things left out"—writings that belong to the genre but are excluded from discussion typically because of provenance. The genre categories and affiliated writings are as follows:

- *Apocalypses*: Primary attention is given to 1 Enoch, 4 Ezra, 2 Baruch, the Apocalypse of Abraham, and Sibylline Oracles 3–5, 11. Secondary consideration is given to 2 Enoch, 3 Baruch, the Apocalypse of Zephaniah, the Testament of Abraham, and fragmentary apocalyptic texts among the Dead Sea Scrolls.
- *Testaments*: Primary attention is given to the Testament of Moses, the Testament of Job, the Aramaic Levi Document, the Testament of Qahat, and the Visions of Amram. Secondary consideration is given to the Testament of Solomon, the Testaments of the Twelve Patriarchs, the (Qumran) Testament of Naphtali, and various testamentary Dead Sea Scrolls fragments.
- *Expansions of biblical narratives and rewritten scripture*: Primary attention is given to Jubilees, Biblical Antiquities, the Genesis Apocryphon, the Letter of Aristeas, and Joseph and Aseneth. Secondary consideration is given to the Life of Adam and Eve, 4 Baruch, Ezekiel the Tragedian, and the Book of Giants.
- *Poetic literature, Wisdom literature, and prayers*: Primary attention is given to Psalms 151–155, the Psalms of Solomon, and Pseudo-Phocylides. Secondary consideration is given to the Hellenistic Synagogue Prayers, the Prayer of Joseph, and the Prayer of Nabonidus (4Q242).

Apocalypses

The word "apocalypse" is derived from the Greek *apokalypsis*, meaning simply "revelation." As a genre, however, it describes a type of literature dating from around 200 BCE to 200 CE[1] that depicts the reception of some divine disclosure to a person—typically a famous figure from the Hebrew Bible—alongside its interpretation by a heavenly figure such as an angel.[2] The manner in which one receives such disclosures is typically by a vision or dream directly conveyed by a heavenly being, or the visionary is taken on an otherworldly journey, often with an angelic guide.

Though apocalypses exhibit some variety, there are some points of commonality: an appeal to heavenly revelation, the importance of angelic mediators, and an expectation of a judgment of individuals after death. Typically apocalypses exhort readers/hearers to perceive the present life "in light of impending judgment and to adopt one's values and lifestyle accordingly."[3]

1. J. Collins, *Apocalyptic Imagination*, 3–4.
2. John J. Collins has defined the term in his seminal work as follows: "'Apocalypse' is a genre of revelatory literature with a narrative framework, in which a revelation is mediated by an otherworldly being to a human recipient, disclosing a transcendent reality which is both temporal, insofar as it envisages eschatological salvation, and spatial, insofar as it involves another, supernatural world." "Introduction," 9.
3. J. Collins, "Apocalypse," 344–45.

19

Or, more poignantly, an apocalypse is "intended to interpret present, earthly circumstances in light of the supernatural world and of the future, and to influence the understanding and behavior of the audience by means of divine authority."[4] Apocalypses are saturated with symbolic language and images of a wide variety, using these images as communicative devices for their messages. They use symbols as metaphors for the purpose of referring to concrete objects or events as well as abstract ideas, often expressed in specific, nonliteral language, typically using imagery drawn from a set of recognizable symbols that were often understood to represent things beyond themselves.

Apocalypses are found in portions of the Hebrew Bible, such as the book of Daniel (chaps. 7–12; cf. Ezek. 40–48; Isa. 24–27, 34–35, 56–66; Zech. 9–14). Apocalypses within the Pseudepigrapha include 1 Enoch, which is composed of a set of distinct apocalypses, including the Book of Watchers (chaps. 1–36), the Similitudes of Enoch (chaps. 37–71), the Astronomical Book (chaps. 72–82), the Dream Visions (chaps. 83–84), the Animal Apocalypse (chaps. 85–90), and the Epistle of Enoch (chaps. 91–108). Also discussed in the coming chapters are 4 Ezra, 2 Baruch, Sibylline Oracles 3–5, 11, and the Apocalypse of Abraham.

4. A. Collins, "Introduction," 7.

1

1 Enoch

Introduction

First Enoch, also known as the Ethiopic Apocalypse of Enoch, is a collection of five originally independent writings dating from the fourth century BCE to the first century CE (see table 1.1). As a whole 1 Enoch represents the oldest of three works associated with the biblical Enoch, who was born in the seventh generation from Adam (Gen. 5:21–24). Aramaic fragments of all portions of 1 Enoch—except the Similitudes—discovered in Qumran Cave 4 confirm Aramaic as the original language.[1] Today the work is extant in full only in Ethiopic, which was translated from Greek between the fourth and sixth centuries. The oldest of the about ninety surviving Ethiopic manuscripts are from the fifteenth century. The first component of 1 Enoch is the Book of Watchers (chaps. 1–36). It describes righteous Enoch's reception of heavenly visions; the rebellion of angels, or Watchers; and the work of Azazel, the rebellion's leader. Enoch ascends to the heavenly throne room and is commissioned as a prophet of judgment. Accompanied by an angelic entourage, he travels throughout the earth and receives visions of judgment. The second component of 1 Enoch is called the Similitudes of Enoch, or Book of Parables (chaps. 37–71). It, like the Book of Watchers, is a record of Enochic visions and angelic interpretations as the prophet travels through God's throne room and the universe. Aside from Enoch, the main figure here is an eschatological judge, mostly called "Chosen One" but also "Son of Man" and other titles. The Astronomical Book, or Book of the Heavenly

---

1. Alongside Jubilees, 1 Enoch is the best-attested pseudepigraphon at Qumran. Fragments from some eleven manuscripts contain portions of 1 Enoch.

Luminaries (chaps. 72–82), describes the role and structure of heavenly and earthly bodies and addresses the importance of the solar calendar of 364 days. This is followed by the Book of Dreams (chaps. 83–90), which contains two visions: the first (chaps. 83–84) is a vision of the coming flood, followed by a prayer; the second (chaps. 85–90), also called the Animal Apocalypse, recounts an apocalyptic vision of human history, using animals to represent people and people to represent angels. The Epistle of Enoch (chaps. 91–108) is a compilation of several writings, only one of which is a letter (Epistle of Enoch [92:1–5; 93:11–105:2]). It is preceded by an Exhortation (91:1–10, 18–19) and followed by the Apocalypse of Weeks (93:1–10; 91:11–17), which gives a visionary account of human history from the time of Enoch to the end of days. The Birth of Noah (106:1–107:3) provides a fictitious account of that biblical figure and is followed by the Eschatological Admonition (108:1–15).

Table 1.1

Components of 1 Enoch

Book of Watchers (1 En. 1–36)
Book of Parables (1 En. 37–71)
Astronomical Book (1 En. 72–82)
Book of Dreams (1 En. 83–90)
  • Dream Visions (1 En. 83–84)
  • Animal Apocalypse (1 En. 85–90)
Epistle of Enoch (1 En. 91–108)
  • Exhortation (1 En. 91:1–10, 18–19)
  • Epistle of Enoch (1 En. 92:1–5; 93:11–105:2).
  • Apocalypse of Weeks (1 En. 93:1–10; 91:11–17)
  • Birth of Noah (1 En. 106:1–107:3)
  • Eschatological Admonition (1 En. 108:1–15)

The Book of Watchers (1 En. 1–36)

Introduction

The Book of Watchers (1 En. 1–36) is among the oldest writings that to-gether make up 1 Enoch and may serve as an introduction to the whole work. On its own, the Book of Watchers is an expansion of the biblical account from Genesis 6. The vaguely referenced "sons of God" (בְּנֵי־הָאֱלֹהִים, bənê-hā'ĕlōhîm) who take human wives in the Hebrew Bible (Gen. 6:2) are given names in the Book of Watchers (e.g., Shemihazah; 1 En. 7:1–2). The enigmatic description of their activities in seemingly neutral tones in the Hebrew Bible (Gen. 6:2) gives way to explicit condemnation of the Watchers for their sin (e.g., 1 En. 6:1–10:16a). Where the ensuing narratives of Genesis depict God's judgment against *humans* in the flood (Gen. 6:6–7), the Book of Watchers lays blame elsewhere. In the Shemihazah narrative (1 En. 7–8) the flood is in response to the violence against humans enacted by the children of the Watchers. The Azazel[2] account (chaps. 10–13) includes this but adds human sin as part of the occasion as well. Despite its present form as a single unit, the Book of Watchers is a composite document often studied in its constituent parts (chaps. 1–5, 6–16, and 17–36). Yet there is some debate among scholars about whether the component parts in their current form can be adequately identified, as well as the profitability of examining these parts for their respective dates and provenances. First Enoch 1:1–12:6 is extant as a unified whole in the earliest fragment of the Book of Watchers (4QEn[a]). Furthermore, the entirety of the Book of Watchers (chaps. 1–36) seems to be established as a whole by the time the book of Jubilees is written mid-second century BCE.[3]

Language and Manuscripts

The Book of Watchers is widely held to be composed originally in Aramaic and then rendered into Greek and then Ethiopic (Ge'ez). Like the remainder of 1 Enoch, the Book of Watchers is found complete only in the Ethiopic version but is attested in fragmentary form in other languages as well.[4] The earliest manuscripts of the Book of Watchers are found among the Dead Sea Scrolls and are written in Aramaic. These include five manuscripts: 4Q201 (also referenced as 4QEn[a]) contains 1 Enoch 1–10 and possibly chapter 12. The manuscript dates from early in the second century BCE but may have been copied from an older manuscript.[5] 4Q202 (4QEn[b]) contains a number of very small, indistinct fragments, but it can be seen to contain 1 Enoch 5–10 and 14 and dates from perhaps the middle of the second century BCE.[6] 4Q204 (4QEn[c]) is also fragmentary and contains portions of the Book of Watchers from chapters 1–6, 10, 13–15, 31–32, and 35–36. It dates from the end of the first century BCE.[7] 4Q205 (4QEn[d]) seems to date from the same period as 4Q204 and contains fragmentary portions of chapters 22 and 25–27.[8] 4Q206 (4QEn[e]) dates from early in the first century BCE and contains fragmentary portions from chapters

---

2. The name is variously spelled. "'Asa'el" is in the Aramaic (and Greek). The Ethiopic has "Asael" (6:7) but more commonly "Azazel."

3. VanderKam, "Enoch Traditions," 1:235.

4. Knibb, *Ethiopic Book of Enoch*, 2:21–22. See also VanderKam, "Textual Base."

5. Milik, *Books of Enoch*, 140–63; Stuckenbruck, "4QEnoch[a]," 3–7.

6. Milik, *Books of Enoch*, 164–65.

7. Milik, *Books of Enoch*, 178–79.

8. Milik, *Books of Enoch*, 5, 217.

20–22, 28–29, and 31–34 of the Book of Watchers.[9] In full the manuscript evidence from Qumran provides compelling evidence for both an early date for the Book of Watchers (prior to 175 BCE) and Aramaic as the original language.[10]

Perhaps before the turn of the era, the Book of Watchers was rendered into Greek. The principal manuscripts include Codex Panopolitanus, which dates from the fifth or sixth century CE and contains, among other things, 1 Enoch 19:3–21:9 followed by a wording that is nearly identical to the fuller Ethiopic version—where they overlap—of 1 Enoch 1:1–32:6a. The ninth-century *Chronography* of George Syncellus contains excerpts from the Book of Watchers (6:1–9:4; 8:4–10:14; 15:8–16:1). And so, though only about 28 percent of the entirety of 1 Enoch survives in Greek (n. 10), the majority of the Book of Watchers is preserved in that language.[11] A portion of the Book of Watchers (6:1–6) is preserved in Syriac in a twelfth-century *Chronicle* of Michael the Syrian.[12] Of the forty-nine Ethiopic manuscripts, however, none date earlier than the fifteenth century. The diversity of manuscripts means that translators follow different traditions. Some utilize a single Ethiopic manuscript as a basis,[13] whereas others utilize an eclectic text informed by the best evidence of Ethiopic, Greek, and Aramaic.[14]

Provenance

The provenance of the Book of Watchers is simplified by its attestation at Qumran—an unambiguously pre-Christian Jewish context. Like other works, the Book of Watchers depicts Jerusalem as singularly important (1 En. 25:4–6; 26:1–2; cf. 89:50; 90:20–36). But additional attention to regions in Galilee, specifically Dan and the region of Mount Hermon, suggests that area as the likely origin of the work.[15]

Date

Manuscript evidence from Qumran indicates the Book of Watchers should be dated to prior to 175 BCE,[16] though there is general agreement that it prob-

9. Milik, *Books of Enoch*, 225.

10. Milik, *Books of Enoch*, 6, 25, 140.

11. Nickelsburg, *1 Enoch 1*, 12.

12. Brock, "Fragment of Enoch."

13. Isaac, "1 (Ethiopic Apocalypse of) Enoch," 1:10–12.

14. Knibb, *Ethiopic Book of Enoch*, 2:28–37; Uhlig, *Das äthiopische Henochbuch*, 470–91; Nickelsburg, *1 Enoch 1*, 18.

15. Nickelsburg, *1 Enoch 1*, 230–31.

16. Milik, *Books of Enoch*, 6, 25, 140.

ably took shape as early as the third century BCE.[17] The Book of Watchers is a composite document sometimes dated according to its constituent parts, which may be arranged as follows:

- Chapters 1–5: Presumably these chapters form the first segment, as they function as an introduction, foreshadowing the message of the remainder of the book. Manuscript evidence from Qumran (4QEn[ab], see below) dating from the first half of the second century BCE contains at least 1 Enoch 1–11, indicating a date from around 200 to 150 BCE.

- Chapters 6–11: These chapters contain the account of the fallen angels, led by Shemihazah (1 En. 6:3–7), forming the nucleus for the remainder of the Book of Watchers. Therefore, the section's date provides a key starting point for dating the entire book. Again manuscript evidence from Qumran (4QEn[ab]) suggests a date from around 200 to 150 BCE.

- Chapters 12–16: These chapters presume chapters 6–11.

- Chapters 17–19: These chapters seem to have evolved over time, yet in their present form they are later than chapters 12–16 and presupposed by chapters 20–36. Furthermore, 1 Enoch 6–19 is known to the author of the Animal Apocalypse (1 En. 85–90), written by 165 BCE. Therefore, it is dated to the second half of the third century BCE.

- Chapters 20–36: These chapters presume chapters 17–19. The attestation of 1 Enoch 20–36 in 4QEn[a] (late third century BCE), the book of Jubilees (4:18–20; 175–150 BCE), and perhaps Daniel 12:2 point to a late third-century-BCE date for chapters 20–36. Moreover, that 4QEn[a] represents the end of a staged development pushes the date early within that window.

The tradition of the Shemihazah myth may date well before 200 BCE, at least from the early third century. This may suggest an earliest date of approximately 300 BCE for chapters 6–11, and chapters 12–16 thereafter, no later than 250 BCE.[18] This leads to a date for the complete Book of Watchers in its present form somewhere by the mid to late third century BCE.

Contents

As a whole the Book of Watchers describes how rebellious fallen angels came to earth and introduced evil into the world and how God and his heavenly

17. Stokes, "Watchers, Book of the," 1334.
18. Nickelsburg, *1 Enoch 1*, 132, 169–70, 230, 279–80, 294.

forces will bring about judgment against those angels and sinful humans. The book is typically divided into three large units: chapters 1–5 serve as an introduction to the Book of Watchers and perhaps the entirety of 1 Enoch; chapters 6–16 expand on the "sons of God" account from Genesis 6; finally, chapters 17–36 recount Enoch's travels.

1 ENOCH 1–5

First Enoch 1–5 presents the book as the product of a revelation received by Enoch from God. The primary intent is to bless "the elect and the righteous who would be present on the day of tribulation at (the time of) the removal of all the ungodly ones" (1:1–2; cf. Deut. 33:1; Num. 24:3–4). The message is one of the coming of God to judge the wicked (1 En. 1:2b–7, 9) but preserve and bless the righteous (1:8). Enoch observes that nature follows its intended course in accord with the purposes of God (2:1–5:3), in stark contrast to the transgressions of the wicked (5:4). The wicked will experience God's judgment for their iniquity (5:5–6), whereas the elect will be blessed and preserved (5:7–10; cf. Isa. 65).

1 ENOCH 6–16

The text of 1 Enoch 6–16 begins with an expanded account of the fall of disobedient angels (Gen. 6:1–4). It develops the cryptic narration of the "sons of God" (בְּנֵי־הָאֱלֹהִים, bənê-hā'ělōhîm) taking the daughters of men for wives in order to describe how the (named) angelic figures—called Watchers—conspire together to sire children by human women (1 En. 6:1–8). Led by Shemihazah, the Watchers also teach their wives various magical crafts (7:1–2; 8:1–3) and sire giants who wreak havoc on the earth (7:2–5). The earth (7:6) and people (8:4) cry out and are heard by the angels Michael, Surafel, and Gabriel, who in turn report it to the Most High (9:1–11). The Most High sends angelic figures to act in response. First, Asuryal is to warn the son of Lamech (Noah) about the coming deluge (10:1–3). Second, Raphael is to bind Azazel and imprison him until the final judgment (10:4–8). Third, Gabriel is instructed to destroy the wicked, including the giants (10:9–10). Fourth, Michael is sent by God to inform the fallen Watchers of their doom and God's intent to rid the world of their wickedness (10:11–16a). God will then restore righteousness and purity, and his people will experience prosperity (10:16b–20). All the nations will come to worship God, and the earth will be cleansed from its pollution forever (10:21–22; 11:1–2). Curiously, no mention of Enoch is made in chapters 6–11.

Enoch returns in 1 Enoch 12–16, where he is commissioned to inform the fallen Watchers of God's judgment against them (12:1–13:1). First, though, he narrates his experience of being hidden with the Watchers (12:1–2). He was blessing the Lord when the Watchers called to him and charged him to tell the fallen Watchers that their sin brought defilement on the earth and they will therefore have neither peace nor forgiveness (12:3–6). Enoch obeys his commission and confronts Azazel and the other fallen Watchers with the message (13:1–3a). They respond in fear (13:3b) and beg for Enoch's (written) intercession to the Lord (13:4–5). Enoch writes the prayer and falls asleep while reading it (13:6–7). In a vision he is commissioned to reprimand the fallen Watchers (13:8–14:1), and he then recounts the vision to them (14:2–7). Their prayers will not be heard (14:2–4, 7), and they will be unable to ascend to heaven and will remain imprisoned for all eternity (14:5). They will observe the destruction of their loved ones (14:6). Then Enoch recounts his heavenly ascent (14:8), wherein he enters the heavenly sanctuary (14:9–17) and sees the Great Glory sitting on a lofty throne (14:18–23). The Lord then calls him (14:24–25) and commissions him to deliver a message to the Watchers that immortal beings are not to intermix with mortals (15:1–7). As a result, their progeny—the giants—will yield evil spirits from their bodies to wreak havoc on the earth (15:8–12; 16:1–2). Enoch is to announce to these fallen Watchers their impending doom (16:3).

1 Enoch 17–36

First Enoch 17–36 is an extensive description of Enoch's heavenly travels and accompanying visions. Chapters 17–19 begin with Enoch being lifted up by angels and given a tour—in a westerly direction—of the mythical world (17:1–18:9), including the prison where the fallen Watchers are to be kept (18:10–19:1a) until their final demise (19:1b–3). The final section of the Book of Watchers (chaps. 20–36) describes a second account of Enoch's heavenly ascent. It begins (chap. 20) with a list of the names of his angelic guides. A cyclical pattern of the ensuing visions is thereafter observable as follows: arrival ("I came to . . ."), vision ("I saw . . ."), question ("I asked the angel . . ."), angelic interpretation ("he said . . ."), and blessing ("Then I blessed the Lord").[19]

The final section continues by repeating (chap. 21) the description of the prison from 18:10–19:2. This stands in stark contrast to chapter 22, where Enoch is given a vision of the existence of the souls of the righteous dead anticipating heavenly bliss (22:1–9) and the sinners their torment (22:10–14). In 1 Enoch 23:1–24:1, Enoch travels west and sees another vision of a river of

19. Nickelsburg, *Jewish Literature*, 51–52.

fire, the function of which is unclear. He then travels to see seven mountains adorned and picturesque, configured as a throne (24:2–3), where he sees the tree of life (24:4–6). The angel Michael explains the vision to Enoch (25:1–4) and the ensuing blessings for the righteous in the new Jerusalem (25:5–7). Enoch then travels to the center of the earth, where he marvels (26:6) at the lush mountains and valleys (26:1–3) within which is another, barren valley (26:4–5). His angelic guide—this time Uriel—explains that the accursed valley is reserved for the gathering of the accursed for judgment in the last days (27:1–2), while the righteous receive blessings (27:3–5).

Then Enoch's travels take him east, to the center of a mountain, and he sees a lush wilderness (28:1–3), the tree of judgment (29:1–2), a lush valley (30:1–3), and a forest of fruitful trees (31:1–3; 32:1–2). This easterly journey culminates in Enoch's arrival in paradise (32:3–6) and at the ends of the earth (33:1–36:4). Within this final segment Enoch describes the opening of the gates of heaven (33:2–4; in reference to chaps. 72–82) and then his journey to the north (34:1–3), west (35:1), and south (36:1–3; cf. chap. 76). The book concludes (36:4) with a blessing to God.

Contribution and Context

The Visionary Experiences of Enoch in the Book of Watchers

The narrative framework and the conveyance of a heavenly revelation from the supernatural world that have come to form the foundational definition of an apocalypse[20] play a vital role in the Book of Watchers.[21] The entire work is introduced in the first of Enoch's visions (1 En. 1–5), where his eyes are opened (1:2) and he receives a vision (1:2) concerning the elect of a future generation who will experience the day of tribulation (1:1–2). Enoch's role is typically that of an intercessor for the fallen Watchers, even though he, like the biblical Ezra, is depicted as a "scribe" (12:3–4; cf. Ezra 7:6, 11; Neh. 8:1, 4; etc.). In his role Enoch is given access to God, is commissioned to announce judgment (1 En. 12:3–13:6),[22] and is charged to communicate judgment upon the Watchers (1:1–2; 12:4b–6; 13:8b).

Enoch receives his visionary experiences through both dreams (13:8a, 10; 14:1–2) and visions (1:2; 13:8a, 10; 14:1, 2, 8a, c, 14b). He also experiences heavenly ascent (14:8c, 25; 15:1; 17:1, 2, 4; cf. 18:14–19:3) and the opening of the gates of heaven (33:2–5). He has these experiences in a variety of settings, such as while blessing God (1:1–2; 12:3a), interceding in prayer (12:3), and

---

20. J. Collins, *Apocalypse*.
21. The following is developed from Gurtner, "Revelatory Experiences," 31–44.
22. Nickelsburg, *1 Enoch 1*, 229.

sleeping (13:7b; cf. 14:2; 83–90). He is also found in a posture of fear, falling on his face (14:14a); in the sanctuary (12:3; 14:9–23); and by a river (13:7; cf. Ezek. 1:1; Dan. 10:2–12:11).

The centerpiece of Enoch's heavenly vision in the Book of Watchers is the "throne vision" (1 En. 14), in which Enoch sees God himself enthroned, "great in glory," brighter than the sun and whiter than snow (1 En. 14:20). Here God is the object of worship for countless worshipers (14:22; cf. Dan. 7), and it is here where Enoch receives his commission and charge against the fallen Watchers (1 En. 14:24–16:4). In this respect the visions in general and the throne vision in particular point to the coming judgment of God.

Eschatological Judgment in the Book of Watchers

The Book of Watchers addresses several interrelated themes in its overall message. These include the origins and nature of sin, its spread throughout humanity, and its ultimate consequences. While some of these components are familiar from other Second Temple writings, the Book of Watchers is among the oldest and most explicit with respect to some of the most important facets.

At the center of the Book of Watchers lies the myth of fallen angels, or Watchers. It is their rebellion against God, not the disobedience of Adam and Eve, that accounts for the origin of sin. But even here the Book of Watchers retains two distinct traditions pertaining to the original culprit for the rebellion and ensuing havoc wreaked on humanity. On the one hand, Shemihazah leads the fallen Watchers to take human wives and sire giant offspring (1 En. 6:3, 7; 9:7; 10:11; 15:3–7). These giants bring about violence and bloodshed, transforming the earth into a state of impurity (10:20–22). On the other hand, sin enters the world through Azazel revealing heavenly secrets to humans (8:1; 9:6; 10:4–8). These include metallurgy, from which humans make weapons for shedding blood, as well as cosmetics and jewelry used for sexual seductions. Still other skills imparted by the fallen Watchers include magical incantations and astrology (7:1; 8:2–3). Presumably both the author of the Book of Watchers and those who preserved it were content to allow this disparity to stand.[23]

The sin of the fallen Watchers introduces violence, bloodshed, and religious impropriety into the human sphere of existence. As told in 1 Enoch 12–16, the story of angelic rebellion is cast in the form of priests who abandon their ministry in the heavenly sanctuary and become defiled by intercourse with human women (cf. 15:4–7a). They sire giants, who continue to lead humans

23. Nickelsburg, *1 Enoch 1*, 46.

into sin and plague them with sickness (15:8–16:1). In both instances the condition of human sin and suffering is attributed to the continuing influence of fallen Watchers in the world.[24] In this framework God himself is not culpable for human sin, and people are as much victims as perpetrators (e.g., 1:9; 5:4; 27:2).

With the entrance of sin into the human condition, people are generally placed into one of two categories: the wicked or the righteous. The latter are surely those with whom the original audience of the Book of Watchers was to identify. The wicked, or "sinners," are the objects of stern warnings, similar to those issued to Israel (e.g., Deut. 33; Judg. 5; Hab. 3; Mal. 1). They will ultimately be destroyed because of their sins (1 En. 1:9). In stark contrast to the natural created order, the wicked do not observe the laws of God and will receive their due judgment (chaps. 2–5).[25] They join the fallen Watchers in their cursing and ultimate condemnation (5:6–7; 16:1). They commit adultery and become corrupt by the arts taught by Azazel (8:1–2). At their death they are set apart, buried to await the judgment they did not receive in their lifetime (22:10). They will be plagued by eternal pain and retribution (22:11a), and, as with other criminals, their souls will endure but will not rise from death (22:13–14).

The righteous avert the fate of the wicked. They are coupled with the "chosen" (5:7, 9), the "elect" (1:1), the "blessed" (1:2), and the "pious" (25:5), and the entire vision of the Book of Watchers is for their benefit (1:2). Enoch himself is counted among them (1:2; 15:1; cf. 12:4). They will enjoy light, joy, and (eternal) peace and will inherit the earth (5:7, 9; cf. Isa. 65:17–25). They are present at the day of tribulation when the ungodly are removed (1 En. 1:1). They receive (divine) wisdom and will not do wrong again (5:8; 8:8). They will complete the natural number of the days of their lives (5:9). Most of what is explicitly said of them pertains to their future: they will pass through judgment with peace (1:7, 8a; 10:17) since they will be preserved by God (1:8b). Their souls will be separated from their bodies and will avoid judgment (22:9, 13). God will show them kindness, prosperity, and the light of God (1:8b). They will be blessed when God comes to visit the earth (25:2–6), and they will enjoy the fruit of a fragrant tree prepared for them (25:5, 7).

Judgment itself seems to occur in stages. Initially Raphael is instructed to bind Azazel and cast him into darkness in anticipation of the day of judgment when he will be hurled into fire (10:4–6). Likewise Shemihazah and his entourage are bound under the earth until judgment occurs, when they will

24. Nickelsburg, *1 Enoch 1*, 46–47.
25. Some see here a reference to the law of Moses.

be shut up in the torment of eternal fire (10:12–13). Elsewhere, prior to final judgment, fallen Watchers are kept in "prison" until the great day of judgment (18:14). There are places where the "spirits of the souls of the dead" are kept until judgment (22:3) and a "cursed valley" where all the godless, cursed people are kept until judgment (27:2–3). The Book of Watchers depicts a typological understanding of the flood as judgment on the wicked, a perspective shared among other Second Temple writings (e.g., CD-A II, 17–21; Matt. 24:36–41; 2 Pet. 2:4–5). Beyond judgment lies restoration. Early on Raphael is told to "restore the earth which the angels have ruined" (1 En. 10:7). But it is not clear whether the earthly restoration is terminated or at all affected by the final judgment.[26]

CONTEXTUAL INFLUENCES

Some scholars (e.g., P. Grelot) have suggested that the Book of Watchers shares important similarities with Babylonian traditions from the Gilgamesh Epic, such as the "waters of life" (1 En. 17:4).[27] More recently scholars have suggested that the description of the giants (esp. in 7:2–5; cf. 15:11) is modeled after the violent behavior of demons in Mesopotamian literature (*Utukkū Lemnūtu*).[28] Yet some find difficulties in comparing the journeys of Gilgamesh and Enoch, which differ both in content and sequence. Others suggest Enoch's travels are drawn from a Greek tradition, such as Odysseus's journey to the underworld.[29] Perhaps it is best to acknowledge affinities with several of these settings while observing the distinctive manner in which the Book of Watchers brings them together[30] using a model of depicting Enoch's journeys that draws from ancient Near Eastern diplomacy intended to impress and intimidate (cf. 2 Kings 20).

Purpose

Determining the original setting of the Book of Watchers is notoriously challenging. The difficulty arises in that the pseudepigraphic nature of the work veils historical referents. Finding the setting is further complicated by the consensus that the Book of Watchers is not a single composition but a compilation of several traditions, each—at least potentially—with distinct

26. J. Collins, *Apocalyptic Imagination*, 71.
27. P. Grelot, "La Géographie mythique."
28. Drawnel, "Mesopotamian Background."
29. Homer, *Odyssea* 11.576–600; cf. also Plato, *Respublica* 10.614–21; Plutarch, *Moralia* 563–68.
30. J. Collins, *Apocalyptic Imagination*, 71–72.

social settings. Therefore, while some scholars advocate a search for the work's setting in its current form, others have carefully examined the polemical nature of portions of the Book of Watchers to posit possible settings (see below). A matter of a more general nature throughout the work is the conspicuous absence of Torah. Though the reader is repeatedly advocated to pursue righteousness and avoid sin, there remains strikingly little indication of obedience to Torah. This is sometimes seen as an indication that whatever identification of the author (or authors) can be inferred from the text, Torah is not central to it. Some scholars have taken this, coupled with the polemic against the Jerusalem priesthood and its temple, to posit a unique form of Judaism known today as "Enochic Judaism."[31]

For 1 Enoch 1–5 some have suggested a situation in which new converts are addressed on issues of judgment and salvation. The history of the eschatological remnant is rehearsed, and the hearers are co-opted into that history through a set of appeals to obey God's commandments. In this reading, 1 Enoch 1:1 indicates insiders of the religious group, which includes those previously numbered among the "sinners."[32] However, the nature of the sins and the identity of the sinners cannot be identified with any clarity (e.g., 1:9; 5:4; cf. 27:2). Nevertheless, the edification and admonition are not thereby lost since the message is to the "ideal readers," the elect, to affirm that they are God's righteous people. Despite all their hardships, God controls their fate, and they as his elect people—addressed in these chapters in the third person—are blessed for their faithfulness to God's covenant. The wicked—addressed in the second person—face divine retribution, and the contrasts between the righteous and the sinner and blessing and cursing run throughout with God as the principal actor.

The setting for 1 Enoch 6–11 has been seen in terms of the author casting his own context in the last days typologically upon the events of primordial times. Its retelling of the fall of the angels from Genesis 6:1–4 is placed into the author's own setting, in which depravity, led by the fallen angels, notably Shemihazah, incites divine judgment. These angels are sometimes identified with a corrupted Jerusalem priesthood of the original audience.[33] In this respect the judgment recorded in the Book of Watchers against the fallen Watchers is a veiled condemnation against the priestly establishment overseeing the Jerusalem temple.[34] The nature of their corruption pertains to illicit marriages in which the wayward priests marry women forbidden to the

31. See esp. Boccaccini, *Beyond the Essene Hypothesis*.
32. Nickelsburg, *1 Enoch 1*, 132–34.
33. Suter, "Fallen Angel, Fallen Priest."
34. For a more recent summary, see Suter, "Revisiting 'Fallen Angel, Fallen Priest.'"

priesthood (cf. Lev. 21), thereby polluting the sanctity of the temple and its cult. Another component of this segment of the Book of Watchers has been identified in terms of its political rather than cultic setting.[35] The violence of the giants described in chapters 6–11 is thought to reflect the tumultuous events after the death of Alexander the Great. These are the wars of the Diadochi (successors), in which Alexander's generals fought with one another over the succession of his dynasty. In this reading, the giants correspond to Macedonian chieftains of that era, pointing to a geographical origin of Galilee.[36] A similar conclusion has been drawn pertaining to chapters 12–16,[37] where heaven is found to be depicted as a temple, its angels are priestly in function, and by his passing through the heavenly sanctuary, Enoch is himself likely a priestly figure. Finally, some have argued that chapters 17–19 depict the scribal origin of a social group traveling between Jerusalem and Galilee, perhaps under temporary duress, during the third century BCE, prior to the influx of Hellenism.[38]

Some have responded with caution to an antipriestly polemic in the Book of Watchers. On the one hand, it is unclear whether the Book of Watchers is sufficiently transparent to identify such a polemic.[39] More generally, the Book of Watchers in particular and apocalypses in general exhibit what has been called the "essential polyvalence of apocalyptic symbolism," which "enables it to be re-applied in new historical situations."[40] This necessitates caution in drawing firm conclusions about the social settings of a document from the symbolic descriptions it contains. In other words, "by telling the story of the Watchers rather than of the Diadochi or the priesthood, *1 Enoch* 1–36 becomes a paradigm which is not restricted to one historical situation but can be applied whenever an analogous situation arises."[41] This means that the setting may depict the wars of the Diadochi or the Jerusalem priesthood and that the author chooses to avert explicit references and, as John J. Collins argues, transpose the *specific* historical crisis onto a mythical plane, wherein 1 Enoch 1–36 becomes a "paradigmatic model" that can be applied "whenever an analogous situation arises."[42] This necessarily frustrates one's attempt to identify a single *Sitz im Leben* and favors notions of a social setting in a broader sense.

35. Nickelsburg, "Apocalyptic and Myth."
36. Nickelsburg, "Enoch, Levi, and Peter."
37. Nickelsburg, "Enoch, Levi, and Peter."
38. Bautch, *Geography of 1 Enoch 17–19.*
39. Himmelfarb, "Book of the Watchers."
40. J. Collins, "Apocalyptic Technique," 98.
41. J. Collins, *Apocalyptic Imagination*, 64.
42. J. Collins, "Apocalyptic Technique," 98–99.

The ambiguity of the setting serves the overall purpose(s) and function(s) of the work rather well. The transcendent perspective of the Book of Watchers, implicit in its genre and explicit in its outlook, subverts the earthly crises (whatever they may be) to the transcendent plan of Israel's God.[43] The work as a whole, then, provides a "lens through which any crisis can be viewed": "By evoking a sense of awe and instilling conviction in its revelation of the transcendent world and the coming judgment, the apocalypse enables the faithful to cope with the crises of the present and so creates the preconditions for righteous action in the face of adversity."[44]

The punishment of the Watchers may distract attention from earthly troubles, equipping the readers to endure any further hardships. They are offered both consolation and, perhaps implicitly, exhortation to be faithful to Israel's God. After all, the suffering of the righteous amid the proliferation of sin is not new to the readers (1 En. 6–16). This must not be taken to mean the perspective of the righteous is wrong. On the contrary, the righteous are affirmed.

Their cry is heard by God, who sends judgment on the earth. God is attentive to the plight of his people, addressing wickedness and injustice in the heavenly realm in a manner that will one day be replicated on earth. The wicked and their offspring will be destroyed, their judgment will be completed, and the righteous will be restored. For the readers of this text, it is a statement about the demonic powers behind the evil in their own contemporary experiences. They can take comfort in that God and his angelic forces are aware of their plight and will bring it to an end, which may well be the "essence of this author's message."[45] The nature of the book's use of apocalyptic symbols both conceals aspects of the book's provenance and lends to its ability to be applied to a variety of situations.[46]

The Similitudes of Enoch (1 En. 37–71)

Introduction

The Similitudes of Enoch, or Book of Parables (1 En. 37–71), is likely the latest of the five segments that compose 1 Enoch. It dates from between the first century BCE and the end of the first century CE and clearly depends on earlier portions of 1 Enoch (the Book of Watchers and the Epistle of Enoch). It

---

43. J. Collins, "Apocalyptic Technique," 109.
44. J. Collins, *Apocalyptic Imagination*, 75.
45. Nickelsburg, *1 Enoch 1*, 232.
46. J. Collins, "Apocalyptic Technique," 97–98.

likely originates from a distinct Enochic writing concerned with vindication of the righteous and judgment on mighty rulers and is the only major portion of 1 Enoch not attested among the Dead Sea Scrolls. Like the Book of Watchers, the Similitudes records Enochic visions and angelic interpretations as Enoch is borne up by clouds and wind (39:3; cf. 52:1) through God's throne room—where he sees the "Son of Man" enthroned (46:1–8; 61:8)—and the universe (41:3–8). In these experiences, Enoch learns the fate of the righteous and the wicked, and about the new order that is to come. Furthermore, Enoch sees the "Son of Man" (also called the "Anointed One" and "Elect One") acting as God's agent of judgment against the wicked. Finally (chap. 71), Enoch ascends to the heavenly throne room, where he is told that he himself is the "Son of Man."[47] The terms *similitudes* and *parables* draw from prophetic literature and indicate the book's revelatory nature, though the work itself is introduced as a "vision of wisdom" (37:1).

Language and Manuscripts

With no portions of the Similitudes found at Qumran, it is extant today only in Ethiopic (Ge'ez). Like other portions of 1 Enoch, it may have been written originally in Aramaic or Hebrew and then translated into Greek and from Greek into Ethiopic. It is possible that it was in its Greek form that the Similitudes was enveloped into the corpus of 1 Enoch, perhaps early in the second century CE. Its rendering into Ge'ez likely occurred in the fifth or sixth century, with the translation of biblical texts into that language. Manuscript evidence in Ge'ez, however, is no older than the fifteenth century.

Provenance

The absence of the Similitudes alone among 1 Enoch from Qumran may give indications as to its origins.[48] It may well have been rejected because of its apparent sympathies with equating the sun and moon (e.g., 1 En. 41:3–9), indicating a recognition of a lunar-solar calendar, whereas the Scrolls—and the remainder of 1 Enoch—exhibit particular favor toward the solar calendar.[49] This provides a better explanation for its absence at Qumran but also suggests an authorship for the Similitudes by a Jewish group that is distinct from

---

47. Stuckenbruck, "1 Enoch or Ethiopic Enoch in Outline."
48. The suggestion by J. T. Milik (*Books of Enoch*, 89–98) for a late (third-century CE) Christian provenance was largely discredited shortly after publication. See Knibb, "Date of the Parables of Enoch"; Mearns, "Dating the Similitudes of Enoch."
49. Greenfield and Stone, "Enochic Pentateuch."

that which composed other Enochic writings. It is in any case likely that the
Similitudes comes from Jerusalem or the surrounding area, perhaps Galilee.[50]

Date

Determining a date of origin for the Similitudes is made difficult because
of the very few allusions to historical events found within it. A reference to
the Parthians and the Medes (1 En. 56:5–8) is typically taken to refer to the
Parthian invasion of Palestine in 40 BCE.[51] The reference to springs that serve
the kings and the mighty but will become an instrument of judgment (67:5–13)
is typically taken to refer to Herod the Great's attempts to find healings in
the hot springs of Callirhoe (Josephus, *Ant.* 17.6.5 §§171–173; *J.W.* 1.33.5
§§657–658).[52] This locates the Similitudes after Herod's rise to power in 37
BCE.[53] Others take mention of "the kings and the mighty" to suggest Roman
authorities,[54] which may place the Similitudes in the late first century CE. A
common view is that it originates prior to the outset of the Jewish revolt in
66 CE, to which no clear reference is made.[55]

Contents

The Book of Parables is thought to be composed of material written over
a period of time. Yet in its present form it exhibits a clear structure. An
introduction (1 En. 37:1–4) is followed by three sets of parables or similitudes (38:1–44:1; 45:1–57:3; 58:1–69:29), each of which begins with a chapter
presenting the subject matter of the whole. These, along with a conclusion
(70:1–71:17), recast some material from the Book of Watchers (1 En. 1–36). It
is woven with wisdom material, which serves the book's message of unraveling
the mysteries of eternal life given to Enoch (37:4).[56]

INTRODUCTION (37:1–4)

The *introduction* (37:1–4) identifies the work as the second of Enoch's
visions (37:1), which are words of wisdom (37:2; cf. 37:3, 4) announced to

---

50. Charlesworth, "Books of Enoch," xiii–xv; cf. Aviam, "Book of Enoch."
51. Greenfield and Stone, "Enochic Pentateuch," 58; Walck, *Son of Man*, 45.
52. See Sacchi, "2005 Camaldoli Seminar," 511. Alternatively, see Erho, "Ahistorical Nature
of *1 Enoch* 56:5–8," 23–54.
53. See Charlesworth, "Date and Provenience," 40.
54. Knibb ("Date of the Parables of Enoch") prefers a date after the destruction of Qumran,
ca. 70–135 CE.
55. J. Collins, *Apocalyptic Imagination*, 221.
56. J. Collins, *Apocalyptic Imagination*, 222–23.

all who dwell on the earth (37:2, 5). It is taught in accord with the Lord of Spirits (37:2, 4), who has given the lot of eternal life to Enoch (37:4). Enoch is charged to impart the three ensuing parables (37:5).

THE FIRST PARABLE (38:1–44:1)

The *first parable* (38:1–44:1) introduces the main figures of the work and generally follows the structure of the opening chapters of the Book of Watchers. It begins with an announcement of the coming judgment on the wicked (chap. 38). They are sinners judged for their sins and driven from the earth (38:1; cf. 38:3). They have denied the name of the Lord of Spirits (38:2; cf. 1:3–9), and it would be better for them had they not been born (38:2). Their fate of destruction (38:6) is juxtaposed with that of the righteous, the elect, and the holy when the Righteous One appears (38:2–3). Chapter 39 begins by recounting—in the future tense—the fall of the angels and their siring of children with humans (39:1; cf. chaps. 6–7). Then Enoch is introduced alongside an announcement of judgment on the fallen angels (39:2; cf. 14:1). Enoch ascends to heaven (39:3) and sees the dwelling places of the holy ones (39:4–5; cf. chap. 14). He also sees the Elect One (39:6a) and countless righteous and elect caught up in praise of the Lord of Spirits (39:6b–7). Enoch joins in the heavenly worship (39:8–14) and enters the innumerable company of those who stand before the Lord of Spirits (40:1; cf. chap. 14). In this setting Enoch has a vision of four angels (40:2–7), whom his angelic guide identifies as Michael, Raphael, Gabriel, and Phanuel (40:8–10).

Enoch then sees the secrets of heaven (41:1–2a), where "sinners" are identified as those who "deny the name of the Lord of Spirits" (41:2b) and are expelled (41:2c). He sees heavenly secrets of the universe (41:3–8a) displaying the incomparable power of the Lord of Spirits (41:8b–9). This is followed by a poetic section on Wisdom (42:1–3; cf. Sir. 24; 1 Bar. 3:9–4:4; 1 En. 94:5), who finds no place to dwell on earth, so she returns to heaven. Then Enoch has another vision of the cosmic secrets of lightning and stars (43:1–3) in which he learns from his angelic guide that they are the names of those who dwell on the earth and believe in the Lord of Spirits (43:4–44:1).

THE SECOND PARABLE (45:1–57:3)

The *second parable* (45:1–57:3) concerns judgment on those who will deny the Lord (45:1–2) when the Elect One is enthroned (45:3), dwells among his people, and transforms the earth for the righteous (45:4–6a). In contrast, the wicked will be destroyed from the earth in judgment (45:6b; cf. 10:16–11:2; 91:14). Enoch then has a vision of the Chosen One (46:1–3), the Son of Man (cf. Dan. 7:9, 13; Isa. 49) who will open hidden storerooms (1 En. 46:3b) and will execute judgment on kings and mighty ones (46:4–8; cf. chaps. 62–63; Isa. 13–14; 52–53). In the days of judgment on the wicked, the prayers of the righteous—as well as their blood—will ascend to heaven and occasion God's vindicating judgment (1 En. 47:1–4).

After Enoch sees a "fountain of righteousness" (48:1; cf. Wis. 2, 4–5), the discussion of the Son of Man resumes. He is called "Before Time" (1 En. 48:2–3) and variously described as a "staff for the righteous" (48:4a), the "light of the gentiles" (48:4b; cf. Isa. 49:6; 1 En. 10:21; 90:38; 91:14), and the hope of those who are sick (48:4c). He shall be worshiped (48:5), though he was concealed prior to creation (48:6). He reveals the wisdom of the Lord of Spirits (48:7a). He preserves the righteous but will humiliate the kings of the earth (cf. Ps. 2:2) and the mighty landowners (1 En. 48:8), who will be delivered to the elect ones and face judgment (48:9–10a) since they have denied the Lord of Spirits and his messiah (48:10b). The vision returns to the flow of Wisdom (chap. 49), which dwells in the Elect One (49:2b–3; cf. Isa. 11:2), who will judge secret things (1 En. 49:4; cf. 62:3; Isa. 42:1).

Chapter 50 begins with a contrasting account of the fate of the righteous and the wicked (50:1–2a) and introduces a new category: the wicked who repent of their sins (50:2b–5; cf. 100:6). The future outlook of this section anticipates the resurrection of the dead (51:1–2), the enthronement of the Elect One (51:3), and the eschatological bliss of the righteous elect on the earth (51:4–5). More secret things of heaven and the future are seen in Enoch's travels to the west (52:1; cf. 39:1), where he experiences visions of various mountains (52:2; cf. chap. 18). These visions, his angelic guide explains, depict things that will happen by the authority of God's messiah (52:3–4, 6–9; cf. 8:1; 63:10), when all the secret things will be revealed to him (52:5). There will be judgment in which the kings of the earth are chained for their destruction (53:1–5). As for the righteous, they will be vindicated by the coming of the Righteous and Elect One (53:6–7; cf. 38:2). The kings of the earth are thrown into a deep valley (54:1–2) where they are bound with iron fetters (54:3). The angelic guide explains that the prisoners are being prepared for the armies of Azazel to cast them into the abyss for judgment (54:4–6; cf. chap. 18)—a great flood on the earth that will destroy the wicked oppressors (54:7–10). But the Antecedent of Time regrets the destruction and swears not to do so again (55:1–2). For the present, however, God will have his Elect One seen as he (the Elect One) executes judgment upon Azazel and his angelic company (55:3–4). The army of angels gathers the elect in nets of iron and bronze (56:1–4), and the angels turn against the wicked, who will be swallowed up in Sheol (56:5–57:3).

THE THIRD PARABLE (58:1–69:29)

The *third parable* (58:1–69:29) seems to focus on the righteous and their future. It begins (chap. 58) with a poetic blessing on the righteous elect (58:1–2), who shall enjoy innumerable days (58:3, 6), peace (58:4, 6), and light (58:4, 5, 6). Enoch then (59:1–2a, 3) describes a vision of lightning and thunder for blessings or curse, "according to the word of the Lord of Spirits" (59:2b). A great shaking and agitation of the forces of the Most High begins chapter 60 (60:1). The enthroned Antecedent of Time is surrounded by angels and the righteous (60:2), and Enoch himself falls down in fear (60:3). An angel is sent to raise him up (60:4), and Michael tells him that so far God has been patient with humanity, but the day of his judgment is coming (60:5–6). Enoch then has a vision of two monsters (60:7a), the Leviathan and Behemoth (60:7b–8). When he asks an angelic host about them (60:9–10), Enoch is shown many hidden things of the universe (60:11–23) and told that the monsters will turn into food when the Lord's punishment comes on the wicked (60:24–25).

The Son of Man and judgment are the primary subjects of 1 Enoch 61–64. Enoch sees angels lifting long ropes to make measurements, preparing for the resurrection of the righteous in the day of the Elect One (61:1–5). This gives way to a wide acclaim of praise to the Lord from those in heaven (61:6–13). The Lord announces his condemnation of the ruling class (62:1–6; cf. 49:3; Isa. 11:2, 4), whereas the elect will be blessed by the Most High (1 En. 62:7–8). The rulers will beg for mercy in their panic and shame (62:9–10) and will be delivered to angels for punishment (62:11). The righteous and elect shall be vindicated and blessed by the Lord of Spirits (62:12–16; cf. Isa. 52:1). The governors and kings will plead for an opportunity to worship God and confess their sins (1 En. 63:1–5; cf. Isa. 53:1–6; Wis. 5:6–8), but they will not find it (1 En. 63:6–8). Instead they will vanish from before God because of their deeds (63:9–10); they will be filled with shame, be driven out, and experience God's judgment (63:11–12; cf. 62:10, 12; Gen. 3:24). Chapter 64 describes mysterious faces, said to be angels who led people astray (1 En. 64:1–2).[57]

Noah is said to witness the destruction (65:1–2a) and to cry out to Enoch (65:2b), who explains that doom has come on the earth because people have acquired the secrets of angels (65:3–8). Enoch exhorts Noah to flee God's coming judgment on the earth, yet Noah and his righteous seed will be preserved for kingship and great glory (65:9–12; cf. chaps. 83–84; 106–7). Noah then becomes a visionary, seemingly guided by his grandfather Enoch. He sees the angels of punishment who will be responsible for the flood (66:1–2) and is told by God that his blamelessness gained him God's favor and protection

---

57. The connection of chap. 64 to the context is unclear.

(67:1–3; cf. 10:1–3; 84:5). While some angels will aid in the construction of the ark (67:2a), others will be judged with water and eternal fire as a testimony to the rulers of the earth (67:4–13; cf. chap. 52).

Noah is even given instructions about the secrets of Enoch's parables (68:1), primarily concerning the judgment of fallen angels (chaps. 68–69). Michael tells Raphael of the coming judgment (68:2–5), and the names and offenses of the fallen angels are listed (69:1–12; cf. 6:7). This is followed by enigmatic references to an oath, of which a certain Kasb'el is executor (69:13) and before which people will tremble (69:14–15a). The Evil One places this oath in Michael's hand (69:15b). The oath is said to be the means by which the world is created and sustained (69:16–26). Surprisingly, this is followed by a scene of great joy at the revealing of the Son of Man (69:27). Yet those who have led the world astray will be judged and banished from the earth (69:28), after which time nothing corruptible will be found on earth (69:29a). This is because of the appearance of the Son of Man, who seats himself on the throne and before whom all evil disappears (69:29b).

CONCLUSION (70:1–71:17)

In the *conclusion* to the Similitudes (70:1–71:17), Enoch is removed from the earth and placed between two winds, where angels measure a place for him among the elect and righteous (70:1–3). There he sees the first humans and righteous people (70:4) before his final heavenly ascent (71:1–17; cf. chaps. 14–16; 46). His spirit passes into heaven, where he sees angels (71:1) and two rivers of fire (71:2), and Michael shows him heavenly secrets (71:3–4). He is lifted to the heaven of heavens (71:5a) and sees a building of crystals and fire (71:5b), encircled by a ring of fire (71:6) and angelic guards (71:7), with innumerable angels surrounding the house (71:8–9). He falls prostrate before the Antecedent of Time (71:10–11a), to whom he cries out in praise (71:11b–12). Finally, one of God's angelic hosts addresses Enoch as the righteous Son of Man (71:13–14), whose righteousness establishes peace for all who follow his example (71:15–17).

Contribution and Context

THE SIMILITUDES IN THE CONTEXT OF 1 ENOCH

The authors of the Similitudes exhibit clear dependence on the Book of Watchers at numerous points throughout the book. The general structure of the first parable follows that of the opening chapters of the Book of Watchers (cf. chap. 37 and 1:1–3; chap. 38 and 1:3–9; 39:1 and chaps. 6–11; 39:2;

40:1–10 and chap. 14). It is clear from the outset that the authors saw the Similitudes as, in some sense, a continuation of the earlier experience of Enoch. The Similitudes is introduced as Enoch's "second vision" (37:1) following upon the heels of the first (1:2). There the earlier vision is expressly called a parable (1:2); the Similitudes employs the term to describe its own visions (37:5; 38:1; 45:1; 58:1). The term *parable* or *similitude* is best conceived of in a broad context (e.g., Num. 23:7, 18; Ezek. 17:2; 20:49; Mic. 2:4) where the concept of a "figurative discourse" is in view.[58] Enoch's revelatory episodes are parables or similitudes "insofar as they involve a complex set of analogies: between the fate of the righteous and that of the wicked, the holy on earth and the holy ones in heaven, the mysterious order of the cosmos and the lot of the righteous."[59]

The macro-genre of the Similitudes is that of an apocalypse. It contains features common to apocalypses in general but also exhibits affinities with other portions of 1 Enoch. Enoch's experience is one of heavenly ascent and a series of journeys with accompanying reports on these experiences. He is raised to the heavenly throne room (39:2–41:2). As in the Book of Watchers (17:1–18:5; 33–36), Enoch sees an array of cosmic phenomena (41:3–8; 43:1–44:1; 59:1–3; 60:11–22) and places of punishment (52:1–56:4). Throughout he sees things that require explanation by an angelic guide. The subject matter is the heavenly realm and the inevitable judgment on the wicked oppressors of God's righteous people (48:2, 7, 8–10; 50:1–5; 63:1–12). In some instances judgment evokes the narratives of Noah and the flood (54:7–55:2; 60:1–25; 65:1–67:3) in a manner found elsewhere in the Enochic corpus (chaps. 6–11; 106–7). Despite the repeated references to the political interests of the Similitudes found in the "kings" and the "mighty," Collins is careful to point out that one finds little review of historical material in comparison to what one finds in the so-called historical apocalypses.[60]

THE RIGHTEOUS IN THE SIMILITUDES

Much of the outlook of the Similitudes as a whole is concerned with judgment and the fate of the righteous, especially in contrast with that of the wicked. The righteous suffer persecution at the hands of the wicked (1 En. 53:7; 62:11), and their cry for vengeance gains God's attention (47:1–2; cf. 48:7). Their lot is one of blessing, including resurrection (51:1; 62:15) and eternal life on a transformed earth with the Son of Man (45:4–6; 51:4–5;

58. See Knibb, "Enoch, Similitudes of," 586.
59. J. Collins, *Apocalyptic Imagination*, 224; Suter, "Masai in the Similitudes."
60. J. Collins, *Apocalyptic Imagination*, 225; cf. J. Collins, "Jewish Apocalypses," 39.

58:2–6; 62:13–16). Correlating these heavenly blessings with tangible human experience is notoriously difficult.[61] This is due in part to the terminology used. "Righteous" in the Similitudes is often used interchangeably with "chosen" and "holy."[62] Moreover, it has been shown to take on a quasi-technical sense as a title for a religious community.[63] A few aspects, though, can be inferred. The righteous are people who believe in the name of the Lord of Spirits (43:4). They also hate this world and reject its evil works in the name of the Lord (48:6). That they likely experienced persecution is indicated by a reference to their blood (47:2). Nothing is explicit about observance of the law, which may be presumed. More can be inferred about the righteous by contrastive statements made with respect to their wicked opponents.

The wicked are enemies of the righteous—people of power, described as kings of the earth and mighty men (46:4; cf. 38:4; 48:8; 53:5; 54:2; 62:1, 9; 63:1). They commit sin and evil (45:5) and deny the name of the Lord of Spirits (38:2; cf. 41:2; 45:1). All their deeds are oppression (46:7a), and "their power (depends) upon their wealth. And their devotion is to the gods which they have fashioned with their own hands. But they deny the name of the Lord of the Spirits" (46:7b). They have placed their hopes "upon the scepters of [their] empires" (63:7). When judgment comes, these sinners will be punished (38:3–5; 41:2; 45:2; 53:2; 69:27–29) and will burn in the fires of gehenna (48:9; 54:2; 63:3).

The distinction between the righteous and the wicked, then, is their belief in or denial of the Lord of Spirits. The latter misplace trust in their earthly powers, whereas such facets of this world are disdained by the righteous. Cumulatively, this suggests that the Similitudes come from a group oppressed by ruling powers and authorities. Even though the righteous are Jews and the wealthy, idolatrous oppressors are gentiles, the polemic between the righteous and the wicked is not couched in language of Jews and gentiles.[64]

SON OF MAN IN THE SIMILITUDES

Another important aspect of the Similitudes is the extensive material on the "Son of Man" (1 En. 46:3, 4; 48:2; 62:5, 7, 9, 14; 69:29; 70:1; 71:14, 17), also called the "Chosen One" (48:6) or "Elect One" (39:6; 40:5; 45:3, 4, 5;

61. J. Collins, "Heavenly Representative."
62. J. Collins, *Apocalyptic Imagination*, 225.
63. Hill, "Dikaioi."
64. J. Collins, *Apocalyptic Imagination*, 226–27.

49:2, 4; 51:3, 4; 52:6, 9; 53:6; 55:4; 61:5, 8, 10; 62:1) and "Messiah" (48:10; 52:4). His importance is evident when one observes that the Similitudes is unique among Jewish apocalypses in the attention given to a single individual.[65] This figure first appears in 1 Enoch 46:1 with a vivid description: "I saw the One to whom belongs the time before time. And his head was white like wool, and there was with him another individual, whose face was like that of a human being. His countenance was full of grace like that of one among the holy angels."

The language here draws from the Son of Man vision in Daniel (Dan. 7:9–10, 13–14).[66] While the presentation does not presuppose "Son of Man" to be a well-known title,[67] the Enochic introduction of the figure does seem to presuppose some familiarity with its Danielic source. The Enochic Son of Man also resembles figures from the Hebrew Bible such as the Isaianic servant and the Davidic king (e.g., 1 En. 48:1–7 and Isa. 49:1–6; 1 En. 49:1–4 and Isa. 42:1; 49:7; 1 En. 48:8a, 10 and Ps. 2:2; 1 En. 49:3–4; 51:3 and Isa. 11:3–4).[68] Particularly intriguing about the Son of Man in the Similitudes is that his role throughout is inextricably linked to the "righteous," for whom he will be a staff upon which they can lean (1 En. 48:4, 5). He is revealed to the righteous by the wisdom of the Lord of Spirits (48:5). He will dwell with the righteous forever after the day of judgment (62:14). In short, the Son of Man's role is as eschatological revealer and judge, who vindicates the righteous and judges the wicked.[69]

The identification of the Son of Man with Enoch in the Similitudes (70:1; 71:14) has generated some discussion among scholars. Though 1 Enoch 70:1 clearly equates him with Enoch ("his name was lifted up into the presence of that Son of Man and into the presence of the Lord of Spirits"), some dispute this identification on textual grounds. The difficulty lies in the omission of "into the presence of" in one manuscript (Abbadianus 55 [U]). The result reads: "his [Enoch's] name was lifted up, that Son of Man . . . to the presence of the Lord of Spirits." The second text (71:14) is more clear: "You (are) that Son of Man who was born for righteousness."[70] Scholars typically observe that references to "that Son of Man" elsewhere in the Similitudes (41:2; 62:5, 9, 14; 63:11; 69:29 [2x]) give no indication that Enoch himself is

---

65. J. Collins, *Apocalyptic Imagination*, 227.
66. See esp. Casey, "Use of the Term 'Son of Man'"; Casey, *Son of Man*, 99–112; VanderKam, "Righteous One."
67. J. Collins, *Apocalyptic Imagination*, 227.
68. See esp. Nickelsburg, *Resurrection, Immortality, and Eternal Life*, 83–107.
69. J. Collins, *Apocalyptic Imagination*, 229.
70. Nickelsburg and VanderKam, *1 Enoch*, 95.

in view. Collins offers three potential solutions to the tension of identifying Enoch with "that Son of Man." The first potential solution, and perhaps the most straightforward approach, is to identify Enoch as the Son of Man throughout, even though it does not become known to either the reader or him until the end of the book (e.g., Morna Hooker, Maurice Casey, James VanderKam). Several objections could be raised. The first objection is that the preferred reading at 70:1 makes a clear distinction between Enoch and the Son of Man. The second objection is that nowhere else in apocalyptic literature does one find a visionary who fails to recognize himself in his own visions. A third objection, John J. Collins observes, is that the preexistence of the Son of Man elsewhere (1 En. 48:2; cf. 48:6; 62:7) precludes anything attested about Enoch.[71] A possible solution to these three objections may be found in the notion of a "heavenly counterpart,"[72] in which Enoch functions as a prototype for the righteous, analogous to the Son of Man's function as the heavenly counterpart for the righteous community. This has been found in the Prayer of Joseph and 3 Enoch. In the latter—which dates not earlier than the fifth century CE—Metatron is a figure enthroned, called the "Prince of the Divine Presence," and even likened to YHWH himself (3 En. 12:5). He is likewise identified with Enoch (3 En. 4:1–5), though whether such correspondence between Enoch and a heavenly figure is present in the Similitudes is not entirely clear.[73]

Collins's second possible solution regarding the identification of Enoch with the Son of Man is to read "Son of Man" in 71:14 as a common noun ("that man who").[74] In this manner the alleged identifications of Enoch as the "Son of Man" (e.g., 60:10; 71:16) instead single him out "as the human being most closely associated with the heavenly counterpart."[75] Collins's third and final possible solution to the question of Enoch's identification with the "Son of Man" is to regard chapter 71 as a secondary addition to the Similitudes.[76] This understanding, substantiated on literary grounds, recognizes that the redactional addition of chapter 71 introduces an incongruity foreign to the remainder of the Similitudes.

71. J. Collins, *Apocalyptic Imagination*, 232–36.

72. VanderKam, "Righteous One," 182–83.

73. J. Collins, *Apocalyptic Imagination*, 234. It is possible the prior Enochic material (esp. 1 En. 15:1–2) provides "building blocks" for such an evolution that make the explicit claim about Enoch in 1 En. 71 conceivable. See Stuckenbruck, "Building Blocks for Enoch," 325.

74. J. Collins, *Apocalyptic Imagination*, 235, citing Mowinckel, *He That Cometh*, 443, and J. Collins, "Son of Man in First Century Judaism," 451–59.

75. J. Collins, *Apocalyptic Imagination*, 235.

76. J. Collins, *Apocalyptic Imagination*, 235, citing Müller, *Messiahs und Menschensohn*, 54–59; Nickelsburg and VanderKam, *1 Enoch 2*, 330–33.

The solution that regards Enoch's identification with the Son of Man throughout, though only made known later, seems the most probable. Yet what motivated the author of the Similitudes to identify Enoch with the Son of Man remains a mystery. Collins theorizes that it may have been a response to early Christian use of that title for Jesus. Yet as Collins himself observes, chapter 71 is otherwise void of any anti-Christian polemic.[77]

The Son of Man in the Similitudes has been compared with other heavenly beings and messianic figures, such as the messiah (4 Ezra 11–13), Melchizedek (11QMelch), and the Son of God (4Q246). In 4 Ezra the Danielic fourth beast is recast as the Roman Empire (4 Ezra 12:11), and the Son of Man figure is hidden in the presence of God (4 Ezra 12:32; 13:26; cf. Isa. 49:3; 1 En. 48:6; 62:7). For this author, writing after the destruction of the temple in Jerusalem in 70 CE, the Son of Man is the Davidic messiah (4 Ezra 12:31–32) who executes judgment on the enemies of God's people with fire (4 Ezra 13:3–4; cf. Dan. 7:13; Pss. Sol. 17:35; 1 En. 51:3).

The title also gains prominence in early Christianity, where Jesus is identified as "Son of Man" (e.g., Mark 2:10, 28; 8:31, 38; 9:9, 12, 31; 10:33, 45; 13:26; 14:21, 41, 62; and parr.).[78] Aside from its four occurrences outside the Gospels (Acts 7:56; Heb. 2:6–8; Rev. 1:13; 14:14), the term is always attributed to Jesus in reference to himself. It seems likely that the Markan use of the title derives from Jesus's own usage, itself influenced by Daniel 7, independent of Jewish texts of the Second Temple period, including the Similitudes of Enoch.[79] The titular ascription is best seen as an appropriation of Daniel 7 with respect to Jesus as the Son of Man coming on the clouds of heaven rather than influence from the Similitudes.[80] Some point of similarity is found in the enthronement of the Son of Man (Matt. 19:28; 25:31; 1 En. 61–62). It is probably best to conceive of the "Son of Man" beyond the confines of a titular usage but within the more fluid depiction of supernatural beings evident in a number of texts, such as the preeminent place of angelic figures like Michael (in Daniel and the War Scroll [1QM]), Melchizedek (in 11QMelch), and the Angel of Truth (in the Rule of the Community [1QS]). The Son of Man of the Similitudes is likely best ranked among these figures while superior to archangels.

The Son of Man is explicitly identified as the messiah (1 En. 48:10). Depending on the date of this tradition, it may have prepared for subsequent

---

77. J. Collins, *Apocalyptic Imagination*, 236.

78. See most importantly B. E. Reynolds, *Son of Man*.

79. Dunn, "Son of Man in Mark."

80. See Collins, "Son of Man in First Century Judaism," and Slater, "One Like a Son of Man."

developments of the messiah as a supernatural being found in Jewish apocalypses of later dates. In this respect the Similitudes may have a point of commonality with early Christianity in its appropriation of messianic categories
with a figure that is distinctly more than human. The significance with regard
to messianism and law observance is difficult to pinpoint. On the one hand,
there is a palpable absence of explicit law observance as a means of identification with the righteous and procurement of God's eschatological redemption.
On the other hand, there is no trace of polemic against the law.

Purpose

From the above material, several things can be inferred as to the function
of the Similitudes in the community of the righteous. The work seems at
least in part designed to encourage the righteous that their destiny is bound
up with the Son of Man, who dwells in heaven and prepares a place for the
righteous. They in turn are exhorted to trust and believe. The setting of the
work provides no clear historical material to make points of contact with
known events. The application can be as broad as any situation where the
kings and the mighty are oppressing the righteous. Rather than a particular
crisis, the righteous community could be experiencing pressures from known
first-century-CE sources, such as the pagan imperialistic ambitions of Rome
or the impious reign of the Herods. Regardless of its original setting, "the
Similitudes offered to the powerless the assurance of a special destiny guar-
anteed by a heavenly patron. The heavenly world would furnish the respect
and dignity denied them in the present."[81]

The Astronomical Book (1 En. 72–82)

Introduction

The Astronomical Book (1 En. 72–82) describes the role and structure of
heavenly and earthly bodies and addresses the importance of the solar calendar of 364 days. Yet the presentation of this material creates some unique
challenges for the reader. Unlike other apocalypses, including those within the
Enochic corpus, readers are given no account of the process of the revelation
through a dream or heavenly ascent. Instead, the entire work is a report of
the revelation that Enoch receives while guided by Uriel.[82] More difficult still
is the manner in which the revelation is described. George W. E. Nickelsburg

---

81. J. Collins, *Apocalyptic Imagination*, 236–39.
82. J. Collins, *Apocalyptic Imagination*, 76.

explains it well: "With monotonous repetition and with calculations and predictions ad infinitum, the treatise demonstrates the uniformity and order of God's creation as it is evidenced in the movements of the luminaries and the blowing of the winds."[83] The purpose is to advocate for a solar calendar of 364 days, in contrast with competing views.

Language and Manuscripts

First Enoch 72–82 is extant in its entirety only in Ethiopic, which is a translation from a Greek rendering of an original Aramaic.[84] The Astronomical Book is attested in the four fragmentary Aramaic manuscripts (4Q208–211), which contain more detail than the shorter Ethiopic version, including an otherwise unattested ending to chapter 82. The manuscripts are as follows: 4Q208 dates from the late third to the early second century BCE and resembles 1 Enoch 73:1–74:9; 4Q209 dates from around 30 BCE to 70 CE and corresponds roughly to 1 Enoch 76–79, 82; 4Q210 dates from the mid-first century BCE and corresponds to 1 Enoch 76–79; and 4Q211 dates from 50 to 1 BCE and bears no correspondence with the Astronomical Book. These important fragments are listed in terms of correspondence with the Astronomical Book because they differ from the fuller text attested in Ethiopic.

For example, 4Q208 contains details of calendrical material that is much more extensive than the corresponding material in Ethiopic (1 En. 73:1–74:9). Similarly, 4Q209 contains portions of an amalgamated calendar and aspects that overlap with 1 Enoch 76–79, 82. Since 4Q211 has no overlap with the extant Astronomical Book, some have conjectured that it contained an alternative ending, now lost, that belongs at the end of the present chapter 82.[85] This hypothesis regards the mention of "winter" in this fragment as an indication that the alleged longer ending provides discussion of seasons and concluding observations about the stars. Yet the connection between this reading and the present chapter 82 is uncertain. How this and other material relates to the Ethiopic is explored below.

Evidence of a Greek version of 1 Enoch 72–82 is sparse. It seems likely that Greek fragments from the Oxyrhynchus papyri, dating from the fourth century CE, contain material from the Astronomical Book.[86] Second Enoch

---

83. Nickelsburg, *Jewish Literature*, 44.
84. See also Nickelsburg, *1 Enoch 1*, 15–17.
85. Milik, *Books of Enoch*, 19.
86. P.Oxy. XVII 2069, frag. 3, corresponding to 1 En. 77:7–78:1; 78:8. See Chesnutt, "Oxyrhynchus Papyrus."

11–16 may depend on a Greek text of the book, but 2 Enoch survives only in
Slavonic, and its antiquity is disputed (see more below). Some have suggested
Christian authors writing in Greek exhibit awareness of this material.[87]

The ambiguity created by the similarities and differences between the Aramaic (Qumran) and Ethiopic material requires attention to the textual history
of the respective texts. The latter is based on a Greek translation, now almost
completely lost, of something similar to the Aramaic text from Qumran. If
the current Ethiopic version is indeed based on a Greek text derived from
an Aramaic original, then "something drastic happened in the journey from
one to the other."[88] Nevertheless, the Ethiopic and extant Aramaic traditions
have some important points of similarity. They share, for instance, concern
for topics such as the calendar,[89] the gates and their winds,[90] the four quarters
and their names,[91] the heavenly bodies and their rules,[92] the seasons,[93] and the
so-called paternal report in which Enoch addresses his son.[94] At the same time,
their differences are worth noting.[95] First, the Qumran fragments (e.g., 4Q208,
4Q209) contain considerably more detail than the Ethiopic, and it is estimated
that the full text—of which the Qumran evidence is only a small fragment—
was quite extensive. No extant Ethiopic traditions preserve this vastly expanded
material, particularly the lengthy lunar sections found among the Qumran
texts.[96] Second, there are differences in the wording between the accounts on
the twelve gates and their winds (4Q210 1 II, 1–10; 1 En. 76:3–14) and the
four quarters and their names (4Q209 23 3–10; 4Q210 1 II, 14–20; cf. 1 En.
77:1–4). There is an incomplete correspondence between 4Q209 28 and 1 En.
82:9–13, and 1 En. 82:15–20 deals with only two of four seasons (cf. 4Q211).

The Ethiopic is thus an abbreviated version of what was most likely a much
longer work. One can only conjecture why some material was omitted whereas
other tedious elements were preserved. Perhaps for its literary location only
summaries of the astronomical material were necessary, with the details available for consultation elsewhere.[97] But the Ethiopic of 1 Enoch 72–82 contains

87. E.g., Anatolius, bishop of Laodicea (d. ca. 282; cited in Eusebius, *Hist. eccl.* 7.32.6, 19
[cf. 1 En. 72:6, 9, 31, 32]), and Origen (185–254; *Homiliae in Numeros* 28:2 [cf. 1 En. 82]). See
Nickelsburg and VanderKam, *1 Enoch 2*, 348–50.
88. Nickelsburg and VanderKam, *1 Enoch 2*, 351.
89. 4Q208; 4Q209 1–22, 26, 29–41 (?); cf. 4Q210 1 III, 3–9; cf. 1 En. 73:4–8; 74:3–10; 78:6–8.
90. 4Q209 23 1–2; 4Q210 1 II, 1–10; cf. 1 En. 76:3–14.
91. 4Q209 23 3–10; 4Q210 1 II, 14–20; cf. 1 En. 77:1–4.
92. 4Q209 28; cf. 1 En. 82:9–13.
93. Cf. 4Q211; 1 En. 82:15–20.
94. 4Q209 26 6; cf. 1 En. 79:1. Nickelsburg and VanderKam, *1 Enoch 2*, 352.
95. Nickelsburg and VanderKam, *1 Enoch 2*, 352–56.
96. Drawnel, "Moon Computation"; Drawnel, *Aramaic Astronomical Book*.
97. Nickelsburg and VanderKam, *1 Enoch 2*, 357.

no evidence of the synchronistic calendrical material found in 4Q208. The synchronistic calendar in 4Q209 adds material to 1 Enoch 72–82. The result is that the Aramaic Qumran evidence implies a more extensive synchronistic calendar than that found in any Ethiopic manuscript.

Additional challenges unique to the Astronomical Book pertain to its ending. Whereas the entire work is concerned with the intricate details of astronomical matters, chapter 81 contains no cosmological interest at all. Instead it introduces the tablets of heaven (81:1–2), blessings on the righteous (81:4), and Enoch's return home to instruct Methuselah and his progeny (81:5–10). This leads scholars to conclude the entire chapter was likely a later addition that explains how Enoch disseminates his instruction and provides ethical direction for his revelation. Another problem in the ending of the Astronomical Book is found in chapter 82. After Enoch names the four leaders who distinguish the four seasons (82:10–20), only two are described (82:15–20). This leads most scholars to presume some material after verse 20 is lost. But even in its incomplete state the chapter plays an important role: it employs features from testamentary literature in that Enoch offers some parting wisdom to Methuselah, pronouncing blessings on the righteous who adhere to the correct number of days. In this respect chapter 82 bears more correspondence with the remainder of the Astronomical Book than chapter 81.[98]

Provenance

The Astronomical Book is a Jewish work concerned with the importance of the correct, solar calendar. As such it stands in unison with other Jewish works from antiquity (select Qumran texts and the book of Jubilees). It is unclear what further can be said about its provenance, though some speculate its traces of polemical tones suggest an association with traditional intellectual groups of scribes and priests.[99] Its affinities with astronomical concerns from Babylonian literature may suggest an origin in the eastern diaspora (see "Critical Issues" below).

Date

Early work on the Astronomical Book from Qumran has suggested it is among the oldest of the Enochic compositions, perhaps from the late third or early second century BCE. Subsequent analyses of the manuscripts themselves suggest, for example, that 4Q208 was copied somewhat later in the

---

98. See J. Collins, *Apocalyptic Imagination*, 76, 78.
99. Nickelsburg, *Jewish Literature*, 46.

second century BCE.[100] This requires a date of composition prior to that, which is supported by secondary references to the Astronomical Book. In the early- to mid-second century BCE, Pseudo-Eupolemus identifies Enoch as discovering astrology and perhaps relating it on to Methuselah.[101] Possible references to Enoch's astronomical affiliations are found in Sirach (Sir. 44:16; 49:14), circa 200–167 BCE, though the allusions are much too vague to offer any firm determination.[102] Perhaps more definitive is the influence of astronomical material on subsequent Jewish works. For example, the book of Jubilees, which dates from the mid-second century BCE, likely refers to the Astronomical Book in its mention of an astronomical composition by the seventh patriarch (Jub. 4:17, 18, 21).[103] Finally, scholars have recognized material from the Astronomical Book in the Book of Watchers (esp. 1 En. 2–4, 33–36),[104] which places the Astronomical Book at least into the third century BCE and likely among the earliest Enochic material.

Contents

The book is a revelation of the movements of celestial bodies—the sun, moon, and stars. It gives account of the positions of heavenly bodies until the eternal, new creation comes. Throughout these chapters Uriel reveals to Enoch—who then relates to his descendants—the movements of the sun through heavenly gates, six to the east and six to the west, in accordance with the annual calendar. The sun remains in each of these six gates for thirty days in each of its two annual movements through them (1 En. 72:2–24). At the end of each of the four seasons an extra day is added—making thirty-one days—to arrive at a 364-day solar year (72:25–37). (The failure to account for the four extra days by some is later criticized [75:1–3; 82:4–8]). The travels of the moon are likewise described (73:1–8), with its waxing and waning and movements like those of the sun (73:3, 5–8).

Uriel then shows Enoch the rotation of the stars, which, like the sun, measures a year of 364 days (74:1–13), whereas the moon reflects a shorter year of 354 days (74:14–17). These are the fixed positions for the heavenly luminaries (75:1–2), shown to Enoch by Uriel (75:3). Uriel also shows Enoch the openings of the sky through which the rays of the sun shine and give heat

---

100. Jull et al., "Radiocarbon Dating of Scrolls."

101. Pseudo-Eupolemus is a source quoted by Eusebius in his *Preparation for the Gospel.* See Holladay, *Historians,* 157.

102. See Moshe Segal, *Complete Book of Ben Sira,* 307–8.

103. See VanderKam, *Book of Jubilees* (2001), 17–21; VanderKam, "Enoch Traditions," in VanderKam, *From Revelation to Canon,* 313–14.

104. Nickelsburg, *Jewish Literature,* 45.

(75:4, 6–9), which affects the winds and dew (75:5). Then Enoch sees twelve gates and their corresponding winds, three going in each of the four directions of the compass and associated with different weather (76:1–13). These Enoch reveals to his son, Methuselah (76:14). The four directions are named (77:1–4); then Enoch sees seven high mountains (77:5) and seven great rivers (77:6–8), as well as seventy-two large islands in the sea (77:9). Enoch gives the names for the sun (78:1) and moon (78:2), which are compared to each other (78:3–4) prior to a description of the latter's waxing and waning in its cycles and seasons (78:5–17). In chapter 79 Enoch again addresses his son (79:1; cf. 76:14), indicating he has revealed to him the rules of all the stars of heaven, rules that Uriel showed him for every day of every season (79:2–80:1).

Then the narrative turns polemical in tone. It introduces "the sinners," whose days, like the days of winter, are cut short (80:2a; cf. 75:2) and whose labors are futile (80:2b). "He" will appear and withhold rain (80:2c), though the identity of the figure is unclear. At his appearance, crops shall be lacking, and the heavenly luminaries will depart from their normal courses (80:3–6) against "the sinners" (80:7a), who will in turn regard the heavenly luminaries as gods (80:7b). As a result, they will experience judgment (80:8). Uriel then instructs Enoch to read and understand the tablets of heaven, which describe the deeds of humanity for all generations of the world (81:1–2). Enoch utters a blessing to God (81:3) and then pronounces the person blessed who is righteous and does not receive judgment "on that day" (81:4). After this, seven angels bring Enoch home and instruct him to tell Methuselah and all his children that "no one of the flesh can be just before the Lord; for they are merely his own creation" (81:5). Enoch is given one year for the task (81:6). He is told that the righteous will be blessed (81:7, 9a) whereas the "sinners" and "the apostate" will be judged (81:8, 9b). When the angels conclude their instruction, Enoch returns home blessing the Lord (81:10).

In the final chapter Enoch explains to Methuselah (82:1a) that he will write all that was revealed to him concerning these things and exhorts his son to preserve it for generations to come (82:1b–3). Enoch pronounces a blessing on the righteous "in the computation of the days in which the sun goes its course in the sky" (82:4)—whereas others err in their computation of days (82:5)—which is recorded forever as 364 days (82:6). This is the true computation recorded by Enoch as instructed by Uriel concerning the luminaries and the months, festivals, years, and days (82:7–9). Then Enoch names the four leaders who distinguish the four seasons (82:10–20). The book seems to anticipate a description of these seasons, though only two are described (82:15–20), with the remainder likely contained in the lost material thought to follow verse 20.

Critical Issues: Sources for the Astronomical Book

Scholars have observed similarities between the Astronomical Book and cuneiform documents from Babylonian astronomy, which share both general and particular features.[105] These include the sun's yearly movements, the names and numbers of stars as well as their times, and the correspondence of the sun's travels with other celestial and meteorological activities. From this, several conclusions may be inferred.[106] First, much of the background for the astronomy of the Astronomical Book is attested in the Babylonian material. Second, the 360-day calendar opposed in the Astronomical Book (1 En. 75:1–2; 82:4–6) is known in Mesopotamia. Third, the points of correspondence between the Astronomical Book and the Babylonian literature may suggest an origin in the eastern diaspora. Despite these similarities, the numerous places in which stars are present in the Astronomical Book have no relation to astronomy in other ancient Near Eastern contexts[107] and may stand in opposition to it.[108]

The Astronomical Book also makes use of texts from the Hebrew Bible.[109] It identifies the two great luminaries, the sun and the moon (1 En. 78:3), of Genesis 1:16, where they are identified only as the greater and lesser lights. In the Enochic material the sun is the "great luminary" (72:4, 35, 36) and the moon the "smaller luminary" (73:1). Like the Genesis text, the Astronomical Book plays a pivotal role for the demarcation of seasons, days, and years (75:2–3; 82:7–10). The Astronomical Book also draws from Genesis the ruling function of the luminaries (Gen. 1:16, 19; 1 En. 72:1; 75:3; 79:2; 82:10, 15–20). The luminaries also play a role of separation (Gen. 1:14, 18; 1 En. 82:4, 11–14). In addition to Genesis, the Astronomical Book looks to Isaiah 30:26 to explain how the moon can be one of the great luminaries while also being small. The Enochic material indicates that the greater and lesser status pertains to brightness (1 En. 72:37; cf. 78:3–4).

Contribution and Context

THE ASTRONOMICAL BOOK IN THE CONTEXT OF 1 ENOCH

The Astronomical Book contains points of correspondence with other material from 1 Enoch. Aramaic material from Qumran suggests the Astronomical Book stands alongside the Book of Watchers (1 En. 1–36) as one of the

---

105. See Ben-Dov, *Head of All Years*.
106. Nickelsburg and VanderKam, *1 Enoch 2*, 373–83.
107. Neugebauer, *Ethiopic Astronomy*, 216.
108. Nickelsburg and VanderKam, *1 Enoch 2*, 388–89.
109. See VanderKam, "Scripture in the Astronomical Book."

earliest Enochic compositions. It seems likely, especially from 1 Enoch 76–77, that the former is older and bore some influence on the latter.[110] This may be seen with matters such as aspects of mythical geography (chap. 77 in chaps. 17–19),[111] the placement of the heavenly gates, the role of Uriel, and Enoch's praise to God (chaps. 72–82; 33–36).[112] The Astronomical Book contains some similarities as well as differences with respect to the Similitudes of Enoch (chaps. 37–71).[113] On the one hand, the works have some common features, such as Enoch's presence with angelic figures and the inclusion of items such as winds, mists, the sun, and the moon. On the other hand, the secrets and storehouses in the Similitudes (41:3–8) are absent in the Astronomical Book, which employs instead the terminology of gates. The lightning, thunder, and clouds so important in the Similitudes (e.g., chap. 41) are absent in the Astronomical Book. And the matters of stars, calendrical issues, mountains, and so on in the Astronomical Book are absent from the Similitudes (again, chap. 41). These and numerous other points of comparison suggest that these two works share concern for the same subject matter at several points. Shared features between the Astronomical Book and other portions of 1 Enoch are sparse. The Epistle of Enoch (chaps. 91–108) references the respective luminaries (e.g., 100:10–13; 101:2; 102:2; 104:2) and the one (i.e., Enoch) who looks into such things (93:11–14) but is more concerned with judgment. The Book of Dreams (chaps. 83–90) contains no astronomical material and only loosely relates to the Astronomical Book in its eschatological outlook after a season of judgment. The fragmentary material from the Book of Giants is concerned only with angelic matters.[114]

COSMOLOGY AND ESCHATOLOGY IN THE ASTRONOMICAL BOOK

The central concern of the Astronomical Book is cosmology—the order of God's created celestial bodies depicted in their movements and corresponding calendrical concerns. God's angels remain active agents in the execution of these movements and therefore appropriate guides for Enoch's vision. Enoch's conception of the heavenly realms is a large "hemispherical vault stretched over the flat disk of the earth and set upon its outer edge."[115] Where the heavenly realm intersects with the earth, Enoch describes a series of twelve gates through which the sun and moon travel in their monthly and

---

110. Nickelsburg and VanderKam, *1 Enoch 2*, 390.
111. Bautch, *Geography of 1 Enoch 17–19*, 201–5.
112. Nickelsburg and VanderKam, *1 Enoch 2*, 391–94.
113. VanderKam, "Book of Parables."
114. Nickelsburg and VanderKam, *1 Enoch 2*, 394.
115. Nickelsburg, *Jewish Literature*, 44.

annual cycles. There are also scores of other openings through which the stars come and go.

These cosmological laws are unchanging and remain the same from creation until the establishment of a new creation (see, e.g., 72:1). The point of the steadfastness of creation observing the laws of the Creator stands in sharp contrast to human waywardness in the Book of Watchers (e.g., 2:1–5:4). This contrast is absent in the Astronomical Book. Instead, the constancy of the travels of the sun, moon, and stars seems to underscore the endurance of the 364-day solar calendar. As long as these patterns endure, the calendar they establish endures. Changes in God's created order are couched in the author's eschatological framework, some of which are reflective of similar anticipations in the Hebrew Bible. The prophets foresee that the heavens will vanish and the earth will wear out (Isa. 51:6). The sun and moon will no longer give their light (Isa. 13:10; Ezek. 32:7–8; Joel 2:10) but will be replaced by the radiance of the Lord (Isa. 60:19). The Astronomical Book sees the pattern of the heavenly luminaries retained until the establishment of a "new creation" (1 En. 72:1; cf. Isa. 65:17; 66:22). Also in the eschatological future, Enoch foresees a time when the years become shorter, the leaders of stars go astray, people take the stars for gods, evil overtakes them, and punishment destroys them (1 En. 80:2–8). The constancy of God's created order is thereby disrupted.

Purpose

The function of the Astronomical Book lies in its advocacy for a 364-day calendar (1 En. 72:32). It is on this matter that its polemical tone is introduced. Typically the importance of calendrical issues lies in the correct days for observing religious festivals.[116] Yet the Astronomical Book does not criticize the observance of festivals according to other calendars (cf. 82:7); rather, its polemic is against the 360-day calendar for its failure to account for the additional four days (e.g., 75:1–2; 82:4–6).[117] The importance of a 364-day calendar (72:32) in the Astronomical Book is shared with and likely influences the book of Jubilees and the Qumran scrolls.[118] Calendrical material from Qumran evidences the two calendrical systems likely influenced by the Astronomical Book: the solar year of 364 days and lunar year of 354 days (see esp. 4Q317–330). The author of the book of Jubilees also knew and drew on astronomical material associated with Enoch.[119] Jubilees shares the Astronomical Book's specific calendrical

---

116. See Beckwith, "Earliest Enoch Literature."
117. So also Nickelsburg and VanderKam, *1 Enoch 2*, 367.
118. See Nickelsburg, *Jewish Literature*, 46.
119. Nickelsburg and VanderKam, *1 Enoch 2*, 398–403.

concerns and explicitly references Enoch writing a book concerning heavenly signs that pertain to the cycles of months and seasons and accounting for the months and days of the year (e.g., Jub. 4:17–19).

A related polemic occurs against "sinners" (1 En. 80:2; cf. 75:2), who will worship the heavenly luminaries as gods (80:7). Such atrocities, said to be done by the wicked Manasseh (2 Kings 21:3; cf. 2 Kings 23:4–12), were strictly forbidden (Deut. 4:19–20) and punishable by death (Deut. 17:3–5; cf. Job 31:26–28; Zeph. 1:5; Jer. 19:13; Ezek. 8:16). Likewise the sinners and the "apostate" in the Astronomical Book will experience God's judgment (1 En. 80:2; 81:8). Employing features of testamentary literature, the Astronomical Book depicts Enoch instructing Methuselah (82:1) with what becomes the main purpose of the work as a whole: to exhort its audience to avoid the lot of sinners who err in their computation of days (82:4b–5) and to take heart at the anticipated celebration of the righteous (81:7).

The Book of Dreams: Dream Vision (1 En. 83–84)

Introduction

The Book of Dreams (1 En. 83–90) contains two visions. The first, called the Dream Vision (chaps. 83–84), contains an account of the coming flood, followed by a prayer. The second, called the Animal Apocalypse (chaps. 85–90), offers an allegorical recounting of human history, using animals to represent people and people to represent angels. Israel is symbolized by sheep, and God himself is the Lord of the sheep. Both visions are experienced by Enoch, who relates them to Methuselah (83:1). Both occur in the house of Enoch's grandfather, Mahalalel, and pertain to intercession either on behalf of all humanity (chaps. 83–84) or for Israel (chaps. 85–90). They are distinguished by the fact that the first is received while Enoch was learning to write (83:2a) and the second prior to his marriage to Methuselah's mother (83:2c). These two components of the Dream Vision are typically preserved together in manuscript evidence, and therefore presented together here.

Language and Manuscripts

It is widely recognized that the discovery of Aramaic material from Qumran affirms the origin of the Dream Vision in that language, though Hebrew sources are likely.[120] Among the Aramaic manuscripts from Qumran, those

120. Nickelsburg, *1 Enoch 1*, 9.

preserving portions of the Dream Vision are as follows: 4QEn^c (4Q204) contains 1 Enoch 89 and dates from the last third of the first century BCE; 4QEn^d (4Q205) contains 1 Enoch 89 and seems to be a contemporary copy of 4QEn^c; 4QEn^e (4Q206) contains 1 Enoch 88–89 and dates from the first half of the first century BCE; and 4QEn^f (4Q207) contains fragments from 1 Enoch 86:1–3 and dates from 150–125 BCE.[121]

Among the Greek witnesses, Oxyrhynchus Papyrus 2069 (frags. 3, 1), dating from the fourth century CE, contains portions of 1 Enoch 85:10–86:2; 87:1–3.[122] Written into the margins of an eleventh-century manuscript (Codex Vaticanus Gr. 1809) is a text identified as "an excerpt from the book of Enoch," which contains the Greek text of 1 Enoch 89:42–49. As is the case with the Book of Watchers, the Dream Vision is most fully attested in Ethiopic (Ge'ez), translated from the Greek sometime between the fourth and sixth centuries.

The Dream Vision (1 En. 83–84) is unique in the corpus of 1 Enoch for several reasons. First, it is composed almost entirely of prior material from elsewhere within 1 Enoch. Second, it makes no clear reference to any historical event or person, which makes rendering its date of composition, setting, and relation to the Animal Apocalypse possible only by inference (chaps. 85–90). At the same time, it introduces unique material in the narrative, such as Enoch's grandfather, Mahalalel. He is an otherwise unknown figure and may have been placed in the account to emphasize the youth of Enoch, perhaps to imply this is his first revelation. Finally, through chapter 84 and in portions of 83 (vv. 3a, 5, 6a, 7a, 8a) the Dream Vision exhibits a parallelism that suggests a poetic literary style.[123] Though brief and absent of any identifiable historical referent, the Dream Vision presents a vision of the utter destruction of the world and its complete dependence on God.[124]

Contents

The Dream Vision, sometimes called the Vision of the Flood (1 En. 83:3–84:5), is described as a "terrible vision" (83:2d).[125] In it, Enoch sees heaven thrown down upon the earth, and the earth, hills, and trees swallowed up (83:3–4). Enoch's grandfather, Mahalalel, explains that Enoch has seen the sins of the world (83:5–7) and exhorts him to pray for a remnant to remain

121. Milik, *Books of Enoch*, 5, 178–79, 217, 225.

122. Milik, "Fragments grecs du livre d'Hénoch"; presented in Hunt, "2069. Apocalyptic Fragment," 6–8.

123. Nickelsburg, *1 Enoch 1*, 347–48.

124. J. Collins, *Apocalyptic Imagination*, 85–86.

125. Translations, headings, and divisions throughout are taken from Nickelsburg and VanderKam, *1 Enoch*, unless otherwise indicated.

in light of the impending destruction from heaven (83:8–9). Enoch writes his prayers for generations to come (83:10–11) and recounts them to God (84:1–3). He warns of God's coming judgment (84:4) and implores God to sustain a generation to succeed him (84:5–6).

Contribution and Context

THE DREAM VISION IN THE CONTEXT OF 1 ENOCH

Most of the Dream Vision is adapted from earlier material found elsewhere in 1 Enoch.[126] Its account of the sun, moon, and stars (1 En. 83:11) is drawn from the Astronomical Book (chaps. 72–82). The judgment on fallen angels at the day of judgment (84:4) comes from the Book of Watchers (chaps. 1–36). As is the case in the Book of Watchers (esp. 13:4–7) and the Animal Apocalypse (89:57; 90:3), the person of Enoch functions not only as the visionary but also as the intercessor (83:8, 10; 84:1–6). Furthermore, his prayer (84:1–6) recalls the angelic prayer in the Book of Watchers (e.g., 1 En. 9), and his dream resembles those found in that earlier writing (83:3–4 [cf. 1:6–7]; 83:11 [cf. 2:1–2]).

FLOOD AND FINAL JUDGMENT IN THE DREAM VISION

The Dream Vision depicts the flood as the final judgment, which likely draws from the Book of Watchers (cf. 1 En. 6–11, esp. 10:1–2). In this respect, the typology resembles the narratives of Noah found in other places in the Enochic corpus (chaps. 65–67; 106–7). Despite the coming judgment, Enoch prays for a remnant to be preserved (83:8; 84:5; cf. 10:16–17), recalling the similar assurance Noah receives in Genesis (Gen. 8:20–9:15). Yet unlike the Book of Watchers, all humanity is guilty of the sin that occasions this judgment (as in Genesis). The deliverance expected by the remnant is not from the consequences of fallen angels and the ensuing violence (as in 1 En. 6–11) but from a judgment of a more universal nature. Some have observed a natural progression in this regard: while the fallen angels introduce sin through the revelation of forbidden secrets (chaps. 6–11), humanity nonetheless acts on such knowledge and is punished accordingly (10:7; cf. 65:6; 84:4; 106:13–18).[127]

Purpose

While the Dream Vision draws from prior material within the Enochic tradition, it has modified that material in such a way as to emphasize that

126. Nickelsburg, *1 Enoch 1*, 346.
127. Nickelsburg, *1 Enoch 1*, 346–47.

God has long stood ready to bring judgment through the waters of the flood. In this respect, its function is to bring earlier material together to provide a companion of sorts to the Animal Apocalypse.[128] It may also serve to remind its audience that Enoch's prayers for the preservation of a righteous remnant are indeed heard, evidence for which is found in the harmony of the celestial bodies (cf. 1 En. 83:11).

The Book of Dreams: Animal Apocalypse (1 En. 85–90)

Introduction

As in the Dream Vision (1 En. 83–84), the Animal Apocalypse is recounted to Methuselah and pertains to the vision in which Enoch sees "all the deeds of humanity" (90:41). The narrative is a symbolic depiction of events from Adam into the Hellenistic time and of the ensuing final judgment and the establishment of a newly created order.[129] In this allegory the fallen Watchers are fallen stars, humans are depicted as various kinds of animals, and angels are white men.

Provenance

The highly symbolic nature of the Animal Apocalypse makes it difficult, if not impossible, to gain a clear indication of its origin. The imagery of the Israelite lambs who see, in contrast to others who are deaf and blind (1 En. 90:6–7), is an important starting point. The opening of eyes and seeing connote the reception of a revelation from God. The lambs' crying out to other sheep is seemingly an appeal to a religious renewal to overturn the blindness (apostasy) of prior generations (esp. Manasseh; 89:54, 74). That the other sheep are deaf and blind to the prophetic exhortation of the younger sheep suggests the rejection of their message (cf. 89:17–19, 30–34, 41, 51–53). The specific nature of their exhortation is not expressed. There is no clear indication from the text that the recipients of the revelation receive a "new Torah" or even "right insight about the old Torah."[130] Yet it seems likely that the prophetic concern of the younger Israelites pertains to the pollution of the temple cult (89:73–74).

Some scholars observe a militant component or ideology in the author's perspective, including the killing of idolaters (89:35) and the wars of the kings

128. Nickelsburg, 1 Enoch 1, 347.
129. Nickelsburg, 1 Enoch 1, 354.
130. Nickelsburg, 1 Enoch 1, 361.

David and Saul (89:42–43, 49). Militant components are present within what is presumably the author's own community, among which horns arise (90:9) and a sword is given to the sheep (90:19). This may be taken as God's intervention in the warfare of Judas Maccabaeus.[131] From the internal information, a profile of the author's community may be proposed: they are a younger generation within the elders of Israel, perhaps learned scribes. While concern for the sanctuary and its cult may not imply priestly interests, attention to Moses, Aaron, and the Levites may connote Levitical associations.[132] There is concern about oppression from gentiles (90:8), but there is also an anticipation that all the animals on earth (gentiles) will worship in a new temple (90:30; cf. Dan. 7:14, 27).

Date

Dating the Animal Apocalypse is facilitated by the generally recognized reference to the Maccabean conflicts (1 En. 90:9b–16). The anticipation of God's dramatic intervention in this affair (90:17–19) would suggest a date between 164 BCE (the battle of Beth-zur; 1 Macc. 4:29–34) and 160 BCE (Judas Maccabaeus's death; 1 Macc. 9:11–18).[133]

Contents

The narrative can be divided into three segments of redemptive history: from creation to the flood (1 En. 85:3–89:8), from the flood to the final judgment (89:9–90:27), and a final renewal into a new beginning (90:28–42).[134]

FROM CREATION TO THE FLOOD (85:3–89:8)

It begins with a symbolic depiction of Adam and Eve and their children (85:3–10; cf. Gen. 2–5). In this vision Enoch sees a white bull (Adam), followed by a young heifer (Eve), then two bull calves, one black and the other red (Cain and Abel) (85:3). The black calf strikes the red (85:4), grows, and has offspring like himself (85:5). The female grieves the absence of the red calf (85:6–7) and bears another white bull (Seth) and many more black bulls

131. Nickelsburg, *1 Enoch 1*, 362. Alternatively, Daniel Assefa suggests the ram (90:9b–12, 16) is not Judas Maccabaeus but a spiritual leader of a group behind the Animal Apocalypse. For this reading, he sees 90:13–15 as a later interpolation inserted to support the Maccabean revolt. Assefa, *L'Apocalypse des animaux (1 Hen 85–90)*, 332.

132. Nickelsburg, *1 Enoch 1*, 362.

133. So also J. Collins, *Apocalyptic Imagination*, 85; Nickelsburg, *1 Enoch 1*, 361; Tiller, *Commentary*, 61–82.

134. Nickelsburg, *1 Enoch 1*, 354.

and cows (85:8). That white bull grows and bears other white cattle like himself (85:9–10).

The next segment (86:1–88:3) provides a symbolic account of the fall of the Watchers (cf. Gen. 6:1–4; 1 En. 6–11), their begetting children with human women, and the ensuing violence. Enoch sees a star fall from heaven (Azazel; cf. 10:4), which then rises and grazes among the cattle (86:1). He sees large black cattle, which exchange their pastures and calves and then moan (86:2). Enoch then sees many stars descend and become bulls in the midst of the calves; they pasture with them (86:3) and sire elephants, camels, and asses (giants) (86:4). These bring violence and fear on the bulls (86:5–6), drawing the attention of heaven (87:1). Seven figures like white men (angels) come (87:2), three of which instruct Enoch to see what happens to the violent animals, the stars, and the cattle (87:3–4). One of the white men seizes the first fallen star, binds it, and casts it into the abyss (88:1). The elephants, camels, and asses are armed with a sword, with which they strike one another (88:2). Another one of the white men seizes all the great stars (fallen angels), binds them, and casts them into the abyss as well (88:3).

The account of Noah and the flood is the subject of the next symbolic account (89:1–8). One of the white men goes to a white bull (Noah) and teaches a mystery: he is born a bull but becomes a man (89:1a). He builds a vessel for himself and three other bulls (89:1b). Enoch then sees the great deluge overtaking the earth (89:2–5). The vessel floats safely while the bulls, elephants, camels, and asses perish (89:6), after which the waters recede, the vessel comes to rest, and darkness gives way to light (89:7–8).

From the Flood to the Final Judgment (89:9–90:27)

The next major section begins (89:9–27) with the white bull (Noah) departing the vessel along with the three other bulls—one white (Shem), one red (Ham), and one black (Japheth) (89:9; cf. the depiction of Adam and his sons in 85:3, 8). These beget a variety of (unclean) wild beasts. From the one white bull (Shem) come other white bulls (Abraham and Isaac). One of these sires a black wild boar (Esau) and a white sheep (Jacob), who then begets twelve sheep (the twelve tribes of Israel) (89:10–12). The movement from bulls to sheep marks a transition from the time of the patriarchs to Israel's history.[135] These twelve sheep (the sons of Jacob) hand over one of their own (Joseph) to wild asses (Ishmaelites), who in turn hand him over to wolves (Egyptians) (89:13). That sheep (Joseph) becomes a ram and cares for the other eleven among the wolves (89:14).

135. J. Collins, *Apocalyptic Imagination*, 86.

Eventually the wolves begin to fear the sheep and oppress them, and the sheep's cry reaches the Lord (89:15–16). The Lord summons one of the sheep (Moses) to testify against the wolves on behalf of the sheep (89:17). That sheep, accompanied by another sheep (Aaron), speaks to the wolves on behalf of the sheep (89:18). The wolves deal still more harshly with them despite the Lord striking the wolves (89:19–20). The sheep depart and the wolves pursue them to a swamp of water (89:21–23), which splits before the sheep and devours the wolves (89:24–27). The sheep enter a desert, where the Lord cares for them (89:28). The lead sheep (Moses) goes up a high rock, and the Lord of the sheep appears (89:29–31), yet the rest of the sheep are blinded and go astray (89:32). The Lord's anger burns against them, but the lead sheep returns all the straying flock to their fold (89:33–35). The lead sheep builds a house for the Lord (89:36) and leads them to a river before all the large sheep fall asleep (89:36–38).

The description continues with the succession of Moses to the building of the temple (89:39–50). Two sheep (Joshua and Caleb) arise to lead the flock to a pleasant land (89:39–41). There the flock is devoured by wild animals until the Lord raises up a ram (King Saul) from among the sheep to lead them (89:42) and defeat those who harm the flock (89:43), until he himself is led astray (89:44). The Lord appoints another sheep to be the ram and rule the flock, but the first ram pursues the second ram until the former falls before the dogs (89:45–47). The second ram (David) leads the sheep (89:48), who have become numerous and feared among animals (89:49). The ram sires other sheep and then falls asleep. One of those sheep becomes a ram (Solomon) and rules the sheep (89:48b) and builds a house (the temple) for the Lord of the sheep (89:50).

The sheep abandon the house of the Lord and go astray, so they fall into the hands of wild beasts (89:51–58; around the time of Manasseh). The Lord then appoints seventy shepherds (guardian angels)[136] to pasture the sheep and keep a record of their deeds (89:59–64; cf. 90:5; Deut. 32; Dan. 10; Jer. 25), each in their own period of time (roughly the Babylonian, Persian, Ptolemaic, and Seleucid rules).[137] The first account of the disobedient shepherds (89:65–68a) runs from Manasseh (ca. 671/661 BCE) to the destruction of Jerusalem by Nebuchadnezzar and exile to Babylon (587/577 BCE).[138] These shepherds abandon the sheep to lions (89:65), who, along with leopards and boars, devour and destroy them (89:66–67; cf. 2 Kings 25:1–20; 2 Chron. 36:17–20). This is followed by the writing of a report of these events (1 En. 89:68b–72a).

136. So *APOT* 2:255; cf. Tiller, *Commentary*, 325.
137. J. Collins, *Apocalyptic Imagination*, 87.
138. The dates are suggested by Nickelsburg, *1 Enoch 1*, 393.

The second period of the shepherds' activities (89:72b–90:1) covers the
return from exile and the rebuilding of the temple to the time of Alexander
the Great. Led by three sheep (Zerubbabel, Jeshua [Ezra 5:2; 1 Esd. 6:2], and
likely Sheshbazzar [Ezra 1:8–10; 5:14–16; 1 Esd. 2:12–15; 6:18–20]), the exiles
return and commence rebuilding the temple (1 En. 89:72b). The temple is
rebuilt, but its sacrifices are polluted (89:73). Both the sheep and their shepherds are blind (89:74a; cf. Mal. 1:7–8, 12; CD-A IV, 17–V, 19), and the sheep
are scattered (1 En. 89:75; cf. Ezek. 34:12). The one writing the book shows
his account of the deeds of the shepherds to the Lord, but to no avail (1 En.
89:76–77; 90:1). In the third period (90:2–5) the conquests of the Macedonians
are recounted, though Alexander the Great is not explicitly identified. The
birds of heaven come, led by eagles (Macedonians), and devour and blind the
sheep (90:2). The ensuing violence (90:3–5) reflects the wars of the Diadochi
(323–301 BCE), followers of Alexander fighting with one another to succeed
him after his premature death.[139]

The fourth period then commences (90:6–19). This is the era of Seleucid
rule (after 198 BCE). The lambs are born (a new generation of Israelites) and
begin to see Israel's errors and cry out to their elders, who remain deaf and
blind (90:6–7; cf. Jub. 23:16–20). Ravens (gentile rulers) arrive and devour the
lambs (1 En. 90:8),[140] but a "great horn" (Judas Maccabaeus) arises (90:9–11;
cf. Dan. 11:14; 1 Macc. 2:42–48; 7:13; 2 Macc. 14:6) and engages in battle
(1 En. 90:12–16; cf. 2 Macc. 11:6–12). Next, the vision leaves the historical
narrative for a vision of God's anticipated future intervention with a large
staff to strike the enemies of the sheep (1 En. 90:17–18); the sheep are armed
with a large sword to do the same (90:19). This is followed by a vision of
judgment (90:20–27) in which the Lord of the sheep summons the white men
to bring various figures before him for judgment. Judgment begins with the
first fallen star (fallen angels) (90:21b–24), then the disobedient shepherds
(90:25), and finally the blinded sheep (apostate Jews) (90:26–27; cf. 10:14).

A FINAL RENEWAL INTO A NEW BEGINNING (90:28–42)

The final vision begins with the "old house" (Jerusalem) being folded up
and the Lord bringing a new house (Jerusalem),[141] where all the sheep are
present (90:28–29; cf. 2 Bar. 4:2–7). All the sheep (Israel) as well as all the

139. Nickelsburg, *1 Enoch 1*, 394, 396.
140. The killing of "one of these lambs" (90:9) is often taken as a reference to the murder
of the high priest Onias III (J. Collins, *Apocalyptic Imagination*, 87–88; see 2 Macc. 4:33–35
and Dan. 9:26; cf. Tiller, *Commentary*, 349).
141. The temple is identified as a "tower" (1 En. 89:50, 54, 56, 66, 67, 73).

animals on earth (gentiles) worship there (1 En. 90:30; cf. Dan. 7:14, 27). Enoch is taken before the sheep and finds that all those dispersed were gathered at the house (1 En. 90:31–33). The sword given to the sheep (90:19) is now sealed up (90:34). Warfare is no longer necessary.[142] All whose eyes are open see good things (90:35), and Enoch sees the vastness of the temple (90:36). Then a white bull—whose identity is debated but is likely messianic—arrives on the scene (90:37a) and is feared by all the other animals (gentiles) (90:37b). Strikingly, these animals change to become white bulls (90:38). The sheep are restored to their (new) house, and enmity with other animals is ended.

The entire Animal Apocalypse concludes with a summary of the vision and Enoch's response to it (90:39–42). Enoch awakens and blesses the Lord (90:39–40) but then weeps over the deeds of humanity and the judgment it incurs (90:41–42).

Critical Issues: The Sources of the Animal Apocalypse

Naturally the Animal Apocalypse, in its concern for the history of the Israelites, draws considerably from the Hebrew Bible, especially Genesis. Some estimate that fully one-sixth of 1 Enoch 85:3–89:8 corresponds to Genesis 1:1–8:7, whereas the remainder of Genesis is treated in only five verses (1 En. 89:9–14). The nature of sin and judgment in the Animal Apocalypse is modified from the Genesis narrative to shift emphasis from the origins and activities of humanity to God's judgment itself. Divine judgment is estimated to comprise some 29 percent of the Genesis account (Gen. 1–8) but swells to 54 percent in the Animal Apocalypse (esp. 1 En. 85:3–89:8). This is seen specifically in its account of the flood (86:1–89:1), which draws from the Genesis narrative supplemented by that of 1 Enoch 6–11. The Animal Apocalypse differs from the Genesis narrative in identifying Cain's murder of his brother, Abel, as the first sin. Furthermore, the primary source of evil in the first place is not human behavior but the fall of the heavenly Watchers. It is *after* their initial fall that the line of the white bull is corrupted and the flood ensues. The widespread violence and ensuing judgment likewise follow the stars intermingling with the cows.[143]

In the author's recounting of the biblical narrative, the cycle of sin, punishment, repentance, and restoration rings of Deuteronomic conceptions, dividing history into three distinct eras. In addition to narrative material, one finds echoes of prophetic texts from the Hebrew Bible in the Animal Apocalypse.

---

142. Nickelsburg, *1 Enoch 1*, 406.
143. See Nickelsburg, *1 Enoch 1*, 354.

Nickelsburg observes as the most obvious the metaphorical depiction of Israel as a victimized flock (e.g., Ezek. 34, 37; Zech. 11). Points of similarity are found with Daniel 9, where, as in the Animal Apocalypse, the seventy years of Jeremiah 25 are interpreted as seventy weeks of years, or 490 years. The new Jerusalem (1 En. 90:28–38) of Isaianic tradition (Isa. 60, 65–66) resembles other material (cf. 1 En. 10; Jub. 23; Dan. 12:1–3).[144]

The Animal Apocalypse shows affinities with and makes use of other Enochic material, particularly the Book of Watchers. In the author's demarcation of time, key events that are *future* in the Book of Watchers (e.g., 1 En. 6–11) are presented as *past* events in the Animal Apocalypse (the fall of the Watchers, the siring of giants, the binding of angels, the destruction of giants, and the flood). Other events that are past in the Book of Watchers are moved to the eschatological future in the Animal Apocalypse (89:76; 90:3, 12–14, 20–38), such as people's cry for help (8:4), intercession by angels (9:1–11), and the new earth (10:7–11:2).[145] Also drawn from the Book of Watchers is Enoch's travel to the heavenly temple (87:3–4; cf. chaps. 12–16) along with archangels (chap. 81; cf. chaps. 17–36).

Though clearly dependent on the Hebrew Bible, the author of the Animal Apocalypse is also familiar with traditional expositions of those narratives, such as Cain's demonic affiliation (85:3), Eve's grief over Abel's death (85:4, 6), and the expansive flood story (86:1–89:1), among others.[146] The Animal Apocalypse may have drawn on other sources (e.g., Jub. 4:23–24; T. Ab. 11:3–9), which, like the Animal Apocalypse (e.g., 1 En. 87:3–4; 90:31), depict Enoch's designation as the heavenly scribe charged with recording human deeds for final judgment.

Contribution and Context

The Animal Apocalypse in the Context of 1 Enoch

Perhaps the closest conceptual parallels to the Animal Apocalypse within the Enochic corpus are found in the Apocalypse of Weeks (93:1–10; 91:11–17). Both works narrate God's history with humanity from creation to the new creation. Both divide history into distinct periods, though the Animal Apocalypse is more concerned with the later stages of that history than is the Apocalypse of Weeks. Other points of similarity have been noted,[147] including an indication of apostasy beginning during the time of Manasseh

---

144. Nickelsburg, *1 Enoch 1*, 359.
145. Nickelsburg, *1 Enoch 1*, 355.
146. Nickelsburg, *1 Enoch 1*, 359.
147. Nickelsburg, *1 Enoch 1*, 359.

and continuing into the Hellenistic era. This apostasy is checked only when a select few Israelites experience a religious awakening of sorts, and it occasions the final judgment.

Genre, Plot, and Characterization in the Animal Apocalypse

Though the Animal Apocalypse—as its name suggests—belongs decidedly to the genre of apocalypse, it bears some unique features within that genre that raise distinct interests. Most scholars find the Animal Apocalypse shares features with the visions of Daniel, such as its dream visions (Dan. 2:1; 7:1–2, 7, 13; 8:1–2, 17–18), its recounting a sequence of historical events leading to the end of days (2:32–45; 7:1–27; 8:3–26; 11:2–12:4), its use of animals to symbolize people or nations (Dan. 7, 8), and its relation of these events to events in heaven (7:9–10, 13–14; 8:10–12; 10:20–21). But there are also some important differences between them. First, whereas the Danielic visions require an interpreter (Daniel himself in chap. 2; angels in chaps. 7 and 8; cf. Dan. 10–12), Enoch seems to understand the vision quite well without any interpreter (1 En. 90:39–42). Second, Daniel's vision is limited to the historical settings of the Babylonians, Medes, Persians, and Macedonians (chaps. 2, 7) and specific instances with Alexander and Darius and conflict between the Ptolemies and Seleucids (chaps. 8, 11). The author of the Animal Apocalypse shares Daniel's interest in the four kingdoms of Daniel 2 and 7, but expands his interests to the entire breadth of human history. His scope transcends, then, the limited interests of Daniel. Third, the animal symbols in the Animal Apocalypse look more specifically to Israel's sufferings under oppressive gentile rulers, and it becomes a "full-blown allegory."[148] This is an integral component of the Animal Apocalypse, and identifying the symbols is important for understanding the message of the work as a whole (see below).

The Animal Apocalypse also recounts God's dealings with Israel as the center of its plot. This accounts for a full two-thirds of the narrative, focusing on sin, judgment, and deliverance with Israel at center stage. Violence introduced on the earth by the fallen Watchers extends to Israel time and again. Yet the hardships of Israel are often the consequences of its own sin. It is the apostasy of Manasseh that plunges Israel into sin, resulting in exile. Instead of repentance, Israel continues in blindness to the point of corrupting the temple cult itself. This occasions still further hardships for Israel, this time in the Hellenistic period. But the narrative extends beyond

148. Nickelsburg, *1 Enoch 1*, 357.

Israel in its hope for re-creation, which entails all humanity in its return
to an era before the formation of Israel, back to the garden itself. In this
respect Enoch's vision shows that though sin and corruption seemed to
frustrate God's ultimate plan for humanity, in the end his purpose will be
accomplished.[149]

Table 1.2

Symbolism in the Animal Apocalypse

Symbol	Referent
white bulls	Adam, Sethites
black bulls	Cain, Japheth
red bulls	Abel, Ham
stars	fallen Watchers
white men	holy ones
sheep	Israel
beasts (general)	gentile oppressors
lions	Babylonians
leopards	Syrians
wolves	Egyptians
dogs	Philistines
hyenas	Moabites
wild boars	Edomites, Amalekites
foxes	Ammonites
vultures	Macedonians
wild ass	Ishmael
shepherds	(negligent) leaders

Adapted from Nickelsburg, *1 Enoch 1*, 358,
table 5.

Perhaps the most distinctive feature of the Animal Apocalypse is its characterization of people and nations as animals of various kinds. Some of the
symbolic depictions may be outlined as follows (see table 1.2): Humans are
first depicted as bulls and cows, which may suggest their longevity in earliest biblical accounts (1 En. 85:3–89:8).[150] The depiction of Israel as sheep
is a common biblical metaphor (Num. 27:17; 2 Sam. 24:17; 1 Kings 22:17;
1 Chron. 21:17; 2 Chron. 18:16; Pss. 44:11, 22; 49:14; 74:1; 78:52; 79:13;
95:7; 100:3; 119:176; Isa. 13:14; 53:6, 7; Jer. 12:3; 23:1; 50:6, 17; Mic. 2:12;

149. Nickelsburg, *1 Enoch 1*, 356–57.
150. Nickelsburg, *1 Enoch 1*, 354.

Zech. 10:2; 13:7), especially in Ezekiel (34:2, 3, 6, 8, 10, 11, 12, 15, 17, 19, 20, 22, 31). In the Animal Apocalypse Israel's depiction as sheep entails, on the one hand, blindness and wandering, describing their propensity toward unbelief and apostasy (1 En. 89:32–33, 41, 51–54, 74; 90:8). On the other hand, their depiction as sheep is also indicative of their vulnerability to predatory wild beasts (gentiles; cf. 89:13–21, 42, 55–57; 90:2–4, 11–13, 16).[151] The predatory animals (esp. in 89:9–90:27) are depicted as *unclean* animals (gentiles), so the Israelite sheep are victims of the unclean, gentile predators.

SIN AND JUDGMENT IN THE ANIMAL APOCALYPSE

Sin is an ever-present reality in the narrative of the Animal Apocalypse, in which humans are both its victims and perpetrators. The origins of sin are less developed here than in the Book of Watchers. It does seem clear that Cain's murder of Abel, rather than the disobedience of Adam and Eve, is the first sin. This facilitates the author's laying blame for the origin of sin at the feet of the fallen Watchers rather than with humanity. It is also the case that violence ensues only after the stars (fallen Watchers) mingle with the cows (human women) and in later times is perpetrated by gentiles but not Israelites. Though the Israelites are the victims of such violence, the violence done to them is typically divine punishment for their own sins. And so the cycle continues.

In general, sin is depicted as blindness and straying from God's righteous path, the law. Specifically, the path of God is the appropriate use of the temple cult, as is evidenced by references to the tabernacle (1 En. 89:36), the Solomonic temple (89:50, 54, 66), and the second temple (89:73). It also entails specific matters, such as the worship of the golden calf (89:32–35), the Israelites' "blindness" during the time of the judges (89:41), Saul's sin (89:44), the abandonment of Jerusalem (89:51) and the temple (89:54), and the temple's pollution (89:73).[152]

More specifically still, the abandonment of the Jerusalem temple by the Northern Kingdom and subsequent cultic apostasy by Manasseh lead to God's abandonment of the flock (89:9–90:27). In his place are angelic shepherds whose failures exacerbate gentile oppression. The task of these shepherds is temporary (89:64; 90:5), and their misdeeds are recorded by still another angel (89:61–64, 68–71, 76–77; 90:14, 17, 20, 22; perhaps Michael; cf. Dan. 12:1). God appears to judge (1 En. 90:20) the rebellious angels (90:24; cf. 10:7, 12),

151. Nickelsburg, *Jewish Literature*, 84.
152. Nickelsburg, *1 Enoch 1*, 355–56.

disobedient shepherds (90:25), and apostate Jews, all of whom are cast into
a fiery abyss (90:26–27; cf. 10:14; 27:1–3).[153]

As discussed above, this work shares with other documents (T. Mos.; Jub.
23; Dan. 7–12) attention to particular events of the Seleucid rule (198–167
BCE; cf. 1 En. 90:2–15; Jub. 23:16–20). This makes the omission of a particular cultic matter all the more curious. It is well known that during this
time Antiochus IV Epiphanes, a Seleucid ruler, sought to quell tumult in Jerusalem by force, by striking at the heart of Judaism. In 167 BCE he issued
a royal edict forbidding distinctive customs under his jurisdiction, including
circumcision and festival and Sabbath observances, so that the Israelites defiled
themselves and the cult (1 Macc. 1:41–50; cf. 2 Macc. 6:1–11). There was even
a "desolating sacrilege" erected on the altar of burnt offering (1 Macc. 1:54).
Extant copies of the law were destroyed (1 Macc. 1:55). Violators were put to
death (1 Macc. 1:50, 57). Through a series of battles and negotiations, Judas
Maccabaeus led Israel to purify the sanctuary and resume its cult by the end
of 164 BCE (1 Macc. 4:52–55). Why this situation is not addressed in the
Animal Apocalypse is unclear. This may suggest that from the perspective of
the author of the Animal Apocalypse, the second temple was polluted from
its inception (1 En. 89:73; cf. T. Mos. 4:8), mitigating the significance of the
desecration.[154] The Animal Apocalypse is not explicit in some instances as
to the causes of sin, such as why Cain is a black bull spawning other black
bulls, or who precisely the active agent is when the Israelites are "blinded."
Perhaps the implied subject is the angelic figure Sammael.[155]

God's judgment on sin seems to be presented as a dividing structure for
the author's presentation of history into its three respective eras. So despite
God's judgment on sin in the first era (e.g., 1 En. 88:1–3; 89:2–6), it recurs at
the beginning of the second (89:11). Objects of judgment are both heavenly
(fallen Watchers) and human, with only the righteous Israelites escaping it. The
third and final era is one of restoration, a new beginning (90:28–38) in which
a new Jerusalem and temple greater than the first are established (90:28–29).

Purpose

It is generally recognized that the Animal Apocalypse was written to address a crisis that had arisen in the events leading up to the Maccabean revolt.
The author presents his symbolic review of history so as to place that crisis
within a broad context. Though many of the symbolic depictions of events

153. Nickelsburg, *Jewish Literature*, 85.
154. Nickelsburg, *Jewish Literature*, 86.
155. Nickelsburg, *1 Enoch 1*, 356.

and people can be discerned, the allegorical nature of the presentation suggests a typical rather than particular treatment. As in other facets of the Enochic writings, the message is one of judgment against Israel's oppressors. Yet here it is particularly the gentile rulers who, like the fallen Watchers, will be disposed of by God's angelic host.[156] The readership is aligned with the righteous in their militant resistance, while being encouraged by God's ultimate intervention and the promise of resurrection in a new earth. In this sense the elect are given both hope in an eschatological future and encouragement amid their present plight. Further clarity on the purpose of the work may be evident if, in fact, the author had the Apocalypse of Weeks at hand. Nickelsburg suggests that the author of the Animal Apocalypse may have achieved advantages from his revision of the other apocalypse.[157] Among other things, this would include a revision of the story line that underscores Israel's suffering at the hands of its enemies. Furthermore, the Animal Apocalypse brings the eschatological future near to the readers.

The Epistle of Enoch (1 En. 91–108)

Introduction

In its present form the Epistle of Enoch (1 En. 91–108) is a compilation of several writings, only one of which, by far the longest, is an actual epistle (though the epistle itself is composed of two distinct units). The literary segments begin with an Exhortation (91:1–10, 18–19), followed by the Epistle of Enoch (92:1–5; 93:11–105:2). Then comes the Apocalypse of Weeks (93:1–10; 91:11–17), the Birth of Noah (106:1–107:3), and the Eschatological Admonition (108:1–15). There are many challenges to this portion of 1 Enoch, the most obvious of which entails its sequence. For example, though the segment 91:11–17 occurs in the middle of the Exhortation (91:1–10, 18–19), it belongs rather to the Apocalypse of Weeks. Similarly, the segment 93:1–10 occurs in the middle of the Epistle of Enoch (92:1–5; 93:11–105:2) but belongs likewise to the Apocalypse of Weeks. Another difficulty with this work is that its component parts are, in their present form, not in their (rough) chronological order. A general chronology of the origins of the respective units is as follows:

Apocalypse of Weeks (93:1–10; 91:11–17)
Epistle of Enoch (92:1–5; 93:11–105:2)

156. J. Collins, *Apocalyptic Imagination*, 88.
157. Nickelsburg, *1 Enoch 1*, 360.

Exhortation (91:1–10, 18–19)
Birth of Noah (106:1–107:3)
Eschatological Admonition (108:1–15)[158]

With the exception of the Eschatological Admonition, which originates in the late first century CE, each of these sections dates from the second century BCE, like other portions of 1 Enoch (e.g., the Book of Dreams [83:1–84:6], the Animal Apocalypse [85:1–90:42], the Astronomical Book [81:1–82:4a]). Though these segments differ in their historical settings and theological outlooks, they share dependence on earlier strands of Enochic traditions from the Book of Watchers (1 En. 1:1–36:4) and the Astronomical Book (1 En. 72:1–80:8; 82:4–20). Perhaps this was among the factors that brought the constituent parts together soon after their composition into a collection of "revelatory disclosures made by Enoch to his son Methuselah,"[159] with the final chapter appended at a later date.

As we have seen with other portions of 1 Enoch, elements of Enochic literature were written quite early, surely before the composition of the constituent parts of the Epistle of Enoch. It also seems clear that prior to their redaction and collection into their present shape, chapters 91–108 were composed independently. Therefore, it is important to distinguish between the respective dates of composition, the dates of the manuscripts in which they are preserved, and the dates of their early redaction and literary histories.[160]

How the constituent parts came together into their present form is a literary puzzle, the solution to which may be facilitated by the Aramaic manuscripts from Qumran (e.g., 4Q204, 4Q212), which date from shortly after the composition of the original work. Portions of chapters 91 and 92–94 are evident in 4QEn^g (see table 1.3), while chapters 1–36, 85–90, the end of the epistle itself, and chapters 106–7 are present in 4QEn^c, though the latter offers no evidence of literary shape or cohering principles.[161]

Manuscript evidence does provide a means of identifying the oldest Enochic material toward establishing a theory of the emergence of the collection of the earliest Enochic material. The earliest are the Astronomical Book and the Book of Watchers, both from the third century BCE; while distinct from each other, they overlap in form and content. Additional independent material— including the Apocalypse of Weeks, portions of Epistle A (92:1–5; 93:11–94:5;

104:9–105:2), and Epistle B (94:6–104:8)—likely originates prior to the Maccabean era (on the distinction between Epistle A and Epistle B, see below). These writings share a common interest in wisdom (93:10; 98:3; 99:10) associated with Enoch and made known through heavenly writings (93:2; 103:2; 104:9–13). In its current form the compilation exhibits signs of editorial handling to bridge material. What bridged the earlier and later material seems to be the addition of the account of Enoch's return to earth to relate information to Methuselah and his children (81:1–82:4a) and the ensuing admonition and predictions Enoch conveys to Methuselah and his brothers (91:1–10, 18–19). These additions, accompanied by further revisions (e.g., 92:1–5; 94:1–5), seem to have constructed the testamentary features evident in the collection's current form.[162] While some suggest the collection was "shaped into a literary unity as a testamentary collection of Enochic writings,"[163] Loren T. Stuckenbruck is less certain about this terminology. He prefers instead to view the testament-like material (e.g., scenes in 81:5–82:3; 91:1–3; 94:1) as later developments as compilers of the respective materials sought to "find a literary or narrative rationale for the additions they were making."[164]

The result is that the material was organized around the revelatory experiences of Enoch, which he subsequently discloses to Methuselah, his son (91:1–2; 92:1; 106:1, 7; 107:1–3). In this respect it exhibits a testamentary character found in other, roughly contemporary Enochic material (Book of Dreams [83:1], Animal Apocalypse [85:1–3], and Astronomical Book [81:5–6; 82:1]), with the Eschatological Admonition likely added later to an extant collection.[165]

Languages and Manuscripts

The material from the Epistle of Enoch in its constituent parts is preserved in Aramaic among the Qumran material (see table 1.3).

Table 1.3

Qumran Aramaic Manuscripts of the Epistle of Enoch

Apocalypse of Weeks (93:1–10; 91:11–17)	4QEn^g (= 4Q212; mid-first century BCE)
Epistle of Enoch A (92:1–5; 93:11–14; 94:1–5; 104:9–105:2)	4QEn^c (= 4Q204; last third of first century BCE) 4QEn^g (= 4Q212; mid-first century BCE)
Epistle of Enoch B (94:6–104:8)	Not attested

162. Stuckenbruck, 1 Enoch 91–108, 9–10.
163. Nickelsburg, Jewish Literature, 114.
164. Stuckenbruck, 1 Enoch 91–108, 16.
165. Stuckenbruck, "Enoch, Epistle of," 583.

Exhortation (91:1–10, 18–19)	4QEn^g (= 4Q212; mid-first century BCE)
Birth of Noah (106:1–107:3)	4QEn^c (= 4Q204; last third of first century BCE)
Eschatological Admonition (108:1–15)	Not attested

Evidence of this material in Greek is scant. Though not attested among the Aramaic material from Qumran, portions of the Epistle of Enoch B (94:6–104:8) may be preserved in Greek fragments from Qumran Cave 7 (e.g., 7Q4 1 = 1 En. 13:3–4; 7Q4 2 = 1 En. 98:11; 7Q8 = 1 En. 103:7–8). A papyrus codex from the fourth century CE contains the Greek of 1 Enoch 97:6–104:13; 106:1–107:3. These are from preserved leaves of the Chester Beatty-Michigan papyrus, which may have originally contained 1 Enoch 91/92–107.[166] To this one could add the Antinoe (Coptic) fragment (1 En. 93:3–8) and the Latin Royal MS 4 E XIII (1 En. 106:1–18).[167]

As elsewhere in 1 Enoch, the full text of the Epistle of Enoch is extant only in Ethiopic. Here, however, scholars have observed two distinct versions, or recensions, of the text that have been transmitted: the first (Ethiopic I) is an older text-form, whereas the second (Ethiopic II) is a later reworking of the texts by copyists.[168] The former contains ten or eleven parchment manuscripts dating from the fifteenth to eighteenth century. The latter contains more than fifty manuscripts, most of which date from the eighteenth or nineteenth century, though a few date earlier and some later.[169]

Exhortation (1 En. 91:1–10, 18–19)

INTRODUCTION

The opening segment of the larger collection that makes up the Epistle of Enoch begins with what some scholars identify as a "bridge" in the narrative. Previously, the Animal Apocalypse (1 En. 85–90) described the conclusion of Enoch's instruction to Methuselah, his son. The present Exhortation (91:1–10, 18–19) returns to that testament-like setting at least in part to set what follows—the Epistle of Enoch (92:1–5; 93:11–105:2)—in the context of what preceded.

PROVENANCE AND DATE

Because the Exhortation bridges and makes use of other material (e.g., the Epistle in 92:1–5; 94:1–5; and the additions to the Astronomical Book

---

166. Nickelsburg, "Two Enochic Manuscripts," 255–59.
167. Stuckenbruck, *1 Enoch 91–108*, 17.
168. Fleming, *Das Buch Henoch*, ix.
169. Stuckenbruck, *1 Enoch 91–108*, 21, 23–26.

in 81:1–82:3), it is generally dated from the middle to the second half of the second century BCE.[170]

Contents

This brief document begins with Enoch's appeal to Methuselah, exhorting him to gather his brothers to hear Enoch's account of what will happen to them in the future (91:1–2). In Enoch's speech, which comprises the remainder of the document (91:3b–10, 18–19), he is said to discourse on righteousness (91:3a). Specifically, he exhorts them to walk in truth and righteousness and to avoid a double heart (91:4). He warns that violence and iniquity will escalate (91:5a) but will be cut down (91:5b) only to prevail again (91:6). At that time God himself will bring judgment on the earth (91:7), removing violence, iniquity, and idolatry (91:8–9). The righteous will be raised and given wisdom (91:10). The segment concludes (91:18–19) with Enoch's final exhortation to heed his instructions in the paths of righteousness.

Contribution and Context

Because the Exhortation makes use of prior Enochic material, it naturally shares some of its interests and resembles some of its forms. Like the final chapter of the Astronomical Book (chap. 82), the setting is like that of a testament in which Enoch relates instructional information to Methuselah (91:1–2). Exhortations themselves are generally presented as the alternatives of two ways, acting righteously and rejecting wrongdoing (91:3–4, 18–19), a familiar trope in the Hebrew Bible (e.g., Deut. 30:15–30; Ps. 119; Prov. 1:15–16; 2:12–13, 18–19; 4:10, 14–19; 5:56; 7:27) and other Second Temple writings (Tob. 1:3–9; 4:5–6, 10, 19; 5:21–22; 1QS III, 15–IV, 26; CD-A I, 10–II, 14; cf. Sir. 15:11–17:24).[171] In the Exhortation these contrasts frame an anticipated eschatological sequence of an increase in wickedness and consequent punishment (91:5), a sequence that will escalate until it is brought to a dramatic end, at which time the righteous will be rewarded as they arise from sleep (91:6–10). Since these anticipate themes taken up later (cf. the Epistle at 1 En. 92:3a and the Birth of Noah at 106:19–107:1), the Exhortation was likely composed in order to integrate these later works into the prior Enochic writings.[172]

---

170. Stuckenbruck, *1 Enoch 91–108*, 584.
171. See Nickelsburg's "Excursus: The Two Ways" in *1 Enoch 1*, 454–56; Nickelsburg, "Seeking the Origins."
172. Stuckenbruck, *1 Enoch 91–108*, 2.

Epistle of Enoch (1 En. 92:1–5; 93:11–105:2)

INTRODUCTION

This important work is, despite its name, not an epistle. This designation was added in the Greek tradition, which references "the words of this epistle" (1 En. 100:6) and the title "Epistle of Enoch" after the end of the Greek text (which ends at 107:3). The work purports to be written by Enoch to his descendants. In that respect it has been likened to a testament. Throughout it bears assertions of authority, placing on Enoch's lips statements like "I swear to you" and "I say to you." The author's authority derives from his knowledge of heavenly secrets, read from tablets in heaven (cf. 103:1–2), and forms the basis for his exhortations throughout.[173]

PROVENANCE

Nothing is known about the author of the Epistle except what can be gleaned internally from the letter itself. Some suggest the criticism of those who "alter and distort the words of truth" and "write books in their (own words)" (104:10; 98:15) implies Hellenistic Jews who acclimated their ancestral traditions to Greek language and customs.[174] It is possible that a reference to the sea (101:4–9) implies a maritime city as the work's origin.[175] But the general lack of specificity both inhibits a precise identification and lends the work to application in several settings.[176] Some clues may be found in the accusations against the wicked, who are accused of blasphemy and idolatry (94:9; 96:7; 99:7) and, more prominently, acts of social oppression against the righteous (e.g., 94:8; 96:5; see below). This sort of class division is suitable within the setting of the Hellenization of Palestine prior to the Maccabean revolt (167–160 BCE).

The prophetic tone of the Epistle suggests the author perceives himself within that tradition as an advocate for the otherwise helpless righteous. He is given prophetic oracles pertaining to the suffering righteous (103:2) in terms of both the present (in reference to their unjust sufferings) and the future (in reference to eschatological blessings and vengeance on their oppressors). For the author these concerns are indeed personal: not only does he align himself with the righteous community, but their experiences are identical to his own (cf. 103:9–15). Yet here the author differs from the implied authors of other Enochic material, who are given visions of the cosmos (cf. chaps. 17–36;

173. J. Collins, *Apocalyptic Imagination*, 83.
174. J. Collins, *Apocalyptic Imagination*, 84.
175. Milik, *Books of Enoch*, 49–51.
176. J. Collins, *Apocalyptic Imagination*, 85.

72–80; 82:4–20) and significant historical events (e.g., 1 En. 85–90; 93:3–10; 91:11–17). Furthermore, while there are a number of statements about angels (e.g., 97:2; 99:3; 100:4–5; 102:3; 104:1, 4; cf. 104:6), Enoch's message is not received from angels. The author also seems to take a unique place in his chastisement of the wicked. His repeated emphasis that their deeds will not be forgotten (e.g., 96:4, 7; 97:2, 7; 99:3, 15; 103:4; 104:1) may suggest he sees himself as providing a record of the indictment against them for when God's eschatological judgment arrives.[177]

DATE

Since the Epistle makes use of the Book of Watchers (see below), it can be written no earlier than the third century BCE—but how much later has occupied more recent discussion. Manuscript evidence from Qumran (e.g., 4QEn^g and 4QEn^c) indicates on paleographic grounds a date no later than the middle to the end of the first century BCE. The Epistle is likely known by the author of the book of Jubilees, which dates from the mid-second century BCE. If this is the case, then the Epistle dates from before approximately 150 BCE.[178] Recent scholarship has tied the date of composition for the Epistle to that of the Apocalypse of Weeks, since the latter is preserved within the former and there is no evidence they circulated independently. The Apocalypse of Weeks is typically regarded as being written prior to the Maccabean era (before 167 BCE),[179] suggesting the Epistle was likewise written then. Furthermore, the charges of idolatry seem more suited to before or during the Maccabean revolt (cf. 1 Macc. 1:43, 47; 13:47; 2 Macc. 12:40),[180] and the Epistle exhibits traits consistent with conditions prior to the Maccabean revolt[181] and lacks any allusion to the revolt itself. The Epistle most likely dates from just prior to 167 BCE.

CONTENTS

The introduction (1 En. 92:1–94:5) begins with Enoch exhorting his descendants and the last righteous generations not to be troubled by the present times

177. Stuckenbruck, *1 Enoch 91–108*, 216.
178. Jubilees refers to a testimony written by Enoch against all the children of men and their generations (Jub. 4:19; cf. 1 En. 91:3; 96:5; 97:4; 99:3; 100:11; 104:11; 105:1). Scholars take this as an indication that the author of Jubilees knew of the Epistle in its entirety (Stuckenbruck, *1 Enoch 91–108*, 214–15).
179. Stuckenbruck, "Enoch, Epistle of," 584.
180. VanderKam, *Enoch and the Growth of Apocalyptic Tradition*, 144; Stuckenbruck, *1 Enoch 91–108*, 213n382.
181. Stuckenbruck, *1 Enoch 91–108*, 215.

(92:1–2). God will bless the righteous, who will arise from sleep to everlasting mercy (92:3–4), whereas sin will be destroyed (92:5). This hope is grounded in the incomparability of God (93:11–14; cf. Deut. 5:26). This is followed by an exhortation to follow the path of righteousness and avoid that of iniquity pursued by sinners, and to hold out hope for ultimate vindication (1 En. 94:1–5).[182]

The body of the work consists of three main units that encompass (1) woes pronounced against sinners (94:6–100:9); (2) a description of creation's agency in God's judgment against the sinner (100:10–102:3); and (3) a refutation of the fallacious claims of the wicked (102:4–104:8).

This first segment is an interwoven series of woes and exhortations (94:6–100:9). It begins with a first set of woes against those who are violent, profit from sin, and trust in riches (94:6–8); they will be overthrown by God (94:9–10; 95:1–2). The righteous are exhorted not to fear the sinners (95:3), who are condemned in a second set of woes for their blasphemy, deception, and injustice (95:4–7). The righteous are then exhorted to hope because they will be blessed (96:1–3), while the rich and powerful who oppress them are condemned in a third set of woes (96:4–8). The righteous are then charged to take courage (97:1–2), and sinners are condemned with warnings of impending judgment (97:3–6). This is followed by a fourth set of woes directed against those who gain wealth unjustly and err in placing their security in it (97:7–10). Following this is an oath sworn to the wise (98:1–3) and to the sinner (98:4–8). The fifth set of woes chides the sinners as fools (98:9–99:2) who oppose the righteous (98:13–14), deceive, and will have no lasting peace (98:15–99:2). The righteous are then encouraged to pray for judgment on the unrighteous (99:3–9) standing in contrast to the righteous, who heed the words of the wise and will be saved (99:10; cf. 94:1–5). This gives way to a sixth collection of woes (99:11–16), leveled against those who spread evil (99:11–13) and practice lawlessness (99:14–16). The text then turns to a description of the future impending judgment on the wicked (100:1–4) and blessings on the righteous (100:5–6).

In the next major portion of the Epistle, one reads an account of how creation functions as a divine agent in affirming the hopeless state of the sinner (100:10–102:3).[183] The moon and stars bear witness to their wickedness (100:10); rain will be withheld as a testimony against them (100:11–12), while snow and frost will be hurled against them in judgment (100:13). This is because the creation does the bidding of the Most High, and he uses it to execute judgment as he sees fit (101:1–9; 102:1–3a). The sinner will have no place to hide and will be cursed forever and without peace (102:3b).

182. Nickelsburg, *Jewish Literature*, 110.
183. Stuckenbruck, "Enoch, Epistle of," 584.

A lengthy discourse ensues (102:4–104:8) in which the souls of the righteous who died are exhorted to have hope (102:4–5) since they, unlike the sinner (102:6–11), are promised good things (103:1–3). They will come to life and rejoice (103:4), whereas misery will fall on the sinner (103:5–8). The piety of the righteous is not in vain (103:9–15), and their sufferings are seen by God (104:1). They are to take courage in a hope that lies in the future (104:2, 4–5) and in impending judgment for the wicked oppressors (104:3, 6–8).

In the conclusion to the Epistle (104:9–105:2), Enoch exhorts his audience to avoid error and deceit and to not alter the words of truth, as the sinners do (104:9–10). These words must not be altered (104:11) and will be given to the righteous and pious (104:12) to learn all the paths of truth (104:13; 105:1–2).

CONTRIBUTION AND CONTEXT

The Epistle of Enoch in the context of 1 Enoch. Within the corpus of 1 Enoch, the Epistle of Enoch borrows from the Book of Watchers, primarily concerning the themes of the transgressions of sinners and their punishments, the role of angels in relating the laments of the suffering righteous, and the placements of human souls. The punishment of the wicked after their death (1 En. 102:4–104:8) recalls a scene from the Book of Watchers where Enoch sees four chambers holding the souls of the dead (22:3–9), three of which contain the souls of the wicked awaiting judgment (22:10–13). Similar classifications of souls recur in the Epistle (cf. 102:6b; 103:5–8; 104:7–8) and, as in the Book of Watchers, address the matter of how the wicked experienced no punishment during their lifetime. Furthermore, the Epistle seems to draw on a tradition early in the Book of Watchers (e.g., chaps. 1–5) aligning the fallen angels with the wicked activities of "sinners" (e.g., 94:6; 95:4; 97:9; 98:1, 2, 4; 100:9; 103:1). Furthermore, while the Epistle exhibits familiarity with the Book of Watchers, on several points it does so in distinct contrast to it. Whereas in the Book of Watchers angels descend as rebels against God (6:6), in the Epistle angels descend as agents of God (100:4). Whereas God— through his angels—intercedes on behalf of the righteous in the Book of Watchers (e.g., 8:4–9:3), in the Epistle the righteous find no justice against their oppressors (103:14).[184] Finally, the Epistle indicates that sin was created by humanity (98:4), whereas fallen angels introduce sin into the world in the story line of the Book of Watchers.[185]

Prophetic nature of the Epistle of Enoch. Scholars typically observe that, perhaps more than any other facet of the Enochic corpus, elements of the

---

184. Stuckenbruck, *1 Enoch 91–108*, 210–11.
185. J. Collins, *Apocalyptic Imagination*, 85.

Epistle of Enoch communicate directly to both the righteous and the wicked in the second person. Yet these statements are more than mere predictions of eschatological punishments and rewards.[186] Furthermore, the experiences and circumstances of the righteous and sinners in the past or present are framed in terms of predictions of the future (1 En. 94:1–5; 104:9–105:2).[187] The author seems to infer that his denunciations play a role in actually bringing the expected judgment into effect. In this way, he takes on a prophetic role as one who champions the cause of the victimized righteous of his community. This is embedded in the text within the exhortations to the righteous themselves, in which they are called to courage, faith, and hope in view of the impending judgment on the sinner on the one hand (e.g., 95:2–3; cf. 1 En. 91:12; Num. 21:34; Deut. 3:2; Josh. 8:1) and the promise of vindication and eternal life for the righteous on the other (e.g., 1 En. 104:2).[188]

In the author's perspective, the sinners in the present world prosper in wealth and social standing at the expense of the righteous. The difficulty is that the wicked not only prosper at the expense of the righteous but also seem to be receiving the blessings of God's covenant with Israel (Deut. 28:1–14), whereas the righteous gain only its curses (Deut. 28:15–68; cf. 1 En. 103:9–15). This problem is addressed most substantially in the "woe oracles" throughout the document, which both outline the crimes committed by the sinners and pronounce their ensuing judgment. The prophetic nature of the Epistle is also borne out in its "disclosure formulae," statements whereby the author claims to know and make known special revelations from God. The author knows the special mysteries of heaven (103:2; 104:12), that sinners will tempt the righteous (94:5), and that God is mindful of their plight (97:2). He also knows that God will overturn the fortunes of the wicked (94:10), whose deeds are recorded for judgment (98:8; cf. 98:10, 12; 100:10; 103:7–8).[189]

Righteous and sinners in the Epistle of Enoch. The relation between the righteous and sinners is an integral part of the Epistle of Enoch. The author draws on themes from the Hebrew Bible to invoke matters pertaining to the unjust suffering of the righteous and the inevitable judgment anticipated for their wicked oppressors. Much of this is borne out in the woe oracles, which show that the wicked will experience a reversal of fortune at the final judgment (e.g., 1 En. 96:4, 7; 97:7), a time in the eschatological future when the blessings and curses of the Deuteronomic covenant will finally be realized (cf. 103:9–15; 104:1–6). It seems the author's prophetic role in these instances

186. Stuckenbruck, "Enoch, Epistle of," 584.
187. Stuckenbruck, *1 Enoch 91–108*, 192.
188. Nickelsburg, *Jewish Literature*, 112.
189. Stuckenbruck, *1 Enoch 91–108*, 192, 201–2.

aligns him with prophets from the Hebrew Bible who lay similar charges against disobedient Israel. In contrast to the wicked, the righteous will have a place in bringing about judgment on the sinners (95:3; 96:1; 98:12; 99:11), and the righteous will also enjoy the eschatological rewards of future life (92:3; 103:4; cf. 96:3a; 104:2b, 4, 6b).[190]

But the document precludes vague generalizations about who these people are. For the author, the righteous are members of his own community, while the sinners are the ones oppressing them. Specifically, the righteous are the victims of the oppression of the sinners. They are the ones with whom the author identifies, people without influence or power who are yet recipients of Enoch's revealed wisdom. They "receive the words of the wise and understand them and do the ways of the Most High" (99:10).

Frequent charges of wickedness and oppression are expressed in prophetic tones in woe oracles directed toward "sinners," who are variously identified as the wealthy, the elite, idolaters, and propagators of false teachings.[191] They lack understanding (98:3) and are fraught with falsehood (95:6; 98:15; 99:1, 2, 9, 12). Their lot is generally expressed in temporal phrases such as "then" or "in those days," with stronger formulas such as "know!" and "be it known!" and "I say to you." The strongest condemnatory invocation employs an oath formula: "I swear to you." The several woes are directed toward them and provide charges against them for which they will be judged. These charges fall into one of two types: religious and social. The religious charges (esp. 99:8–10) include accusations of idolatry (99:7), consuming blood (98:11), blasphemy (94:9; 96:7), and cursing (95:4). The sinners pervert God's law (98:9; 99:2, 14) and lead many astray in their false teaching (98:15). Most of the charges against the sinners, however, are social in nature, especially pertaining to their wealth and power and exploitation of the righteous who lack the means to repel the oppression of the wicked. The sinners build their homes at the expense of others (94:6–7; 99:3) and lavish in their wealth (96:5–6; 97:8–9), which they flaunt publicly (98:1–3). The comforts and security that they have found in their wealth will be snatched from them in judgment.

Purpose

Scholars generally recognize that the author wrote this letter in the name of Enoch, ostensibly addressed to Enoch's children. Yet historically it is directed to the author's contemporaries: "the future generations that will practice

---

190. Stuckenbruck, *1 Enoch 91–108*, 187, 200, 204–6.
191. Stuckenbruck, *1 Enoch 91–108*, 3.

righteousness and peace" (1 En. 92:1; cf. 1:1–2; 37:2).[192] The message is one of consolation: it recognizes the hardships of the righteous at the hands of the wicked. But it also offers consolation in the ultimate vindication and blessings the righteous will experience. Moreover, the righteous are assured that the wicked oppressors, despite their affluence and power at present, will be the objects of God's swift and righteous judgment.

The work also exhibits sapiential features to extend moral exhortations (94:1, 3–4) alongside warnings that the readers will be enticed away from the path of wisdom (94:2, 5). It uses the familiar framework of two ways—righteous and wicked paths (92:3; 94:1–4; 104:13; 105:2)—as in the Exhortation (91:18–19) and the Apocalypse of Weeks (91:14).[193] In words similar to those of Moses (Deut. 30:11–20), the author anticipates rewards for those who heed his instructions (1 En. 94:4; 104:12–13; 105:1), who will in turn instruct future generations (104:13–105:1). Couched in apocalyptic language, the Epistle offers consolation and exhortation to the righteous, whose efforts do not appear to be paying off. Enoch explains, on heavenly authority, that the plight of the righteous in the present world will one day be reversed.[194]

Apocalypse of Weeks (1 En. 93:1–10; 91:11–17)

INTRODUCTION

Embedded within the Epistle of Enoch (1 En. 92:1–5; 93:11–105:2), the Apocalypse of Weeks (93:1–10; 91:11–17) is an account of the world's history from the author's own time to the end of days placed on the lips of Enoch. In this respect it is like the Animal Apocalypse (85:1–90:42), yet shorter and likely earlier.[195] In it Enoch offers exhortation to his sons, appealing to divine revelation, and summarizes history in ten (uneven) lengths of time designated "weeks." These are further divided into seven parts, creating seventy units in all. The arrangement of the material requires some explanation, for in its present form the conclusion (91:11–17) precedes the beginning (93:1–10). Not only does the flow of the text fit better in this transposed way (93:1–10 followed by 91:11–17), but an ancient fragment from Qumran (4Q212; mid-first century BCE) confirms this arrangement and suggests the segment 91:11–17 was somehow displaced in the Ethiopic tradition.[196]

192. Nickelsburg, *Jewish Literature*, 110–12.
193. Stuckenbruck, *1 Enoch 91–108*, 191.
194. J. Collins, *Apocalyptic Imagination*, 85.
195. Stuckenbruck, *1 Enoch 91–108*, 2.
196. J. Collins, *Apocalyptic Imagination*, 79.

PROVENANCE AND DATE

Manuscript evidence (4Q212) requires a date of composition prior to the middle of the first century BCE. Most scholars think the lack of any reference to the Maccabean revolt, the persecution under Antiochus IV Epiphanes, or any events thereafter implies a date prior to 167 BCE.[197] If this is so, then the "perverse generation" in week seven (1 En. 93:9) may correspond to Jews succumbing to the pressures of Hellenization in Jerusalem that accompanied Antiochus's rise to power (175–170 BCE).[198] Since the Apocalypse of Weeks alludes to features of the Book of Watchers, it dates from later than the third century BCE.

CONTENTS

The apocalypse commences by attributing it to a discourse recited by Enoch (1 En. 93:1). At the outset the subject matter is identified as the "sons of righteousness" (93:2a), those chosen from eternity, and is addressed to Enoch's sons (93:2b). The author claims a threefold source for his revelation: a vision of heaven shown to him, words taught to him by angels, and words read from the heavenly tablets (93:2c). The entirety of the remainder of the apocalypse recounts history in terms of "weeks," spanning from Enoch's own time in the first week (93:3) to a future time when there will be "many weeks without number forever" (91:17).

Enoch was born in the first week, prior to which righteousness endured (93:3). Subsequent weeks are spoken of in terms of future events. In the second week, deceit will arise and there will be the "first end." In it a man will be saved (Noah), after which iniquity will increase and a law will be established for sinners (presumably the covenant with Noah; 93:4). At the conclusion of the third week (93:5) a man will be chosen as "the plant of righteous judgment" (Abraham), after whom the plant of righteousness will go forth in perpetuity. This group of elect, righteous people remains the focus for the duration of the apocalypse and represents the origins and history of the author's community. After the fourth week (93:6), visions of the holy and righteous will be seen, a covenant will be established (Mosaic law), and a tabernacle will be made. The temple, built forever, will arise after the fifth week (93:7). A turning point is reached during the sixth week (93:8), in which apostasy ensues. A man will ascend (Elijah), after which the temple will be burned and Israel, the "race of the chosen root," will be dispersed. In the seventh week (93:9) a perverse

197. Charles, "1 Enoch," 2:171.
198. So also Stuckenbruck, *1 Enoch 91–108*, 62.

generation will emerge, after which witnesses of righteousness will be chosen from the everlasting plant of righteousness (93:10a). These will receive sevenfold wisdom and knowledge (93:10b) and will uproot the foundations of violence (91:11). These first seven weeks correspond to events known to the author and his community, whereas the remaining three speculate about the eschatological future in which righteousness triumphs over the wicked.[199]

Righteousness will emerge in the eighth week (91:12) when the righteous—Enoch's own group—will take up the sword against the wicked. At the end of this week (91:13), the righteous will acquire possessions and a temple will be built for all subsequent generations. Righteous law will be revealed to all the sons of the earth in the ninth week (91:14a). All wickedness will be eradicated from the earth, and humanity will pursue the path of everlasting righteousness (91:14b). This gives way to the climactic seventh part of the tenth and final week (91:15), in which there will be judgment on the fallen angels. A new heaven will replace the first heaven (91:16a), and the powers of heaven will shine (91:16b). After this final week there will be innumerable weeks in which righteousness will prevail and no sin will be found (91:17).

Contribution and Context

Among the distinct features of the Apocalypse of Weeks is its lack of any description of a revelatory disclosure of any kind—a heavenly ascent, vision, or dream. Instead, Enoch himself indicates he received his message in a vision, in words from angels, and from heavenly tablets (1 En. 93:2). In this respect the wisdom Enoch receives is acquired by revelation, though not a direct revelation from God but one that is mediated through other sources. Whereas the Animal Apocalypse recounts history through the depiction of peoples as distinct animals, the Apocalypse of Weeks does this with a distinct emphasis on the division of time organized into ten "weeks." The significance of this scheme lies in its understanding of history as carefully ordered and controlled by God. The audience of this work is thereby encouraged by God's control of their present events and able to locate themselves within the overall account of history. Moreover, the ancient readers, in identifying themselves in the seventh week, recognize that God's great breakthrough and overturning of their unjust circumstances is at hand in the eighth week.[200]

Within the Apocalypse's schematization of history, a number of patterns emerge. First, the narrative begins with the sons of righteousness (93:2) and a time when righteousness endures (93:3), and concludes with a time that foresees

199. Stuckenbruck, 1 Enoch 91–108, 2.
200. J. Collins, Apocalyptic Imagination, 79, 81.

an enduring righteousness (91:17). Second, the advent of a wicked generation in the seventh week (93:9), the author's own time, corresponds to that of the second week (93:4). This suggests the writer sees his own time as in some sense recapitulating the generation leading up to the flood and suggests the author likewise sees judgment on the wicked as imminent. Similarly, third, there are significant reversals in the fortunes of the author's community at hand. The oppressed righteous (93:9) will themselves punish their oppressors (91:11–12). The Solomonic temple (93:7; week five), destroyed by fire (93:8; week six), will be restored (91:13; week eight). Fourth, the elect descendants of Abraham (93:5; week three) produce a perverse generation from within their own ranks (93:9), and the chosen from that week, the seventh, are heirs of Abraham (93:10). The cumulative effect of these and other features seems to be that the author sees himself and his community as among the righteous recipients of Abrahamic election. And they see themselves on the cusp of a turn in their fortune from hardship to salvation. This is even more pronounced when God's rule is established on earth (91:12–14; weeks eight and nine), in judgment (91:15) and in the new heaven (91:16; week ten). Yet this reversal of fortunes for the righteous and the onset of innumerable weeks of sinless bliss (91:17) are accomplished without reference to the agency of any messianic figure.[201]

Whereas the Animal Apocalypse was distinct in its portrayal of peoples in the guise of animals, the Apocalypse of Weeks, as its name suggests, contributes an understanding of the significance of the number seven. Its periodization of history into seven-day units ("weeks") is presented as a set of ten weeks, for a total of seventy days. This may be derived from the "seventy generations" during which the fallen Watchers are to be bound (1 En. 10:12),[202] though the correlation is not entirely clear. Biblical interest in the number seventy suggesting seventy years of rest (e.g., Jer. 25:11–12; 29:10; 2 Chron. 36:21) or years that the temple lies in ruins (e.g., Zech. 1:12–17) does not provide evident points of correspondence. Instead, Stuckenbruck looks to the seventy weeks of years from Daniel 9, which, he suggests, understands a period of 490 years ($70 \times 7 = 490$) extending from the exile (596 BCE) to the author's present time. A similar articulation of seventy weeks (490 years) is attested elsewhere (e.g., 4Q181 1 1; 2 3; 4Q383–384; 4Q385a–b; 4Q387b; 4Q389a; 4Q390; cf. 1 En. 93:2). If this analogy is more appropriate, then the Apocalypse of Weeks may use a 490-year scheme after the exile (93:8) and within the seventh week (93:9–10), extending into the author's own time.[203]

201. Stuckenbruck, 1 Enoch 91–108, 59–60.
202. J. Collins, Apocalyptic Imagination, 81.
203. Stuckenbruck, 1 Enoch 91–108, 54–55.

The Apocalypse of Weeks finds natural affinities within the Epistle of Enoch as a whole (1 En. 91–108), particularly with respect to the Exhortation (91:1–10, 18–19) and the Epistle of Enoch proper (92:1–5; 93:11–105:2). A number of distinctive features are shared among them, including contrasts between the righteous and sinners on the one hand, and righteousness and wickedness on the other. They also share an interest in heavenly tablets, the use of "I make known to you" as a means of relating revealed material, judgment on sinners with the sword, the removal of wicked deeds done by sinners, and the understanding, even conversion, of non-Israelites. Because of these and other commonalities, it is sometimes suggested that the works all stemmed from a single author.[204]

Nevertheless, the ideological similarities suggest an affinity that may account for the merging of these works but need not point to common authorship. The contrasts between the righteous and sinners, righteousness and wickedness, are familiar from other Enochic writings as well as other literature from the Second Temple period in general. Furthermore, the particular identification of sinners as oppressors of the righteous in the Epistle is absent in the Apocalypse. Likewise, the mention of heavenly tablets is sufficiently attested outside this literature (Jub. 3:10; 5:12; 6:17; 15:25; 16:3, 9; 18:18; 19:9; 23:32; 24:33; 28:6; 30:9, 19, 20, 22; 31:32; 32:10, 15; 49:8; 4Q537 1–3 3; 1 En. 81:1–2; 103:2–3; etc.) to allow for other options besides common authorship. The disclosure formulas are in different contexts between the Apocalypse and the Epistle, and the Apocalypse's indication that the sword of judgment is borne by the righteous is absent from the Epistle. Finally, the removal of wicked deeds and the extension of understanding to all humanity may depend on earlier material (e.g., 1 En. 10:21). The implication seems to be that while material from the Apocalypse of Weeks on the one hand and material from the Epistle and Exhortation on the other share sufficient ideologies to warrant their melding into a common document, their distinctions would suggest different authors.[205]

Birth of Noah (1 En. 106:1–107:3)

INTRODUCTION

In this work Enoch tells the story of Noah's birth. Yet the work is less interested in Noah's angelic features and ability to speak (in praise of God) than the significance of his name etymologically. The name "Noah" is said to

---

204. VanderKam, *Enoch and the Growth of Apocalyptic Tradition*, 145; Stuckenbruck, *1 Enoch 91–108*, 62–64.

205. Stuckenbruck, *1 Enoch 91–108*, 64.

mean "rest" (1 En. 106:18; cf. Gen. 5:29), "relief" (107:3; cf. Gen. 5:29), and "to be left as a remnant" (1 En. 106:16).[206] Noah's name, and his accompanying story, is used to hold out the promise of hope to the righteous, who will experience an upsurge of evil before their allotted eschatological blessing.

Date

The presence of the Birth of Noah segment at Qumran (4QEn^c = 4Q204), which dates from the end of the first century BCE,[207] requires a prior date of authorship. Its use of the Exhortation (91:5–9) requires a date later than the mid-second century BCE.

Contents

At the beginning of the narrative Enoch relates the marriage of his son, Methuselah, and the birth of his grandson Lamech (1 En. 106:1a), who grew to have a son himself (106:1c). Prior to Lamech, righteousness was "brought low" (106:1b). Lamech's son (Noah; Gen. 5:28–29), born both white and red and bearing a glorious face (1 En. 106:2), immediately stands and praises the Lord (106:3). In fear, Lamech flees to Methuselah (106:4) and reports to his father that his newly born son is more like an angel than a human, with eyes like the rays of the sun and a glorious face (106:5). Lamech suggests the child comes from angels and, fearing calamity (106:6), implores Methuselah to inquire of Enoch, whose "dwelling is with the angels" (106:7). Methuselah goes to Enoch (106:8) and inquires about "a terrible vision" (106:9). He describes the child to his father (106:10) and recounts his standing and praising the Lord at birth (106:11). He also explains to Enoch Lamech's fears and that he has come to Enoch because he learns from angels the exact facts and the truth (106:12). Enoch replies that the Lord will renew his commandment since the present generation has transgressed the word of the Lord (106:13) by sinning with women and siring fleshly children (106:14). As a result, there will be wrath and destruction by a flood for a year (106:15). The child and his three children alone will be saved from this calamity (106:16–17). Enoch confirms to Lamech that the child is his, instructs him to name the son Noah, and informs him of the corruption Noah and his progeny will escape (106:18). Afterward, Enoch announces that there will be even greater iniquity (106:19), which will continue until a generation of righteousness arises (107:1a). During this generation violence will give way to good (107:1b).

206. Stuckenbruck, "Enoch, Epistle of," 584–85.
207. Milik, Books of Enoch, 178–79.

At Enoch's instruction (107:2), Methuselah tells Lamech that the child is indeed his (107:3a). The child is called Noah, "he who gladdens the earth from destruction" (107:3b).

CRITICAL ISSUES: SOURCES

Scholars generally recognize that the Birth of Noah text (1 En. 106:1–107:3) derives from an earlier document, similar to the Genesis Apocryphon, shaped by the Exhortation (1 En. 91:5–10). Such reshaping, according to Stuckenbruck, resulted in the narrative being told from the perspective of Enoch (106:1, 8–9, 13) and depicting the flood as a type for judgment and salvation (106:13b–17; 106:19–107:1).[208]

CONTRIBUTION AND CONTEXT

The Birth of Noah (1 En. 106:1–107:3) text stands out among the Enochic literature for its placement of Enoch in the unique position to identify Noah's father and significance. Despite the extraordinary aspects of his birth, Noah's name is explained in terms of the fact that he and his sons will survive God's forthcoming judgment on evil and endure into the coming age. Elsewhere Noah is merely alluded to as "the son of Lamech" (10:1–3). In the Book of Giants (cf. 2Q26; 6Q8 2, 26) Noah is saved from the great flood, and Enoch is an interpreter of dreams. The story of Noah is recounted in the Animal Apocalypse (e.g., 1 En. 89:1–9) and, along with related accounts, in the Similitudes of Enoch (54:7–55:2; 60:1–10, 24–25; 65:1–67:3; 67:4–68:5; 69:1–26[?]) and the Book of Dreams (83:1–84:6).[209]

PURPOSE

The presentation of Noah and his sons among the righteous few may serve as an exhortation to the readers. Like Noah, the righteous elect will be rescued from divine judgment on the wicked whose iniquities are part of the readers' present experience.

Eschatological Admonition (1 En. 108:1–15)

INTRODUCTION

The Eschatological Admonition (1 En. 108:1–15) is an appendix to the corpus extant only in Ethiopic, functioning in part as a summary and interpretive

208. Stuckenbruck, *1 Enoch 91–108*, 4, 606–7.
209. Stuckenbruck, *1 Enoch 91–108*, 608–9.

conclusion to the whole work. Its concern is the pious who keep the law in the last days.

PROVENANCE

The text, preserved only in Ethiopic, derives from a Greek *Vorlage*,[210] and its affinities with Jewish conceptions of the Second Temple period and the absence of Christian redaction indicate a Jewish writing appended to a prior Enochic collection.[211]

DATE

The Admonition's familiarity with both the Book of Watchers and the Epistle (see below) requires a date after the end of the second century BCE. The latest possible date is more challenging. Though manuscript evidence in Ethiopic dates from the fifteenth century CE, there is no reason to doubt a much earlier origin for the Admonition, and the text was surely part of the Enochic collection when it took shape in the fourth century CE. Furthermore, the vague description of a "deserted place" in which the wicked are to be punished (108:3c–6) suggests a date prior to the developed articulations of retribution on sinners prevalent from the second century CE.[212] In this respect the text aligns more closely with the end of the first century CE.

CONTENTS

The work describes itself as a book by Enoch for Methuselah and those after him who keep the law in the last days (1 En. 108:1), and therefore it is written in the first person addressed to the second (I-you). Enoch says that his audience, who has observed the law, awaits the end of those who transgress it (108:2). This is a time when sin passes away (108:3a); the sinners, their descendants, and the memory of them will perish (108:3b). Furthermore, their spirits will be slaughtered as they cry out in a desolate place of fiery judgment (108:3c). Enoch then describes a vision in which he sees something like a cloud, flames, and a glorious mountain shaking (108:4). When Enoch asks an accompanying angel about it (108:5), he is told it is the place where the wicked will be punished in accordance with the utterances of the prophets

210. "Vorlage" is a German technical term used to designate a textual tradition in one language from which a text in another language is derived. Here the *Vorlage* is Greek from which the Ethiopic is derived.

211. Stuckenbruck, *1 Enoch 91–108*, 691.

212. Stuckenbruck, *1 Enoch 91–108*, 693–94, citing Apoc. Zeph. 2:1–8; 4:1–7; 10:1–14; 2 En. 7:1–5; 10:1–5; 3 Bar. 2:1–3:8; 4:3–5; T. Ab. 12:1–18 [Rec. A]; 9:1–10:16 [Rec. B].

(108:6). Heavenly records, to which angels may refer, keep accounts of the afflicted and their oppressors (108:7). The righteous victims are described as ones who love God, forsake wealth and their physical well-being (108:8), deny worldly food, and consider their life but a breath (108:9a). These are tested by God and found pure that they might bless his name (108:9b). Enoch claims to have recounted their blessings "in the books" (108:10a) and that God has recompensed them for their lives (108:10b). Despite their hardships, they have "blessed me" (108:10c)—here the speaker seems to switch from Enoch to God. God—speaking in the first person—announces that he will summon the spirits of the pious, transforming those among them who died (108:11), and enthrone each of them (108:12). They will shine, because God is faithful (108:13), and witness the punishment of sinners (108:14), who in turn will see the righteous shine (108:15).

CONTRIBUTION AND CONTEXT

The Admonition shares with other Enochic writings the presentation of Methuselah as the first of Enoch's descendants to receive his message (1 En. 108:1; cf. 81:1–82:4; 91:1–4; 93:1–2). Similarly, the wicked are presented as punished and destroyed (108:3–7), as they are in the Book of Watchers (e.g., 17:1–22:14) and in the Epistle (e.g., 102:4–104:8). The Admonition also shares with the Epistle explicit concern for obedience to the law (108:1; cf. 99:2a) and the path of the righteous (91:18–19; cf. 94:1–5; 108:12–13, 15; cf. 104:2b). Notably, the Admonition recognizes an authoritative tradition aside from Enoch in "the prophets" (108:6). Stuckenbruck observes unique features in the Admonition as well,[213] such as a punishment for the wicked that is not delayed to the eschaton (e.g., 22:10–13; 103:7–8) but takes place immediately after death. For their part, the righteous are said to be "lowly" (108:7); they "love God" (108:8, 10) and are tested by him (108:9), belong to "the generation of light" (108:11), and even sit on a throne of God's glory (108:12).

PURPOSE

The author's community is among the righteous who "keep the law in the last days" (1 En. 108:1), though in the present life they are trampled down by men and reproached (108:10). Nevertheless, they are indeed the "generation of light" (108:11a) who have not yet received recompense appropriate for their faithfulness (108:11b). They will shine (108:12a, 13a, 14a, 15a), be enthroned (108:12b), and see the faithfulness of God (108:13b). The wicked

213. Stuckenbruck, *1 Enoch 91–108*, 692–93.

both misinterpret the prophets (108:6) and oppress the righteous (108:7, 10). Their lot is judgment in darkness (108:14–15). The unique concern in the Admonition that the wicked will be judged immediately after death and that the righteous will themselves witness this judgment (108:13–15) suggests a readership concerned that justice is done. Enoch's vision (108:6–15) provides much-needed assurance that vindication is imminent.

Reception History of 1 Enoch

While noting the disparity of the collection called 1 Enoch outlined above, a survey of the reception of 1 Enoch can be divided into the various parts of the work in Jewish and Christian traditions as well as the Ethiopic context in which the whole of the work is preserved.[214]

In the context of Second Temple Judaism, discussion begins with the preservation of various portions of 1 Enoch among the Dead Sea Scrolls, including the Book of Watchers, the Astronomical Book, the Book of Dreams, the Epistle of Enoch, and the Birth of Noah (though nothing is found among the Scrolls from the Book of Parables or the Eschatological Admonition). But at Qumran the reception of 1 Enoch transcends the manuscript witness of the document itself to its influence on other works found there. It has also influenced Aramaic works such as the Aramaic Levi Document, Testament of Qahat, Pseudo-Daniel, Genesis Apocryphon, and other works such as the Pesharim, Apocryphal Psalms, and the book of Jubilees. It is also likely that 1 Enoch influences the language of other Qumran texts in their depiction of "angels of destruction" (e.g., 1QS IV, 12; CD-A II, 6; 1QM XIII, 12).[215]

Jubilees adopts from the Enochic material its understanding of the revelation of the ordering of the cosmos and history before the time of the flood. And so Jubilees recognizes Enoch as the recipient of divine revelation who "functions as a calendrical sage."[216] This is an important observation, for it not only is taken from the Enochic Astronomical Book (cf. Jub. 4:17–18) but also expands, from either the Apocalypse of Weeks or the Animal Apocalypse, to see Enoch as one who is able to foretell human events until the final judgment (cf. Jub. 4:19) and to testify against the evil of humanity (Jub. 4:19, from the Epistle of Enoch). Jubilees also draws especially from the Book of Watchers (1 En. 6:1–9:3; 15:3–16:1) its Enochic tradition about the myth of

---

214. Stuckenbruck, "*Book of Enoch*," 7–40.
215. Stuckenbruck, "*Book of Enoch*," 11–14.
216. Stuckenbruck, "*Book of Enoch*," 13.

the rebellious angels (cf. Jub. 5:1–11; 7:21–25; 10:1–6, 7–14).[217] Outside of the Scrolls, influence of the Enochic traditions, or at least literary parallels, is found in the Wisdom of Solomon in its argument about the fate of the righteous dead (Wis. 2:1–4:9; cf. 1 En. 102:6–103:15) and its attention to Enoch as one whose piety before God led to his exalted status (Wis. 4:10–15). And finally, Philo of Alexandria, like the Enochic materials, regards the "sons of God" (Gen. 6:2, 4) as angels (1 En. 6:2; 19:2; 21:10; 100:4; 106:5, 12).[218]

Influence of 1 Enoch can also be found in the writings of early Christianity, and the material here is quite vast.[219] Even limiting the discussion to the Book of Watchers (1 En. 1–36) yields a notable amount of material.[220] Some familiarity with Enochic traditions is suggested in the writings of Paul (1 Cor. 11:10), Peter (1 Pet. 3:18–22; 2 Pet. 2:4–5), the Revelation of John (Rev. 4:1; 12:8), and the Letter of Jude (Jude 6, 14–15). Jude cites the Book of Watchers (1 En. 1:9), in which Enoch, the seventh from Adam, predicts divine judgment (Jude 14; cf. 1 En. 37:1; 60:8), which attests to the widespread dissemination of Enochic traditions by the first century CE.[221]

While it is unclear to what degree Enochic (1 Enoch) traditions circulated beyond the first century in exclusively Jewish contexts, it is evident in Christian texts. First among these is the Jewish-Christian Testaments of the Twelve Patriarchs, where appeal is made explicitly to the writings (or words) of Enoch (T. Sim. 5:4; T. Levi 10:5; 14:1; T. Jud. 18:1; T. Dan 5:6; T. Naph. 4:1; T. Benj. 9:1; cf. T. Zeb. 3:4) in contexts in which sins to be committed by the sons of Jacob are said to be predicted, though no actual text is indicated. The writings of Enoch are cited as "scripture" in the Epistle of Barnabas (130s CE; Barn. 16:5–6; cf. 1 En. 89:56, 60, 66–67; 91:13–18). Augustine (354–430) knows the Enochic writings, but while he draws on them for some of his own writings,[222] he insists that they not be regarded as scripture.[223] After Augustine, there is little evidence for explicit interest in Enochic traditions in the West.[224]

The story is quite different in the East, particularly in the Ethiopic tradition, where the Book of Enoch (*Mäshafä Henok*), alongside works like Jubilees,

217. See Stuckenbruck, *Myth of the Rebellious Angels*, 36–57.
218. Cf. Philo, *Giants* 2–4; Philo, *QG* 1.92. Stuckenbruck, "*Book of Enoch*," 14–15. See esp. Stuckenbruck, "To What Extent," 131–42.
219. See, for example, Stuckenbruck and Boccaccini, *Enoch and the Synoptic Gospels*; deSilva, *Jewish Teachers of Jesus*, 101–40.
220. For more focused studies, see Harkins, Bautch, and Endres, *Watchers in Jewish and Christian Traditions*.
221. Stuckenbruck, "*Book of Enoch*," 16–17.
222. Augustine, *Civ.* 15.23, 18.38.
223. Stuckenbruck, "*Book of Enoch*," 17–20.
224. Nickelsburg, *1 Enoch 1*, 94.

retained a place in sacred Ethiopian Christian tradition.[225] Although prior to the fifteenth century the status of the Book of Enoch in the Ethiopian church is unknown, it was likely valued in that context as early as the fourth century. But it is clear that the fifteenth century saw not only a recognition of the value it held in Ethiopia but also an elevation of its status. There was, to be sure, discussion about the formal inclusion of the Book of Enoch among the Ethiopian scriptures that revolved around its use in liturgical settings, its use in theological and mystical texts, its manuscripts, and whether it was to be included among the eighty-one sacred writings said to compose this canon. For many in Ethiopia today, 1 Enoch is one of the most important books in the tradition of the Ethiopian church.[226]

---

225. The most complete discussion of this tradition is Stuckenbruck, "*Book of Enoch*," 21–39.
226. Stuckenbruck, "*Book of Enoch*," 22–24, 40.

2

4 Ezra

Introduction

Nested within the book of 2 Esdras is a Jewish apocalypse from the end of the first century CE known as 4 Ezra. The fictional setting of this work is thirty years after the destruction of Jerusalem by the Babylonians (ca. 557 BCE). The real setting, though, is shortly after the destruction of Jerusalem by the Romans in 70 CE. Israel is forced to come to terms with this tragedy, and much of the narrative of 4 Ezra depicts the very real angst experienced by Jews who survived these events. Amid the turmoil, the author of 4 Ezra deals with the culpability not only of Israel's gentile oppressors but of Israel itself. The author also wrestles with the notion of God's justice in allowing these events to happen to Israel, with whom God himself made a covenant. Curiously, the main figure of the vision, Ezra, is generally regarded to have lived over one hundred years after the fictional setting. It may be for this reason that Ezra in 4 Ezra is also known as Salathiel, father of Zerubbabel (Shealtiel; 4 Ezra 3:1), who is more aptly suited chronologically for this setting (cf. 1 Chron. 3:17). Ezra is likely chosen as the protagonist for this work because of his role in restoring the instruction of Torah to Israel (4 Ezra 14). In the story line of the book, Ezra develops from one who mourns over the destruction of Jerusalem and questions God's justice to one who is granted understanding of God's ways through a series of revelations and offers comfort to Israel.[1]

1. Nickelsburg, *Jewish Literature*, 270–71.

92

Languages and Manuscripts

Partly on the basis of extensive evidence of Hebrew syntax, terms, and idioms, most scholars recognize that 4 Ezra was originally written in Hebrew.[2] It is curious, though, that no portion of 4 Ezra is extant in Hebrew, nor is there any evidence of its use in other literature from the Second Temple period. Even its Greek translation from antiquity has not survived in full but only in early Christian quotations.[3] A more extensive Greek version can be reconstructed, though, from other versions translated from the Greek (Latin, Syriac, Ethiopic, Georgian, Armenian, Coptic, and Arabic). Technically, two independent Greek translations were produced from the Hebrew original. The Latin and Syriac derive from one Greek translation, and the Ethiopic and Armenian (as well as two Arabic versions, portions of the Georgian, and a Coptic fragment) from the other.

In its present form 2 Esdras is composed of three works: a Christian apocalypse known as 5 Ezra (= 2 Esd. 1–2), the Jewish apocalypse known as 4 Ezra (= 2 Esd. 3–14), and another Christian apocalypse, known as 6 Ezra (= 2 Esd. 15–16). The Christian writings were appended to the Latin text of 4 Ezra. A preface, perhaps dating from the second century CE, includes two chapters known as 5 Ezra but referenced as 4 Ezra 1–2 (or 2 Esd. 1–2). Contrary to the earlier, Jewish material, these chapters assert that God has forsaken Israel (4 Ezra 1:24–26, 33–37; 2:10–11) and replaced "Mother Zion" with the "Mother Church" (2:1–7, 15–17, 30–32). Additional chapters dating from the third or fourth century were appended to the end of the earlier, Jewish material as 6 Ezra, referenced as 4 Ezra 15–16 (or 2 Esd. 15–16), which addresses Christian persecution.[4]

Table 2.1

4 Ezra Embedded in 2 Esdras

2 Esdras chapters	Other names
2 Esdras 1–2	5 Ezra
2 Esdras 3–14	4 Ezra
2 Esdras 15–16	6 Ezra

2. Violet, *Die Esra-Apokalypse*, 2.xxxiv–xxxvii.
3. E.g., the Apostolic Constitution (2.14.9 resembles 4 Ezra 7:103; 8.7.6 quotes 4 Ezra 8:23) and Clement of Alexandria (*Strom.* 3.16 quotes 4 Ezra 5:35; *Strom.* 1.22 quotes 4 Ezra 5:5a). Stone, *Fourth Ezra*, 4–5.
4. Nickelsburg, *Jewish Literature*, 277.

Provenance

The exact provenance of 4 Ezra is unknown. Some see an affinity with the rabbis in Yavneh, though there is no evidence of its influence on later rabbinic writings.[5] The place of composition is also unclear. References to Babylon (e.g., 4 Ezra 3:1, 29) suggest to some that the author was in Rome, though this is difficult to substantiate. The work's affinities with 2 Baruch and a Hebrew *Vorlage* yield a consensus that it was written in Palestine (see discussion below).[6]

Date

With the fictional setting of thirty years after the Babylonian destruction of Jerusalem in 587/586 BCE, it may be that 4 Ezra was written thirty years after the Roman destruction of 70 CE—namely, about 100 CE.[7] It is widely agreed that, like 2 Baruch, the author of 4 Ezra is writing in response to the destruction of the temple in 70 CE.[8] Specifically, the Roman symbol of the eagle is prominent in the Eagle Vision (4 Ezra 11–12), and its three heads represent the three Flavian emperors, Vespasian (r. 69–79 CE), Titus (r. 79–81 CE), and Domitian (r. 81–96 CE).[9] This suggests a date around or shortly after the end of the latter's reign. Quotations found in the writings of Clement of Alexandria require a Greek version of 4 Ezra no later than 190 CE.[10] Some have attempted to identify items within the book with known historical events, equating the "unexpected ruler" (4 Ezra 5:6) with Herod the Great or the Roman emperor Octavian (Augustus). Likewise, the splits of the earth (4 Ezra 5:8) have been identified with the earthquake of 31 BCE or the eruption of Mount Vesuvius in 79 CE. Yet the general nature of the signs here and elsewhere likely precludes such specific identifications.[11]

Contents

Fourth Ezra is a collection of seven units, each with its own central revelation (3:1–5:20; 5:21–6:35; 6:36–9:26; 9:27–10:59; 11:1–12:51; 13:1–58; 14:1–48).

5. Nickelsburg, *Jewish Literature*, 276.

6. Stone, *Fourth Ezra*, 9–10; J. Collins, *Apocalyptic Imagination*, 242.

7. Nickelsburg, *Jewish Literature*, 270. However, Stone (*Fourth Ezra*, 8–9) sees this as a merely typological reading of Ezek. 1:1 and therefore of little value for identifying the date of composition.

8. See Stone, *Fourth Ezra*, 9.

9. Alternatively, Lorenzo DiTommaso has argued for later revisions of an earlier original of the Eagle Vision (chaps. 11–12) from as late as ca. 218 CE in the reign of Septimus Severus. DiTommaso, "Dating the Eagle Vision."

10. Clement of Alexandria, *Strom*. 3.16, quotes 4 Ezra 5:35.

11. Stone, *Fourth Ezra*, 8.

Each of the first three segments begins with a prayer regarding God's justice, after which an angel responds and dialogue on the subject ensues (cf. 1 En. 12:3; Dan. 9).

The First Section (4 Ezra 3:1–5:20)

The setting is the thirtieth year after the destruction of Jerusalem, during which Salathiel (Ezra) is in Babylon (4 Ezra 3:1a). He lies in bed, troubled because of the desolation of Zion and uttering prayers to God (3:1b–3). In his prayer Ezra complains about the sinful condition that was introduced into humanity by Adam and brought about death (3:4–7a). The pattern of sin and punishment continued with Adam's offspring through the time of Noah and the flood (3:7b–11) and that of the patriarchs from Abraham through Moses (3:12–19). Yet, Ezra complains, God did not by the law remove evil from the human heart (3:20–22). Even with the establishment of David's kingdom in Jerusalem and subsequent sacrifices offered there, the evil heart in humanity remained unchanged from the time of Adam (3:23–27). Ezra himself witnesses the wickedness of Babylon and cannot fathom why it is treated as more righteous than Zion (3:28–36).

The response to Ezra's prayer comes not from God himself but from the angel Uriel (4:1). Rather than answering Ezra's question directly, Uriel poses problems for him to solve as a means of illustrating to him that God's ways are incomprehensible (4:2–4). First Uriel instructs Ezra to weigh fire, measure wind, or call back the past (4:5). When Ezra acknowledges his inability to do so (4:6), Uriel rebukes him for having the audacity to think he can ascertain things even more lofty in the ways of God (4:7–12). The second problem posed to Ezra is a parable: If he were to judge in a fictitious story between the waves of the sea and the trees of the forest, which would he favor (4:13–18)? When Ezra points out the foolishness of both in their desire to transgress their natural boundaries (4:19), Uriel turns the same charge on him for demanding to know the ways of God (4:20–21).

In response to these rebukes Ezra complains that his inquisitive nature is given by God (4:22–24), and his concern is for God's very reputation (4:25). Uriel then concedes information to Ezra, telling him that he is witnessing the sadness sown in the world, which will one day be harvested (4:26–32). When Ezra inquires about how long it will be until the matter is resolved (4:33), Uriel responds that God's timing cannot be hastened (4:34–37). Though Ezra speculates that the delay is caused by human sin (4:38), Uriel says this is not the case (4:39–41). By further inquiries (4:44–46) Ezra learns that more time has passed than is yet to come (4:47–50), though he does not learn whether he shall live to see those days (4:51–52). Ezra then learns that particular signs will occur prior to the end (5:1–13). When Ezra awakens from his vision, he is approached by a leader of Israel, who suggests Ezra has abandoned the people and exhorts him to return to care for the flock (5:14–18). Ezra dismisses the man and commences a seven-day fast to prepare for the next vision (5:19–20). This concludes the first vision.

The Second Section (4 Ezra 5:21–6:35)

This vision begins after a seven-day reprieve (4 Ezra 5:21) when Ezra recovers and speaks to God (5:22). He asks why God has allowed the nations he has not chosen to punish the one he has (5:23–29). For Ezra, it would be better to be punished by God himself (5:30). In an ensuing dialogue with the angel, Ezra affirms that though he does not love Israel more than God does, he longs to understand the ways of the Most High (5:31–34). The angel illustrates that God's ways are incomprehensible to people in general and Ezra in particular (5:35–40). Undeterred, Ezra asks why God does not arrange matters so that his judgment comes sooner (5:41–43). Again through analogies, the angel counters that God arranges his creation as he sees fit (5:44–49). When Ezra returns to the question of the nearness of the end (5:50), the angel reveals that they are nearer the end than the beginning (5:51–55) and describes signs of its coming (5:56–6:24). Survivors of those events will see God's salvation (6:25–28). The vision concludes with a command for Ezra to fast another seven days in preparation for the next revelation (6:29–35).

The Third Section (4 Ezra 6:36–9:26)

Like the second vision, Ezra's third vision begins after a seven-day fast with a prayer to God (4 Ezra 6:36–37). Here Ezra asks, If all creation is made for Israel, why does Israel not yet possess it, and how long will it be until it does (6:37–59)? In response the angel says to Ezra that Israel must pass through the dangers it faces before claiming its inheritance (7:1–16). When Ezra inquires about what hope the wicked may have (7:17–18), the angel explains that they have only themselves to blame for their fate because they scorned God's law (7:19–25). This is followed by a description of what will occur in the last days (7:26–44). The new city will appear (7:26), and the righteous will see God's wonders (7:27). The messiah, God's son, will appear and reign four hundred years (7:28). He and all humanity will die (7:29), and the world will lay silent for seven days, as at the beginning (7:30). After this the world will be awakened and the dead will rise (7:31–32). Then the Most High will appear in judgment (7:33), with blessings to the righteous (7:34) and recompense for the wicked (7:35). Particular attention is given to the furnace of hell, which lies opposite the paradise of delight (7:36) and into which the wicked nations are to be cast (7:37–44).

Ezra is then concerned that nearly everyone has sinned and that therefore God's blessings will be enjoyed by only a few (7:45–48). To this the angel retorts that God will rejoice over the few that are saved and not grieve over the many who perish (7:49–61). This gives way to Ezra's lament, where he bemoans the fact that humans are capable of understanding their impending judgment (7:62–69). The angel responds that the human capacity to understand renders them culpable for the sins they commit and the consequential torment (7:70–74).

Ezra takes the inquiry further by asking about what occurs to a person immediately after death (7:75). The angel responds that first a spirit leaves the body and returns to God to give him praise (7:76–78). The wicked then go immediately to unending torment in seven distinct ways (7:79–87). Those who have kept God's ways will be separated from their bodies and have rest in seven orders (7:88–101). Ezra then asks if the righteous may intercede for the ungodly (7:102–3). When he receives a negative answer (7:104–5), he again commences a lament for the human condition caused by Adam's sin (7:106–26). But, according to the angel, the sinful condition is not the fault of Adam but is a contest waged by every person (7:127–31). Ezra then appeals to mercy like God showed to Moses (7:132–40), but the angel again affirms it is but a few who will be saved (8:1–3).

This is followed by two lengthy prayers to God for mercy on the wicked (8:4–19a; 8:19b–36). Ezra is then reminded that just as not all seeds sown take root, so also not all people will be saved (8:37–41). God responds to Ezra's frequent identification with the unrighteous that he is among the praiseworthy and hence a beneficiary of God's promised blessings (8:42–54). Therefore, Ezra is instructed not to ask any more about the many who perish (8:55–62a) but simply to know that the signs will indicate the nearness of the judgment (8:62b–9:12). Again Ezra is instructed to ask no more about the fate of the wicked (9:13). Nevertheless, Ezra again complains that there are more who perish than are saved (9:14–16). Again Ezra is told that God created all humans and supplied them with all their needs, yet they have turned corrupt and will perish while the few righteous will be saved (9:17–22). Then Ezra is instructed to prepare for the next revelation another seven days, not by fasting but by praying and eating only flowers (9:23–26).

The Fourth Section (4 Ezra 9:27–10:59)

Like the previous revelations, the fourth occurs after seven days of preparation (4 Ezra 9:27) and extended prayer to God affirming the endurance of the
law (9:28–37). This is followed by a vision in which Ezra takes on a very different
role, from complaining to comforting. In his vision he sees a woman mourning
(9:38–39), telling Ezra that after thirty years of barrenness she gave birth to a
son (9:40–45a). She and her husband rejoiced, and when the child grew up, she
found him a wife and prepared the marriage feast (9:45b–46). Yet as he entered
his wedding chamber, the son died, and she entered her mourning (10:1–4).
Ezra responds that she should trust in the justice of God, anticipate receiving
her son back at the resurrection, and conceal her mourning (10:5–17). When
she refuses (10:18), Ezra again exhorts her to lay down her grief by comparing
her sorrows, and correspondingly her hope, to those of Zion (10:19–24). Suddenly the woman's face begins to shine; then she disappears and in her place
is the heavenly Jerusalem (10:25–27). Ezra calls on the angel Uriel to interpret
the vision (10:28–32). From him Ezra learns that the woman mourning, whom
Ezra consoled, is no less than Zion herself (10:33–44). Her thirty years of
barrenness correspond to the three thousand years before the world made its
first offerings in the temple of Solomon (10:45–46); her raising the son was
the time of residence in Jerusalem (10:47); the son's death corresponds to the
destruction of Jerusalem (10:48); and her glorification is a vision of what Zion
will one day be (10:49–54). Ezra is then told that in his next vision he will see
what God will do to those on the earth in the last days (10:55–59).

The Fifth Section (4 Ezra 11:1–12:51)

The next vision begins with the appearance of an eagle with twelve wings
and three heads (4 Ezra 11:1).[12] The eagle spreads its wings over the earth
and sprouts other wings, leaving all things subject to him (11:2–6). Then a
voice comes from the midst of its body (11:7–10), and eight smaller, opposing
wings become visible (11:11). Each of the eight opposing wings arises but
only three of them rule (11:12–21). Then the twelve wings and two smaller
wings disappear, leaving only the eagle's body, the three heads, and the six
smaller wings (11:22–23). The two smaller wings separate from the rest and
set themselves up but disappear (11:24–27). When two other wings plan to
reign together, one of the heads awakes and joins with the other two heads
and devours the two smaller wings (11:28–31). The one head gains control

---

12. These represent the three Flavian Roman emperors, Vespasian, Titus, and Domitian; cf.
2 Bar. 36–40; Rev. 13 (Nickelsburg, *Jewish Literature*, 275).

of the whole earth and dominates its inhabitants (11:32), after which one of
the remaining heads disappears (11:33) and another is devoured (11:34–35).
Then Ezra sees a lion arise and rebuke the eagle, informing him that the
Most High has heard of his insolence and that his end is near (11:36–46).
After this Ezra sees the remaining eagle head and two wings disappear and
its body burned (12:1–3a).

When Ezra asks for an interpretation of the vision (12:3b–9), he learns
that the eagle is the fourth kingdom in the vision of Daniel (12:10–12). The
twelve wings correspond to twelve kings that will reign in succession over a
kingdom that will emerge (12:13–16). The voice that comes from the midst
of the eagle represents the struggles that will arise in the midst of the time of
that kingdom (12:17–18). The eight small wings correspond to eight kings
that shall arise (12:19–21), and the three heads represent three kings that will
come to power in the last days (12:22–25). The heads that disappear are the
deaths of successive kings (12:26–30). The lion is the messiah who will come
to rebuke the eagle (12:31–32). He will destroy them and deliver the remnant
(12:33–34). After Ezra receives this interpretation, he is told to wait seven
more days (12:35–39). Then the people gather and bemoan Ezra's absence
(12:40–45a). Ezra exhorts them with the message he has heard (12:45b–50).
He then sits in the field seven days and eats only flowers (12:51).

The Sixth Section (4 Ezra 13:1–58)

The next vision begins with a dream in which Ezra sees the sea and a
man coming up out of it (4 Ezra 13:1–3a). The man flies with the clouds and
speaks with an imposing voice (13:3b–4). Then a multitude of men from all
directions converge on the man from the sea, who carves out a great mountain
and flies up on it (13:5–7). When the opponents press their attack, they are
burned to ashes by the breath of the man's mouth (13:8–11). He then comes
down from the mountain and calls another multitude to him, some joyful and
bringing offerings, others sorrowful and bound (13:12–13a). Ezra awakes from
his vision and asks God for an interpretation (13:13b–20a). It is explained
that the man coming out of the sea is the one the Most High has kept for
many ages to deliver God's creation and deliver the righteous who are left at
the end of days (13:20b–26). The wind and storm coming from his mouth
anticipate the day when the man, the son of the Most High, will rebuke the
nations and destroy them (13:27–38) and save the righteous within his borders
(13:39–50). All these things have been revealed to Ezra alone because he has
devoted himself to wisdom (13:51–56a). Ezra is then told that he will be told
more things after three days (13:56b–58).

The Seventh Section (4 Ezra 14:1–48)

The final vision begins with Ezra, who is sitting under an oak tree, being summoned by the Lord (4 Ezra 14:1–3). Ezra is told that he, like Moses, is given heavenly secrets (14:4–8). Ezra will be taken up from among men to live with God's son until the times are ended (14:9–12). Therefore, he is instructed to set his house in order and instruct the people (14:13–18). Ezra then prays that God will send the Holy Spirit to enable him to write the things written in the law for the instruction of future generations (14:19–22). God grants this request and tells Ezra to make preparations (14:23–26), which include addressing the people with a charge to discipline their hearts so that they may receive mercy at the judgment (14:27–35). Ezra concludes his message with a charge for them not to seek him for forty days (14:36) while he gathers five men and proceeds to a field where he is to remain (14:37). The next day the voice instructs Ezra to drink a curious substance, and instantly his heart is given understanding (14:38–41). The five men with Ezra are given understanding to write what Ezra dictates for forty days, culminating in ninety-four books (14:42–44). Of these, Ezra is to make public only twenty-four, and the remaining seventy are only for the wise among the people (14:45–48).

Critical Issues: Sources and Structure

The transformation of Ezra in the story line of 4 Ezra suggested to some scholars (G. H. Box and W. O. E. Oesterley) that the document was a collection drawn from distinct sources. Since Hermann Gunkel, most scholarship has held that there is a unity to the book and attributes its disparities to the state of mind of the author, who was troubled by the disaster of Jerusalem's recent destruction. Debate remains, however, about how the dialogues (4 Ezra 3:1–9:26) relate to the visions (9:27–13:58) and the epilogue (14:1–48). Some suggest the dialogues depict debates current among the original setting of the book, with the author's views aligned with Uriel. For Michael E. Stone, the figure of Ezra experiences a conversion of sorts, which is cognitive in the dialogues and culminates in a more extensive religious experience in the visions.[13] For some, the shift from dialogue with Uriel to visions represents the author's sympathy with Ezra's distress in posing his questions and, at the same time, the inadequacy of a dialogical means of resolution. For Karina Martin Hogan, "the shift from dialogue to vision form represents the author's conviction that the questions of theod-

13. Stone, Fourth Ezra, 31–32.

icy he raises through Ezra in the dialogues cannot adequately be addressed through rational discourse, but only through the religious symbolism of the visions."[14]

Contribution and Context

Theodicy

Two fundamental concerns drive the movement of the book through a series of questions and answers, or dialogues, between Ezra and the angel Uriel. The first question pertains to why God created human beings with an inclination to evil. The second asks why Israel was given over to its enemies when Israel is more righteous than them in terms of obedience to God's statutes. Initially Uriel's answers are unsatisfactory in that he simply appeals to the notion that God's ways are incomprehensible to humans (4 Ezra 4:11; 5:35). Eventually, as the discourses unfold successively, Uriel acknowledges that a seed of evil was planted in Adam from the beginning (4:30). Nevertheless, God has provided his law by which people should live and thereby avert the requisite punishment for evil (7:20–21). Furthermore, Uriel rejects Ezra's contention that Israel has kept God's commands better than other nations on the grounds that most of Israel has been unfaithful to the covenant (7:22–24, 129–31). Naturally this implies that the vast majority of people will be punished in the final judgment and a very small minority in the end will be saved (7:61–62, 89; 8:3). Ezra appeals to God's mercy toward his created beings (8:4–36) and by this point remains unconvinced that God's justice must result in so few passing through judgment.[15]

Midway through the book, beginning in the fourth vision, Ezra experiences a transformation of sorts. First he begins to realize that the culmination of Israel's hope lies in a future intervention of God (10:27; cf. 10:44; 13:36) and the emergence of God's messiah, who will pronounce judgment on the Roman Empire (the eagle; 11:36–46). This messiah is "one like the son of man" (cf. Dan. 7:13; 4 Ezra 13:3, 25–26), whose role is to execute God's righteous judgment on wicked nations by means of fire (the Torah; 4 Ezra 13:38) and gather to himself a multitude of dispersed tribes and of those who remained in Palestine (13:12–13, 39–50). Finally, Ezra himself transitions from one who questions God's justice to one who defends it, exhorting the faithful to heed God's commandments and receive his mercy (14:34).

14. Hogan, "Ezra, Fourth Book of," 626.
15. Hogan, "Ezra, Fourth Book of," 624.

Torah and Inspiration

At the close of the book (4 Ezra 14) Ezra is portrayed as a Moses-like figure, restoring the lost Torah by means of inspiration (14:1–8).[16] This is important for several reasons. First, Ezra is said to receive his message by divine revelation. Ezra asks God to send the Holy Spirit to him that he may write "everything that has happened in the world from the beginning" (14:22a), with the purpose that people may find a path of life (14:22b). For this task God will "light in [his] heart the lamp of understanding, which shall not be put out until what [he is] about to write is finished" (14:26).[17] And so Ezra's task of writing is undertaken under the inspiration of God himself. Second, Ezra is explicitly instructed to rewrite scripture that had been burned (14:19–26),[18] a role in which he is equated with Moses (14:13; cf. 12:37–38; 14:5, 8, 27–35).[19] Third, in his reception of this revelation Ezra gains not merely the twenty-four books of the Hebrew Scriptures; he also receives revelation to dictate to his scribes another set of seventy books intended only for the wise (14:44–47; cf. 12:37–38). The designation of twenty-four books of the Hebrew Bible is a familiar way of accounting for the collection (cf. b. Ta'an. 8a; Num. Rab. 13:15–16), though some sources count twenty-two (Josephus, Ag. Ap. 1.8 §38). More curious is the revelation of these additional, secret books. Nothing is said of what these books are, but they may be apocalyptic works such as 4 Ezra itself.[20]

Purpose

Discerning the overall setting, purpose, and function of 4 Ezra is complicated by the problem of its literary unity and the dialogical nature of the text. Those who espouse distinct, even contradictory sources account for the tensions raised by the opposing views of Ezra and Uriel earlier in the book by appealing to prior sources or even conflict within a community that may simply be exhibited in the conflict within the narrative. Yet Stone advocates "a very distinct overall progressive development in Ezra's position," which supersedes the structural underpinnings assumed by prior

16. Some regard the terminology for "the law" in 4 Ezra more broadly than the Mosaic law, taking it to mean rather "divine instruction." See Hogan, "Meaning of *tôrâ*."

17. For further consideration of the nature of inspiration in 4 Ezra 14:37–38, see Stone, *Fourth Ezra*, 119–24.

18. Najman, "Ezra, Fourth Book of."

19. Stone, *Fourth Ezra*, 416.

20. Stone, *Fourth Ezra*, 441.

scholars and accounts for the framework and structure of the book as a whole, which is presented in seven visions.[21] This rubric sees the dialogues not as contradictions between opponents in a community but as a natural progression for a Jew who questions God's justice in the destruction of Jerusalem by Titus in 70 CE, which must be "absolutely central to the author's thought."[22]

The social setting of 4 Ezra has generated some discussion. Some see the author as a member of an apocalyptic community that considered itself to be the faithful remnant of Israel, while the rest of the people had been led astray by unfaithful leaders.[23] Others suggest 4 Ezra is the text of a sectarian community, the members of which considered themselves to be the righteous remnant because of their faithfulness before God, while the rest of the people, especially those in power, had fallen away from God's law.[24] Yet such isolationist readings contradict the work's affinities with other Second Temple texts, not to mention its concerns for theodicy (Apocalypse of Abraham; 2 Baruch; cf. Biblical Antiquities).[25] Another theory averts this problem by suggesting the author is a Jewish leader writing after the destruction of Jerusalem, trying, in some sense, to reformulate Judaism.[26] Perhaps in recognition that apocalyptic works need not be generated by disenfranchised religious groups,[27] some have argued that 4 Ezra was likely composed by learned Jews informed by the Hebrew Scriptures, producing an interpretive writing in some sense.[28] This coheres with the notion of Jewish leaders trying to articulate "a Jewish way of life in a time when the temple was not functioning."[29] In this regard Ezra's meeting with Phaltiel, "a chief of the people" (4 Ezra 5:16–19) suggests an affiliation with leadership looking for divine guidance for God's people.

The pessimism of the first three sections and the limited scope of those experiencing salvation suggest a restricted readership. In addition to Ezra's affinities with the leadership, his instruction is to reveal eschatological secrets to the wise, not the general population (as in, e.g., Jub. 1:4–7; 1 En. 82:1–3). This is not for public consumption. Whether the "public-private" distinction here is a literary device or an indication of social setting, Bruce Longenecker

21. Stone, *Fourth Ezra*, 28.
22. Stone, *Fourth Ezra*, 10.
23. Kee, "'The Man' in Fourth Ezra."
24. Overman, *Matthew's Gospel and Formative Judaism*, 27–34.
25. Longenecker, *2 Esdras*, 102.
26. Grabbe, "Chronography in 4 Ezra."
27. Grabbe, "Social Setting"; Davies, "Social World."
28. Knibb, "Apocalyptic and Wisdom."
29. Longenecker, *2 Esdras*, 102–3.

suggests it appears to function as the latter—it was "written for a consciously distinct group within the general population of Israel."[30]

The author, then, was a Jewish leader writing after the destruction of Jerusalem for a distinct group of Jewish leaders, who may "have recognized something of themselves in the figures of Ezra and Phaltiel."[31] That is, the questioning of God's justice throughout may depict the real angst of the authors. In 4 Ezra God's justice is questioned early on by Ezra and affirmed by Uriel. It is also the issue that Ezra comes to terms with in the second half of the book—not by a reasoned conclusion but by a "volitional decision to subscribe to the assessment of God as the benevolent and righteous sovereign of the world."[32] The transition occurs in the fourth section (4 Ezra 9:27–10:59), where, after the perspectives of Ezra and Uriel play out in an even-handed exchange, Ezra "internalizes and articulates the sentiments that Uriel had voiced earlier, affirming the justice of God without complaint."[33] It may be that this resolution to accept the justice and sovereignty of God is among the messages of 4 Ezra as a whole. This confidence escalates in the book to the final section (4 Ezra 14:1–48), where faithfulness to the law is espoused in a confident hope in God's ultimate salvation. The progression of Ezra's development of faith in Israel's God likely reflects the pilgrimage of those responsible for the book as a whole.[34]

There may be several ways in which the text was to function within the author's community: advocating steadfast regard for Torah, advocating confidence in God's sovereign plan and their ultimate vindication, and perhaps implicitly advocating caution in taking up arms against Rome as a means of national reconstitution. An important indication of this reading is how Uriel's repeated attempts in the first three sections undermine Ezra's interest in the reversal of Israel's fortunes in the present world. This, alongside Uriel's attempts to redirect Ezra's focus to the vindication of the righteous in the world to come, lays the prerogative for Israel's fortunes squarely on God. There is no role for the righteous in overthrowing evil or establishing justice.[35] This is affirmed in the role of the messiah, who himself overthrows evil (4 Ezra 13:38). The people themselves are not combatants; they are peaceable (13:12, 39, 47).

As opposed to other texts in which the righteous execute justice on the wicked (Apoc. Ab. 29:18–19; cf. 1QM), 4 Ezra encourages a degree of passivity.

30. Longenecker, 2 Esdras, 104.
31. Longenecker, 2 Esdras, 104.
32. Longenecker, 2 Esdras, 95.
33. Longenecker, 2 Esdras, 95.
34. Longenecker, 2 Esdras, 94, 96.
35. Longenecker, 2 Esdras, 105.

Yet even here the author extends instruction on eschatological matters to the select few who are charged to handle it responsibly. "Matters concerning the end of this age when God will overthrow all other claimants to power and eradicate all evil—these matters are not to be the object of speculation within the ranks of the general population, but only among the wise. The people of Israel need only to be instructed in the ways of the law in an attitude of complete confidence in God."[36] This message fell on deaf ears for those who saw fit to initiate revolt against Rome under Bar Kokhba (132–135 CE). But for the author the question of theodicy ultimately remains unresolved and becomes peripheral to his main purpose. This, it seems, is to call Jews who survived the 70 CE tragedy to live faithfully in accordance with Torah and, at the same time, to exhort them implicitly to a patient trust in God in the political setting in which they live.

Reception History

There is no evidence that 4 Ezra bears any influence on ancient Jewish literature. Instead, reception of 4 Ezra is first evident in Greek-speaking Christianity. The work influenced later Christian apocalyptic works (Greek Apocalypse of Ezra [Esdras] and the Apocalypse of Sedrach) and is quoted in a few early Christian writings. It is most important in the Latin church, where it is augmented by two prior chapters (chaps. 1–2; 5 Ezra) and supplemented by two later chapters (chaps. 15–16; 6 Ezra). The work as a whole is included as an appendix to the Latin Vulgate. The Vision of Ezra (*Visio Bead Esdrae*) is a later Latin composition, seemingly derived from the Greek Apocalypse of Ezra and the Apocalypse of Sedrach. The Armenian language preserves two recensions of the Questions of Ezra, which is concerned with the ultimate fate of the righteous as well as sinners in a question and answer form patterned after that of 4 Ezra.[37]

36. Longenecker, *2 Esdras*, 106.
37. Stone, *Fourth Ezra*, 5, 45.

Comparing 4 Ezra and 2 Baruch

Fourth Ezra and 2 Baruch share a number of distinct features. Both are Jewish apocalyptic writings composed after the destruction of Jerusalem in 70 CE, likely in Hebrew and in the environs of Judea. Both are written to Jews in response to the Roman destruction and address the problems it creates. Both are also set within the fictitious context of the destruction of the Solomonic temple by the Babylonians in the sixth century BCE. Both present a scribe anxious to understand God's justice in allowing gentiles to destroy the Holy City and the sanctuary of God's people. The form of revelations and dialogues is very similar in both documents, as are many formal, thematic, and verbal parallels. Both protagonists are scribal figures from the Hebrew Bible who engage in a dialogue with God or his angel in their respective formative journeys.

The dominant models for analyzing the nature of the relationship between these two documents have been literary in nature. Some suggest that 4 Ezra is dependent on 2 Baruch, or that 2 Baruch is dependent on 4 Ezra;[1] that both are dependent on a common source or even a common author;[2] or that the direction of interdependence cannot be determined.[3] More recently Matthias Henze has advocated a model that allows for the complicated interrelationship between text and transmission on the one hand and composition and oral performance on the other. Henze argues that the similarities between the documents originated at a time prior to their present, final form, and that their respective compositions were both oral and written in nature.[4]

---

1. See Bogaert's list in Bogaert, *Apocalypse de Baruch*, 1:26; Box, "*4 Ezra*," 2:553; Metzger, "Fourth Book of Ezra," 1:522.

2. Klijn, "2 (Syriac Apocalypse of) Baruch," 1:620.

3. Charles, "2 Baruch," 2:477; Stone, *Fourth Ezra*, 39; Nickelsburg, *Jewish Literature*, 287.

4. Henze, "4 Ezra and 2 Baruch"; Henze, *Jewish Apocalypticism*, 148–86.

3

2 Baruch

Introduction

Second Baruch is an ancient apocalypse featuring Baruch, the scribe of Jeremiah, who is called from his role as companion and secretary to the prophet (Jer. 36:4–10, 26, 32) and placed as a nobleman (2 Bar. 21:12; 43:2–3; 51:59). In 2 Baruch he becomes the recipient of a prophetic revelation—perhaps even as the successor to Jeremiah,[1] who is an apocalyptic visionary and crucial leader of God's people in a time of crisis. Like 4 Ezra, this work is written after the destruction of the temple in 70 CE and is trying to process the inexplicable tragedy that befell the people of God.

Languages and Manuscripts

The superscript to 2 Baruch 1:1 indicates the Syriac is a translation from the Greek, which is widely recognized to be the case.[2] Though a few scholars have held that Greek is the original language of composition,[3] most argue for a Hebrew or even Aramaic original. The reasons are several: 2 Baruch's references to texts from the Hebrew Bible follow the Hebrew rather than the

1. J. Wright, "Baruch," 266.
2. See Klijn, "2 (Syriac Apocalypse of) Baruch," 1:616.
3. Whitters, *Epistle of Second Baruch*, 15n46, 17n56; Bogaert, *Apocalypse de Baruch*, 1:353–80. See Zimmerman, "Textual Observations"; Charles, *Apocalypse of Baruch*, xliv–lii; and esp. Violet, *Die Apokalypsen des Esra und des Baruch*, 344–50.

Greek traditions (LXX); some Syriac expressions are only intelligible when retroverted to Hebrew; numerous Hebraisms appear throughout; and affinities with rabbinic writings abound. For Bruno Violet, the primary reason for favoring a Semitic origin is that the extant Syriac tradition does not coalesce with the extant Greek fragment.[4]

Second Baruch is found in the earliest surviving manuscript of the entire Syriac Bible, Codex Ambrosianus (MS 7a1),[5] which dates from the sixth or seventh century,[6] though some texts of 2 Baruch were preserved fragmentarily in lectionaries. Codex Ambrosianus was found under A. M. Ceriani's curatorship of the Ambrosian Library in 1855. In it, the text 2 Baruch is composed of about 8,800 Syriac words in all. It consists of two parts, the Syriac Apocalypse (2 Bar. 1–77) and an epistle (2 Bar. 78–87). The text of the Syriac Apocalypse is persevered primarily in that language. In addition to Codex Ambrosianus, 2 Baruch is found in four Syriac-language Jacobite lectionaries. It is also preserved partially in Greek (2 Bar. 11:1–13:2; 13:11–14:3) from the Oxyrhynchus papyri cache of the fourth or fifth century.[7] A Latin excerpt (2 Bar. 48:36, 33–34) is found in a single citation from Cyprian.[8] An Arabic manuscript from the tenth or eleventh century (Sinai No. 589)[9] contains all of the Syriac Apocalypse and is likely a translation from a Syriac text slightly different from that found in Ambrosianus. The Epistle of 2 Baruch is preserved in thirty-six Syriac manuscripts,[10] including Codex Ambrosianus, generally in two recensions with slight differences.[11]

Provenance

Second Baruch is widely recognized as a "boundary-maintaining" Jewish document with characteristics such as the centrality of Torah, a robust nationalistic identity, and an eschatology that all suggest authorship by a "Torah-observant Jew."[12] The consensus, then, is that the work was written by a Torah-observant Jewish author between the First and Second Jewish Revolts against Rome.

---

4. Violet, *Die Apokalypsen des Esra und des Baruch*, lxii–lxiv.
5. Whitters, *Epistle of Second Baruch*, vii, 4.
6. Klijn, "2 (Syriac Apocalypse of) Baruch," 1:615.
7. Whitters, *Epistle of Second Baruch*, 8 and n. 17.
8. *Ad Quirinum testimonia adversus Judaeos* 3.29.
9. Van Koningsveld, "Arabic Manuscript."
10. Klijn, "2 (Syriac Apocalypse of) Baruch," 1:615–16.
11. Whitters, *Epistle of Second Baruch*, 14.
12. Davila, *Provenance of the Pseudepigrapha*, 128. Rivka Nir's contention that 2 Baruch is a Christian document has not been widely accepted. See Nir, *Destruction of Jerusalem*.

Date

Most scholars have recognized that because the destruction of the temple in 70 CE seems to be alluded to in 2 Baruch (32:2–4) and since there is no apparent indication of the Bar Kokhba revolt (ca. 135 CE), the writing of 2 Baruch occurred somewhere in between these two events. Some argue that 2 Baruch's relationship to 4 Ezra, coupled with the apparent nearness of the 70 CE tragedy, suggests a date sometime toward the end of the first century CE.[13] The only clear indication of the date of composition (1:1) indicates "the twenty-fifth year of Jeconiah." This expression is borrowed from the Hebrew Bible and refers to the reign of Jeconiah (Jehoiachin; 1 Chron. 3:17), who took the throne of Judah at age eighteen and reigned in Jerusalem for three months (2 Kings 24:8) prior to being taken to Babylon (2 Kings 24:12). Second Baruch's reference to the twenty-fifth year of his "reign" places him in captivity in Babylon (cf. 2 Kings 25:27), which seems to suggest the author may see himself likewise within a time of exile. The designation of the "twenty-fifth" does not appear to have any symbolic value, which may suggest it is to be taken literally. If so, then the book dates from the twenty-fifth year after the Babylonian captivity (i.e., the destruction of 70 CE)—that is, 95 CE.[14]

Contents

Second Baruch is typically divided into seven sections, though there is much less consensus on where they are. Most scholars see divisions at chapters 20/21 and 52/53; divisions within chapters 1–20, 21–52, and 53–77 are more disputed. The difficulty lies in the fact that there are many points of transition throughout the book—speeches, prayers, locations of Baruch, fasts, revelations—that could serve as points of division. Perhaps a reasonable approach centers on the sections delineated by fasts, for which the divisions by R. H. Charles and a few others (which are followed below) can be useful.[15]

The first section (2 Bar. 1:1–5:7) places Baruch's narrative before the destruction of 70 CE. Baruch is provided with a warning of the coming disaster and some explanation. This involves punishment for the sins of the Southern tribes, who will be removed from God's favor "for a time." God himself will destroy Jerusalem (cf. 5:1–4) because of the sins of the people, yet God commands Baruch and Jeremiah to depart because their prayers and good

13. Nickelsburg, *Jewish Literature*, 283. See Gurtner, *Second Baruch*, 16–18.
14. See Gurtner, "'Twenty-Fifth Year of Jeconiah.'"
15. Klijn, "2 (Syriac Apocalypse of) Baruch," 1:616; Charles, *Apocalypse of Baruch*, 1, 9, 13, 20, 36, 74.

deeds are protecting the city from the destruction that must come (2:2). When Baruch protests (3:4–9), he learns that the destruction is only a temporary chastisement rather than a final judgment (4:1). Furthermore, the city of Jerusalem is a mere shadow of the heavenly Jerusalem (4:2–7), but Baruch still responds in lamentation and the first fast (5:5–7).

In the second section (6:1–9:1) the destruction itself is described (6:1–8:5). Baruch sees angels burning the walls of Jerusalem, though the temple vessels are removed first to ensure their subsequent reuse at the restoration (6:5–10). Baruch and Jeremiah again respond with lamentations of grief (cf. 5:6; 6:2) and the next fast (9:1).

The third section (10:1–12:5) begins with an extended lament, reiterating the temporary duration of the catastrophe and the impending judgment on the Babylonian (Roman) perpetrators (11:1–7; 12:1–4). This is followed by another fast (12:5), anticipating another revelation in the fourth section (13:1–20:6). Here one finds an extended dialogue between God and Baruch on theodicy: "Why has the mighty God brought upon us this retribution?" (13:4). Baruch learns that God's punishment is intended to bring about repentance and forgiveness (13:10), though both Israel and the nations have been ungrateful for God's benefits and grace (13:12). Baruch's objections (14:1–19) are not immediately answered by God (15:1–8), though God does assert humanity's responsibilities in light of the law, the justice of God's judgment (15:1–16:1), and for the righteous, the new things to come (chaps. 17–20).

The fifth section (21:1–47:2) begins with another extended dialogue concerning the "consummation of times" (21:1–30:5). Here Baruch's prayer about the duration of Israel's hardships (21:1–26) is answered by God in terms of his plans for the redemption of the righteous (22:1–24:2). They will endure a season of tribulation, after which the messiah will come to establish eschatological bliss (24:3–30:5). Baruch then assembles Israel for instructions based on the revelation just received (chaps. 31–43). The temple will be destroyed and rebuilt in the new creation (32:3–6), Baruch himself will depart (32:7–33:30), and the people are exhorted to obey the law (32:1–2) in preparation for the coming judgment of God (40:1–43:3). Next, Baruch gathers the people for another instruction about the law (44:1–47:2), which he informs them will inaugurate the incorruptible world to come (44:8–45:3).

The sixth section (48:1–77:26) completes the apocalypse proper. After fasting and praying (48:1–49:3), Baruch is told that those who have been faithful to the law will enjoy eschatological bliss (50:1–51:13; 52:3–7), whereas the wicked will be separated and face judgment (51:14–52:3).

The next segment of section six (53:1–77:26) begins with a vision of bright and dark waters (53:1–12), followed by a request for its interpretation

(54:1–22). The angel Ramial explains that the vision pertains to Israel's history in alternating seasons of righteousness ("bright waters") and wickedness ("dark waters"), beginning with Adam (56:5–16) through the disaster that has "now befallen Zion" (67:1–9), and ultimately a season of restoration and rebuilding (68:1–8). The final "bright water" of vindication and eschatological bliss (72:1–74:4) is followed by a series of praises to God (75:1–6) and exhortations to Israel to obey (75:7–77:19).

The seventh and final section of 2 Baruch (chaps. 78–87) is a letter sent to the nine and one-half tribes. First (78:1–80:7) it recounts the narrative of 2 Baruch 1–9. This is followed by words of consolation (81:1–82:9) and exhortations to obey the law, especially in light of imminent judgment (83:1–87:1).

Critical Issues: Epistle of 2 Baruch and the Apocalypse

As noted above, some manuscript evidence indicates the Epistle circulated independently of the Apocalypse, raising the question as to whether it should be considered part of the Apocalypse of Baruch[16] or distinct from it.[17] Recent work utilizes literary analysis to demonstrate that the letter is an integral part of the overall message of 2 Baruch as a whole, especially with respect to time and geography.[18]

Contribution and Context: Eschatology and Torah in 2 Baruch

Torah observance is central to the message of the book as a whole,[19] but it is couched in an overriding eschatological outlook. This takes shape early on when God announces to Baruch that the days are coming, and are very near, when God will visit the world (2 Bar. 20:1–2, 6; cf. 24:4; 48:33–37; 54:17; 82:2). This is the end of days—also described as "the completion of all things" (83:23; cf. 27:14–15; 49:5; 83:6; 85:12), which is already prepared (21:17)—in which God's power may be made known to those who think God's forbearance is weakness (21:20). At that time the Most High will bring about a new world (44:12; cf. 32:6; 83:1) and accomplish good works (69:4). This is driven by Baruch's assessment of the past, frustration at the present crisis, and anticipation of the future reward for the faithful. The latter is a "time of

---

16. Charles, *Apocalypse of Baruch*, lxv–lxvii; Charles, "2 Baruch," 2:476; Whitters, *Epistle of Second Baruch*, 8.

17. Sayler, *Have the Promises Failed?*, 98–101.

18. Whitters, *Epistle of Second Baruch*, 33, 64.

19. Gurtner, "On the Other Side." Cf. Gurtner, "Eschatological Rewards."

redemption," which extends from the establishment of the messianic reign to the final actualization of the other world. This time includes the messianic era that restores and transforms the world, as well as resurrection, judgment, and the appropriation of the other world. In this scheme, the messianic era "has one foot in each world," culminating in the ultimate "salvation" for God's people.[20]

Within 2 Baruch's eschatological scheme the rewards for the righteous are found after the onset of tribulations (25:1, 3; cf. 13:3). The destruction of Jerusalem and its temple are, of course, integral parts of the tribulations. Yet that particular catastrophe is wrought by God himself, who instructs his angels to carry it out (7:1–2) and has himself abandoned the temple (8:2; cf. 32:3). Through the tribulations, the righteous receive a kind of purging; that is, tribulations occur "in order that, in the last times, you may be found worthy of your fathers" (78:5). Yet tribulations give way to rewards in an imminent (23:7) season of God's redemption (ܦܘܪܩܢܐ, *purqānā*; 23:7) and consolation (44:7). Moreover, the present season of tribulation pales in comparison to the bliss of those who persevere and do not forget the law (44:7–8). Here we catch a glimpse of 2 Baruch's conception of end-time blessing for the righteous. In 2 Baruch's view, people are divided with respect to how they have or have not observed the covenant and the law. This makes Torah observance the central theme. The difference between the righteous and the wicked "comes down to a fundamental acceptance or rejection of the Law."[21] The righteous are those "who have forsaken their vanities and fled for refuge beneath [God's] wings" (41:4). They "make straight [their] ways" (77:6). They are "those who have drawn near" (48:19),[22] which may include gentiles who have taken on the yoke of the law (cf. 41:3).[23] They will not "fall" as long as they keep God's statutes (48:22). They find security and safety as a result of law observance (48:24). Indeed, those who have now been made righteous have been made so by observance of God's law (51:3; cf. 15:5; 21:9), for the righteous are defined as "those who have been saved by their works" (51:7a; cf. 14:7). Indeed, "they have a store of (good) deeds laid up in treasuries" (24:1; cf. 4 Ezra 4:35; 7:77; Matt. 6:19, 20). For them, "the Law has been a hope" (2 Bar. 51:7b). They have acquired "treasuries of wisdom" and "stores of understanding." They have "not withdrawn from

20. Lied, *Other Lands of Israel*, 3–4.

21. Bauckham, "Apocalypses," 180.

22. This is an expression often associated etymologically with προσήλυτος, *prosēlytos*. Donaldson, *Judaism and the Gentiles*, 188.

23. Donaldson, *Judaism and the Gentiles*, 185–93; cf. Deut. 32:21; Ruth 2:12; 1 Kings 16:13, 26; 2 Kings 17:15; Jer. 2:5; 8:19; Jon. 2:8.

mercy" and have "preserved the truth of the Law" (44:14). They are those characterized by faithfulness (54:21) and belief (59:2).

Purpose

George W. E. Nickelsburg helpfully observes that the author of 2 Baruch is still grieved over the 70 CE tragedy and, unlike the author of 4 Ezra, engages not in theodicy but pastoral exhortation: "His own grief has given way to consolation. His admonitions to 'prepare your souls' are part of that consolation and, together with his exhortations to heed God's sages and teachers, they focus on the practical task of reconstruction."[24] The challenge for 2 Baruch's readers is that though they live in the present world, they are told that the future world was created for and promised to Israel (2 Bar. 14:13; 21:25; 83:5; cf. 4 Ezra 6:55–59). As Frederick J. Murphy rightfully claims, Baruch, "and eventually all the righteous, are to escape from the sphere of mortality to one of immortality."[25] Attaining this eschatological bliss is their reward (2 Bar. 52:7; cf. 48:48–50; 54:16–18), acquired to a large extent on the basis of their adequate observance of the law. The book, then, is written "to persuade people to follow a certain theological program promoting obedience to Torah."[26]

Reception History

Much remains unknown about the reception of 2 Baruch. It was once thought that the book was preserved and read among Syriac-speaking Jews recalling the destruction of Jerusalem.[27] But its preservation in exclusively Christian contexts complicates this theory. As a whole it is preserved only in Codex Ambrosianus (MS 7a1), and in part in select Jacobite lectionaries. The lectionaries may show that excerpts from 2 Baruch (44:9–15; 72:1–73:2), and in some instances portions of an original whole, can be extracted and take on their own lives in faith communities in both liturgical collections.[28] Also in lectionaries one finds epithets that read, for example, "from Baruch, the prophet" (lect. 1213).[29] The preservation of 2 Baruch alongside canonical texts

24. Nickelsburg, *Jewish Literature*, 283.
25. Murphy, *Structure and Meaning of Second Baruch*, 56.
26. J. Wright, "Social Setting," 86.
27. Bogaert, *Apocalypse de Baruch*, 1:448–51.
28. Lied, "*Nachleben* and Textual Identity," 428.
29. Lied, "Die Syrische Baruchapokalypse," 329–40.

of the Hebrew Bible may suggest that in some instances communities regarded 2 Baruch as belonging to that corpus of sacred Scripture.[30] Yet even its inclusion in the Syriac Codex Ambrosianus may be an expression of interest in its role to fill "a void in the chronological organization" of the codex.[31] This is because, as in other early Syriac codices, Codex Ambrosianus organizes its books chronologically, "with primary reference to the main protagonists of the books in question."[32] In Liv Ingeborg Lied's estimation, the organizing theme and focus of the codex is on Jerusalem, its falls, and the destruction of its temples. What remains puzzling, however, is the absence of 2 Baruch in other Syriac contexts, suggesting that it was either less known or, perhaps, less important.

30. Lied, "Die Syrische Baruchapokalypse," 329–40.
31. Lied, "2 Baruch and the Codex Ambrosianus," 83.
32. Lied, "2 Baruch and the Codex Ambrosianus," 87.

4

Apocalypse of Abraham

Introduction

Like both 4 Ezra and 2 Baruch, the Apocalypse of Abraham is a Jewish apocalyptic written after the destruction of the temple in 70 CE. Unlike those other works, however, and more like the book of Daniel, this text consists of a first-person narrative of the patriarch's youth and pilgrimage from the idolatry of his fathers (Apoc. Ab. 1–8) and an apocalypse proper in which God makes revelations to him (chaps. 9–32). It is preserved only in the Slavonic translation and is the earliest writing of what evolves into mystical writings in the medieval *hekhalot* traditions.[1]

Language and Manuscripts

The Apocalypse of Abraham is preserved in Old Slavonic, which, when its six constituent manuscripts are collated,[2] provides a full text of the document. It was translated directly from a Semitic original (Hebrew or Palestinian Aramaic)[3] early in the twelfth century and preserved in manuscripts from the fourteenth century or later.

1. Kulik, *Retroverting Slavonic Pseudepigrapha.*
2. These manuscripts date from the fourteenth to seventeenth century. Rubinkiewicz, "Apocalypse of Abraham," 1:681–83.
3. The Semitic origin of the work is seen in its inclusion of numerous Hebrew words and phrases. See Rubenstein, "Hebraisms in the Slavonic 'Apocalypse of Abraham'"; Rubenstein, "Hebraisms in the 'Apocalypse of Abraham'"; Rubenstein, "Problematic Passage."

Provenance

The preservation of the Apocalypse of Abraham in a Slavonic context, its expression of dualistic views, and Christian interpolations complicate clear identification of its provenance. Some have found in its dualism affinities with the Dead Sea Scrolls and posit an Essene provenance,[4] while others suggest such dualism could be attributed to its preservation in Slavonic contexts.[5] Most scholars agree, however, that linguistic evidence and subject matter point to a Jewish original, likely from Palestine. However, its outlook, particularly with regard to the temple, is distinct from that of 2 Baruch and 4 Ezra.

Date

The Apocalypse of Abraham is typically dated from shortly after the destruction of the Jerusalem temple in 70 CE, which is the event of central importance to the work (esp. Apoc. Ab. 27:1–5).[6] Some suggest that the centrality of the temple (e.g., 1:2–3; 25:4; 27:1–5; 29:18; cf. 9:9), as well as a possible reference to events circa 38 CE (1:9), may point to composition prior to the temple's destruction.[7] Regardless of its origin, since the Apocalypse of Abraham is likely first cited in the second century CE, it must have been written prior to that date.[8]

Contents

Narrative (Apoc. Ab. 1–8)

The book begins with Abraham's narration of his observing the gods of his father and brother to see which was strongest (Apoc. Ab. 1:1). In the course of his story Abraham encounters a stone god, Marumath, fallen to the ground (1:2–4). Abraham, with the help of his father, Terah, lifts it to its place only for its head to fall off in Abraham's hands (1:5–6). Thereupon Terah fashions a new god Marumath without a head from another stone and smashes the remains of the first one (1:7–9). Terah then makes five other gods and instructs Abraham to sell them (2:1–3). Along the way three of them break

4. Box, *Apocalypse of Abraham*, xxi–xxiv.
5. Rubinkiewicz, "Apocalypse of Abraham," 1:683.
6. J. Collins, *Apocalyptic Imagination*, 279.
7. Kulik, "Apocalypse of Abraham."
8. Pseudo-Clementine, *Recognitions* 32–33. Rubinkiewicz, "Apocalypse of Abraham," 1:663.

(2:4) and are thrown into a river (2:9). The remaining two are sold at a price suitable for all five (2:5–8). While returning to his father, Abraham ponders the legitimacy of man-made idols being gods (3:1–8).

Upon his return to his father (4:1–2), Abraham explains to Terah that he, Terah, is in fact god to the idols that he himself fashioned (4:3–5). Terah responds in anger (4:6) and instructs Abraham to gather woodchips lying about from his fashioning of gods from fir (5:1–3). Among the remains Abraham finds a small god called Barisat (5:4–5), whom Abraham instructs to tend a fire set to prepare Terah's food in his absence (5:6–8). Later, to his amusement, Abraham finds Barisat ablaze and consumed by the fire (5:9–11). Abraham himself prepares Terah's meal on the fire and encourages his father to praise Barisat, who threw himself on the fire to cook the food (5:12–15). Presumably missing the humor and irony, Terah indeed praises Barisat and vows to create another to make his food the next day (5:16–17). Perplexed with a mixture of laughter, bitterness, and anger (6:1), Abraham questions his father's sensibility (6:2–7:10). Abraham then appeals to the one true Creator God to make himself known (7:11–12). God answers that prayer, makes himself known to Abraham (8:1–2; cf. Gen. 12:1) as the Creator, and instructs Abraham to leave his father's house, which subsequently burns to the ground (8:3–6).

Apocalypse (Apoc. Ab. 9–32)

Then God himself calls to Abraham, in a scene set in Genesis 15, and identifies himself as the one true Creator God (Apoc. Ab. 9:1–4). He instructs Abraham to offer a sacrifice, at which time God will make known to him great and guarded things (9:5–10). Abraham, hearing the voice but seeing no one, is terrified (10:1–3a). God instructs an angel, Iaoel, to strengthen Abraham and show him the land of his inheritance (10:3b–12). He appears to Abraham and accompanies him to offer the prescribed sacrifices, after which the angel will be invisible forever (10:13–11:6). Abraham and his companion travel to Mount Horeb for forty days and nights, neither eating nor drinking (12:1–3). Abraham is then instructed to prepare the sacrifices with the animals that had been following him without his knowledge (12:4–10). Abraham is doing this (13:1–3) when an unclean bird of prey comes down on the carcasses and speaks, exhorting Abraham to flee (13:4–5). Abraham learns from the angel that the bird is Azazel (cf. 1 En. 6–16), whom the angel rebukes and sends away (Apoc. Ab. 13:6–14). The angel then teaches Abraham how to rebuke Azazel himself (14:1–8) and instructs him not to answer Azazel when he speaks to him (14:9–14).

As the sun is setting, Abraham sees smoke from which the angel comes to him (15:1). The two of them ascend to the edge of the flames, where Abraham sees a strong light (15:2–5) in which a fiery gehenna is kindled and a crowd in the likeness of men is changing forms, running about, prostrating, and crying out (15:6–7). Abraham is told that the Eternal One is approaching him and the angel will strengthen him in his weakness (16:1–3). God's fiery presence approaches them as an ethereal voice (17:1) as the angel and Abraham bow in reverence (17:2–3). Abraham recites a song of praise taught to him by the angel (17:4–19), which turns into a prayer for God to accept and instruct him (17:20–21).

Abraham sees the fire rising and underneath it a throne with angelic figures singing the song of praise (18:1–7). When they finish their song, they exchange threatening looks with one another, which is abated when the angel who is with Abraham intercedes and teaches them the Eternal One's song of peace (18:8–11). Then Abraham sees a chariot with fiery wheels covered with eyes that bears the fiery throne (18:12–13). From the throne Abraham hears the voice of God (18:12–14; 19:1–2; cf. Ezek. 1), who reveals himself as the only god who commands the heavens and heavenly beings (Apoc. Ab. 19:3–9).

Then the Mighty One tells Abraham that like the number of the stars and their power, God will grant to Abraham's seed the nations and men set apart with Azazel (20:1–5; cf. Gen. 15:5–6). When Abraham objects to Azazel's involvement (20:6–7), the Eternal One commands him to look beneath his feet, where he sees the heavens, the earth, and the things therein (21:1–7) that God had created good (22:1–2). There he also sees people divided into two groups, which, he learns, are those prepared for judgment on one side and those set apart with Azazel on the other (22:3–5a). It is the latter, God says, that have been prepared to be born of Abraham and called to be God's people (22:5b).

Then God instructs Abraham to gaze into the garden of Eden, where he sees a man great in height, breadth, and aspect entwined around a woman (23:1–5). They are standing beneath the tree of Eden, which has fruit that looks like bunches of grapes (23:6). Behind the tree stands a figure like a dragon, with hands, feet, and wings, feeding the grapes to the entwined couple (23:7–8). God identifies the couple as Adam and Eve, and the dragon-like figure as Azazel (23:9–11). In astonishment, Abraham asks why God gave Azazel such dominion on earth (23:12). God explains that Azazel is given dominion (only) over those who desire evil (23:13). In response Abraham asks why God should even allow such evil to come about (23:14), which God answers by showing Abraham what will be in the last days (24:1–3). Abraham witnesses the extent of perdition brought about by the lawless one—murder, fornication, theft—leading to destruction (24:4–9). Then he sees the idolatrous practices of Israel, led by a man slaughtering in the temple who makes the Lord angry (25:1–6). Then Abraham sees that heathens will come and kill the people of Jerusalem and destroy its temple (26:1–27:5). He learns that it is his own seed that has provoked God to such judgment (27:6–12) and that his wayward seed will live under God's judgment until the end of time (28:1–29:2).

Next Abraham sees a man from among the heathens worshiped by a crowd of heathens, joined by Azazel but abused by others (29:5–7). The man is identified as the descendant of Abraham who will be the liberation from the heathen (29:8–10). God explains that the worshiping means that many heathens will trust in him, while those abusing him are offended by him (29:11–12). He is the one who will test Abraham's seed from which God will bring forth a select number of righteous ones (29:13–20).

Abraham returns to earth, and God explains to him the ten plagues he has prepared against the heathen (29:21–30:8; cf. 2 Bar. 27). God will sound a trumpet and send his "chosen one," empowered to summon God's people who were humiliated by the heathen (Apoc. Ab. 31:1). These God will burn in his fiery wrath, and those who favored a foreign god will burn in the fires of Azazel's tongue (31:2–8). Finally, God informs Abraham that his offspring will be enslaved in a foreign land, but God will be judge of that nation (32:1–6; cf. Gen. 15:14).

Critical Issues

The fact that the apocalypse (Apoc. Ab. 9–32) refers back to the previous narrative (chaps. 1–8) suggests the unity of the work. There are, however, some instances of later insertions (chap. 7) or Christian interpolations (29:3–13).[9] In places there are gnostic-like inferences suggesting the God of the Old Testament is evil (20:5, 7; 22:5); these are later and unique to the Slavonic tradition.[10]

Contribution and Contexts

With Abraham as its central figure, the Apocalypse of Abraham naturally has affinities with the book of Genesis, where the account of Abraham (Abram) runs from his call at Genesis 11:26 to his death at Genesis 25:8. The

9. Rubinkiewicz, "Apocalypse of Abraham," 1:684.

10. This may originate in the tenth-century Slavonic tradition of the Bogomils. Rubinkiewicz, "Apocalypse of Abraham," 1:684.

apocalypse in particular is "woven around the story of Abraham's sacrifice in Genesis 15."[11] So it is natural that there are biblical quotations (Apoc. Ab. 8:4 = Gen. 12:1; Apoc. Ab. 9:1–4 = Gen. 15:1; Apoc. Ab. 9:5 = Gen. 15:9; Apoc. Ab. 15:1 = Gen. 15:17; Apoc. Ab. 21:1–4 = Gen. 15:13–14; Apoc. Ab. 32:1–4 = Gen. 15:13–14) and allusions (Apoc. Ab. 20:4 = Gen. 18:27; Apoc. Ab. 20:6 = Gen. 18:30). In his vision Abraham sees things drawn from the book of Ezekiel, such as the four living creatures (Apoc. Ab. 18:5–11 = Ezek. 1:10; 10:14), the wheels full of eyes (Apoc. Ab. 18:3, 12 = Ezek. 1:18; 10:12), the throne (Apoc. Ab. 18:3 = Ezek. 1:26), and the divine chariot (Apoc. Ab. 18:12 = Ezek. 10:6). Some adjustments are made to the Old Testament source, such as the promise to Abraham that his fourth generation will go with him into the land (Gen. 15:13–14), which becomes in the Apocalypse of Abraham the seventh (perfected) generation (Apoc. Ab. 32:1–4).[12]

The Apocalypse of Abraham shares a number of features with other Second Temple texts, such as the conversion of Abraham (Jub. 11:16–12:31; LAB 6; Josephus, *Ant.* 1.7.1 §154; Philo, *Abraham* 15) and his ascent into heaven (4 Ezra 3:13–14; 2 Bar. 4:5; LAB 18:5). Like both 4 Ezra and 2 Baruch, the Apocalypse of Abraham belongs to an apocalyptic tradition established in the wake of the destruction of Jerusalem and its temple in 70 CE and shares their concern for theodicy, though to a lesser extent.[13] The figure Azazel (Apoc. Ab. 13:6–7; 14:5; 20:5, 7; 22:5; 23:11; 29:6–7; 31:5) is known as the chief of the fallen angels from the Book of Watchers (1 En. 1–36; cf. Gen. 6:1–4). He reveals heavenly secrets and is banished to the desert. Here the Apocalypse of Abraham draws on the Book of Watchers.[14] Abraham, like Enoch, rebukes Azazel (Apoc. Ab. 13:6–14; 14:1–14), who is given dominion over people with evil desires (23:12–13) and becomes an agent of God's judgment (31:2–8).[15]

The Apocalypse of Abraham is unique in its cultic focus, which is missing from 4 Ezra and scant in 2 Baruch (cf. 2 Bar. 1–8; 64–66).[16] As the center of the Apocalypse's concern, the temple, with its defilement and anticipated restoration to righteous sacrifices, is of critical importance. This may indicate an implicit critique of the priesthood, with the author belonging to a priestly group alienated from the mainstream.[17] But the Apocalypse of Abraham is

11. J. Collins, *Apocalyptic Imagination*, 280.
12. Rubinkiewicz, "Apocalypse of Abraham," 1:684.
13. J. Collins, *Apocalyptic Imagination*, 279, 288.
14. Rubinkiewicz, "Apocalypse of Abraham," 1:684.
15. J. Collins, *Apocalyptic Imagination*, 284.
16. J. Collins, *Apocalyptic Imagination*, 279; Nickelsburg, *Jewish Literature*, 288.
17. J. Collins, *Apocalyptic Imagination*, 288.

unique in its indictment of the cult itself, resembling the tradition blaming Jerusalem's fall in 587/586 BCE on the sin of Manasseh (2 Kings 21:10–15) but cast within a context of its own setting. For this author, the impropriety of cultic activity in his own day—which he construes as idolatry—was the cause of the tragic events of 70 CE, and the distinction between right and wrong in cultic practices lies at the heart of the author's conception of Abraham's election, heavenly ascent, and eschatological hope.[18]

In the text's apocalyptic setting, Abraham is given a view of the garden of Eden and questions why Azazel was given dominion over the earth. God responds by showing him what will happen in the last days (Apoc. Ab. 24:1–3). This triggers an eschatological outworking for the book, in which Abraham sees gentiles come to Jerusalem, kill its people, and destroy its temple (26:1–27:5). Yet it was his own people who incited God's judgment (27:6–12), and the wayward among them will live under God's judgment until the end of time (28:1–29:2). Abraham's seed will be tested, and from them God will bring forth a select number of righteous (29:13–20). But his wrath will nonetheless fall on those who abuse God's people (29:21–30:8; 32:1–6; cf. 2 Bar. 27), and those who favored a foreign god will burn in the fires of Azazel's tongue (Apoc. Ab. 31:2–8). This eschatological outlook can be seen in terms of an age of ungodliness that endures twelve periods (29:2).[19] After this comes judgment in the form of ten plagues (29:15; 30:2–8), through which the righteous will endure and then be gathered by God's "chosen one" (31:1). The righteous will participate in God's punishment of the wicked (cf. 31:2, 6), and the temple and its sacrifices will be restored (29:17–18).

Integral to the eschatology of the Apocalypse of Abraham is its depiction of God's ordering of history and human affairs. The division of history into twelve hours reflects God's ordering of events, while the periodizing of gentile oppression as four hours, each a hundred years in length, reflects the four kingdoms of Daniel (Dan. 7:17; cf. 2 Bar. 6:4; 64:3; 4 Ezra 11:38), likely culminating in the destruction of the temple. In this respect, the Apocalypse of Abraham shows that "the course of events is predetermined and that the end is near."[20] God's ordering extends to humanity, which is depicted as half on the right as God's chosen people, the descendants of Abraham, and half on the left, the gentiles. The role of the descendants of Abraham is explained only in eschatological terms, in which it can be inferred that the destruction of the temple leaves a purified remnant in Israel. Yet this remnant, the

18. Nickelsburg, *Jewish Literature*, 288.
19. Rubinkiewicz, "Apocalypse of Abraham," 1:684.
20. J. Collins, *Apocalyptic Imagination*, 285.

"righteous," will be gathered. The Apocalypse envisions a man coming from the left, worshiped by the heathens but beaten by the readers' own seed (Apoc. Ab. 29:11–13). The "chosen one" will be sent by God to gather his people and bring judgment on their oppressors (31:1–7). That their acceptance is tied to sacrifices (29:18) suggests a return to a restored Jerusalem cult.

The message or messages of the work are enigmatic. Its attention to the destruction of the temple lays blame on Jewish idolatry, with an interest in cultic activity absent in both 2 Baruch and 4 Ezra. It lacks, however, those works' attention to Torah observance in general. The concern for idolatry "may reflect the proliferation of idols in Judea because of an increasing Gentile population after the destruction of Jerusalem."[21] There may be two main themes in the Apocalypse of Abraham: first, the tension between Israel's status as God's covenant people and its fate at the hands of the gentiles; and second, the practice of idolatry[22] and the special role of Abraham and his descendants in rejecting it.[23] Abraham is the patriarch of Israel with whom God made the covenant, and Israel is identified as Abraham's descendants (Gen. 15). The distinction between Israel and the gentiles "is fundamental to the book, as is evident from the graphic division of the picture of the world into a left side and a right side."[24] The gentiles are the antagonists of Israel, and the Apocalypse of Abraham, like 4 Ezra and 2 Baruch, traces the problem of God's permission of this state of affairs back to the fall. Also like those works, the author here, according to George W. E. Nickelsburg, finds his solution in the future—judgment that fits the respective sins, a restored temple and sacrificial system, and eschatological bliss for Israel.[25]

Purpose

The purpose of the Apocalypse of Abraham can be found in two unifying themes.[26] First, the author stresses the fundamental distinction between the gentiles and Israel, who are inextricably identified as descendants of Abraham. Second, the book stresses the rejection of idolatry and presents its ancient readers' idolatry, particularly within the temple cult, as an abandonment of Abraham's calling in favor of the idolatrous practices of Terah.

21. J. Collins, *Apocalyptic Imagination*, 287.
22. Nickelsburg, *Jewish Literature*, 287–88.
23. J. Collins, *Apocalyptic Imagination*, 282.
24. Nickelsburg, *Jewish Literature*, 287.
25. Nickelsburg, *Jewish Literature*, 288.
26. Nickelsburg, *Jewish Literature*, 287–88.

Reception History

The reception of the Apocalypse of Abraham is obscure. It was virtually unknown for ten centuries. It first surfaced in Bulgaria, then circulated in Russia, with little influence on other writings. Its preservation in Slavonic means that whatever can be discerned about the reception of the Apocalypse of Abraham must be drawn from that context. This can be attributed to the literary productivity under the reign of Simeon of Bulgaria (893–927), whose efforts to elevate his kingdom included translating Greek writings into Old Church Slavonic. It is from this context that the six extant manuscripts, the earliest of which dates from the early fourteenth century, originate.[27]

27. Rubinkiewicz, "Apocalypse of Abraham," 1:686–88.

5

Sibylline Oracles 3–5, 11

Introduction

Whereas the apocalypses discussed throughout this volume belong to a genre native to Second Temple Judaism, the genre of the Sibylline Oracles was used in non-Jewish contexts as early as the fifth century BCE[1] and was subsequently utilized by Judaism[2] and Christianity. The Sibyllines, however, are presented as oracles given not in a vision but through the inspired speech of the Sibyl,[3] a woman in the ancient world who uttered oracles of future events while in a trance-like state.[4] Allusions and references to the Sibyllines are made by Josephus (*Ant.* 1.4.3 §118), the Shepherd of Hermas (4), Justin Martyr (*1 Apol.* 20, 44), Theophilus (*Ad Autolycum* 3, 31), and Clement of Alexandria (*Protrepticus* 2.27; 4.50, 62; *Strom.* 1.15.70; 1.21.108). The Sibylline Oracles are analogous to apocalypses in that they are historical in nature, meaning that they reflect on the course of history.[5] However, they are notably different from the formal apocalypses studied here. These are diaspora writings, and the Jewish diasporic apocalypses (e.g., 2 Enoch, 3 Baruch, Testament of Abraham) do not contain reviews of history but do contain heavenly ascents of the visionary figure. They represent, then, "a

---

1. Parke, *Sibyls and Sibylline Prophecy*.
2. J. Collins, "Jewish Adaptation of Sibylline Oracles"; J. Collins, *Sibylline Oracles of Egyptian Judaism*, 1–19.
3. See J. Collins, *Apocalyptic Imagination*, 290, 300.
4. Nickelsburg, *Jewish Literature*, 194–95.
5. J. Collins, *Apocalyptic Imagination*, 143.

strand of political prophecy that had a considerable impact on one aspect of apocalyptic thought."[6]

Though this phenomenon originated in Ionia with a single woman, similar traditions multiplied among pagans, Jews, and Christians. Typically, the Sibyllines were composed in Greek poetic verse (hexameter) and mentioned explicit political events in specifically named locations.[7] The genre came to be utilized among Hellenized Jews of the diaspora, those for whom syncretism with non-Jewish practices was perhaps more commonplace. But there are additional features of the Sibyllines that enabled Jews to utilize them for their own literary purposes. Romans consulted the Sibyls in times of crisis, so Jews in crisis in a Romanized/Hellenized context may have found the Sibyl a suitable voice for their views. In some instances, the Sibyl was said to be the daughter-in-law of the biblical Noah (Sib. Or. 3:824–27) and is presented as "a prophetess of the high God" (3:818–19) analogous to prophetesses of biblical tradition, such as Deborah (Judg. 4:4) and Huldah (2 Kings 22:14–20). Finally, the similarities of Hellenistic oracles to Old Testament prophecies against foreign nations "may have encouraged the Jewish-hellenistic author to borrow the form and language of the Sibylline Oracles in order to present his own message."[8]

Nevertheless, the Jewish adaptations of the Sibyllines studied here often retain Jewish concerns for the end of time and the primacy of Israel's God over against pagan idolatry and accompanying practices of immorality.[9] Their primary background is the oracles of the Hellenistic era with political interest particular to the restoration of native Egyptian rule and the fall of the Greeks.[10] The fundamental distinction between typical Jewish apocalypses and the Sibylline Oracles is that the former are attributed to revered figures of Israel's past, whereas the Sibylline Oracles are ascribed to the pagan Sibyl and so share in the thought world of Hellenistic propaganda.[11] Of the entire collection of twelve books,[12] only books 3–5 and 11 are Jewish texts from the time between the Maccabees and Bar Kokhba.[13]

6. J. Collins, *Apocalyptic Imagination*, 157.

7. Nickelsburg, *Jewish Literature*, 194–95.

8. Bartlett, *Jews in the Hellenistic World*, 36–37.

9. Cf. Plutarch, *De Pythiae oraculis* 9; Livy, *Ab urbe cond.* 42.2–6; Tibullus 2.5.67–74; 6; Dionysius of Halicarnassus, *Antiquitates romanae* 4.62.6; 7; Strabo, *Geogr.* 17.1.43. Nickelsburg, *Jewish Literature*, 194–95.

10. J. Collins, *Apocalyptic Imagination*, 145.

11. J. Collins, *Apocalyptic Imagination*, 145; J. Collins, "Sibylline Discourse."

12. These are numbered 1–8 and 11–14. The disparity of numbering comes from the collection of manuscripts. See J. Collins, "Development of the Sibylline Tradition."

13. Book 8 is a Christian expansion of a Jewish original. Books 6 and 7 are Christian writings. Books 12–14 are Jewish writings from later periods. See J. Collins, *Apocalyptic Imagination*, 145–46. The extant version of Sibylline Oracles 1–2 is a Christian work that is really a single,

Sibylline Oracles 3

Introduction

Sibylline Oracles 3 is the oldest of the Sibylline tradition, a collection of oracles dating from the second century BCE through the early first century CE and stemming from various settings.[14] A major theme of the entire collection is the ancient struggle for kingship and sovereignty.[15] The collection likely developed in three main stages,[16] identified as the main corpus (vv. 97–349 and 489–829), oracles against various nations (vv. 350–488), and a seemingly misplaced conclusion to a different work (vv. 1–92).[17] Each segment in the main corpus begins with an exclamation by the Sibyl in which she claims God's inspiration for her prophecy.

Sibylline Oracles 3:1–92

INTRODUCTION

Verses 1–92 are topically unrelated to the rest of Sibylline Oracles 3, a verdict corroborated by manuscript evidence. Verses 1–45 resemble the writings of Theophilus of Antioch (d. ca. 183/185 CE)[18] and may date as early as the second century BCE. It is unclear when and how they became associated with verses 46–92, to which they otherwise seem unrelated. The three distinct oracles of verses 46–92 can be dated with some clarity. The first, verses 46–62, is marked by the defeat of Antony at the Battle of Actium (31 BCE). Rome has control over Egypt (v. 46), and the second triumvirate is in place (v. 52). Verses 63–74 pertain to the coming of "Beliar," who will come from the "Sebastēnoi," which is often taken as the line of Augustus, thereby identifying Beliar with the Roman emperor Nero. It describes his rise to power and ultimate downfall and was likely added to the Sibyllines sometime after 70 CE. Cleopatra is the central figure in verses 75–92, described as a defeated widow (v. 77), no longer a glorious queen (vv. 78–80), who brought calamity on the world (after ca. 31 BCE), implying the despair of diaspora Jews living in Egypt. Evidence from this disparate collection suggests authorship after 31 BCE to sometime around 70 CE, most certainly by Egyptian Jews.

---

continuous work and may come from a Jewish original. Wassmuth, "Sibylline Oracles 1–2"; Watley, "Sibylline Identities"; Wassmuth, *Sibyllinische Orakel 1–2*. Some claim Sibylline Oracles 1–2 are Christian compositions entirely. See, e.g., Lightfoot, *Sibylline Oracles.*

14. Buitenwerf, "Sibylline Oracles 3."
15. J. Collins, *Apocalyptic Imagination*, 148.
16. J. Collins, "Sibylline Oracles," OTP 1:354.
17. Buitenwerf, *Book III of the Sibylline Oracles*, 137–43.
18. Theophilus, *Ad Autolycum.*

CONTENTS

Verses 1–45 deal with the uniqueness and immutability of God (vv. 1–7), exhorting people to praise him and denounce idolatry (v. 8). God has made humankind, not the other way around (vv. 9–28). Idolaters worship not God but what he has created; they rejoice in evil, forget divine judgment, and ravage booty without shame (vv. 29–45). Verses 46–92 are composed of three distinct oracles. Verses 46–62 describe the rule of Rome over Egypt (vv. 46–48) and the establishment of the second triumvirate (Antony, Lepidus, and Octavian; v. 52) as times of calamity (vv. 53–62). Verses 63–74 describe the rise of "Beliar" (Nero), who will come to great power, perform signs, but ultimately be destroyed. Verses 75–92 describe the rise of Cleopatra, whom the author praises at first but whose failure leaves the author in despair. A final oracle, seemingly unrelated to the rest, lauds the rising of the sun (vv. 94–95).

CONTRIBUTION AND CONTEXT

This section of Sibylline Oracles 3 provides readers with a unique slant on diaspora Judaism. Although the utilization of the pagan guise of the Sibyl suggests a degree of syncretism, the author affirms the eternality and invisibility of God (vv. 11, 15) and the folly of idolatry. The eschatology of these Egyptian Jews couches the end times in terms of despair surrounding the defeat of Cleopatra (vv. 46–62, 75–92).[19] But the Sibyl anticipates a savior who will hold influence over the whole earth, not just Egypt (v. 49; cf. 3:75–92; Isa. 47:8–9; Sib. Or. 5:512–31; Rev. 6:13–14).

Sibylline Oracles 3:93–294

INTRODUCTION

The oldest and main unit of Sibylline Oracles 3 contains verses 97–349 and 489–829. The reference to the seventh king of Egypt (vv. 193, 318, 608) suggests Ptolemy VII (Neos Philopator, r. 145–144 BCE) or Ptolemy VI (Philometor, r. 181–146 BCE),[20] though ambiguity in how kings were counted and whether Alexander was reckoned the first king complicates the matter. It is generally held that the Sibyl's confidence in the Ptolemaic kings and the overall positive view of the king's relationship with Egyptian Jews suggest a date of composition from 163 to 45 BCE. The references to the seventh king of Egypt and the mention of Egypt throughout (e.g., vv. 155–61) indicate an Egyptian origin for Sibylline Oracles 3. Typically, scholars look to Alexandria, the locus of a

---

19. J. Collins, "Sibylline Oracles," *OTP* 1:361.
20. Bartlett, *Jews in the Hellenistic World*, 37.

significant Jewish population in antiquity, for the particular place of origin. But the strong political inclinations of Sibylline Oracles 3 differ widely from the allegorical literary milieu characteristic of Alexandria.[21] Moreover, the concern for cultic matters in general and the temple in particular (see vv. 286–94, 564–67, 657–59, 715–18) may suggest instead the city of Leontopolis, where a Jewish temple was constructed under the priestly auspices of Onias.[22] This is supported by the work's acclamation of the Ptolemaic king as a savior who establishes a peaceful rule. This suggests a date of composition circa 160–50 BCE.[23]

CONTENTS

The first of the series of oracles (Sib. Or. 3:93–161) recounts episodes from primeval history.[24] It describes the fall of the Tower of Babel (vv. 97–104), followed by a narrative of the mythical war between the Titans and Cronos (father of Zeus) as the first of the wars of all mortals (vv. 105–55). Finally, the Sibyl explains that in God's judgment the descendants of the Titans and Cronos all died, and new empires arose (vv. 156–61).

The second series of oracles in this unit (3:162–95) is an utterance from God regarding the future kingdoms of the world, beginning with the house of Solomon (v. 167). Others include the "overbearing and impious Greeks" (v. 172) and the Macedonians (v. 173), who will be destroyed by God (v. 174). Then "another kingdom" will arise that is "many-headed" and "from the western sea" (vv. 175–76). This kingdom, which is Rome, will rise in might and haughtiness but is rebuked by the Sibyl for injustice and impiety (vv. 177–84), particularly homosexuality (vv. 185–93). But it will be overthrown when a king from Egypt, of the Greek race, will rule (vv. 192–93), and the people of God will again be strong (vv. 194–95).

The third section (3:196–294) is headed "A prophecy of various woes." It anticipates God's judgment on the Titans (v. 199) and the Greeks (v. 202), the latter by tyrannical and proud kings (vv. 202–5). Other nations will likewise be judged with similar calamities (vv. 206–17). The oracle breaks with an

---

21. J. Collins, "Sibylline Oracles," *OTP* 1:355.

22. Onias IV (or Onias III), son of the high priest, fled from Jerusalem to Egypt (Josephus, *Ant.* 12.9.7 §§383–388; *J.W.* 1.1.1 §§31–33; 7.10.2 §§423–425), where he implored Ptolemy (Ptolemy VI Philometer) to allow him to build a Jewish temple in Egypt (ca. 172 BCE). Ptolemy granted his request and assigned him the city of Leontopolis in the region of Heliopolis (Josephus, *Ant.* 13.10.4 §285). There he was to build his temple and ordain Levites and priests (Josephus, *Ant.* 13.3.1–2 §§62–71; 20.10.3 §§235–237) in service for local populations of Jews (Josephus, *J.W.* 7.10.3 §430), all amply funded by local revenue (Josephus, *J.W.* 7.10.3 §430).

23. J. Collins, "Sibylline Oracles," *OTP* 1:356.

24. Buitenwerf, "Sibylline Oracles 3." See Buitenwerf, *Book III of the Sibylline Oracles*, 61–64.

account of the Jews (vv. 213–19), followed by an extended praise for their goodness and nobility largely depicted in terms of pagan practices that they do not observe (vv. 220–47). This is followed by an account of the exodus and the covenant at Sinai (vv. 248–64). But even Israel will experience the hardship of exile because of idolatry (vv. 265–82). But God promises a "good end and very great glory" for Israel, who is exhorted to trust in God's laws (vv. 283–84). God will send a king (v. 286) from an unwavering royal tribe (v. 288) who will raise up a new temple of God (v. 290) and restore the temple to what it was before (v. 294).

CONTRIBUTION AND CONTEXT

The entirety of 3:97–161 is an introduction to the remainder of the book, presenting the key theme of world kingship and the conflict it causes and thus providing a context for the oracles that follow pertaining to the end times. The remaining four sections of the main corpus (vv. 162–95, 196–294, 545–656, and 657–808) depict the pattern of sin (typically idolatry) that leads to judgment and tribulation, which in turn is brought to an end by the rise of a new king or kingdom.[25]

Sibylline Oracles 3:295–488

INTRODUCTION

While most of this segment (Sib. Or. 3:295–488) deals with affairs in Egypt, the first oracle (vv. 350–80) relates an anticipated vengeance of Asia on Rome. The entirety of this section (vv. 295–488) is "essentially a string of very brief pronouncements of doom against a wide range of peoples and places, many of them in Asia."[26] There is only very brief mention of anything Jewish (e.g., Babylon at the beginning, and Gog and Magog at v. 319).

CONTENTS

This segment begins with a collection of woes against Babylon, Assyria, Egypt, Gog and Magog, and Libya (vv. 295–349). The next part is an oracle (vv. 350–80) in which Asia takes vengeance on Rome. The downfall of the Macedonian kingdom after its conquest of Babylon is predicted next (vv. 381–87). Then (vv. 388–400) the oracle anticipates the coming of Alexander the Great on Asia, but Alexander himself and his race (Macedonians) will be

25. J. Collins, "Sibylline Oracles," *OTP* 1:354.
26. J. Collins, *Apocalyptic Imagination*, 147.

destroyed. A collection of catastrophic prophecies largely pertaining to the Trojan War makes up verses 401–88.

Contribution and Context

The oracle dates from after the Battle of Actium (31 BCE) and was likely written in Egypt. It is curious that there is nothing decidedly Jewish about this segment, making it equally plausible that it was adopted by Jews rather than written by them. Nevertheless, it exhibits some harmony with the positive sentiments toward Ptolemaic (Egyptian) rulers in the main segments of Sibylline Oracles 3.[27] In this respect its importance lies in the presence of anti-Roman sentiment among Egyptian Jews. The prophecies of verses 401–88 are attributed to the Sibyl of Erythrae, who allegedly prophesied the fall of Troy[28] and sang of Helen and the Trojan War.[29] The majority of verses 350–480 depicts little interest in ethical concerns but relates to the other oracles of Sibylline Oracles 3 by virtue of their prophecies of destruction uttered against other cities.

Sibylline Oracles 3:489–656 and 3:657–808

Contents of Sibylline Oracles 3:489–656

This segment begins with a series of prophetic woes against the Phoenicians, Crete, Thrace, Gog and Magog, and Greece (vv. 489–544), followed by an exhortation to the Greeks (vv. 545–72), rebuking them for idolatry and exhorting them to revere the one true God. The oracle then turns to a prophecy of a resurgence of Jews, who honor the Most High, his temple, and his law, unlike the idolatrous nations (vv. 573–600). This gives way to a prophecy of judgment on immoral and idolatrous humanity (vv. 601–18), a judgment after which God will bless the earth (vv. 619–23). Appeal is made to the "devious mortal" to repent and turn to God and his ways (vv. 624–34), which is followed by the threat of eschatological tribulations (vv. 635–51). Hope at last is offered (vv. 652–56) when the Sibyl announces that God will send "a king from the sun"—presumably Egypt—who will put an end to evil war and rule according to the "noble teachings of the great God" (v. 656).

Contents of Sibylline Oracles 3:657–808

The oracle describes the wealth of the temple, over which the kings of the earth will fight and to which they will lay siege (vv. 657–68). God will

---

27. J. Collins, "Sibylline Oracles," *OTP* 1:358.
28. Lactantius, *Divinarum institutionum libri VII* 1.6.
29. Pausanias, *Descr.* 10.2.2.

respond in mighty judgment against the assailants (vv. 669–76) so that even creation will be shaken (vv. 676–81) and complete desolation is accomplished (vv. 682–701). Only the "sons of the great God" will live (v. 702), shielded by God and living peacefully around the temple (vv. 703–17). They will be free to worship at the temple and ponder the law of God, living in repentance from former deeds (vv. 718–31). The Sibyl then rebukes Greece for its pride and demands its loyalty to "the great God" (vv. 732–40). There will come a day of great judgment from God on mortals (vv. 741–43), which will be accompanied by abundant blessings and peace (vv. 744–59), and God will establish his solitary rule (vv. 760–61). The Sibyl exhorts readers to shun idolatry and immoral practices (vv. 762–66). God will raise up a kingdom where people from every land will bring offerings to God (vv. 767–73). There will be only one God; hardships, warfare, and injustice will cease; and all will live in eschatological bliss (vv. 774–95). Signs from heaven will be given that the end is at hand (vv. 796–808). The Sibyl concludes by identifying herself as a prophetess of God whose utterances are true (vv. 809–29).

Importance of Sibylline Oracles 3

There are a several important contributions made by the oldest and main unit of Sibylline Oracles 3 (vv. 97–349 and 489–829). As with other portions of Sibylline Oracles 3, the primary contribution here is its witness to a Jewish community in Egypt. In particular, it affirms the rule of the Ptolemaic king, whom it regards as a savior figure. Furthermore, it casts its eschatological time frame in terms of the reign of the seventh king (vv. 193, 318, 608, 652–56). Collins observes that the most striking epithet is the phrase "a king from the sun" (vv. 652–56), which is also found in the closely contemporary Egyptian Oracle, where it reflects the Egyptian mythology that its king was an incarnation of the sun god, utilizing a gentile myth to cast the Ptolemaic king in messianic terms (cf. Isa. 45:1).[30] Sibylline Oracles 3 is also important for its ethical stances against pervasive practices in its Hellenized, diaspora context. It shares with other writings, for instance, a repugnance for sexual vices (cf. Philo, *Abraham* 135; *Spec. Laws* 2.50, 3.37; Let. Aris. §152; Rom. 1:26) and pagan practices associated with divination and astrology (esp. Sib. Or. 3:220–28; cf. Jub. 12:16–18; 1 En. 80:7).[31]

For all its syncretistic features, Sibylline Oracles 3 elevates the Jews alone for their adherence to the law (vv. 246, 580), which other nations fail to observe

---

30. J. Collins, *Apocalyptic Imagination*, 150–52.
31. J. Collins, "Sibylline Oracles," *OTP* 1:357.

(vv. 599–600). The misfortunes for their sins can be reversed by trust in the law (vv. 283–84), but always in general terms or at best with reference to their refraining from idolatry and sexual aberration—practices that can be shared with enlightened gentiles[32]—not the Jewish distinctives of circumcision, dietary laws, or even Sabbath observance.[33] To the Greeks (Seleucids), however, there is an exhortation to participate in sacrificial worship to Israel's God (vv. 545–72), and there is a hope that other gentiles will send gifts to the temple and reflect on God's laws (vv. 702–31). At this time Onias has not yet established a temple in Egypt, but the reference here still presumes the primacy of the temple in Jerusalem.

Sibylline Oracles 4

Introduction

Like other Sibylline Oracles, book 4 is a composite work of a political nature from a Hellenistic context that may have developed in stages. The first stage (vv. 49–101) divides history into two segments of ten generations and four kingdoms. This entails the rule of the Assyrians (six generations), the Medes (two generations), and the Persians (one generation). The tenth generation corresponds to the fourth kingdom, the Macedonian Empire. The first stage's discontinuity with verses 1–48 and 102–72 suggests the latter two segments are secondary additions, verses 102–72 bringing the older material up to date and verses 1–48 providing the moral and religious teachings of the author.[34]

The inclusion of the Macedonian Empire and the absence of any mention of the death of Alexander the Great and the rise of Rome suggest a date shortly after the advent of his reign (ca. 336 BCE). And it is possible to read Macedonia as the object of God's judgment in the earliest portion of the work (vv. 49–101). The larger segment (vv. 102–72) dates from around 80 CE, as indicated by its reference to the destruction of the temple in Jerusalem in 70 CE (v. 116), the legend of Nero's (d. 68 CE) flight to the Parthians (vv. 119–24, 138–39), and the eruption of Mount Vesuvius in 79 CE (vv. 130–35). The location is probably Syria or the Jordan Valley.[35]

32. J. Collins, *Apocalyptic Imagination*, 153; J. Collins, *Between Athens and Jerusalem*, 160–65.
33. Cf. J. Collins, *Apocalyptic Imagination*, 152–53.
34. J. Collins, "Sibylline Oracles," *OTP* 1:381.
35. J. Collins, "Sibylline Oracles," *OTP* 1:381–82.

Contents

SECTION 1 (VV. 1–48)

This oracle begins with an address to Asia and Europe by the Sibyl as a prophecy from the "great God" (vv. 1–7), who neither is made by humans nor dwells in human-made temples (vv. 8–11) and who inspires the words of her oracle (vv. 12–23). This leads to a statement of blessing on those who renounce idolatry for the "great God" and follow his ways (vv. 24–39). The ungodly will face the judgment of God, whereas the righteous will experience his blessings (vv. 40–48).

SECTION 2 (VV. 49–101)

As we have seen, this section divides history into two segments of ten generations and four kingdoms. This entails the rule of the Assyrians (vv. 49–53), the Medes (vv. 54–64), and the Persians (vv. 65–66). This is followed by an introduction of the evils that will befall humanity (vv. 67–85). When the tenth generation, the fourth kingdom of the Macedonians, comes, it will add to these woes the burden of slavery (vv. 86–101).

SECTION 3 (VV. 102–72)

This section begins with a prediction of the downfall of Macedonia at the hands of the Italians (vv. 102–4), who will also subdue Corinth, Carthage, Laodicea, Myra, and Armenia (vv. 105–14). The oracle then depicts the calamity to come on Jerusalem and its temple (vv. 115–27) followed by natural disasters wrought by the hand of God (vv. 128–51). Then the Sibyl predicts wickedness in the last days—impiety, injustice, murder (vv. 152–58)—to which God will respond in righteous anger (vv. 159–70). She warns of destruction by great fire for those who do not heed her exhortations (vv. 171–78). But after this God will resurrect the ashen bones, pronounce judgment on the impious (vv. 179–86), and bless the pious with life (vv. 187–92).

Contribution and Context

As with other oracles, Sibylline Oracles 4 exhibits some unique traits among diaspora Jews. On the one hand, it seems to reject temple worship (vv. 5–12, 27–30); God does not live in a temple of stone (vv. 8–11), and the pious reject all temples and sacrificial cults (vv. 27–30; cf. Acts 7). On the other hand, it depicts the eruption of Vesuvius as just punishment for the destruction

of Jerusalem and its temple (v. 135).[36] This Jewish response is quite different
from that of 4 Ezra and 2 Baruch or even Sibylline Oracles 5.[37]

The later redactions, perhaps dating from the first century CE (vv. 1–48),
exhibit more familiar Jewish conceptions, such as monotheism and the immutability of God, as well as the rejection of idolatry (vv. 6–7), sexual immorality
(vv. 33–34), and injustice (vv. 152–58). Dividing time into ten generations is
also found in Jewish apocalyptic texts (Apocalypse of Weeks [1 En. 93:1–10;
91:11–17]; Melchizedek [11QMelch]; Sibylline Oracles 1 and 2). The view of
the end time of Sibylline Oracles 4, with its emphasis on bodily resurrection,
finds its closest parallel in Sibylline Oracles 2.

Other aspects of its Jewish origin are more complicated. While enu-
merations of world kingdoms are familiar from the book of Daniel, none
of those mentioned here (Assyria, Media, Persia, Macedonia) derive from
that book.[38] The reference to baptism in the context of judgment is curious here since it resembles early Christian texts associated with John the
Baptist, whereas scholars generally agree that there are no signs of Christian
authorship in Sibylline Oracles 4.[39] The baptism is dissimilar to familiar
Jewish ritual washings (Sib. Or. 3:592–93) and those of the sectarians at
Qumran.[40] Collins suggests it derives from a Jewish baptist movement in
the Jordan Valley.[41]

Sibylline Oracles 5

Introduction

Book 5 of the Sibylline Oracles is comprised of six oracles (vv. 1–51, 52–110,
111–78, 179–285, 286–433, 434–530), the first of which (vv. 1–51) serves as
an introduction reviewing history from Alexander the Great to Hadrian (or
Marcus Aurelius).[42] Throughout, the emperors are mentioned not by name but
by numbers corresponding to their initials (a method known as gematria).[43]
The following four oracles contain similar patterns, beginning with oracles
against various nations like Egypt (in oracles 2 [vv. 52–110] and 4 [vv. 179–
285]) or Asiatic nations (in oracles 3 [vv. 111–78] and 5 [vv. 286–434]). They

---

36. J. Collins, "Sibylline Oracles," *OTP* 1:382.
37. J. Collins, *Apocalyptic Imagination*, 300.
38. J. Collins, "Sibylline Oracles," *OTP* 1:381–82. See Flusser, "Four Empires."
39. J. Collins, *Apocalyptic Imagination*, 299.
40. J. Collins, "Sibylline Oracles," *OTP* 1:383.
41. J. Collins, *Apocalyptic Imagination*, 299.
42. J. Collins, "Sibylline Oracles," *OTP* 1:390.
43. See Helyer, "Gematria."

then present Nero as an "eschatological adversary." This is followed by the appearance of a savior and destruction, usually by fire.[44] The sixth and final oracle (vv. 434–530) pertains to affairs in Egypt, particularly the destruction of the Jewish temple there and the subsequent destruction of the Ethiopians.

Though portions of Sibylline Oracles 5 may derive from different times and contexts, its present form dates somewhere between 70 and 132 CE. The former year is determined by the prominence of legends pertaining to Nero (oracles 2–5), whereas the latter year is suggested by positive references to Hadrian (vv. 46–50), implying a date prior to the Second Jewish Revolt (132–135 CE). The bitterness of the complaints about the destruction of the temple (esp. vv. 398–413, but in general, oracles 2–5) may imply a date not long from the fall of Jerusalem in 70 CE.[45]

Sibylline Oracles 5 was written in Egypt, which not only is the primary subject matter of oracles 2 and 4 but also is reflected in the author's familiarity with Isis (vv. 53, 484), Cleopatra (vv. 17–18), and Sarapis (v. 487). The Sibyl also anticipates a temple to God in Egypt (vv. 501–3). Mention of its destruction by the Ethiopians is ambiguous, since elsewhere (3:319–20) the Ethiopians are associated with Gog and Magog, suggesting the possibility of a general eschatological adversary, and the temple at Leontopolis was actually destroyed by the Romans by order of Vespasian in 73 CE (Josephus, J.W. 7.10.2 §421).[46]

Contents

Oracle i (vv. 1–51)

The first oracle reviews the history of the Latin race (v. 1), beginning with the first prince (Alexander),[47] who will conquer long in wars (v. 13), establish laws, and bring people into subjection under him (v. 19). Then will come another king (Tiberius, v. 20), followed by Gaios (Caligula, v. 24), then Klaudios (Claudius, v. 25), who will campaign against Britain (vv. 26–27). Then comes Nero (v. 28), a "terrible snake" (v. 29), who will slay his own family and throw everything into confusion and declare himself equal to God (vv. 30–34). The three princes after him, who will perish at each others' hands (v. 35), are

---

44. J. Collins, "Sibylline Oracles," *OTP* 1:390.
45. J. Collins, "Sibylline Oracles," *OTP* 1:390.
46. J. Collins, "Sibylline Oracles," *OTP* 1:390–91. See Piotrkowski, *Priests in Exile*. For recent arguments on the provenance of various portions of Sibylline Oracles 5, see Felder, "What Is the Fifth Sibylline Oracle?"
47. Sib. Or. 5:1–11 is a summary of the entirety of Sib. Or. 11, but otherwise they have few similarities.

Galba, Otho, and Vitellius. The "great destroyer of pious men" (v. 36) is Vespasian, who conducts the war against the Jews in the First Jewish Revolt (66–73 CE) and is followed by his son, Titus (vv. 37–39),[48] then the "cursed man" Domitian (v. 40). He is followed by a "revered man," Nerva (v. 41), then Trajan (vv. 42–45). Then comes a man after whom a sea is named (Hadrian, for the Adriatic Sea, vv. 46–47)—an "excellent man" (vv. 48–50)—and last of all Marcus Aurelius (v. 51).

ORACLE 2 (VV. 52–110)

This oracle is primarily a series of prophetic utterances concerning the destruction of Egypt (vv. 52–92), who "raged against my [the Sibyl's] children who were anointed by God" (v. 68). Furthermore, Egypt's sins of idolatry have aroused the anger of God (vv. 77–87), and the luxuries of Alexandria will come to an end (vv. 88–92). This judgment is described in terms of the conquests of "the Persian," who is Nero returning from the Parthians to bring destruction on Alexandria and destroy all life (vv. 93–103).[49] With help from the West (Rome; cf. v. 139) he will lay waste to the entire land (vv. 104–5) but will himself be judged by a king sent from God (vv. 106–10).

ORACLE 3 (VV. 111–78)

The third oracle is uttered primarily against eastern, Asiatic nations: the Persians, Iberians, Babylonians, and Massagetae will all burn (vv. 111–18). Also to be destroyed are Pergamos (v. 119), Pitane (v. 120), Lesbos (v. 121), Smyrna (vv. 122–23), Bithynia (v. 124), Syria (v. 125), and Lycia (vv. 126–29). Phrygia will experience wrath (vv. 130–31), the people of Tauri and Lapith will be destroyed by the sea (vv. 132–33) and Thessaly by a river (vv. 134–35). The Sybil's attention turns next to Nero (vv. 137–54), "a godlike man" (v. 138), who destroys men and flees to Babylon (Rome, vv. 139–46; cf. Rev. 14:8). He appoints rulers among the Medes and Persians and is charged with seizing the Jerusalem temple and burning the citizens (vv. 147–54). But judgment will come on Babylon (Rome, v. 159) because of the plight of God's people (vv. 155–61). This gives way to an oracle specifically against Rome (vv. 162–78), who murders and claims divinity (vv. 172–73), and whom God himself will destroy (vv. 174–78).

48. Cf. Suetonius, *Divus Titus* 5
49. J. Collins, "Sibylline Oracles," *OTP* 1:395. A tradition spread that Nero had escaped to the Parthians and would return to reclaim his rule with their aid (Tacitus, *Historiae* 2.8; Suetonius, *Nero* 57; Dio Chrysostom, *De pulchritudine* 21.10). See van Henten, "*Nero Redivivus* Demolished."

ORACLE 4 (VV. 179–285)

The fourth oracle returns attention to Egypt, announcing the destruction of its cities (vv. 180–99). Then follows an oracle against the Gauls for the evil they did to the children of God (vv. 200–205) and a prophecy of the destruction of the Ethiopians (vv. 206–14). Corinth also will fall (v. 214) at the hands of Nero, who is given strength by God to enact judgment (vv. 215–27). The Sibyl then denounces the arrogance of kings (vv. 228–37) before turning to her praise of the Jews as a light shining among men (vv. 238–85).

ORACLE 5 (VV. 286–434)

The fifth oracle is a scathing set of condemning woes on the nations of "wretched Asia" (vv. 286–87) and cities destroyed by earthquakes (vv. 288–91). The shrine of Artemis of Ephesus likewise will fall headlong into the sea (vv. 292–97). And God himself will act in further deeds of vengeance through nature to bring calamity (vv. 298–305). The Sibyl then names cities that will also fall: Smyrna, Cyme, Lesbos, Cibyra, Hierapolis, Tripolis—all will be utterly destroyed by God (vv. 306–27). The Sibyl prays for grace toward Judea (vv. 328–32) before launching into another series of woes, this time against the regions of Europe (vv. 333–45). God himself will bring about calamity (vv. 346–60). In the next oracle (vv. 361–80) the Sibyl predicts a great work, with a man (Nero) coming from the ends of the earth to destroy every land and conquer all. This war will bring an end to war, and only a wise people will be left (vv. 381–85). An admonition to the Romans (vv. 386–96) is followed by a lament over the destruction of Herod's Temple (vv. 397–402), which fell though the people honored God (vv. 403–7). It was cast down by "a certain insignificant and impious king" (Titus, vv. 408–13), who himself perished. This gives way to the depiction of a savior figure, sent from heaven, who restores Jerusalem and a magnificent temple, establishing peace for the holy people of God (vv. 414–33).

ORACLE 6 (VV. 434–530)

The sixth and final oracle begins with a woe against Babylon, who will pay a bitter price for her wrongs (vv. 434–46). There is then a predication of dramatic eschatological upheavals—swellings of the sea, famine, wintry blasts of freezing air, wild animals turning on humankind, and darkness (vv. 447–81). But good men will be led by the light of God, singing praises to him (vv. 482–83). Even Egyptians will turn from their idols, "turning their attention to the imperishable God" (vv. 484–91). A priest clad in linen will erect a sanctuary to the true God and lead worship at a temple in Egypt (vv. 492–503). But then the Ethiopians will come and destroy that temple (vv. 504–11). The oracle concludes with a vision in which the stars are engaged in battle, constellations against constellations (vv. 512–27), until heaven itself intercedes (vv. 528–31).

Contribution and Context

Sibylline Oracles 5 continues things found in Sibylline Oracles 3 (vv. 75–92, 611) concerning the temple, the advent of a savior, and an eschatological adversary, and therefore Sibylline Oracles 3 and 5 can be taken as the two extremities of one tradition in Egyptian Judaism.[50] But as Collins observes, Sibylline Oracles 5 responds to the destruction of the temple "not by pondering divine justice (like 4 Ezra) or seeking to fill the gap it left in religious life (like 2 Baruch) but by venting its outrage against the heathen power that was responsible."[51]

Yet, presuming Egyptian provenance for both, it seems that the enthusiasm toward Ptolemaic (Egyptian) rule found in Sibylline Oracles 3 has turned to antagonism in Sibylline Oracles 5, where one finds hostility (vv. 82–85, 484–96) and evidence of the persecution of God's children by the Egyptian ruler (vv. 68–69). And so much of sections 2 and 4 are devoted primarily to oracles of retribution against Egypt. But Rome also shares in the Sibyl's rebuke (vv. 162–78) because of its immorality (v. 166), destruction of Jerusalem (vv. 160–61), and especially claims to divinity (v. 173). So it comes as no surprise to the reader that the eschatological enemy of God is none other than Nero,[52] legends about whom are plentiful in Sibylline Oracles 5.[53]

The savior figure features prominently in the four main oracles (oracle 2 [vv. 108–9], oracle 3 [vv. 155–61], oracle 4 [vv. 256–59], and oracle 5 [vv. 414–25]). He is said to come from heaven (vv. 256, 414), from God and against Nero (v. 108). He is depicted as a "great star" (vv. 158–59), which is common for savior figures in Hellenistic contexts and may indicate an angelic or heavenly savior analogous to the role of Michael in the book of Daniel (Dan. 10:13, 21; 12:1; cf. 1QM XVII, 6–8) or Melchizedek in 11QMelch (II, 9, 13, 25). This stands in stark contrast to the savior of Sibylline Oracles 3, who is a Ptolemaic ruler. While Sibylline Oracles 5 anticipates a restored, massive Jerusalem (vv.

50. J. Collins, "Sibylline Oracles," OTP 1:391.
51. J. Collins, Apocalyptic Imagination, 292.
52. J. Collins, "Sibylline Oracles," OTP 1:391.
53. See van Henten, "Nero Redivivus Demolished."

249–55, 420–27) that extends as far as Joppa (v. 251) and will be admired by the nations, the emphasis lies on its destruction.[54] The Judaism found in Sibylline Oracles 5 is similar to what is found elsewhere: sharp polemics against idolatry (vv. 75–85, 278–80, 353–56, 403–5, 495–96) and sexual immorality (vv. 386–93, 430).

Sibylline Oracles 11

Introduction

Sibylline Oracles 11 heads a collection of four books (Sib. Or. 11–14) that presents a general narrative of historical events from the time of the flood to the Arab conquest, with book 11 itself ending with the death of Cleopatra (30 BCE).[55] As in book 5, historical figures are identified by numbers representing their names or initials (gematria). In this respect Sibylline Oracles 11 collates a series of kingdoms, though with varying degrees of historical veracity and chronology (cf. Sib. Or. 3:159–61).[56] The author has made some notable adjustments to sequence, such as inserting a Hebrew kingdom ruled by Moses (vv. 33–41) between the first Egyptian rule (vv. 19–32) and the Persian rule (vv. 47–50).[57] Surprisingly, the Assyrians (vv. 80–103) are presented positively as champions of the law of Moses (vv. 81–92) who rebuild the temple (v. 87). The narrative trajectory changes (vv. 109–71) with accounts of Romulus and Remus (vv. 109–21), the Trojan War (vv. 122–43), Aeneas (vv. 144–62), and Virgil (vv. 163–71). An account of the Persian invasion of Greece (vv. 179–82) resumes the narrative, which culminates in a lengthy account of the Ptolemies during Cleopatra's rule in Egypt (vv. 243–60), which is finally conquered by Rome (vv. 277–314).

Though scholars have suggested a variety of dates for the origin of Sibylline Oracles 11, it most likely dates from no later than the first century CE. Items that are typically of interest to the Sibyl—the destruction of the temple, persecutions, and hostilities with peoples in the second century—are absent in this book. There is no antagonism toward Rome; instead, it is toward Egypt (vv. 298–314). Mention is made of Cleopatra (Cleopatra VII Philopator, d. 30 BCE), and it is possible that the book was written shortly after her death. Some suggest that it was during the reign of Augustus (27 BCE–14 CE) or Tiberius (14–37 CE), before relations between the Jews and Romans in Egypt

54. J. Collins, "Sibylline Oracles," OTP 1:392.
55. J. Collins, "Sibylline Oracles," OTP 1:430.
56. Kurfess, Sibyllinische Weissagungen, 333.
57. J. Collins, "Sibylline Oracles," OTP 1:434.

began to deteriorate during the time of Caligula (37–41 CE).[58] Furthermore, the fact that Sibylline Oracles 5:1–11 summarizes Sibylline Oracles 11 requires the latter to predate the former. With Sibylline Oracles 5 likely dating shortly after 70 CE, Sibylline Oracles 11 dates perhaps around the turn of the era.[59] The prominence of Egypt at both the beginning and the end of the narrative, as well as the focus on its destruction because of its oppression of Israel (v. 307), indicates an Egyptian origin for the work, particularly Alexandria (vv. 219–20, 232–35).

Contents

At the outset of Sibylline Oracles 11 the Sibyl announces her disastrous tidings to the diverse languages and kingdoms wrought after the Tower of Babel (vv. 1–18). The first oracle pertains to Egypt, which will receive its royal dominion but be governed by a "terrible man" (Pharaoh) who will oppress Israel and be visited with plagues (vv. 19–34). The Sibyl then introduces the "people of the twelve tribes" (Israel), who are given God's law and led by a "great, great-spirited king" (Moses) before succumbing to the empire of the Persians, when "there will be darkness upon the Jews" (vv. 35–46). But the Persian rule will come to an end (vv. 47–50) at the hand of the Medes (vv. 51–60). A wealthy Indian will subdue the Medes (vv. 61–64) and cause the Medes to serve the Ethiopians (vv. 65–67). There will come a great peace (v. 79), but only after nations have willingly subordinated themselves to the Indian king (vv. 68–78). A great king will rule over the Assyrians (v. 80); he will reign in accord with the laws of God, build a temple to God, cast down idols, and rule over other kings (vv. 81–103) until the rise of Macedonia (vv. 104–8). A series of digressions follows this narrative, first pertaining to Romulus and Remus (vv. 109–21), then the Trojan War (vv. 122–43), Aeneas (vv. 144–62), and Virgil (vv. 163–71). The Sibyl returns to her narrative with a prophecy about infighting caused by God among the Greeks and other nations (vv. 172–77). The Assyrians will invade Greece (vv. 178–85), after which the Macedonians will come upon Greece (vv. 186–194) and will be ruled by Alexander the Great (vv. 195–223). After his death the Diadochi will vie for power (vv. 224–31). The narrative returns its attention, for a second time, to the rule of Egypt (vv. 232–60) and the reign of Cleopatra (vv. 243–60). The focus then turns to Rome, where Julius Caesar will rise to power (vv. 261–314; Gaius Julius Caesar, r. 49–44 BCE). He will conquer Egypt (vv. 277–97) and punish Egypt with slavery (vv. 298–314). The Sibyl concludes with an affirmation of the truth of her oracles (vv. 315–24).

---

58. Kurfess, *Sibyllinische Weissagungen*, 339; J. Collins, "Sibylline Oracles," *OTP* 1:430.
59. J. Collins, "Sibylline Oracles," *OTP* 1:432.

Contribution and Context

Book 11 stands out among the other Sibylline Oracles for what it omits. Here one finds no depiction of eschatological judgment, interest in the temple, or polemic against sexual immorality and idolatry. Furthermore, its review of history carries no ethical or religious exhortation as one finds in Sibylline Oracles 4 and 5. More astounding is the author's erroneous presentation of history, in which he mistakenly presents the Persian, Median, and Ethiopian Empires prior to the reign of Solomon and omits any reference to the Babylonians.[60]

Sibylline Oracles 11 is relatively thin on theological and historical contributions. It acknowledges Egypt's oppression of the Jews prior to the exodus (vv. 307–10), which may suggest tensions between the Jewish community for which the Sibyl speaks and the Egyptian rule under which they live.[61] Its Jewish origins are found in its references to figures such as Joseph (vv. 29–30), Moses (vv. 38–40), and Solomon (vv. 80–103). This is affirmed by its claim that Egypt will be destroyed for its treatment of God's people (v. 307). It fits with the general attitude of Alexandrian Judaism, which was favorable toward Egyptian rulers while hostile toward native Egyptians.[62] But the religious advocacy is muted when compared to the other oracles, suggesting its concerns had less to do with religious promotion than with advocating hostility toward Egypt.

---

60. J. Collins, "Sibylline Oracles," *OTP* 1:432–33.
61. J. Collins, "Sibylline Oracles," *OTP* 1:432.
62. J. Collins, "Sibylline Oracles," *AYBD* 6:4.

6

Additional Writings

2 Enoch, 3 Baruch, Apocalypse of Zephaniah, Testament of Abraham, and Apocalyptic Material in the Dead Sea Scrolls

Introduction

The writings discussed above represent the majority of apocalypses, or apocalypse-like writings, that date from the Second Temple period. In addition to these writings there are additional ancient texts of a similar nature. These are either fragmentary or of disputed provenance and so do not fit neatly into the category of Second Temple Jewish apocalypses we aim to cover here. Instead, we will provide a brief overview of each text, try to articulate the nature of the debates that render them outside our purview, and provide readers with a suitable bibliography to explore matters further.

2 Enoch

Introduction

Among the apocalypses outside the immediate purview of this volume, pride of place belongs to 2 Enoch, a diaspora writing also known as the Slavonic Apocalypse of Enoch. It narrates the life of Enoch to the onset of the flood, amplifying the narrative of Genesis 5:21–32. The main text (2 En. 1–68) describes Enoch's ascent to the seven heavens, where he encounters God enthroned, after which he returns to earth to exhort his family and others with messages from God. The remainder of the book (chaps. 69–73) describes Enoch's successors and the miraculous birth of Melchizedek.

Contents

Second Enoch is generally an apocalypse but begins as a "testament," setting a narrative framework for the subsequent heavenly ascent and visions. Enoch, toward the end of his life, is in bed when confronted by two angels, who instruct him to summon his household to his bedside for instruction (chaps. 1–2). Enoch then ascends into heaven where, in the seventh heaven, he sees the enthroned deity and receives his commission (chaps. 3–37).[1] Enoch is transformed into a heavenly being when he enters God's presence in a process that suggests a priestly investiture (21:2–22:10).[2] He is commissioned to write 360 books of cosmological and ethical teaching, dictated by an angel (chap. 23). After this Enoch is given an account of the secrets of creation, unknown even to angels (chaps. 24–30), which differs considerably from the narrative of Genesis 1. God explains that he alone is the sole creator and sovereign of the heavens (chap. 33) and, since humanity refuses to recognize this—through their injustice, idolatry, and fornication[3]—a great flood will come upon the earth (chap. 34). God tells Enoch that he will raise up a descendant who will read from these books and learn from them (chap. 35), and Enoch will be sent to impart this knowledge to his sons and should prepare to be taken up again at a later time (chaps. 36–37). So Enoch is returned to earth and passes on instructions, which are to be the means of salvation after the flood, to his children (chaps. 38–56), to Methuselah's family and to the elders of the people (chaps. 57–63), and finally to all his people (chaps. 64–66) before he is taken up again to heaven (chap. 67). The work concludes with a narrative tracing the priestly succession from Enoch, who is presumed to be a priest (cf. 2 En. 59; 64:6), to Melchizedek (chaps. 68–73). This final section is best seen as a summary of the entire work in which Enoch's revelations and exhortations are rendered into a cultic framework that furnishes humanity after the flood with direction.[4]

Contribution

While apocalypses are generally known for ascents through heaven, the enumeration of heaven originates in the first century CE. Second Enoch may

---

1. For discussion of how the layout of 2 Enoch is patterned after that of 1 Enoch, see Nickelsburg, *Jewish Literature*, 221–24.
2. Himmelfarb, "Revelation and Rapture," 83.
3. J. Collins, *Apocalyptic Imagination*, 306.
4. Böttrich, "Enoch, Slavonic Apocalypse of."

be one of the first texts to designate seven heavens.[5] Whereas most apocalypses are thought to be born out of crisis, there is little evidence of this in 2 Enoch.[6] Readers are not told why Enoch is weeping and grieving in the opening chapter. It may be inferred from the words attributed to God in chapters 33–35 that the underlying problem is the sinful conduct of humanity, which will provoke the flood. Enoch is uniquely presented as one who carries away the sin of humanity (2 En. 64:5). He is best understood in terms of his role as a revealer whose revelation deals with human sin.[7] The instructions imparted by Enoch are more ethical than theological, exhorting his sons to care for the needy since they, as all humanity, are created in God's likeness (44:1). In this respect the *imago Dei* is understood in distinctly ethical rather than metaphysical terms.[8] Similarly, Enoch's instructions to Methuselah pertain to the treatment of animals as established at creation. And so God's created order is the scale of justice by which the coming judgment will be assessed. There is no mention of the Sinai covenant with Moses,[9] Israel's history, or legal matters particular to Judaism, such as purity, circumcision, Sabbath observance, or dietary regulations.[10] And yet there is something similar to the law, long before the Sinai encounter of Moses, that is revealed to Enoch in the heavenly books.[11] This and other factors suggest to some that Enoch and Moses are set up as rivals,[12] or at least that in the late first century CE Moses was not the only figure utilized as a model of Judaism.[13] Overall the author of 2 Enoch combines biblical traditions with philosophical concepts to furnish his Alexandrian Jewish readers with instructions for living as Jews in a non-Jewish environment.[14]

Text and Provenance

Second Enoch is preserved in two Slavonic traditions, or recensions, dating from the fourteenth to the eighteenth century.[15] Four Coptic fragments, dating from the eighth to the tenth century, favor the shorter recension.[16] The

5. J. Collins, *Apocalyptic Imagination*, 303.
6. Vaillant, *Le livre des secrets d'Hénoch*, 3; J. Collins, *Apocalyptic Imagination*, 307.
7. Macaskill, *Revealed Wisdom*, 225.
8. Andersen, "2 (Slavonic Apocalypse of) Enoch," 1:97.
9. Macaskill, "Personal Salvation and Rigorous Obedience."
10. Cf. J. Collins, *Apocalyptic Imagination*, 302.
11. Geller, "Heavenly Writings."
12. Alexander, "From Son of Adam to Second God," 110.
13. J. Collins, *Apocalyptic Imagination*, 309.
14. Böttrich, "Enoch, Slavonic Apocalypse of."
15. Böttrich, "Enoch, Slavonic Apocalypse of"; see Macaskill, *Slavonic Texts of 2 Enoch*.
16. Hagen, "No Longer 'Slavonic' Only."

relationship between these two recensions is disputed. Some have argued for the priority of the shorter,[17] others for the priority of the longer,[18] and still others that the matter is too complicated simply to favor one over the other.[19] Regardless, both recensions likely come from a Greek original.[20]

Second Enoch is generally thought to be a Jewish work that may date as early as the first century CE. The importance of animal sacrificial practices throughout the work suggests active participation in temple worship.[21] It was likely written in Egypt, largely because of its familiarity with Egyptian mythology and close points of correspondence with other diaspora writings, especially Philo of Alexandria.[22] It may have been composed by a wealthy, well-educated Jew living in Alexandria in the first century CE.[23] Though this is likely the case for the origins of 2 Enoch, it is evident that in the course of its transmission over numerous centuries it accumulated elements foreign to the original, including Christian, later Jewish, and mystical traditions. So in its extant form it is difficult to designate 2 Enoch a Second Temple Jewish pseudepigraphon, as it is not a matter of simply peeling off layers of mysticism or other later traditions to arrive at an original core document. Therefore, further treatment will not be undertaken here. Instead, readers may consult the extensive introduction and translation by F. I. Andersen,[24] an important collection of essays edited by Andrei A. Orlov and Gabriele Boccaccini,[25] or the commentary by Orlov.[26]

3 Baruch

Introduction

Like 4 Ezra and 2 Baruch, 3 Baruch is an apocalypse dealing with the destruction of Jerusalem but cast in the setting of the first temple. For its readers,

---

17. See, recently, Navtanovich, "Provenance of 2 Enoch."

18. Charles and Morfill presuppose the priority of the longer recension (*Book of the Secrets of Enoch*).

19. See Andersen, "2 (Slavonic Apocalypse of) Enoch," 1:92–94; Böttrich, *Weltweisheit, Menschheitsethik, Urkult*, 59–144.

20. See Macaskill, "2 Enoch," 83–101, who collates an abundance of Semitisms.

21. See esp. Orlov, "Sacerdotal Traditions of 2 Enoch," 107.

22. J. Collins, *Apocalyptic Imagination*, 302.

23. Böttrich, *Weltweisheit, Menschheitsethik, Urkult*, 192; Böttrich, *Das slavische Henochbuch*, 810–12. The notion that 2 Enoch was composed by Christians is helpfully refuted by Nickelsburg, *Jewish Literature*, 225.

24. "2 (Slavonic Apocalypse of) Enoch."

25. *New Perspectives on 2 Enoch.*

26. *2 Enoch.*

the destruction of the temple in 70 CE is fresh, and the mysteries of God "allay the original grief and fear."[27] The visionary ascends to the fifth heaven, is given a message from God, and returns to earth to relate the message to others.

Contents

Third Baruch, like 2 Baruch, presents Baruch, the scribe of Jeremiah, as its central figure. At the beginning of the book, Baruch is mourning the destruction of Jerusalem and its temple (3 Bar. 1:1–2). The angel of the Lord appears, intent to show Baruch the mysteries of God on the condition that he will recount them without addition or omission (1:3–8). Then the angel leads Baruch through the five heavens.[28] In the first heaven (chap. 2) Baruch is shown a plain where those waging war against God are being punished. In the second heaven (chap. 3) Baruch sees another plain that holds those who forced others to build a tower to heaven to learn of what it is made. The third heaven (chaps. 4–9) contains a plain with a serpent on a stone mountain that drinks from the sea and eats the earth (chap. 4). Baruch is also shown the vine from which Adam was deceived by the serpent. The angel explains that the serpent can drink great quantities from the sea because its stomach is as great as Hades (chap. 5). Then (chaps. 6–8) Baruch sees a bird named Phoenix that guards the world from the burning rays of the sun with its wings. In chapter 9 Baruch is told the moon is beautiful, like a woman, but when Adam sinned it always shone and never hid, angering God. The fourth heaven (chap. 10) contains a wide mountain with a large lake and a variety of birds, which the angel explains is the gathering place for the souls of the righteous.[29] Then Baruch is taken by the angel to the fifth heaven (chaps. 11–16). There he sees large gates that cannot be opened until Michael, the keeper of the keys, comes (11:1–2). Baruch then sees Michael descending, holding a large receptacle with which prayers are gathered (11:3–9). Following this, Baruch sees angels who are in the service of people placing gifts into the receptacle, and Michael weeping because the receptacle is not filled (chap. 12). Other angels are also weeping, imploring Michael to allow them to be transferred from their service to disobedient, unreasonable humanity (chap. 13). Michael brings the prayers to God (chap. 14) and returns with angels full of mercy (which represent the prayers of the righteous, 15:1–2) and angels with lesser gifts (which represent prayers of insufficiently righteous people, 15:3). In chapter 16, Michael

27. J. Collins, *Apocalyptic Imagination*, 313.
28. There is debate as to whether the original number was the more common seven rather than five (cf. Origen, *Princ.* 2.3.6). See Harlow, *Greek Apocalypse of Baruch*, 34–76.
29. Gaylord, "3 (Greek Apocalypse of) Baruch," 1:653.

summons other angels, who bear petitions that are ignored, and he commands them to bring judgment on the people (16:1–3). Then Baruch is shown the resting place of the righteous and the anguish of the damned (16:4–8). The angel is told to bring Baruch back to earth, where he is exhorted to tell all that he has seen and heard (chap. 17).

Contribution

Some features of 3 Baruch are unique among Jewish apocalypses. It is notable that Baruch never ascends to the throne room of God personally, nor is Baruch transformed into any kind of heavenly, angelic figure.[30] A final farewell by the visionary, such as that found in 2 Enoch, is absent in 3 Baruch. Whereas testaments like 2 Enoch are utilized to convey exhortations to the reader, 3 Baruch weaves its exhortations into the tapestry of its revelations. Judgment is decidedly individualized rather than corporate.[31] Though a Jewish writing (see below), 3 Baruch has little interest in distinctive features of Judaism, such as circumcision, idolatry, Sabbath observance, or temple worship. Unlike works such as the Sibylline Oracles, there is little concern for other nations, or even Israel's history.[32] There are numerous angels in 3 Baruch. The main ones are Phanael, who is the interpreter of revelations (3 Bar. 11:7 [Greek]; cf. 2:6 [Greek]; 10:1), and Michael, who is head of all the angels (cf. 11:4), holds the keys to the gates of heaven (11:2), and, in a priestly role, carries prayers to the heavenly sanctuary. The presence of the phoenix is not unique to 3 Baruch,[33] but only here is it depicted as a protector of the world. The twelve Slavonic manuscripts that attest to 3 Baruch suggest its importance in that context, though it is sparsely cited in other literature and little used in Western settings.

Text and Provenance

Third Baruch is found in twelve Slavonic manuscripts that represent translations of a lost Greek original. The Slavonic is preserved in two manuscript families (A and B [thirteenth to eighteenth century]), with A generally providing more original readings and B exhibiting revisions and redactions.[34]

30. Himmelfarb, *Ascent to Heaven*, 87; J. Collins, *Apocalyptic Imagination*, 311–12; Kulik, "Baruch, Third Book of," 1:125.
31. J. Collins, *Apocalyptic Imagination*, 312–15.
32. Kulik, "Baruch, Third Book of," 1:125.
33. Ezek. Trag. 245–69; cf. Herodotus, *Historiae* 2.73.
34. Gaylord, "3 (Greek Apocalypse of) Baruch," 1:654. See Gaylord, "Slavonic Version of III Baruch"; Gaylord, *Slavonic Version of III Baruch*, xxi–xvii; Kulik, *3 Baruch*, 7–8.

It is also attested in two manuscripts dating from the fifteenth or sixteenth century written in Greek, which is likely the original language of 3 Baruch.

Determining the date and provenance of 3 Baruch is complicated. It may be cited by Origen,[35] making it no later than 231 CE. But there are some indications of Christian influence, or at least Christian redactions of an earlier Jewish text, in chapters 11–16 in the Greek version only. These features are absent in the Slavonic version. H. E. Gaylord suggests it could be a Christian composition using Jewish traditions, or a Jewish composition that has undergone Christian reworking, probably in the first two centuries CE.[36]

The book is likely a Jewish composition[37] whose author wrote in Greek but had some rudimentary knowledge of Hebrew. The text is deeply rooted in Jewish lore and is incomprehensible without some context within Judaism, and yet it offers no indication of specifically Jewish matters as basic as the dichotomy of Israel and the nations.[38] The situation of 3 Baruch strongly suggests a date of composition after 70 CE, and its affinities with other writings of diasporic Judaism point to Egypt as its place of origin.[39] At the same time, although its core composition is Jewish, the Christian redaction is made to such an extent that it "constitutes a rereading of the book."[40] This ambiguity means that no further attention will be given to 3 Baruch here, and readers are instead encouraged to consult the excellent work by Daniel C. Harlow and the more recent commentary by Alexander Kulik.[41]

Apocalypse of Zephaniah

Introduction

The Apocalypse of Zephaniah is unique among the writings treated here in that it is attested only in a brief fragment in Coptic (Sahidic), a quotation from Clement of Alexandria (150–215 CE),[42] and eighteen fragmentary pages of text in another dialect of Coptic (Akhmimic). According to one estimate, only about one-fourth of the original apocalypse survives, with its beginning particularly poorly attested. Yet enough text is attested to identify it as an

---

35. Origen, *Princ.* 2.3.6.
36. Gaylord, "3 (Greek Apocalypse of) Baruch," 1:656–57.
37. Harlow, *Greek Apocalypse of Baruch*, 90–96.
38. Kulik, "Baruch, Third Book of."
39. J. Collins, *Apocalyptic Imagination*, 311; cf. Picard, *Apocalypsis Baruchi Graece*, 77–78.
40. J. Collins, *Apocalyptic Imagination*, 311.
41. Harlow, *Greek Apocalypse of Baruch*; Kulik, *3 Baruch*.
42. Clement of Alexandria, *Strom.* 5.11.77.

apocalypse.[43] It is not clear why the text is identified with Zephaniah. However, the Sahidic manuscript makes it clear that, for whatever reason, the work is identified with Zephaniah where it states: "Truly, I, Zephaniah, saw these things in my vision" (v. 7).[44] In all, it is likely that the original Apocalypse of Zephaniah presented the seer's heavenly journey, view of the final judgment, and descent into and vision of hell.[45]

Contents

The segment from Clement recounts the seer's ascent into the fifth heaven, where he sees angels sitting on radiant thrones and adorned by the Holy Spirit with diadems.[46] They dwell in the temples and sing hymns to God. The Sahidic fragment contains a description of the seer's vision of a soul in torment (vv. 1–7) and another of a broad place with countless figures (angels?) surrounding it (vv. 8–9).

More coherent material is found in the Akhmimic text, showing that the text is organized into a series of seven travel episodes (chaps. 1–8) and four trumpet scenes (chaps. 9–12). The Apocalypse of Zephaniah begins with a fragmentary text (two verses) about what the speakers will do with a man for his burial (chap. 1). In chapter 2 the seer observes Jerusalem from heaven, discusses with an angel the light that shines from the righteous, and witnesses the souls of men in torment. In chapter 3 the angel takes the seer to Mount Seir, where he is shown how angels record the deeds of people on a manuscript for the time of judgment.[47] Chapter 4 depicts scenes outside the heavenly city, where the seer sees unsightly angels who bring the souls of the ungodly to their eternal torment. Zephaniah himself is spared from this fate. Chapter 5 turns to scenes within the city, which the seer enters with his angelic guide (who is mysteriously transformed) and where he admires the city square and its gates. Chapters 6 and 7 depict scenes from Hades. First (chap. 6) the seer sees a great sea of fire from which a hideous angel comes bearing a manuscript with an account of Zephaniah's sins and another angel, Eremiel, with an account of his good deeds (chap. 7). In the seventh scene (chap. 8) the seer enters a boat with his host, dons an angelic garment, and makes a parting comment to the reader, addressed as "my sons," indicating this is the manner in which good and evil are to be weighed (8:5).

43. Wintermute, "Apocalypse of Zephaniah," 1:497.
44. Wintermute, "Apocalypse of Zephaniah," 1:499.
45. Diebner, "Zephanjas Apokalypse"; Sommer, "Zephaniah, Apocalypse of."
46. Clement of Alexandria, *Strom.* 5.11.77.
47. Wintermute, "Apocalypse of Zephaniah," 1:498.

The remainder of the book (chaps. 9–12) contains a series of four episodes introduced by an angel blowing a golden trumpet. In the first (chap. 9) the trumpet announces Zephaniah's triumph over his accuser. In the second scene (chap. 10) the trumpet announces the opening of heaven, and Zephaniah again sees sinners in anguish in a fiery sea. The trumpet in the third scene (chap. 11) calls the righteous to intercede in prayer for those in torment. The fourth and final trumpet (chap. 12) indicates the beginning of the end, in which Zephaniah is told that there will again be a trumpet blown in the future coming of God's wrath. Four pages are missing from the manuscript after this segment.[48]

Contribution

The central theme is one of divine judgment that all people face, the righteous and the wicked. The lot of the wicked is depicted in terms of eternal torment by hideously distorted angelic beings. The apocalypse depicts the manner in which evidence is gathered for and against a person, with written records preserved of good and evil alike. In the end, they are weighted against one another. Yet Zephaniah himself is able to plead for mercy and receives it. Furthermore, the righteous are able to plead for the souls of the tormented sinners. Readers see a God who has compassion (Apoc. Zeph. 2:9), faithfulness (6:10), and mercy (7:8; 11:2). And so the mercies of God, the allowance of intercession, and the opportunity for repentance suggest a "strong appeal for repentance" in the message of the Apocalypse of Zephaniah.[49]

The author's depiction of angels is important for his narrative and understanding of the work of God, who is absolutely sovereign (Akhmimic ⲡⲭⲁⲉⲓⲥ ⲡⲧⲟⲕⲣⲁⲧⲱⲣ [pjaeis pantokrator] = Greek κύριος παντοκράτωρ [kyrios pantokratōr], "Lord Almighty"; 2:8; 3:5, 7; 4:9; 6:4, 10, 13, 14; 7:8; 11:2, 6; 12:5) but whose works are carried out by angelic figures. Angels are depicted either as beautiful creatures aiding the righteous and praising God or as hideous figures who usher the souls of the wicked to eternal torment. They record the deeds of people, for good or ill, but all judicial authority lies with God (cf. 1QS III, 13–IV, 26). People are judged by God according to their deeds. The righteous are delivered from the torment of Hades, have their names written in the book of the living (9:2), participate in angelic worship, and share communion with other righteous people. The wicked experience eternal punishment in Hades (4:6–7) but have the freedom to

---

48. Wintermute, "Apocalypse of Zephaniah," 1:515.
49. Wintermute, "Apocalypse of Zephaniah," 1:502.

embrace repentance, with both the angels and the righteous interceding in prayer for them toward that end.

Text and Provenance

The earlier of the two manuscript traditions, written in Akhmimic, may date from as early as the fourth century CE. The Akhmimic manuscript consists of four pages of the Apocalypse of Zephaniah. The later of the two, written in Sahidic, dates from the early fifth century CE and contains only two pages of the Apocalypse of Zephaniah. In addition to Clement's citation in Greek,[50] there are three ancient witnesses that mention an Apocalypse of Zephaniah, but the relationship between the texts in Coptic and citations in later works is unclear.[51] It may be that all four of these sources refer to the same text, whereas the Coptic manuscripts represent two versions of that same text. The text was likely written in Greek, with some access to Hebrew, which the author may not have understood very well (cf. Apoc. Zeph. 6:7).[52]

The date is also problematic. The citation by Clement means it originated no later than 215 CE. At Apocalypse of Zephaniah 6:10, an appeal is made to the account of Susanna, an addition to the book of Daniel, the date of which itself is uncertain. However, Susanna was surely known in Alexandria in the first century BCE, suggesting to some scholars a date between 100 BCE and 175 CE.[53] On the other hand, others suggest that features of the work's eschatology and points of correspondence with later Jewish and Christian writings make possible a date as late as the early third century CE as well.[54] The apocalypse contains elements of Judaism—judgment for sin, prayer, afterlife—that bear nothing distinctly Christian.[55] O. S. Wintermute therefore concludes it is a Jewish work. B. J. Diebner suggests it was a Jewish writing originally but became appropriated in some sense by Christians. It is true that the Apocalypse of Zephaniah, like nearly all Jewish apocalypses, was preserved in a Christian context. But it is also true that some Jewish distinctives that are absent—circumcision, Sabbath observance, calendar—are

---

50. Clement of Alexandria, *Strom.* 5.11.77.

51. E.g., Nicephorus, patriarch of Constantinople (806–815); *Synopsis scripturae sacrae* of Pseudo-Athanasius (perhaps sixth century); and the anonymous *Catalogue of the Sixty Canonical Books*.

52. Wintermute, "Apocalypse of Zephaniah," 1:499–500.

53. Wintermute, "Apocalypse of Zephaniah," 1:501–2.

54. Diebner, "Zephanjas Apokalypse"; Sommer, "Zephaniah, Apocalypse of."

55. Wintermute, "Apocalypse of Zephaniah," 1:501—though he notes close parallels to the Akhmimic text at 2:1–4 (cf. Matt. 24:40–41; Luke 17:34–36) and 6:11–15 (cf. Rev. 1:13–15; 2:18; 19:10; 22:8–9).

sometimes absent from Jewish works of the diaspora. So it seems best to
see it as a Jewish work. Portions exhibit familiarity with Exodus and Daniel
(LXX)[56] and perhaps Ezekiel 40–48.[57]

That it was written in Greek suggests a location outside Judea/Palestine.
Its preservation in Coptic and by Clement of Alexandria, among other factors, suggests Egypt as its place of origin. These ambiguities create problems
for placing it within the context of Second Temple Judaism. There is little
comprehensive work done on the Apocalypse of Zephaniah. To date the most
complete resource remains that of Wintermute.[58]

Testament of Abraham

Introduction

The Testament of Abraham is technically not a testament but an apocalypse.[59] It lacks the key feature of a testament, in which the main character,
on his deathbed, imparts his lifelong wisdom to his progeny for ethical and
eschatological instruction.[60] Instead, it contains a narrative and an apocalypse
combined into a single work that deals with the fear of death itself and
one's attitudes about death's relationship to God's judgment.[61] Furthermore,
whereas most pseudepigraphic apocalypses discussed in this volume depict
the first-person narrative of the named figure, the account here is in the third
person and therefore is not strictly pseudepigraphic.[62]

Contents

Of the two ancient versions, or recensions, of the Testament of Abraham
that have been transmitted, Recension A furnishes readers with the most
complete account. At the beginning of the work, Abraham is near death
when Michael is instructed by God to inform Abraham that his end is near so
that he can get his affairs in order (T. Ab. 1:1–7). Michael comes to Abraham
(2:1–12) and together they arrive at the patriarch's house, where only Isaac
recognizes the companion as an angel (3:1–12). Michael returns to heaven,

56. Sommer, "Zephaniah, Apocalypse of."
57. Himmelfarb, *Tours of Hell*, 56–58.
58. Wintermute, "Apocalypse of Zephaniah."
59. Allison, *Testament of Abraham*, 12–27; Ludlow, *Abraham Meets Death*, 152–80.
60. Nickelsburg, *Jewish Literature*, 325; Kolenkow, "Genre Testament and the Testament of Abraham."
61. Nickelsburg, *Jewish Literature*, 325.
62. J. Collins, *Apocalyptic Imagination*, 315.

explaining to God that he cannot bring himself to tell such a righteous man about his impending death (4:6). God explains that he will inform Abraham of his coming death through a dream given to Isaac, which Michael is to interpret (4:7–11). When he returns and Isaac has the dream, it is interpreted by Michael, whom only Sarah recognizes as an angel (5:1–6:8). When Michael (who throughout is called "the Commander-in-chief") explains that he was sent to bring Abraham's soul to God, the patriarch (who is often identified as God's "friend") refuses to go with him (7:1–12). Michael asks God what he should do and is told that God could send Death to force the issue (8:1–12). Abraham begs Michael to first see all creation before he is taken away, to which God agrees (9:1–8).

Abraham and Michael begin a tour of the inhabited world on a heavenly chariot, from which he witnesses people engaging in various sins. At Abraham's request, they are destroyed immediately (10:4–11). But God insists that Abraham not see the entire inhabited world or it would all be destroyed (10:12–15).

Michael then turns the chariot toward the first gate of heaven, where Abraham sees two ways corresponding to two gates—one broad and spacious and the other straight and narrow—with a man seated on a golden throne at the entrance (11:1–4). Angels are taking the souls of many through the broad gate and only a few through the narrow, causing the man on the throne, whom Michael identifies as Adam (11:8–9), to weep (11:5–7, 10–12). Then Abraham sees two fiery angels relentlessly beating souls, driving them into the broad gate for destruction (12:1–2). As Abraham and Michael follow, they again see a wonderous man on a throne between the gates, before whom is a table with a thick book on it (12:3–7). Angels flank the table, holding papyrus, ink, and pen to record the deeds of the souls (12:8, 12). Another angel holds a balance in his hand to weigh the souls (12:9, 13) while the one on the throne judges and sentences the souls (12:11). The fiery angels test the souls (12:10, 14) that are judged by the man, who Abraham learns is Abel (12:15–13:3). This will be followed by "perfect judgment" at the "glorious parousia" (12:4). At a second parousia they will be judged by the twelve tribes (12:5–6) and then by God (12:7) through three tribunals (12:8). Then the role of the recording angels and the judging angels is explained, as well as the nature of the test by fire (12:9–13:14). Abraham prays for the souls of those with equal sins and righteous deeds to receive their salvation and be borne into paradise (14:1–15).

God then instructs Michael to return Abraham to his house, for his end is near (15:1–3). There Michael implores Abraham to make his final testament before his family and servants (15:4–7). Abraham again refuses and Michael

again returns to God to ask for further instructions (15:8–15). God instructs
Death to bring Abraham peacefully (16:1–5). Death masquerades as an angel
and goes to Abraham to claim his soul, but again Abraham refuses (16:6–16).
Death then follows Abraham and refuses to leave until he takes the patriarch
with him (17:1–8). When Abraham asks to see the fullness of Death's feroc-
ity, Death removes his disguise and shows his true horror, at which many die,
to the trembling Abraham (17:9–19). Abraham and Death together pray for
the restoration of those who prematurely died (18:1–11). Death continues to
follow Abraham (19:1–3) and recounts for him the different ways in which he
appears to claim souls (19:4–16; 20:1–2). Death again implores Abraham to
follow, again Abraham refuses (20:3–5), and his household enters, weeping
(20:6–7). Death simply asks Abraham to kiss his right hand to be strengthened,
but it is a trick. Abraham is taken (20:8–9). Michael appears with a multitude
of angels who bear Abraham's soul away and tend to his body (20:10–12).
Abraham then joins the angelic hosts in singing praises to God with undefiled
voice in paradise (20:13–14).

Contribution

Perhaps the most unique aspect of the Testament of Abraham is Abraham's reluctance to die despite God's clear instruction. This is coupled
with statements about Abraham's piety and righteousness alongside God's
surprising tolerance of the patriarch's disobedience. For John J. Collins
this allows the otherwise ethereal Abraham to become a figure with whom
readers can relate and through whom they come to terms with their own
mortality. The illocutionary function of the work as a whole, then, is one
of consolation. Abraham sees the wickedness of people, and his prayers for
retributive justice are swiftly answered—a deed of which he later repents;
no doubt the fear of facing judgment himself is at play in the portrayal of
Abraham.[63]

Despite the condemnation of so many souls, intercession can be made on
their behalf.[64] Specifically, the prayer of Abraham tips the balance of righteous deeds versus sins in favor of the soul, thus securing their salvation into
paradise. It is curious that the narrative portrays Abraham being so harsh
toward the sinners he observes, while presenting God as patient with the
presumptuousness of Abraham.

There are some notable absences in the Jewish character of the Testament
of Abraham. Though Abraham is celebrated for his righteousness and piety,

---

63. J. Collins, *Apocalyptic Imagination*, 317–18.
64. This is explicitly denied in 4 Ezra. J. Collins, *Apocalyptic Imagination*, 318.

nothing is said about his obedient faith.[65] There is no mention of Torah or covenant. Even the sins enumerated are rather general, without mention of Sabbath observance, dietary restriction, circumcision, or even idolatry (cf. 2 En. 10:6; 3 Bar. 13:4). E. P. Sanders rightly observes that the Testament of Abraham is unique among Egyptian Jewish writings in that it neither gravitates toward the philosophical interpretations associated with Alexandria (e.g., Philo) nor advocates for Jewish distinction from pagan Egyptian practices (e.g., Joseph and Aseneth; Sibylline Oracles).[66] The outlook of the Testament of Abraham is also distinct in its developed personification of Death and detailed judgment scenes that reflect common features in Egyptian burial texts.[67] Also notable is its rather broad soteriology. Nothing is clearly indicated about the parameters of Israel, or even a distinction between Jews and gentiles.[68] There is mention of Adam, Abel, Isaac, and Sarah, but Abraham views the behavior of the entire inhabited world (T. Ab. 10:1; 12:2).[69] Judgment and salvation are presented clearly: sin must be repented of or else be punished by premature death. If sins are found to outweigh righteous deeds at judgment, the soul departs to punishment. Those for whom righteous deeds outweigh evil go to paradise. If sins and righteous deeds are balanced evenly, intercessory prayer can intervene and tip the scales in the person's favor (14:6). But even here there are levels of judgment—the judgment of individual souls after death, the judgment of the wicked by the righteous, and the final judgment of God.

Text and Provenance

The text of the Testament of Abraham is preserved in two recensions that likely share a common ancestor.[70] The longer of these (Rec. A) contains the more complete account of the narrative[71] and is attested in several Greek manuscripts and a Rumanian version, whereas the shorter (Rec. B) is found also in several Greek manuscripts, a single Rumanian version, and texts in Slavonic, Coptic, Arabic, and Ethiopic. It was most likely written in Greek.[72] Similarities with Egyptian mythology and Egyptian Jewish literature, such as

---

65. Nickelsburg, *Jewish Literature*, 325; Ludlow, *Abraham Meets Death*, 69–72; Reed, "Construction and Subversion"; Wills, "*Testament of Abraham*."

66. E. P. Sanders, "Testament of Abraham," 1:877.

67. Ludlow, "Abraham, Testament of," 1:95.

68. Only in T. Ab. 13:6 does one find distinctive Israelite identity in the mention of the role of the twelve tribes in judgment.

69. E. P. Sanders, "Testament of Abraham," 1:877.

70. E. P. Sanders, "Testament of Abraham," 1:871. On the relationship between the textual traditions, see most recently Allison, *Testament of Abraham*, 12–27.

71. Nickelsburg, "Structure and Message," 92.

72. Some argue for a Hebrew original to Rec. B. See Schmidt, *Le Testament grec d'Abraham*.

the Testament of Jacob, suggest Egypt as the place of origin.[73] Like nearly all Jewish pseudepigrapha, the Testament of Abraham was transmitted among Christians. Some suggest it could have been written by a Jew, a gentile Christian, or even a Godfearer.[74] Yet it is generally presumed to be Jewish, notably because of places that either contradict known Christian beliefs or have no Christian parallels.[75] It seems unlikely that a Christian writer would place Abel at the seat of judgment rather than Christ.[76] A date in the first century CE is suggested by comparable Hellenistic Jewish writings,[77] but nothing in the text gives any clear indications of historical referents. Dale C. Allison Jr. suggests it is unlikely to be later than the Diaspora Revolt (115–118 CE).[78] These important uncertainties suggest caution about the Testament of Abraham's placement within the context of the notable Second Temple apocalypses discussed in this volume. For further consideration, readers are well served by the thorough commentary by Allison.[79]

Dead Sea Scrolls

Introduction

Among the Dead Sea Scrolls there is no single, complete apocalypse preserved. Many manuscripts represent portions of apocalyptic literature from Daniel and the Enochic corpus, as we have seen before. And apocalypticism in general permeates much of the thought world of the Qumran texts.[80] What we are left with in terms of apocalypses aside from Daniel and the Enochic texts are fragments.[81] But the book of Daniel warrants further consideration since it is particularly influential among the apocalyptic literature from Qumran. Eight manuscripts of Daniel[82] were discovered among the Dead Sea Scrolls in Qumran Caves 1, 4, and 6 (1QDan^{a–b}, 4QDan^{a–e}, 6QpapDan). Daniel is

73. J. Collins, *Apocalyptic Imagination*, 316; Allison, *Testament of Abraham*, 32–33.

74. Davila, *Provenance of the Pseudepigrapha*, 205–7.

75. Allison, *Testament of Abraham*, 29.

76. Nickelsburg, *Jewish Literature*, 327.

77. Reed, "Testament of Abraham," 1672.

78. Allison, *Testament of Abraham*, 38–39.

79. Allison, *Testament of Abraham*.

80. See esp. J. Collins, *Apocalypticism and the Dead Sea Scrolls*.

81. Nickelsburg ("Apocalyptic Texts," 1:34, following García Martínez, *Qumran and Apocalyptic*) lists apocalyptic works composed at Qumran: Elect of God (4Q534); Prayer of Nabonidus (4Q242); Pseudo-Daniel (4Q243–245); Aramaic Apocalypse (4Q246); and New Jerusalem (1Q32, 2Q24, 4Q232, 4Q554–555, 5Q15, 11Q18).

82. This segment draws in part from Gurtner, "Danielic Influence at the Intersection." The most complete analysis of Daniel among the Scrolls is that of Mertens, *Das Buch Daniel*.

also noted for its literary influence on the pseudepigraphic materials that emerged around the figure of Daniel. One, the Prayer of Nabonidus (4Q242), will be dealt with in chapter 22. The "Pseudo-Daniel" texts are three Aramaic documents from Qumran (4Q243–245 = Pseudo-Daniel[a–c]) in which Daniel is mentioned, but they are not part of the book of Daniel itself. Also like their Danielic counterpart, these texts share a setting in a royal court and an apocalyptic review of history.[83]

The Vision of Daniel

Pseudo-Daniel[a–b] (4Q243–244) comprises two documents of a single composition that together encompass fifty-four fragments (forty and fourteen, respectively) in a Herodian script dating from the late first century BCE. Together they are sometimes called the Vision of Daniel.[84] The beginning seems to give a setting in which Daniel is speaking to Belshazzar (cf. Dan. 5; 4Q243 1–2; 4Q244 1–3), and mention is made of something written (4Q243 6). Daniel appears to give an account of Israel's history, beginning with Noah (Gen. 6–9; 4Q244 8) through the Tower of Babel (Gen. 11; 4Q244 9; 4Q243 10). Brief mention is made of the prediction to Abraham of captivity in Egypt for four hundred years (Gen. 15:13; 4Q244 12 1) followed by a prediction of the exodus itself (Gen. 15:14; Exod. 15–16; 4Q244 12 2–3). The text then discusses Israel's apostasy in language drawn from the Psalms (4Q244 13 1–3; 12 3–4). After seventy years of punishment in exile, the Israelites will be brought back (4Q244 16). Then Daniel describes a series of kingdoms to succeed Babylon (4Q244 19–21). The text concludes with a description of some kind of gathering, potentially an eschatological battle (4Q244 24–25).[85] The text is intriguing but too fragmentary to be of much service for our purposes.

The Second Vision of Daniel

The Second Vision of Daniel[86] (4Q245; Pseudo-Daniel[c] or 4QpsDan[c] ar) is a separate work concerned with the internal affairs of Israel's history.[87] In all, Pseudo-Daniel[c] is composed of four fragments that date to the early first century CE, with a date of composition not earlier than the late second century BCE. A major theme of the work is the restoration of the elect, who walk in

---

83. Bledsoe, "Daniel, Pseudo-Texts."
84. Wise, Abegg, and Cook, *Dead Sea Scrolls*, 342–44. The summary presented here generally follows that of Wise, Abegg, and Cook.
85. Wise, Abegg, and Cook, *Dead Sea Scrolls*, 344.
86. Wise, Abegg, and Cook, *Dead Sea Scrolls*, 344
87. Collins and Flint, "4Q243–245," 133.

the way of truth, at the eschaton.[88] This fragmentary text presents Daniel, seemingly in a foreign court (4Q245 I, 1–4), when he is handed a book from which he reads names of priests (I, 5–11) and kings (I, 11–14), numbering the kings prior to the "cessation of evil" at twenty-two and the priests at thirty-five (I, 15–16). Some, the text remarks, walked in error and others in truth (I, 16–17). The text ends with "Then shall arise [the Elect of God, and they shall receive the h]oly [kingdom], and restore [. . .]." The priests listed here end at Judah Aristobulus I (d. 103 BCE). After him, Alexander Jannaeus came to the high priesthood and kingship as well (Josephus, *J.W.* 1.4.1 §85; *Ant.* 13.12.1 §320), which suggests the author's own time, when he envisions the coming of God's intervention being imminent.[89]

Aramaic Apocalypse

The Aramaic Apocalypse (4Q246) or "Son of God" text is a single fragment dating from the late first century BCE, composed perhaps as early as the mid-second century BCE. Though Daniel is not named in this document, its court setting, eschatological outlook, and mention of the "Son of God" suggest affinity with the biblical book.[90] At the outset of the fragment, the spirit comes upon a man who falls before a throne and begins an interpretation, seemingly of a vision had by a king (4Q246 I, 1). He predicts that a cruel tyrant will come to power, bringing about tribulation on the world (I, 2–5). After this "a prince of nations" will arise and rule (I, 5–8). Then the son of the tyrant will arise and be designated "Son of God," but his rule will only be temporary (I, 9; II, 1–3). Deliverance comes only when the people of God arise and establish peace (II, 3). They will establish an eternal kingdom, end warfare, judge justly, and be honored by all nations (II, 4–7). God will help them, fighting for them, putting people in power, and establishing his eternal rule (II, 8–10). Verbal parallels to Daniel throughout may suggest the use and adaptation of Daniel 7, or else a contemporary work with shared language.[91]

88. Similarly see the Animal Apocalypse (1 En. 83–90), the Apocalypse of Weeks (1 En. 93:1–10; 91:11–17), the Damascus Document, and Pseudo-Moses[c] (4Q390). J. Collins, "Daniel, Book of," 1:176–77.

89. Wise, Abegg, and Cook, *Dead Sea Scrolls*, 344–45.

90. The identity of this figure has eluded scholars, with some suggesting he is Antiochus IV Epiphanes (Puech, "4QApocryphe de Daniel ar"), Melchizedek or the angel Michael (García Martínez, "Eschatological Figure of 4Q246"), an obscure messianic figure (J. Collins, "Background of the 'Son of God' Text"), or a heavenly counterpart to the fourth kingdom in Daniel (Michael Segal, "Who Is the 'Son of God'").

91. Puech, "Fragment d'une apocalypse en araméen."

Apocryphon of Jeremiah

The Apocryphon of Jeremiah is a collection of manuscripts dating from the mid-first century BCE,[92] though the texts are fragmentary and lack clear context.[93] The content is sparse, but it suggests a third-person narrative in which Jeremiah appears in three settings. First, he appears on the shores of a river with the residents of Jerusalem on their way to exile in Babylon (4Q385a 18 I). Second, he is presented among a community of Jews in Tahpanes, Egypt (4Q385a 18 II). Third, Jeremiah is seen writing from Egypt to exiled Jews in Babylon (4Q389 1).[94] The text is replete with first-person statements by the visionary in conversation with God. Much of it is an apocalyptic review of Jewish history from the exile up to the author's own time, utilizing the temporal designation of "jubilee" (cf. 4Q387 1–3).[95] In it one finds repeated statements by God in which he rebukes people for forsaking his covenant, temple, and festivals and profaning God's name (esp. 4Q385a 3a–c; 4Q388a 3; 4Q387 1). It also anticipates Israel forsaking God and experiencing judgment by its enemies, but God will preserve a remnant to escape from his wrath, ruled by the angels of Mas[t]emah (4Q390 1 2–12).[96] There is a lengthy prophecy about a blasphemer who will come after the destruction of the temple, probably in reference to the Seleucid (Syrian) king Antiochus IV Epiphanes (168 BCE), whose profaning of the temple triggered the Maccabean revolt (4Q387 2; 4Q385a 4; 4Q388a 7 II; 4Q389 8 II). The priests likewise engage in disobedient acts that will lead to judgment (4Q385a 5a–b; 4Q387 3; 4Q387 4 I; cf. 4Q390 2 I, 2–12; II, 4–11). An exhortation by Jeremiah for them to keep the covenant of their fathers while in exile (4Q385a 18a–b I, 2–11) is followed by a fragmentary narrative of Jeremiah among Jews in Tahpanes, Egypt (4Q385a 18 II, 1–10).[97] Kipp Davis summarizes the content by emphasizing Jeremiah's dialogues as a review of Israel's past glories and sins, which "culminates into an apocalyptic vision about the corruption of the priesthood in the 2nd cent. BCE and the resulting judgment of God in the last days."[98]

92. Dimant, *Qumran Cave 4, XXI*, 129–253.
93. K. Davis, "Jeremiah, Apocryphon of." The manuscripts (4Q383, 4Q384, 4Q385a, 4Q387a[?]; 4Q387, 4Q388a, 4Q389) are distinguished as Apocryphon of Jeremiah A, B, and C.
94. K. Davis, "Jeremiah, Apocryphon of."
95. K. Davis, "Jeremiah, Apocryphon of." The sequence of the episodes represented in the fragments is not entirely clear. The present discussion follows that of Dimant, *Qumran Cave 4, XXI*, 129–253.
96. The inclusion of 4Q390 is debated. See Davis, "Jeremiah, Apocryphon of," 271; Dimant, *Qumran Cave 4, XXI*, 235–54.
97. Wise, Abegg, and Cook, *Dead Sea Scrolls*, 439–46.
98. K. Davis, "Jeremiah, Apocryphon of." See also K. Davis, *Cave 4 Apocryphon of Jeremiah*.

4Q390

A similar and perhaps related text is 4Q390 (sometimes called 4QPseudo-Moses[e]), which may have been part of the Apocryphon of Jeremiah C[99] or a later interpretation of it.[100] Regardless, it provides a historical overview found in other apocalyptic writings,[101] here by dividing history into jubilees.[102] The text describes the sons of Aaron ruling over Israel, which will nonetheless do evil in God's eyes and will forget the law, including its festivals, the Sabbath, and the covenant (4Q390 1 1–9). God will deliver them into the hands of their enemies in judgment. But he will preserve survivors who will be ruled by angels of destruction, who will again lead them in evil (lines 9–12). After some fragmentary mention of the temple (4Q390 2 I, 2), the text anticipates the coming dominion of Belial to deliver them to the sword (lines 3–4). Seemingly during that time they will break God's laws and be delivered to the hands of the angels of destruction, who will rule over them (lines 5–7). They will again violate the laws of God (lines 7–10).

Apocryphon of Ezekiel

The Apocryphon of Ezekiel (4Q385, 4Q385b, 4Q386, 4Q388) comes from the same time as the Apocryphon of Jeremiah. It purports to contain the words of Ezekiel concerning the coming destruction of the gentiles (esp. Egypt; 4Q385b 1 1–6). It also recounts the prophecy of the dry bones (Ezek. 37), interpreting it as one of the earliest depictions of bodily resurrection (4Q385 2 1–9; 4Q388 7; 4Q386 1 I) and as a promise that Israel will again possess the land (4Q385 3 1–7). God promises to preserve a remnant from the oppression of Belial (4Q386 1 II, 1–10) and judge Babylon for oppressing Jerusalem (4Q386 1 III, 1–6; 4Q385 4 1–7). The text ends with Ezekiel's vision of the chariot (4Q386 6 1–16; cf. Ezek. 1).[103]

Book of Giants

The so-called Book of Giants (4Q203, 4Q530–532, 6Q8, 1Q23, 2Q26) includes one manuscript (4Q530) that has a throne vision similar to that of Daniel 7 and 1 Enoch 14.[104] Among the fragmentary statements found in

99. B. H. Reynolds, *Between Symbolism and Realism*, 268.
100. C. Davis, "Torah-Performance and History," 468–72.
101. See DiTommaso, "Development of Apocalyptic Historiography."
102. J. Collins, *Apocalyptic Imagination*, 181.
103. Wise, Abegg, and Cook, *Dead Sea Scrolls*, 447–49. See Strugnell and Dimant, "4Q Second Ezekiel."
104. See Stuckenbruck, "Daniel and Early Enoch Traditions"; Stokes, "Throne Visions of Daniel 7."

4Q530, one finds mention of "the death of our souls" (II, 1), dreaming of dreams (line 4) and something coming to people in their dreams (lines 5–6), watching tongues of fire (line 9) and interpreting the dream (lines 14–15, 23). Then the seer narrates in the first person seeing something in his dream: "The Ruler of the heavens came down to earth, and thrones were erected and the Great Holy One sa[t down" (lines 16–17). The Holy One is surrounded by countless attendants, and books are opened from which sentences are proclaimed in an apparent judgment scene (lines 17–20).

Four Kingdoms

The fragmentary Four Kingdoms text (4Q552–553; 4QFour Kingdoms[a–b] ar) is written in Aramaic and depicts kingdoms as trees.[105] In this respect it resembles the symbolism used in the book of Daniel (chaps. 2, 7) for its depiction of Babylon, Media, Persia, and Greece. Though, in the Four Kingdoms text only Babylon is clearly identified where it rules over Persia,[106] and perhaps a reconstructed Greece is identified as well.[107] At the outset the text mentions angels, a king, and the seer, who speaks in the first person, apparently seeing four trees (4Q552 2 I, 5–12; II). The first tree is Babylon (II, 2–6), the second is perhaps Greece (lines 6–10), and the third (line 11) may be Rome. The fourth tree is not mentioned (4Q553 8 I, 1–5; II, 1–4; 4Q553 9–10).[108]

Messianic Apocalypse

The Messianic Apocalypse (4Q521; 4QMessianic Apocalypse) was copied in Hebrew around 100–80 BCE from an earlier manuscript that probably dates from the second half of the second century BCE.[109] It contains a complete statement that the heavens and earth will listen to "his anointed one" (4Q521 2 II, 1). It promises care for the poor and pious and the performance of marvelous acts (4Q521 2 II, 4–11). It is understood by some as an account from a miracle-working messianic tradition similar to Jesus.[110] Its mention of the "messiah" or "anointed one" in the context of both eschatological miracles and resurrection (4Q521 7 + 5 II, 6) has generated some discussion. But its fragmentary nature complicates interpretation.[111] And, though designated an

105. Puech, *Qumrân Grotte 4, XXVII*, 57–90.
106. J. Collins, *Apocalyptic Imagination*, 182.
107. B. H. Reynolds, *Between Symbolism and Realism*, 200.
108. Wise, Abegg, and Cook, *Dead Sea Scrolls*, 555–57.
109. Becker, "Messianic Apocalypse (4Q521)."
110. Tabor and Wise, "4Q521."
111. Becker, "Messianic Apocalypse (4Q521)."

"apocalypse" by its principle editor,[112] it is uncertain whether it contains any characteristics of an apocalypse.[113]

New Jerusalem Text

The New Jerusalem text (4Q554–555, 5Q15, 11Q18, 1Q32, 2Q24), preserved in seven fragments written in Aramaic, describes a heavenly Jerusalem modeled after Ezekiel 40–48.[114] Hugo Antonissen remarks that the manuscripts were copied between the first half of the first century BCE and the first half of the first century CE, while the original was likely composed in the second quarter of the first century BCE or earlier.[115] Despite its fragmentary nature, it is most likely an apocalypse.[116] The book begins with a description of the gates of the new Jerusalem, each of which is named after one of the twelve tribes of Israel (4Q554 2 I, 9–22; II [= 2Q24, 5Q15], 1–11; cf. Ezek. 48:30–35; Rev. 21:12–13).[117] It then describes an angelic guide leading the visionary to show the layout of the streets (4Q554 2 II, 12–23). Next, the angel shows the walls, towers, and stairs (5Q15 1 I, 7–14; cf. 4Q554 3 II, 13–18). Then the angel shows more details about the city blocks (4Q554 2 III, 12–22; 5Q15 1 I, 4–5) and the houses on each block (5Q15 1 II, 6–15). Within the temple the visionary sees the work of the priests (11Q18 15) as well as their clothing (11Q18 14 II) and their work of offering sacrifices (11Q18 13; cf. 2Q24 4 [+ 11Q18 13]). The text concludes (4Q554 3 III) with a prophecy of an eschatological battle between Israel and gentile nations in which Israel is victorious.[118]

Conclusion

While the Qumran texts are sometimes frustratingly incomplete, collectively they indicate that a significant amount of apocalyptic literature was extant during the Second Temple period. Moreover, some have suggested that the fact that most of these were written in Aramaic rather than Hebrew implies that they were composed not within the *yaḥad*[119] at Qumran but else-

112. Puech, *Qumrân Grotte 4, XVIII*, 1–38.

113. Becker, "Messianic Apocalypse (4Q521)."

114. J. Collins, *Apocalyptic Imagination*, 182–83.

115. Antonissen, "New Jerusalem Text"; Puech, "554–554a–555." Cf. Antonissen, "Visionary Architecture."

116. DiTommaso, *Dead Sea New Jerusalem Text*, 110.

117. The outline here closely follows that of Wise, Abegg, and Cook, *Dead Sea Scrolls*, 557–63.

118. Wise, Abegg, and Cook, *Dead Sea Scrolls*, 557–63.

119. The term *yaḥad* is a Hebrew word meaning, generally, "community" and is the term by which the Jewish community at Qumran identified themselves in the Dead Sea Scrolls.

where.[120] Furthermore, these and other apocalypses dealt with throughout this volume have influenced a plethora of other apocalypses in later Jewish and Christian contexts that are beyond our purview. Titles such as the Apocalypse of Ezra and the Apocalypse of Daniel suggest the manner in which figures and scenes from the Hebrew Bible cast long shadows of influence into later traditions beyond the Second Temple period.

120. Dimant, "Qumran Aramaic Texts"; J. Collins, *Apocalyptic Imagination*, 183.

Testaments
and Related Texts

Readers of the Hebrew Bible are familiar with the last words of figures like Jacob (Gen. 49) and Moses (Deut. 33–34).[1] In these scenes a revered figure, typically a father or leader, delivers a discourse to his sons, his people, or his successor in anticipation of his imminent death. This setting has evolved into a specific category of literature known as a testament. Testaments typically present the discourse of the main figure in the first person, followed by an account of his death in the third person. Testaments can also occur as segments of larger Jewish works that themselves belong to another genre.[2] At least part of their importance lies in the notion that a person nearing death is likely to convey ideas of utmost importance to their progeny, whether information received on an otherworldly journey, ethical teachings, or the distribution of inheritance.[3] A history of scholarship is outlined by Anitra Bingham Kolenkow,[4]

1. Cf. the words of Joshua (Josh. 23–24), Samuel (1 Sam. 12), and David (1 Kings 2:1–9; 1 Chron. 28–29).
2. J. Collins (*Apocalyptic Imagination*, 158) notes Tob. 14; 1 Macc. 2:49–70; Jub. 21, 36; LAB 19, 23–24, 33; 2 En. 39–55; 2 Bar. 43–47.
3. See Kolenkow, "Literary Genre 'Testament,'" 259.
4. Kolenkow, "Literary Genre 'Testament,'" 259–62.

who observes that the considerable work done on the Testaments of the Twelve Patriarchs lends particular insight. Though the provenance of the Testaments of the Twelve Patriarchs is disputed, the twelve distinct testaments contained therein, as well as the presence of the word "testament" in its title, furnish readers with substantial material for identifying testamentary characteristics. The genre seems to have emerged in the Hellenistic era[5] and, following its Old Testament pattern, exhibits some defining characteristics. In addition to the discourse delivered in anticipation of imminent death, the testament typically begins by describing in the third person the situation in which the discourse is delivered, and it ends with an account of the speaker's death.[6] One finds a generally consistent pattern in the Testaments of the Twelve Patriarchs of three common elements: first, a historical narrative retrospectively accounting for the patriarch's life; second, a moral or ethical exhortation to the figure's progeny; and third, a prediction of the future in Deuteronomistic fashion in which a pattern of sin-exile-restoration is evident.[7] These patterns may be exhibited to varying extents in other testaments. For instance, the Testament of Moses is nearly all prediction, with little exhortation and no historical retrospection. By contrast, one finds primarily retrospection on the life of Job in the Testament of Job, only brief exhortation, and no prediction.[8] The testament genre, then, is best identified in terms of its central figure nearing death with ancillary features varying from one text to another.[9] This allows for some flexibility in identifying works belonging to this category, though our usual parameters of being demonstrably Jewish and dating from the Second Temple period remain. Among the challenges in the study of testaments is that, of the six or seven that survive from antiquity, all contain substantial Jewish material, but only a few are Jewish in their present form.[10] These are limited to the Testament of Moses, the Testament of Job, the Visions of Amram, Aramaic Levi Document, and Testament of Qahat. This means that our analyses of respective testaments must pay careful attention to their provenance, but because these texts can be so disconnected and fragmentary, they sometimes fall outside the strict parameters of Second Temple Jewish pseudepigrapha. Still, they illustrate some important aspects of the literature and so are included here.

5. J. Collins, "Testaments," 325.
6. J. Collins, "Testaments," 325.
7. J. Collins, "Testaments," 325. Such restrictions lead Collins ("Testaments," 326) to allow for only the Testament of Moses, the Testament of Job, the Testaments of the Twelve Patriarchs, and potentially the Visions of Amram to fit within this genre.
8. J. Collins, "Testaments," 325–26.
9. So also Hillel, "Testaments."
10. J. Collins, *Apocalyptic Imagination*, 158.

7

Testament of Moses

Introduction

Also known as the Assumption of Moses,[1] the Testament of Moses is a farewell exhortation given to Joshua by Moses before the transfer of leadership of the people of Israel. The ending of the book has been lost, and it is generally assumed that Moses's death was narrated at some point in the earlier text.[2] The narrative is almost entirely attributed to Moses in the form of a prediction regarding Israel's people from their entrance into Canaan until the end of days.[3]

Language and Manuscripts

The Testament of Moses survives in a single Latin palimpsest from the sixth century CE, which likely dates from the fifth century. This text was discovered by A. M. Ceriani in 1861 in the Ambrosian Library (Milan) in a fragmentary form, with estimates of one-third to one-half being lost.[4] John Priest observes that the remaining portions are often fragmentary, illegible, and at times replete with orthographical and grammatical irregularities, requiring editors

1. The designation "Assumption of Moses" was given by A. M. Ceriani (1861) even though the bodily assumption of Moses is not described. J. Collins, *Apocalyptic Imagination*, 159. See also Tromp, *Assumption of Moses*, 281–85.
2. Hillel, "Testaments"; J. Collins, *Apocalyptic Imagination*, 159.
3. Priest, "Testament of Moses," 1:919.
4. Priest, "Testament of Moses," 1:919.

and translators to derive emendations and reconstructions. A number of factors suggest the Latin text was translated from Greek, such as Greek words transliterated into Latin and syntactical constructions that clearly reflect Greek conventions.[5] Yet there are other phenomena for which Greek syntax cannot account.[6] Whether the Greek behind the Latin text was translated from a Hebrew (or Aramaic) original cannot be discerned on available evidence.

Provenance

Most presume the Testament of Moses was written in Palestine,[7] though with little discussion. Johannes Tromp helpfully observes that Jerusalem is the only city mentioned in the work and suggests that diaspora Jews seem to have no role. Furthermore, the threat to the temple and its sacrifices likely affirms this suggestion.[8] Priest contends that, of the diverse array of proposals for the Jewish community that lies behind the Testament of Moses, three are particularly worth consideration: the Hasidim, a branch of the Pharisees, and the Essenes.[9] The Hasidim were known during the Maccabean time, but what is known of their beliefs is too general to be able to identify them with a particular ideology. The notion of Pharisaic authorship was espoused by R. H. Charles, who claimed the author was resisting the burgeoning nationalism within the party.[10] Still others suggest the sectarians of Qumran, commonly regarded as Essenes, for the origins of the book, and Priest cautiously affirms that the Testament of Moses "does appear to have closer affinities with the Essenes than with any other *known* group in the Judaism of the period."[11] And yet he prefers to regard the work as reflecting the "general outlook" of the Hasidic movement with a particular emphasis on apocalyptic motifs. The work recognizes a division within Israel between those who observe the law and those who do not (T. Mos. 12:10–11), but there is no recognizable organization into a distinct community. The indication that two tribes lament because they are unable to offer sacrifices to the Lord (T. Mos. 4:8) is generally read as a rejection of worship at the second temple (cf. 1 En. 89:73; T. Levi 16:1),[12] though it is

5. Priest, "Testament of Moses," 1:920. See also Tromp, *Assumption of Moses*, 78–81.
6. Tromp, *Assumption of Moses*, 79–80, 85.
7. Priest, "Testament of Moses," 1:921.
8. Tromp, *Assumption of Moses*, 117.
9. Priest, "Testament of Moses," 1:921.
10. Charles, "The Assumption of Moses," 2:411.
11. Priest, "Testament of Moses," 1:921.
12. J. Collins, *Apocalyptic Imagination*, 164–65.

also possible that the tribes are in exile and so prevented from participation in cultic worship.[13]

Date

The date of the Testament of Moses has been the subject of some dispute.[14] Initially Charles suggested it was written shortly after the attack on Jews by Varus (4 BCE; Josephus, *Ant.* 17.10.9–10 §§286–298; *J.W.* 2.3.1–5.3 §§39–79) and dated the work from shortly after the turn of the era.[15] Others argued that this was the date of the work's revision, whereas its composition dates from the persecutions under Antiochus IV Epiphanes (175–164 BCE; cf. 2 Macc. 4–6).[16] More recently it has been argued that the material after Antiochus and the Maccabean revolt (T. Mos. 6–7) is a later insertion, creating a two-stage understanding to the development of the book.[17] However, some scholars dispute a stage in the time of Antiochus and date the whole document to the first century CE.[18] There is clear evidence of earlier material, such as the Hasmonean rulers ("powerful kings . . . [who] will be called priests," 6:1) and Herod the Great ("a powerful king from the west," 6:8).[19] The persecutions in the Testament of Moses 8 resemble those under Antiochus IV Epiphanies— forced idolatry and blasphemy, punishment for circumcision, and surgical reversal of circumcision (cf. 1 Macc. 1:48, 60–61; 2 Macc. 6:6, 9, 10).[20] So it is generally safest to conclude that in its present form the Testament of Moses dates from early in the first century CE.

Contents

The surviving material begins in the middle of a sentence, since the beginning of the text is missing. It is presumed that three lines of text began the document, likely referring to the year of Moses's life when he conveyed his

---

13. Schwartz, "Tribes of As. Mos. 4:7–9."

14. J. Collins, "Testamentary Literature," 277.

15. Charles, "Assumption of Moses," 2:407.

16. Licht, "Taxo." Cf. Nickelsburg, *Resurrection*, 43–45.

17. Nickelsburg, "Assumption of Moses as a Testament"; J. Collins, "Some Remaining Traditio-Historical Problems"; J. Collins, "Testamentary Literature," 277; so also A. Collins, "Composition and Redaction."

18. Priest, "Testament of Moses," 1:920–21; Tromp, *Assumption of Moses*, 120–23.

19. Some also see the campaigns of Varus (4 BCE; T. Mos. 6:8–9; J. Collins, *Apocalyptic Imagination*, 160), though this is contested by Tromp, *Assumption of Moses*, 117.

20. Tromp, *Assumption of Moses*, 217–18.

farewell speech to Joshua (cf. Deut. 31:2; 34:7). It is sometimes regarded as a loose rewriting of Deuteronomy 31–34.[21] The extant text identifies the setting—after the exodus and when Israel had crossed the Jordan—and identifies what follows as the prophecy of Moses in the book of Deuteronomy (T. Mos. 1:2–5). Moses summons Joshua to minister in the tabernacle and lead Israel to the promised land (1:6–9). He addresses Joshua with exhortations to obey God's commandments blamelessly (1:10), since God created the world on behalf of his people (1:11–12) but concealed his purposes from the guilty nations (1:13). Furthermore, Moses claims that he was prepared from the beginning of the world to be the "mediator of his covenant" (1:14). And so he informs Joshua of his impending death (1:15) and instructs him to preserve the books with which he is entrusted (1:16–18).

Chapters 2–9 give an extensive prophecy of the history of Israel,[22] beginning with Moses predicting the entry into the promised land under Joshua (2:1–2) and moving on to the time of the judges, the united monarchy (2:3–4), and the divided monarchy (2:5–9), acknowledging that some of the tribes will violate their covenant with God. This will lead to God's just punishment for sin by a king from the East who will overrun their land, burn their city and temple, and carry off its vessels and its people into exile (3:1–3), where they will all cry out to God for deliverance (3:4–9). They will recognize that their punishment is in accord with the prophecy of Moses, and they shall be slaves for about seventy-seven years (3:10–14).

Dramatically, "one who is over them" (perhaps Ezra)[23] will arrive and pray for Israel's restoration (4:1–4). Moses predicts that God will remember his covenant with Israel and inspire a king to have pity on them and send them home (4:5–6). They will rebuild Jerusalem, and two tribes will return to their former faith in repentance and with sacrifices (4:7–8), but ten tribes will spread among the nations during their captivity (4:9). Moses then predicts a time in which kings will arise who will share in the ten tribes' punishment, and they will again fall into sin (5:1–2) by polluting temple worship with foreign customs and foreign gods under illegitimate priests (5:3–6). This is typically associated with the hellenizing priests appointed during Seleucid rule (198–167 BCE) or the priest-kings in place during the Hasmonean rule (142–37 BCE).[24]

Then there will arise kings who will be called priests (a clear reference to the Hasmoneans; 6:1). They are followed by a "wanton" or "petulant" king (*rex*

---

21. J. Collins, *Apocalyptic Imagination*, 161; Harrington, "Interpreting Israel's History."
22. J. Collins, *Apocalyptic Imagination*, 159.
23. For discussion of the identity of this intercessor, see Tromp, *Assumption of Moses*, 175–76.
24. Priest, "Testament of Moses," 1:927.

petulans) who is not of a priestly line (6:1; Herod the Great, r. 37–4 BCE). He is described as rash and perverse, shattering leaders, exterminating others, and killing both young and old without mercy (6:2–4). He will rule for thirty-four years and beget heirs to rule in his stead (6:5–7). This is a clear reference to Herod's sons Antipas (r. 4 BCE–39 CE), Philip (r. 4 BCE–34 CE), and Archelaus (r. 4 BCE–6 CE).[25] After his death will come a "powerful king of the West" who will subdue them, carry away captives, burn part of the temple, and crucify opponents around their city (Jerusalem; 6:8–9). This is held to be the activity of Varus, Roman governor of Syria, whose assaults on Jerusalem occurred in 4 BCE (Josephus, *J.W.* 2.3.2–5.2 §§45–75; *Ant.* 17.10.2–10 §§254–298).

In chapter 7 Moses foresees a crucial time of destructive rulers (T. Mos. 7:1–4), though verse 2 is illegible. Regardless, it seems that the events of chapters 5 and 6 are now coming to a climax, and likely at the readers' own time. The author does not identify the rulers particularly but lists common qualities among them: they are godless, they claim to be righteous, and they are deceitful, self-pleasing, false, devouring, and gluttonous (7:3–40). Verse 5 is composed of five largely illegible lines of text, perhaps continuing the list of accusations,[26] as one reads in the following verses (7:6–10). Here it is said that they exploit the poor, neglect justice, and handle impure things hypocritically.

Moses then (chap. 8) predicts a time of unprecedented persecution by a king who will crucify those who confess their circumcision (8:1–2). Their wives will be given to foreign gods, and their sons will have their circumcision surgically removed (8:3), and still others will experience torture and be compelled to blaspheme their laws and cultic worship (8:4–5). Then a Levite named Taxo will appear with his seven sons, who would rather die than transgress the laws of their ancestral God (9:1–7).

Chapter 10 is a prophecy of the advent of God's kingdom in hymn form. The kingdom will appear throughout creation; the devil and sorrow will come to an end (10:1). Then there will be an appointed "messenger" (*nuntius*), or angel, perhaps Michael, who will avenge the enemies of God's people (10:2). God himself will appear dramatically and bring about vengeance on the nations (10:3–7), and Israel will be exalted (10:8–10). After this Moses exhorts Joshua to keep the words of the book and be strong in light of his impending death (10:11–15). At this Joshua mourns (11:1–4) and asks Moses how the remains of such a revered figure as Moses should be honored after his death (11:5–8). Before Moses replies, Joshua laments his own inability to lead Israel (11:9–15) and his anticipation that Israel's enemies will grow bold when they learn that

---

25. Atkinson, "Moses, Assumption of."
26. Tromp, *Assumption of Moses*, 206, 211.

Moses is gone (11:16–12:1). Moses encourages Joshua by affirming that God is sovereign in all things (12:2–5) and that the mercies of God that sustained Moses's leadership will sustain Joshua's also (12:6–9). Finally, Moses promises good to those who observe God's commands and evil to those who neglect them (12:10–11). Regardless, there will remain a segment of Israel through whom God will establish his ancient covenant (12:12–13). Then the text breaks off in the middle of a sentence, and the remainder of the manuscript is lost.[27]

Critical Issues

The proposed redactional layering of the text of the Testament of Moses (see "Date" above) is its most important critical issue, which George W. E. Nickelsburg explains in some detail. He suggests the original was composed during the time of Antiochus IV Epiphanes,[28] with chapter 5 referring to events leading up to his persecution of Jews, chapter 8 describing the persecution itself, chapter 9 exhibiting God's vengeance, and chapter 10 describing the ushering in of the end. When the persecution ended and Antiochus died, the Testament of Moses "was shelved" and almost two centuries later was "dusted off and revised to make it relevant for new times."[29] The later editor then updated the work by inserting a sketch of events that would bring the reader to the present time (between chaps. 5 and 8). So after mention of the Hasmonean high priests (6:1), the remainder of the chapter is devoted to Herod and his sons. Testament of Moses 6:7 predicts their rule will be shorter than that of their father, which was thirty-four years (6:6). Since Herod's sons succeeded him at his death in 4 BCE, the latest date for the revision is 30 CE. Only before that time could any of Herod's sons have had a rule shorter than that of their father, since we know that both Antipas and Philip exceed the rule of their father. The burning around the temple (6:9) may be identified with the activity of Sabinus, commander under Varus, who crucified Jews following the death of Herod the Great. The descriptions in chapter 7 are difficult to identify. The editor(s) during the time of Herod, writing in the years following his death, updated and reissued the work to encourage readers with an apocalyptic message in the face of hardships suffered under the Roman Empire, now supplanting that of the Seleucid Empire of the earlier recension.[30]

27. Priest, "Testament of Moses," 1:934.
28. Nickelsburg, *Jewish Literature*, 74–76.
29. Nickelsburg, *Jewish Literature*, 247.
30. Nickelsburg, *Jewish Literature*, 248.

Several scholars have attempted to reconstruct the sizable material that must have composed the now lost ending of the Testament of Moses.[31] But only a small amount can be said with much certainty. First, the original ending must have contained some account of Moses's death by virtue of the dialogues and the testament form. Second, statements indicating that Moses expected his death (1:15; 10:14) suggest that some account of the event itself must have been in the original ending. Third, the concern about how Joshua could care for the body of such a revered figure as Moses (11:7) again suggests his death. And fourth, fragments of the lost ending (see below) suggest Michael the archangel may have been involved in the burial or perhaps transported Moses's body to heaven.[32]

Fragments of Greek texts provide some indication of the lost ending, and the most important of these are from the *Ecclesiastical History* of Gelasius Cyzicenus (d. ca. 476) and the Letter of Jude. Gelasius, who elsewhere quotes from Testament of Moses 1:14, includes additional quotations in reference to the dispute between the devil and Michael that are almost verbatim to that found in Jude. The Gelasius account in *Ecclesiasical History* reads, "In the book of the Assumption of Moses, the archangel Michael, in a discussion with the devil, says: 'For by his Holy Spirit, all of us have been created,' and further he says: 'God's spirit went forth from his face, and the world came into being'" (2.21.7). The quote from Jude 9 reads, "And the archangel Michael, when he was in a dispute with the devil over Moses's body, did not dare to declare him guilty of slander, but said: 'May the Lord rebuke you.'" Tromp observes that the interchanges between Michael and the devil are nearly identical in Greek, suggesting that the original ending did indeed contain a dispute between Michael and the devil regarding the body of Moses.[33]

As noted at the beginning of this chapter, the present work is also known as the Assumption of Moses, though it is not entirely clear why it is known by two names. Ancient sources list both titles,[34] though the "Assumption of Moses" is the preferred name in early Greek and Latin writings. Others cite material, though not by name, that would be suitable for a record of the death and assumption of Moses. The identification of the present text as the Assumption of Moses was based on a passage from the *Acts of the Council of Nicea* that appears to cite 1:14 (and perhaps 1:6, 9) as belonging to the "Assumption of Moses," even though the extant text itself does not describe his assumption. And so it is not entirely clear that the present text should be identified as the

31. See esp. Bauckham, *Jude, 2 Peter*, 73–76.
32. Tromp, *Assumption of Moses*, 270–71.
33. Cf. Origen, *Princ.* 3.2.1. Tromp, *Assumption of Moses*, 272–75.
34. For the primary source references, see Russell, *Method and Message*, 391–95.

"Assumption of Moses."[35] Charles posits that there were two works—the Testament and the Assumption—that were merged into a single work in the first century CE.[36] Tromp prefers to use the title "Assumption of Moses" and dismisses the identification of the work with the Testament of Moses.[37]

Contribution and Context

The primary theological interest of the Testament of Moses is that of "apocalyptic determinism."[38] This, coupled with the view that the righteous will be rewarded and sinners punished (T. Mos. 12:10–11), is found in other works from that time. All that God revealed to Moses and all that has happened in the past were orchestrated by God (3:11–12; 12:4–5). This allows Moses to have a high degree of confidence in God's promises of intervention and in his covenant fidelity both amid hardship (10:1–12; 12:3–13) and, inferentially, to the readers as well. Likewise, Israel's hope lies not in the strength of Moses (12:7) or the piety of Israel (12:8) but entirely in the covenant fidelity of God (12:13; cf. 1:8–9; 3:9; 4:2–6; 12:7–13).

Moses's role is of course central to the narrative. It is likely that he is utilized for the deeply covenantal interest of the book in terms of Deuteronomy (esp. Deut. 31–34). But as we have seen, even Moses attributes his success to God (T. Mos. 12:7). He indicates that he himself was designed and prepared by God before the beginning of the world as "the mediator of his covenant" (*arbiter testamenti*, 1:14). It seems uncertain that he is presented here as preexistent, as one could suggest for the "Son of Man" (1 En. 48:2, 3, 6; 62:7; cf. 4 Ezra 12:32; 13:26), but at the very least it seems that Moses's role as mediator was within the sphere of God's deterministic plan. Priest observes that the role of mediator is not used of Moses in the Old Testament (it only occurs at Job 9:33), but he is designated that role in first-century literature (cf. Philo, *Moses* 3.19; Gal. 3:18; Heb. 8:6; 9:15; 12:21).[39]

Taxo is an enigmatic figure in the Testament of Moses whose role in the narrative generates debate about his identification with historical figures.[40] Some have suggested he was a suffering messiah whose death brings about the consummation of the ages.[41] This has not been widely accepted, but

35. Priest, "Testament of Moses," 1:925.
36. Charles, "Assumption of Moses," 2:409.
37. Tromp, *Assumption of Moses*, 115
38. Priest, "Testament of Moses," 1:922.
39. Priest, "Testament of Moses," 1:922.
40. So also Priest, "Testament of Moses," 1:922–23.
41. Lattey, "Messianic Expectation."

there is something to be said for his role as one who "precipitates the divine vengeance that inaugurates the end-time."[42] That is, his death and that of his sons provoke God's vengeance and thus trigger the commencement of the eschaton. For his part, in light of martyrdom accounts elsewhere in Second Temple texts, Priest suggests a softened approach whereby the author uses a typical martyrdom story merely to introduce his pronouncement of the end of time, not to provoke it per se. In this way Taxo is a "singular example" of the hardships that fall upon the people of God.[43] The importance of the Taxo account is indicated by its placement in the narrative at the transition from persecution to the advent of God's kingdom, where the people of God undertake fasting as a means of invoking God's intervention (T. Mos. 9:6–7; cf. Deut. 32:35–43). They then *permit* themselves to be martyrs, not actively provoking God's reaction, and so die in innocence (cf. 1 Macc. 2:29–38). In so doing, according to John J. Collins, they advocate a policy of nonviolent fidelity to the law even at the price of death.[44] Another view is taken by Kenneth Atkinson, who views the role of Taxo through the lens of "shedding of innocent blood by an intermediary figure to save humanity."[45] For him Israel stands in a sort of wilderness between Moses's past redemption and the fulfillment of God's eschatological promises. Taxo then functions as Moses's "ultimate successor," since he is the final intercessor for Israel.[46] These are by no means all the options, as Tromp counts nearly thirty proposals for the identification of Taxo in Testament of Moses 9:1 and surveys many of them at length.[47] Some have seen the Greek origin of the name, *taxori*, as corresponding to the Hebrew *meḥōqēq*, "orderer," corresponding to the designation as "one who is over them."[48] For his part, Tromp finds merit in a proposal from the nineteenth century that observes that the Latin word *taxo* means "badger," as an allusion to the account in 2 Maccabees 10:6 in reference to the Jews celebrating the Feast of Tabernacles in caves like animals (cf. T. Mos. 9:6; 2 Macc. 5:27; 1 En. 96:2).[49]

Some scholars identify the figure praying (T. Mos. 4:1) with Daniel[50] and note the similarities between the hymn in Testament of Moses 10 and the

42. Priest, "Testament of Moses," 1:923.
43. Priest, "Testament of Moses," 1:923.
44. J. Collins, *Apocalyptic Imagination*, 162.
45. Atkinson, "Taxo's Martyrdom," 475.
46. Atkinson, "Taxo's Martyrdom," 476.
47. Tromp, *Assumption of Moses*, 124–28.
48. Mowinckel, "Hebrew Equivalent of Taxo."
49. Tromp, *Assumption of Moses*, 128.
50. Charles, *Assumption of Moses*, 14; Tromp, *Assumption of Moses*, 175.

judgment scene in Daniel 12.[51] The Testament of Moses also shares with Daniel the view that the course of history is mysterious and revealed only through a special revelation from God. Furthermore, both documents culminate history with the advent of the heavenly kingdom, and their historical overviews are positioned to support the notion of martyrdom. Yet the Testament of Moses differs from an apocalypse in that it is presented as a prophecy by Moses, not an angelic revelation that he receives.[52]

Purpose

The purpose of the Testament of Moses may simply be to assure faithful Jews that the world was created for them, despite present appearances to the contrary.[53] More to the point, however, is the contention that the book aims to strengthen readers in their faithfulness to the conditions attached to the covenant, which are inextricably linked to Israel's eschatological fate. Secondarily, Tromp provides another poignant purpose—to comfort readers despairing over the conditions of Israel (politically and religiously) by casting the present as the final stage in redemptive history and indicating that their eschatological redemption is at hand.[54]

Reception History

A number of New Testament texts are said to reflect the Testament of Moses (e.g., Jude 9, 12–13, 16; 2 Pet. 2:13; Acts 7:36–43; Matt. 24:19–21 and parr.). The most important of these is Jude 9, which refers to the dispute between Satan and Michael over the body of Moses. As we have seen, this is not found in the extant text of the Testament of Moses but most likely draws from the now lost ending.[55] Metaphors and descriptions from Testament of Moses 10:5–6 and elsewhere are likely reflected in Jude 12–13, 16.[56]

---

51. Priest, "Testament of Moses," 1:923–24.
52. J. Collins, Apocalyptic Imagination, 162.
53. J. Collins, Apocalyptic Imagination, 162.
54. Tromp, Assumption of Moses, 123.
55. See esp. Bauckham, 2 Peter, Jude, 47, 65–76.
56. Priest, "Testament of Moses," 1:924; cf. Tromp, Assumption of Moses, 275–81.

8

Testament of Job

Introduction

The Testament of Job is an embellishment of the biblical book of Job. As a testament it presents Job imparting wisdom to his progeny prior to his impending death, with particular emphasis on the virtue of patient endurance. Most of the work (T. Job 1:4–45:4) is Job's first-person account of the cause and consequences of his hardships,[1] and the testament concludes with Job's death, the ascent of his soul, and his burial (chaps. 51–53).

Language and Manuscripts

The most important manuscript witnesses of the Testament of Job are four Greek texts from the eleventh to the fourteenth century, a version in Old Church Slavonic, and an incomplete version written in Coptic (Papyrus Cologne 3221; fifth century CE). Most scholars are content to recognize Greek as the language of composition,[2] especially because of the linguistic affinities with the Septuagint of Job. A few have posited a Semitic original, though this must remain speculative.[3] Although some have theorized that various sections of the Testament of Job were added later to the original,[4] most recognize a

1. Spittler, "Testament of Job," 1:833.
2. Davila (*Provenance of the Pseudepigrapha*, 196–97) says that the Greek text is about thirty-five hundred words long.
3. See Spittler, "Testament of Job," 1:830.
4. Spittler, "Testament of Job," 1:834.

literary unity on the basis of a common theme of revealed knowledge versus Satanic deception[5] or recurring literary features that structure the text.[6]

Provenance

Some have regarded the Testament of Job as a Christian writing, but there are no undisputed Christian (or Jewish) distinctive features. The interest in glossolalia may be attributed to Christian interests (e.g., 1 Cor. 13:1; 14:1–33; 2 Cor. 12:1–5) and is quite at home in later Egyptian Christianity, as attested in the Nag Hammadi library. James R. Davila concludes, therefore, that he sees no "compelling reason to move backward from the context of late antique Egypt (early fifth century CE) to a putative earlier origin for the Testament of Job in Jewish circles."[7] But this method requires a "default" position in which the provenance is identified with the earliest manuscript attestation unless proven otherwise. In an important rebuttal to the method in general and Davila's treatment of the Testament of Job in particular, Richard Bauckham points out Davila's failure to illustrate in what manner the work belongs to and could be composed by fifth-century Egyptian Christians. Moreover, Bauckham questions the utility of the need for any such "default position" in the first place, contending instead that works preserved by Christians in antiquity naturally would date earlier, and that there is no need to presume either Jewish or Christian provenance on the basis of traditions of manuscript preservation alone.[8] Some have argued that the work was a pre-Christian folk presentation of Jewish piety that informed the New Testament portrayal of Jesus as a sufferer,[9] or a pre-Christian work designed according to missionary interests of Hellenistic Judaism.[10] Still others argue the disguise of Satan (T. Job 17:1–2) points to Pacorus, the Persian general who invaded Palestine in 40 BCE.[11] Some attribute it to a Jewish sect known as the Therapeutae (cf. Philo, *Contempl. Life* 1.1–90),[12] though this view is not widely held. Others argue for a Jewish provenance with specific identification with Essenes.[13]

5. J. Collins, "Structure and Meaning."
6. Schaller, "Zur Komposition und Konzeption"; Cioată, "Job, Testament of."
7. Davila, *Provenance of the Pseudepigrapha*, 198.
8. Bauckham, "Continuing Quest," 22–24.
9. Spitta, "Das Testament Hiobs"; Spittler, "Testament of Job," 1:833.
10. Rahnenführer, "Das Testament des Hiob," 68–93; Spittler, "Testament of Job," 1:833.
11. Delcor, "Le Testament de Job."
12. Spittler, "Testament of Job," 1:833; Philonenko, "Le Testament de Job."
13. Kohler, "Testament of Job."

Date

There is nothing explicit in the text of the Testament of Job that helps deter-mine its date. Its clear dependence on the Septuagint of Job suggests a date no earlier than the first century BCE.[14] Most scholars attribute the Testament of Job to an Egyptian Jew writing at the turn of the era, primarily because of its affinities with other Jewish writings from that time.[15] A context of the diaspora uprisings (115–117 CE) may be suitable for the composition of the Testament of Job (esp. chaps. 1–27), since there are similarities between Job's destruction of the idol's temple and the destruction of the temple of Serapis in Alexandria.[16] Some take the account of Job offering sacrifices for his chil-dren (15:4) as evidence for the work being written before the destruction of the temple in 70 CE.[17]

Contents

The Testament of Job is introduced as the words of Job, also called Jobab (T. Job 1:1; 2:1; cf. Job 42:17b LXX). It may be that Job is identified as Jobab, the descendent of Esau (Gen. 36:33–34), before he is named "Job" by God.[18] This would locate the narrative to the time of the patriarchs, which is reflected in Job's own genealogy (T. Job 1:6; cf. Job 42:17 LXX).[19]

Job and the Revealing Angel (T. Job 1:2–5:3)

The narrative depicts the setting of the work, in which Job is falling ill, settling his affairs, and calling his children to his side to tell them of the Lord's dealings with him (T. Job 1:2–4). He explains that he has endured and that they are of the chosen race of Israel (1:5–7). Job, then called Jobab, was observing the worship at an idol's temple and was perplexed by how the deity within could really be the God who made all things (2:1–4). In a dream Jobab is told by an angel that the true God will make himself known to him and that what is really worshiped in the temple is the devil (3:1–3). Jobab asks for permission to purge the pagan temple (3:4–7). He is told that he may purge the temple, but if he does, Satan will strike him with all manner of hardships, save only

14. J. Collins, "Testamentary Literature," 276.
15. J. Collins, "Structure and Meaning." Cf. Kee, "Satan, Magic and Salvation."
16. W. Gruen, "Seeking a Context."
17. Rahnenführer, "Das Testament des Hiob."
18. Spittler, "Testament of Job," *OTP* 1:829.
19. Spittler, "Testament of Job," *OTP* 1:839nb.

death (4:1–5). If Jobab is patient through this, his name will be renowned and his possessions will be restored twofold; the angel also promises him resurrection to show how the Lord deals with his elect ones (4:6–11). Then Jobab replies that he will endure the hardship, proceeds to destroy the temple of the idol, and retreats to his home to prepare for Satan's reprisal (5:1–3).

Job and Satan (T. Job 6–27)

Having secured himself in his home, Jobab instructs his doormen to turn away any visitors (T. Job 6:1–3). Satan soon appears at the door dressed as a beggar, only to be told off by the door maid (6:4–6), but not before receiving a burned loaf of bread (7:1–11). Satan replies with a threat of retributive devastation (7:12–13) before receiving authority from God to take away all Jobab's wealth (8:1–3).

Satan looks to take advantage of Job's generosity and other virtues, which are documented at length (T. Job 9–15). This includes his kindness to others (chap. 9), hospitality (chap. 10), and support of charities (chaps. 11–12). He is also known for his wealth (chap. 13), musical abilities (chap. 14), and acts of piety on behalf of his family (chap. 15). This lengthy account of Job's wealth and virtue is followed by a longer account of his losses (chaps. 16–26). He loses his cattle (chap. 16), his children (chaps. 17–19), his health (chap. 20), and finally his wife (chaps. 21–25). The account of Job's wife, Sitis, begins with her enslavement to a nobleman so that she may get bread for Jobab (21:1–22:2). In her desperation she sells her own hair to Satan (22:3; 23–24). Sitis laments with much remorse (chap. 25), to which Job responds with fortitude (chap. 26). He finally confronts Satan, who, unlike Job, is weary in light of Job's fortitude and leaves him, ashamed, for three years (chap. 27).

Job and the Three Kings (T. Job 28–45)

Three men, Eliphas, Baldad, and Sophar, identified as kings, appear and express their astonishment at Job's hardships (T. Job 28–45). Job has now endured the plague for twenty years (28:1), and the kings come looking in Ausitis (cf. Job 1:1 LXX) for Jobab, whom they call "the king of all Egypt" (T. Job 28:7). They are told he has sat on a dung heap outside the city for twenty years, and they approach him to learn about his hardships (28:8–9; 29–30). When he finally confirms Jobab's identity (31:1–6), Eliphas laments for Jobab's losses (31:7; 32). Job retorts to Eliphas—hoping to silence the three kings (34:1)—that all possessions will pass away but that his reward, his "throne in the holy land," will endure (chap. 33). Eliphas is enraged, taking Jobab's response as an insult, and leaves (chap. 34). For his part, Baldad challenges Jobab's sanity (35:1–38:5). Shophar even offers the services of his royal physicians (38:6–8). Finally, Jobab's wife, Sitis, arrives, having fled her servitude (39:1–3). She laments the death of her children (39:4–13), while Job arises—with help—and sings praise to God (40:1–3), joined by Sitis in repentance (40:4). She departs and dies "in good spirits" (40:5–6) and then is buried (40:7–14).

When Elihu speaks, he rebukes Jobab's boastful words and audacity of claiming a heavenly throne (41:1–4), though readers learn that Elihu's words were inspired by Satan and insult Jobab (41:5–6; 42:1–3). God then speaks, rebuking the kings and instructing them to help Jobab offer intercession for their sin (42:4–8). When Eliphas, Baldad, and Shophar recognize their sin, Eliphas raises a hymn against Elihu and the curse that falls upon Elihu (43:1–17). Then Jobab, as promised, is restored and resumes his good and charitable works (chap. 44) before counseling his progeny to remember the Lord and do good to those in need and before disseminating inheritance to his sons (chap. 45).

Job and His Three Daughters (T. Job 46–51)

Jobab's distribution of the inheritance among his male children causes his daughters to inquire about their share (T. Job 46:1–2). Jobab, here called Job (cf. 1:5; 2:1; 6:4; 7:2; 41:3; 46:3; 51:3; 52:1, 8), presents them with three golden cords from heaven, which, he says, is an inheritance superior to that of his sons since it bestows lifelong blessings to them (46:3–7). When one daughter questions the value of the cords, Job explains that these were the cords the Lord used to heal him of his infirmities (cf. Job 38:3) and therefore implores them to wear the cords as protective "amulets" (T. Job 47).[20] When each of the daughters takes her strings in turn, she loses interest in earthly things and speaks in an angelic tongue in hymnic praise to God (chaps. 48–50), which is recorded by Job's brother, Nereus, who speaks in the first person (chap. 51).

Job's Departure (T. Job 52–53)

Three days later, Job falls ill, though without pain, and gives a lyre, censer, and kettle drum to his daughters that they may bless those who come for his soul (T. Job 52:1–5). Then a gleaming chariot comes, and the daughters glorify God in their own distinct dialects (52:6–7) while Job's soul is taken away and his body taken for burial (52:8–12). The work concludes with a final lament for Job, led by Nereus (T. Job 53).

20. Importantly, the word literally means "phylactery," the Greek word for tefillin (Deut. 6:8; Attridge, "Testament of Job").

Critical Issues

The Greek text of the Testament of Job has many affinities with the Septuagint of Job, which itself is considerably shorter (approximately 20 percent) than the Hebrew Masoretic Text but is more expansive on several points.[21] This is particularly evident in the speech of Job's wife, where the two sentences in Hebrew (Job 2:9) become an extended paragraph in the Greek, which is amplified further still in the Testament of Job, where her name (Sitis) is given (T. Job 24–25). The Septuagint of Job also has an extended account of Job's homeland and ancestors (Job 42:17b–e LXX) not found in the Hebrew but corresponding with elements of the Testament of Job. Though the Testament of Job is primarily dependent on the narrative of the Septuagint of Job (Job 1–2; 42:7–17 LXX), it also draws on Job 29–31 (LXX) for its description of Job's affluence (T. Job 9–16).[22]

Contribution and Context

A number of features stand out in the Testament of Job. R. P. Spittler observes theological traits that align with Hellenistic Judaism.[23] First, God is the living and just creator of all things (T. Job 2:4; 37:2; 43:13) who is often addressed as a "father" (33:3, 9; 40:3; 47:11; 50:3; 52:9). He is a healer (38:8) and rightful recipient of praise (14:3; 48–50; 51:2), to be worshiped at the exclusion of all other rivals (idols) regardless of the cost (chaps. 2–5). Second, Satan is the fundamental adversary as both the figure that stands behind idolatry and the disguised antagonist of Job himself throughout much of the text (chaps. 6–27), though with authority strictly limited by God (8:1–3; cf. Job 1:12; 2:6). The main angel is called an "interpreting" angel, and Job's daughters speak the angels' language of praise. Angelic figures also take Job's soul away after his death (T. Job 52:6–10; cf. 47:11).

The notion of cosmic dualism is evident where Job asserts that his throne is in the "upper world" (33:3) whereas the present world passes away (33:4, 8). Job's daughters not only speak in angelic tongues but also have their affections turned from earthly to heavenly affairs (chaps. 48–50). There is a particular concern for the proper burial of the dead in accord with Jewish custom. This is said of Job's body (53:5–7) and also of his wife (40:6–14) and her children (39:1–10). A number of women play prominent roles in the

21. See Cox, "Job," 385–400.
22. Spittler, "Testament of Job," 1:831.
23. Spittler, "Testament of Job," 1:835.

Testament of Job. Job's first wife (Sitis) and second wife (Dinah) are both named, the former playing an important role not found in the biblical book of Job with her extensive speech (24:1–25:10). Sitis becomes a lamentable figure who is driven to slavery and sells her hair to Satan (chaps. 21–26). She later mourns the passing of her children (chaps. 39–40). Job's daughters are also named and receive an inheritance superior to that of Job's sons (chaps. 46–50). Yet scholars debate whether these women are presented in contrasting perspectives of negative and positive,[24] entirely negative,[25] or generally positive.[26] At the very least it seems evident that women play an important role in the narrative in a way unlike any of the male characters. Indeed, Job's dialogue with the three kings presents these males as largely negative until they finally reach repentance. Sitis is a figure who evokes empathy, and Job's daughters are unequivocally favorable in the narrative.

Job's legendary endurance and patience are emphasized throughout. He is patient at the outset (1:5), and his enduring patience will be rewarded with restored fortunes (4:6; 27:4). He exhibits patience to those who owe him (11:10), and not even Satan can cause him to forego his patience (20:1). This occurs while he is seated on a dung heap (26:5; cf. 24:1), from which he exhorts his progeny to patience (27:7).

A unique feature of the Testament of Job that finds elaborate expression in later Judaism is the appearance of the chariot (*merkabah*). This becomes the basis for Jewish speculation focused on God's chariot known as Merkabah mysticism. The dualism (esp. in chap. 43) resembles sectarian interests from Qumran.[27]

It is often recognized that the Testament of Job bears strong similarities of form with the Testaments of the Twelve Patriarchs. These include (1) a deathbed scene at the outset, (2) the celebration of a particular virtue, (3) moral exhortations by the central figure, and (4) the death and burial of the key figure followed by lamentation. But the Testament of Job is unique in that the key figure is from Wisdom texts rather than the Pentateuch, and its source from the Old Testament undergoes more adjustments here than in the Testaments of the Twelve Patriarchs.[28] Unlike some other testaments, the apocalyptic elements are comparatively sparse: there is an angelic interpreter (T. Job 3–5), and heavenly threads are given to Job's daughters (46:7–8), but there is no heavenly ascent or bodily assumption.

24. Van der Horst, "Images of Women," 95.
25. Garrett, "'Weaker Sex,'" 57.
26. Chesnutt, "Revelatory Experiences," 118.
27. Spittler, "Testament of Job," 1:833, 836.
28. Spittler, "Testament of Job," 1:832.

There are similarities between the Testament of Job and the book of Jubilees, where Abraham recognizes the folly of idols, defeats Satan, and destroys idolatrous temples (Jub. 11:15–12:15). The interest in heavenly realities and revealed knowledge is found elsewhere in Second Temple Jewish texts (e.g., 1 En. 37–71; 92–105; 2 Bar. 4:2–4).[29]

Purpose

It seems that the Testament of Job is addressed to Jews pressured to assimilate under Roman rule in Egypt, offering a lesson to receive enduring honor from God rather than temporary honor from people.[30] The primary exhortation is one of patience and endurance in an unstable world, noting the permanence and stability of heavenly matters (T. Job 33:2–9; 36:4–6).[31] But it seems that the polemic against idolatry around which the entire narrative revolves should play more of a role in discerning its purpose. As we have seen in other diaspora (Egyptian) texts addressing idolatry, the polemic is strong here. Idolatry is attributed to Satan, and the sufferings of Job throughout are attributed to Satan's retaliatory response to Job's destruction of an idolatrous temple. And so the work may serve to advocate opposition to idolatry among diaspora (Egyptian) Jews in recognition of the heavenly benefits that result from it.

Reception History

As we have seen, the Testament of Job, like nearly all pseudepigrapha, was preserved in Christian environments, and it is in those contexts where one finds hints of influence and reception. The reference to Job's endurance (ὑπομονή, *hypomonē*) in James 5:11[32] may allude to the Testament of Job, though this is uncertain (cf. Heb. 10–12; 1 Pet. 5). Furthermore, it was likely known by the third-century Christian Tertullian of Carthage when he wrote his work on patience (*De patientia*). Harold W. Attridge suggests that the work was seemingly popular in Christian circles in late antiquity given its preservation in Greek, Coptic, and Slavonic; it was regarded as extracanonical in the sixth century by the decree of Pope Gelasius I, who served as bishop of Rome from 492 to 496, and was largely ignored in the West through the Middle Ages.[33]

29. Nickelsburg, *Jewish Literature*, 321–22.
30. Kugler and Rohrbaugh, "On Women and Honor," 43–62.
31. Nickelsburg, *Jewish Literature*, 320.
32. See Allison, *James*, 714–17.
33. Attridge, "Testament of Job," 1872.

Maria Cioată contends that, with most manuscripts of the Testament of Job being preserved in monasteries, it is perhaps not surprising that Job is in some contexts regarded as a saint, even suggesting that the work may have been read on the day of Saint Job (May 6 for the Eastern Orthodox tradition; May 10 for the Roman Catholic tradition).[34] It may have also influenced traditions that connote Job as the patron saint of musicians and healer of skin diseases.[35]

34. Cioată, "Job, Testament of."
35. See Cioată (Haralambakis), *Testament of Job*, 141–72.

9

Aramaic Levi Document

Introduction

The Aramaic Levi Document is a testament-like text recounting the life story of the patriarch Levi. But the work extends beyond his life and advice to his progeny, elements that one finds in a formal "testament." Instead, the work gives particular attention to Levi's establishment of the Levitical priesthood, long before the time of Aaron, and the sacred laws for sacrifices that he received from his grandfather Isaac.[1] As Levi was the head of the priestly tribe, the exhortations in this document articulate the responsibilities and prerogatives of the priests. The text presents the ideal priest as a "combination of a zealous warrior for God, a punctilious observer of ritual purity, an inspiring teacher, and a recipient of divine revelation through dreams and prophecy."[2] The entire work is presented as a first-person narrative attributed to the biblical Levi.[3] It is the most extensive of three works, including the Testament of Qahat (4Q542) and the Visions of Amram (4Q543–549), that contain distinct instructions for the Levitical priesthood, set in an autobiographical narrative (see Visions of Amram below).[4]

Language and Manuscripts

A number of editions, texts, and translations of the Aramaic Levi Document have been published, the most accessible of which is that of James R.

1. Davila, "Aramaic Levi," 121.
2. Wise, Abegg, and Cook, *Dead Sea Scrolls*, 304.
3. Davila, "Aramaic Levi," 121.
4. Drawnel, "Aramaic Levi Document."

Davila.[5] The text is necessarily a composite document, reconstructed from manuscripts preserved in Aramaic, Greek, and Syriac.[6] None of these are complete, and some overlap, allowing for more certain reconstruction. However, the beginning and ending are both lost and of uncertain length.[7] The work was likely composed in Aramaic. With this plurality of traditions there are a number of ways to configure some of the fragments that comprise the Aramaic Levi Document. For convenience, the present discussion adopts that of Davila.[8]

The Aramaic Levi Document is attested in Aramaic in eight manuscripts. The first was found in a repository of disused medieval Jewish texts in a synagogue in Cairo, Egypt (the "Cairo Geniza").[9] It dates from the late ninth or early tenth century and contains three (damaged) leaves (pages). Each page is written on both sides in three columns of about twenty-three lines per column. The lines are well preserved but exhibit some signs of updating of grammar and spelling.[10] 1Q21 (1QLevi ar) contains six small fragments that overlap somewhat with the Cairo Geniza text and dates from the late Hasmonean era (150–30 BCE).[11] 4Q213 (4QLevi[a] ar) contains five fragments and overlaps with a portion of the Cairo Geniza text (§§82–95) and 4Q214a. It dates no later than the early Herodian period (30 BCE–70 CE).[12] 4Q213a (4QLevi[b] ar) has six fragments, two of which overlap with a Greek fragment from the Mount Athos text (see below). It dates from the late Hasmonean period. 4Q213b (4QLevi[c] ar) is a single fragment overlapping the Cairo Geniza text at §§6–9. It dates from the late Hasmonean period. 4Q214 (4QLevi[d] ar) is four fragments with some overlap with the Cairo Geniza text at §§25–30 and a possible variation of §§20–23. The fragments were written in the Hasmonean period. 4Q214a (4QLevi[e] ar) is eleven fragments, three of which seem to overlap with the Cairo Geniza text at §§24–25 and §§69–71, while others overlap with 4Q213 and 4Q214b. It dates no later than the early Herodian period (30 BCE–70 CE). 4Q214b (4QLevi[f] ar) contains eight fragments in

5. Davila, "Aramaic Levi." The most recent, aside from Davila's, are those of Drawnel, *Aramaic Wisdom Text*, 353–73, and Greenfield, Stone, and Eshel, *Aramaic Levi Document*, 56–109.

6. For a complete account and description of the extant manuscripts, see Drawnel, *Aramaic Wisdom Text*, 21–32.

7. Davila, "Aramaic Levi," 122.

8. Davila, "Aramaic Levi," 129–42.

9. Greenfield and Stone, "Remarks on the Aramaic Testament of Levi"; Bohak, "New Geniza Fragment."

10. Davila, "Aramaic Levi," 122. Today these are housed in the Cambridge University Library (T-S 16.94), the John Rylands Library in Manchester (P1185), and the Oxford Bodleian Library (Ms Heb c 27 f. 56r.–v.).

11. See Barthélemy and Milik, "Testament de Lévi."

12. Stone and Greenfield, "Aramaic Levi Document."

Hasmonean script, some of which overlap with the Cairo Geniza text at §§22–27 and others with 1Q21 and 4Q214a.

Two excerpts from the Aramaic Levi Document are preserved in a Greek translation housed at the Mount Athos (Greece) Monastery of Koutloumous (Codex 39; catalogue no. 3108). The manuscript is an eleventh-century copy of the Greek Testaments of the Twelve Patriarchs with portions of the Aramaic Levi text inserted at three places.[13] It is unknown whether the rest of Aramaic Levi was translated into Greek and why these texts were inserted into the Greek of the Testaments of the Twelve Patriarchs where they are.[14]

A quotation from the Aramaic Levi Document corresponding to the Cairo Geniza text §§78–81 is found in Syriac and is introduced as a quotation from Levi's testament.[15]

Date, Provenance, and Purpose

The date, provenance, and purpose of the Aramaic Levi Document are intimately intertwined and subject to debate. The earliest manuscript (4Q213a) dates from the second half of the second century BCE, so the Aramaic Levi Document dates prior to 100 BCE. The text's restrictions for Levitical priestly marriages and facets of the metrological section may align with the reforms enacted by Ezra (Ezra 7:12)[16] and brought to Palestine by the returning exiles under Ezra's leadership. Furthermore, the writings of Hecataeus of Abdera (ca. 300 BCE) speak of the Levitical priesthood in terms of royal leadership, congruent with what is found in the Aramaic Levi Document (§§3c, 99, 100; cf. §67). Also, in the late fourth century BCE, according to Josephus (*Ant.* 11.7.2–8.7 §§302–347), the brother of a high priest was expelled because of his marriage into a Samaritan family, which exhibits some of the hostility toward Samaritans implicit in the description of the Shechemites' destruction in the Aramaic Levi Document (cf. Gen. 34).[17] The lack of polemic against illegitimate priesthood corresponding to the time of Antiochus IV Epiphanes suggests a date prior to that,[18] which some think points to the late fourth or

13. On the insertions, see Davila, "Aramaic Levi," 123, 123n2.
14. Davila, "Aramaic Levi," 123.
15. B. Add. 17, 193, British Museum, London, catalogue number 861; Davila, "Aramaic Levi," 123.
16. Drawnel, "Aramaic Levi Document."
17. Drawnel, *Aramaic Wisdom Text*, 63–75.
18. Greenfield, Stone, and Eshel, *Aramaic Levi Document*, 19–22; Drawnel, *Aramaic Wisdom Text*, 63–75.

early third century BCE.[19] Others contend that the Aramaic Levi Document was a source for the book of Jubilees and hence dates from the third or early second century BCE. They find evidence in such features as the sectarian solar calendar (ALD §§65–72); royal components attributed to the line of Levi (§§xxiii, 67, 99–100); emphasis on the Levitical line and transmission of priestly tradition; distinctive notions of exorcism, demonology, and dualism; and Joseph as a figure of wisdom.[20] Robert A. Kugler agrees to a third-century-BCE date but argues that Jubilees and Aramaic Levi draw on a common, lost source (the "Levi-apocryphon").[21] James Kugel dates the work to the end of the second century BCE (shortly before 4Q214b).[22] In his view it was a Hasmonean composition advocating the merger of the priestly and royal authority that the Hasmonean rulers utilized (142–63 BCE). He sees the book of Jubilees as a source for the Aramaic Levi Document and two theoretical documents.[23] This theory requires that the reference to "priests and kings" and "your kingdom" (ALD §§99–100) refer to Levi's line, despite the fact that this passage in particular is poorly preserved.[24] Davila finds none of the arguments compelling: the alleged relationship with Jubilees or a putative Levi source, royal elements, and alleged Samaritan interests could potentially be evident in priestly circles anywhere from the fourth through the second century BCE, likely in Palestine.[25]

Contents

The narrative is presented as a first-person account of Levi. The beginning is lost, so the fragmentary account begins with a narrative of the vengeance on Shechem for the rape of Dinah (Gen. 34). In it is found the familiar account of the Israelites' request for the Shechemites to circumcise their males when really their intent was to enact vengeance on them (ALD §§1–2). This is followed by a scene that, though too fragmentary to provide any coherent account, involves Shechem and Levi (again in the first person), along with

19. Drawnel, "Aramaic Levi Document."

20. Greenfield, Stone, and Eshel, *Aramaic Levi Document*, 19–22, 189–90.

21. Kugler, *From Patriarch to Priest*, 131–35.

22. Kugel, "Levi's Elevation to the Priesthood"; Kugel, *Ladder of Jacob*, 115–68.

23. These Kugel designates "Levi's Apocalypse" and "Levi's Priestly Initiation." Kugel, "Levi's Elevation to the Priesthood," 62.

24. Davila, "Aramaic Levi," 126. Kugler's view has not been well received—nor has his contention that Aramaic Levi is a "protest document" standing in contradiction to the Pentateuch (Kugler, *From Patriarch to Priest*, 109–10). See Schiffman, "Sacrificial Halakhah"; Himmelfarb, "Earthly Sacrifice and Heavenly Incense."

25. Davila, "Aramaic Levi," 126.

Judah, Simeon, Reuben, and Asher (§3). This is followed by a prayer, before which Levi purifies his clothes and himself (§§i–iv). In his prayer Levi requests that the Lord turn him from any unrighteousness and sexual immorality (§§v–vii, xiv–xv) and asks for wisdom to do things pleasing to God (§§viii–x). He prays for God's mercy and peace as well as the removal of lawlessness from the earth (§§xi–xiii). He reminds God that a righteous seed was promised to Abraham and Sarah and prays that his own sons would participate in God's words so as to accomplish true judgments for all generations (§§xv–xix).

Then, while setting out from Abel Mayyin, Levi has a vision of the heavens in which he comes to the gate of heaven, where a single angel is present (§xx). This segment (4Q213 2 11–18) is too fragmentary to discern anything else from the narrative. In what appears to be a second vision, the text speaks of the shame a woman has brought on her family (§§xxi–xxii), though again the fragmentary text makes it difficult to gain much clarity (4Q213a 3–4; 1Q21 1). The remainder of the vision speaks of the horrors involved with "the kingdom" (§§4–6); then it becomes clear that this was part of a vision in which seven figures (angels?) were present (§7). In the next episode (§§8–10) Levi receives a tithe from his father Jacob, who clothes him in priestly garments and ordains him as priest for eternity. Levi then blesses his father and brothers, who in turn bless him, and he presents offerings at Bethel.

When they depart Bethel, they go to the "fortress of Abraham" with Isaac (§11), and there Isaac blesses his sons (§12). Isaac then begins to instruct Levi in the laws of the priesthood, telling him to guard himself from impurity and that his law is of a higher standard than that for all other flesh (§§13–15).

Isaac's admonitions pertain to sexual immorality and include an exhortation to Levi to marry within his father's own clan (§§16–18). He also instructs Levi on the proper procedures for entering the house of God with respect to bathing, dressing, washing of hands and feet, and making offerings (§§19–22). When making offerings, Levi is to inspect the wood carefully for worms, taking pains as Abraham did, and Isaac explains what kinds of wood would be suitable for offering the holocaust on the altar (§§22–25). When the fire kindles, Levi is to sprinkle the blood on the sides of the altar, wash again, then lift up the salted limbs for the offering—head, neck, forelegs, breast, thighs, and so on (§§26–30). The next section (§§31–47) pertains to measurements of respective offerings, concluding with an exhortation to Levi to heed these commands with all due diligence and likewise pass them on to his sons (§§48–49): "For so father Abraham commanded me to do and to command my sons" (§50).

Isaac's admonitions conclude with a mixture of encouragement and reminder, repeating some of the instructions he already said as well as rejoicing in his son's calling (§§51–56, 58–61). Isaac says this was passed to him from Abraham, who himself found regulations concerning blood in "the Book of Noah" (§57). In pronouncing a blessing on his son, Isaac says that Levi's seed will be preserved for all ages "in the Book of Remembrance of Life" (§59).

The rest of Levi's life story is narrated in the next section (§§62–80), beginning with his marriage at the age of twenty-eight to Milcah from the kin of Abraham (§62). She gives birth two years later to a son, Gershon, who, as Levi saw in his vision, will, with his seed, be expelled from the priesthood (§§63–65). Six years later Milcah bears a second son, Qahat, whom Levi says will be the great high priest of all Israel (§§66–68). Four years later, when Levi is forty years old, Milcah bears a third son, Merari, who nearly dies at birth (§§69–70). Then, at the age of sixty-four, Levi fathers a daughter, Jochebed, born seven months after they entered Egypt (§§71–72). Levi then recounts his entry into Egypt with his children and grandchildren (§§73–77). His grandson Amram, son of Qahat, marries his daughter Jochebed when Levi is ninety-four years old (§75). Levi then recalls that he was eighteen years old when he came to Canaan and killed Shechem, nineteen when he became a priest, and twenty-eight when he married. He was forty-eight when he entered Egypt, where he lived eighty-nine years to the age of 137 (§§78–80).

Levi reports that when he was 118 years old, his brother Joseph died, and he calls together his sons and grandsons to tell them his last wishes (§82), which pertain to his progeny exhibiting truth and righteousness (§§83–87) but above all wisdom (§88). This is to be passed on from father to son, and Levi instructs them at length of wisdom's benefits (§§89–97). In the final extant section, which is highly fragmentary, there is further exhortation to Levi's sons, a reference to a vision, and perhaps a reference to Dinah (§§98–104 = 4Q214b 8; 4Q213 3–5; 4Q214 3). The end of the work is lost.

Critical Issues

In addition to its place in the so-called priestly trilogy (see Visions of Amram below), the Aramaic Levi Document presents other critical issues that require consideration.

Genre

Formally speaking, the Aramaic Levi Document is not a testament, since that genre contains a deathbed scene by an ancient figure who imparts ethical instruction and sometimes apocalyptic and eschatological reflection. The instructions imparted by Levi to his sons (§§82–83) seem to be occasioned not by Levi's own impending death but rather by the death of Joseph. Though the work is cast as Levi's words toward the end of his life, it lacks the testamentary framework evident in other testaments in what remains of the work. Instead, Davila regards the Aramaic Levi Document as an example of "rewritten scripture," a genre in which a narrative from the Hebrew Bible is retold with the object of resolving particular problems and contemporizing the account for a later audience, similar to that of Jubilees, the Genesis Apocryphon, and Pseudo-Philo's Biblical Antiquities.[26] Henryk Drawnel contends that the Aramaic Levi Document is "a pseudepigraphic text written not only to tell the story of Levi's life, but also to transmit well defined wisdom ideals pertinent to Levitical priestly and scribal instruction."[27] Because it utilizes a combination of recasted scriptural narratives, poetic laments, heavenly visions, distinctively priestly instructions, and wisdom materials, Drawnel simply calls it a "pseudepigraphic composition with an educational thrust."[28] Or, perhaps more specifically, "a pseudo-epigraphic autobiography with a didactic poem and prophetic speech at its end."[29]

Visions

Another issue in the Aramaic Levi Document pertains to how many visions Levi had. The Greek Testament of Levi, which uses Aramaic Levi as its primary source, recounts two. The first vision (T. Levi 2:5–5:7) occurs at Abel-Maoul, when Levi is taken by an angel through the seven heavens to the throne of God and instructed to take revenge on the Shechemites (cf. chaps. 6–7). The second vision (chap. 8) occurs after the Shechem incident, at Bethel, where seven angels are present. The Aramaic Levi Document is fragmentary at precisely this point. It does contain a vision involving a single angel when Levi departs from Abel Mayyin (ALD §xx), but this is followed by a gap in the extant manuscript. The account continues with the end of a vision, though its location is not stated, and it is unclear whether it is the same vision or a second one. In this continuation there are seven figures, which may be angels.[30] Some have argued for a single vision only that belongs after the Shechem incident and that was creatively divided into two for the Greek Testament of Levi.[31] The assumption here is that the seven-heaven cosmology of the

26. Davila, "Aramaic Levi," 124.
27. Drawnel, Aramaic Wisdom Text, 87.
28. Drawnel, Aramaic Wisdom Text, 96.
29. Drawnel, "Aramaic Levi Document," 1:108.
30. Davila, "Aramaic Levi," 124.
31. Kugler, From Patriarch to Priest, 45–51.

first vision did not exist at the time when Aramaic Levi was composed, and
so it was expanded by the Greek Testament of Levi when such a view was
more prevalent. This view is not widely held.[32] Others refrain from preferring
one or two visions and place the relevant sections (§§1–3) before the prayer.[33]
Still others prefer two visions, which can be reconstructed with the relevant
section (§§1–3) placed in the gap between sections xx and 4.[34] Finally, others
are inclined to think there were two visions originally, the first of which is
expanded in the Greek Testament of Levi.[35]

Prayer

The fragmentary nature of the Aramaic Levi Document makes it unclear
whether Levi's prayer belongs before or after the incident with Shechem. If
there was only one vision, as some contend (above), the incident of Shechem
(§§1–3) would come first and the prayer would follow, perhaps functioning
as a prayer of purification following the various defilements associated with
the incident. Or it may belong elsewhere, such as between sections xx and
4. Consensus remains allusive, and here we follow Davila's placement of the
prayer after the Shechem account.[36]

Length

The problems of genre, number of visions, and placement of prayer outlined above together suggest there is uncertainty as to the length of the original
Aramaic Levi Document. As Michael E. Stone explains, there is evidence that
the work was longer, perhaps substantially so, than the extant material indicates.[37] He enumerates several points. First, there is potentially more than one
prayer of undetermined length (specifically T. Levi 3:2 and 4Q213a). Second,
since some of the Aramaic Levi texts from Qumran have no overlap with the
extant material from the Cairo Geniza and Greek material, the original of the
Aramaic Levi must have been longer than the most complete manuscript, that
of the Cairo Geniza. Third, the possible citation of Aramaic Levi by Ammonas
(see below under Reception History) is also unattested in the extant Greek,

---

32. See, e.g., Davila, "Aramaic Levi," 124–25; Jonge, *Pseudepigrapha of the Old Testament*,
110, 131–34.
33. Greenfield, Stone, and Eshel, *Aramaic Levi Document*, 11–19; so also Kugler, *From
Patriarch to Priest*, 57.
34. Drawnel, *Aramaic Wisdom Text*, 43–49.
35. Davila, "Aramaic Levi," 125. Davila presents a helpful chart (pp. 130–31) outlining the
various ways in which the text is arranged and presented by different scholars.
36. Davila, "Aramaic Levi," 125.
37. Stone, "Levi, Aramaic," 1:487.

Aramaic, or Syriac witnesses, indicating yet another unique piece of material that must be added to the whole. Finally, it is possible that other Qumran manuscripts (4Q540–541), with close affinities to Testament of Levi 18, may be part of Aramaic Levi.[38] Again this would add to the unique material not otherwise attested of the Aramaic Levi Document and thus increase the length of the original text.[39]

Stone rightly observes that the sequence of these fragments is important because it determines the order of the events in the original text, but this ordering is necessarily frustrated by the fragmentary nature of the extant witnesses. In addition, where there are gaps in the texts, it is impossible to know not only what was once there but also how much material was there in the first place.[40]

Contribution and Context

Sources

The Aramaic Levi Document is obviously a recasting of the biblical book of Genesis, including the accounts of Abraham, Isaac, Jacob, and Joseph, as well as the vengeance by Levi and Simeon on Shechem for the rape of Dinah, their sister (Gen. 34; ALD §§1–3). The account of Jacob's promise to tithe to God (Gen. 28:20–22) is cast as fulfilled in the consecration of Levi to the priesthood and payment of the tithe to him (ALD §§9–10). The genealogical account of Levi and his family (Gen. 46:11; Exod. 6:16–20; Num. 3:17–20; 26:59; 1 Chron. 6:16–18) becomes the "narrative scaffolding" for Levi's account of his life and descendants (ALD §§62–81). Priestly instructions (esp. from Leviticus) compose the priestly regulations (§§11–61). The account of Levi and Simeon taking revenge on Shechem for the rape of Dinah is found in both Aramaic Levi and the book of Jubilees (30:1–32:9). The works also share the account of Jacob's visit to Isaac, Isaac's consecration of Levi, Levi's dream of his priestly consecration, and Jacob's tithe to Levi at Bethel, though there is debate as to whether Jubilees depends on Aramaic Levi or whether they share a common lost source. Aramaic Levi appeals to a "Book of Noah" for cultic regulations concerning blood (ALD §57), which may be the same book by that name cited elsewhere (e.g., Jub. 10:13; 21:10; Genesis Apocryphon V, 29).[41]

38. Puech, "Fragments d'un apocryphe de Lévi."
39. Stone, "Levi, Aramaic," 1:487.
40. Stone, "Levi, Aramaic," 1:487.
41. Davila, "Aramaic Levi," 127–28.

Presentation of Levi

The centrality of Levi to the entire document warrants some consideration of the manner in which he is presented. The author of the Aramaic Levi Document has worked his biblical sources in a fashion to present Levi as a pious Jew, an ideal priest, a student of priestly law, and a wisdom teacher. This is particularly noteworthy since Levi is only sparsely mentioned in the book of Genesis (Gen. 29:34; 34:25, 30; 35:23; 46:11; 49:5). Furthermore, the incident with Shechem is condemned by Jacob in Genesis (Gen. 34:30; 49:5–7) but revered in the Aramaic Levi Document (cf. ALD §§1–3). The ordination of Levi (ALD §§8–10) recalls portions of the same account in the Hebrew Bible (e.g., Gen. 28:20; Exod. 29:9, 33, 35) but also contains allusions to the priesthood of Melchizedek (Gen. 14:18–20). One also finds amplifications of biblical traditions that exhibit the distinct interests of the author of the Aramaic Levi Document. Levi's priesthood is characterized by a studious posture with respect to the priestly law (ALD §§19–61), exhibiting strict purity and holiness with respect to endogamy (§17) and fastidious attention to the measurements of sacrificial elements (§§32a–47). Levi's wisdom is both imparted and exhibited (§§82–98) and bears some indication of an apocalyptic perspective (§§99–104).[42]

Reception History

The Aramaic Levi Document was the primary source behind the composition of the Greek Testament of Levi in the Testaments of the Twelve Patriarchs. There is debate as to whether the Aramaic Levi Document is cited in the Damascus Document (CD-A IV, 15, 17–18; cf. ALD §§16–17b).[43] Two quotations attributed to "Levi" are quoted by a fourth-century Egyptian monk, Ammonas, writing in Greek, which bear some resemblance to portions of Aramaic Levi (§§i–xx).[44] The Aramaic Levi Document is widely understood to have informed the other components of the priestly trilogy of Qumran: the Testament of Qahat (4Q542) and the Visions of Amram (4Q543–549).[45]

---

42. Drawnel, "Aramaic Levi Document."
43. Greenfield, "Words of Levi."
44. Tromp, "Two References to a Levi Document."
45. Stone, "Levi, Aramaic," 2:487. There is some debate about the inclusion of 4Q548 and 4Q549. See Puech, "4Q543–4Q549," 283; Duke, "Amram, Visions of," 1:104.

10

Testament of Qahat

Introduction

Qahat (or Kohath) is named in the Old Testament as the son of Levi (Gen. 46:11; Exod. 6:16; Num. 3:17) and father of Amram (Exod. 6:18; Num. 3:19, 27) who lived to 133 years (Exod. 6:18). The Testament of Qahat, along with the Visions of Amram and the Aramaic Levi Document, is part of a trilogy of priestly testaments, or testament-like texts, attested among the Dead Sea Scrolls. As an ancestor of the high priests, Qahat is portrayed as one encouraging his progeny to be faithful to their priestly duties with all due care. The work is sometimes called the Admonitions of Qahat since Qahat's exhortations, sustained throughout, are addressed to his sons, concentrating on priestly traditions and preserving the books that contain them.[1] The Testament of Qahat was unknown until the discovery of the Dead Sea Scrolls, and the extant text (4Q542) is missing its beginning and end, so whether it contained a narrative and/or prophetic vision, like other testaments, is unknown.[2]

Language, Date, and Manuscripts

The Testament of Qahat (4Q542), like the other texts of the so-called priestly trilogy (Aramaic Levi Document [4Q213–214] and the Visions of Amram

---

1. Drawnel, "Qahat, Admonitions (Testament) of," 1125.
2. Wise, Abegg, and Cook, *Dead Sea Scrolls*, 545.

[4Q543–549]) is written in Aramaic. Paleographically it dates from 125–100 BCE[3] and is preserved in one large fragment with two columns (4Q542 1) and two smaller fragments with little text preserved (4Q542 2 and 3).[4]

Provenance and Purpose

The setting and purpose of the Testament of Qahat are uncertain. It may be that the warnings about giving priestly traditions to "strangers" and the inheritance to "assimilationists" refer to the crisis under Jason the high priest (r. 174–171 BCE).[5] Jason was not a legitimate priest but solicited his position from Antiochus IV Epiphanes (r. 175–164 BCE) with a significant bribe (2 Macc. 4:7–9) and promptly introduced Greek customs and Greek ways of life into Jerusalem contrary to Jewish laws (2 Macc. 4:10–17).[6] Furthermore, his appointment replaced the legitimate Zadokite priest, Onias III. And so Qahat's exhortations may be addressed to legitimate priestly figures to resist the pressures of Hellenization and assimilation.[7]

Contents

The text of the Testament of Qahat begins in the middle of the account and ends without the typical resolution of a testament; the beginning and end of the text are missing. The extant text starts with a blessing pronounced by Qahat to his sons and descendants (4Q542 I, 1–4).[8] He then exhorts his sons to be careful with their inheritance (the priestly office) and not to give it away to "strangers" or "assimilationists" (4Q542 I, 4–7a). He exhorts them to honor their ancestors and keep themselves pure (4Q542 I, 7–13; II, 1) and so reap eternal blessings while the sinners and wicked will be punished by fire (4Q542 II, 2–8). Qahat then charges Amram, his son, directly to guard the sacred writings as he, Qahat, guarded them after his father Levi (4Q542 II, 9–11). These sacred writings are seemingly passed along in Qahat's writings as a testimony (כול כתבי בשהדו, *kôl ktbê bśhdû*; 4Q542 II, 12–13).[9]

3. Puech, "Testament de Qahat."
4. Drawnel, "Qahat, Admonitions (Testament) of," 1125.
5. Wise, Abegg, and Cook, *Dead Sea Scrolls*, 545.
6. See VanderKam, *From Joshua to Caiaphas*, 199–203.
7. Wise, Abegg, and Cook, *Dead Sea Scrolls*, 545. See also Cook, "Remarks on the Testament of Kohath."
8. The language here alludes to the priestly benediction from Num. 6:24–26. Gross, "Testament of Kohath," 1870.
9. Wise, Abegg, and Cook, *Dead Sea Scrolls*, 545–46.

Contribution and Context[10]

In the context of the so-called priestly trilogy (see Visions of Amram below), the Testament of Qahat shares several characteristics with the Aramaic Levi Document and the Visions of Amram. These include, first, the use of the first-person singular in the narrative, which yields an autobiographical character to the entire document. Second, all three texts employ a patriarch of the priestly line addressing his children with instructions pertaining to a distinctly priestly inheritance. Third, the priestly instruction is passed to sons who are carrying on the priestly lineage. Finally, this knowledge is distinctly for priestly usage and priestly instruction.[11]

Reception History

The notion that books of the patriarchs were transmitted through Levi and his descendants (Jub. 45:15–16) may have been derived from the Testament of Qahat[12]—though this idea itself likely stems from the tradition that priests were to transmit the law (Lev. 10:11; Deut. 17:18). The priestly judgment of the wicked found in the Testament of Qahat resembles the presentation of the righteous as eschatological judges (1 En. 91; Dan. 7; Matt. 19:28; Rev. 20:4). Furthermore, the judgment also resembles that of 1 Enoch 22:8–11 in that it involves an abyss and caves, though Qahat does not indicate that the punishment is either postmortem or eternal (cf. Dan. 12:2).[13]

10. See esp. Cook, "Remarks on the Testament of Kohath."
11. Drawnel, "Qahat, Admonitions (Testament) of"; Drawnel, "Priestly Education."
12. Milik, "4QVisions d'Amram."
13. Penner, "Qahat, Testament of."

11

Visions of Amram

Introduction

Visions of Amram is the third of three testaments in a series composed of the Aramaic Levi Document and the Testament (or Admonitions) of Qahat that together form a corpus of priestly didactic literature that grew out of the experience of Levitical teachers.[1] Of these texts, the Visions of Amram alone preserves the opening paragraph containing its ancient title,[2] though its conclusion is missing. Amram is the father of Moses, Aaron, and Miriam, though he is little known in the Old Testament, where he is only mentioned in genealogical lists as the son of Qahat, or Kohath (Exod. 6:18; Num. 3:19; 26:58; 1 Chron. 5:28; 6:3; 23:12). He married his father's sister Jochebed, with whom he fathered Aaron, Moses, and Miriam (Exod. 6:20; Num. 26:59), whose descendants were in the Levitical line (1 Chron. 5:29; 6:2–3, 18; 23:12–13; 24:20, 26:23). The Visions of Amram presents his words pertaining to a vision in the form of a book delivered to his sons on the day of his death.[3]

Manuscripts, Language, and Date

The Visions of Amram is extant in five fragmentary manuscripts from the Dead Sea Scrolls (4Q543–547), all written in Aramaic. Two additional

1. Drawnel, *Aramaic Wisdom Text*; Drawnel, "Literary Form and Didactic Content."
2. Wise, Abegg, and Cook, *Dead Sea Scrolls*, 547.
3. J. Collins, "Testaments," 326.

manuscripts (4Q548–549) are so similar to the five primary fragments paleo-graphically and thematically that they may have been part of the original, though the fact that they do not overlap with the five means that their con-nection to them is hypothetical.[4] The manuscripts date from the second half of the second century BCE (4Q543, 4Q544, 4Q547), the first half of the first century BCE (4Q545, 4Q546), and the second half of the first century BCE (4Q548, 4Q549).[5] This means the work was written not later than the first half of the second century BCE.[6] And since the book of Jubilees (mid-second century BCE) seems to know the Visions of Amram (Jub. 47:8), the latter may date as early as the third century BCE (cf. Jub. 46:9–11; 4Q544 1 1–9).[7]

Provenance and Purpose

The origins of the Visions of Amram are not entirely clear. J. T. Milik and Émile Puech argue for a Samaritan provenance.[8] Robert R. Duke argues for a group of disenfranchised priests living in Hebron, south of Jerusalem.[9] He observes a growing scholarly consensus ascribing the text to priestly circles with the intent to strengthen the connection between Levi as founder of the Levitical priesthood and later exalted figures.[10] Its purpose is to address con-cerns about non-endogamous marriages of priests and priestly involvement in international affairs. In this context, where priests ruled, marriages were important facets of international diplomacy, and so the Visions of Amram was written to advocate for priestly purity in this context.[11]

Contents

The fragmentary Visions of Amram is reconstructed to comprise four epi-sodes[12] after an introductory heading. This introduction identifies the work

4. Drawnel, "Amram, Visions of," 326.
5. Puech, "4Q543–4Q549," 285–87.
6. Drawnel, "Amram, Visions of," 326.
7. Puech, "4Q543–4Q549," 287; Duke, "Amram, Visions of."
8. Milik, "Milkî-sedeq et Milkî-reshaʻ"; Puech, "4Q543–4Q549," 287.
9. Duke, Social Location, 110–11.
10. Duke, "Amram, Visions of"; Angel, Otherworldly and Eschatological Priesthood, 53–55; Perrin, Dynamics of Dream-Vision Revelation, 162–70.
11. Duke, Social Location, 110–11.
12. Duke, Social Location, 12–27. The present arrangement follows that of Wise, Abegg, and Cook, Dead Sea Scrolls, 547–50.

as "a copy of the book 'The Words of the Vision of Amram'" (4Q543 1 1), who is the son of Qahat, the son of Levi, and explains its contents: everything that he told his sons and commanded them on the day of his death during the 136th year of his life, which is the 152nd year of the "exile" of Israel in Egypt when he settled in the land (4Q543 1 I, 1–4; 4Q545 1a 4). In the first episode, Amram gives his daughter Miriam, age thirty, to his younger brother Uzziel in marriage (4Q545 1a 1). The second episode takes place after the wedding festival (4Q545 1a 7–8 = 4Q543 1–2). Amram calls for his son Aaron, age twenty, who is to summon Moses, here called Malachiyah, meaning "angel of the Lord" (4Q545 1a 8–9). The following text is considerably fragmented (4Q545 1a 9–14), but it appears to be a prophecy uttered by Amram, foretelling that his son—it is unclear whether he is referring to Aaron or Moses—will rise up to be God's messenger (4Q545 1a 14–19; cf. 4Q543). In the third episode Amram relates how he went to Hebron (in Canaan) from Egypt with his father Qahat and extended family to build tombs for those who died during their time in Egypt. From Canaan, Qahat returns to Egypt when he learns of the threat of war, while Amram remains in Hebron to finish building the tombs (4Q545 1a–b II, 11–19). Amram learns of the Philistines' defeat of Egypt and the closing of Egypt's borders, preventing Amram from returning to Egypt and to his wife, Jochebed, for forty-one years (4Q545 1a–b II, 19; 4Q544 1 5–9).

In the fourth episode Amram has a vision of two angelic figures who compete for influence on him (4Q544 1 10–15; 2 11–16).[13] Amram is told that he may choose which one will have influence on him (4Q544 2 9–12a). He sees that one is dark and hostile while the other is pleasant and smiling (4Q544 2 12b–14); all the human race falls under the sway of one or the other (4Q544 2 12). The next section is fragmentary (4Q545 2 III) but appears to describe Amram's choice of the light angel and his asking the angel questions about the vision.[14] The angel explains that the dark angel is Melki-Resha "ruler of wickedness," whose deeds are darkness and who leads people to darkness and rules over darkness (4Q545 2 III, 13–15). The light angel, who is likely Melchizedek,[15] is the ruler of all light (4Q545 2 III, 16). In answer to Amram's question (4Q545 3 IV), Melchizedek explains that those who follow light will be healed, delivered from death and destruction, and experience blessings, whereas those who follow darkness will go to destruction and receive just judgment (4Q548 1 II, 2–16).

13. Duke, "Amram, Visions of."
14. Wise, Abegg, and Cook, *Dead Sea Scrolls*, 549.
15. Milik, "Milkî-sedeq et Milkî-reshaʿ"; Kobelski, *Melchizedek and Mechiresha*; Wise, Abegg, and Cook, *Dead Sea Scrolls*, 549. The text itself is fragmentary.

Melchizedek then predicts the coming of what appears to be a priestly clan led by Moses and, presumably, Aaron (the text is fragmentary; 4Q545 4 14). Moses will be "a holy priest," as will all his descendants forever (4Q545 4; 4Q547 9 2–7a). When he awakens, Amram writes down the vision and seemingly returns to Egypt, where he gives the writing to his family (4Q547 9 7b–9) and particularly to his sons (4Q546 14).[16] Any additional ending is missing.

Critical Issues

In his critical edition, Émile Puech advanced the view that the Visions of Amram was part of a trilogy of priestly works pertaining to Amram (Visions of Amram), Levi (Aramaic Levi Document), and Qahat (Testament of Qahat).[17] In addition to the priestly lineage they all share, one of the Amram texts (4Q547) was written in a hand similar to that of a text from the Testament of Qahat (4Q542). The similar shape of these two fragments may suggest they were once part of the same scroll. Finally, stitching before the first column in 4Q543 indicates there were once preceding columns.[18] When compared with other texts from Qumran, the manuscripts of the Visions of Amram are consistently early.[19]

Contribution and Context

The Visions of Amram belongs to a unique assortment of narrative texts from the Dead Sea Scrolls that address people and events prior to the exodus (e.g., Jubilees, Aramaic Levi Document, and Testament of Qahat). It shows an interest not only in the events from this time but more particularly in the seven generations from Abraham to Moses, which would lend continuity to God's covenantal dealings with Israel. Amram himself appears in the rewritten account of Exodus in Pseudo-Philo's Biblical Antiquities. Amram appears in the time of the persecution of Egypt prior to the birth of Moses (Exod. 1:22) when the elders resolve to have no children, reasoning it is better to die without sons than to have the wombs of their wives defiled and offspring that serves idols (LAB 9:1–2). Amram rejects this resolution, instead appealing to the covenant promises made to Abraham, in anticipation of God's intervention on their behalf (9:3–6). Amram's plan is pleasing to God, who in turn

---

16. Wise, Abegg, and Cook, *Dead Sea Scrolls*, 547–50.
17. É. Puech, "4Q543–4Q549," 283–405. See Duke, *Social Location*, 119–22.
18. Puech, "4Q543–4Q549."
19. Duke, "Amram, Visions of."

promises that Amran's offspring will serve before God forever, that he will do marvelous things in the house of Jacob through Amran, and that he will reveal his law to him (9:7–8). And so Amram takes a Levite wife, with whom he has Aaron, Miriam, and Moses (9:9–10). A similar account is found in Josephus, where Amram is described as "a Hebrew of noble birth" who prays for God's intervention in the same persecution (Exod. 1–2) of those who in no way transgressed in their worship of God (*Ant.* 2.2.1–2 §§10–11). God hears his prayer and, answering him in a vision, promises Amram a son who will be a deliverer and another who will be a priest (*Ant.* 2.2.2–4 §§10–19).[20]

Reception History

It seems plausible that the Visions of Amram was known to the author of Jubilees (Jub. 47:8), and perhaps Josephus.

20. Duke, "Amram, Visions of."

12

Additional Writings

Testament of Solomon, Testaments of the Twelve
Patriarchs, Testament of Naphtali (4Q215), and Other
Testamentary Material in the Dead Sea Scrolls

In addition to the works explained above, there were several other testaments in the ancient world. Some of these are extremely fragmentary, such as those from the Dead Sea Scrolls, while others are of questionable provenance. As we have seen before, the transmission of ancient Jewish texts by hand and by Christians frequently serves to obscure the Jewish original, sometimes beyond recovery. The texts described here are among the most important that are debated, but for various reasons they do not receive full treatment here.

Testament of Solomon

Introduction

The Testament of Solomon only loosely belongs to the genre of testament, despite suggestions that it is Solomon's final testament prior to his death (T. Sol. 15:14; 26:8). But it lacks the deathbed scene and the imparting of wisdom to his progeny and seems primarily concerned with demonic lore. Furthermore, in its present form it is a Christian document from around the third century CE, which may be based in part on Jewish material from the first century CE.[1]

1. J. Collins, "Testaments," 327.

Contents

The narrative begins with the story of a boy, the son of the master work-man overseeing the building of the temple, being tormented by a demon named Ornias (T. Sol. 1:1–2). Solomon, speaking in the first person, learns of this (1:3–4) and prays for authority over the demon (1:5). In response the archangel Michael arrives and gives Solomon a magical seal ring that he can use to imprison demons and help build the temple (1:6–7). Solomon directs the boy to use the ring to bring back the demon (1:8–13), whom Solomon interrogates and commands to work on the temple (2:1–7). When Ornias resists, the archangel Ouriel is summoned to aid Solomon in subjecting Or-nias (1:8–9). Then Solomon directs Ornias to use the ring to bring to him Beelzeboul (2:8–9), whom Solomon then interrogates and orders to bring him unclean spirits that are bound (3:1–6). Beelzeboul shows him several demons, each with unique traits and means of tormenting humanity, and explains the means by which each may be thwarted and their respective assignments for building the temple. First comes Onoskelis, with the body of a woman and legs of a mule, who lives in caves but comes out to torment men. It travels by the moon (4:1–9) and is commanded to spin hemp for robes used in the construction of the temple (4:10–12). Beelzeboul next brings Asmodeus, a demon of the Great Bear constellation (5:1–10), who is to mold clay for all the vessels of the temple (5:11–13). Solomon learns that Beelzeboul is a fallen angel, after which Beelzeboul is directed to cut marble (chap. 6). Lix Tetrax, a wind demon with a star near the moon, is next interrogated by Solomon, who directs it to throw stones to the heights of the temple for the workmen (chap. 7). Seven evil spirits—Deception, Strife, Fate, Distress, Error, Power, and the Worst—appear to Solomon and are directed to dig the foundation for the temple (chap. 8). The headless demon called Murder is commanded to stay with Beelzeboul (chap. 9). Scepter is a doglike demon who helps Solomon acquire an emerald for the temple and is instructed to join Murder in cutting marble (chap. 10). A demon in the shape of a lion rules over a "legion" of demons, which will be driven over a cliff by Emmanouel (cf. Mark 5:13). The legion is instructed to carry wood, and the lion-shaped demon is to saw it and fuel the burning kiln (T. Sol. 11). A three-headed dragon demon, called the Head of Dragons, is thwarted by the Place of the Skull (cf. Mark 15:22) and the Wonderful Counselor (cf. Isa. 9:6) on the cross. He is instructed to make bricks for the temple (T. Sol. 12). Then Solomon interrogates a female demon, Obyzouth, who is bound by her disheveled hair and hung in front of the temple (chap. 13). A winged dragon who burns wood for constructing the temple is thwarted and condemned to cut marble for constructing the temple (chap. 14). Enepsigos is a two-headed female demon who hovers near the moon and, when bound by Solomon, prophesies the destruction of the kingdom, the temple, and Jerusalem, as well as the coming of the Son of God, Emmanouel, who will be born of a virgin and crucified (15:1–13). Solomon explains that he writes this testament so that Israelites may know the forms in which demons appear, as well as their powers, and how they may be overcome (15:14–15). The sea-horse demon, Kunepegos, turns himself into a wave to wreak his havoc on mankind but is sealed by Solomon in a bowl and stored in the temple (chap. 16). Solomon interrogates a "lecherous spirit" who appears in the shadowy form of a man with gleaming eyes and who is conquered by the Savior or the sign of the cross on the forehead. He is locked up with the other demons (chap. 17). Thirty-six heavenly bodies, which are demonic divisions of the Zodiac, are bound and ordered to bear water to the temple (chap. 18).

The narrative then breaks from its pattern of demonic interviews with Solomon's account of the honors bestowed on him by the kings of the earth, including Sheeba, the Queen of the South, who is a witch (chap. 19). Then Solomon learns of a conflict between an old man and his son, (20:1–5) which Ornias, the demon, predicts will end in the son's death (20:6–10), and in fact it does (20:18–21). Ornias explains that demons overhear God's decisions since they are really fallen angels who fell because they had no place to rest (20:11–17). Sheeba, the Queen of the South, is so impressed with the new temple that she contributes ten thousand shekels to it (chap. 21). Adarkes, the king of Arabia, writes to Solomon asking for help with a wind demon, Ephippas (22:1–5), which is brought to the temple and interrogated by Solomon, who learns that he can be thwarted by the one who will be born of a virgin and crucified by the Jews (22:6–20). Solomon directs the demon to put the cornerstone of the temple in its place, fulfilling the prophecy of the stone rejected by builders becoming the keystone (Ps. 118:22; T. Sol. 23). The demon also, with the aid of the demon who lives in the Red Sea, lifts up the pillar in the Red Sea and offers to put it wherever Solomon wishes (23:2; 24:1). But Solomon tricks them, and so they are trapped into holding the pillar aloft in perpetuity (chap. 24). When Solomon interrogates the demon from the Red Sea, Abezethibou, he learns that this demon was called to aid Egypt against Moses, to harden Pharaoh's heart, and to pursue Israel to the Red Sea. There, with the Egyptian army, he was trapped in the waters of the Red Sea (25:1–7). The demon is instructed to continue holding up the pillar (25:8). In the end (chap. 26) Solomon falls in love with a Shummanite woman and sacrifices to the foreign gods Raphan and Molech to obtain her (26:1–5). Then the spirit of God departs from Solomon, who then builds temples to the woman's idols and becomes a laughingstock to the idols and demons (26:6–7). And so,

Solomon says, he writes the testament "in order that those who hear might pray about, and pay attention to, the last things and not to the first things, in order that they might finally find grace forever" (26:8).

Contribution

Naturally the Testament of Solomon has a number of affinities with the Hebrew Bible as well as the New Testament, though only one biblical text is actually quoted (Ps. 118:22 at T. Sol. 23:4).[2] Solomon's wisdom (1 Kings 4:29–34) and building of the temple (1 Kings 6–7) are central to the entire narrative. The Queen of Sheeba (1 Kings 10) appears twice in the Testament of Solomon (T. Sol. 19:1–3; 21:1–4). Solomon's many foreign wives (1 Kings 11) lead to his downfall (T. Sol. 26), and prophetic texts are presented in eschatological contexts (Isa. 7:14 in T. Sol. 6:8; 11:6; 15:11; Isa. 9:6 in T. Sol. 12:3). Affinities with New Testament texts give the Testament of Solomon its obviously Christian character, such as the prevalence of Beelzeboul (cf. T. Sol. 3; 4:2; Mark 3:22), the Gerasene demoniacs (cf. T. Sol. 11; Mark 5:1–13), the "virgin" (cf. T. Sol. 15:10; 22:10; Matt. 1:18–25), references to the crucifixion (cf. T. Sol. 6:8; 12:3; 17:4), and the titular use of "Son of David" for Solomon (T. Sol. 1:7; 20:1; cf. Matt. 9:27; 12:23; 15:22; 20:30–31; 21:9, 15; 22:42).

The Testament of Solomon evidences the burgeoning traditions surrounding Solomon, such as the Wisdom of Solomon, which claims Solomon knew about astrology and spiritual forces (Wis. 7:15–22), and Josephus, who says that Solomon wrote incantations (*Ant.* 8.2.5 §§42–49).[3] Later we will see that other works become associated with his name, including psalms (Psalms of Solomon) and odes (Odes of Solomon).

Some of the Testament of Solomon's outlooks are shared with other Jewish and/or Christian texts, such as the division of the cosmos into heaven above, earth between, and hell below (T. Sol. 18:3). It also holds that demons are fallen angels (cf. Gen. 6:1–4; T. Sol. 5:3; 6:2) and names angels known by other texts, such as Michael, Ouriel, Raphael, and Gabriel (cf. T. Sol. 1:6; 2:4; 5:9; 8:9; 13:6; 18:4–8).[4] Yet unlike other texts discussed here, there is a unique depiction of magic. Solomon is given a magic ring, and the indications of what binds certain demons resemble formulaic magical incantations utilized to alleviate certain medical conditions (cf. T. Sol. 18:14, 32). The use of a fish liver and gall smoking on coals resembles a similar incident in the book of Tobit (Tob. 6:4–7, 16; 8:2) also in the context of exorcism.

2. Duling, "Testament of Solomon," 1:954–56.
3. Duling, "Testament of Solomon," 1:945.
4. Duling, "Testament of Solomon," 1:953.

Text and Provenance

The text of the Testament of Solomon is attested in eighteen Greek manuscripts, some dating from the fifth or sixth century CE, but most from the fifteenth or sixteenth century.[5] Though there may be elements of Semitic language material behind some of its sources, the Testament of Solomon is widely recognized to have been composed in Koine Greek.[6] The date for the Testament of Solomon is uncertain because of its lack of references to historical events.[7] Its linguistic affinities with the New Testament suggest the first century CE or later, perhaps to the fourth century. F. C. Conybeare argued that the present Testament of Solomon may stem from such a later date, but it is a Christian reworking of a Jewish original from about 100 CE.[8] C. C. McCown contended that the earlier Jewish material may have been a collection of Jewish interpretive stories about Solomon and the demons, originating in Palestine and subsequently undergoing revisions.[9] There remains today debate about the so-called evolution of the text of the Testament of Solomon, but there is a general consensus that it was written by a Greek-speaking Christian who used Jewish traditions, or perhaps a Greek-speaking Jew whose work was rewritten with unquestionably Christian elements. The use of magic complicates identification of a geographical location, and Babylonia, Asia Minor, Palestine, and Egypt have all been proposed.[10] The Christian nature of the document means that further inquiry can be made elsewhere, particularly the complete introduction and text by D. C. Duling[11] and the more recent monograph by Todd E. Klutz.[12]

Testaments of the Twelve Patriarchs

Introduction

The Testaments of the Twelve Patriarchs is composed of twelve distinct testaments woven into a single unit, modeled after Jacob's last words (Gen.

5. Klutz, *Rewriting the Testament of Solomon*, 19–34; Duling, "Testament of Solomon," 1:937–39. The most important critical edition and most extensive collation of manuscripts is that of McCown, *Testament of Solomon*.

6. McCown, *Testament of Solomon*, 42–43.

7. See Duling, "Testament of Solomon," 1:940–43, and Klutz, *Rewriting the Testament of Solomon*, 34–37.

8. Conybeare, "Testament of Solomon," 1–15.

9. McCown, *Testament of Solomon*, 83–86.

10. See McCown, *Testament of Solomon*, 110; Duling, "Testament of Solomon," 1:943–44.

11. Duling, "Testament of Solomon."

12. Klutz, *Rewriting the Testament of Solomon*.

49; cf. Deut. 33).[13] They are perhaps the most important examples of the testament genre from the Second Temple period and early Christianity. They have received the most scholarly attention in part because they, uniquely, contain the word "testament" (διαθήκη, *diathēkē*) in their titles and also contain deathbed speeches from each of the twelve sons of Jacob addressing ethical matters all framed, with the exception of Asher, within a narrative of the figure's life.[14] They each conclude with predictions about Israel's future, utilizing the rubric of sin-exile-restoration, and instructions for the patriarch's burial, which are then followed at the end.[15] And yet the Testaments of the Twelve Patriarchs is widely regarded as a work originally written in a Jewish context[16] from the Second Temple period but, in its present form, has been thoroughly reworked by Christians so as to become a Christian text.[17] Furthermore, there is considerable debate as to whether the later Christian interpolations can be recognized and excised so as to arrive at the earlier Jewish text.

Contents

Testament of Reuben

The Testament of Reuben takes place in the patriarch's 125th year, two years after the death of Joseph (T. Reu. 1:1–2). It deals with Reuben's sexual relations with his father's concubine, Bilhah (Gen. 35:22; 49:4).[18] Reuben speaks to his brothers and his sons from his deathbed, exhorting them not to indulge in the sexual promiscuity that he did and from which he repented (T. Reu. 1:3–10). He warns them of the influences of the spirits of deceit (chap. 2) and error (chap. 3). He also warns them against devoting attention to the beauty of women (chap. 4), who are evil and entice men to promiscuity (chap. 5) and must be avoided (6:1–4). Reuben then predicts his sons' hostility with Levi but exhorts them to submit to the latter's God-given authority over them (6:5–12). He then dies and is carried from Egypt to Hebron, where he is buried (chap. 7).

Testament of Simeon

The Testament of Simeon is set at Simeon's 120th year, at the time of the death of Joseph (T. Sim. 1). Simeon is near death and speaks to his sons, primarily addressing his jealousy that caused him to hate his brother Joseph

---

13. Hillel, "Patriarchs."
14. Hillel, "Testaments." See also J. Collins, *Apocalyptic Imagination*, 168.
15. Cf. Kee, "Testaments of the Twelve Patriarchs," 1:775.
16. Kugel, "Some Translation and Copying Mistakes."
17. Kugler, *Testaments of the Twelve Patriarchs*, 31–38.
18. Kugler, *Testaments of the Twelve Patriarchs*, 41.

(Gen. 37:26–28).[19] He recounts the consequences of his envy (T. Sim. 2) and exhorts his sons to beware of deceit and envy (chap. 3). Simeon also exhorts his sons not to succumb to jealousy but to love each other (chap. 4). Joseph was faultless, and his integrity should be imitated in Simeon's sons (chap. 5) so that they will be a blessing to their father even when he is gone (chap. 6). Simeon then exhorts his sons to obey Levi and Judah (chap. 7) before Simeon himself dies (chap. 8) and is lamented by his sons (chap. 9).

TESTAMENT OF LEVI

The Testament of Levi begins and ends with the subject of the priesthood and arrogance (T. Levi 1:1–2:1; 19:1–5) but otherwise departs from the bio-graphical rubric of a testament in favor of parenesis and future prediction.[20] The setting is Levi's decree to his sons about future events in light of Levi's impending death. Surprisingly, Levi is in good health (chap. 1). He recounts his background to the time of the incident with the Shechemites and his sister Dinah (2:1–2; cf. Gen. 34). While tending flocks, he has a vision in which he observes and laments the sins of humanity and prays for his own deliverance (T. Levi 2:3–4). He falls asleep and finds himself on a mountain, where heaven is opened and an angel implores him to enter (2:5–6). He is told he will be near to God as his priest and will tell of God's mysteries to humankind (2:7–12). Then he is instructed about heavenly things and the Lord's observance of the sins of people (chap. 3) and God's impending judgment that Levi and his progeny can avoid (chap. 4). Levi is then commissioned to the priesthood by God before he returns to earth, takes vengeance on Shechem, and awakens from his dream (chaps. 5–7). Levi has another vision in which he is commis-sioned for his priestly task by angels and then awakens (chap. 8). Levi then settles at Hebron, where Isaac continually reminds him of the laws of the priesthood (chap. 9), which he passes on to his sons (chap. 10). Levi recounts his marriage and the birth of his children (chap. 11) and other significant events of his life (chap. 12) before exhorting his children to walk according to God's law and to teach their own children to do the same (chap. 13). Levi predicts the impiety of his children toward the Lord, which he knows from the writings of Enoch (chaps. 14, 16), and the consequential destruction of the sanctuary (chaps. 15, 17). Then the Lord will raise up a glorious new priest who will minister to the nations and bind evil (chap. 18). The work ends with Levi's sons' commitment to follow the ways of the Lord. After he witnesses this, Levi himself dies at the age of 137 and is buried in Hebron (chap. 19).

19. Kugler, *Testaments of the Twelve Patriarchs*, 44.
20. Kugler, *Testaments of the Twelve Patriarchs*, 47.

Testament of Judah

The Testament of Judah is set just prior to his death, when he gathers his sons, to whom he explains that his father declared him to be king (T. Jud. 1). The majority of the text (1:1–20:5) is devoted to matters of courage, love of money, and impurity. When it shifts to the future (21:1–25:5), attention turns to the royal line that comes from Judah's seed that will produce a savior for Israel.[21] Judah recounts his miraculous feats with animals in the wild (chap. 2) and in the field of battle (chaps. 3–7). Judah marries Saba, who bears him three more sons; only one of whom, Shelom, lives (chap. 8). Judah indicates that his father Jacob had lived at peace for eighteen years with his brother Esau when the latter came against Jacob and his sons (9:1–2). Jacob killed Esau, and Jacob's sons pursued Esau's sons, who were taken captive and paid tribute to Jacob's sons until they all went to Egypt during the famine (9:3–8). When Judah's son Er married Tamar of Aram, she bore no children (chap. 10) until Judah, drunk and led astray, slept with her (11:1–12:4). Judah, who had left his pledge with her, was exposed for what he had done (12:5–10). Then Judah went to Egypt because of the famine at the age of forty-six (12:11–12). Judah addresses his children, exhorting them first not to succumb to their lusts with women (chaps. 13, 15), then not to get drunk with wine (chaps. 14, 16). He adds to that avoiding sexual promiscuity and the love of money (chaps. 17–19). After an exhortation to abide by the spirit of truth rather than that of error (chap. 20), Judah charges his progeny to be humble toward Levi, who has received the priesthood, whereas to him, Judah, belongs the kingship (chap. 21). Yet Judah predicts that his rule will be terminated by an alien race until the coming of God and the establishment of Judah's eternal kingship (chap. 22). His children will turn from the Lord, who will in turn discipline them until they repent (chap. 23). Then a "Star from Jacob" will arise from Judah's posterity who will raise the scepter of his kingdom and save those who call on the Lord (chap. 24). Abraham, Isaac, and Jacob will be raised from the dead, and Judah and his brothers will rule in Israel (chap. 25). At the end, Judah exhorts his children to observe the whole law; then he dies at the age of 119 years and is taken to Hebron for burial (chap. 26).

Testament of Issachar

The focus of the Testament of Issachar is simplicity, with much of the work lauding the virtue of a farmer's simple life (T. Iss. 3:1–8; 7:2–6).[22] At the outset

21. Kugler, *Testaments of the Twelve Patriarchs*, 57.
22. Kugler, *Testaments of the Twelve Patriarchs*, 57.

Issachar recounts his birth to his sons, specifically his conception associated with the account in Genesis (30:14–18), in which Jacob sires Issachar with Leah (T. Iss. 1–2), and his life as a farmer (chap. 3). And so Issachar exhorts his children to live in integrity, in a way pleasing to the Lord (chap. 4), and to keep the law of God (chap. 5). He warns his children that their sons will abandon the commands of the Lord and warns them to teach their children to repent (chap. 6). At the age of 122, Issachar rehearses his piety and instructs his children to bury him at Hebron upon his death, which occurs at the very end (chap. 7).

TESTAMENT OF ZEBULON

Zebulon is 114 at the outset of the Testament of Zebulon (T. Zeb. 1), which is primarily concerned with compassion and mercy.[23] Zebulon recounts to his children how he was a blessing to his parents from birth (1:3) and has committed no sin, except in his mind (1:4–5) and except for keeping secret from his father his brothers' plans to kill Joseph (1:5–7). He narrates the account of his brothers' intent to do harm to Joseph, clarifying that he played no part in the plot (chap. 2) and did not share in the price received for selling Joseph (chap. 3; cf. Gen. 37). After Joseph was gone, his brothers ate while Zebulon, along with Judah, fasted (T. Zeb. 4). So Zebulon exhorts his children to exhibit mercy and compassion to all (chap. 5). Because of his compassion Zebulon was preserved from calamity (5:3–5) and became a successful fisherman (chap. 6). Zebulon recounts other deeds of his own compassion (chap. 7) and exhorts his children to follow his example (chap. 8) in undivided fidelity (9:1–4). He tells his sons that the writings of the fathers predict they will defect from the Lord toward idolatry, and they will be punished accordingly (9:5–9). At the end he exhorts his children again to fear the Lord; then he dies and is buried at Hebron (chap. 10).

TESTAMENT OF DAN

Anger (θυμός, thymos) is the primary subject matter of the Testament of Dan.[24] The setting is the 125th year of Dan's life, where his children are gathered, confessing that he rejoiced over the death of Joseph (T. Dan 1). Dan announces his impending death and entreats his children to avoid the ensnarement of anger (chap. 2). Anger is evil and weakens a person (chap. 3), and Dan explains how it exercises its senseless power (chap. 4). In poetic fashion Dan exhorts his children to avoid wrath and lying (5:1–3) and then predicts that they will defect from the

---

23. Kugler, Testaments of the Twelve Patriarchs, 64.
24. Kugler, Testaments of the Twelve Patriarchs, 67. Kugler observes that the prevalence of the subject is suggested by the frequent use of the noun θυμός, thymos (T. Dan 1:8; 2:2, 4; 3:1, 4, 5; 4:1, 2, 3, 6, 7; 5:1; 6:8).

Lord, live by every evil deed (5:4–7), and be led into captivity (5:8). And so he exhorts them to repent and turn to the Lord (5:9) and predicts that the Lord's salvation will arise from the tribes of Judah and Levi (5:10–11) to refresh the saints in Eden and that the righteous will rejoice in a new Jerusalem (5:12–13). Dan exhorts his children to fear God and draw near to God, to the interceding angels, and to the righteousness of the law of God (6:1–10). Dan dies and is buried near Abraham, Isaac, and Jacob (6:11; 7:1–2), but the work concludes that Dan prophesied to his children that they would go astray and be estranged from their inheritance and Israel, which in fact occurred (7:3).

TESTAMENT OF NAPHTALI

The Testament of Naphtali is unlike other testaments in that its subject matter is "natural goodness" and, apart from the account of his birth (T. Naph. 1:4–11) and a single verse (2:1), has nothing to do with Naphtali's own life narrative.[25] It is set in the patriarch's 132nd year (1:1), when he was in good health and gathered with his sons (1:2). The next morning he announces his impending death (1:2–5) followed by an account of his birth to Bilhah (1:6–8) and then Bilhah's birth (1:9–12). He explains that he was as fast as a deer and then launches into an extended discourse on the wisdom of God creating the human form (2:1–8) and exhorts his sons to live in accord with the good purpose of God (2:9–10) and not to alter the created order of God (chap. 3). Naphtali claims to have read in the writings of Enoch that his children will stray from the Lord (chap. 4). He then recounts a dream from his fortieth year in which he saw on the Mount of Olives that the sun and moon stood still; Levi seized the sun and Judah the moon, thereby achieving their greatness (chap. 5). In another dream Naphtali, along with his father and brothers, boards a ship that survives a storm, whereas Joseph escaped on a small boat (chap. 6). When Naphtali recounts these dreams to his father, Jacob concludes that Joseph is still alive (chap. 7). Naphtali commands his children to be in unity with Levi and Judah, since salvation will arise for Israel from Judah (chap. 8). Then Naphtali dies and is buried by his sons at Hebron (chap. 9).

TESTAMENT OF GAD

The Testament of Gad is similar to the Testament of Dan in its concern for anger, but the language is different.[26] The setting is Gad's 127th year

---

25. Kugler, *Testaments of the Twelve Patriarchs*, 71.
26. Kugler, *Testaments of the Twelve Patriarchs*, 74. Dan uses the term θυμός, *thymos*, whereas Gad uses μῖσος, *misos*.

(T. Gad 1:1), when he recounts to his sons how, when shepherding his father's herd, Joseph misleadingly accused him to Jacob of killing and eating
the flock, causing Gad to nurse a grudge against Joseph (1:2–9). Though
Gad is careful to explain his innocence, he nonetheless confesses his desire
to kill his brother (chap. 2) and exhorts his children not to fall prey to such
hatred (chaps. 3–5). They are to love and forgive one another (chap. 6) and
not harbor jealousy at the success of another (chap. 7). They are to instruct
their children accordingly, and honor Judah and Levi, from whom the Lord
will raise up a savior for Israel. Then after five years Gad dies and is buried
by his sons in Hebron (chap. 8).

TESTAMENT OF ASHER

There is almost no biography in the Testament of Asher, which is concerned primarily with a single-minded obedience to God's commands.[27] It is
set in Asher's 125th year, when he is still healthy and calls his sons to show
them what is right in the sight of God (T. Ash. 1:1–2). He explains to them
that there are two ways—good and evil (1:3–9)—exhorting his sons to be
uniformly devoted to good in all aspects of their lives (chaps. 2–5). They
are to pursue the Lord's commands with the same singleness of mind (chap.
6). Asher then predicts they will sin and be delivered into the hands of their
enemies but will be gathered in faith through God's compassion and because
of Abraham, Isaac, and Jacob (chap. 7). At the end Asher dies and is buried
at Hebron (chap. 8).

TESTAMENT OF JOSEPH

The Testament of Joseph is a lengthy and complicated work that utilizes
a diversity of sources and emphasizes Joseph's endurance as the key to his
salvation/exaltation.[28] Joseph is near death and calls his brothers and children to him (T. Jos. 1:1–2), first recounting that he was hated by his brothers and sold into slavery but loved by God (1:3–7). He then recounts how
he was unjustly accused of abusing a woman in Egypt, was imprisoned but
remained steadfast, and was not forgotten by God (chap. 2). Joseph goes on
at length about the chidings of the Egyptian woman and his responses to
her with words from God to divert her desires (chaps. 3–7). Even when in
prison Joseph worshiped God, though the woman grieved (chap. 8) and continued to try to entice him (chap. 9). Joseph then explains to his children the

27. Kugler, *Testaments of the Twelve Patriarchs*, 77.
28. Kugler, *Testaments of the Twelve Patriarchs*, 80.

merits of patience and prayer (chap. 10) and exhorts them to fear the Lord, for by doing the law of the Lord they too will be loved by God (11:1). Next Joseph returns to his account of his enslavement by describing how he was taken by the Ishmaelites, to whom he was sold, to an Egyptian trader who prospered while Joseph was with him (11:2–7). Word of the good fortune he brought to his master spread to a high-ranking official in Egypt, Pentephris (chap. 12), who did not believe that Joseph was really a slave (chap. 13). The Egyptian's wife, referred to as "the Memphian woman," pleaded for Joseph's release as a well-born man who should not be imprisoned, but to no avail (chap. 14). After a few weeks the Ishmaelites returned, asking Joseph why he said he was a slave when he was not, but Joseph simply affirmed his slavery in order to protect his brothers from disgrace (chap. 15). Joseph was then purchased by an Egyptian eunuch on behalf of the Memphian woman and her husband (chap. 16). With this Joseph exhorts his sons to endure in the face of adversity (chap. 17) and live according to God's commands (chap. 18). Then he tells his children of a dream vision in which he sees twelve stags grazing, grouped into nine in one place and three in another. He sees a virgin born from Judah who bears a spotless lamb and angels rejoicing, explaining these things will occur in the last days and exhorting his sons to honor Levi and Judah, since from them will come the savior (chap. 19).[29] Joseph also predicts that the Egyptians will oppress his sons but God will lead them into the promised land. When he dies, his sons take his bones and bury him in Hebron (chap. 20).

Testament of Benjamin

The Testament of Benjamin is unique among the Testaments of the Twelve Patriarchs because it primarily concerns Joseph, not Benjamin, and because it summarizes what other testaments in the collection say about ethics, eschatology, and theology.[30] At the outset Benjamin is 125 years old and recounts to his sons his birth to Rachel and Jacob (T. Benj. 1). He tells his gathered sons about his meeting with Joseph in Egypt, who told of his abuse at the hands of the Ishmaelites (chap. 2). Benjamin then tells his sons to follow the pattern of the good and pious life of Joseph (3:1–5; 4), who urged their father to pray for his brothers and was told by Jacob that prophecy concerning the savior would be fulfilled through Joseph (3:6–8). Benjamin lauds the virtues of setting one's mind toward good (chap. 5) and avoiding evil, corruption, and

29. There is a longer Armenian version and a shorter Greek account of the same vision. See Kugler, *Testaments of the Twelve Patriarchs*, 83.
30. Kugler, *Testaments of the Twelve Patriarchs*, 83.

hatred (chaps. 6–8). Benjamin states that he learned from the works of Enoch that his sons will be sexually promiscuous and go astray, but the twelve tribes will be united again through a "unique prophet" (chap. 9). Benjamin tells his sons that he is dying and exhorts them to do the truth to their neighbors and to pass the law on to their own children as an inheritance (10:1–4); then they will see and experience resurrection (10:5–11). He predicts that from the lineage of Judah and Levi will rise up the "beloved of the Lord," who will bring salvation for Israel and dwell among gentiles (chap. 11). Then Benjamin dies and is buried by his sons in Hebron (chap. 12).

Contribution

Perhaps the most prominent contribution of the Testaments of the Twelve Patriarchs is its ethics, the moral terms of which are broadly categorized as Hellenistic-Jewish.[31] Surprisingly, obedience to the law, which is equated with wisdom (T. Levi 13:1–9), is seldom regarded in their ethical instruction, where there is a tendency to avert distinctive Jewish elements such as circumcision, dietary laws, and Sabbath.[32] Instead, the command to love God and one's neighbor seems to set the standard for behavior (Deut. 6:5; Lev. 19:18; Matt. 22:37–40; cf. T. Sim. 4:7; T. Iss. 5:2; T. Dan 5:3).[33] Some see a connection between Stoicism and the particular ethical concerns of integrity (T. Sim. 4:5; T. Levi 13:1; T. Iss. 3:2; 4:6; 5:1; 7:7; T. Jud. 23:5), piety (T. Reu. 6:4; T. Iss. 7:6; T. Levi 16:2), uprightness (T. Iss. 4:1, 6; T. Gad 7:7; T. Sim. 5:2), honesty (T. Dan 1:3), generosity (T. Iss. 3:8; 4:2; 7:3), compassion (T. Iss. 7:5; T. Jud. 18:3; T. Zeb. 2:4; 5:1–3; 7:1–4; 8:6), hard work (T. Iss. 5:3–5), and self-control (T. Jos. 4:1–2; 6:7; 9:2–3; 10:2–3). Sexual promiscuity is particularly loathsome (e.g., T. Reu. 3:10–4:2; T. Levi 9:9; 14:6; 17:11; T. Sim. 5:3; T. Iss. 4:4; 7:2; T. Jud. 11:1–5; 12:1–9; 18:2–6) but is incited by evil spirits (T. Reu. 4:7, 10; 5:6) as well as by the enticement of women (T. Reu. 5:1–7; T. Jud. 10:3–5; 15:5–6). Other sins are likewise produced by the influence of evil spirits, but also by negative ethical behaviors, including vices such as anger (T. Dan 2:1–5:2), envy (T. Dan 1:4; T. Gad 7:1–7; T. Sim. 4:5, 7, 9; 6:2), and greed (T. Jud. 17:1; 19:1–3). The Torah does not provide the resources for right living but rather one's conscience does (T. Reu. 4:3; T. Jos. 20:2), as does God's spirit and his fidelity (T. Sim. 4:4; T. Jos. 9:2) and the "inherent power of good to overcome evil" (T. Benj. 5).[34]

31. Hillel, "Patriarchs."
32. So also Hillel, "Patriarchs"; Kee, "Testaments of the Twelve Patriarchs," 1:779.
33. Hillel, "Patriarchs."
34. Kee, "Testaments of the Twelve Patriarchs," 1:779.

The utilization of Jewish traditions in the Testaments of the Twelve Patriarchs is exhibited by its affinities with other Second Temple Jewish texts.[35] Many examples can be enumerated, such as the activities of Judah (T. Jud. 3–7 and Jub. 34:1–9), the similarities between the Testament of Naphtali 1:6–12 and the Hebrew Testament of Naphtali from Qumran (4Q215), and the affinities between the Testament of Levi (esp. chaps. 8–13) and the Aramaic Levi Document. The work also draws on the writings of Enoch eight times (T. Sim. 5:4; T. Levi 10:4; 14:1; T. Jud. 18:1; T. Dan 5:6; T. Naph. 4:1; T. Benj. 9:1; 10:6), yet none of these come from identifiable texts in extant Enochic literature.[36]

A distinct feature of the testaments is their association of eschatological events with both Levi and Judah, who have prominent roles throughout (e.g., T. Jud. 25:1; T. Reu. 6:7; T. Gad 8:2; T. Iss. 5:7), though not always consistently.[37] Sometimes God will save the nations through a chief priest of Levi and a king of Judah (T. Sim. 7:2; cf. T. Jos. 19:6; T. Levi 18; T. Jud. 24). Though Judah is king (T. Jud. 1:6; 24:1–6), Levi is God's anointed agent of eschatological redemption (T. Levi 18:1–12) and superior to Judah (T. Jos. 19:4).[38] H. C. Kee notes that, in additional to Levi and Judah, another prophetic figure appears in the eschatological temple (T. Benj. 9:2), while elsewhere it is a singular agent "from Levi and Judah" who accomplishes redemption (T. Dan 5:10; T. Gad 8:1; T. Benj. 11:2). Whatever may have been the case in the works' sources or prior recensions, in their present Christian form the testaments envision a single messiah, Jesus, associated with both Levi and Judah.[39]

Text and Provenance

The Testaments of the Twelve Patriarchs is preserved in fourteen Greek manuscripts (the most important of which dates anywhere from the tenth to the eighteenth century),[40] twelve Armenian manuscripts, and a few Latin and Slavonic texts.[41] The Armenian is perhaps the most significant and dates from the sixth or seventh century.[42] The Qumran Testament of Naphtali (4Q215) and the Aramaic Levi Document are not regarded as manuscript witnesses to the Testaments of the Twelve Patriarchs but may contribute to our understanding of the sources they used. Some have theorized that the testaments

35. J. Collins, *Apocalyptic Imagination*, 166.
36. Hillel, "Patriarchs"; Hillel, "Demonstrable Instances."
37. J. Collins, *Apocalyptic Imagination*, 173; so also Hillel, "Testaments."
38. Kee, "Testaments of the Twelve Patriarchs," 1:779.
39. J. Collins, *Apocalyptic Imagination*, 174; Jonge, "Two Messiahs."
40. Hillel, "Patriarchs."
41. See Kee, "Testaments of the Twelve Patriarchs," 1:776.
42. Hillel, "Patriarchs"; see Stone, *Testament of Levi*.

were originally written in Hebrew because of alleged Hebrew idioms and awkward constructions.[43] Most today recognize Greek as the language of composition, with the Semitic features exhibiting traces of models, sources, or both,[44] though a Semitic text can be reconstructed to a date no earlier than the ninth century.[45] The Christian interpolations may date from the early second century CE, the original being composed by a Hellenized Jew.[46] But being more specific is difficult. Its affinities with the Septuagint require a date after 250 BCE. Some take the combination of prophetic, priestly, and kingly roles (T. Levi 18:2) as a reference to John Hyrcanus, pointing to a date during his reign from 137 to 107 BCE.[47] While the presence of similar testaments among the Dead Sea Scrolls has suggested an Essene origin for the Testaments of the Twelve Patriarchs,[48] this view is not widely held today. Nevertheless, proponents of this view naturally see Palestine as the place of origin. Others suggest Egypt, particularly the literary output of Alexandria, given the Testaments' alleged special interest in Joseph, as the place of origin. Kee contends Syria as the place of origin, presuming the Syrians (Seleucids) to be the ruling power at the time of the composition of the original Testaments.[49]

The provenance of the Testaments of the Twelve Patriarchs has been debated for some time.[50] It was typically thought to be a Christian work; then in the nineteenth century the view emerged of a Jewish composition with Christian interpolations. M. de Jonge championed the view of Christian authorship in an initial publication[51] and subsequent work.[52] But most scholars today view the work as a Christianized Greek expansion of a prior Jewish work. The discovery of testamentary material at Qumran has given rise to the view that the Testaments was originally an Essene text. Though few hold this view today, there remains no consensus regarding the composition history of the Testaments, except perhaps that the Christian elements cannot simply be excised by means of textual criticism. Two helpful conclusions can be drawn regarding the Christian character of the Testaments of the Twelve Patriarchs.[53]

43. Charles, *Greek Versions of the Testaments.*
44. Kee, "Testaments of the Twelve Patriarchs," 1:776.
45. Jonge et al., *Testaments of the Twelve Patriarchs,* 19, 27–29.
46. Kee, "Testaments of the Twelve Patriarchs," 1:777.
47. Charles, *Greek Versions of the Testaments,* xlii–xliii.
48. Dupont-Sommer, *Essene Writings from Qumran,* 301–5.
49. Kee, "Testaments of the Twelve Patriarchs," 1:777.
50. See Slingerland, *Testaments of the Twelve Patriarchs.*
51. Jonge, *Testaments of the Twelve Patriarchs.*
52. Jonge, *Studies on the Testaments;* Hollander and Jonge, *Testaments of the Twelve Patriarchs.*
53. Nickelsburg, *Jewish Literature,* 315.

First, these works should not be used uncritically to illustrate pre-Christian aspects of Judaism. Second, there is a place for these writings in illustrating the diversity of religious expression for historical inquiries into second-century Christianity. The impasse as to the origins and language of composition of the Testaments of the Twelve Patriarchs has caused many scholars to direct attention instead to the themes and motifs of the work in its present form.[54] The most complete and accessible source for current study of the Testaments of the Twelve Patriarchs is that of Robert A. Kugler.[55]

Testament of Naphtali

Introduction

Only the autobiographical material of Naphtali remains in the fragmentary Testament of Naphtali (4Q215), with no moral exhortation or prophetic word to round out the features typical of a testament. The document recounts the narrative of the birth of Naphtali (Gen. 30:7–8), the fifth son of Jacob, born to Jacob and Bilhah—one of the two handmaidens, along with Zilpah, of Jacob's wives, Rachel and Leah (Gen. 29–30).[56]

Contents

This brief and fragmentary but sequential text recounts the affairs of Naphtali's mother, Bilhah (4Q215 1–3 1) and her birth to her mother Hannah (lines 2–5).[57] Then it explains how Rachel bore no children and asked that her maidservant, Bilhah, bear children for her (lines 6–8). And so Bilhah bore for Jacob first Dan and then Naphtali (lines 9–10).[58] This text names the maids Zilpah and Bilhah as sisters, and Bilhah's father as 'Ahiyot, brother of Deborah, the nurse of Rebecca (Gen. 35:8).[59]

Text and Provenance

The Testament of Naphtali is preserved in three fragments (4Q215 1–3) written in eleven lines in Hebrew from the late Hasmonean[60] or Herodian

54. Hillel, "Patriarchs." See also deSilva, "Testaments of the Twelve Patriarchs."
55. Kugler, *Testaments of the Twelve Patriarchs.*
56. Wise, Abegg, and Cook, *Dead Sea Scrolls,* 314–15.
57. See Stone, "Genealogy of Bilhah."
58. Wise, Abegg, and Cook, *Dead Sea Scrolls,* 314–15.
59. Stone, "Naphtali, Testament of (4Q215)."
60. Kugler, "Naphtali, Testament of," 2:603.

period, copied no later than the latter part of the first century BCE.[61] The Testament of Naphtali is also the name given to a portion of the Testaments of the Twelve Patriarchs (see above). Like the rest of the latter work, the provenance and date of the version found in the Testaments of the Twelve Patriarchs are debated, ranging from Jewish authorship from 200 BCE to Christian authorship as late as 200 CE. Furthermore, although the version of the Testament of Naphtali found in the Testaments of the Twelve Patriarchs is extant in Hebrew and Greek, the relationship is likewise debated.[62] The fragments of 4Q215 were initially identified as a Hebrew version of the Testament of Naphtali because a portion of the text (frag. 1, lines 2–5) resembled the Greek Testament of Naphtali (1:6–12) in its treatment of the birth of Bilhah, Naphtali's mother.[63] Kugler, however, explains that these fragments lack the narrative framework of a testament and exhibit no parallels otherwise with the Greek Testament of Naphtali.[64] Instead, Kugler suggests they provide additional information pertaining to Bilhah,[65] but he leaves the question as to the interest in an otherwise obscure figure of Naphtali unanswered.[66] Finally, Kugler considers it best to regard 4Q215 as a potential source for the Greek Testament of Naphtali and the Hebrew Testament of Naphtali, and to regard it as among the Qumran sect's collection of documents written in the name of ancient biblical figures.[67]

Dead Sea Scrolls

Other fragmentary works from the Dead Sea Scrolls have been suggested as "testaments," including the Testament of Jacob (4Q537), the Testament of Judah (3Q7, 4Q484, 4Q438), and the Testament of Joseph (4Q539).[68] First, 4Q537 is an Aramaic text in three fragments often designated a "testament" (e.g., 4QTestament of Jacob? ar). It seems to present a vision of Jacob dealing with apocalyptic and priestly matters, with no evidence of features characteristic of a testament.[69] The so-called Testament of Judah is made up of three

61. Stone, "Naphtali, Testament of (4Q215)."

62. See Jonge, *Testaments of the Twelve Patriarchs*, 52–60; Korteweg, "Meaning of Naphtali's Visions."

63. Milik ("Écrits préésséniens de Qumrân") describes 4Q215 as a Hebrew Testament of Naphtali.

64. Kugler, "Naphtali, Testament of," 2:603.

65. Cf. Stone, "4Q215."

66. Kugler, "Naphtali, Testament of," 2:603. See also Stone, "Why Naphtali?"

67. Kugler, "Naphtali, Testament of," 2:603.

68. Hillel, "Testaments."

69. Kugler, "Testaments," 2:935.

texts. First, 3Q7 is a fragmentary Hebrew text with a list of tribes and mention of "the Angel of the Presence" that together resemble the Testament of Judah (25:1–2). Second, 4Q484 is composed of twenty small fragments, two of which (frags. 1, 7) may relate to the Testament of Judah (25:1–2). Third, 4Q538, which consists of two Aramaic fragments, was once thought to correspond to the Testament of Judah (12:11–12).[70] A text sometimes called the Apocryphon of Joseph (4Q539) was once identified as a version of the Testament of Joseph,[71] though that identification may be questionable.[72]

70. Milik, "Écrits préesséniens de Qumrân," 97–98. Milik saw the work corresponding to the second trip by Jacob's sons to Egypt and Joseph (cf. Gen. 44:1–45:10; Jub. 42:25–43:18).
71. Milik, "Écrits préesséniens de Qumrân," 101–2. He identifies T. Jos. 14:4–5 with frag. 1 and T. Jos. 15:1–17:2 with frag. 2.
72. Kugler, "Testaments," 2:935.

Legends
and Expansions
of Biblical Traditions

A variety of narrative texts relating in various ways to the Hebrew Bible were
written and preserved among Jews of the Second Temple period. However,
defining a single genre to which they belong fails to deal adequately with the
nature of the respective documents. To a large extent they are narratives that
do not simply intend to narrate. In his introduction to many of these writings,
James H. Charlesworth calls them "expansions of the 'Old Testament' and
legends,"[1] explaining that early Judaism "was a religion bound to and defined
by the Book, the Torah," and that the "biblical narratives were clarified, en-
riched, expanded, and sometimes retold from a different perspective."[2] And
this aptly describes many of these writings, though Charlesworth goes on to
explain how some, like the Letter of Aristeas, are not about a biblical narrative

1. Charlesworth, "Expansions of the 'Old Testament,'" 2:5.
2. Charlesworth, "Expansions of the 'Old Testament,'" 2:5. The exception, he notes, is the
Letter of Aristeas.

223

at all but about the Greek translation (Septuagint) of the Hebrew Scriptures, while others, like the book of Jubilees, though containing narrative elements, are also clearly related to apocalyptic writings.[3] Daniel J. Harrington employs a general approach for his use of the term "rewritten Bible," identifying this literature as "those products of Palestinian Judaism at the turn of the era that take as their literary framework the flow of the biblical text itself and apparently have as their major purpose the clarification and actualization of the biblical story."[4] For his part, George W. E. Nickelsburg categorizes such writings generally as "stories of biblical and early post-biblical times,"[5] noting the commonality of narrative literature related to situations and characters known from Israelite history. Some expand, paraphrase, and implicitly comment on biblical texts. Like Charlesworth, Nickelsburg notes the ambiguity, stating that these "narrative writings do not admit of easy classification, and some of them could, with good reason, have been grouped with [other genres of] texts."[6] Some have regarded these works as "parabiblical," which constitute the largest category of the Dead Sea Scrolls.[7] However, many would object to the use of the term "biblical" at this time, since it is often held among scholars that the notion of a fixed and complete "canon" of unique, clearly defined, and authoritative texts was not in place during the Second Temple period. For his part Daniel K. Falk uses the term "parascriptural," which, in his view, serves "as an umbrella term for a broad class of texts that in various ways extend the authority of Scripture by imitation and interpretation."[8]

With such cautions in mind, we proceed with both writings that are narrative and those that are not. While the genres may defy simple categorization, all are in some way or another, as Nickelsburg says, "loosely connected with biblical traditions about Israel's past."[9] Or, as Falk puts it, they "in various ways extend the Scriptures in terms of content, meaning and/or application."[10] For each of these works, matters pertaining to genre will be addressed on an individual basis, as suits the diversity of texts here addressed. However, there is one kind of literature that is more particularly identifiable within this wide swath of writings, often called "rewritten scripture." Here Nickelsburg uses the nomenclature of "the Bible rewritten and expanded," which he says relates to literature expanding and paraphrasing biblical texts and implicitly com-

---

3. Charlesworth, "Expansions of the 'Old Testament,'" 2:5.
4. Harrington, "Bible Rewritten (Narratives)," 239.
5. Nickelsburg, "Stories," 33.
6. Nickelsburg, "Stories," 33.
7. Falk, *Parabiblical Texts*, 1.
8. Falk, *Parabiblical Texts*, 7.
9. Nickelsburg, "Stories," 33.
10. Falk, *Parabiblical Texts*, 1.

menting on them, and he includes in this category such works as 1 Enoch, the Book of Giants, Jubilees, and the Genesis Apocryphon, among others.[11] More recent scholarship has advanced understanding of the phenomena involved.

In an important recent essay on the subject with respect to the Dead Sea Scrolls, Molly M. Zahn explains that the term "rewritten scripture" is typically used "to denote a group of texts which reproduce substantial portions of one or more biblical books, but modify the scriptural text by means of addition, omission, paraphrase, rearrangement, or other types of changes."[12] Scholarly debate continues regarding a terminology suitable for expressing the conceptual models that account for the development, interpretation, and status of biblical texts.[13] From the Dead Sea Scrolls, Zahn discusses four key texts usually seen as paradigmatically representing rewritten scripture—Jubilees, the Genesis Apocryphon, the Temple Scroll, and the Reworked Pentateuch (4QRP, composed of five manuscripts). She notes the problematic overlaps between expanded and revised copies of biblical books, including translations, on the one hand and the body of Jewish literature that builds on themes or expands on stories of biblical narratives on the other, which necessarily complicates a clear delineation of this kind of literature.[14] In other words, how does one distinguish, particularly among the Dead Sea Scrolls, between a copy of a biblical book that may include some variation from other extant traditions[15] and a document in which an author deliberately adds, rearranges, or paraphrases a text so as to create or elucidate a distinct meaning? Some have sought to alleviate the problem by categorizing texts not according to the genre of their final form but according to the procedural manner in which they were composed.[16] Here is not the place to pursue these complex issues, except to note that Zahn and others have observed that the flexibility of genre theory offers a helpful way forward.[17] It is also debated to what degree a rewritten text is regarded as authoritative. Though cases may vary, Zahn cites the example of the books of Chronicles, which she regards as a form of rewritten scripture based on the books of Samuel and Kings, and yet they are

11. Nickelsburg, "Bible Rewritten and Expanded," 89.

12. Zahn, "Rewritten Scripture," 323. The expression "rewritten Bible" was coined in 1961 by Geza Vermes (*Scripture and Tradition in Judaism*, 95), who describes this material as the insertion of "haggadic development into the biblical narrative" to resolve interpretive questions raised by the text.

13. Zahn, "Rewritten Scripture," 324.

14. Zahn, "Rewritten Scripture," 326.

15. See, e.g., Ulrich, *Dead Sea Scrolls*, 23–33.

16. Harrington, "Bible Rewritten (Narratives)," 243; Brooke, "Rewritten Bible," 2:780; Falk, *Parabiblical Texts*, 17.

17. See most helpfully Zahn, "Rewritten Scripture," 326–30.

preserved as canonical.[18] Another problem with the phenomena of rewritten scripture is the relation of the rewritten text to that which it rewrites. Whether it replaces or merely supplements is the subject of considerable discussion.[19] Sidnie White Crawford notes that with respect to the book of Jeremiah, which has a version found in the Septuagint as well as among the Qumran manuscripts, there is evidence that scribes are not creating new compositions but "rework[ing] the existing tradition into a new, perhaps updated, edition."[20]

Crawford's work is expansive and distinct in several respects. First, she contends that a "rewritten scripture" is first of all an exegetical work that can be distinguished from other exegetical works.[21] Building on the work of other scholars,[22] Crawford contends that rewritten scriptures constitute a distinct category or group of writings that "are characterized by a close adherence to a recognizable and already authoritative base text (narrative or legal) and a recognizable degree of scribal intervention into that base text for the purpose of exegesis."[23] She also suggests that the rewritten texts often—though not always—make a claim to an authority equal to that of its base text, though not all receiving communities would accept this claim.[24] The breadth of this definition compels Crawford to introduce the concept of a four-tiered "spectrum of texts." At one end are texts that are recognizably authoritative across groups and use nothing from outside the existing base text. Next are rewritten texts whose scribal interventions do incorporate material outside the base text but without the intention of creating new compositions (e.g., 4QRP). Third in Crawford's spectrum are texts that exhibit such extensive scribal manipulation of the base text that they create recognizably new works (e.g., Jubilees and the Temple Scroll). Finally, at the opposite end of her spectrum, Crawford places works with a recognizable authoritative base text reworked using a variety of techniques of inner-scriptural exegesis but without claiming the authority of the base text (e.g., Genesis Apocryphon). Helpfully, Crawford explains a kind of literature that she regards as beyond the spectrum

18. Zahn, "Rewritten Scripture," 329. Michael Fishbane calls this type of interpretive rewriting "inner biblical exegesis." See Fishbane, *Biblical Interpretation in Ancient Israel*; Fishbane, "Inner Biblical Exegesis."

19. Zahn, "Rewritten Scripture," 331; Brooke, "Temple Scroll," 41–42; Levinson, *Deuteronomy and the Hermeneutics of Legal Innovation*; Najman, *Seconding Sinai*, 46–50; Stackert, *Rewriting the Torah*, 211–24.

20. Crawford, *Rewriting Scripture*, 4, citing the further discussion in Ulrich, *Dead Sea Scrolls*, 34–120.

21. Crawford, *Rewriting Scripture*, 9.

22. Alexander, "Retelling the Old Testament," 116–18; Bernstein, "'Rewritten Bible'"; Brooke, "Rewritten Bible," 2:777; Tov, "Rewritten Bible Compositions," 334.

23. Crawford, *Rewriting Scripture*, 12–13.

24. Crawford, *Rewriting Scripture*, 13.

of rewritten scripture but that nonetheless has a place in our discussion for this volume. These are works that use a passage, event, or character from a scriptural work as a jumping-off point to create a new narrative or work. For these she uses the term "parabiblical" and includes writings such as the Life of Adam and Eve as well as Joseph and Aseneth.[25] While the categories of literature—"rewritten scripture"[26] or "parabiblical"—may be allusive, the identification of which texts to discuss will follow our familiar pattern. Again, we will follow our familiar rubric of texts that are demonstrably Jewish from the Second Temple period and allocate those that are marginal to a brief discussion at the end of this section.

---

25. Crawford, *Rewriting Scripture*, 14.

26. Typically, the works considered "rewritten scripture" are limited to a few—the Book of Jubilees, the Genesis Apocryphon, and Pseudo-Philo's Biblical Antiquities—though some scholars include other writings in this category. Harrington ("Bible Rewritten [Narratives]," 239) also includes the Qumran Temple Scroll (11QTemple), Josephus's *Jewish Antiquities*, and, secondarily, Paralipomena of Jeremiah, Life of Adam and Eve/Apocalypse of Moses, and Ascension of Isaiah.

13

Jubilees

Introduction

The book of Jubilees is largely a retelling of the biblical book of Genesis and early parts of Exodus (chaps. 1–24). It is valued for its exhibition of biblical interpretation and was preserved at Qumran in twelve (fragmentary) manuscripts. Some scholars contend that it may be the most important and influential book written by Jews prior to the turn of the era.[1] It claims to have been dictated to Moses on Mount Sinai by the "Angel of the Presence" (Jub. 1:29; 2:1) alongside the law at his first ascent up the mountain (Exod. 24:12–18). After the introductory scene (Jub. 1), the remainder of the book constitutes the content of the revelation (chaps. 2–50). The repeated interpositions by the angel (e.g., 2:1, 26; 6:13, 20, 32, 38; 23:32; 30:11; 33:18) remind the reader throughout that the message is related through the angel by God himself.[2]

The book of Jubilees is typically regarded as a classic example of "rewritten scripture" in its recasting of the biblical narrative. However, it also answers many questions about those accounts, such as how humanity developed if Adam and Eve only had sons, when God chose Israel, where Abraham was when first spoken to by God, and why Levi was chosen for the priesthood in Israel. All of this is couched in an exhortation to the author's strict interpretation of the law.[3] The narrative generally follows the order of the biblical text,

1. Kugel, "Book of Jubilees," 272.
2. VanderKam, *Jubilees*, 1:1.
3. Kugel, "Book of Jubilees," 272.

sometimes reproducing the text verbatim, at other times omitting segments,[4] condensing stories,[5] explaining,[6] supplementing,[7] or entirely recasting biblical episodes,[8] but typically recasting the narrative or making additions to it in light of the author's own interests.[9] Its most distinctive characteristic is its chronological framework, including numbered months, 364-day years, seven-year periods ("weeks of years"), and units of seven seven-year periods (forty-nine years) called "jubilees." The entire book of Jubilees traces biblical history from creation until the entry into the promised land as fifty jubilees (2,450 years).[10] Jubilees is a massive document, taking up nearly fifty-five thousand words in its English translation (*OTP*). By way of comparison, the biblical text on which it is based uses approximately forty-nine thousand words in its English translation (ESV).

Language and Manuscripts

It is widely recognized that the book of Jubilees was originally composed in Hebrew, from which it was translated into Greek and from Greek into Ethiopic and Latin. A Syriac translation may have been made from either Hebrew or Greek.[11] The full text of the book, however, is preserved only in Ethiopic.[12]

The discovery of manuscripts of Jubilees at Qumran[13] confirms Hebrew as the original language of the work. Fourteen manuscripts were found among the discoveries between 1947 and 1956, in Caves 1, 2, 3, 4, and 11. The Qumran manuscripts, their contents, and their dates appear in table 13.1.[14] The date of

4. E.g., Gen. 12:11–15a, 18–19a at Jub. 13:12; Gen. 13:5–10 at Jub. 13:17; Gen. 20 at Jub. 16:10; Nickelsburg, "Bible Rewritten and Expanded," 97.

5. E.g., the plagues on Pharaoh: Exod. 7–10 = Jub. 48:4–11; Wintermute, "Jubilees," 2:35.

6. E.g., Reuben's apparent incest: Gen. 35:22 = Jub. 33:2–20; Wintermute, "Jubilees," 2:35.

7. E.g., tales of Abraham's youth: Jub. 12:1–8, 12–14, 16–21, 25–27; Wintermute, "Jubilees," 2:35.

8. E.g., Isaac's covenant with Abimelech: Gen. 26:23–33 = Jub. 24:21–33; Wintermute, "Jubilees," 2:35.

9. Nickelsburg, "Bible Rewritten and Expanded," 97n35.

10. VanderKam, *Jubilees*, 1:1.

11. Nickelsburg, *Jewish Literature*, 74; van Ruiten, "Jubilees, Book of"; VanderKam, *Jubilees*, 1:1.

12. Nickelsburg, "Bible Rewritten and Expanded," 104.

13. See VanderKam, "Manuscript Tradition of Jubilees." See also Stökl, "List of the Extant Hebrew Text," 97–124.

14. The date designations are adapted from Cross, "Development of the Jewish Scripts." On 1Q17 and 1Q18, see Milik, "Livre des Jubilés," pl. XVI; for 2Q20 see Baillet, "Livre des Jubilés (i, ii)," pl. XV; for 3Q5 see Baillet, "Une prophétie apocryphe," pl. XVIII; Baillet, "Remarques sur le manuscrit du Livre des Jubiles"; for 4Q176 see Allegro, "*Tanḥûmîm*"; Kister, "Newly-Identified Fragments"; for 4Q223–224 see "4QJubilees^a" and "4QJubilees^c" in VanderKam and

Hebrew manuscripts from Qumran is determined by the handwriting, or paleography, classified in terms of Hasmonean and Herodian eras (see table 13.1).

Table 13.1
Qumran Manuscripts of the Book of Jubilees

1Q17	ca. 30–1 BCE	Jub. 27:19–20
1Q18	ca. 50–25 BCE	Jub. 35:8–10
2Q19	ca. 20–50 CE	Jub. 23:7–8
2Q20	first century CE	Jub. 46:1–3
3Q5 3, 1	first century CE	Jub. 23:6–7, 12–13
4Q176 19–21	ca. 20–50 CE	Jub. 23:21–23, 30–31
4Q216	ca. 125–100 BCE / 50 BCE	Prologue; Jub. 1:1–2, 4–7, 7–15, 26–28; 2:1–4, 7–12, 13–24
4Q218	ca. 30–1 BCE	Jub. 2:26–27
4Q219	ca. 50–25 BCE	Jub. 21:1–2, 7–10, 12–16; 21:18–22:1
4Q220	ca. 30–1 BCE	Jub. 21:5–10
4Q221	ca. 50–1 BCE	Jub. 21:22–24; 22:22, 30(?); 23:10–13; 33:12–15; 37:11–15; 38:6–8; 39:4–9
4Q222	ca. 50–25 BCE	Jub. 25:9–12; 27:6–7; 48:5(?)
4Q223–224	ca. 50–25 BCE	Jub. 32:18–21; 34:4–5; 35:7–22; 36:7–23; 37:17–38:13; 39:9–40:7; 41:7–10; 41:28(?)
11Q12	ca 50 CE	Jub. 4:6–11, 13–14, 16–18(?), 29–31; 5:1–2; 12:15–17, 28–29

Though no Greek manuscripts of Jubilees are extant, it is certain that one
existed. First, it is widely held that both the Latin and the Ethiopic text are translations of a Greek *Vorlage*. Second, fragmentary quotations and summaries of
Jubilees are found in other Greek works. A Greek text from the fourth century
CE (Oxyrhynchus Papyrus 4365) refers to Jubilees as "The Little Genesis" (τὴν
λεπτὴν Γένεσιν, *tēn leptēn Genesin*).[15] Epiphanius of Salamis (ca. 315–403 CE)
used Jubilees in two of his writings, the *Panarion* (ca. 375 CE) and *Measures and
Weights* (392 CE).[16] In the former, he mentions Jubilees by name in reference to
texts in Jubilees (Jub. 4:9–11, 15, 16, 27, 28, 33) regarding Seth to refute a Sethian
view of the origin and nature of Seth.[17] In the latter text, preserved in both Greek
and Syriac, Epiphanias cites Jubilees 2 (though not by name) for its articulation

Milik, "Jubilees," 1–22, 35–140 (pls. I–II, IV–IX); for 11Q12 see Tigchelaar and van der Woude,
"11QJubilees," pl. XXVI.

15. See Franklin, "Note on a Pseudepigraphical Allusion."
16. Van Ruiten, "Jubilees, Book of."
17. VanderKam, *Jubilees*, 1:11; Reed, "Retelling Biblical Retellings," 304–21.

of a biblical unit of measurement. Also, a series of Christian Greek expositions on Genesis, called Catenae, string together a number of allusions to Jubilees.

Jubilees was translated into Latin, about one-third of which is preserved in a fifth or sixth-century palimpsest alongside the Assumption of Moses (Ambrosiana C 73 Inf.) and published in 1861 by A. M. Ceriani.[18] This places the Latin text about one thousand years earlier than the extant Ethiopic text, and despite its corruptions, the Latin text has been used to emend and clarify the Ethiopic text.[19]

The book of Jubilees is preserved in full in more than forty-seven copies in Ethiopic (Ge'ez),[20] dating from the fourteenth to the twentieth century. Though it was translated from the Greek, which itself was translated from the original Hebrew, careful comparison of the Ethiopic manuscripts with the Qumran fragments exhibits a "very close correspondence between the Hebrew and Ge'ez readings,"[21] suggesting the complete text in Ethiopic is a "very accurate" form with respect to the original.[22]

As with the Greek, there is no extant manuscript of Jubilees in Syriac. Unlike the Greek, however, it is unclear whether there ever was such a text. Some have held to its existence because Jubilees is cited in Syriac sources. These include a Syriac manuscript (BM Additional 12.154), which draws from Jubilees for a list of the names of the wives of the patriarchs, and a Syriac chronicle of the world that cites perhaps as many as seventeen units of Jubilees.[23] However, there is insufficient data to determine whether there was a Syriac text of Jubilees, and so it is typically thought that Syriac authors drew from Greek texts.[24]

It is evident from the traditions in which the book is mentioned that it came to be known by a few titles, including Jubilees (ܝܘܒܠܡ, *yublēm*, or ܝܘܒܠܬ, *yublāt*, in Syriac; οἱ ἰωβηλαιοι, *hoi iōbēlaioi*, in Greek), the Little Genesis (τὴν λεπτὴν Γενεσιν, *tēn leptēn Genesin*, in Greek), and the Book of the Divisions of the Times (Hebrew [CD-A XVI, 3–4]; Ge'ez).

Provenance

The exact provenance of the book of Jubilees is unclear. However, its preservation among the Dead Sea Scrolls, citation as an authoritative text (CD-A

18. Ceriani, "Fragmenta Parvae Genesis."
19. Wintermute, "Jubilees," 2:42.
20. VanderKam's earlier 1989 edition collated only twenty-seven. Since then more than twenty more have surfaced. VanderKam, *Book of Jubilees: A Critical Text*.
21. VanderKam, *Jubilees*, 1:15–16; cf. VanderKam, *Textual and Historical Studies*, 1–95.
22. VanderKam, *Jubilees*, 1:16.
23. Tisserant, "Fragments syriaques due Livre des Jubilés."
24. VanderKam, *Jubilees*, 1:10.

XVI, 3–4), shared interests in priestly concerns, and similar religious ideas indicate a close affinity with the Qumran sectarians.[25] However, the book is too early to have been written at Qumran, and there are differences between Jubilees and the Qumran sectarian texts. It may be that the Qumran sect was simply an heir of the book of Jubilees, though the historical relationships between the author (or authors) of Jubilees and the Qumran sectarians are now obscure. Regardless, the Palestinian Jewish provenance seems clear, as its composition in Hebrew alone suggests.[26]

The author's report that Abraham had to learn Hebrew, which was essential for the study of sacred books (Jub. 12:25–27), may imply that not all within his readership knew Hebrew as a first language. Other affirmations may be found as well, such as his praise for the land from Jordan to the sea (10:29), the holiness of Jerusalem (1:28), and the identification of Zion as the navel of the earth (8:19). The author also shows his geographical familiarity with the region of Canaan from the Jordan to the Mediterranean (10:29), including detailed knowledge of many cities and towns in the area.[27]

In most scholars' view, the style and outlook of the book indicate a uniformity that points to a single author.[28] A few have argued that in its present form the work is the product of multiple authors,[29] arguing for eschatological expansions to an original text,[30] suggesting that later interpolations were inserted to correct the earlier version,[31] or theorizing that to an original document were added legal sections that were then shaped into the present chronological framework.[32] Jacques T. A. G. M. van Ruiten concedes the possibility of the evolution and growth of the document but also indicates that inconsistencies and contradictions in the document, often taken as the starting point for identifying redactional layers, do not necessarily indicate multiple authors.[33]

The work is of course anonymous, so interpreters are left to derive characteristics of the author on the basis of what can be known of him from the contents and emphases of the book. There are three primary traits.[34]

25. Nickelsburg, *Jewish Literature*, 74.

26. Wintermute, "Jubilees," 2:45.

27. Wintermute, "Jubilees," 2:45.

28. Van Ruiten, "Jubilees, Book of."

29. Michael Segal, *Book of Jubilees*, 35.

30. Davenport, *Eschatology*.

31. Testuz, *Les idées religieuses*; Kugel, *Walk through "Jubilees."*

32. Michael Segal, *Book of Jubilees*.

33. Van Ruiten, "Jubilees, Book of." For a complete and recent survey of the differing theories, see VanderKam, *Jubilees*, 1:25–28.

34. VanderKam, *Jubilees*, 1:38.

The author is, first, a learned student of Israel's ancient literary traditions,[35] which he knows well and interprets in light of other scriptural texts. Yet he also exhibits a degree of boldness in his presumption to—in varying degrees and in different ways—modify the ancient text, perhaps seeing himself as "setting forth the real message of Genesis-Exodus."[36] Second, the author holds strongly to the joining of God and Israel in an unbreakable covenant, establishing Israel as distinct among the nations, from which they are to keep themselves separate. And yet Israel could face the same destructive fate of the nations for failure to obey the laws of the covenant. Third and finally, the author holds the priesthood in high regard. This can be seen from the author's handling of the text of Genesis, where key figures—Adam, Enoch, Noah, Abraham, Isaac, Jacob, and Levi—all take on a priestly function. Levi himself, though generally presented in a negative light in Genesis (e.g., Gen. 49:5–7), is "rehabilitated" in Jubilees (cf. Mal. 2:4–7), where he is generally praised and affirmed in his priestly office (e.g., Jub. 30:17–20; 31:13–17; 32:1–9; 45:16).[37] This has led many scholars to view the author as a member of the clergy, likely a priest (cf. Jub. 30:18; 32:1, 3, 9).[38] Some have sought to adduce evidence to be even more specific, such as identifying the author as an Essene,[39] though even if the author were an Essene, he would have belonged to the sect prior to its settlement at Qumran. Nevertheless, it seems clear that the author and the Jews at Qumran shared some beliefs and likely belonged to a similar tradition.[40] Wintermute asserts that the author was "part of a zealous, conservative, pious segment of Judaism which was bound together by its own set of traditions, expectations, and practices."[41] Finding a proliferation of such groups during the Maccabean era (e.g., 1 Macc. 2:29–42) suggests to him that the author of Jubilees belonged to either the Hasidim or the Essenes.

More particularly, the legal perspective of the author has been the subject of some discussion. Notably, his legal material differs widely from Pharisaic and subsequent rabbinic traditions,[42] suggesting to some that he was a figure from outside Pharisaism. Opinions here are diverse, with some suggesting

---

35. Kugel ("Jubilees," 272) believes it was composed in Hebrew by a learned Jew who likely lived in the environs of Jerusalem.

36. VanderKam, Jubilees, 1:38.

37. VanderKam, Jubilees, 1:38.

38. VanderKam, Jubilees, 1:38–39; Charles, Book of Jubilees, lxxiii.

39. Jellinek, Bet ha-Midrasch, 3:xi.

40. VanderKam, Jubilees, 1:39.

41. Wintermute, "Jubilees," 2:45.

42. Nevertheless, some scholars, such as Charles (Book of Jubilees, lxxiii), still contend he was a strict Pharisee.

he was a part of the Dositheans, a Samaritan sect in Egypt.[43] Others argue
that he was a priest in the Jewish temple at Leontopolis, Egypt.[44] Still others,
surprisingly, suggest he was a Pharisee or some undesignated sectarian group.[45]
Since the discovery of the Dead Sea Scrolls, however, it has become evident
that the author of Jubilees "belongs in the same stream of legal thinking,
most likely as a predecessor to the scrolls literature."[46]

Date

Jubilees' attestation at Qumran reveals fragments dating from the last quarter
of the second century BCE, requiring a date of composition before then.[47]
Most scholars believe Jubilees was written early in the second century BCE,
perhaps earlier. Prior to evidence discovered among the Dead Sea Scrolls,
scholars dated Jubilees as early as the fifth century BCE and as late as the
first century CE.[48] A fixed point by which Jubilees can be dated can be found
in the Jubilees material among the Dead Sea Scrolls (4Q216 V–VII), which,
since it dates from 125–100 BCE,[49] requires a date of composition prior to
then. And so most scholars recognize it was written sometime in the second
century BCE. Debate today pertains to Jubilees' location early or late in
that century.

Some argue for an early second-century date, suggesting that the command
for all humanity to cover themselves (Jub. 7:20; cf. 3:31) corresponds to the
introduction of the gymnasium in Jerusalem, in which youth participated
naked according to a Greek custom introduced by the hellenizing program
of the high priest Jason (175 BCE; cf. 1 Macc. 1, 14; 2 Macc. 4, 11).[50] This
view also sees the reference to the "sinful nations" and an "evil generation"
(Jub. 23:14–32) corresponding to the sacking of Jerusalem by Antiochus IV
Epiphanes (169 BCE).[51] These and other factors that seem to correspond to
events leading up to the Maccabean crisis, suggest an authorship between
175 and 167 BCE.[52]

43. Beer, *Das Buch der Jubiläen*, 56–80; Beer, "Noch ein Wort."
44. Frankel, "Das Buch der Jubilaen."
45. Albeck, *Das Buch der Jubiläen*.
46. VanderKam, *Jubilees*, 1:83.
47. Kugel, "Jubilees," 272.
48. VanderKam, *Jubilees*, 1:25.
49. VanderKam and Milik, "Jubilees," 2–3.
50. Cf. Finkelstein, "Pre-Maccabean Documents."
51. Finkelstein, "Pre-Maccabean Documents," 24; Goldstein, "Date of the Book of Jubilees."
52. Cf. Finkelstein, "Pre-Maccabean Documents." VanderKam (*Jubilees*, 1:33) is less convinced that the text points to the pre-Maccabean events with such clarity.

Others argue for a date in the mid-second century BCE, seeing the decree by Antiochus IV Epiphanes (167 BCE) as the upper limit, and seeing evidence of the Maccabean revolt in Jubilees 23 and in the wars of Israel against the Amorites and Edomites (Jub. 34, 37–38),[53] though these identifications are tenuous.[54] Similarly, scholars have looked to datable texts to which Jubilees refers, or that cite Jubilees, as a means of dating the book of Jubilees, but the only certain one comes from the citation of Jubilees in the Damascus Document (CD-A XVI, 3–4), which dates to the first half or middle of the first century BCE[55] and so adds no information not already obtained by the dating of 4Q216.[56]

Finally, some scholars contend for a date in the last third of the second century BCE, the most important being Cana Werman.[57] This date is based first on a rather general observation of the hellenizing practices under John Hyrcanus (134–104 BCE) that would facilitate the kinds of literature with which Jubilees is familiar. Furthermore, Werman suggests the author of Jubilees was familiar with issues contemporary with the Hasmonean rulers and writes against it. This, however, provides rather general and thin evidence on which to establish a date for Jubilees.[58] James C. VanderKam cautiously concludes that evidence enables us to date Jubilees with confidence sometime between the 170s and 125 BCE.[59]

Contents

In its title the book of Jubilees describes itself as an account of the division of days as the Lord gave Moses on Sinai. The first chapter sets the scene for the entire book. The narrative begins in the first year of the exodus from Egypt, when Moses is summoned up Mount Sinai, where he stays forty days and nights (Jub. 1:1–4a). There the Lord reveals to Moses the past and the future, the account of the division of all days "of the Law and the testimony" (1:4b). Moses is instructed to write in a book what God tells him for his descendants as witness that God has not abandoned them (1:5–6). First Moses is told that Israel will enter the promised land but nonetheless will turn to foreign gods and abandon the commandments of God (1:7–11). Then God will send

---

53. E.g., Charles, *Book of Jubilees*, lxii–lxiii; Mendels, *Land of Israel*, 57–88.
54. VanderKam, *Jubilees*, 1:34.
55. Yardeni, "4QDamascus Document," 26.
56. VanderKam, *Jubilees*, 1:35.
57. Werman, *Book of Jubilees*.
58. So also VanderKam, *Jubilees*, 1:35.
59. VanderKam, *Jubilees*, 1:37–38.

witnesses whom Israel will reject and murder, and so Israel will be cast into captivity, during which they will be removed from the land and forget God's ordinances (1:12–14). God then promises that when Israel repents, they will be restored and their sanctuary rebuilt (1:15–18). Moses prays that Israel will not be ensnared by their sin and pleads for God's mercy (1:19–21), and the Lord predicts their restoration (1:22–25). God tells Moses to write all that he will be told on the mountain from beginning to end (1:26) and tells the angel to write, or perhaps "dictate,"[60] the history for Moses (1:27–28). This angel, identified as the one that accompanied Israel from Egypt (cf. Exod. 14:19), takes the tablets that tell of the divisions of years from the time of creation to the time of the new creation (Jub. 1:29; cf. Isa. 65:17; 66:22).

Chapters 2–4 pertain to the creation accounts and stories pertaining to Adam, beginning with a recounting of the six days of creation (Jub. 2:1–16) and culminating in the Sabbath and a detailed explanation of its significance (2:17–24) and regulations (2:25–33). Then comes the naming of animals (3:1–3; cf. Gen. 2:18–20a) and the creation of Eve (Jub. 3:4–7; cf. Gen. 2:20b–25), which is followed by a protracted teaching on the purification of women after childbirth (Jub. 3:8–14). Adam and Eve care for the garden for the first week of the first jubilee—seven years (3:15–16). In Jubilees' account of the fall (3:17–25; cf. Gen. 3) and subsequent expulsion (Jub. 3:26–29), Adam offers sacrifices, the animals become mute, and God's clothing of Adam becomes the basis for a law prohibiting nudity that distinguishes humankind from animals (3:30–31). So they leave Eden and dwell in 'Elda, where Adam tills the land, but they have no son until after the first jubilee (3:32–35).

In the second jubilee Eve bears Cain, in the fourth, Abel, and in the fifth, a daughter, 'Awan (4:1). Cain kills Abel in the third jubilee over a sacrifice (4:2–4), which occasions a prohibition against murder written in the heavenly tablets (4:5–6). After a season of mourning, the narrative resumes with an account of the other descendants of Adam through the tenth jubilee, when the angels of the Lord—called Watchers—come to earth to teach the sons of man and do unrighteous deeds among them (4:7–15).

Jubilees then turns to the account of Enoch, who is born in the fourth year of the eleventh jubilee (4:16). He is among the first to learn writing and writes a book of the signs of the heaven as a testimony to all the earth; in it he recounts the days of the years and the Sabbaths according to jubilees and foresees the judgment to come (4:17–20). Enoch is with the angels of God six jubilees of years, when he is shown everything on earth, in heaven, and in the dominion of the sun, being witness to the Watchers and writing

60. Kugel, "Jubilees," 288.

everything down (4:21–22). He is taken to the garden of Eden, which, because of him, is unharmed by the flood (4:23–24). He also offers incense to the Lord at one of God's holy places on earth (4:25–26). After an account of the generations from Enoch to Noah (4:27–28), Adam dies in the nineteenth jubilee (4:29–30). At the end of that jubilee Cain is killed in retribution for his murder of Abel (4:31–32); then the birth of Noah's sons is recounted in the twenty-fifth jubilee (4:33).

Chapters 5–10 relate to Noah, beginning with the account of fallen angels mating with humans, bearing giants, and corrupting all humanity (5:1–2). The Lord pledges to send the flood to punish the angels and destroy their offspring (5:3–11). But he also promises to make a "new and righteous nature" for all his works, that they may not sin, and God will judge impartially and forgive the righteous (5:12–19). The flood comes in the twenty-second jubilee of years (5:20–32). Immediately afterward, Noah leaves the ark, builds an altar, and makes atonement for the land (6:1–3). This is followed by God's covenant with Noah, in which laws pertaining to the eating of blood are introduced (6:4–16). The covenant, written on the heavenly tablets, is to be observed as the Feast of Shebuot each year (6:17–31). Israel is also warned of the perils of failing to observe the 364-day calendar (6:32–38). Then Noah offers up burnt offerings to the Lord, offering their flesh on an altar he built and drinking wine from his own vineyard (7:1–6). When drunk and naked, Noah is seen by Ham, whose son Canaan is then cursed while Shem is blessed (7:7–19). This is followed by a testament of Noah in which he warns his progeny against fornication, blood pollution, and injustice and instructs them on regulations on reserving the firstfruits for the Lord (7:20–39). Beginning in the next chapter, the twenty-ninth jubilee, Cainan is born and comes upon a writing containing the astrological teaching of the Watchers, which he copies (8:1–4). The narrative then recounts his descendants (8:5–9) and, in the thirty-third jubilee, the allocation of the land between Shem, Ham, and Japheth (8:10–30) and their sons (9:1–15). Then Noah himself prays against the demons (10:1–6), after which nine-tenths are bound (10:7–14) before Noah finally dies (10:15–17). When people build the Tower of Babel, God mixes up their languages so they cannot understand one another, and the building ceases (10:18–26). Canaan sees that the land allotted for Shem is good, and so seizes it for himself (10:27–34), while Japheth and his sons settle in the land of their portion (10:35).

The primary attention of Jubilees then turns to Abraham (11:1–23:10). In the thirty-fifth Jubilee, Seroh (Serug) is born, and with the help of evil spirits people fight and enslave one another (11:1–6). Then Nahor is born, and the Chaldeans begin practicing divination and astrology (11:7–8). When Terah is born in the thirty-seventh Jubilee, Mastema sends crows to bring devastation on the earth (11:9–13). Abram is born in the thirty-ninth jubilee, learns to write, and begins to turn from idolatry and pray to the Creator for salvation from the strayings of people (11:14–17). Abram is able to turn the devouring crows away and save the harvest (11:18–24). He pleads with his father, Terah, to turn from idolatry and worship the God of heaven (12:1–11) before burning the house of idols (12:12–14) and departing for Haran (12:15). There he spends the whole night praying to God, asking where he is to settle (12:16–21). God speaks to him through the narrating angel and directs him to the promised land (12:22–24). Then God instructs the angel to teach Abram Hebrew, "the tongue of creation" (12:25–26). Abram copies his father's books (in Hebrew), studies them, and is given understanding of them (12:27). When Abram tells his father that he is leaving Haran for Canaan, Terah blesses him (12:28–31).

Abram leaves Haran for Shechem, where he builds an altar and offers a burnt offering to the Lord (13:1–3) before doing the same thing at Bethel (13:4–9). He spends two years at Hebron and then goes to Egypt for five years (13:10–15). He is sent by Pharaoh back to Bethel in the forty-first Jubilee, and there he offers a burnt offering, calls on the name of the Lord, and is promised a bountiful land (13:15–21). Abram then goes to Hebron, where he learns of the capture of Sodom and his nephew, Lot (13:21–25). Jubilees here inserts a law regarding the tithe (13:25–27; cf. Gen. 14:20; Lev. 27:30–33; Deut. 14:22–23), though there is no clarity as to who gave a tithe to whom and the purpose of its placement here.[61] Abram then restores booty to the king of Sodom (Jub. 13:28–29).

The Lord speaks to Abram in a dream and promises him numerous descendants (14:1–5) before instructing him to offer a sacrifice at Mamre (14:6–15). God establishes a covenant with Abram (14:17–20), who, at the age of eighty-six, fathers Ishmael by Hagar, his wife Sarai's maid (14:21–24). Nothing is said in this account, or anywhere in Jubilees, of Sarai's cruel treatment of Hagar (cf. Gen. 16:4–14). To celebrate his harvest of grain, Abram observes the Feast of Firstfruits (Jub. 15:1–4; cf. Lev. 23:18; Num. 28:27) and receives the covenant, for which his name is changed to Abraham (Jub. 15:5–10). Abraham is instructed to circumcise all his males as a sign of the eternal ordinance between himself and God (15:11–24) and receives extensive laws for circumcision (15:25–32). He is told that the sons of Israel will one day deny this ordinance and experience the wrath of God with no hope for forgiveness (15:33–34). Abraham is told he will have a son—Isaac (16:1–4)—by Sarah, and that same month Sodom is destroyed (16:5–6). The sin of Lot's daughters in sleeping

61. See Kugel, "Jubilees," 342–43.

with their father is in violation of commands engraved in the heavenly tablets (16:7–9). Isaac is born on the Feast of Firstfruits and of course circumcised according to the stipulations of the covenant (16:9–14). Next Abraham has a theophany, not found in the Hebrew Bible, in which angels instruct him on what will become of Isaac (16:15–19). Furthermore, Jubilees has Abraham celebrate the Feast of Tabernacles (or Booths [Sukkoth]; 16:20–31), which does not occur in the Hebrew Bible until long after the death of Abraham (Exod. 23:14–17; 34:18, 22–24; Deut. 16:1–17).[62] Still another feast is celebrated at the weaning of Isaac (Jub. 17:1–3) before Hagar is banished (17:4–14). The circumstances behind Abraham's testing are recounted in a narrative not found in Genesis, when "Prince Mastema" requests permission to test Abraham's faithfulness (17:15–18; cf. Job 1–2). Abraham is then called by the Lord and told to offer his son Isaac on an altar (18:1–8). But, the narrating angel says, God instructs the angel not to let Abraham harm the child (18:9–11). Mastema is shamed by the obedience of Abraham, who offers a ram as an offering instead of his son, and the location is identified as Mount Zion (18:12–13). Then Abraham departs and celebrates this event as "the feast of the Lord" in accordance with what is ordained in the heavenly tablets (18:14–19). Then Sarah dies and is buried in Hebron (19:1–9), after which Isaac marries Rebecca, who bears Jacob and Esau. Jacob learns writing, whereas Esau learns warfare (19:10–14). Abraham, in his favoritism of Jacob over Esau, blesses Jacob (19:15–30) and gives his farewell testimony to all his children (20:1–13) and then privately to Isaac (21:1–26). Abraham then celebrates the Feast of Firstfruits (22:1–9) and blesses Jacob twice (22:10–30) before his own death and burial (23:1–10).

After the death of Abraham, wickedness grows and pollutes the land, and the author predicts still further decline in future generations (23:11–21). They will be punished for their sins but will ultimately repent and receive God's blessing (23:22–31). All of this Moses is to write on heavenly tablets as a testimony for future generations (23:32).

Chapters 24–29 turn to Jacob, displaying him in the highest regard and justifying Rebecca's favoritism. Conversely, Esau is depicted as a disobedient, disloyal son.[63] Isaac's family travels to the Well of the Vision and dwells there seven years, when Jacob acquires Esau's birthright (24:1–7); then Isaac travels to Gerar (24:8–13). There among the Philistines Jacob and Isaac prosper and dig wells from Gerar to Beersheba (24:14–26) before Isaac curses the Philistines with whom he is compelled to swear an oath (24:27–33). Rebecca instructs Jacob to find a wife from among her father's family (25:1–3), to which Jacob

62. Abraham dies in Gen. 25:8.
63. Wintermute, "Jubilees," 2:36.

agrees, informing his mother that Abraham gave him the same instructions. He tells his mother that he has not yet taken a wife from among other peoples but intends to marry within his father's family, as both his parents request (25:4–10). Rebecca then blesses Jacob (25:11–23). The account of Jacob gaining the blessing intended for Esau (26:1–34) follows the biblical narrative closely, to the point where Rebecca dresses Jacob in Esau's clothing in order to get the latter's blessing from their father (26:1–24; cf. Gen. 27:1–29). Then Esau comes to his father and learns of the trickery of his brother. Isaac, rather than giving Esau the blessing of the firstborn, pronounces his lot in life to live by the sword, serve his brother, "sin completely unto death," and have his seed rooted out from under heaven (26:25–34; cf. Gen. 27:30–40). Esau breathes murderous threats against his brother Jacob (26:35). Rebecca learns of this in a dream and sends Jacob to Haran and prompts Isaac to counsel the same to Jacob (27:1–12). Jacob departs and Isaac consoles Rebecca with assurances of his safety and well-being (27:13–18). Now in the forty-fourth jubilee, Jacob travels to Bethel, where he has a dream of a staircase to heaven on which angels are ascending and descending (27:19–21). The Lord promises Jacob and his seed the land on which he is then sleeping (27:21–25). When he awakens, Jacob anoints a stone pillar and vows to honor the Lord as his God (27:26–27). When Jacob marries Leah (28:1–5), Laban explains that the elder daughter is to marry before the younger, and so Jacob serves Laban for seven years for the hand of Rachel (28:6–8). Leah and Rachel, as well as Bilhah, Rachel's attendant, all bear children to Jacob (28:9–24). Jacob agrees to continue working for Laban (28:25–30) only to flee secretly to Gilead (29:1–4). When Laban at last catches up with Jacob, they swear an oath and go their separate ways (29:5–13). Then Jubilees inserts a unique account that depicts Jacob sending goods to his father and mother four times per year, whereas Esau marries an Ishmaelite, takes his father's flocks, and abandons his father (29:14–20).

Further additions are found in chapters 30–32, which first focus on Simeon and Levi and their revenge on Shechem for the rape of Dinah (30:1–6). This is followed by a law prohibiting marriage to non-Israelites (30:7–17; cf. Gen. 34:8–23; Lev. 18:21). Jubilees then announces that Levi and his seed are chosen for the priesthood because of their zeal to do righteousness and take vengeance on those who rise up against Israel (30:18–20; cf. ALD §§3–20).[64] There is a warning not to violate the covenant written in heaven on the day Israel took vengeance on Shechem (30:21–23), after which the narrative involving Shechem concludes (30:24–25). In preparation for his travels to Bethel, Jacob instructs his household to purify themselves and put away their idols, which

64. Kugel, "Jubilees," 397.

he takes and destroys (31:1–2). Jacob then visits his father and mother with his sons Levi and Judah (31:3–10, 21–25). Levi and Judah come near to their grandfather Isaac, who prophesies a blessing on Levi (31:11–17) and Judah (31:18–20, 31–32). Jacob tells Isaac about his vow to build an altar and offer a sacrifice to the Lord at Bethel (31:26). Isaac again blesses Jacob and sends Rebecca with him (31:27–30). While at Bethel, Levi dreams that he and his sons are ordained priests forever, after which he awakes and gives a tenth of all he has (32:1–2).[65] Then Jacob makes priestly garments for Levi and makes an offering to the Lord (32:3–9). This is followed by the explanation of the law of the tithe, as decreed in the heavenly tablets (32:10–15). Jacob plans to build a wall around the court and sanctify it to the Lord, but the Lord intercedes in a dream and prevents it (32:10–26). Then Jacob offers another sacrifice, which he calls the "Addition" feast day, an extension to the Feast of Tabernacles (32:27–29).[66] Rebecca's nurse, Deborah, dies (32:30), and this is followed by Rebecca's departure (32:31–32) and Rachel's death while giving birth to Benjamin (32:33–34).

Jubilees 33 is regarded as a "midrash" on Reuben's sin (Gen. 35:22),[67] in which Reuben sleeps with Bilhah, Rachel's attendant, and flees when she screams (Jub. 33:1–6). Bilhah finally tells Jacob, for whom she is rendered unclean (33:6–9). This is followed by an explanation of the laws in the heavenly tablets forbidding incest under pain of death (33:10–17). Moses is instructed to warn Israel of laws pertaining to sexual defilement (33:18–20), after which the children of Jacob appear before Isaac and are blessed by him (33:21–23).

The wars of Jacob, supplementing the biblical narrative, are found in Jubilees 34–38. First, Jacob's sons successfully defeat a coalition of Amorites (34:1–9). The account of Joseph, thought dead, being sold into slavery is highly condensed (34:10–14) and commemorated (34:18–19) and is followed by the death and burial of Bilhah and Dinah (34:15–17) and an account of the names of the wives of Jacob's sons (34:20). Rebecca then predicts her death to Jacob (35:1–8). She also implores Isaac to make Esau swear not to harm Jacob (35:9–17) and makes the same request to Esau himself (35:18–27). Isaac calls Esau and Jacob to himself and gives them parting words of advice and blessing before dying at the age of 180 (36:1–18). Esau then travels to Edom to dwell on the mountain of Seir, while Jacob goes to Mount Hermon, where he worships the Lord with all his heart (36:19–20), and then Leah dies (36:21–24). On the day Isaac dies, the sons of Esau rebuke their father for yielding to

65. The text does not say to whom he gave the tithe.
66. VanderKam, *Jubilees*, 2:893.
67. Wintermute, "Jubilees," 2:36.

Jacob (37:1–8), and so they hire mercenaries to wage war against their uncle (37:9–10). Esau's sons threaten to kill their father if he does not lead them all into battle against Jacob, but he is soon embittered with the recollection of his own fury (37:11–13). Jacob, still lamenting the death of Leah, knows nothing of the threat until it is upon him (37:14–16). Jacob withdraws to a gated tower and, with Esau outside, the two engage in dialogue in which Esau is clearly presented as the aggressor who violates his oath to do no harm to his brother (37:17–23). It is only when Jacob realizes that Esau is unmoved in his intent to kill him that he mobilizes his forces against him (37:24) and defeats him and his allies from Edom (38:1–11), reducing them to servitude (38:12–14). This is followed by a list of the kings who ruled in Edom prior to the establishment of the kingship in Israel (38:15–24).

Chapters 39–45 are the author's condensed account of the stories of Joseph (Gen. 39–50), beginning with the arrival of Joseph, at the age of seventeen, to Egypt to work in the house of Potiphar, where he is falsely accused of impropriety with Potiphar's wife (Jub. 39:1–10; cf. Gen. 39:1–23). He is imprisoned for two years, during which he interprets the dreams of two of Pharaoh's eunuchs, a chief butler and chief baker (Jub. 39:11–18; cf. Gen. 40:1–23). Joseph is summoned to Pharaoh, who also has a dream. When Joseph interprets it (Jub. 40:1–5; cf. Gen. 41:1–36), Joseph is put in charge of storing grain for a coming famine and is made the second-highest official in Egypt (Jub. 40:6–13; cf. Gen. 41:37–55). Jubilees records the account of Judah and Tamar (Jub. 41; cf. Gen. 38), beginning in the forty-fifth jubilee (Jub. 41:1–21), after which the full harvest of seven years about which Joseph told Pharaoh is completed (41:22). Judah then repents of his actions with Tamar and is told in a dream that he is forgiven because of his remorse (41:23–25a). But, the author adds, anyone who commits a sexual indiscretion like this will burn under the wrath of God (41:25b–28).

When the years of famine come, in the forty-fifth jubilee, Joseph is able to feed Egypt with the grain he stored (Jub. 42:1–3; cf. Gen. 41:56–57). The sons of Jacob also travel to Egypt for food (Jub. 42:4–8; cf. Gen. 42:1–28) and upon their return to Canaan recount their experience to their father (Jub. 42:9–12; cf. Gen. 42:29–39). When the famine in Canaan becomes more severe, the sons of Jacob return to Egypt with Benjamin (Jub. 42:13–19; cf. Gen. 43:1–14) and appear before Joseph (Jub. 42:19–21a; cf. Gen. 43:15). Joseph recognizes Benjamin, his brother, and brings his family to a banquet at his house, where they present him with gifts and eat and drink together, though Benjamin receives more than his brothers (Jub. 42:21b–24; cf. Gen. 43:16–34). Though in Genesis the portions were five times those of the brothers (Gen. 43:34), in Jubilees it is seven times (Jub. 42:23). Then Joseph tests his brothers, which,

Jubilees explains, is to determine whether their intentions are peaceful or not (Jub. 42:25). Joseph accuses the brothers of theft and instructs them to leave Benjamin and go (Jub. 43:1–13; cf. Gen. 44:1–34). But Jubilees makes no mention of Joseph's statement that he could find such things out by divination (Gen. 44:15) and instead has Joseph claim to fear the Lord and really like the cup they allegedly stole (Jub. 43:10). According to Jubilees, it is when Joseph sees that the hearts of his brothers are united with one another for good that he chooses to reveal himself to them and instructs them to bring their father to Egypt (Jub. 43:14–20; cf. Gen. 45:1–24). So the brothers return to Canaan to retrieve Jacob (Jub. 43:21–24; cf. Gen. 45:25–28). When Jacob sets out from Haran toward Egypt, he celebrates the Feast of Firstfruits at Beersheba, where the Lord appears to him and instructs him to go to Egypt without fear (Jub. 44:1–10; cf. Gen. 46:1–7). Then there is a detailed list of all the children of Jacob who came to Egypt (Jub. 44:11–34; cf. Gen. 46:8–27). Joseph greets his father, whom he settles in the land of Goshen (Jub. 45:1–7; cf. Gen. 46:28–47:12). In the severity of the famine, Joseph proves to be an able administrator, caring for all in the land (Jub. 45:8–12; cf. Gen. 47:13–26). Jacob dies in the forty-fifth jubilee, having lived in Egypt seventeen years and having lived three jubilees, and he gives the books of his fathers to his son Levi (Jub. 45:13–15; cf. Gen. 47:27–49:33).

Jubilees 46–50 primarily concerns Moses, with chapter 46 serving as a transition from the flourishing life under Joseph to the harsh slavery in Egypt; the mention of Moses's father introduces the shift of focus, and conflict between Egypt and the Canaanites accounts for the deteriorating conditions for Israel.[68] After Jacob dies, the Israelites become numerous in Egypt, and "there was no Satan or anything evil all the days of the life of Joseph," because the Egyptians honored the Israelites (46:1–2). Then Joseph and all that generation die in the forty-sixth jubilee (46:3–10). Whereas Jacob's bones are carried immediately for burial in Canaan (Gen. 50:2–5), Jubilees explains this is not possible in the case of Joseph since, by that time, war with Canaan prevented travel in and out of Egypt (Jub. 46:7; cf. Gen. 50:22–26; Exod. 1:1–7).[69] Then the king of Canaan defeats Egypt and compels the Egyptians to reduce Israel to slavery (Jub. 46:11–16; cf. Exod. 1:8–14). Moses's life is summarized briefly (Jub. 47–48), with the exodus story revised to show how Mastema tried to assist the Egyptians.[70] In the forty-seventh jubilee Moses's father comes from Canaan, and during the following jubilee Moses is born (Jub. 47:1; cf. Exod.

68. Wintermute, "Jubilees," 2:36.
69. See Kugel, "Jubilees," 439–40.
70. Wintermute, "Jubilees," 2:36.

2:1–2). When Pharaoh decrees the murder of the male Israelite children, the infant Moses is hidden and later placed among the reeds of the river (Jub. 47:1–4; cf. Exod. 2:3). The daughter of Pharaoh, Tharmuth, discovers him and, at Miriam's suggestion, fetches his mother, Jochebed, to nurse him (Jub. 47:5–8; cf. Exod. 2:4–9). When Moses is grown, he is brought to the daughter of Pharaoh as her son, and he is taught writing by his father Amram (Jub. 47:9–10a; cf. Exod. 2:10). When Moses kills an Egyptian abusing an Israelite, his deed becomes known and he flees (Jub. 47:9–12; cf. Exod. 2:11–15).

In the forty-ninth jubilee Moses goes to the land of Midian, and he returns to Egypt in the fiftieth jubilee (Jub. 48:1). The narrative then implies that it was in Midian that Moses went up Mount Sinai, which may allude to the account of God's encounter with Moses at the burning bush on Mount Horeb (Exod. 3:1–4:19).[71] Where Exodus 4:24 mentions the Lord's intent to kill Moses, Jubilees attributes that plan to Prince Mastema to save the Egyptians from Moses's hand (Jub. 48:2–3). But God delivers Moses and sends him to Egypt to perform signs against Pharaoh (48:4), which are recounted in the plagues (48:5–8; cf. Exod. 7:1–11:10). But Prince Mastema tries to make Moses fall into the hand of Pharaoh by aiding the latter's magicians (Jub. 48:9–12). But the revealing angel stands between Egypt and Israel to deliver Israel by binding Mastema to prevent Egypt from pursuing Israel out of Egypt (48:13–15). Then Mastema is released so that the Egyptians might pursue Israel and be trapped in the midst of the sea (48:16–19). Moses's story ends in Jubilees 49–50, which contains a collection of laws pertaining to the Passover (chap. 49), jubilees (50:1–5), and the Sabbath (50:6–13).[72] The book ends by declaring the "account of the division of days is finished here" (50:13).

Critical Issues

As noted above, the identification of a work as "rewritten scripture" is anything but straightforward. But Jubilees is typically regarded as among the most exemplary of this kind of text, and indeed it defines the category into which it falls.[73] Yet, as will become evident, in its recasting of biblical accounts Jubilees utilizes a number of genres, and debates about genre illustrate its complexities. Some have regarded the book as an apocalypse,[74] and in some respects it suits this model well, with its revelatory nature, narrative

71. Kugel, "Jubilees," 442.
72. Wintermute, "Jubilees," 2:36.
73. VanderKam, *Jubilees*, 1:19.
74. Dillmann, "Das Buch der Jubiläen," 74.

framework, mediation by a heavenly being, human recipient, eschatological outlook, and spatial interests in the supernatural world.[75] But it is best regarded as a marginal member of this genre,[76] since much of its attention looks back to Israel's history rather than forward to eschatological judgment and is void of symbolic dreams and angelic interpretations. While either rewritten scripture or apocalypse is a reasonable genre for Jubilees, interpreters must not lose sight of the presence and functions of other genres interspersed throughout the book.[77] For instance, Jubilees naturally bears the narratives familiar from Genesis and Exodus, but it also gives painstaking attention to chronological matters, such as the dates of events and ages of key people, all within the consistent rubric of "jubilees" (forty-nine-year units), weeks of years (seven-year units), and years. Speeches are also prominent, sometimes taking the form of testaments (e.g., Jub. 7:20–39; 20–21; 22:10–30).[78] There are considerable amplifications of legal matters that, the author claims, were known and written on stone tablets long before Moses but only revealed with the Decalogue. These include expansions of the Sabbath (Jub. 2:16–33; cf. Gen. 2:2–3; 50:6–13) and purifications for mothers giving birth (Jub. 3:8–14; cf. Lev. 12:2–5).[79] Finally, Jubilees contains geographical units (e.g., Jub. 8–9) that explain the partition of the world among Noah's sons (cf. Gen. 10–11).[80]

It is the author's task of "rewriting" biblical accounts that has most intrigued scholars. In general, the author's interpretive methodology is unlike other methods, such as midrash or pesher, in that here the author quotes his source, but not to set it off as distinct from his own contribution; the source and contribution are melded into a new text entirely, all placed within the new setting of Moses at Sinai (Jub. 1). And so the Angel of the Presence, commanded by God, dictates the narrative to Moses in place of the anonymous narrator of Genesis[81] and sets the whole within an explicit chronology. The modifications are generally of two kinds—additions and omissions—some of which function as what James C. VanderKam calls enhancements and "defamation of characters."[82] Additions take a number of forms, such as the clarification that the sin introduced by the fallen angels was so heinous as to justify the extent of God's judgment in the flood (5:1–19). And even after the flood the offspring of the fallen angels continue to lead humanity into sin (10:1–13). The account

75. VanderKam, *Jubilees*, 1:20.
76. J. Collins, "Genre of the Book of *Jubilees*," 754.
77. VanderKam, *Jubilees*, 1:21.
78. VanderKam, *Jubilees*, 1:21; Hayward, "Genesis and Its Reception," 398–401.
79. VanderKam, *Jubilees*, 1:21.
80. VanderKam, *Jubilees*, 1:21.
81. See Michael Segal, "Between Bible and Rewritten Bible," 21–23.
82. VanderKam, *Jubilees*, 1:23.

of the land allocated to Noah's descendants provides a basis for Israel's territorial claims (8:8–9:15; 10:28–34). After recounting the Genesis narrative of Abram's origins (11:27–32), Jubilees furnishes accounts of his youth in which he exhibits hostility toward idolatry while embracing monotheism (Jub. 11:15–12:21), thereby explaining that he merited the ensuing favor with God (cf. Gen. 12:1–3). Also, though Abraham and Jacob are contemporaries in Genesis, they never meet. Jubilees, however, depicts Abraham's recognition of Jacob as his promised heir, whom he blesses and instructs (19:16–29; 22:10–30). Levi's negative depiction in Genesis (Gen. 34; 49:5–7) causes the author of Jubilees to try to improve his reputation. His vengeance on Shechem is seen as a righteous act (Jub. 30:17–20). He is blessed by Isaac (31:13–17) and learns by a dream of his appointment to the priesthood (32:1), for which he is anointed by Jacob (32:2–9). Jubilees also inserts an account of a war between Egypt and Canaan to explain why Joseph's bones remained in Egypt until after the exodus (46:4–11; cf. Gen. 50:24–26; Exod. 13:19; Josh. 24:32).[83] Jubilees adds a number of speeches not found in the Hebrew Bible, such as the dialogue between Moses and God (Jub. 1), the legal topics explained by the angel (2:17–33; 5:13–19; 6:10–38; 15:25–34; 16:28–31; 23:8–31; 30:5–23; 32:10–15; 33:9–20; 41:23–28; 49:7–23; 50:6–13), and speeches or "testaments" from parents to their progeny (7:20–39; 20:1–22:30; 25; 35; 36).[84] Still other additions pertain to characterization, both positive and negative. Jacob, for instance, is an obedient and respectful son (Jub. 25; 29:15–20; 35–36), whereas Esau breaks his pledge to his parents and wages war against Jacob (37:1–38:14).[85]

It is worth considering why the author would introduce more laws into his narrative than are found in Genesis and Exodus. First, the author may have intended, in part, to enumerate and identify the laws and commands that Abraham is said to have obeyed (Gen. 26:5). Second, Jubilees may try to resolve problems created by punishments indicated in Genesis for violating laws that were not yet revealed.[86] Finally, the ascription of additional laws in the narratives and the attribution of them to the heavenly tablets establish the eternality of the Torah. Its statutes did not simply originate with Moses; rather, Moses was recording something that was established long beforehand.[87] The author of Jubilees omitted material from his sources that did not suit his purposes or that perhaps conflicted with them. These include the expulsion of Hagar (Gen. 16:6–14) and

83. VanderKam, *Jubilees*, 1:22–23.

84. VanderKam, *Jubilees*, 1:23.

85. VanderKam, *Jubilees*, 1:23–24. See more extensively VanderKam, *Book of Jubilees* (2001), 109–14.

86. VanderKam, *Jubilees*, 1:79–80.

87. VanderKam, *Jubilees*, 1:80.

two accounts of Abimelech (Gen. 20; 21:22–34). Additionally, the lengthy search for a wife for Isaac (Gen. 24) and the preparations for Esau and Jacob to meet (Gen. 32:1–33:17) are each reduced to a single verse (Jub. 19:10; 29:13).[88] Also omitted are negative portrayals of people whom the author prefers to cast in a positive light, such as Abraham (Gen. 12:13, 19) and Jacob (Gen. 27:19).

Contribution and Context

As a large and extensive text, the book of Jubilees touches on many subjects, only the principal of which can be treated here.[89] Most of these, however, fall into an overarching category of God's deliberate ordering of creation. Everything, it seems, has a way in which it is to operate in a manner ordained by God (cf. Jub. 5:13). This is most prevalent in the author's relation of scriptural narratives within a distinct chronological framework. The author divides all history into jubilees (seven weeks of years, or forty-nine years), which are times of liberation from slavery and of restoration of property that are drawn from Leviticus 25. All of history from creation to the entrance to the promised land is fifty jubilees, or 2,450 years. The final and fiftieth jubilee, then, is the climax of the system, when the Israelites are liberated from bondage in Egypt and so return to their ancestral land.[90]

Within this rubric it is notable that the author pays fastidious attention to matters regarding the calendar revealed to Moses by the angel (6:23, 29; 30).[91] Each year is divided into four seasons of thirteen weeks, yielding a 364-day calendar (fifty-two weeks; 6:32, 38). The concern with the calendar pertains to the author's concern to celebrate prescribed festivals at the correct times, according to the "prescribed pattern" (6:23–32) and "divisions of times" recorded on heavenly tablets (6:35).[92] The sun, rather than the moon, is the proper luminary for such determinations (2:8–10; 6:36). The determination of a 364-day solar calendar is shared with other works (e.g., 1 En. 72:32; 74:10, 12; 75:2; 86:2) in a similarly contentious tenor (cf. 1 En. 75:1–3; 82:4–7), though the Astronomical Book (1 En. 72–82; cf. 4Q208–211) does not reject the moon from its calendrical calculations.[93]

In addition to the calendar, Jubilees exhibits an interest in the ordering of creation in terms of geographical parameters for the nations, depicted

---

88. VanderKam, *Jubilees*, 1:23.
89. VanderKam, *Book of Jubilees* (2001), 120–33.
90. Van Ruiten, "Jubilees, Book of."
91. VanderKam, *Jubilees*, 1:44–47.
92. VanderKam, *Jubilees*, 1:45.
93. VanderKam, *Jubilees*, 1:45. See VanderKam, *Calendars in the Dead Sea Scrolls*.

most explicitly in Jubilees 8–9. Apparently the allocation is so important that participants are made to promise not to violate its boundaries (9:14–15).[94]

While numerous angels are found throughout the book of Jubilees,[95] the most distinctive are the "angels of the Presence," which perform seven distinct functions in the narrative. These include a liturgical function of praising and blessing God (2:3; 30:18; 31:14), being made privy to God's plans (2:19; 3:4–5; 10:22–23) and conveying information to others (3:15; 4:18; 10:10–13; 16:1–4, 15–19; 41:24, 27; 50:2), and leading people into the garden of Eden (3:9, 12; 4:23; cf. 3:1; 5:23). Furthermore, they can exercise power over fallen angels and demons (5:6; 10:7; 48:10–11, 16–19), rescue people (16:7; 48:13–14), either accept or reject sacrifices (4:2), and participate in a covenant (14:20). Finally, there are some instances where these angels take on the role God has in the biblical context, such as placing Adam and Eve in the garden (Jub. 3:9; cf. Gen. 2:15), bringing out Adam to name the animals (Jub. 3:1; cf. Gen. 2:19), and accepting or rejecting a sacrifice (Jub. 4:2; cf. Gen. 4:4–5). As revered as these figures are, the revealing Angel of the Presence is distinct, participating in all activities in which the other angels of the Presence are present but exhibiting an elevated status perhaps indebted to the "angel of the Lord" in Exodus (cf. Jub. 1:29; Exod. 14:19). As an agent or intermediary figure, the revealing angel takes roles that in Genesis are attributed to God (e.g., Gen. 12:1 // Jub. 12:22).[96]

There are also evil spirits and demons,[97] the principal of which is Mastema (Jub. 10; cf. 4Q225 2 I, 9; II, 13–14),[98] who is also called "Satan" (23:29; 40:9; 46:2; 50:5). He is described as the leader of the evil spirits, and he pleads with God for the preservation of these spirits to carry out punishment on the evil of humankind (10:8). And so Mastema carries out his task through these evil spirits, one-tenth of which God agrees to preserve for that purpose. As human behavior deteriorates, it is revealed that it is the exertions of "Prince Mastema" that lay behind them (11:4–5). When Mastema sends birds to ravage the harvest of farmers (11:11–13), which marks a high point in his activities, the young monotheist Abram is able to intercede and save the crops (11:15–24).[99] Mastema appears again later at the binding of Isaac (17:15–18:16), where in a scene reminiscent of Job (Job 1–2), Mastema exhorts God to tell Abraham to sacrifice his beloved son Isaac to see whether he is truly faithful to God in

94. VanderKam, *Jubilees*, 1:45.

95. See Dimant, "Sons of Heaven"; Hanneken, "Angels and Demons"; van Ruiten, "Angels and Demons."

96. VanderKam, *Jubilees*, 1:48–49; see VanderKam, "Angel of the Presence."

97. See VanderKam, "Demons in the Book of Jubilees."

98. See VanderKam, "Mastema in the Qumran Literature."

99. VanderKam, *Jubilees*, 1:50–51.

everything (Jub. 17:16; cf. Gen. 22:1; Jub. 18:9–12).[100] Mastema also features prominently in the narrative of the plagues on Egypt and Israel's exodus (Jub. 48); here he tries to thwart God's plans of deliverance, first by trying to kill Moses (48:2; cf. Exod. 4:24–26), then by aiding the Egyptian magicians in their attempts to replicate the plagues (48:9–12; cf. Exod. 7–9). Toward the end of the book readers are told that Mastema was temporarily bound (48:15) only to be released to deploy the Egyptians in their fatal pursuit of the Israelites to the Red Sea (48:17).[101]

Jubilees is concerned with Israel and the nations, and van Ruiten is careful to point out that this stems from the author's deep concern for purity.[102] The notion of ritual purity is scarcely mentioned (e.g., 3:8–14; 32:3) in favor of a kind of moral impurity—idolatry, murder, sexual aberrations—that characterizes other (gentile) nations.[103] Israel itself is a people separated from among the nations for God, chosen and blessed (2:19–21). Though the nations belong to the Lord (2:19; 15:31), they are associated with impurity and idolatry (1:9; 11:2–5; 15:30–32; cf. 9:15; 16:5–6; 21:21–23; 22:16–22; 30:11–15). And so the relation of Israel to these nations comes to the very heart of the book by virtue of Israel's separation from them and their impurities, especially with respect to marriage.[104] Marriage within Israel is esteemed, whereas intermarriage is strongly prohibited (e.g., 2:19–21; 12:1–8, 12–14; 15:21–34; 20:4; 22:20–22; 25:1–3; 30:7–17).[105]

Also integral to Israel's identity is its covenantal relationship with God.[106] It is often noted that the covenants and promissory passages in Genesis and Exodus (e.g., Gen. 9; 12:1–3, 7; 13:14–17; 15; 17; Exod. 19–24) are a new setting, and the covenantal relationship between God and Israel is articulated in Jubilees 1 (esp. vv. 5–6), which underlies the entirety of the book. Much of what Moses is to record in the book of Jubilees is the way in which God demonstrates covenant fidelity whereas Israel continues to fail. Yet Israel's covenant is to be renewed annually at the Festival of Weeks (Jub. 6:17–19). Subsequent ceremonies entail the promise of land (14:1; 15:1–14), and the Sinai covenant becomes the "last and fullest iteration in a single chain of agreements between the Lord and his special people."[107]

100. See van Ruiten, "Abraham, Job and the Book of Jubilees."
101. VanderKam, Jubilees, 1:51–52.
102. Van Ruiten, "Jubilees, Book of."
103. See Werman, "Attitude towards Gentiles."
104. Van Ruiten, "Jubilees, Book of."
105. Cf. Ezra 10:2, 10, 17–18, 44; Neh. 13:27; van Ruiten, "Jubilees, Book of."
106. See Endres, Biblical Interpretation, 226–31; Gilders, "Concept of Covenant in Jubilees."
107. VanderKam, Jubilees, 1:153–55.

Jubilees gives attention to the subject of eschatology in two sections.[108] First, in Jubilees 1 the author predicts a return of Israel from the nations; the people will be gathered by God and blessed with peace (1:15–18). He also predicts that they will not listen to God but then will ultimately return with circumcised minds and be purified, swearing eternal allegiance to God's commands (1:22–25). Furthermore, God will dwell with them in an eternal temple, and all creation will be renewed (1:27–29). In the second section (chap. 23), the angel explains that future generations will abandon Israel's covenant with God (23:16, 19) and receive judgment at the hands of other nations (23:23–24). Redemption begins with children beginning to study the laws and seeking out commands; people will live longer and peacefully, without Satan or evil, but with healing from God (23:26–31). VanderKam observes that in both sections the emphasis, or turning point, seems to be the return to covenantal obligations on the part of Israel.[109] In the eschaton Israel will be pure from polluting sin and will live in their promised land for all eternity (50:5).

Standing out in the narrative of Jubilees is the place of writing, specifically the identified media of heavenly tablets, the law, and the testimony. The heavenly tablets[110] are referenced by other Jewish writings even before the book of Jubilees[111] and have an extensive history in ancient Near Eastern thought.[112] In the Enochic writings, for instance, they contain information on the heavenly realms (1 En. 81:1–2; 93:2; 103:2; 106:19) as well as the past and future actions of humanity.[113] In Jubilees they are said to contain the law and the testimony (1:26, 29) and thus encompass a breadth of teaching that surpasses that of Torah alone. Their innovation lies in the fact that they claim to contain laws.[114] It may be that the heavenly tablets function in the same way as the Oral Torah in rabbinic Judaism, utilizing a hermeneutic that facilitates the presentation of a "correct" interpretation of the law that adapts it to changing situations.[115] And by placing these interpretations alongside the Pentateuch, they are accorded a similar authority.[116] Others take a slightly different view, noting that Jubilees describes the tablets (1:29) in a manner

108. VanderKam, *Jubilees*, 1:66; Scott, *On Earth as in Heaven*, 19–158.

109. VanderKam, *Jubilees*, 1:66.

110. For the terminology and vocabulary used, see Ravid, "Special Terminology."

111. See Baynes, *Heavenly Book Motif*.

112. VanderKam, *Jubilees*, 1:68–69; see Paul, "Heavenly Tablets."

113. VanderKam, *Jubilees*, 1:69; Nickelsburg and VanderKam, *1 Enoch 2*, 536–37.

114. VanderKam, *Jubilees*, 1:68.

115. García Martínez, "Heavenly Tablets," 258. Their specific contents in Jubilees, according to García Martínez, fall into five categories: the tablets of the law, a heavenly register of good and evil, the "book of destiny," the calendar and feasts, and new halakot.

116. García Martínez, "Heavenly Tablets," 259.

that suggests they include the chronology of all time, divided into units and multiples of seven—a "comprehensive account of history . . . all properly ordered into years, weeks of years, and jubilee periods."[117] More specifically, they contain individual laws (e.g., 3:10, 31; 4:5, 32; 15:25; 28:6; 30:9; 32:10, 15; 33:10) and regulations particular to the calendar and festivals (e.g., 6:17, 28–31, 35; 16:28–29; 18:19; 32:28; 49:8) and, finally, information about people, their characteristics, and their respective destinies (e.g., 5:13; 16:3, 9; 23:32; 24:8; 30:19–22; 31:32).[118]

Mention of the law is also prevalent in Jubilees, sometimes in general references (e.g., 1:12; 6:22; 23:16, 19; 24:11; 30:12; 50:13) but more commonly in specific items of legislation on various topics. The latter entail a wide variety of legal matters, the most common of which pertain to Sabbaths and festivals (2:29; 16:29; 49:7; 50:1, 6), purity/impurity of parturients (3:13), blood (6:14), sexual matters (30:10; 33:16–17; 41:28), tithes (13:26; 32:10), and circumcision (15:25, 33).[119] Language of "testimony" is also common in Jubilees,[120] and there have been a number of views posited for its meaning.[121] VanderKam proposes a meaning encapsulated in the word "message," advocating that "testimony" in Jubilees has several important functions. First, it gives a more complete explanation or clarification of laws, accompanied by reasons that they should be obeyed (e.g., 2:33; 3:14; 4:30; 6:12; 16:28).[122] Second, it provides examples of how God orchestrates history and the activities of people and whole nations (e.g., 23:32; 30:17; 31:32). Finally, testimony is used in Jubilees to depict God's division of time and calendar for events in history.[123]

Beyond the obvious use of Genesis 1 through Exodus 24, Jubilees exhibits familiarity with and usage of other portions of the Hebrew Bible. Teaching on the Sabbath (Jub. 2:17, 25) is drawn from features elsewhere in Exodus (Exod. 31:12–17), and Leviticus is particularly important for regulations used throughout Jubilees pertaining to sacrifices (Lev. 1–7), festivals (chaps. 16, 23), and sexual relations (chaps. 18, 20). Material regarding the dates and offerings pertaining to festivals is utilized in Jubilees (Jub. 49; cf. Num. 9:1–14), as is the priestly blessing (Jub. 31:15; cf. Num. 6:24–26). Deuteronomy serves as a sort of model for Jubilees, which draws from it in statements about the

117. VanderKam, *Jubilees*, 1:70.
118. VanderKam, *Jubilees*, 1:70.
119. VanderKam, *Jubilees*, 1:70, 72.
120. VanderKam (*Jubilees* 1:72) counts twenty-five occurrences (Prologue; 1:4, 8 [twice], 26, 29; 2:24, 33; 3:14; 4:18, 19, 30; 6:12, 23, 32, 37; 10:17; 16:28; 23:32; 29:8 [twice]; 30:17, 19; 31:32; 32:29). See also VanderKam, "Moses Trumping Moses."
121. For a survey of the principal interpretations, see VanderKam, *Jubilees*, 1:74–78.
122. VanderKam, *Jubilees*, 1:78.
123. VanderKam, *Jubilees*, 1:79.

residing presence of God (Jub. 49:21; cf. Deut. 7:1–6) and regulations about tithes (Jub. 32:10–15; cf. Deut. 14:22–27).[124] The author of Jubilees also utilized sources from outside the Hebrew Bible. VanderKam notes a number of texts, especially from the Enochic corpus. The astronomical and calendrical matters from the Astronomical Book (1 En. 72–82) are explicitly said to have been written about by Enoch (Jub. 4:17–18). Furthermore, both books indicate the solar year lasts 364 days (1 En. 72:32; 74:10, 12; 75:2; 82:6, 11; Jub. 6:32, 38) while the lunar year is 354 days (1 En. 74:10–17; 78:15–16; 79:4–5; Jub. 6:36). This suggests that the author of Jubilees likely used a version of the extant Astronomical Book, but there are differences in that Jubilees rejects the lunar calendar for calculating times while the Enochic material accepts it. Also, Jubilees is concerned with the dates for the purpose of observing festivals, whereas the Astronomical Book uses the dates of the calendar for the "scientific" aspect of the 364-day year.[125] Jubilees also exhibits familiarity with the traditions of the fallen angels or Watchers from the Book of Watchers (1 En. 1–36; cf. Jub. 4:22; 5:1–11; 7:21–25; 10:1–13).[126]

The book of Jubilees shares with the Aramaic Levi Document an interest in the role and development of Levi in his priestly office (cf. Jub. 21, 30–32; ALD §8 // Jub. 31:5–30).[127] There are also points of correspondence between Jubilees and the Genesis Apocryphon that are so close that scholars debate which may have influenced the other. Regardless, the agreements are notable for their detail, such as the use of particular names (Batenosh [Bitenosh] as the wife of Lamech [1QapGen II, 3, 8; Jub. 4:28] and Lubar for the mountain on which the ark rested [1QapGen XII, 13; Jub. 5:28, etc.]).[128] Larger units are also similar, such as Noah's sacrifice after the flood (1QapGen X, 13–17; Jub. 6:1–3), the account of Noah's vineyard (1QapGen XII, 13–17; Jub. 7:1–5, 35–37), and the divisions of the earth between Noah's progeny (1QapGen XV?–XVII?; cf. XIV, 15–22; Jub. 8:11–9:15), among others.[129] A similar situation occurs with respect to the Visions of Amram, where the accounts of war between Egypt and Canaan are similar (cf. Jub. 46:6–11).[130] Finally, both Jubilees (Jub. 8–9) and the Genesis Apocryphon (1QapGen XVI–XVII) utilize a map of the world that is generally recognized to be Ionian in origin, though the origins of this map remain unexplained.[131]

124. VanderKam, *Jubilees*, 1:85.
125. VanderKam, *Jubilees*, 1:88–89.
126. VanderKam, *Jubilees*, 1:88.
127. VanderKam, *Jubilees*, 1:90–91.
128. VanderKam, *Jubilees*, 1:92.
129. VanderKam, *Jubilees*, 1:92–93.
130. VanderKam, *Jubilees*, 1:95.
131. VanderKam, *Jubilees*, 1:97.

Purpose

The author of the book of Jubilees is relatively clear on his reasons for writing the book, of which VanderKam focuses on three. First, it seems evident that despite his utilization and "rewriting" of Genesis 1 through Exodus 24, the author did not intend to replace the biblical narrative, which he regards as authoritative and divinely revealed in the same manner as the book he himself penned. VanderKam therefore classifies the book as a "guide" to Genesis-Exodus, "helping the reader derive the correct message from the biblical material and ensuring that the wrong conclusions were not drawn from it."[132] Second, the work claims to be written under the authority of God, serving a legal purpose to demonstrate the justice of God, who maintains covenant fidelity.[133] Third, it advocates the necessity for strict adherence to the law, often taking the form of distancing oneself from other people who "embody impurity," and this, says the author, had always been God's intent and an essential facet of his covenant relationship with Israel.[134]

Reception History

It is generally recognized that Jubilees influenced later writers within Judaism as well as Christianity.[135] Most of its influence in Judaism is found in the Dead Sea Scrolls and perhaps Josephus, whereas Christian usage is found from the fourth century CE. Jubilees is explicitly cited in the Damascus Document in its reference to the determination of times as the "Book of the Divisions of the Times into their Jubilees of Weeks" (CD-A XVI, 1–4; cf. Jub. Prologue; 1:4, 26, 29; 50:13).[136] Furthermore, language found in the "Words of Moses" texts from Qumran (1Q22; 4Q588) closely resembles that found in Jubilees, as does language in other Dead Sea Scrolls (e.g., Pseudo-Jubilees [4Q225–227]; Miscellaneous Rules [4Q265]; and the Hymn to the Creator in 11QPs^a XXVI, 9–15), with one likely citation of the "divisions of the times" (4Q228 1 I, 2, 4, 7).[137] It is evident that the book of Jubilees influenced Josephus in his retelling of Genesis and the beginning of Exodus, by some accounts in as many

132. VanderKam, *Jubilees*, 1:39.
133. VanderKam, *Jubilees*, 1:39–40.
134. VanderKam, *Jubilees*, 1:40.
135. For a complete treatment of this subject, see VanderKam, *Jubilees*, 1:98–121.
136. VanderKam, *Jubilees*, 1:99. For an opposing view, see Dimant, "Two 'Scientific Fictions,'" 246.
137. VanderKam, *Jubilees*, 1:101–6.

as forty-eight instances.[138] Though VanderKam urges caution with respect to
the clear identification of Jubilees as a source and to the number of instances
cited, he nonetheless observes a number of positive examples,[139] but in the
end he suggests that a "wiser course" would be "to say that Josephus is a
witness to the kinds of exegesis of Genesis and Exodus that were current in
his time," rather than requiring direct dependence.[140]

Clear evidence of the influence of Jubilees on Christian literature is ambiguous until the fourth century. There may be some affinities between Jubilees
and the New Testament with regard to an understanding of angels receiving
the law (cf. Acts 7:38, 53; Gal. 3:19; Heb. 2:2) and even to calendrical matters in the Synoptic passion narrative (Matt. 26:17–19; Mark 14:12–16; Luke
22:7–15; cf. John 18:28, 38; 19:14), the account of Pentecost (Acts 2), or
the laws pertaining to the so-called apostolic decree (Acts 15:20–21).[141] Some
have argued for a clear identification of Jubilees as a source for the Pseudo-
Clementine *Recognitions* 1.27–71 (ca. 200 CE).[142] The first Christian writer to
clearly use Jubilees as a source, and cite it as such, is Epiphanius of Salamis
(ca. 315–403 CE).[143] Traces of Jubilees are evident in later Greek and Syriac
writings and chronographies as well as in Ethiopian literature after Jubilees
was translated from Greek into Ethiopic (Ge'ez) in the fifth or sixth century.[144]
Subsequently the work was almost unknown to Western scholarship until a
manuscript was found in Ethiopia among biblical manuscripts in the Abys-
sinian Church by J. L. Krapff, who subsequently brought it to Europe. There
it was studied and translated into German by August Dillmann (1850–1851).
By 1861 A. M. Ceriani found and published a Latin manuscript containing
approximately one-third of Jubilees. To date, the most important edition and
translation of the Ethiopic text, noting all the variations and other manuscripts, is that of James C. VanderKam.[145]

138. Halpern-Amaru, "Flavius Josephus and the *Book of Jubilees*."
139. E.g., Jub. 3:18 // *Ant.* 1.1.4 §40; Jub. 31:2 // *Ant.* 1.19.8 §§310–311; 1.19.10 §§322–323,
343; Jub. 19:10 // *Ant.* 1.16.1 §242; Jub. 42:12 // *Ant.* 2.6.5 §113; 2.6.6 §120; Jub. 47:5 // *Ant.* 2.2.9.5
§§224–225; 2.9.7 §§232, 236; Jub. 13:10–12 // *Ant.* 1.8.3 §170. VanderKam, *Jubilees*, 1:107–10.
140. VanderKam, *Jubilees*, 1:110.
141. VanderKam, *Jubilees*, 1:111–14.
142. Jones, *Ancient Jewish Christian Source*, 138.
143. See Rönsch, *Das Buch der Jubiläen*, 252–65.
144. See VanderKam, *Jubilees*, 1:116–21.
145. VanderKam, *Book of Jubilees* (2001); Kugel, "Jubilees," 273.

14

Biblical Antiquities

Introduction

The Book of Biblical Antiquities, or simply Biblical Antiquities, was transmitted in the name of Philo of Alexandria. However, it is now known that he was not the author, and so scholars refer to the person who composed the work as "Pseudo-Philo." The book is often known by its Latin title, *Liber antiquitatum biblicarum* (abbreviated LAB). Like the book of Jubilees, Biblical Antiquities recasts biblical narratives, but in this case from the time of Adam to King David, with several lacunae in the narrative.[1] Also like Jubilees, the author treats the biblical narrative in a variety of ways, sometimes summarizing briefly or completely omitting text, while at other times quoting specifically or paraphrasing it. In still other instances the author inserts material, such as prayers, speeches, or narrative sections, not found in the Hebrew Bible.[2] In other words, "it interweaves biblical incidents and legendary expansions of these accounts."[3] The unnamed narrator writes from the perspective of a setting prior to the building of Solomon's Temple (LAB 26:12).[4]

Language and Manuscripts

Biblical Antiquities survives only in a Latin translation, which was created from a Greek version of an original Hebrew text. Of the extant Latin

1. Hayward, "Philo, Pseudo- (LAB)," 1:438.
2. Nickelsburg, *Jewish Literature*, 265–66.
3. Harrington, "Pseudo-Philo," 2:297.
4. Hayward, "Philo, Pseudo- (LAB)."

manuscripts, the earliest dates from the eleventh century, and the most recent dates from the fifteenth century.[5] In addition to being two steps removed from the original Hebrew and being replete with corruptions, the Latin is preserved in two distinct recensions, neither of which carries precedent over the other.[6] Eighteen Latin manuscripts are complete, while three are fragmentary. Even with this evidence there are gaps of undetermined length (between 36:4 and 37:2 and between 37:5 and 38:1) and an abrupt ending that suggests the original ending is lost.[7] Daniel J. Harrington observes that the Latin text exhibits particular idioms and characteristic features found in the Old Latin version of the Bible.[8]

There is evidence for a Greek predecessor to the Latin text.[9] One finds likely confusion of Greek words (e.g., ἐρρέθη, *errethē*, "was spoken," and εὑρέθη, *heurethē*, "was found" [LAB 9:3]) and some Greek words left nearly untranslated (*paratecem*, "deposit" [3:10]; *ometoceam*, "miscarriage" [9:2]; *zaticon*, "covenant" [9:15], and *anteciminus*, "adversary" [45:6]).[10]

There is some evidence of Hebrew behind the Latin text as well, notably from mistranslations that seem to refer back to the Hebrew language. For instance, where a correct reading would be "laws," the Latin has "boundaries" (*terminus*), which comes from the Hebrew חֻקִּים (*ḥuqqîm*), which can mean both "boundaries" and "laws" (LAB 15:6). Also, a correct reading, "be deaf," is represented by the Latin "be silent" (*taceat*), which derives from the Hebrew חָרַשׁ (*ḥāraš*), which can mean "be silent" or "be deaf" (53:6). Finally, there is evidence of biblical texts translated from Hebrew into Greek, and from Greek into Latin. For instance, the word "blameless," which in a Latin version of Genesis 6:9 is *inmaculatus*, renders the Hebrew תָּמִים (*tāmîm*). But the Septuagint at Genesis 6:9 renders that Hebrew word with "perfect" (τέλειος, *teleios*). The Greek of Biblical Antiquities must have used "blameless" (ἄμωμος, *amōmos*), which in Latin became *inmaculatus*, introducing a rendering of the Hebrew Bible text independent of the Greek Septuagint rendering (LAB 3:4).[11]

The narrative ends abruptly, with Edabus the Amalekite preparing to kill King Saul (LAB 65:4–5). It has long been recognized that the ending is problematic and so has been presumed that the remainder of the ending is lost.

5. Harrington, "Pseudo-Philo," 2:298.
6. Jacobson, "*Pseudo-Philo*," 470.
7. Harrington, "Pseudo-Philo," 2:298; cf. Jacobson, *Commentary*, 1:257–73.
8. Harrington, "Pseudo-Philo," 2:298.
9. Harrington, "Original Language."
10. Harrington, "Pseudo-Philo," 2:298.
11. Harrington, "Pseudo-Philo," 2:299. For a more complete and updated account of the Hebrew and Greek stages of LAB, see Jacobson, *Commentary*, 1:215–24.

Others, though, see the present ending as genuine, corresponding to the Chronicles narrative (1 Chron. 10) or deliberately ending on a note of repentance and forgiveness.[12]

Provenance

It is generally agreed that Biblical Antiquities was written in Palestine to an audience likely competent in Hebrew and educated in the Scriptures. This is determined from its composition in Hebrew, fluid handling of Scripture, and familiarity with Palestinian geography (e.g., LAB 55:7). Though some think the term "holy land" (19:10) suggests otherwise, the occurrence of the term in the Old Testament (Zech. 2:12) and books like 2 Baruch hints at a Palestinian origin.[13] It may be that the text's familiarity with Judea and Galilee implies the author wrote from one of these locations.[14] Howard Jacobson suggests a location near a Greek city, given the author's familiarity with pagan traditions, Greek folk material, and magic and interest in demons. According to him, Galilee abounded in superstitions, and so he suggests that as its location of origin.[15] Harrington suggests the confusion of authorship with Philo of Alexandria may point rather to that city as the origin of Biblical Antiquities but ultimately dismisses this because of the spurious attribution of authorship. For his part Harrington dismisses the association of Biblical Antiquities with any known specific group or sect in Palestine but favors in general "the milieu of the Palestinian synagogues at the turn of the common era" because of its utilization of motifs frequently found in Jewish traditions.[16]

As noted above, the work was transmitted under the name of Philo of Alexandria, and initially scholars accepted this as fact, though doubts soon arose. It was not until 1898 that scholars recognized that the work's style and literary character are so different from Philo's that he could not have been the author.[17] But how it came to be attributed to Philo at all is a mystery.

---

12. Jacobson, *Commentary*, 1:254.

13. Jacobson, *Commentary*, 1:210.

14. Hayward, "Philo, Pseudo- (LAB)."

15. Jacobson, *Commentary*, 1:210–11, citing b. Avodah Zarah 27b (cf. 17a); y. Avodah Zarah 2.2, 40d–41a; Mark 1:28–42; t. Shabbat 6–7. See also Freyne, *Galilee from Alexander the Great to Hadrian*, 333.

16. Harrington, "Pseudo-Philo," 2:299–300.

17. Cohn, "Apocryphal Work."

Date

Biblical Antiquities is not cited by any ancient authors, and so internal evidence must be utilized to determine its date. Scholars generally agree that it was written between 50 CE and 150 CE.[18] George W. E. Nickelsburg sees "many close and substantial parallels" with 2 Baruch, 4 Ezra, and aspects of Josephus's *Antiquities* pointing to events near 70 CE,[19] though there is some uncertainty as to whether it was before or after the destruction of the temple in 70 CE. Scholars dating the original Hebrew composition often look to Biblical Antiquities 19:7 as a point of departure. This refers to the destruction of "the place where they will serve me [God]" and is sometimes understood as Titus's destruction of Jerusalem and its temple in 70 CE. However, it could just as easily refer to the capture of Jerusalem by Nebuchadnezzar (587/586 BCE), Antiochus IV Epiphanes (169 BCE), or Pompey (63 BCE).[20]

Furthermore, Harrington adopts the notion of a "Palestinian" biblical text evident in Biblical Antiquities, which implies a date no later than 100 CE, when such texts were suppressed. He also looks to Biblical Antiquities 32:3, which references "a lamb of the flock . . . accepted as sacrifice to the Lord," and the mention of offering sacrifices on the altar "unto this day" (LAB 22:8), as though the temple cult were still functioning. Other factors also suggest to him a date prior to 70 CE: a negative attitude toward Jewish rulers not chosen by God, silence on the destruction of the temple, and a free rendering of the biblical text all suggest a date around the time of Jesus.[21]

Thorough research on the subject argues for a post-70 CE origin to Biblical Antiquities by addressing arguments in favor of a date before 70 CE.[22] First, the presence of active cultic function (e.g., LAB 13:1) is to be expected of a text recounting the biblical narrative and need not refer to an active cult. Second, silence about the destruction of the temple is necessarily dubious, and the prediction of its destruction (e.g., 19:7) would seem sufficient. Third, the "unto this day" (22:8) is placed in the setting not of the presumed author but of the persona adopted by the author in his pseudepigraphic context, in which the temple had not yet been built (cf. 26:2). The contention that the author would not take such liberties in handling Scripture after 70 CE presumes a strictness more conducive to a much later time than simply fifty to one hundred

18. Hayward, "Philo, Pseudo- (LAB)."

19. Nickelsburg, *Jewish Literature*, 269.

20. Harrington, "Pseudo-Philo," 2:299.

21. Harrington, "Pseudo-Philo," 2:299; see also Harrington et al., *Pseudo-Philon, Les Antiquités Bibliques*, 2:66–74.

22. Jacobson, *Commentary*, 1:199–210.

years afterward. The "Palestinian biblical text" theory must recognize, on the one hand, that it is dealing with a secondary reconstruction of a Hebrew text via extant Latin manuscripts and, on the other, that 100 CE is hardly a fixed terminus for that tradition and in any case postdates 70 CE as well.[23]

More positively toward a post-70 CE dating, Jacobson points out the long-recognized points of similarity between Biblical Antiquities and the apocalypses of 2 Baruch and 4 Ezra, both of which were written after 70 CE and share with Biblical Antiquities themes, ideas, language, phasing, and imagery, suggesting they must all derive from "the same historical, cultural and social context."[24] Then, building on the work of Leopold Cohn,[25] he argues that the reference to the future destruction of the place where the Jewish people will serve God on the seventeenth of Tammuz (LAB 19:7) does not point to Antiochus IV or Pompey but most resembles teachings of the rabbis (e.g., m. Ta'an. 4:6; y. Ta'an. 68c) that are primarily associated with the Roman destruction of Jerusalem. And so he concludes the reference functions as a prophecy *ex eventu* (Josephus, *J.W.* 6.2.1 §§93–94; cf. t. Ta'an. 4:10).[26] Further, the reference to the removal of the temple's stones, which will not be restored until the eschaton (LAB 26:13), would make little sense prior to the temple's destruction. Jacobson then notes a litany of other evidence, some of which is more persuasive than others. These include the apparent absence of a temple (22:1–6), the alleged presence of a synagogue (cf. 11:8), and the language of "sages" (e.g., 23:7), which is more prominent after the destruction than before, and more. In conclusion, he finds no cogent arguments for dating Biblical Antiquities prior to 70 CE and describes arguments for dating it after as "overwhelming." He finds some evidence in the text of persecutions under Hadrian and the failure of the Bar Kokhba revolt, together suggesting to him a date no later than the mid-second century CE.[27] It is worth noting at the conclusion of Jacobson's extensive work that much of his argument depends on rebuttals of pre-70 CE arguments and largely conjectures for a post-70 CE date. Perhaps it is prudent, then, with scholars like Hayward, to contend the evidence is insufficient to make a clear determination either way,[28] or at least to suggest the matter awaits further, careful scholarly scrutiny. Regardless, a date between 50 and 150 CE provides suitable parameters.

23. Jacobson addresses similar contentions for a pre-70 date, none of which he finds compelling. Jacobson, *Commentary*, 1:201.
24. Jacobson, *Commentary*, 1:201.
25. Cohn, "Apocryphal Work."
26. Jacobson, *Commentary*, 1:202–3.
27. Jacobson, *Commentary*, 1:206–10.
28. Hayward, "Philo, Pseudo- (LAB)"; seemingly also Nickelsburg, *Jewish Literature*, 269.

Contents

Biblical Antiquities begins with material from Genesis (LAB 1–8),[29] starting with lengthy genealogies from Adam to Noah (chap. 1) and from Cain to Lamech (chap. 2; cf. Gen. 5). The account of the flood (LAB 3; cf. Gen. 6:9–9:29) is followed by the genealogy of Noah's descendants to Abraham (LAB 4; cf. Gen. 10; 11:10–32) and a census of Noah's descendants (LAB 5). In the story of the Tower of Babel (cf. Gen. 11:1–9), the people build a tower and they all write their names on the bricks, except twelve men (LAB 6:1–3). These men refuse to participate because they worship the Lord, and they are then threatened to be burned (6:4–5). Jotkan, one of the chiefs, helps the twelve flee to the mountains (6:6–10), but only one, Abram, remains behind (6:11). Abram is taken and thrown into a furnace (6:12–16), but God intervenes, burns up all his accusers, and spares Abram, who rejoins the other eleven men, and together they come down from the mountains and worship God (6:17–18).

Nevertheless, the people yet again seek to build a city and a tower, which is seen by God, who now intervenes and divides their languages and banishes them from the land (7:1–3). Abram alone is brought out of their land to a land of God's choosing, where a covenant will be established between God and Abram (7:4–5; cf. Gen. 11:7–9). And so Abram dwells with Sarai, his wife, in Canaan, where God promises him the land and changes his name to Abraham. There also Abram fathers Ishmael by Hagar and Isaac by Sarah (LAB 8:1–3; cf. Gen. 12:4–5; 13:11–15; 16:1–15; 17:1–8; 21:2–3). This is followed by an account of Isaac, Esau, Jacob, and Jacob's twelve sons (LAB 8:4–8; cf. Gen. 25:20–26; 29:31–30:24; 35:18–26; 36:2–18), a summary of Joseph's slavery in Egypt and subsequent rise to power (LAB 8:9–10; cf. Gen. 41:1–42:8), and an account of the Israelites who went to Egypt (LAB 8:11–14; cf. Gen. 46:8–25; Exod. 1:1).

Biblical Antiquities 9–12 comes from the book of Exodus. After Joseph's death, Israel grows in numbers and is subjected to slavery in Egypt when Amram announces his intent to sire a son in defiance of Pharaoh's decree (LAB 9:1–6; cf. Exod. 1; 6:20). Amram's plan pleases God, and he has three children—Aaron, Miriam, and Moses (LAB 9:7–16; cf. Exod. 2). The entire narrative of the rise of Moses, his confrontation with Pharaoh, and the plagues on Egypt (Exod. 3–13) is summarized in a single verse (LAB 10:1). This is followed by the account of the crossing through the Red Sea (LAB 10:2–6; cf. Exod. 14) and the forty-year wilderness wandering (LAB 10:7; cf. Exod. 15–18).

29. Harrington, "Pseudo-Philo," 2:297.

In the third month of their exodus Israel comes to the wilderness of Sinai, where God tells Moses to ascend the mountain and receive the everlasting law (LAB 11:1–3; cf. Exod. 19). Amid the clamoring of thunder and lightning, Moses brings the people before God, who speaks the Ten Commandments (LAB 11:4–14; cf. Exod. 20). Then Moses himself draws near the cloud where God is and is told statutes and judgments that are detailed to him for forty days and forty nights, including instructions for a tabernacle (LAB 11:15; cf. Exod. 25–31). When Moses descends the mountain, the people do not recognize him in his radiance (LAB 12:1; cf. Exod. 34:29–35). But while Moses was on the mountain, the people implored Aaron to fashion gods for them and, though reluctant, he was forced to do so and so produced a golden calf (LAB 12:2–3; cf. Exod. 32:1–6). The Lord then sends Moses to them to intercede (LAB 12:4–7; cf. Exod. 32:7–30), and so Moses returns up the mountain and prays for God's forgiveness, which he receives along with stone tablets to replace those he broke (LAB 12:8–10; cf. Exod. 32:31–34:1).

At the outset of chapter 13, Moses constructs the tent of meeting and its fixtures (LAB 13:1; cf. Exod. 35–40). The rest of the chapter contains a selection of regulations drawn from the book of Leviticus, beginning with laws pertaining to the use of the altar (LAB 13:2; cf. Lev. 1) and the cleansing of lepers (LAB 13:3; cf. Lev. 14) followed by regulations for festivals (LAB 13:4–10; cf. Lev. 23, 26).[30]

The book of Numbers is the source for Biblical Antiquities 14–18, which begins with an account of the census (LAB 14; cf. Num. 1). Then Moses sends out twelve men to spy out the land (LAB 15; cf. Num. 13–14). The author recounts the rebellion of Korah, who with two hundred men complains about "an unbearable law imposed upon us" (LAB 16:1; cf. Num. 16). God sent a warning through Moses (LAB 16:2–3; cf. Num. 16:5, 22), but Korah and his men remain defiant (LAB 16:2–4). Korah's own sons refuse to join his rebellion (16:4–5), and the earth swallows Korah and his men (16:6–7). Then it is revealed to Moses by the sprouting of the rod of Aaron that to his line belongs the priesthood (chap. 17).

When Moses defeats the kings of the Amorites, Balak rules as king in Moab and summons Balaam, an interpreter of dreams, to curse Israel for him, though the reader is told this is the plan of God (LAB 18:1–3; cf. Num. 21).[31] God speaks to Balaam at night and warns him against cursing whom God has chosen (LAB 18:4–6). The next morning Balaam dismisses Balak but, upon inquiring of God, goes with him, having been told that God will bring ruin

30. Harrington, "Pseudo-Philo," 2:297.
31. For some discussion of this complicated chapter, see Murphy, Pseudo-Philo, 84–89.

on Balak (LAB 18:7–9; cf. Num. 22:21–35). When Balaam comes to Moab, the spirit of God comes upon him, and he exclaims that Israel, as God's planted vine (cf. Isa. 5; Jer. 12), cannot be uprooted (LAB 18:10; cf. Num. 24:2) and prophesies Balak's own destruction (LAB 18:11–12). But then Balaam advises Balak on how to lead Israel into sin and so its own destruction, which Balak does, and Balaam departs (18:13–14).

The book of Deuteronomy is the source of Biblical Antiquities 19,[32] which begins with Moses's announcement of his impending death, Israel's impending sin, and God's consequential anger, punishment, and ultimate restoration of Israel (LAB 19:1–6; cf. Lev. 26:42–45). God then calls Moses up the mountain again to show him the promised land before he dies (LAB 19:7–13; cf. Deut. 34:1–4). Moses asks God to show him how much time remains before the end and learns that 4,500 years have passed since the beginning and 2,500 years remain to the end (LAB 19:14–15).[33] Then Moses, full of understanding and with a glorious countenance, dies (19:16; cf. Deut. 34:5–6).

Biblical Antiquities 20–24 comes from the book of Joshua, beginning with the commissioning of Joshua as Moses's successor (LAB 20:1–5; cf. Josh. 1) and the sending of spies to scout out Jericho, which Israel takes (LAB 20:6–7; cf. Josh. 2; 6:24). Israel conquers and divides the rest of the land (LAB 20:8–10; cf. Josh. 13–23). When Joshua grows old, God tells him there is still much land to conquer and Joshua must bear witness to Israel before he dies because they will be seduced by foreign gods (LAB 21:1; cf. Josh. 13:1). Joshua prays, asking God to give his people a wise heart that they may not sin against him (LAB 21:2–6), and builds an altar to the Lord at Gilgal, where the people present offerings and Joshua blesses the people (21:7–10; cf. Josh. 8:30–35). Joshua learns that the tribes across the Jordan—Reuben, Gad, and the half-tribe of Manasseh—built their own altar and appointed their own priests (LAB 22:1–2), which, they explain, was so that they too may remember the Lord (22:3–4). Joshua exhorts them to destroy their altars and offers sacrifices for their forgiveness (22:5–7; cf. Josh. 22). Then Joshua goes to Gilgal to gather the tent of meeting and the cultic articles before taking them to Shiloh (LAB 22:8–9).

Joshua divides the land and gathers all the people to establish a covenant before them at Shiloh, in which Joshua recounts words spoken to him by the Lord at night, words promising his provision and care if they will heed the words of their fathers (LAB 23:1–13), to which all Israel agrees (23:14; cf. Josh. 24). Joshua again gathers the people and exhorts them to serve the

32. Harrington, "Pseudo-Philo," 2:297.
33. Jacobson, "Pseudo-Philo," 517.

Lord (LAB 24:1–2; cf. Josh. 24:15) and then blesses them (LAB 24:3) before he dies (24:4–6; cf. Josh. 24:28, 30).

The book of Judges is the basis for a large section of Biblical Antiquities (chaps. 25–48).[34] Kenaz, who is only mentioned briefly in the Hebrew Bible (Judg. 3:9–11; cf. Josh. 15:17; Judg. 1:13), is made the leader of Israel (LAB 25:1–2). He gathers the people and discerns who believes in the Lord and who does not. He imprisons 6,110 unbelievers whom God says should be given the opportunity to confess, which they do (25:3–13). Kenaz has these confessions recorded and read before the Lord, who instructs him to place the men and their possessions in a riverbed and burn them (26:1–2). But the book of confessions and some precious stones are to be placed on the top of the mountain beside a new altar, where God will blot out what is written in the book and destroy it with lightning (26:3). But the stones will be swallowed up in the depths of the sea because they have been defiled by the idols of the Amorites (26:4–8). Other stones have the names of the twelve tribes engraved on them, and Kenaz is told to put them into the ark of the covenant in the temple that is to be built (26:9–12; cf. 2 Sam. 7:12–13). When Israel's sins reach their full measure, they will be removed and stored until God visits the earth (LAB 26:13–15).

Then Kenaz musters an army of three hundred thousand men and defeats the Amorites (chap. 27; cf. Judg. 7). Before the end of his fifty-seven-year reign (LAB 27:26), he establishes a covenant with the prophets Jabis and Phinehas, as well as Phinehas the son of Eleazar the priest, that they will stay faithful to the Lord (28:1–2). Phinehas son of Eleazar says the Lord told his father (Aaron) that the people will turn away from God (28:3–5), after which Kenaz has a vision and dies (28:6–10). Then Zebul is anointed leader (chap. 29; cf. Judg. 9:28–41), after whom no one is left to lead Israel (LAB 30:1; cf. Judg. 3:5–6). The Lord is angry with them for abandoning his ways, so he arouses their enemies to rule over them (LAB 30:2–4). The people repent and the Lord sends Deborah, who rebukes them for their disobedience (30:5–6; cf. Judg. 4) and tells them God will intervene because of his covenant (LAB 30:7). So Deborah summons Barak to fight against Sisera, who is killed by Jael (chap. 31; cf. Judg. 4). Deborah leads Israel in rejoicing (LAB 32; cf. Judg. 5). As Deborah nears death, she gathers Israel and implores them to direct their hearts to God. After she dies, the land has rest for seven years (LAB 33).

Then the author introduces Aod, a magician from Midian, who entices Israel to ignore the law in favor of other gods (34:1). With the aid of angels to whom he sacrificed, he shows them the sun by night, which amazes them (34:2–4). But

34. Harrington, "Pseudo-Philo," 2:297.

it turns out to be a test from God, who hands them over to the Midianites (34:5; cf. Judg. 6). Then the angel of the Lord informs Gideon that their oppression by the Midianites is because they have abandoned the promises of God, and so he commissions Gideon to deliver Israel from them (LAB 35; cf. Judg. 6). Gideon defeats the Midianites and requests a portion of the plunder from his people, from which he makes idols (LAB 36:1–3; cf. Judg. 7–8). But God, to preserve his reputation, determines to punish Gideon after his death, and so Gideon dies of old age and is buried (LAB 36:4). Then Abimelech comes to power, which is described in terms of an allegory of trees and vines, and he rules a year and a half (chap. 37; cf. Judg. 9). Then Jair builds a sanctuary to Baal, requiring everyone to offer sacrifices there (LAB 38:1; cf. Judg. 10:3–6). Only seven are unwilling, and Jair has them burned alive (LAB 38:1–3). But the angel Nathaniel extinguishes the fire, burns the servants of Jair, releases the seven men, and strikes the rest with blindness (38:3). Jair himself is rebuked by the angel of the Lord and burned alive. The sanctuary to Baal is destroyed, and a thousand of Jair's men are also burned (38:4). The Ammonites arise against Israel (39:1; cf. Judg. 10), so Jephthah the Gileadite comes from the land of Tob and urges Israel to return to the Lord and his law (LAB 39:2–7; cf. Judg. 11). Jephthah goes to battle against the Ammonites and vows to offer whoever he sees upon his return as a sacrifice to the Lord (LAB 39:8–10; cf. Judg. 11:30–31). But God is angry that Jephthah would vow so carelessly to offer even a dog to the Lord and so determines his firstborn should be offered instead. The author is careful to indicate that the Lord will indeed free his people, but this is because of the prayer of Israel and not because of Jephthah (LAB 39:10). When Jephthah returns from battle, the first to meet him is his daughter, Seila, who implores her father to keep his vow to the Lord and requests she be able to retreat to the mountains with companions to mourn her father's vow (40:1–3; cf. Judg. 11:32–38). So she goes to Mount Stelac, where the Lord praises her for her wisdom (LAB 40:4–7). Then she returns to her father, and all Israel mourns for her (40:8–9; cf. Judg. 11:39–40). This is followed by accounts of the judges Abdon (LAB 41:1; cf. Judg. 12:13–15) and Elon (LAB 41:2–3; cf. Judg. 12:11–13; 13:1). Samson is the next judge featured (LAB 42–43). First the author narrates the extensive account of the announcement of Samson's birth (chap. 42), identifying his mother, Eluma, as pleading to the Lord for a son (42:1–2). The Lord hears her prayer and sends an angel to announce her coming son, whom she is to name Samson (42:3). But her husband, Manoah, does not believe her until it is confirmed to him by an angel, named Fadahel (42:4–8, 10). Then he offers sacrifices to God (42:9–10).

Samson is born, and in addition to his quickly seeking to attack the Philistines, other events are recounted and explicitly attributed to the "Book of Judges" (LAB 43:1–4; cf. Judg. 14–15). Samson takes a Philistine wife, Delilah, a harlot (cf. Josephus, *Ant.* 5.8.11 §306), who betrays the secret of his strength to the Philistines (LAB 43:5–6; cf. Judg. 16). He is then captured and taunted by them, only to bring down the roof of a house upon himself and forty thousand of his enemies (LAB 43:6–8).

At a time when Israel has no leader and everyone does whatever they want, Micah, at the prompting of his mother, fashions silver and gold into idols, gods for whom he would be priest (LAB 44:1–5; cf. Judg. 17). And so all who wish to consult the idol come to Micah (LAB 44:5; cf. Judg. 17) until many Israelites are led astray and provoke the anger of the Lord (LAB 44:6–7), who brings his jealous wrath upon Micah, his mother, and all who violate his laws (44:8–10).

Then a Levite named Beel and his servant go to Nob, in the region of Benjamin, and sit in the open square when another Levite, Bethac, warns him of the wickedness of the city and takes him into his house (45:1–2; cf. Judg. 19). The inhabitants of the city implore Bethac to give up Beel to them; they break in and drag off Beel and his concubine (LAB 45:3). Beel they spare but they kill his concubine, whom he cuts up and sends to the twelve tribes to expose the wickedness done in Israel (45:4–5; cf. Judg. 19:27–20:6). The Lord, speaking to "the adversary," vows to frustrate and destroy the sinners (LAB 45:6). Israel responds to these events in the next chapter (chap. 46). At the suggestion of Phinehas, they use the Urim and Thummim to inquire of the Lord, who instructs them to go into battle against the sinners in Israel. But this is intended to lead them astray (46:1; cf. Judg. 20). They go up on battle to seek the men who had done this from among the people of Benjamin, who route Israel (LAB 46:2). Israel flees to Shiloh, where they inquire of the Lord, who promises they will be victorious next time. But the next time Israel again is routed by Benjamin (46:3) and in desperation asks for answers from the Lord (46:4; 47:1–2).

The Lord answers the prayer of Phinehas with a parable of a lion (47:3–6), explaining Israel's duplicity in benefiting from the sins of Micah while being repulsed at the sin against the concubine (47:7–8) and that their defeat is God's just retribution (47:8). When they realize their sin, they are given victory against the Benjamites of Nob (47:8–12; cf. Judg. 20). When Phinehas is near death, the Lord tells him to go to a mountain in the land of Danaben and, though the 120 years allotted for every man has passed for him, he will dwell there many years. There he will be fed by an eagle until a time of his testing, after which he will be lifted up (48:1–5).

The last section of Biblical Antiquities (chaps. 49–65) comes from the books of Samuel and is primarily devoted to Samuel and David.[35] At the outset Israel

35. Harrington, "Pseudo-Philo," 2:297.

looks for a leader to rule like Kenaz, so they cast lots but to no effect (49:1–2). Then they pray, recognizing their sin has made them hateful to God, and cast lots again, with the lot falling to Elkanah, who is unwilling to lead (49:3–5). So Israel prays again, and God appoints Elkanah's son to rule (49:6–8). Then Elkanah's wife, Hannah, prays (50:1–5; cf. 1 Sam. 1:2–13). Eli the priest tells her that her prayer will be answered (LAB 50:6–7; cf. 1 Sam. 1:14–17), but he does not tell her that her son will be a prophet (LAB 50:8; cf. 1 Sam. 1:18). Hannah gives birth to a son, who is named Samuel (LAB 51:1–2; cf. 1 Sam. 1:20–26), which causes Hannah to pray again (LAB 51:3–6; cf. 1 Sam. 2:1–11), and the people celebrate (LAB 51:7; cf. 1 Sam. 2:11). The sons of Eli, Hophni and Phinehas, have been walking in wickedness and taking the sacrificial offerings (LAB 52:1; cf. 1 Sam. 2:11–16), so Eli rebukes them—but they do not listen (LAB 52:2–4; cf. 1 Sam. 2:23–25). Young Samuel, age eight, does not yet know the oracles of the Lord when God calls to him at night (LAB 53:1–7; cf. 1 Sam. 3:1–11). God tells Samuel that destruction will come on those who transgress the commands given to Moses (LAB 53:8–10), and Samuel relates the message to Eli (53:11–13; cf. 1 Sam. 3:15–18). The narrative then recounts a battle between Israel and the Philistines in which the ark of the covenant is taken into the fray (LAB 54:1–3; cf. 1 Sam. 4:1–11). Saul, son of Kish, and the sons of Eli try to hold back the ark from the Philistine Goliath, who has taken hold of it. But Hophni and Phinehas are killed, and the ark is taken (LAB 54:3). Saul flees and tells the news to Eli, who acknowledges the fulfillment of Samuel's prophecy and dies (54:4–6; cf. 1 Sam. 4:14–21). When Samuel learns that the ark has been taken, God tells him it will be returned and Israel's enemies destroyed (LAB 55:1–2; cf. 1 Sam. 6:4; 7:17). The ark, which was taken by the Philistines to the temple of their god, Dagon, brings destruction on the Philistines and so is returned to Israel (LAB 55:3–10; cf. 1 Sam. 5:2–6:19).

In Biblical Antiquities 56 the people demand a king, which they ask of Samuel (LAB 56:1–3; cf. 1 Sam. 8:4–9). Samuel approaches Saul, tells him he is to rule as king (LAB 56:4–7; cf. 1 Sam. 9:1–10:9), and presents him to Israel (LAB 57; cf. 1 Sam. 12). The Lord sends Saul to destroy Amalek, but though he wins the battle, he allows their king, Agag, to live in order to acquire his treasures (LAB 58:1–2; cf. 1 Sam. 15). God, through Samuel, rebukes Saul, and Samuel at last kills Agag (LAB 58:3–4).

The remainder of Biblical Antiquities relates to David (chaps. 59–65).[36] The Lord tells Samuel that the kingdom of Saul is being blotted out and that Samuel is to anoint the next king (59:1; cf. 1 Sam. 16:1–3). So Samuel goes to

36. Harrington, "Pseudo-Philo," 2:297.

the sons of Jesse at Bethel, where he anoints David as king (LAB 59:2–5; cf. 1 Sam. 16:4–7, 11–13; 17:34–37). The spirit of the Lord leaves Saul and an evil spirit oppresses him, so David is summoned to play his lyre and sing to drive away the evil spirit (LAB 60; cf. 1 Sam. 16).

In his first battle David slays fifteen thousand Midianites (LAB 61:1; cf. 1 Sam. 17:15). Then the Philistine Goliath comes forward to taunt Saul and Israel (LAB 61:2), but David promises to defeat Israel's enemy (61:3–4; cf. 1 Sam. 17:16–36). David draws seven stones, on which he writes the following names: Abraham, Isaac, Jacob, Moses, Aaron, his own name, and "the Most Powerful." God sends an angel named Zervihel, presumably to aid David, and David strikes Goliath (LAB 61:5–7; cf. 1 Sam. 17:49–51). But before he dies, Goliath sees an angel, for God had changed David's appearance so even Saul does not recognize him (LAB 61:8–9; cf. 1 Sam. 17:55–58). When jealousy provokes Saul to seek to kill David, a spirit intercedes and compels him to leave David alone (LAB 62:1–2; cf. 1 Sam. 18:3; 19:18–23). Then David comes to Saul's son, Jonathan, with whom he makes a covenant, and tells him of his father's plan to kill him (LAB 62:3–8; cf. 1 Sam. 20:3–8). Jonathan confirms David's righteousness, and David flees to the wilderness (LAB 62:9–11; cf. 1 Sam. 20:23, 41–42). Meanwhile the priests in Nob profane the name of the Lord.

Doeg the Syrian reports to Saul that Abimelech the priest is making plans with David, so Saul kills all his household—only his son Abiathar escapes to tell David (LAB 63:1–5; cf. 1 Sam. 22:9–21). After the death of Samuel, Saul scatters the wizards from Israel, but God recognizes that he really did this so as to have someone to consult by divination since there was now no prophet in Israel (LAB 64:1; cf. 1 Sam. 28:3). The Philistines, recognizing Israel is divided and weak, plot revenge against them (LAB 64:2–3; cf. 1 Sam. 28:3 –7). In desperation, Saul seeks a witch in Endor to summon the spirit of Samuel (LAB 64:4; cf. 1 Sam. 28:11), who rebukes Saul and tells him he and his sons will die at the hands of the Philistines the next day (LAB 64:5–9; cf. 1 Sam. 28:12–25). So the Philistines attack Israel, and Saul, otherwise apparently uninjured, falls on his sword and is killed by an Amalekite prince (LAB 65; cf. 1 Sam. 31:1–4; 2 Sam. 1:7–10).

Critical Issues

Biblical Interpretation

Biblical Antiquities, as a "rewritten" account of scripture, exhibits its hermeneutic and interests by its handling of the biblical narrative. In so doing, it entirely omits large portions, such as Genesis 1–3, Exodus 3–13, and all the legal material in Exodus except Exodus 20,[37] which it amplifies considerably (LAB 11:6–14; 44:6–7). Indeed, except for the Decalogue, legal material receives very little attention.[38] It also omits almost the entire book of Leviticus, all the legal material in Numbers, Deuteronomy 1–30, Joshua 3–21, and portions of 1 Samuel.[39] It condenses all of Genesis 12–50 into a single chapter (LAB 8). But it generally follows the narrative sequence of the biblical text with respect to chronology and physical setting.[40] There are some instances, however, in which the author relocates some biblical events, such as to Shiloh rather than Mizpah (Judg. 20:1; LAB 45:5) or Bethel (Judg. 20:18; LAB 45:5) or Beth-shemesh (1 Sam. 6:12; LAB 55:9). And there is Ramathaim rather than Gilgal (1 Sam. 15:12, 21, 33; LAB 58:2) and Bethel rather than Bethlehem (1 Sam. 16:4; LAB 59:2).[41] Judges alone is an exception to the author's technique of excision and compression in that the material corresponding to that book (LAB 25–40) constitutes about one-third of the entire work. Judges 1–3 alone is removed, replaced by an expanded account of Kenaz (LAB 25–28), who, though the father of Othniel (Judg. 1:13), takes the place of Othniel as the first judge in Biblical Antiquities (cf. Judg. 3:7–14). Other accounts from the book of Judges— Deborah, Gideon, Abimelech, Jephthah, Samson, Micah, the Levite, and the war between Benjamin and Israel—are preserved but revised.[42] In his thorough discussion of the subject, Jacobson first notes the author's writing is "the result of the author's profound knowledge of the biblical text."[43] With this skill the author is able to weave quotations seamlessly into his own narrative.[44]

Biblical Quotations

Scholars have examined Biblical Antiquities's quotations in an attempt to shed light on the history of the biblical text. Harrington argues that the author of Biblical Antiquities used a distinctive Palestinian text-type that differed from the current Masoretic tradition.[45] Jacobson, however, dismisses

---

37. Nickelsburg, *Jewish Literature*, 266.
38. Hayward, "Philo, Pseudo- (LAB)."
39. Nickelsburg, *Jewish Literature*, 266.
40. Hayward, "Philo, Pseudo-Philo."
41. Jacobson, "Pseudo-Philo," 470.
42. Nickelsburg, *Jewish Literature*, 266.
43. Jacobson, *Commentary*, 1:224–25.
44. Jacobson, *Commentary*, 1:225.
45. Harrington, "Biblical Text."

this entire enterprise because, first, the author of Biblical Antiquities routinely paraphrases rather than quotes and, second, he seems to be working from his recollections rather than from literary traditions. There is, for Jacobson, no compelling evidence for a Hebrew basis distinct from that of today's Masoretic Text.[46] Perhaps yielding more positive results is an analysis of the manner in which the author of Biblical Antiquities utilizes quotations from the Hebrew Bible.[47] Jacobson provides ten ways in which he sees this play out in the narrative, which may be summarized as follows:[48] First, some citations make use of the immediate context of their Old Testament sources, and others, second, are used in a manner distinct from it. A third, related category of citation draws from a different place in the Hebrew Bible that is related to the topic or episode in which it is discussed in Biblical Antiquities. Fourth, sometimes the author alludes to another context by quoting from that context. Fifth, a quotation may be introduced from a different context with no clear explanation as to its suitability in its new context. Sixth, language may be utilized from a different context to establish some link. Seventh, two contexts may even be conflated by the merger of quotations from both. Or eighth, words may be quoted explicitly from one context with a different sense in the new context. Ninth, words may be taken from an immediate context yet slightly altered to meet an exegetical need in a new context. Finally, Jacobson suggests that a quotation may be used that simply does not fit in Biblical Antiquities, not because the quoted text is unsuitable but because the new context is in some sense altered.

Genre

As noted above, Biblical Antiquities belongs properly to that allusive category of "rewritten scripture." Yet within this framework it occupies a unique place that is developed extensively in later Judaism. This place has come to be known as "midrash" (Hebrew מִדְרָשׁ, *midrāš*), which typically refers to a practice used by rabbis from the late first century CE onward to interpret Scripture.[49] Works of a similar nature, such as the Genesis Apocryphon and Josephus's *Antiquities*, resemble Biblical Antiquities in that they imitate and to an extent rewrite biblical texts, but, as Jacobson observes, the method of midrash employed in Biblical Antiquities seems to have come to a standstill

---

46. Jacobson, *Commentary*, 1:255.
47. See Jacobson, "Biblical Quotation and Editorial Function."
48. Jacobson, *Commentary*, 1:257. See also Fisk, *Do You Not Remember?*
49. See Burns, "Midrash."

with that work, only to be revived centuries later in rabbinic literature, such as *Sefer Hayashar*, or still other works like *Pesikta Rabbati*, which likewise present a continuous narrative with embellishment.[50]

Contribution and Context

Jacobson summarizes the primary theme of Biblical Antiquities as follows: "No matter how much the Jewish people suffer, no matter how bleak their situation appears, God will never completely abandon God's people and in the end will grant salvation and triumph to the Jews."[51]

The importance of the law is underscored by its depictions as an eternal light (LAB 9:8; cf. 11:5) and as the foundation of understanding prepared from creation (32:7); it will be the means by which God will judge the world (11:1–2).[52] The law is set out as the eternal covenant (*testamentum*) for Israel (11:5).[53] This is depicted in the obedience of the twelve righteous men who refused to take part in the rebellious tower-building affair (6:3–4), of whom, in the end, only Abram exhibits a faith that adheres fastidiously to the law and trusts God for the outcome (6:11). Similarly, Amram objects to Egyptian demands to cease bearing children in obedience to the law and looks to God to render aid (9:2–5).[54]

Sin is always punished in the end (6:11; 27:7, 15; 45:3; 49:5), and the Biblical Antiquities utilizes the familiar rubric of sin-punishment-salvation (3:9–10; 12:4; 13:10; 19:2–5).[55] Integral here are individual responsibility and repentance (21:6).[56] Violations articulated in Biblical Antiquities are primarily idolatry and intermarriage. Abraham prefers death to idolatry (chap. 6), which is the basis for all sin (44:6–7; cf. 25:9–13). The villains who lead Israel astray do so by idolatry (chap. 34; 36:3; 38; 44:1–5).[57] Yet Jacobson is probably correct to observe that idolatry in the Biblical Antiquities is to be understood not in the restricted, narrow sense of worshiping idols or foreign gods but rather as "faithlessness to God and His Law," which is a primary concern for the author. So "idolatry" is an inclusive term, a reference in the narrow sense to worshiping a (false) foreign god and also a symbol of betrayal of God and

50. Jacobson, *Commentary*, 1:211–13.
51. Jacobson, "Pseudo-Philo," 470. Similarly, Nickelsburg, *Jewish Literature*, 267–68.
52. See Murphy, "Divine Plan, Human Plan."
53. Hayward, "Philo, Pseudo- (LAB)."
54. Jacobson, *Commentary*, 1:245.
55. Harrington, "Pseudo-Philo," 2:301. See Murphy, "Eternal Covenant in Pseudo-Philo."
56. Jacobson, *Commentary*, 1:245.
57. Murphy, "Retelling the Bible."

his law.[58] Tamar is said to have had intercourse with her father-in-law so as to avoid intermarriage with a gentile (9:5). Balaam's scheme for the downfall of Israel began with a plot to seduce them with Midianite women (18:13–14; cf. 9:1; 21:1; 30:1; 43:5; 44:7; 45:3).[59]

Unlike in other writings examined here, angels are not intermediaries of heavenly revelations in Biblical Antiquities. They exhibit traits like jealousy (32:1–2) and grief (19:16). Angels can serve as guardians (11:12; 59:4)—they help Samuel when he is summoned by the witch at Endor (54:6)—but they do not intercede for Israel in their sin (15:5). Only four angels are named: Ingethel (27:10), Zeruel (27:10; called Zervihel in 61:5), Nathaniel (38:3), and Fadahel (42:10). Sparse mention is made of evil spirits, which were created on the second day of creation (60:3) and have assisted people in sorcery (34:3; cf. also 53:3–4; 60:1).[60]

It is generally recognized that eschatology in the Biblical Antiquities deals with the fate of people after death and what occurs at God's coming to earth. All of these occur according to a schedule ordained by God (19:14–15; 56:2; 59:1; 61:3; 62:2, 9),[61] at the fulfillment of time (3:9–10) when the natural order of things ceases, the dead are restored to life, and light and darkness cease to exist.[62] There is no hint of political interests or messianic fervor. Instead, the author compartmentalizes matters into the present and future worlds (e.g., 3:10; 16:3; 19:7, 13; 32:17; 62:9).[63] After death the soul is judged according to the person's deeds (44:10). For the wicked there is no opportunity for repentance after death (33:2–5), and they will inevitably experience divine retribution for their sins (6:3; 23:6; 31:7; 36:4; 38:4; 44:10; 51:5; 63:4). The righteous will rest peacefully until God visits the world (23:13; 28:10; 51:5), at which time all will be raised (3:9–10; 19:12–13; 25:7). The righteous will dwell with God and their fathers (19:12–13; 23:13), whereas the wicked will be destroyed like Korah (16:3).[64]

For all his fidelity to Judaism and Israel's covenant with God, the author of Biblical Antiquities depicts intimate familiarity with pagan contexts. Some have observed that his interests in the origins of certain technologies and the arts, and the association of moral degeneration with the beginning of civilization, among other matters, reflect concerns of a Greco-Roman context.

---

58. Jacobson, *Commentary*, 1:245. Cf. Murphy, "Retelling the Bible," 287.
59. Harrington, "Pseudo-Philo," 2:301.
60. Harrington, "Pseudo-Philo," 2:301.
61. Nickelsburg, *Jewish Literature*, 269.
62. Jacobson, *Commentary*, 1:247.
63. Harrington, "Pseudo-Philo," 2:301.
64. Harrington, "Pseudo-Philo," 2:301.

Others have seen affinities with Greek literary traditions, such as dramas, romances, and mythology.[65] Affinities with such contexts are most evident in the author's mention of magic. Though seemingly effective, the stones that heal and repel demons are rejected for their role in idolatrous worship (25:11–12). Similarly, the sun is made to shine at night by the arts of an evil Midianite wizard (34:4).[66]

Jacobson observes that other works resemble Biblical Antiquities in their rewriting of Scripture in the Hellenistic period, such as the *Exagōgē* of Ezekiel the Tragedian from the second century BCE. Yet unlike Biblical Antiquities, which seeks to present its narrative in a generally biblical format, Ezekiel changes both the form and format of his narrative. Furthermore, Ezekiel presents a single extended narrative of the exodus, whereas Biblical Antiquities utilizes a number of narratives from Genesis to 2 Samuel. Similarly, the narrative of Joseph and Aseneth is more of a spinoff from a biblical narrative than a rewriting of it. The Genesis Apocryphon, though fragmentary, is similar in its imitation of the Bible. Josephus's *Antiquities* is often compared with Biblical Antiquities in that the historian recasts wide swaths of biblical narrative. But Josephus has his own rhetorical flourishes and motives for writing his account of Jewish history in a post-70 CE context. Similarities with the book of Jubilees are also obvious in that both books recount biblical history in a continuous prose, though Jubilees ends its account with Moses rather than David, as in Biblical Antiquities. Furthermore, Jubilees evidences more thorough reworking of material from the outset by its presentation in a framework of a revelation to Moses. Nevertheless, Jacobson regards Jubilees as the "closest cousin" to Biblical Antiquities.[67]

If a date for the Biblical Antiquities after 70 CE is correct, then it shares with other works such as 2 Baruch and 4 Ezra a context in which it reacts to the fall of Jerusalem and the destruction of its temple.[68] In all three, the dead are said to sleep in the earth (LAB 3:10; 19:12; 35:3; 4 Ezra 7:32; 2 Bar. 11:4), and the souls of the righteous are stored in their chambers (LAB 32:13; 4 Ezra 4:35; 2 Bar. 21:23; 42:7–8). Death is "sealed up" (LAB 3:10; 33:3; 4 Ezra 8:53; 2 Bar. 21:23; 42:7–8), Sheol restores its debt (LAB 3:10; 4 Ezra 4:41–43; 2 Bar. 21:23), and the nations are likened to spittle (LAB 7:3; 12:4; 4 Ezra 6:56; 2 Bar. 82:5). Other portions of Biblical Antiquities resemble similar accounts of 4 Ezra, such as the description of events at Sinai (LAB 23:10; cf. 4 Ezra 3:18)

---

65. Jacobson, *Commentary*, 1:213–15. See Jacobson, "Marginalia to Pseudo-Philo."
66. Jacobson, *Commentary*, 1:215.
67. Jacobson, "Pseudo-Philo," 471.
68. Jacobson, "Pseudo-Philo," 471; Harrington, "Pseudo-Philo," 2:302; Hayward, "Philo, Pseudo- (LAB)."

and the darkness and silence before creation (LAB 60:2; cf. 4 Ezra 6:38–39). Still others resemble 2 Baruch, such as God showing paradise and its mysteries to Adam (LAB 13:8; 26:6; cf. 2 Bar. 4:3), God's shortening of the times before the end (LAB 19:13; cf. 2 Bar. 20:1), and the exclusion of intercession of the dead for the living (LAB 33:5; cf. 2 Bar. 85:12). There are noteworthy affinities with 1 Enoch, such as God's plan to visit the world (LAB 19:12–13; cf. 1 En. 25:2), and there are explicit references to other documents (LAB 26:1–3; 35:7; 43:4; 56:7; 63:5).[69]

A number of expressions find clear parallels in the New Testament, though these need not suggest any kind of literary dependence except, in some instances, the utilization of common traditions. These include statements such as "may your blood be upon your own head" (LAB 6:11; cf. Matt. 23:34–35; 27:25) and discussion of "the restrainer" (LAB 51:5; cf. 2 Thess. 2:6–7). The birth accounts of Moses (LAB 9:9–16) and Samson (42:1–10) resemble the infancy narratives of Jesus (cf. Matt. 1–2; Luke 1–2).[70]

Purpose

Few scholars discuss the purpose of Biblical Antiquities at any length. In his later and shorter work, though, Jacobson, seeing the book written after the destruction of the temple in 70 CE, naturally articulates its purpose in that light.[71] In his view, the author was dealing with a community whose past was filled with trauma and whose present circumstances offered no better prospects. His aim, then, was to give his readers reasons for hope and optimism. This he did by recasting the biblical narrative, in which God is the "prime mover in history," for their present circumstances and by seeing even their disasters as God's own doings. Furthermore, God's doings are always reasonable, consistent, and in keeping with his promise to bring about the ultimate salvation of the Jews. That this salvation will come is without question, but when it comes will be determined largely by Israel turning from sin and toward devotion to God and the law (cf. LAB 21:6).[72] Additionally, the author was striving to combat idolatry and other pagan influences[73] and to advocate the necessity of good leadership.[74] Leaders are highlighted when, for instance, their idolatrous behavior leads to disaster for Israel (e.g., Jair

69. Hayward, "Philo, Pseudo- (LAB)."
70. Harrington, "Pseudo-Philo," 2:301–2.
71. Jacobson, "*Pseudo-Philo*," 470.
72. Jacobson, "*Pseudo-Philo*," 470.
73. Jacobson, *Commentary*, 1:253.
74. Nickelsburg, "Bible Rewritten and Expanded," 109.

in LAB 28:1–29:1; cf. 27:7; 38:4; 44:10; 49:5). Leaders who dispute among themselves are ultimately ineffective (e.g., 10:3), whereas Moses is approved by God (10:3).[75]

Reception History

A work that was translated from Hebrew to Greek, and from Greek into Latin, and survives in about twenty manuscripts today must have had some popularity. Yet, as Jacobson observes, evidence of its influence is surprisingly scarce. There is no evidence of Biblical Antiquities in any Hebrew writings, and scant shadows in Greek. The Latin text is more easily recognized, but even these writings are sparse and late. It is likely that the discussion of the descendants of Noah by Petrus Comestor (twelfth century CE) derives from Biblical Antiquities. Similarly, the elaborations on the Bible by Albertus Magnus (thirteenth century CE), attributed to Philo, also come from the Biblical Antiquities. To this one could add the fourteenth-century *Chronicles of Jerahmeel* and the first two citations in the work of Rabanus Maurus (ninth century CE).[76]

---

75. Hayward, "Philo, Pseudo- (LAB)."
76. Jacobson, *Commentary*, 1:273–76.

15

Genesis Apocryphon

Introduction

The Genesis Apocryphon (1Q20 or 1QapGen) was entirely unknown until its discovery on the floor, rather than in jars, in Cave 1 at Qumran in 1947. And it remains today among the most enigmatic texts among the Dead Sea Scrolls.[1] It narrates stories of Enoch, Lamech, Noah, and Abram related to accounts in Genesis 6–15. As a pseudepigraphon it presents many of these accounts in the first person (Lamech, Enoch, and Noah).[2] Yet as a "rewritten scripture" it contains considerable additions, omissions, and various amendments to the biblical account.[3] Abraham's account, also given in the first person, is expanded from the biblical account with his sojourn in Egypt (cf. Gen. 12:10–20).[4] Though later (1Q20 = 1QapGen XXI, 23–XXII, 34), curiously, the narrative adheres closely to Genesis 14 and gives its account of Abraham in the third person.[5]

Language and Manuscripts

The principal manuscript, 1QapGen,[6] is written in Aramaic,[7] which is likely the language of composition as well.[8] It is the longest Jewish Aramaic liter-

1. Becker, "Genesis Apocryphon."
2. See Bernstein, "Pseudepigraphy in the Qumran Scrolls," 15–17.
3. See Falk, *Parabiblical Texts*, 101–2.
4. Zahn, "Rewritten Scripture," 325.
5. Fitzmyer, *Genesis Apocryphon*, 16–20.
6. For an extensive account of its discovery and subsequent publication, see Machiela, *Dead Sea Genesis Apocryphon*, 21–27. For a complete account of the primary manuscript and fragments, see Falk, *Parabiblical Texts*, 26–28; Machiela, *Dead Sea Genesis Apocryphon*, 22–29.
7. For a complete discussion of linguistic aspects of Genesis Apocryphon's Aramaic, see Machiela, *Dead Sea Genesis Apocryphon*, 137–40.
8. Nickelsburg, "Bible Rewritten and Expanded," 106; Fitzmyer, *Genesis Apocryphon*, 25.

ary composition outside the Bible to survive from the Second Temple period.[9] The majority of the document, composed of four sheets of parchment, was purchased for the Hebrew University in 1955, though fragments of it remained in other hands. Infrared photos taken that year exposed some text that was otherwise illegible. When discovered, the scroll was rolled up so that the end of the text was in the center of the roll, and the beginning on the outside.[10] It is the latter portion from which material is lost, though how much is impossible to know. Though the former portion, the end of the document, is sufficiently preserved, it is notably abrupt in its ending in the middle of a sentence in the last preserved column (XXII).[11] Furthermore, this column is followed by evidence of sewing for an additional sheet, suggesting there was more to the original document.[12] But even what remains of the document is badly fragmented. Of the twenty-two columns that survive, only five (cols. II, XIX–XXII) are substantially legible.[13] Fragments comprise an additional column, labeled "column 0" and are placed at the beginning, though its proper location is uncertain.[14]

Provenance

Some scholars have seen the Genesis Apocryphon as belonging to the Qumran sect, arguing for a direct connection between that text and the Community Rule, the War Scroll, and the Pesharim.[15] Since Joseph A. Fitzmyer's critique, the consensus has been that the Genesis Apocryphon is a nonsectarian text.[16] And so most scholars recognize the text betrays no evidence of distinctive Qumran (sectarian) beliefs.[17] This view gains further support by the fact that all the sectarian (Essene) writings from Qumran were written in Hebrew, whereas the Genesis Apocryphon was written in Aramaic.[18] Though not a sectarian document composed at Qumran, it was certainly read and used there, and scholars are able to explain its appeal to that Jewish group. Daniel A.

9. Morgenstern and Segal, "Genesis Apocryphon," 238.

10. Morgenstern and Segal, "Genesis Apocryphon," 237.

11. Becker, "Genesis Apocryphon."

12. Falk, *Parabiblical Texts*, 28.

13. Nickelsburg, "Bible Rewritten and Expanded," 103.

14. Becker, "Genesis Apocryphon."

15. Notably Vaux, review of *The Genesis Apocryphon*; Dupont-Sommer, *Le Ecrits esseniens*, 293.

16. Fitzmyer, *Genesis Apocryphon*, 23; Harrington, "Bible Rewritten (Narratives)," 244–45; Nickelsburg, *Jewish Literature*, 177; Falk, *Parabiblical Texts*, 29.

17. Nickelsburg, "Bible Rewritten and Expanded," 106; Fitzmyer, *Genesis Apocryphon*, 11–14; Falk, *Parabiblical Texts*, 29.

18. Machiela, *Dead Sea Genesis Apocryphon*, 8.

Machiela urges that the Apocryphon's apocalyptic perspective, emphasis on Israel's exclusive claims to the land, discussion of divine mysteries, and reverence for the patriarchs, among other features, all would appeal to the Qumran sectarians.[19] Finally, the notion of Abram viewing the land from Mount Hazor (1QapGen XXI, 8) suggests the author lived in Palestine.[20] Today there is a general recognition that the author possessed an extensive knowledge of the geography of the region, and so there is a consensus that it was authored in Palestine.[21] The missing elements of the Genesis Apocryphon obscure any further inferences, save perhaps Machiela's astute observation that "behind our scroll was a community aware of the culture around it, but eminently concerned to uphold its own traditions and system of beliefs."[22]

Date

The Genesis Apocryphon is dated by the handwriting of the scribe responsible for producing the manuscript (paleography). The manuscript's use of a formal "Herodian" script suggests the second half of the first century BCE or the first half of the first century CE.[23] A number of features distinctive to scrolls found at Qumran, including 1QapGen, further support this date.[24] These include a deliberate system of blank spaces inserted to divide the text into thought units, dots placed above letters that are to be deleted, other dots placed at the beginning and end of each sheet to mark the lines for ruling, and a fuller spelling that uses extra consonants to indicate the pronunciation of certain vowel sounds.[25] Some argue that the language suggests a much earlier date for the original, indicating that the manuscript 1QapGen is not the autograph but a copy, though no other copies have been found. Other evidence likewise suggests an earlier date for the composition of the original (see below).

Scholars suggest linguistic features of the manuscript are helpful for dating[26] it just slightly later than the Targum of Job from Qumran (11QtgJob).[27]

19. Machiela, *Dead Sea Genesis Apocryphon*, 135–36.

20. Fitzmyer, *Genesis Apocryphon*, 220.

21. Machiela, *Dead Sea Genesis Apocryphon*, 8.

22. Machiela, *Dead Sea Genesis Apocryphon*, 142.

23. Avigad, "Paleography of the Dead Sea Scrolls," 71–74; Fitzmyer, *Genesis Apocryphon*, 25–26; Falk, *Parabiblical Texts*, 28. For a thorough account of the various scholarly views on the date of the manuscript, see Machiela, *Dead Sea Genesis Apocryphon*, 136–37.

24. Falk, *Parabiblical Texts*, 28. These features are part of what is sometimes called the "Qumran scribal school." See Tov, "Further Evidence."

25. Falk, *Parabiblical Texts*, 28–29; Fitzmyer, *Genesis Apocryphon*, 261–71.

26. Most importantly Kutscher, "Language of the 'Genesis Apocryphon.'" See also Fitzmyer, *Genesis Apocryphon*, 27–28.

27. Rowley, "Notes on the Aramaic."

And so this allows for a date for the Genesis Apocryphon of the late third or early second century BCE.[28] But Machiela finds more compelling evidence in linguistic factors for dating the Apocryphon from other Aramaic texts from Qumran. The majority of these documents date from the second century BCE and are sufficiently similar to the Genesis Apocryphon to come from a similar date. Linguistic evidence alone, then, may locate the last possible date to the early second century BCE.[29] In addition, though it was discovered among the Qumran cache, the work betrays little evidence of distinctive traits of the Qumran sectarians, suggesting the original predated the formation of the Qumran sect.[30]

Linguistic data and the absence of sectarian interests point to an earlier date of composition. Another factor is the Genesis Apocryphon's relationship with other Second Temple texts, notably its incorporation of traditions from both the book of Jubilees and 1 Enoch. All this evidence (and perhaps some other points[31]) suggests a date not later than the mid-second century BCE. The concern with parentage, marriage, and violence toward women by foreign people may fit a context during the transition from Ptolemaic to Seleucid dominance in Israel during the early years of the second century BCE.[32]

Contents

The extant text outlines simply into three main sections containing the account of the miraculous birth of Noah (cols. 0–V), the life of Noah and an account of the flood (cols. V–XVIII), and a narrative about Abram, which is incomplete (cols. XIX–XXII?).[33]

Birth of Noah (cols. 0–V)

As noted above, the beginning of the document is badly fragmented, and surely substantial material existed prior to the beginning of the extant text.[34] It is thought that the earliest portions of the manuscript (cols. 0–I) describe a time before the flood (Gen. 6–9). Its sparse language of "wrath," "curse,"

---

28. Machiela, *Dead Sea Genesis Apocryphon*, 140.

29. Machiela, *Dead Sea Genesis Apocryphon*, 140. Cf. Cook, "Remarks on the Testament of Kohath," 218–19.

30. Becker, "Genesis Apocryphon."

31. Machiela (*Dead Sea Genesis Apocryphon*, 141–42) enumerates seven reasons that, cumulatively in his estimation, point to a date of early to mid-second century BCE.

32. Becker, "Genesis Apocryphon."

33. Becker, "Genesis Apocryphon."

34. The outline here will follow that of Wise, Abegg, and Cook, *Dead Sea Scrolls*, 89–105.

"wickedness," "magicians," and ". . . with women," among other features, suggests that it describes human depravity prior to the flood, with particular reference to the elsewhere-known account of the illicit marriages between fallen angels, or Watchers, and human women (cf. Gen. 6:2–4; 1 En. 6–7).[35] Lamech, speaking in the first person, is concerned that his newborn son, Noah, may be the offspring of one of these fallen Watchers and his wife, Bitenosh (1QapGen II, 1–7). Bitenosh assures Lamech that the child is his own (II, 8–18). Though convinced, Lamech nonetheless seeks reassurance about the child, so he consults his father, Methuselah, asking him to inquire of his grandfather, Enoch, a friend of God to whom the holy ones reveal everything (II, 19–25). Columns III and IV are highly fragmentary but likely contained Enoch's dialogue with Methuselah, which then continues in line 2 of column V.[36] Enoch is replying to Methuselah about Noah, recounting that Lamech's fears about Noah pertain to his appearance, and, though fragmentary, Enoch seems to affirm Lamech's paternity and foretell calamity in the days of Noah (V, 2–23). Methuselah then returns to Lamech, telling him that Enoch confirmed Noah is truly his son (V, 24–27; cf. 1 En. 106; Jub. 4).

Life of Noah and the Flood (cols. V–XVIII)

A heading at 1QapGen V, 29, after a blank space, reads, "a [c]o[p]y of the Book of the Words of Noah," who is the subject throughout this section (cols. VII–XVIII; cf. Gen. 5–10). Noah speaks in the first person in testament-like form.[37] At the outset Noah announces that he was born for righteousness, which he practiced all his days (VI, 1–5). He then describes his marriage to Emzara and the birth of their children, whom he married to the children of his brothers "in accordance with the law of the eternal statute"—then he calculates the completion of ten jubilees (VI, 6–10). Noah is told by a Watcher about coming judgment according to the calculated time (VI, 11–24). The flood is narrated, though in very fragmentary text, over the next several columns (presumably cols. VI–IX), in which Noah, who stands out as the one righteous man on earth, rejoices and shouts for joy (VI, 25; VII, 1–8). Columns VII, 8 through X, 9 are highly fragmentary. However, the new readings and reconstructions give some sense.[38] It seems Noah rejoices at God's words and perhaps receives instructions for sacrifices in a dream, since he mentions blood rendering purity and

---

35. Wise, Abegg, and Cook, *Dead Sea Scrolls*, 90–91. For a complete account of parallels with the book of Genesis, 1 Enoch, and the book of Jubilees, see Falk, *Parabiblical Texts*, 29–41.

36. Wise, Abegg, and Cook, *Dead Sea Scrolls*, 92.

37. Wise, Abegg, and Cook, *Dead Sea Scrolls*, 94.

38. Machiela, *Dead Sea Genesis Apocryphon*, 47–52.

building something according to a dream (VII, 8–23). Column VIII continues with Noah's narration in the first person, referencing the duration of the flood and possibly instructions for after the flood subsides (VIII, 1–36). Column IX seems to be God speaking to Noah, giving him authority and perhaps instructions for the allocation of the land (IX, 1–10). At the beginning of column X, Noah blesses the Lord for keeping him safe, presumably through the flood, and seems to send forth the animals from the ark (X, 1–10).

When the ark comes to rest on Ararat, Noah first offers sacrifices to the Lord (X, 11–18) and then leaves the ark (XI, 8–11). Then, walking the length and breadth of the earth, he praises and blesses God (XI, 11–14; cf. Gen. 8:20; Jub. 6:1–3). The Lord appears to Noah (who narrates the affair in the first person), promising to be with him and giving him and his sons dominion. He also gives the command prohibiting the consumption of blood and establishes a covenant with Noah (XI, 15–24; XII, 1–8). Then Noah descends to the foot of the mountain with his sons and grandsons, observing the devastation from the flood (XII, 8–9) and recounting the names of his sons and daughters (XII, 9–12; cf. Jub. 7:18–19). Noah plants a vineyard on Mount Lubar, where he celebrates the first festival with his family (XII, 13–18; cf. Gen. 9:20; Jub. 7:1–6). Presumably falling asleep drunk,[39] Noah has a vision in which he sees something—the text is too fragmentary to be certain what it is, presumably a cedar (cf. XIV, 9)—being cut down and consumed (XIII, 8–12), an olive tree in full bloom (XIII, 13–15), and then four winds from heaven bringing destruction on the olive tree (XIII, 15–18; cf. Gen. 9:21–23; Jub. 7:7–13).

An explanation of the vision follows (XIV, 9–XV, 22) in which Noah is identified as the cedar, and its shoots are his three sons (XIV, 9–27). It appears—again the text is fragmentary—that some will apostatize and turn evil, only to experience judgment at the hands of a man from the south who will destroy those who rebel (XV, 8–20). Then Noah awakens from his sleep, and his own blamelessness is affirmed (XV, 21–23). Column XVI (lines 8–20) recounts the division of the earth between the sons of Noah—Japheth, Shem, and Ham (cf. Gen. 10; Jub. 8:10–30)—followed by further divisions among their own sons (XVII, 7–15; cf. Gen. 10; Jub. 9:1–19). (Though column XVIII is missing, Becker explains that it contained the transition from Noah to Abram.)[40]

The Account of Abram (cols. XIX–XXII?)

The remainder of the Genesis Apocryphon (cols. XIX–XXII) features Abram (Abraham) as the central figure and follows closely the narrative of

39. Wise, Abegg, and Cook, *Dead Sea Scrolls*, 96.
40. Becker, "Genesis Apocryphon."

Genesis 12–15. As noted above, as one nears the end of the account, the better preserved the manuscript is, so much of what follows is presented with few breaks in the narrative. Abram, speaking in the first person, builds an altar, presumably at Bethel,[41] and calls on the name of God (XIX, 6–9; cf. Gen. 12:1–7). Then he travels with his family to Egypt because of famine (XIX, 9–12). Upon entering Egypt Abram has a dream in which a cedar tree and date palm grow from a single root. People try to cut down the cedar and leave the date palm, but the latter objects—and so the cedar is spared because of the date palm (XIX, 13–16). Abram tells his wife Sarai of his dream, explaining that she is to say Abram is her brother so that he will be treated well on her account (XIX, 16–20). For five years Sarai avoids the notice of anyone attached to the Pharaoh of Zoan, until three of the ruler's men come to Abram and shower him with gifts (XIX, 21–24). They also ask him for knowledge, and so Abram reads to them from the "Book of the Words of Enoch" (XIX, 24–26). When Pharaoh's men, one of whom is named Hyrcanos, return to their master, they describe Sarai's incomparable beauty (XX, 2–8), and so Pharaoh has her brought to him and marries her (XX, 8–9). Abram, who Sarai said was her brother, is spared because of her but mourns her seizure and prays for her protection (XX, 12–16). In response God sends a spirit to afflict every man of Pharaoh's household; the affliction is so severe that Pharaoh is prevented from having sexual relations with Sarai (XX, 16–18). This goes on over the course of two years, during which even the Egyptian healers, magicians, and wise men are unable to help their master (XX, 18–21).

Abram is asked to pray for the king by Hyrcanos, who learns from Lot that Sarai is Abram's wife. When Pharaoh learns of this, he orders her restored to her husband (XX, 21–27). So Abram prays for Pharaoh, "that blasphemer" (XX, 28), and the plague is removed and Pharaoh healed (XX, 27–29). Pharaoh gives Sarai and Abram many gifts and has them escorted out of Egypt (XX, 30–32). Accompanied by Lot, they depart for Canaan, and Abram returns to Bethel, where he rebuilds the altar and offers sacrifices to God (XX, 33–XXI, 4). Lot departs to live near Sodom, while Abram remains at Bethel (XXI, 5–7; cf. Gen. 13:6–7). Then God tells Abram to survey the land that will be given to him and his descendants (XXI, 8–14). So he surveys the land (XXI, 15–19) and settles near Hebron, where he builds an altar and makes offerings to the Lord (XXI, 19–22).

The Apocryphon then narrates in brief the battle between the king of Elam and his allies against the king of Sodom and his allies, the former proving stronger than the latter and imposing tribute on them for twelve

41. Wise, Abegg, and Cook, *Dead Sea Scrolls*, 99.

years (XXI, 23–27; cf. Gen. 14). In the thirteenth year the king of Sodom
rebels but is routed and put to flight (XXI, 27–34). Abram's nephew Lot, who
had been living in Sodom, is taken captive, and his captors take him along
with the rest of their plunder toward Damascus (XXI, 34–XXII, 5). Abram
pursues them to an area near Damascus, where he rescues Lot and all the
plunder and captives from Sodom (XXII, 5–12). The king of Sodom comes
to meet him, and Abram goes to Salem (Jerusalem), where Melchizedek,
its king, provides food and drink for Abram and his men (XXII, 12–15).
Melchizedek blesses Abram, who gives him a tithe of the plunder (XXII,
15–18). The king of Sodom then asks Abram for what was taken from him
and leaves the rest of the plunder to Abram, who refuses it (XXII, 18–26).
Then God appears to Abram and asks him to take account of all he has
acquired since God called him from Haran (XXII, 27–32). When Abram
raises his concern that he has no sons to be his heir, God tells him that he
will have a son to be his heir in place of Eliezer, a member of his household
(XXII, 32–34; cf. Gen. 15:1–4).

Critical Issues

In addition to the matters of provenance and date discussed above, other
critical matters pertain to genre. Though presented here as "rewritten Bible,"
the precise genre of the Genesis Apocryphon requires some further attention.[42]
Since in places it resembles an Aramaic translation of the Hebrew book of
Genesis in a style similar to the targumim, it is sometimes said to belong to
that genre.[43] But this only accounts for part of what the Apocryphon is doing
since the text is not always consistent in its rendering of the Genesis base and
is more expansive and free with it than one observes in the targumim.[44] Others
use the term "midrash" for the methods employed by the author.[45] But again
this fails to satisfy, since the midrashim make a distinction between the scripture and its commentary, which one does not find in the Genesis Apocryphon.
Its most natural category seems to be that of "rewritten scripture," given its
affinities with Pseudo-Philo's Biblical Antiquities. Both share an extended
presentation of the old biblical text into a new narrative that "seamlessly
incorporates interpretation, clarification, harmonization, and supplementary

42. For a complete discussion of its genre, see Fitzmyer, Genesis Apocryphon, 16–25;
Machiela, Dead Sea Genesis Apocryphon, 1–5.
43. Black, Scrolls and Christian Origins, 193–95; Falk, Parabiblical Texts, 41.
44. Fitzmyer, Genesis Apocryphon, 18.
45. Following Zeitlin, "Dead Sea Scrolls," 247; Vermes, Scripture and Tradition, 95–96, 124.

traditions" and "interprets by means of a new telling of the story."[46] And so many scholars follow this designation of "rewritten scripture."[47]

Contribution and Context

Theological Interests

Some scholars, such as Geza Vermes, suggest the Genesis Apocryphon is void of any theological tendencies—interpretive activity motivated by the author's religious or ideological interests.[48] By this such scholars do not mean that there is no theological interest but rather that all the theological interest is inextricably linked to the biblical source. The author "never attempts to introduce unrelated or extraneous matter."[49] His objective is not innovation but explanation of the biblical narrative by bringing together other material from Genesis or utilizing outside material to illustrate the biblical text. Other scholars find some ideological motivation, such as an anti-Samaritan prejudice.[50] More positively, one may find a number of theological tendencies and methodological techniques for the Apocryphon's recasting of the Genesis narratives.[51] Though working with a limited text,[52] George W. E. Nickelsburg identifies four factors, including, first, what he calls an "Enochic" perspective found in the references to the words of Enoch (1QapGen XIX, 25). Similarly, he suggests an eschatological interest, potentially based on the end-time typology from 1 Enoch, in which the sinful generation of Noah and its ensuing punishment is associated with the author's own age.[53] Third, there are "channels of divine revelation"[54] used in the Apocryphon not found in Genesis, including Enoch and dream visions. Finally, there is a distinct interest in presenting dialogue between patriarchs and their wives (e.g., Lamech and Batenosh [Bitenosh], Abram and Sarai).[55] Still other factors could be enumer-

---

46. Falk, *Parabiblical Texts*, 41.

47. Falk, *Parabiblical Texts*, 41; Alexander, "Retelling the Old Testament"; Evans, "Genesis Apocryphon"; Crawford, "'Rewritten' Bible at Qumran"; Bernstein, "Contours of Genesis Interpretation."

48. Vermes, *Scripture and Tradition*, 124–26.

49. Vermes, *Scripture and Tradition*, 126.

50. Winter, "Note on Salem-Jerusalem"; R. Meyer, review of N. Avigad and Y. Yadin, *A Genesis Apocryphon*, *Deutsche Literaturzeitung* 80 (1959): 586–87, cited in Machiela, *Dead Sea Genesis Apocryphon*, 6.

51. Nickelsburg, "Patriarchs Who Worry."

52. Machiela, *Dead Sea Genesis Apocryphon*, 6–7.

53. Nickelsburg, "Patriarchs Who Worry," 182.

54. Machiela, *Dead Sea Genesis Apocryphon*, 6–7.

55. Nickelsburg, "Patriarchs Who Worry," 183–84, 188–89.

ated here, but Machiela is surely correct to affirm the presence of theological interests and literary techniques utilized by the Genesis Apocryphon.[56]

Relation to Genesis

Machiela observes that while the Apocryphon's treatment of Genesis overlaps with Enochic writings (e.g., 1 En. 106–7 and the Book of Giants) and the book of Jubilees (e.g., the chronology of Abram and Sarai in Egypt and the division of the earth), the work is largely unique. The author's interpretations of Genesis are best regarded as "interpretive reworkings, intended to alleviate difficulties in Genesis."[57] It is "mostly a relatively free paraphrase that is often expansive but sometimes abbreviated."[58] But there are exceptions, such as instances of a literal rendering of the Hebrew[59] resembling the tradition of the Samaritan Pentateuch and Septuagint more than the Masoretic Text.[60]

In his treatment of Genesis, the author also exhibits some unevenness in the handling of material.[61] Though there is a similar amount of material between the two, Noah receives considerably more attention than Abram in the Genesis Apocryphon. Furthermore, Noah's presentation draws from Genesis but is supplemented by a great deal of external material, much of which is known from other ancient sources. And there are very few translations from the Genesis account in the Noah narratives (e.g., 1QapGen VI, 23; X, 12; XI, 11, 18; XII, 1, 9, 10, 13).[62] In contrast, the accounts of Abram are much less developed, though the extrabiblical material is unique to the Genesis Apocryphon[63] and there are many instances of translation.[64]

Noah Texts

The "birth of Noah" account (cols. 0–V) is an extensive narrative only loosely connected to the biblical narrative (Gen. 5:28–29; 6:1–5), which it expands by an estimated 300 percent. It contains no translation of Genesis but rather expands on and rewrites the narrative of 1 Enoch 106–7. The subsequent "Book of Noah" text (1QapGen V–XVIII) corresponds to Genesis

56. Machiela, *Dead Sea Genesis Apocryphon*, 7.
57. Machiela, *Dead Sea Genesis Apocryphon*, 131.
58. Falk, *Parabiblical Texts*, 94.
59. Fitzmyer, *Genesis Apocryphon*, 38–45.
60. VanderKam, "Textual Affinities"; VanderKam, *Textual and Historical Studies*, 278–79.
61. Machiela, *Dead Sea Genesis Apocryphon*, 131.
62. Fitzmyer, *Genesis Apocryphon*, 39; Falk, *Parabiblical Texts*, 95.
63. Machiela, *Dead Sea Genesis Apocryphon*, 131.
64. Falk, *Parabiblical Texts*, 95.

6–11 generally in order. Yet there are some additions derived from Genesis and elsewhere (notably Jubilees), as well as rearrangements and omissions. The Apocryphon contains eight Aramaic translations of the Hebrew text of Genesis, which it expands approximately 250 to 300 percent.[65] The result of this creative work on the part of the author is a striking and revered status for Noah. Even Noah's drunkenness is spun in a positive manner as the context for his reception of divine revelation.[66] The myth of the fallen angels, or Watchers,[67] is utilized to clarify some apparent ambiguities in the brief account of Noah's birth (Gen. 5:28–29).[68] Noah is explicitly presented as one who practices Torah (1QapGen VI, 1–5) in terms of his marriage (VI, 7; cf. Jub. 4:33), sacrifices (1QapGen X, 12–13; cf. Gen. 8:20; Jub. 6:1–3), and laws pertaining to fruit trees and festivals (1QapGen XII, 27; XV, 7–18?; cf. Jub. 8:1–9:15).[69] Noah, like Enoch and perhaps Lamech, receives visions and dreams (1QapGen XI, 15; cf. VI, 9–22; XII, ?–XV, 20; XXII, 27; Jub. 5:1–18; 7:20–24; 10:3–14; 1 En. 7; 60:1–6; 65:1–68:1). Among the roles played by Noah is that of apportioning the habitable earth, here emphasizing the right of the Israelites to inhabit and rule the land of Israel (1QapGen XVI–XVII).

Abram Texts

Like Noah, Abram receives editorial attention from the author of the Genesis Apocryphon, who presents him as a blameless patriarch.[70] The beginning of the account of Abram up to his settlement in Canaan (1QapGen XIX, ?–XXI, 22; cf. Gen. 12–13) follows the Genesis account closely, with twenty-two short translations from the Hebrew. It expands the biblical text by an estimated 350 to 400 percent, with additions from other sources, notably the book of Jubilees. The account of Abram's wars to the end of the narrative (1QapGen XXI, 23–XXII, ?) closely follows the biblical text (Gen. 14:1–15:4) with substantial translation and minimum expansion of about 130 to 140 percent.[71] Also notable in the latter section is the switch from Abram's narration in the first person to the third person. The accounts of Abram and Sarai in Egypt (Gen. 12) and later with Abimelech (Gen. 20), which present the patriarch in a negative light, are conflated to a single, more

65. Falk, *Parabiblical Texts*, 95–96.
66. Machiela, *Dead Sea Genesis Apocryphon*, 132.
67. 1 En. 6–7; 106–7; Jub. 4:15, 22; 5:1–11; 7:21–24, 27; 8:3; CD-A II, 17–19; 4Q180 1 7–9; cf. 1 Pet. 2:4; Jude 6.
68. Falk, *Parabiblical Texts*, 42.
69. Falk, *Parabiblical Texts*, 68–76.
70. Machiela, *Dead Sea Genesis Apocryphon*, 132.
71. Falk, *Parabiblical Texts*, 96.

positive account in the Genesis Apocryphon (1QapGen XIX, 10–XX, 32). Several examples could be cited, but the account of Abram and Sarai is most instructive. First, readers learn that the scheme to identify Sarai as his sister originates with God (XIX, 14–21; cf. Gen. 12:11–12). Second, Sarai avoids other men entirely for five years (1QapGen XIX, 23). Third, Abram is sought by the Egyptian noblemen as a wise teacher, and he teaches them (XIX, 24–25). Fourth, Abram is powerless to stop Sarai's abduction by Pharaoh (XX, 8–9; cf. Gen. 12:15). Fifth, Abram, weeping, prays for God's judgment on Pharaoh and protection for Sarai (1QapGen XX, 10–16). Sixth, when Sarai is taken by Pharaoh, Abram does not profit from it. Seventh, God's protection of Sarai entails Pharaoh's inability to approach her sexually (XX, 16–18). Eighth, when Pharaoh learns Abram is Sarai's brother, his rebuke is accompanied by his request for prayer and healing (XX, 26–28; cf. Gen. 12:18–19). Ninth, Abram prays to God to heal Pharaoh, and he does (1QapGen XX, 28–29). Finally, tenth, Pharaoh bestows gifts on Abram for the healing, thus alleviating the problem created in Genesis 12 that he profited by his deception (1QapGen XX, 29–30). Daniel K. Falk argues that the concern here is, first, to defend the integrity of Abram as a "model of piety and wisdom" and, second, to defend Sarai's purity as "the model of the chaste wife who sought to avoid the attention of other men."[72] This is by no means all. To the Genesis account the Genesis Apocryphon adds Abram's prayers (XIX, 7–8; XX, 12–16, 28–29), explicit ascriptions of unique, sought-after wisdom (XIX, 23–25), and Abram's reception of divine revelation (XIX, 14–19, 25; XXI, 8; XXII, 27; cf. Gen. 15:1).[73]

Relation to Other Jewish Texts

A number of affinities could be drawn between the Genesis Apocryphon and other Second Temple Jewish texts, such as the Biblical Antiquities of Pseudo-Philo and even Josephus's *Jewish Antiquities*. However, two in particular stand out for their specific points of correspondence: 1 Enoch and the book of Jubilees. With respect to the former, the account of the birth of Noah (cols. 0–V) resembles that of 1 Enoch (chaps. 106–7) but differs in several notable ways. Here four can be identified. First, the speaker in the Genesis Apocryphon, as elsewhere in the work, is the person of immediate concern, which here is Lamech, whereas in 1 Enoch it is Enoch. Second, Lamech's suspicion that Noah was conceived by an angel, which occasions a lengthy appeal to his wife (1QapGen II, 4–18), is absent in 1 Enoch (cf.

72. Falk, *Parabiblical Texts*, 84.
73. Falk, *Parabiblical Texts*, 87–89.

1 En. 106:6). Yet such emotionally expressive additions are in keeping with other additions to Genesis found in the document (e.g., 1QapGen II, 25; VII, 7; XIX, 21; XX, 8–9, 10, 12, 16; XXI, 7; XXII, 5).[74] Third, the appearance of Noah repeated twice in 1 Enoch (106:5–6, 10–12) may only appear once in the Apocryphon, at the bottom of column II, which is now lost. Finally, Lamech's speech to Methuselah (1 En. 106:5–6) is eliminated in the Genesis Apocryphon (1QapGen II, 19).[75]

The Genesis Apocryphon also bears a number of affinities to the book of Jubilees, in both biblical and nonbiblical material. In the biblical material, one finds points of correspondence such as Abram's sojourn to Bethel (Gen. 12:8–9; cf. 1QapGen XIX, 7–10a; Jub. 13:8–10)[76] and in Egypt (Gen. 12:10–20; cf. 1QapGen XIX, 10–XX, 32; Jub. 13:11–15).[77] A number of nonbiblical parallels between the Genesis Apocryphon and the book of Jubilees, of which there are many, are noted in chronological order.[78] These include Noah's sacrifice after the flood as atoning and as drawn from Leviticus (1QapGen X, 13–17; cf. Jub. 6:2–3) and Noah's obedience to the law regarding fruit trees (1QapGen XII, 13–14; cf. Jub. 7:1–2). Also shared in these two traditions is the manner in which Noah divides the land among his sons (1QapGen XV; XVI, ?–XVII, 6; cf. Jub. 8:10–24) and they in turn among their own sons (1QapGen XVII, 7–?; cf. Jub. 9:1–13; Gen. 10:2–31). There are also minor points of similarity, such as the naming of Lamech's wife as Bitenosh (1QapGen II, 3–18; cf. Jub. 4:28) and Noah's wife as Emzara (1QapGen VI, 6–7; cf. Jub. 4:33a) and the translation of "creeping things" (Gen. 6:7) as "wild beasts" (1QapGen VI, 24–?; cf. Jub. 5:2, 20–21). Despite all these similarities, there are sufficient differences that the question of one text's use of the other, or their use of a common source (a "Book of Noah"), is the subject of some debate.[79]

Purpose

Few scholars elaborate on the purpose of the Genesis Apocryphon, rendering the observations of Machiela all the more important. For him, the work is by no means intended to replace the book of Genesis. It is an exegetical work based on that book and "was meant to be read *alongside* the authoritative

---

74. Nickelsburg, "Bible Rewritten and Expanded," 105.
75. See Falk, *Parabiblical Texts*, 96–97.
76. Fitzmyer, *Genesis Apocryphon*, 105.
77. Nickelsburg, "Bible Rewritten and Expanded," 105.
78. See Fitzmyer, *Genesis Apocryphon*, 99–105; Falk, *Parabiblical Texts*, 97–100.
79. Falk, *Parabiblical Texts*, 98–100.

text."[80] The work tends to fill in material not explicit in the text, address particular interpretative uncertainties, and draw connections between people and events in the narrative and so becomes the "proper lens through which to read Genesis."[81] Falk struggles at this point, for explanations such as Machiela's fail to explain the function of the Genesis Apocryphon and so, for him, problematize the categorization of its genre as "rewritten scripture." For his part, Falk acknowledges the work served to make the scripture more clear, systematic, and lively, but the context in which it did so—a school, synagogue, or home, whether it was educational or liturgical, for educational or apologetic purposes—remains unclear.[82]

80. Machiela, *Dead Sea Genesis Apocryphon*, 142; italics original.
81. Machiela, *Dead Sea Genesis Apocryphon*, 142.
82. Falk, *Parabiblical Texts*, 41–42.

16

Letter of Aristeas

Introduction

The Letter of Aristeas is usually regarded as a fictitious account of the origins of the Greek translation of the Torah from the Hebrew. It is presented as a letter from a certain Aristeas, a (gentile) figure of some importance in the court of Ptolemy II Philadelphus, king of Egypt (283–247 BCE), to his brother, Philocrates, whose interest in religious matters furnishes the occasion for writing (§§1–8).[1] It claims that the Egyptian king instructed his librarian, Demetrius of Phalerum, to collect books for the library in Alexandria. Demetrius, desiring to include the law of the Jews in Greek translation in this collection, dispatched a letter to the high priest in Jerusalem requesting men for the task. A delegation from Alexandria delivered the letter and secured the participation of seventy-two Jews from that region to return to Egypt to undertake the task of translation. Aristeas claims to be among that delegation. But in truth the letter was written by an unknown Jew from Alexandria.[2] The work as a whole exhibits signs that its author was familiar with details of the Egyptian court and the environs of Judea, but it is of dubious value as a historical account of the events it purports to describe.

Language and Manuscripts

The Letter of Aristeas is written in a Greek style consistent with that of literary Koine Greek,[3] though it is sometimes cumbersome and inelegant.[4]

1. Nickelsburg, "Stories," 75–76.
2. B. Wright, "Aristeas, Letter of."
3. Tcherikover, "Ideology," 63; Hadas, *Aristeas to Philocrates*, 55; and esp. Meecham, *Letter of Aristeas*, 44–168.
4. Shutt, "Letter of Aristeas," 2:8.

Yet the author is seemingly well read in some important writings of classical and Hellenistic antiquity.[5]

The Letter of Aristeas survives from antiquity in twenty-three Greek manuscripts, as well as paraphrases and excerpts in the works of Josephus and Eusebius of Caesarea, respectively. The Greek manuscripts date from the eleventh to the sixteenth century[6] and are divided into groups for reconstruction of the Greek text.[7] In all these manuscripts, the Letter of Aristeas is joined to a *Catena on the Octateuch*, which may have originated in the library at Caesarea.[8] Josephus paraphrases a considerable portion of the work (*Ant.* 12.2.1–15 §§11–118, using Let. Aris. §§9–46, 51–81, 172–87, 292–305, and 308–21). There are portions that he omits seemingly as unnecessary, such as the prologue (§§1–8) and the names of the translators (§§47–50). He omits the travelogue (§§82–120), Eleazar's words (§§121–71), the symposia (§§188–291), the mention of ritual washing (§§306–7), and the epilogue (§322). His paraphrasing and selective use of the text makes Josephus of little value for reconstruction of the Greek text of Aristeas. Excerpts of Aristeas are also preserved by Eusebius of Caesarea, who cites the work in his discussion of the life of the Jews.[9]

Most scholars refer to this writing as the Letter of Aristeas or, more complexly, the Letter of Aristeas to Philocrates. But this designation does not occur until a Greek manuscript from the fourteenth century (Q; Paris, Bibliotheque Nationale 950), where it is called "the book of Aristaios" (see also Josephus, *Ant.* 12.2.12 §100). Most Greek manuscripts simply read "Aristeas to Philocrates." Its oldest title, preserved by Eusebius, is "On the Translation of the Law of the Jews."[10]

Provenance

The author himself was clearly a Jew, as indicated by his interests and sympathies,[11] such as his knowledge of Jewish practices and temple worship (e.g.,

---

5. Nickelsburg, "Stories," 78. E.g., Demetrius of Phalerum (§§9–11), Hecataeus of Abdera (§31), Theopompus (§314), and Theodectes (§316). Cf. Hadas, *Aristeas to Philocrates*, 47–59; Tcherikover, "Ideology," 63–69.

6. For a complete list of the manuscripts and their dates, see B. Wright, *Letter of Aristeas*, 28; Pelletier, *Lettre d'Aristée*, 8–9. For a description of most of the manuscripts, see Thackeray, "Appendix," 504–13.

7. Shutt, "Letter of Aristeas," 2:8; B. Wright, *Letter of Aristeas*, 30–31.

8. Pelletier, *Lettre d'Aristée*, 9.

9. Eusebius, *Praep. ev.* 8.2–5, 9; 9.38; B. Wright, *Letter of Aristeas*, 33–34.

10. Eusebius, *Praep. ev.* 9.38; B. Wright, "Aristeas, Letter of"; B. Wright, *Letter of Aristeas*, 30.

11. Nickelsburg, "Stories," 78; Hadas, *Aristeas to Philocrates*, 5–6.

Let. Aris. §§83–120).[12] Furthermore, his writing in several places exhibits a familiarity with the Septuagint that could have come only from a Jewish author.[13] The author's knowledge of Alexandria (§301), particularly his familiarity with Ptolemaic bureaucratic terminology and royal ideology,[14] suggests that as the city of origin.[15] The writing, particularly the author's Greek style, exhibits familiarity with a range of Greek literary traditions.[16]

It is widely recognized that the readership is also Jewish,[17] since the author deals with detailed matters of biblical texts related to animals that chew the cud and part the hoof while ignoring more foundational questions regarding circumcision, Sabbath observance, and the prohibition of pork.[18] Confirmation of a Jewish readership can be seen in the book's aim to justify the translation of the Law into Greek, which is presented with the support of the Jerusalem high priest and the Jewish community in Alexandria.

The primary readership is surely the Alexandrian Jews, since Eleazar's explanation of the significance of the clean and unclean beasts is directed toward the Hellenized Jew, for whom such aspects of the Law are obscure. For Alexandrian Jews, the writing would encourage them to be loyal citizens to their gentile rulers and educated elite. But if the work reached Jerusalem, it would reassure the Jewish leaders that one of their own, Eleazar, endorsed the enterprise of the translation and cooperation with gentiles, and affirm that Alexandrian Jews, too, live in conformity with the Law. One could add that the miraculous nature of the results achieved underscores for a potentially skeptical readership that not only is the Law from God but its translation into Greek is of divine origin as well. The outlook, then, is one in which the author is advocating for the authority of the Greek translation of the Law made in Alexandria, perhaps against the attitude of Palestinian Jews who may already look askance at the complacency of diaspora Jews.[19] But this tells only part of the story.

12. Shutt, "Letter of Aristeas," 2:9. Notably, the author uses the Septuagint (Greek) translation of the law for his depiction of the showbread table (§§51–72) and the high priestly vestments (§§96–99).

13. B. Wright, *Letter of Aristeas*, 16.

14. B. Wright, *Letter of Aristeas*, 17; Hadas, *Aristeas to Philocrates*, 6; Nickelsburg, "Stories," 78.

15. Nickelsburg, *Jewish Literature*, 196; Shutt, "Letter of Aristeas," 2:7; Hadas, *Aristeas to Philocrates*, 26–27; Honigman, *Septuagint and Homeric Scholarship*, 128–30; B. Wright, "Aristeas, Letter of."

16. B. Wright, *Letter of Aristeas*, 17.

17. Hadas, *Aristeas to Philocrates*, 65–66; Tcherikover, "Ideology," 60–63; B. Wright, *Letter of Aristeas*, 63; Barclay, *Jews in the Mediterranean Diaspora*, 148.

18. Nickelsburg, "Stories," 77; Hadas, *Aristeas to Philocrates*, 65–66; Tcherikover, "Ideology," 62.

19. Similarly, Bartlett, *Jews in the Hellenistic World*, 11–13, 16.

More specifically, as Victor Tcherikover argues, the Alexandrian Jewish readership was likely made up of educated members of the elite with some concerns about assimilation within their Hellenistic context. This suggests that at least part of the author's purpose is to address these concerns, which he does in ways that are sometimes strikingly accommodating to Jewish assimilation to Hellenistic contexts. The respect Ptolemy shows to the Law suggests to a Jewish readership not only that gentiles can recognize the homage due to the things of Israel's God but also that coexistence between Jews and gentiles can be maintained with mutual respect. For John R. Bartlett, "Aristeas finds gentile rule agreeable and accommodating."[20] From the author's perspective, Jewish beliefs in their one God are not inconsistent with Greek philosophy (§§121–22).[21] But there is a tension inherent in the author's presentation between respect for Greek culture and learning and a tenacious insistence on the distinctiveness of Israel as God's people. The author's respect for Greek culture and learning is reflected both in the Greek style of the author and in his presentation of the translators, who are revered for their role in translating the sacred text, as astute in Greek culture and philosophy. They are able to express their ideas in terms of Hellenistic ideals, similar to the allegorical devices used in Eleazar's speech (§§148–51, 168). Furthermore, whereas other literature rails against idolatry, the criticism of idolatry in the Letter of Aristeas is less divisive between Jews and Greeks (§§134–38; cf. §§15–16). Yet the author is a steadfast Jew, asserting that the Law has established an impenetrable barrier between the Jews and other nations (§139). In short, the Jews may participate in Greek culture and even utilize their language but remain bound to the laws "that are uniquely theirs and that differentiate them from the gentiles."[22]

Date

It is evident that the work does not date from the time of Ptolemy II Philadelphus, as claimed. Instead, archaizing statements, anachronisms, and historical inaccuracies point to a later time.[23] The actual date is debated and ranges from 250 BCE to 33 CE. The inaccuracies and ambiguities are curious. References to the administration of the Ptolemies (§§128, 182) in Egypt are little help, since this reign took place from 303 to 30 BCE. External sources indicate that Aristeas's librarian, Demetrius of Phalerum, was not a librarian at Alexandria

---

20. Bartlett, *Jews in the Hellenistic World*, 16.
21. Bartlett, *Jews in the Hellenistic World*, 14.
22. Nickelsburg, "Stories," 77–78.
23. Nickelsburg, "Stories," 78; Hadas, *Aristeas to Philocrates*, 6–9.

and died out of favor with the Egyptian rulers soon after the beginning of Ptolemy II's reign (283 BCE).[24]

Historical references are of some help. The decree by Philadelphus that frees Jewish slaves (§§12–27) refers to an event from 262 to 261 BCE. The account is otherwise familiar with protocol of the Ptolemaic court (§§295–300) and economic realities from the late third or early second century BCE in Egypt (§109). Some of the author's Greek expressions were once thought to point to a date in the second half of the second century BCE but now could be dated to the third century BCE. He clearly uses the Greek translation of the Law (§§51–72, 96–99, 155) and quotes from an author, Hecataeus of Abdera, who lived in the days of Ptolemy I Soter (r. 303–285 BCE). There are affinities with the work of Aristobulus, who writes to Ptolemy VI Philometor (r. 180–145 BCE), but it is unclear whether Aristobulus uses Aristeas or the other way around.[25] Most agree that by the first century CE, Philo and probably Josephus knew of the Letter of Aristeas.[26] Most scholars date the Letter of Aristeas to the middle to the latter part of the second century BCE because of its chronology with respect to Aristobulus and its familiarity with Ptolemaic bureaucracy and court protocol of that time.[27] George W. E. Nickelsburg argues that linguistic and other factors point to the end of the second century BCE, during the reign of Ptolemy VIII Euergetes (145–116 BCE), and dates the work between 138 and 130 BCE.[28] Benjamin G. Wright III shows that the linguistic evidence, when all factors are considered, places Aristeas in the second century BCE, sometime between 160 and 100 BCE. He is probably correct to suggest the possibility of an earlier date, from the 150s BCE to the last decade of the second century BCE.[29]

Contents[30]

Introduction (§§1–8)

The Letter of Aristeas, addressed to a certain Philocrates, regards the author's meeting with Eleazar, the high priest of the Jews, giving a clear

24. Cf. Strabo, *Geogr.* 9.1.20; Diogenes Laertius, *Vit. phil.* 5.36; Diodorus Siculus, *Bibliotheca historica* 19.78; Plutarch, *Demetrius* 8–9; Polybius, *Historiae* 12.13; Aelian, *Varia historia* 3.17.

25. Bartlett, *Jews in the Hellenistic World*, 17. Some, however, argue for no literary dependence between them (B. Wright, *Letter of Aristeas*, 28–30).

26. Bartlett, *Jews in the Hellenistic World*, 17.

27. B. Wright, "Aristeas, Letter of."

28. Nickelsburg, *Jewish Literature*, 196.

29. B. Wright, *Letter of Aristeas*, 27–28.

30. For a discussion of the structure of the Letter of Aristeas, see B. Wright, *Letter of Aristeas*, 53–55.

explanation of it because of the recipient's interest in such matters (§1–2). The purpose of this meeting was to devote the things of God to special study, with a view to translate the Law from Hebrew (§3) with an entourage coming to Egypt from Judea for the purpose (§4)—all of which Aristeas writes about for the interest of Philocrates (§§5–8).

Request for a Translation of the Law (§§9–82)

Demetrius of Phalerum, appointed keeper of the king's library, aimed to expand the library's holdings to include all the books in the world, having already attained over two hundred thousand (§§9–10). He informs the king, in Aristeas's hearing, of his intent to expand the holdings to five hundred thousand, including the lawbooks of the Jews (§10). When he learns that the prospect only lacks a translation in their language, the king gives orders for letters to be written to the high priest of the Jews to undertake the project (§11). Aristeas seizes on the opportunity and convinces King Ptolemy to free all Jewish slaves in his kingdom (§§12–20). The king issues a decree of emancipation, which Aristeas quotes at length (§§21–25) and may be based on a genuine decree by Ptolemy II calling for the registration of slaves in Egypt.[31] The slaves are released (§§26–27), and the king instructs Demetrius to draft a memorandum requesting that the translation should be made, which Aristeas recounts in full (§§28–32). It describes the Law as "very philosophical" (cf. 4 Macc. 1:1) and of "divine nature" (§31), views that are said to be affirmed by Hecataeus of Abdera (§31). The king orders the letter addressed to Eleazar and prepares gifts to be sent for the temple in Jerusalem (§§33–34). Aristeas then reproduces in full both Ptolemy's letter to the high priest Eleazar in Jerusalem requesting the production of the translation (§§35) and Eleazar's response acceding to the request and furnishing the names of the seventy-two men who are dispatched to Alexandria to undertake the task (§§41–51). This is followed by a detailed and lengthy description of the gifts sent to Jerusalem by Ptolemy (§§51–82).

The Scene in Jerusalem (§§83–171)

Aristeas first describes Judea and Jerusalem, along with the temple, its cult, and the priestly vestments (§§83–106; cf. Sir. 50:1–21). He also undertakes idealized and vivid descriptions of the surrounding region, including its inhabitants and agriculture (§§107–20), before returning to the business of the translation (§§120–27). Here he lauds the skills of the translators for

31. Nickelsburg, *Jewish Literature*, 196.

their proficiency in Jewish and Greek literature as well as their abilities to converse, with both learning and wisdom, about the Law. This is followed by a lengthy speech by Eleazar on the Law, which Aristeas records in its entirety (§§130–71). First he asserts the justice of the Law and the omniscience of God, which undergirds the entire legislation (§§130–33). Eleazar then explains, with surprising diplomacy, the difference between the God of Israel, creator of all things, and the idols and idolatry of Egypt (§§134–38). Jewish food laws are then explained allegorically, showing the Greek audience that they are both rational and compatible with their own views (§§139–49), and all such laws become allegories for matters revered by the Greeks (§§161–64, 168–71). So, for example, the cloven hoof of kosher animals represents the Jews' discernment of good actions, especially setting themselves apart from people who participate in illicit sexual behaviors (§§150–52). The chewing of cud symbolizes the pious recollections of God (§§153–60), and the weasel, a forbidden animal, symbolizes sinful practices of deceptive speech and gossip (§§165–67).

Ptolemy's Reception of the Jewish Delegation (§§172–300)

Eleazar offers sacrifices, gives gifts for Ptolemy, and sends the delegation on its way to Egypt (§172). Upon their arrival at Alexandria, Aristeas presents Eleazar's letter to the king, who immediately summons the delegation (§§173–75), though it is unprecedented. They bestow their gifts to the king, who convenes a banquet in their honor, complete with requisite kosher protocols (§§176–86). This is followed by a lengthy—about one-third of the entire book—and tedious account of the king's questions to the translators and their replies during the seven days of the banquet (§§187–294). After he apologizes to Philocrates for the length of his account, Aristeas concludes this section with laudatory praise for the translators and repeated affirmation of the veracity of his narrative (§§295–300).

The Translation and Its Reception (§§301–21)

The account of the translation itself is quite brief (§§301–7). Three days after the banquet ends, Demetrius takes the seventy-two translators to an island, where they assemble in a house suitable for their task (§301) and lay out plans for their daily work (§302–4). As each undertakes his translation, the results are compared and harmonized, before completing the task in seventy-two days (§§305–7). The translation is read to an assembled community of Jews, who approve it with great adulation and pronounce a curse on any alterations to it (§§308–11). When King Ptolemy receives word of the completion of the translation, he too rejoices and expresses his admiration for Moses (§312), and Aristeas recounts reports of the misfortunes that have befallen those who misuse or distort the holy text (§§312–16). And so the king instructs that the sacred books be preserved with special care (§317). The translators are then sent home with an effusion of praise and gifts for both themselves and Eleazar (§§318–21).

Epilogue (§322)

At the end Aristeas closes his narrative to Philocrates and implicitly affirms the trustworthiness of the account and the merits of the translated Law of the Jews.

Critical Issues

Genre

Despite its popular designation, the Letter of Aristeas is not formally a letter.[32] Nor, despite the repeated protests of the author, is the narrative to be taken at face value for its historical veracity. Most scholars recognize there is little or nothing in the account of Aristeas that reflects the beginnings of the translation of the Hebrew Bible into Greek. Instead, the most important scholarship sees the letter as a myth of the origins of the Septuagint intended to bolster its status as the sacred scriptures of diaspora Jews living in Greek-speaking Alexandria. As such it belongs to the Septuagint's reception history rather than its inception (see below).[33]

But exactly what kind of work it *is* requires some consideration. Long ago Moses Hadas observed the repeated reference of "narrative" (διήγησις, *diēgēsis*, §§1, 8, 322), in which the author seems to categorize his own work as a "discourse expository of things that happened or might have happened,"[34] which Hadas regards as imaginative rather than historiographic.[35] But others regard the term as more historical in nature and regard Aristeas as "a kind of historical monograph."[36] For Sylvie Honigman, though the work is furnished with pietistic inclinations uncharacteristic of such history, it is

32. For analysis of its epistolary features, see most recently White and Keddie, *Jewish Fictional Letters*.
33. B. Wright, "Aristeas, Letter of"; Honigman, *Septuagint and Homeric Scholarship*, 37–63.
34. Hadas, *Aristeas to Philocrates*, 56–57.
35. Hadas, *Aristeas to Philocrates*, 57; see B. Wright, *Letter of Aristeas*, 44.
36. Honigman, *Septuagint and Homeric Scholarship*, 30.

nonetheless a true history (as opposed to myth telling), written for intellectual and philosophical rather than political motives.[37] While others concur with the historiographic designation for Aristeas, Wright observes that this is complicated by the fact that the work begins and ends with a vocative address to Philocrates, suggesting that "at the least *Aristeas* takes on the trappings of a letter."[38] Though he differs on the meaning and role of διήγησις, *diēgēsis*, Lutz Doering holds that both the vocatives of direct address and the "sustained addressee contact" throughout the document favor an epistolary presentation to the whole document.[39] But its inclusion of material such as official documents may suggest a blending of this genre with its historiography.[40] If it is a merger of sorts, perhaps Wright is most constructive in his notion of an "epistolary treatise," which acknowledges the author's sustained effort to connote correspondence with Philocrates while unmistakably utilizing features of Hellenistic historiography. This "hybrid" is constructed by the author to exploit the advantages of both genres without falling neatly within either.[41]

Historicity

Throughout we have maintained the tension between the agenda (or agendas) of the author to promote his ideas in a seemingly mythical origin of the Septuagint while acknowledging his clear utilization of historical realities such as the Ptolemaic court and Judean geography. This requires some consideration of the historical veracity of the Letter of Aristeas. For much of its history the Letter of Aristeas has been taken as a factual narrative of the miraculous origin of the Septuagint. It was not called into question until the sixteenth century, and then, by 1684, a full critique of its historical value was produced by Humphrey Hody.[42] Hody regarded it as a Hellenistic Jewish forgery intended to claim authority for the Septuagint, and his views form the basis for most scholars' views today.[43] Most scholars recognize that Aristeas was written in the second century BCE, whereas the Greek translation of the Pentateuch, the earliest translation from Hebrew into Greek, dates from the third century BCE. So this raises the question of Aristeas's historical trustworthiness, should he intend to record history in the first place. Those who advocate some degree of reliability do so with some notion of royal patronage

---

37. Honigman, *Septuagint and Homeric Scholarship*, 33–35.
38. B. Wright, *Letter of Aristeas*, 45.
39. Doering, *Ancient Jewish Letters*, 230.
40. Doering, *Ancient Jewish Letters*, 232.
41. B. Wright, *Letter of Aristeas*, 50–51.
42. Hody, *Contra Historiam*.
43. B. Wright, *Letter of Aristeas*, 7.

behind the translation.[44] Yet Wright is hesitant, suggesting that the astute author of Aristeas may have adopted the persona of a fictional character that may well appeal to historical events without necessarily intending to furnish readers with the actual historical realities pertaining to these events. Furthermore, Wright contends that the historical veracity of Aristeas is contradicted by Aristeas's contention that the Septuagint was intended to replace the Hebrew from the outset, which is not supported by the translations themselves. Pointedly, then, Wright concludes that he does not think "that *Aristeas* has any claim to contain historical recollections of the Septuagint's origins."[45]

Contribution and Context

As noted above, the Letter of Aristeas is unique in its sometimes-striking advocacy of the similarities between Jews and gentiles. At least part of its agenda seems to be to contend for a comfortable integration of law-observant diaspora Jews into a Hellenistic gentile elite or royal court. The Scriptures are presented in a philosophical manner compatible with an Alexandrian gentile context, and its Jewish readers are shown how to navigate the retention of Jewish identity and law observance and the integration into a Hellenistic context with a demeanor of mutual respect.

The Letter of Aristeas is also important in that it is the only document of its kind to survive from antiquity.[46] Though scholars debate its historical veracity, and most are quite skeptical, it nonetheless is unique in its *purported* account of the origins of the Greek translation of the Hebrew Bible. In it are addressed the concerns of diaspora Jews living in Alexandria, Egypt, under Ptolemaic rule and their interaction with Judean Jews and the high priesthood in Jerusalem. No other extant text brings these far-reaching subjects into a single narrative.

Though there are few clear indications of Aristeas's use of books from the Hebrew Bible or other Jewish texts from the Second Temple period, save the obvious affinities with the Greek translation of the Pentateuch, points of correspondence are commonly observed between Aristeas and the Sentences of Pseudo-Phocylides, a portion of the Greek translation of Ben Sira, and 3 Maccabees. The first is a series of parallels regarding moderation (Ps.-Phoc.

44. N. Collins, *Library in Alexandria*; Honigman, *Septuagint and Homeric Scholarship*, 93–144; Rajak, *Translation and Survival*, 64–91.

45. B. Wright, *Letter of Aristeas*, 11–12; cf. B. Wright, "Transcribing, Translating, and Interpreting."

46. Shutt, "Letter of Aristeas," 2:10.

69, 76; Let. Aris. §§223, 237, 284), an Aristotelian ideal that likely emerged from an educated Jewish environment and without any clear indication of literary dependence. The corresponding text from Ben Sira is the prologue in its Greek translation, which was written around the same time as the Letter of Aristeas. The most important similarity is where the translator refers to the theme, also found in Aristeas, of the love of learning (Prologue lines 5, 13, 34; cf. Let. Aris. §§1, 171, 300)—though here too literary dependence is unlikely.[47] More plausible literary connections are found with 3 Maccabees. Sara Raup Johnson has identified six significant thematic commonalities:[48] (1) focused attention on Jewish relations with foreign rulers, (2) a presupposition that Jews are highly placed in the court of the foreign rulers, (3) a setting in which a harmonious relationship between Jews and the foreign rulers seems to be commonplace, (4) an expression of loyalty by the Jews to the foreign rulers, (5) an expression of commitment to the observance of the Jewish law, and (6) a presupposition of some interdependence between the diaspora Jews in Egypt and those in Judea. For her, 3 Maccabees and Aristeas are in agreement on all essential points and are remarkably compatible with each other.[49] Characteristically, Wright is more cautious, suggesting, rather than a literary connection between the two as advocated by Johnson, an origin in a contemporaneous period in Alexandria with similar settings and aims.[50]

Purpose

A clear understanding of the actual purpose of the work remains allusive. Some have argued that its purpose is to advocate one particular revision of an earlier Greek translation.[51] Others argue Aristeas was demonstrating the compatibility of Torah-observant Judaism with Hellenism, enabling Jews to remain Jews while belonging to the elite society of the Greeks.[52] Another view sees the author defining for Alexandrian Jews what their relationship should be with Palestinian Judaism.[53] Still others see it as a statement about the self-sufficiency of diaspora Judaism[54] or Jewish ethnic identity in Egypt.[55]

47. B. Wright, Letter of Aristeas, 59–60.
48. S. Johnson, Historical Fictions, 144–66.
49. S. Johnson, Historical Fictions, 168.
50. B. Wright, Letter of Aristeas, 62.
51. Kahle, Cairo Geniza, 213–15. See the critique by Gooding, "Aristeas and Septuagint Origins."
52. Tcherikover, "Ideology," 81.
53. E.g., Howard, "Letter of Aristeas"; Goldstein, "Message of Aristeas to Philokrates."
54. J. Collins, Between Athens and Jerusalem, 103.
55. Moore, Jewish Ethnic Identity, 363.

Johnson advocates a view in which the translation of the Torah was an accurate, even divinely inspired work, and so, by inference, those who kept the Greek translation of the Law (Alexandrian Jews) are every bit as pious as those who adhere to the Hebrew original (Palestinian Jews).[56] Perhaps the most common understanding of the purpose of the Letter of Aristeas is furnished by Tcherikover, who argued that the work was propaganda intended to facilitate a generation of educated, law-observant Jews to live on equal terms with Greek citizens of Alexandria, perhaps even holding high positions in the Ptolemaic court.[57]

In sorting through the diverse understandings of the purpose of the book, it is perhaps most important to recognize that an author may have several purposes at play at the same time.[58] For his part, Wright underscores two broad and intersecting goals of the work: first, to facilitate a Jewish identity that would provide for educated Jews' participation in the Hellenistic context of Alexandria without compromising their Judaism and, second, to promote an account of the origins of the Greek translation of the Torah as the primary basis for Jewish identity in a distinctly Greek context. Wright views the "major issue" of the work is that of identity—what it means to be "a Jew living in Hellenistic Alexandria and at the same time adhering to specifically Jewish beliefs and practices, such as monotheism and Jewish food restrictions."[59] The audience is key, since they are fellow Jews who, like the author, were comfortable in their Hellenistic environment while confronting problems created by Greek religious worship, affirming there is a fine line that one can walk between participation and separation.[60]

Though not unheard of, it is certainly unusual that a Jewish author would adopt the guise of an educated gentile, such as that of the Letter of Aristeas. This allows the Jewish readers to function amid the Greek elites, knowing that they perceive Jewish practices favorably.[61] In other words, an educated Alexandrian Jew uses the identity of a gentile to write his work to reassure his (educated Jewish) readers that, as Wright says, "the Gentiles who occupy the upper strata of Hellenistic Alexandrian society understand and accept Jews *as Jews*."[62] By this Wright means that these gentiles understand that the Jewish Law (in Greek translation) is a defining element of Jewish identity. So Jews,

---

56. S. Johnson, *Historical Fictions*, 38.
57. Tcherikover, "Ideology," 83–84; Nickelsburg, "Stories," 78–79.
58. B. Wright, *Letter of Aristeas*, 66; E. Gruen, *Heritage and Hellenism*, 220–21.
59. B. Wright, *Letter of Aristeas*, 66.
60. B. Wright, *Letter of Aristeas*, 68–69.
61. B. Wright, *Letter of Aristeas*, 64.
62. B. Wright, *Letter of Aristeas*, 19.

whose practices differ markedly from those of these educated, upper-class gentile neighbors, share central values with those neighbors. In practical terms this means that the author's Alexandrian Jewish readership, who have a Greek education and aspire to assimilation in much of Alexandrian society but who still practice the customs of their ancestors, which are foreign to the gentiles of that city, can allay fears about such participation since "those with whom they will socialize recognize why Jews hold to these practices."[63] And so the Jewish author adopts the gentile guise as a spokesman for gentile acceptance of practicing Jews.[64]

Reception History[65]

As noted above, the Letter of Aristeas has generated the most interest for apologetic purposes in its apparent advocacy for the legitimacy of the Greek translation of the Hebrew Bible. Wright has called this concern a "myth of origins" for the Septuagint that "establishes the foundation for its status as the sacred scriptures of Greek-speaking, Alexandrian Jews."[66] Therefore the account remains inextricably tied to contemporary scholarship in its dealings with the origins of the Septuagint.[67] Its reception largely serves to undergird the authority of the Greek Scriptures, and the very name "Septuagint" ("the Seventy") derives from the number of translators.[68] Hadas has compiled some of the most important accounts of the Septuagint legend in Judaism and Christianity, which are likely in some sense dependent on Aristeas.[69] The most important and discussed of these is that of Philo of Alexandria (*Moses* 2.25–44), whose lengthy account diverges in some ways from that of Aristeas. For the present purposes, we will focus on his statements that bear on the nature of the scriptures that were produced. First, he suggests that the high priest in Jerusalem saw the very undertaking of the task as being initiated by God himself. The Hebrew texts themselves are regarded as "the voice of God" and as "sacred books," and their translation "could not add or take away or transfer anything." Indeed, the translators pray to God that they may

63. B. Wright, *Letter of Aristeas*, 20.
64. See B. Wright, "Pseudonymous Authorship."
65. For a complete account of the reception history of the Letter of Aristeas, see White and Keddie, *Jewish Fictional Letters*, 173–274.
66. B. Wright, "Aristeas, Letter of," 1:110; Honigman, *Septuagint and Homeric Scholarship*, 37–63.
67. B. Wright, "Aristeas, Letter of"; Rajak, *Translation and Survival*, 38–43.
68. Nickelsburg, "Stories," 79–80; Hadas, *Aristeas to Philocrates*, 71–72.
69. Hadas, *Aristeas to Philocrates*, 73–84; Pelletier, *Lettre d'Aristée*, 78–98.

not fail in this task. Their task is done under God's supervision, even "under inspiration," and results in identical translations "as though dictated to each by an invisible prompter."

Justin Martyr (ca. 100–165 CE) records the Septuagint myth in his account of the spread of Scripture among Christians.[70] Yet among his differences from Aristeas he explicitly identifies the text to be translated as "prophecies" and seems to suggest not just the Torah is in view but the entire Hebrew Bible. This marks "a definite stage in the growth of the legend."[71] Pseudo-Justin (fourth century CE) further embellishes the story along the lines of Philo when he insists that the seventy translators, working in isolation, produced identical translations.[72] The story persists with Irenaeus (175 CE), who in his *Against Heresies* repeats the statement about the isolation of the translators and regards the product explicitly as inspired by God.[73] Epiphanius of Salamis (ca. 315–403 CE) elaborates further still on the legend, insisting a pair of translators was shut up morning until evening and yet, without collusion, produced identical texts.[74] Despite the doubts cast by Jerome (348–420 CE) in *Preface to the Pentateuch*, the legend is repeated and expanded in Christian[75] and Jewish[76] circles.

---

70. Justin, *1 Apol.* 31.
71. Hadas, *Aristeas to Philocrates*, 74. Cf. Justin, *Dialogus cum Tryphone* 68.
72. Pseudo-Justin, *Cohortatio ad Graecos* 13.
73. Irenaeus, *Haer.* 3.21.2. Cf. Clement of Alexandria, *Strom.* 1.148; Tertullian, *Apol.* 18; Chrysostom, *Homiliae in Matthaeum* 5.2.
74. Epiphanius, *On Weights and Measures* 3–11.
75. E.g., Augustine, *Civ.* 18.42.
76. E.g., b. Meg. 9a; y. Meg. 1.71d; Massakhet Soferim 1.7–10; Mekilta on Exodus 12.40; Midrash R. Exodus 5; Midrash Tanhuma Exodus 22. Hadas, *Aristeas to Philocrates*, 74, 79–84.

17

Joseph and Aseneth

Introduction

Joseph and Aseneth is a fanciful tale of the patriarch Joseph and his Egyptian wife Aseneth, the daughter of Potiphera, priest of On (Gen. 41:45).[1] She gives birth to two sons, Ephraim and Manasseh (Gen. 41:50; 46:20), but the biblical account says nothing else. Joseph and Aseneth expands on this material to create a narrative that describes Aseneth prior to her marriage to Joseph, how they met and subsequently married.[2] How the esteemed Jew Joseph could marry the daughter of a gentile idolatrous priest, a notion strictly forbidden in Scripture (Gen. 24:3–4, 37–38; 27:46; 28:1; cf. Jub. 20:4; 22:20; 30:7–16), is also a matter Joseph and Aseneth seeks to address. The answer lies in Aseneth's repentance, which is displayed in her rejection of idols and in her prayer to God and is recognized by an angelic visitor who declares her converted. With Pharaoh himself officiating, she marries Joseph, who reigns in Egypt for forty-eight years.[3] These and other tales present Aseneth as an idealized proselyte to Judaism and so places Joseph and Aseneth in a unique place among the Second Temple Jewish pseudepigrapha.

1. The name "Potiphera" (Gen. 41:45) is an English transliteration of the Hebrew (פּוֹטִי פֶרַע). The Greek (LXX) renders his name Πετεφρης (Petephrēs; Gen. 41:45, 50; 46:20; cf. Josephus, Ant. 2.6.2 §91). See C. Burchard, "Joseph and Aseneth," OTP 2:202ni.
2. Standhartinger, "Recent Scholarship," 353–54.
3. Burchard, "Joseph and Aseneth," 2:177.

Language and Manuscripts

Most scholars agree that Joseph and Aseneth was composed in Greek since the Greek style belongs to the author rather than a translator. And so it is regarded as "Hellenistic Jewish literature," a work originating in a Greek-speaking location by a Jewish author[4] heavily influenced by the Septuagint.[5] Its style is regarded as simple Koine Greek, with a decidedly "Semitic" inclination perhaps from its Septuagintal influence.

Joseph and Aseneth is preserved in sixteen Greek manuscripts in at least four groups dating from the tenth to the nineteenth century. From the Greek eight additional versions have arisen, including Syriac (sixth century), Armenian (sixth to seventh century), two Latin traditions (both ca. 1200), Serbian Slavonic (fifteenth century [?]), modern Greek (sixteenth century [?]), Rumanian, and (now lost) Ethiopian.[6] The history and transmission of the text is complicated and the subject of some discussion. Christoph Burchard suggests all textual witnesses share a common archetype dating prior to 500 CE.[7] The various translations and manuscripts fall into four groups based on similarities, with some older and more reliable than others. Furthermore, some are longer or shorter than others, and scholars disagree as to which length is preferred. Marc Philonenko regards the "d" text as the oldest and so bases his text on it.[8] But Burchard, whose English translation is the most popular and accessible, establishes his own reconstructed texts, accounting for similarities and differences between the manuscripts and translations.[9]

Provenance[10]

Joseph and Aseneth exhibits characteristics that may be compatible with a variety of contexts, and it contains sufficient ambiguity that scholars debate its provenance, purpose, readership, and date.

While acknowledging the book's message for Jews (i.e., abstain from idolatry and do not marry an idolater), George W. E. Nickelsburg regards the work as primarily addressed to a gentile readership. He enumerates two primary

4. Burchard, "Joseph and Aseneth," 2:181.

5. Standhartinger, "Recent Scholarship," 354; so also Chesnutt, *From Death to Life*, 69–71, 80–76; Humphrey, *Joseph and Aseneth*, 31–33.

6. For a complete list and description, see Burchard, "Joseph and Aseneth," 2:179–80.

7. Burchard, "Joseph and Aseneth," 2:180.

8. Philonenko, *Joseph et Aséneth*.

9. Burchard, "Joseph and Aseneth," 2:180. See more recently Fink, *Joseph und Aseneth*.

10. For a complete survey, see Standhartinger, "Recent Scholarship," 368–71.

reasons: its syncretism and its presentation from the point of view of a proselyte. Regarding the syncretism, Nickelsburg underscores the affinities with the story of Cupid and Psyche and the "rituals of conversion" (laying on of hands, conveying mysteries, sacred meals, etc.), which indicate non-Jewish initiatory rights. These and other syncretisms, he remarks, are sensible for a gentile readership for which Judaism is made attractive and understandable through familiar motifs and elements. The second reason for seeing a gentile readership is that the entire narrative is told from the viewpoint of the convert Aseneth, who describes her thoughts and emotions throughout and in particular her progress to conversion.[11]

Joseph and Aseneth was long presumed to be a later Christian composition, replete with allegorical presentations, such as Joseph representing Christ and Aseneth the church.[12] Some scholars continue to see it as a Christian text, suggesting a Christian allegorizing of the ancient novel that finds expression in the conversions in Acts, Joseph as the "son of God," and Aseneth as the "bride of God."[13] Others see it as Christian for the literary symbols and metaphors it employs.[14] For others, it is a Christian text in part because of its preservation, as far as is known, only in Christian contexts[15] or the presence of unique features (like kissing, e.g., Jos. Asen. 8:4–7; 19:1–11; 21:7).[16] Others see affinities with incantatory rituals conjuring up divine beings, especially the invocation of Helios, the god of the sun,[17] and of elements of Jewish *hekhalot* literature and Greek magical papyri[18]—which, among other things, place it in a late antique religious environment between Jewish *hekhalot* traditions, mystical Helios adjuration, Neoplatonism, and Christian Joseph stories.[19]

Those who deny a Jewish provenance for Joseph and Aseneth have been criticized for their failure to address points of close correspondence between Joseph and Aseneth and both biblical texts and Second Temple Jewish exegetical traditions.[20] Furthermore, the work's familiarity with non-Jewish

---

11. Nickelsburg, "Stories," 69–70.
12. Humphrey, *Joseph and Aseneth*, 28–29.
13. Price, "Implied Reader Response."
14. Nir, *Joseph and Aseneth*, 4.
15. Kraft, "Pseudepigrapha and Christianity, Revisited," 55; cf. Davila, *Provenance of the Pseudepigrapha*, 190–95.
16. Cf. Penn, "Identity Transformation"; Penn, *Kissing Christians*, 96–98.
17. Kraemer, *When Aseneth Met Joseph*, 99–109.
18. Kraemer, *When Aseneth Met Joseph*, 110–54.
19. Kraemer, "Recycling Aseneth," 263.
20. Standhartinger, review of *When Aseneth Met Joseph*, 488–89; cf. Brooke, "Men and Women as Angels," 172–76.

traditions, such as the god Helios, is already present in Hellenistic contexts,[21] and in any case its utilization of non-Jewish sources would not be unique and is certainly not a strong basis for a non-Jewish origin for Joseph and Aseneth. Finally, it has been pointed out that a Christian reading of Joseph and Aseneth cannot explain the absence of baptism, which is perhaps the most important Christian feature of conversion.[22]

Most interpreters view the work as Jewish, given its exegetical affinities with works like Philo, Josephus, and Judith.[23] Though it is sometimes viewed that the central section (Jos. Asen. 14–17) depicting the heavenly being's appearance suggests a Jewish apocalyptic outlook to the book,[24] more evidence is found in relation to a Jewish wisdom theology. Here the righteous are called "sons of God" (chap. 6; cf. Wis. 5), and eating of the honeycomb is the acquisition of wisdom (Jos. Asen. 16:1–13; 17:3; cf. Sir. 24:20).[25] It is possible that by eating the honeycomb Aseneth shares the food of angels (Wis. 16:20), which grants immortality (Wis. 19:21).[26] Aspects of apocalypticism, which by no means is excluded by wisdom theology, are evident in the presentation of the heavenly being (see below; Dan. 10:5–6; cf. 2 En. 1:5; Rev. 1:13–15).[27]

Gideon Bohak argues that Joseph and Aseneth was written as a Jewish apologetic to other Jews justifying the erection of a temple in Heliopolis, Egypt, by Onias IV and his supportive priests after Onias III had been murdered (ca. 171 BCE; cf. 1 Macc. 4:34; 1 En. 90:8; Josephus, *J.W.* 1.1.1 §§31–33; *Ant.* 12.5.1 §237; 13.3.3 §73).[28] In Egypt Ptolemy granted Onias IV permission to build his temple in the region of Heliopolis (Josephus, *Ant.* 13.10.4 §285), where he was to ordain Levites and priests (*Ant.* 13.3.1–2 §§62–71; 20.10.3 §§235–237) in service for local populations of Jews (*Ant.* 13.3.3 §73), all amply funded by local revenue (*J.W.* 7.10.3 §430). In this reading the Isaianic promises to Jerusalem (cf. Isa. 1:26) are transferred to Egypt, with the key in Joseph and Aseneth being the enigmatic honeycomb passage (Jos. Asen. 16). Bohak requires a degree of allegory, with the bees' attire suggesting a Jewish priest, and the burning of the first honeycomb suggesting the Jerusalem temple

21. Ahearne-Kroll, "Joseph and Aseneth and Jewish Identity," 156–68.
22. So also J. Collins, "*Joseph and Aseneth*," 121.
23. Standhartinger, "Recent Scholarship," 369–70; Humphrey, *Joseph and Aseneth*, 55–57; J. Collins, "*Joseph and Aseneth*," 125–26.
24. Humphrey, *Ladies and the Cities*, 30–56.
25. Standhartinger, "Recent Scholarship," 370.
26. Nicklas, "Food of Angels (Wis. 16:20)," 96–99; Standhartinger, "Recent Scholarship," 370.
27. Standhartinger, "Recent Scholarship," 370; Standhartinger, *Das Frauenbild im Judentum*, 113–14; Ahearne-Kroll, "Joseph and Aseneth and Jewish Identity," 226–39.
28. Bohak, *Joseph and Aseneth and the Jewish Temple.*

(perhaps 70 CE), which is replaced with the new honeycomb on Aseneth's lips, representing the new temple cult in Heliopolis. The bees hostile to Aseneth are the detractors of the Heliopolitan temple, whereas those friendly to her are its supporters. For Bohak, then, Joseph and Aseneth may have been written after the destruction of the Jerusalem temple in 70 CE but before the fall of the Oniad temple, which was destroyed by order of Vespasian in 73 CE (Josephus, *J.W.* 7.10.2 §421).[29] Or more likely, in his opinion, it was written in the mid-second century BCE as an explanation for the newly established temple and cult in Heliopolis. A very different approach is taken by Ross Kraemer, who finds in the incident of the bees a reflection of the fate of the souls from third-century-CE Neoplatonic sources.[30] She finds circularity in the argument for an Egyptian provenance that espouses Egyptian Judaism and suggests with this later date that Joseph and Aseneth may just as easily belong in a Christian (or other) setting. Some scholars regard Bohak's second-century-BCE date as too early because the Septuagint, with which Joseph and Aseneth is familiar, does not come about until later. Edith Humphrey rejects the later date (post-70 CE) as incompatible with the Ptolemaic context of the book. She sees Kraemer's thesis as presuming too much fluidity in religious identity at the time, and in the end Humphrey, along with some other scholars, is content to leave the matter undetermined.[31]

It is often suggested that Joseph and Aseneth was written in Egypt, with Pharaoh and the Egyptian priest acknowledging the God of Israel and Aseneth abandoning her ancestral gods to convert to Judaism and marry an Israelite.[32] Some suggest it belonged to a more popular Jewish culture than that of Philo, perhaps in a rural milieu outside the city of Alexandria, but this is at best a guess.[33]

Date

As we have seen, Joseph and Aseneth has been dated to as early as the second century BCE and as late as the fourth century CE. However, most scholars regard two factors as providing parameters to the date of composition.[34] First, on the early end, the work is largely thought to depict familiarity with the

---

29. See Gurtner, "Historical and Political Contexts."
30. Kraemer, *When Aseneth Met Joseph*, 295.
31. Humphrey, *Joseph and Aseneth*, 35, 37.
32. Nickelsburg, "Stories," 71; similarly Humphrey, *Joseph and Aseneth*, 30.
33. Burchard, "Joseph and Aseneth," 2:188. See further Standhartinger, "Recent Scholarship," 373–74.
34. Hicks-Keeton, "Joseph and Aseneth."

completion of the Septuagint, including the book of Psalms. The second factor, on the late end, is the conjecture that a work espousing Jewish proselytism would have little use after the revolt in Egypt under the Roman emperor Trajan (115–117 CE)[35] or, still later, after 135 CE when Emperor Hadrian's edict against circumcision would make conversion to Egyptian Judaism less appealing.[36] In summary, it seems best to favor the majority view that Joseph and Aseneth was composed in a Jewish community in Egypt between 100 BCE and 135 CE.

Contents[37]

Part 1 (Jos. Asen. 1–21).

The narrative begins (chap. 1) during the first of seven years of plenty (cf. Gen. 41:29, 53), when Joseph is sent out by Pharaoh to gather grain and comes into the region of Heliopolis (Jos. Asen. 1:1–2). There he meets Pentephres, a wealthy priest and chief of all Pharaoh's satraps and noblemen (1:3). He has a daughter, Aseneth, a virgin of eighteen, whose beauty is beyond compare in Egypt, resembling rather the daughters of the Hebrews (1:4–5). All the sons of the noblemen fight for her hand (1:6), and even Pharaoh's son pleads with his father for her (1:7–9). But Aseneth will have none of them, scorning them all in her arrogance from a great tower in her father's house and living in virginal isolation (chap. 2).[38]

JOSEPH'S ARRIVAL AND ASENETH'S RESPONSE

When Joseph arrives in the region, he sends a contingent to request of Pentephres refuge from the noonday sun at his home (3:1–2). The jubilant Egyptian, praising the God of Joseph for the honor of such a visit, orders his house made ready and a meal prepared (3:3–4). Aseneth learns of the hubbub and dresses to meet her parents (3:5–6), whom she greets and from whom she learns of their intent for her to marry Joseph (4:1–8). She vehemently and indignantly refuses this suggestion, calling Joseph an "alien and fugitive," saying she will marry the king's son instead (4:9–12). When Joseph arrives, Aseneth flees to her chamber, from which she can observe Joseph (5:1–2). Joseph enters in all his splendor and is greeted by Pentephres and his family

---

35. Burchard, "Joseph and Aseneth," 2:187–88.
36. Chesnutt, *From Death to Life*, 80–85, 254; cf. Humphrey, *Joseph and Aseneth*, 14, 30, 35.
37. The translation followed here is that of Burchard ("Joseph and Aseneth," 2:200). On the numbering of the verses, see note 16 above.
38. Nickelsburg, "Stories," 66.

(5:3–7), except for Aseneth, who is thunderstruck by the sight (6:1), repents to the God of Joseph for her rash words (6:2–7), and longs to marry Joseph (6:8).

Joseph's Refusal of Aseneth and Prayer for Her Conversion

Joseph enters their house, maintaining his segregation from the Egyptians (cf. Gen. 43:32),[39] and is greeted with all due honors (Jos. Asen. 7:1). Elsewhere in Egypt Joseph was so harassed by the women (married and unmarried) of the land to sleep with them that, upon observing Aseneth, he orders her departure lest she too join in the throngs (7:2–6). When her father explains that she is his virgin daughter, Joseph relents and meets her (7:7–8). When Joseph and Aseneth meet, the maiden's father instructs her to kiss Joseph as a brother (8:1–5), but Joseph refuses, arguing it is unsuitable to kiss a "strange woman" (γυναῖκα ἀλλοτρίαν, *gynaika allotrian*, meaning a non-Israelite) with the very lips that bless God (8:5–7). Aseneth is cut to the heart and moved to tears (8:8–9), at which Joseph blesses her and prays for her conversion (8:9).

Aseneth's Conversion

Aseneth, seemingly recovered from her tears, now rejoices and retreats to her room, where she weeps and repents of her idol worship (9:1–2), while Joseph departs after promising to return in a week (9:3–5; 10:1). Aseneth, alone with seven virgins who try to look after her (10:4–7), prepares for her repentance with weeping and fasting (10:1–3). She dresses herself in black for mourning and casts her royal attire out the window to the poor before doing the same with "all the idols of the Egyptians" and cultic sacrifices (10:8–13). She weeps bitterly day and night for seven days in sackcloth and ashes (10:14–17). On the eighth day she rises from her grief and in the quiet of her own heart expresses her grief at being forsaken by her family and her people for forsaking their gods (11:1–6). But she recognizes that the God of Joseph is jealous and hates idols (11:7–9), and she finds strength and refuge in God (11:10–14) and courage to pronounce his name (11:15–18). Having rallied her courage, she addresses God, confessing her sin and praying for forgiveness for her idolatry and her blasphemy against God's "son," Joseph[40] (11:19; 12:1–15; 13:1–15).

39. Note in Gen. 43:32 it is the Egyptians who do not eat with Hebrews because it is detestable for the Egyptians. Here it is the reverse.
40. Nickelsburg, "Stories," 66.

THE APPEARANCE OF THE ANGEL

After this episode Aseneth, early in the morning, sees the heavens torn
asunder, and a man from heaven appears to her, calling her by name and
identifying himself as "the chief of the house of the Lord and commander
of the whole host of the Most High" (14:1–8). Rising at his instruction, she
sees that he resembles Joseph but with a striking radiance that causes her to
tremble (14:9–10). Again imploring her to rise, the man tells her to retire to
her room, put off her mourning attire, and dress in a new linen robe and then
return to him (14:11–13). This she promptly does (14:14–15).

When she returns to the man, he exhorts her to courage and informs her
that her "name [is] written in the book of the living in heaven," her prayers
have been heard, and she will be renewed, eat the bread of life, drink the cup
of immortality, and marry Joseph (15:1–6). Her name is changed to "City of
Refuge," as many nations will take refuge in her exemplary repentance (15:7–8).
The heavenly man intends to leave for Joseph, who will come to her and marry
her (15:9–10). But first she tries to learn his name, which he tells her is unspeak-
able (15:11–12), and then invites him to take food (15:13–15). For this meal a
honeycomb is miraculously furnished, and Aseneth understands it was brought
forth from the man's mouth (16:1–11). At this the angel declares her blessed
for her understanding and says that all who attach themselves to the Lord God
in repentance will eat of this honeycomb (16:11–14). Together they eat of the
honeycomb, which the man says is the "bread of life," and he pronounces her
blessings from God (16:15–16). Then the man marks the honeycomb and causes
bees to arise from it; the bees encircle Aseneth's mouth, eat of the comb that is
on her mouth, and depart for heaven with none injuring her (16:17–22; 17:1–4).
The man then blesses Aseneth's seven virgins (17:4–6) and departs (17:6–10).

MARRIAGE OF JOSEPH AND ASENETH

When Joseph's return is announced, Aseneth instructs her foster father
(and steward of her house), who notices her crestfallen countenance (18:3–5),
to prepare a meal for his arrival (18:1–2). Aseneth hurries to her chamber,
where she dons her luxuriant bridal attire (18:3–6) and is transformed with
her wonderous, heavenly beauty into a bride for Joseph, God's "firstborn
son" (18:7–11). When Joseph's arrival is announced, Aseneth hurries to meet
him (19:1–3). This time it is Joseph who is thunderstruck, for he does not
even recognize Aseneth, who is compelled to explain to him her conversion
and subsequent transformation (19:4–7). Joseph erupts in praise for God and
admiration for Aseneth, whom he at last embraces and kisses (19:8–11; 20:1).
Aseneth leads Joseph into the house, seats him on her father's throne, and

washes his feet (20:1–5). When Aseneth's family takes in the scene, they "[give] glory to God who gives life to the dead" and celebrate. Pentephres, her father, proposes to hold a marriage feast, but Joseph wants this to be held by Pharaoh instead (20:6–10). (The narrative is careful to note that Joseph did not sleep with Aseneth prior to the wedding, as it does not befit a man who worships God; 21:1.) So Joseph made his desires known to Pharaoh, who promptly calls together the wedding, at which he officiates (the couple again kiss), and hosts a grand marriage feast for seven days (21:2–8). (In the course of time Aseneth conceives and gives birth to Manasseh and Ephraim; 21:9.) Then Aseneth commences a lengthy confession, thanksgiving, and prayer to God (21:10–21).

Part 2 (Jos. Asen. 22–29)

The second part of the narrative (Jos. Asen. 22–29), which is shorter than the first, begins during the seven years of famine (22:1). It is at this time that Jacob learns about Joseph and, with his whole family, goes to Egypt to settle in Goshen during the second year of the famine (22:2). So Joseph and Aseneth go to Goshen to see Jacob (Israel; 22:3–6), who is radiant and youthful despite his old age (22:7–10). The couple is escorted home by Simeon and Levi, who are virtuous and godly, whereas the sons of Zilpah and Bilhah are envious and hostile (22:11–13).

SON OF PHARAOH AND THE PLOT FOR ASENETH

While Joseph and Aseneth are passing by, they are observed by Pharaoh's firstborn son, who still harbors his old affections for Aseneth (23:1). He summons Simeon and Levi and offers them great riches to help him kill Joseph and take Aseneth for his wife (23:2–6). The brothers refuse and, drawing their swords, demand the Egyptian prince not to entertain thoughts of harming Joseph (23:6–16). Fearful but not deterred in his ambitions, Pharaoh's son approaches Dan, Gad, Naphtali, and Asher with the same intent and, through trickery, secures their participation (24:1–19). So the brothers set an ambush (24:20) while Pharaoh's son, after failing to kill his own father, takes up his position against Joseph and Aseneth as well (25:1–4). Naphtali and Asher in the end relent but fail to convince Dan and Gad to do the same (25:5–7).

AMBUSH OF ASENETH AND RESCUE

Early in the morning Joseph and Aseneth part (26:1–4) when her entourage of six hundred men is routed by their assailants, and Aseneth flees (26:5).

She is chased by Pharaoh's son and prays for help (26:7–8). Levi, by means of his prophetic gift, perceives the danger and musters his brothers to the rescue (26:6). Benjamin, who is with Aseneth in her flight, wounds the son of Pharaoh and slays his fifty men with stones (27:1–5). Then Levi, along with his brothers Reuben, Simeon, Judah, Issachar, and Zebulon, fall upon and destroy the men of Dan and Gad (27:6). Dan, Gad, Naphtali, and Asher all flee, but when they come to Aseneth with swords drawn, their weapons fall from their hands and turn to ashes (27:7–11). These four brothers, collectively called "the sons of Bilhah and Zilpah," recognize the Lord's hand coming to the aid of Aseneth, plead for mercy from her, and ask her to intercede with the other brothers on their behalf (28:1–7), which she does (28:1–17). Pharaoh's son, still alive but wounded, is nearly run through by Benjamin, whose hand is stayed by Levi (29:1–6). Three days later the son of Pharaoh dies, then his father, and Joseph is left to reign over Egypt for forty-eight years (29:7–9).[41]

Critical Issues

Genre

Joseph and Aseneth is generally regarded as a kind of ancient romance, with some literary affinities with the books of Ruth, Esther, Tobit, and Judith.[42] And to a degree there are resemblances—the centrality of a female character, the question of marriage, and the relation of Jews and gentiles to name a few. But Joseph and Aseneth is deliberately tethered to a known narrative from the Hebrew Bible and addresses the issue of intermarriage that the book of Genesis itself raises. Some scholars have regarded it, then, as a literary syncretism, melding elements of the romantic genre with forms of the "sapiential novel" (Ahiqar, Tobit, Daniel 1–6) to create a work in many ways unique to the ancient world.[43] More recent research locates it rather within the category of "romantic" Greek novels.[44] Such Jewish novels tend to be shorter and earlier than their Greek and Roman counterparts. But like other novels, the Jewish novel tends to contain entertaining elements typical of popular literature: the emphasis on female protagonists, the testing of the protagonist's virtue, and an interest in the development or change within the character.[45] Jewish

41. Burchard, "Joseph and Aseneth," 2:177.
42. Burchard, "Joseph and Aseneth," 2:186.
43. Pervo, "Joseph and Asenath and the Greek Novel."
44. Standhartinger, "Recent Scholarship," 378.
45. Wills, "Novels."

novels share among themselves a depiction of the protagonist's "courage and fidelity to God, especially as that relates to Jews living in a world ruled by other peoples."[46] Finally, they are clearly depicted as fictitious.[47]

Unity

The summary of contents above serves to illustrate that there is an abrupt change from chapter 21 to chapter 22. While the characters remain the same, the narrative focus of Joseph and Aseneth, with the latter's conversion and their ensuing marriage, turns into a plot by a would-be former suitor to take Aseneth for himself. Some scholars have argued that chapters 22–29 are later additions to an original, shorter text, but this is largely discounted.[48] Indeed, some scholars suggest the second half has little to add to Joseph and Aseneth.[49] But this is to discount what Nickelsburg recognizes as an important point: it shows that the new convert is protected from mortal danger by the God whom she now worships.[50] This is an important point, for it shows that the conversion of Aseneth, which is authenticated by the angel and explained to Joseph, now grants to Aseneth the full providential care of Israel's God that one would expect without question for an Israelite in a similar position (e.g., Esther and Judith).

Contribution and Context

Angels

The heavenly figure, clearly an angel, is actually called a "person" (ἄνθρωπος, anthrōpos) in the original Greek.[51] Scholars have noted its resemblance to the Egyptian sun god Helios.[52] It also seems evident that this humanlike portrayal of angels is attested in the Dead Sea Scrolls, particularly in priestly contexts largely disenchanted with the temple cult leadership in Jerusalem.[53] But a sectarian provenance for Joseph and Aseneth is largely rejected.[54] Furthermore,

---

46. Wills, "Novels," 2:548.

47. Wills, Jewish Novel in the Ancient World.

48. Burchard, "Joseph and Aseneth," 2:182.

49. Kraemer, When Aseneth Met Joseph, 40–41; Humphrey, Joseph and Aseneth, 106–11.

50. Nickelsburg, Jewish Literature, 337.

51. See Stuckenbruck, Angel Veneration and Christology, 168–70.

52. Mach, Entwicklungsstadien des judischen Engelglaubens, 265–78.

53. Fletcher-Louis, All the Glory of Adam, 30–31.

54. Standhartinger, "Recent Scholarship," 371; cf. Chesnutt, From Death to Life, 186–95; Chesnutt, "Dead Sea Scrolls," 401–10.

this feature is found in both sectarian and nonsectarian texts, where there is stress on the communion the Jewish sectarians at Qumran share with angels, including those of human form.[55]

Conversion[56]

Joseph and Aseneth is unique among the works studied here in its explicit depiction of the conversion of Aseneth to Judaism. Some have suggested the entire message of part 1 (Jos. Asen. 1–21) is about conversion to Judaism.[57] As noted above, regardless of her ethnicity, she is protected by God as though she were herself an Israelite (e.g., 26:2; 27:10–11). And her protection is against the plan of Pharaoh's son in partnership with the Israelite brothers of Joseph. Yet the actions of other Israelites—Simeon, Levi, and Benjamin—are lauded as exemplary and befitting a man who worships God. Nickelsburg suggests that integral to her conversion is Aseneth's acknowledgment of Joseph as a "son of God," a designation appropriate in the Egyptian context for the son of Pharaoh, by which she is "adumbrating her conversion from the gods of Egypt to the God of Joseph."[58] Also integral is her purification, but in a distinct way. Her blessing of idols and participating in their cult renders her mouth unclean (cf. 8:5; 11:2, 9, 15; 12:4–5), so she dares not open her polluted mouth for seven days even to address God (11:2–3, 9; 12:5). At her conversion she destroys the sacrificial food and drink (10:12–13) and blesses Israel's God (11:10–18). There are several depictions for her conversion: she has passed from death to life (8:9), has her name written in the book of life (15:2–4), receives the mysteries of God (16:13–14), and is able to partake of the food and drink of immortality (16:13–16). Her transformation upon donning bridal array indicates that the eternal life promised is now hers (chap. 18; cf. Sir. 24:13–17; 50:8–12).[59] That salvation was necessary for her is obvious; obvious too is that there is no redeemer figure by whom it is achieved.[60] To this one could add some other interesting observations: Joseph and Aseneth is not announcing a new salvation but rather illustrating the acquisition of a salvation that was long afforded to converts to Judaism. Furthermore, there is no active proselytizing or zealous missionary activity.

55. Brooke, "Men and Women as Angels," 159–65.
56. On the subject of conversion in Joseph and Aseneth, see most importantly Donaldson, *Judaism and the Gentiles*, 141–51.
57. Burchard, "Joseph and Aseneth," 2:189.
58. Nickelsburg, "Stories," 67.
59. Nickelsburg, "Stories," 68.
60. Burchard, "Joseph and Aseneth," 2:192. Burchard does not make much of this, but surely this is the most important evidence against a Christian provenance.

To be sure, Joseph prays for her conversion, but otherwise makes little if any effort toward its accomplishment. He prays for her, then leaves.[61] Also, while she prays for forgiveness (11:18; 13:13), there is no explicit indication that it is granted and so grants her salvation. Surely turning from idols and casting away her valuables are indications of her repentance, but it is all tied to her recognition that they are false and only Joseph's God is true. Yet her salvation is presented in the individualistic terms of a heavenly afterlife (8:9; 15:7–8; 22:13).[62]

Diversity of Judaism

A final contribution made by Joseph and Aseneth is its attestation to a Judaism that is seemingly quite different from that indicated in other texts. It may be easier to explain what kind of Judaism is not depicted than what kind is.[63] It is not Pharisaism, which utilizes the law as a guideline for personal piety and purity of daily life. Nor is it Sadduceeism with its emphasis on Torah and the Jerusalem temple. Nor is it like Essenism with a priestly community withdrawing from the established cult in Jerusalem in fastidious observance of Torah read in light of its own eschatological identity. Indeed the law has little place here explicitly, though this Judaism is clearly defined against the pagan idolatry of Egypt.

Though Joseph and Aseneth depicts a Judaism distinct from others to some degree, it has some points in common with other works. Like other writings (e.g., Ezekiel the Tragedian, Philo the Epic Poet, Pseudo-Phocylides, and the Sibylline Oracles), Joseph and Aseneth represents an attempt by a Jewish author to adapt a Greek literary form for its own purposes.[64] The attention to Joseph, though here in the shadow of Aseneth, is found in many other writings (Philo, De Iosepho; Josephus, Ant. 2.1.1–16.6 §§1–349; Wis. 10:10–14; Jub. 42:1–46:6; 1 Macc. 2:53; 5:18, 56, 60; T. Jos.). Joseph and Aseneth's insistence that Israel's God is the only true deity, who stands in stark contrast to impotent idols, is found in Jewish (Jub. 12; Apoc. Ab. 1–7; Bel and the Dragon) and Christian texts (e.g., 1 Thess. 1:9; 1 Cor. 8:1–10, 10:14–19, 12:2; 2 Cor. 6:16; Rev. 2:14, 20; 9:20).[65] Finally, as noted above, the presentation of a woman as the central figure is found in Judith, as well as Esther and Ruth.

61. Burchard, "Joseph and Aseneth," 2:192.
62. Burchard, "Joseph and Aseneth," 2:194.
63. Burchard, "Joseph and Aseneth," 2:184.
64. Burchard, "Joseph and Aseneth," 2:195.
65. Hicks-Keeton, "Joseph and Aseneth."

Purpose[66]

These matters are not easily resolved and naturally bleed into questions as to why Joseph and Aseneth was written. Accepting a Jewish provenance as the most likely, it is apparent that Joseph and Aseneth was composed at least in part to address the troublesome issue of Joseph's marriage to an Egyptian woman (cf. Gen. 24:3–4, 37–38; 27:46–28:1).[67] In fact many scholars see the book as principally a story of conversion to the God of Israel, while also developing and enforcing norms about the relationship of Jews to non-Jews and the proper behavior of God-worshipers.[68] But this should be tempered to some degree, since scholars such as John M. G. Barclay have noted that the openness toward gentiles is not unqualified but premised on their conversion, and so some implicit function must be seen for discouraging marriage outside Judaism, though with openness to a mixed ethnic origin.[69] Regardless, it is important that at a literary level the Jewish reader is probably to identify with Joseph, who is steadfast in his adherence to Torah and recoils at the potential of marriage to or even kissing a gentile. He prays for Aseneth's conversion and, because he is righteous, his prayer is heard. And it is only after he learns of her conversion that he agrees to marriage. So while many things can be indicated about a readership from this—the elevation of gentile converts in Jewish communities,[70] the problem of Jewish identity in a gentile context, the presentation of Aseneth as an ideal proselyte,[71] and so on—the thrust seems to be that it is permissible for diaspora (Egyptian) Jews to pray for the conversion of non-Jews and to marry converted gentiles.

Reception History[72]

Burchard regards Joseph and Aseneth among the best-attested and most widely distributed books of the Pseudepigrapha.[73] Though nothing is known of its reception in Judaism prior to the Middle Ages, in Christianity it is probably attested first toward the end of the fourth century CE, in the beginning of

66. For a complete survey, see Standhartinger, "Recent Scholarship," 365–67.
67. Hicks-Keeton, "Joseph and Aseneth."
68. Hicks-Keeton, "Joseph and Aseneth"; Burchard, "Joseph and Aseneth," 2:194–95; Chesnutt, *From Death to Life*.
69. Barclay, *Jews in the Mediterranean Diaspora*, 204–16.
70. Chesnutt, "Social Setting and Purpose," 42.
71. Burchard, "Joseph und Aseneth," 73–75.
72. For a recent and complete survey, see Standhartinger, "Recent Scholarship," 386–88.
73. Burchard, "Joseph and Aseneth," 2:195.

the now lost *Pilgrimage of Etheria* (ca. 382 CE).[74] It is clear why such a work would be transmitted among Christians. Its ritual meals would suggest the Christian Eucharist,[75] and its language of "son of God" and "bread of life" and of conversion from death to life, among many other things, finds points of correspondence in the New Testament and early Christianity. Aseneth was listed among the saints in the fifth-century (?) "Passion of Irene." At some point in its transmission, probably before the sixth century, Joseph and Aseneth was paired with the "Life of Joseph."[76] In this Ethiopic text Aseneth learns of Joseph's dream about his own death.[77]

74. Burchard, "Joseph and Aseneth," 2:187. This evidence itself comes from the writing of Peter the Deacon of Monte Cassino (*On the Holy Places*, ca. 1137 CE).

75. See Nickelsburg, "Stories," 71.

76. Burchard, "Joseph and Aseneth," 2:196.

77. Standhartinger, "Recent Scholarship," 386; Isaac, "Ethiopic History of Joseph," 113–14.

18

Additional Writings

*Life of Adam and Eve (Greek), 4 Baruch,
and Ezekiel the Tragedian*

The Second Temple period gave rise to a number of narratives and expansions
of biblical traditions beyond those discussed above. Some of them, however,
are of questionable provenance or in their current state are incomplete. Here
we briefly survey three such documents that attest to the expansion of an
important biblical tradition (Life of Adam and Eve), the further development
of a work affiliated with a revered figure in the Hebrew Bible (4 Baruch), and,
finally, a Hellenistic Jewish work that utilizes the genre of Greek tragedy to
portray a biblical drama (Ezekiel the Tragedian).

Life of Adam and Eve (Greek)

Introduction

The Life of Adam and Eve is a creative expansion of Genesis 4–5. It is
preserved in two distinct recensions of a single work, a Greek text (preserved
as the Apocalypse of Moses) that is comparatively short and simple, and a
Latin text (called the *Vita Adae et Evae*), about one-half of which overlaps
with the Greek. The narrative of the Greek version, discussed here, expands
on key elements of the biblical narrative pertaining to God's mercy on Adam

319

and Eve, the inevitability of death because of their sin, and their expulsion
from the garden of Eden.

Contents

At the outset the narrative recounts the events after Adam and Eve leave
paradise and have Cain and Abel (LAE 1). Eve has a dream about conflict
between Cain and Abel (chap. 2), and she and Adam discover that Abel was
killed by Cain. From the archangel Michael, Adam learns he will have another
son (chap. 3), Seth (chap. 4), and in total thirty sons and thirty daughters (5:1).
Then Adam becomes ill and summons his sons to him before he dies, which
they do not seem to understand (5:2–5; cf. Gen. 4:1–5:5). Seth and Eve go near
paradise to plead for God to send his angel to give him oil that flows from
the tree for Adam's anointing (LAE 6–9). Seth is confronted by a wild beast
(chap. 10) triggered by the fall to hostile behavior (chap. 11), but Seth rebukes
the beast, which flees (chap. 12). Seth is then joined by Eve, and together they
ask God to send his angel to give them the oil of mercy for Adam (13:1).
But the archangel Michael appears and declines their request, explaining
that in "that great day" Adam will be raised and given every joy in paradise
(13:2–6). The angel departs, and Seth and Eve return to Adam, who asks her
to gather their children and grandchildren and tell them how they (Adam and
Eve) transgressed (chap. 14). Eve then launches into a lengthy account of the
fall and its consequences (15:1–30:1; cf. Gen. 3:1–24), considerably longer
than that of Adam (LAE 6:3–8:2). In it she recounts their temptation by the
serpent (chaps. 15–18), their fall (chaps. 19–21), and the appearance of God
in paradise (chaps. 22–23). God issued the punishments first to Adam (chap.
24), then Eve (chap. 25) and the serpent (chap. 26). God instructed his angels
to expel the couple from paradise, but Adam implored God for forgiveness
and asked to eat of the tree of life (chap. 27). God promised that if Adam
kept himself from evil, God would raise him at the resurrection and then he
could eat of the tree and live forever (chap. 28). And so Adam was expelled
and then repented (chap. 29). Eve concludes her exhortation by imploring
her progeny to understand how they were deceived and to watch themselves
so that they do not forsake good (chap. 30). After this, at Adam's prompting
(chap. 31), Eve repents of her sin to God and Adam dies (chap. 32). Then Eve
sees a chariot drawn by four radiant eagles that alight beside Adam's body
(chap. 33). With the chariot, as Seth explains, are the sun and moon, which are
not able to shine in the presence of God (chaps. 34–36). Then Adam's soul is
taken to the heavenly paradise (chap. 37) and his body buried (chaps. 38–40).
Then God tells Adam's body—still in the ground—that it will be raised on

the last day in the resurrection (chap. 41). Then Eve also dies (chap. 42), and her body is buried, after which Michael explains to Seth that this is how each person who dies is to be buried until the day of resurrection (chap. 43).

Contribution

The overall purpose of the Life of Adam and Eve is to elucidate for subsequent generations the nature of the fall so that they may better grasp the reason for human suffering and eventual death.[1] But more than that, it demonstrates that with sincere repentance and remorse, forgiveness is available and resurrection awaits.[2]

There are several important aspects about the Life of Adam and Eve's depiction of God that differ from the biblical account. Not only does God travel on a chariot throne rather than walk in the garden of Eden (LAE 22:1–4; cf. Gen. 3:8), but he is also accompanied by a company of angelic hosts, notably including Michael (LAE 22:1–4; 27:1–5; 29:1–6). Also, the biblical question by God to Adam, "Where are you?" (Gen. 3:9), becomes in the Life of Adam and Eve, "Where have you gone hiding, thinking that I will not find you?" (LAE 23:1). Finally, God's compassionate provision of garments for Adam and Eve at their expulsion from the garden (Gen. 3:21) becomes a rebuke of the angels, who in compassion stop driving Adam from paradise (LAE 27:4).[3]

Notably, the Life of Adam and Eve not only depicts heaven as "paradise" (e.g., 25:3; 29:1) but uses the same language for the garden of Eden (e.g., 29:2–3; 36:2; 37:5; 40:1). Bodily resurrection from the dead at the end of days is found in several instances as a hope for those who repent (30:2; 42; 47:3).

The obvious expansions on familiar traditions from the Hebrew Bible (e.g., Gen. 1–5) are augmented by some general points of similarity with 4 Ezra, Jubilees, and 2 Enoch (e.g., 2 En. 8:1–5; 22:9; 29:4–5; 33:8–12; 42:3; 65:10).[4] Perhaps more noteworthy are intriguing points of correspondence with the New Testament. These include, for example, the description of Eve as the source of sin and death (LAE 14:2; 32:1–2; cf. 2 Cor. 11:3; 1 Tim. 2:14). In both, Satan masquerades as an angel (LAE 17:1; 2 Cor. 11:14), God is the "father of lights" (LAE 27:3; James 1:17), and paradise is located in the "third heaven" (LAE 37:5; 2 Cor. 12:2).[5] Desire is the root of sin (LAE 19:3; Rom. 7:7), and the exchange of God's glory for mortality (LAE 14:2; 21–22; 39:1–3)

1. Anderson, "Life of Adam and Eve," 1331.
2. Anderson, "Life of Adam and Eve," 1331.
3. Levison, "Adam and Eve, Life of."
4. M. Johnson, "Life of Adam and Eve," 2:255.
5. Levison, "Adam and Eve, Life of"; M. Johnson, "Life of Adam and Eve," 2:254–55.

and natural for unnatural (chaps. 10–12) corresponds to the two exchanges in Romans (Rom. 1:18–25).[6]

Text and Provenance

John R. Levison points out that there is ongoing debate about whether the original text was composed in Hebrew or Greek and whether it was written by a Christian or a Jew.[7] The Greek text of the Life of Adam and Eve is preserved in sixteen manuscripts dating from the eleventh to the seventeenth century, portions of which are classified into three different versions.[8] It has also been translated into Latin, Armenian, Georgian, and Slavonic.[9] Though no Hebrew text of the work has survived, some scholars argue that the Life of Adam and Eve was originally composed in Hebrew and subsequently translated into Greek.[10] Others argue that Greek is the language of composition.[11]

There is no clear indication of the date of composition, prompting scholars to propose a vast range from 100 BCE to as late as 740 CE.[12] The earliest date is generally put forward by those who hold to a Jewish provenance, while the latter is often suggested by those who hold to a Christian provenance. More recently scholars have argued that affinities with Romans (Rom. 1:18–32) suggest an earlier date, though perhaps the work was not composed in its entirety in the mid-first century CE.[13]

The provenance is also debated. While there are notable Christian segments in the text of the Life of Adam and Eve (e.g., burning of incense at LAE 29:4; 33:4; 38:2),[14] this does not require that it is a Christian composition. Some have argued that these elements can be excised from the text without disrupting the flow of the narrative, suggesting they were later (Christian) additions that can be removed to recover an originally Jewish text. There are other reasons scholars argue for an original Jewish text (written in Hebrew) that lies behind the Life of Adam and Eve. First, there is nothing distinctive

6. Levison, "Adam and Eve, Life of"; M. Johnson, "Life of Adam and Eve," 2:254–55. See Levison, "Adam and Eve in Romans 1.18–25."

7. Levison, "Adam and Eve, Life of."

8. Levison, "Adam and Eve, Life of." On their significant variations, see Levison, *Texts in Transition*.

9. Levison, "Adam and Eve, Life of." For a chart depicting the translations, see Jonge and Tromp, *Life of Adam and Eve*, 26–27.

10. M. Johnson, "Life of Adam and Eve," 2:250; Dochhorn, *Die Apokalypse des Mose.*

11. Jonge and Tromp, *Life of Adam and Eve*, 66–67.

12. M. Johnson, "Life of Adam and Eve," 2:252.

13. Levison, "Adam and Eve in Romans 1.18–25."

14. Jonge and Tromp, *Life of Adam and Eve*, 69.

to the Septuagint, and all the concerns of the text relate to the Hebrew Bible. Second, there are alleged rabbinic patterns of interpretation (e.g., LAE 24:1–2; cf. Gen. 3:17) and, third, there are extensive parallels with rabbinic literature.[15] Johannes Tromp takes a rather different view. He sees the burning of incense (LAE 29:4; 33:4; 38:2), the similarities between the tomb of Adam (42:1) and that of Jesus (Matt. 27:66),[16] and the reference to the Lake of Acheron (LAE 37:3; cf. Apocalypse of Peter 14; Revelation of Paul 22) as indications of Christian provenance.

Finally, the location at which the text was composed remains disputed. The reference to the Lake of Acheron (LAE 37:3)[17] has been taken to refer to an Alexandrian provenance. But the absence of notable Alexandrian allegorical features coupled with the known parallels with rabbinic texts create problems. Naturally those who contend it is written in Hebrew suggest a Palestinian origin. Others have even suggested Rome.[18] These complications lead scholars to an impasse on several fronts, and so no further attention will be given to the Life of Adam and Eve here. Readers are instead referred to the accessible introduction by Marinus de Jonge and Johannes Tromp.[19]

4 Baruch

Introduction

Fourth Baruch, attributed to Baruch the scribe and also known as Things Omitted from Jeremiah the Prophet (*Paraleipomena Jeremiou*), describes events at the time of the fall of Jerusalem to Nebuchadnezzar (587/586 BCE) but before the death of Jeremiah by stoning. It is generally agreed that the fall of Jerusalem to "Babylon" is a contextual recasting of the destruction of Jerusalem by the Romans in 70 CE. And so the work as a whole is set after the destruction of the Jerusalem temple in 70 CE and before the completion of the Bar Kokhba revolt (ca. 135 CE).

Contents

As the narrative begins, God explains to Jeremiah his intent to destroy Jerusalem by the host of Chaldean armies (4 Bar. 1). Jeremiah brings Baruch

15. Dochhorn, *Die Apokalypse des Mose*, 152–65.
16. Tromp, *Life of Adam and Eve in Greek*.
17. M. Johnson, "Life of Adam and Eve," 2:252.
18. Levison, "Adam and Eve, Life of."
19. Jonge and Tromp, *Life of Adam and Eve*.

to the temple, where he explains God's message and weeps at the altar (chap. 2). Then, at an hour appointed by God, Jeremiah and Baruch ascend the city walls, from which they see angels coming from heaven to lay siege to the city (3:1–10). Jeremiah is instructed to take the holy vessels of the temple and entrust them to the care of the earth, so that they will be hidden until the coming of the "beloved one" (3:11). Abimelech the Ethiopian, God instructs, is to be sent to "the vineyard of Agrippa," where he will be sheltered in the shadow of a mountain. Jeremiah does as he is instructed and is himself told to go with the people to Babylon (3:17–22).

The next morning the angelic hosts call the Chaldeans to take the city and remove its people to Babylon (4:1–3). But Jeremiah flees with the keys of the temple and casts them into the sun for safe keeping (4:4–5) before both he and Baruch are carted off to Babylon with the other exiles (4:6–12). But Abimelech falls asleep under a tree for sixty-six years and learns from an old man that God prevented him from witnessing the tragedy that befell Babylon (chap. 5). Then Abimelech is transported to Baruch, who is in a tomb and learns that those who obey the commands of the angel of righteousness will be preserved (6:1–10). Baruch then explains this to Jeremiah in a letter, which is delivered by an eagle (6:11–24; 7:1–11). The bird arrives in Babylon and delivers the message to Jeremiah, who gathers the people to hear the message (7:12–17). The eagle causes a dead man to come to life so that the people might believe what is said (7:18–23). Then Jeremiah writes to Baruch, explaining to him the hardships suffered by Israel in captivity and even their own worship of foreign gods (7:24–36). Then the Lord leads the people out of Babylon, and Jeremiah instructs only those who are willing to forsake their idolatrous ways to cross the Jordan to Jerusalem (8:1–5). Those who refuse turn back to Babylon, from which they are turned away only to establish their own city, called Samaria (8:6–12). Jeremiah and his companions rejoice and offer sacrifices and prayers (9:1–6). Then, while standing at the altar, Jeremiah dies, and Baruch and Abimelech mourn (9:7–10). While preparing his body for burial, they are told by a (heavenly) voice that he will rise from the dead (9:11–13). This he does after three days and glorifies God and the Son of God, "Jesus Christ," and announces that there will pass another 477 years before Christ will come to earth and establish eschatological promises (9:14–20). But the people become angry at words about the Son of God, taken from Isaiah, and plan to stone Jeremiah (9:21–24). But God turns a large stone into the image of Jeremiah, which the people then stone, thinking it is him. But the stone rebukes them for their stupidity, after which Jeremiah dies and Baruch and Abimelech use the stone to mark the tomb of Jeremiah (9:25–32).

Contribution

It is clear that the author of 4 Baruch anticipates the restoration of the temple and its sacrifices in Jerusalem, for the sacred vessels are not destroyed but kept hidden until Israel returns from exile to reconstitute cultic worship (e.g., 4 Bar. 3:8–11, 18–19; 4:4–5). Jerusalem's destruction in the first place was a display not of Babylonian (Roman) might but of God's explicit orchestration because of Israel's sins (4:7–8). In this respect S. E. Robinson suggests that the message of the work to its ancient audience was that the Jews would experience this restoration by sufficient adherence to the law. The author of 4 Baruch also supports the notion of resurrection, in which personal and corporate views are closely linked (6:6–10; 7:18; cf. 9:12–14).[20]

Robinson observes that 4 Baruch recounts events found in the Hebrew Bible, notably Jeremiah, 2 Kings, 2 Chronicles, Ezra, and Nehemiah, and is surely intended to be a supplement or addition to Jeremiah in particular. Nevertheless, there are discrepancies, such as 4 Baruch's assertion that Jeremiah and his scribe Baruch led Israelites back to Jerusalem from Babylon, whereas the book of Jeremiah makes it clear that he never went to Babylon but went instead to Egypt (Jer. 43:6–7; cf. Neh. 10:2; 12:1, 12, 34). Furthermore, the contention that Samaritans were Jews who intermarried with Babylonians during the exile is contradicted by the account of Ezra-Nehemiah in which they existed before the return (cf. 2 Kings 17:24–41).[21] It is often noted that there are similarities between 4 Baruch and 2 Baruch, with some debate about literary interdependence.[22] There are also affinities with other texts regarding the prophet Jeremiah (e.g., 2 Macc. 2:1–7; Liv. Pro. 2:11–19).[23]

Text and Provenance

The text of 4 Baruch is preserved in sixty-three Greek manuscripts in two recensions: a longer and shorter version. It is generally agreed that the longer, of which there are twenty-three manuscripts, is older, while the shorter, of which there are forty manuscripts, is an abridgement of the longer recension.[24] The text has been translated into Ethiopic, Armenian, and Old Church Slavonic.[25] There is some debate as to whether it was originally written in Greek

---

20. Robinson, "4 Baruch," 2:416.
21. Robinson, "4 Baruch," 2:416.
22. See Robinson, "4 Baruch," 2:416–17; Bogaert, *Apocalypse de Baruch*, 1:192–221.
23. Nickelsburg, "Stories," 75.
24. Torijano, "4 *Baruch*," 2662.
25. Torijano, "4 *Baruch*," 2662; see Robinson, "4 Baruch," 2:413.

or whether the presence of Semitic influences suggests a Hebrew or Aramaic original.[26]

Generally the work is thought to have been written at a date no later than 136 CE, the year after the Roman emperor Hadrian ended the Second Jewish Revolt (Bar Kokhba revolt) and forbade Jews from entering the new Roman colony at Jerusalem. And so some suggest it was originally written right around the time of the Second Jewish Revolt (ca. 132–135 CE).[27] Its earliest date is clearly established by the mention of Agrippa I (4 Bar. 3:14, 21; 5:22), who rose to power in Judea and Samaria in 41 CE (Josephus, *J.W.* 2.11.1–4 §§204–213; *Ant.* 18.6.10–8.2 §§236–267; 19.5.2 §§279–281). And so the destruction of the city (4 Bar. 1–4) likely reflects the destruction of Jerusalem by the Romans in 70 CE (Josephus, *J.W.* 6.4.1–9.4 §§220–434; 7.1.1–3 §§1–20). Furthermore, the points of correspondence with 2 Baruch require a date after the composition of that text, which was likely completed before 100 CE. It is then theorized that perhaps by the mid-second century CE the work was redacted by a Christian who made at least one interpolation (4 Bar. 6:25) and Christianized the ending (8:12–9:32).[28]

As to its provenance, it is generally agreed that 4 Baruch was originally a Jewish composition with Christian redaction in at least these two places.[29] But the fact that it is the work of at least two authors creates problems. The first was surely a Jew. The references to Agrippa I (3:14, 21; 5:22), the market of the gentiles (6:19), and the traditions about Jeremiah that evolve into a tale of national restoration all support this view.[30] The author's familiarity with Jerusalem and its environs supports the geographical location of Palestine for the location of its composition. For the original, pre-Christian version, its purpose was likely to prepare the readers for this restoration by exhorting them to purify themselves of the pagan influences of their exile ("Babylon") and to abstain from gentile defilements (cf. Ezra 9–10; Neh. 13:23–27). But the second author was a Christian who added to the original text and may have tried to change it into a missionary work to the Jewish people after the failure of the second revolt.[31] But here is where the history of the text becomes problematic, since it likely drew from several sources and was adapted by Christians over time and, like most of the works discussed here, was preserved exclusively in Christian contexts. The combination of these complications

26. See Robinson, "4 Baruch," 2:413.
27. Nickelsburg, "Stories," 75.
28. Robinson, "4 Baruch," 2:413.
29. Robinson, "4 Baruch," 2:415; Torijano, "4 *Baruch*," 2661–62.
30. Torijano, "4 *Baruch*," 2662.
31. Torijano, "4 *Baruch*," 2661–62.

makes clear decisions about authorship, date, and provenance problematic.[32] For further consideration readers are encouraged to consult the most complete and recent study by Jens Herzer, which includes a critical introduction, translation, and commentary.[33]

Ezekiel the Tragedian

Introduction

A work known as the *Exagōgē*, meaning "exodus," is a Greek tragedy composed by a certain Ezekiel, about whom nothing is known[34] save that Eusebius,[35] citing Alexander Polyhistor, calls him "the poet of tragedies."[36] (The plural "tragedies" indicates this is not Ezekiel's only work.)[37] As a play it is modeled on the great classical tragedies of fifth-century-BCE Athens.[38] In its extant 269 lines, which preserve only part of the work, it recounts the story of the exodus from Egypt (Exod. 1–15), which it presents as a Jewish form of Greek tragedy.[39]

Contents

The *Exagōgē* is presented in Greek verse in five distinct episodes. It begins, first, with a prologue speech delivered by Moses that describes his Jewish life in Egypt, including his own birth, his flight from Egypt, and his meeting the daughters of Raguel (lines 1–65).[40] The second episode recounts events in Midian, most importantly Moses's dream and its interpretation by Jethro, his father-in-law (lines 66–89). God appears to Moses in the burning bush, from which he instructs Moses and tells him what he is to tell the people (lines 90–192). Then a survivor from the Egyptians arrives and reports the destruction of the Egyptian armies at the Red Sea (lines 193–242). Finally, Elim, a Jewish scout, reports to Moses on the discovery of a good place to set up camp in the desert (lines 243–69; cf. Exod. 15:27).

32. Kraft, "Baruch, Fourth Book of," 1:127–28, citing Herzer, *4 Baruch (Paraleipomena Jeremiou)*, xxx–xxxvi.
33. Herzer, *4 Baruch (Paraleipomena Jeremiou)*.
34. Lanfranchi, "Ezekiel the Tragedian."
35. Eusebius, *Praep. ev.* 9.28.1
36. Cf. Clement of Alexandria, *Strom.* 1.23.155.1.
37. So also Nickelsburg, "Bible Rewritten and Expanded," 129.
38. Jacobson, "Ezekiel, the Tragedian," 730.
39. Jacobson, "Ezekiel, the Tragedian," 730.
40. Jacobson, "Ezekiel, the Tragedian," 730.

Contribution

The *Exagōgē* is unique in that it incorporates an entirely different genre for its recasting of the biblical narrative,[41] with striking parallels with the Septuagint text of Exodus.[42] The author exercises a degree of literary license in his work, such as the dream of Moses and its interpretation by Jethro and the introduction of new characters, in keeping with the literary standards of Greek tragic drama.[43] It is generally, though cautiously, suggested that the *Exagōgē* is a tragedy intended to be staged and performed.[44] This is evident from the extant material for two main reasons:[45] only scenes that are easily depicted on stage are actually recounted, and God explicitly says that he could be heard but not seen. Both of these factors lend themselves well to a performed drama, perhaps for a Jewish audience during the Passover season.[46] It is the most extensive surviving example of Hellenistic tragedy,[47] and somewhat unique in its utilization of historical events (cf. Aeschylus's *Persians*). It also violates the ideal of a classical Greek tragedy, as expressed by Aristotle,[48] that the entirety of a tragedy should occur within a twenty-four-hour period and in a single geographical location.[49]

Text and Provenance

There is no doubt the *Exagōgē*, written in iambic trimeter, which was commonly used in Greek tragic drama, was originally composed in the Greek language. The fragmentary text is extant only in fragments cited by Eusebius, Clement of Alexandria, and Pseudo-Eustathius.[50] It is generally agreed that Ezekiel's writing comes from Alexandria, Egypt, given its setting in Egypt with the Moses account, its use of the Septuagint, and its sophisticated utilization of the Greek tragic drama.[51] There is, however, nothing definitive about this location. The date in which the *Exagōgē* was composed is determined

---

41. See Jacobson, *Exagoge of Ezekiel*, 23–28.
42. Robertson, "Ezekiel the Tragedian," 2:805.
43. Robertson, "Ezekiel the Tragedian," 2:803.
44. Oegema, *Early Judaism and Modern Culture*, 65–66; Lanfranchi, "Ezekiel the Tragedian."
45. Nickelsburg, "Bible Rewritten and Expanded," 128–29.
46. Nickelsburg, "Bible Rewritten and Expanded," 128; Lanfranchi, *L'Exagoge d'Ezéchiel le tragique*, 64–68.
47. Jacobson, "Ezekiel, the Tragedian," 730.
48. Aristotle, *Poetica* 1.5 (1449b).
49. Robertson, "Ezekiel the Tragedian," 2:805.
50. Eusebius, *Praep. ev.* 9.28–29; Clement of Alexandria, *Strom.* 1.23.155–56; Pseudo-Eustathius, *Commentarius in Hexaemeron*. Robertson, "Ezekiel the Tragedian," 2:803.
51. Robertson, "Ezekiel the Tragedian," 2:804; Jacobson, "Ezekiel, the Tragedian," 730; Lanfranchi, "Ezekiel the Tragedian."

by a couple of factors. First, it exhibits clear use of the Septuagint, which was translated in the third century BCE. Second, excerpts of the *Exagōgē* are found in Alexander Polyhistor, whose *Concerning the Jews* dates from the first century BCE. This indicates a date of composition in the mid-first century BCE.[52] But the incomplete and brief nature of the work does not afford any further specificity, and because of its brevity, no further attention will be given to it here. Instead, readers are encouraged to consult the study by Howard Jacobson, which furnishes readers with a complete yet accessible introduction and commentary.[53]

---

52. Robertson, "Ezekiel the Tragedian," 2:803–4.
53. Jacobson, *Exagoge of Ezekiel.*

Psalms, Wisdom Literature, and Prayers

Introduction

The various expressions of religious piety among Second Temple Jews occasioned a large assortment of psalms, hymns, and prayers.[1] These are often embedded in larger texts and so are part of larger writings rather than, for example, prayers utilized in individual practice.[2] This is especially true for prayers, of which numerous examples survive from antiquity but surprisingly few are unintegrated into larger texts. And yet there is surely some degree to which the surviving texts reflect the "living practices of prayer in terms of form, motifs, occasion, and posture."[3] Yet the actual settings in which such works may have been used in worship or liturgical settings is difficult to

1. Falk, "Hymns, Prayers, and Psalms." See Flusser, "Psalms, Hymns and Prayers."
2. Matlock, *Discovering the Traditions of Prose Prayers*.
3. Falk, "Hymns, Prayers, and Psalms," 2:347.

identify. Of a different nature but with some literary affinities, at least in the
Hebrew Bible, is Wisdom literature. Such writings are in part defined by the
use of the term "wisdom" (Hebrew חׇכְמׇה, *ḥokmâh*; Greek σοφία, *sophia*),
found in works in the Hebrew Bible like Proverbs, Job, and Ecclesiastes, and
also in such Second Temple Jewish works as the Wisdom of Solomon and
Ben Sira.[4] In their original forms wisdom writings were educational in nature,
intended for the training of younger scribes for official service. The intent is
to elucidate a way of life as well as facilitate discussion of pertinent religious
and intellectual questions for the respective contexts in which they emerge.[5]
These three kinds of literature—psalms, prayers, and Wisdom literature—
are discussed in this final major section of this book. Before turning to each,
however, it is instructive to discuss a few matters pertinent to each category.

Psalms

The works discussed in the following chapters, Psalms 151–155 and the Psalms
of Solomon, represent a small cross section of what are widely regarded as
psalms and hymns compiled during the Second Temple period both for corporate worship within the temple and for educational purposes.[6] The popularity of psalms is attested by the discovery of thirty-nine psalms scrolls at
Qumran, including three scrolls (11QPsᵃ, 11QPsᵇ, 4QPsᶠ) that include twelve
texts not found in the Psalter of the Hebrew Bible and six of which were
previously unknown.[7] Other Qumran psalms reflect a diverse collection of
Jewish religious poetry,[8] the most important of which are the Thanksgiving
Hymns (1QHᵃ, 1QHᵇ, 4Q427–432), which at times seem to depict the personal experiences of a sectarian leader. Other thanksgiving psalms include
the Barki Nafshi (Hebrew ברכי נפשי, *brkî npšî*, "Bless my soul"), which
contains pleas for deliverance from persecution and for the acquisition of
certain spiritual qualities.[9] Also significant among the Qumran works is the
Songs of the Sabbath Sacrifice (4Q400–407, 11Q17, Mas1k), a liturgical text
that originally consisted of thirteen units ("songs") corresponding to each
quarter of a 364-day calendar.[10]

---

4. Kampen, "Wisdom Literature."
5. Kampen, "Wisdom Literature."
6. Gillingham, "Levites and the Editorial Composition of the Psalms."
7. Falk, "Hymns, Prayers, and Psalms"; Sanders, Charlesworth, and Rietz, "Non-Masoretic Psalms."
8. Nitzan, *Qumran Prayer and Religious Poetry*, 173–318; Schuller, "Prayers and Psalms."
9. Falk, "Hymns, Prayers, and Psalms." See Schuller, "Barki Nafshi (4Q434–438)."
10. Mizrahi, "Songs of the Sabbath Sacrifice"; see Davila, *Liturgical Works*, 83–167.

Wisdom Literature

Pride of place for Wisdom literature in Second Temple Judaism belongs to two works classified among the apocrypha: Ben Sira and the Wisdom of Solomon. The former identifies Torah as Wisdom (Sir. 24:23). The latter belongs to Roman-era Alexandria and, like the work of Pseudo-Phocylides, which is discussed below, addresses matters of a similar perspective. Wisdom literature is also an important component of the Dead Sea Scrolls, where the book of Instruction (4QInstruction), attested in some eight copies and dating from the second century BCE, is most significant.[11] In this work the addressee is exhorted to search for truth, receive instruction, and gain understanding (e.g., 4Q417 1 I, 25; 2 I, 1–7; 4Q418 81 17) but also to receive revealed wisdom by the "mystery of existence" (רז נהיה; *rz nhyh*, e.g., 4Q416 2 III, 14, 18; 4Q417 2 I, 6; 4Q418 43–45 4, 14).[12]

Prayers

Prayer in ancient Judaism is an act of communication with God with the purpose of getting some result from the interaction.[13] In this respect its function is more important than its form,[14] though prayers can be generally categorized into different types. These include petitionary or penitential prayers, which are typically communal in nature (Ezra 9; Neh. 9; Dan. 9; cf. Pss. Sol. 9; 4 Ezra 8:20–36; 1QS I, 18–II, 18) but can also be individual (Neh. 1:5–11; cf. Tob. 3:1–6; Prayer of Manasseh).[15] These are directed to God to confess sins and ask for forgiveness as an act of repentance.[16] There are also prayers of thanksgiving, typically in response to a specific blessing received, such as provisions, deliverance, or simply occasions for joy. These are embedded within other texts in the Hebrew Bible (e.g., 1 Chron. 16:35–36), the Apocrypha (e.g., Tob. 8:5–8; Sir. 51:1–12; Jdt. 16), the Pseudepigrapha (e.g., Pss. Sol. 2:37; 16:5; Jub. 22:7–9), the Dead Sea Scrolls (e.g., 1QHᵃ IV, 29; 1QS XI, 15; 1QM XIII, 2) and the New Testament (e.g., 1 Cor. 15:57; Rev. 11:17).[17]

11. Kampen, "Wisdom Literature."
12. Uusimäki, "Instruction (4QInstruction)"; see Goff, *4QInstruction*; Kampen, *Wisdom Literature*, 36–190.
13. Falk, "Hymns, Prayers, and Psalms"; Malina, "What Is Prayer?," 215.
14. Newman, *Praying by the Book*, 6–7.
15. Falk, "Hymns, Prayers, and Psalms."
16. Werline, "Reflections on Penitential Prayer."
17. Falk, "Hymns, Prayers, and Psalms"; Schuller, "Some Observations"; Falk, *Daily, Sabbath, and Festival Prayers*, 35–43, 79–84, 182–85.

As indicated above, the majority of prayers from the Second Temple period are not freestanding texts but are embedded within other, larger documents. Some may function as doxologies (e.g., 3 Macc. 7:23) or be attributed to biblical figures like Noah and Abraham (Genesis Apocryphon), Levi (Aramaic Levi Document), Enoch (1 Enoch), Baruch (2 Baruch), Ezra (4 Ezra), or Job (Testament of Job). Others are found in early Christian narratives as models for a community (e.g., Matt. 6:9–13) or as a record of the prayers of Jesus (e.g., Luke 11:1–4; Mark 14:26) or Paul (2 Cor. 1:3–7). Sometimes prayers in Wisdom literature have didactic purposes, perhaps functioning as models (e.g., Sir. 23:1–6; 36:1–17; 51:1–12; Wis. 9).[18] This situation renders the analysis of prayers in the present volume rather difficult. As Judith H. Newman indicates, the only prayers that survive as distinct texts are the Prayer of Manasseh and the Hellenistic Synagogal Prayers.[19] To this one could add samples from among the Dead Sea Scrolls, as we shall see below. The Prayer of Manasseh, discussed capably by David A. deSilva, is preserved in part in the Greek tradition among the Septuagint manuscripts and so belongs formally to the Apocrypha.[20] The so-called Hellenistic Synagogal Prayers is thought to derive from an originally Jewish source with Christian interpolations that, in some instances, can be identified (e.g., 5:4–8, 20–24; 7:4)[21] and perhaps excised to identify its Jewish foundation. This is a challenging task, which we have avoided elsewhere (e.g., Testaments of the Twelve Patriarchs). However, the paucity of free-standing prayers in the literature warrants some consideration. And so here we will address some of the matters pertaining to that document as well as a prayer found in the Dead Sea Scrolls (Prayer of Nabonidus [4Q242]).

18. Falk, "Hymns, Prayers, and Psalms."
19. Newman, *Praying by the Book*, 7–11.
20. DeSilva, *Introducing the Apocrypha*, 324–29.
21. Stuckenbruck, "Apocrypha and Pseudepigrapha," 159.

19

Psalms 151–155

Introduction

According to one of the psalms scrolls (11QPsᵃ = 11Q5), King David wrote an astonishing 4,050 works, including 3,600 psalms, 364 songs for daily offerings, 52 songs for the Sabbaths, 30 songs for the festivals, and 4 songs for "making music over the stricken" (11QPsᵃ XXVII, 2–11).[1] At the end (11QPsᵃ XXVII, 11) the author claims that David spoke all these through prophecy from God.[2] This same scroll, which is "the largest and best preserved of all Psalms manuscripts" from Qumran,[3] contains forty biblical psalms (between Pss. 101 and 150) in an order that varies from the Masoretic tradition, as well as eight poems not found in the biblical Psalter.[4] Among these psalms preserved partially in Hebrew in 11QPsᵃ are six psalms from the Second Temple period beyond the 150 collected in the Hebrew Bible (Pss. 151A, 151B, 152, 153, 154, 155).[5] The earliest of these psalms are incompletely preserved among fragmentary Dead Sea Scrolls manuscripts, and their content is sometimes supplemented by surviving Greek and Syriac translations.

Language, Manuscripts, and Date

Originally Psalm 151 was two separate psalms, 151A and 151B.[6] 11QPsᵃ contains all of Psalm 151A (XXVIII, 4–13) and the first two lines of Psalm

---

1. Schuller, "Apocryphal Psalms," 2095.
2. Schuller, "Apocryphal Psalms," 2095.
3. Flint, *Dead Sea Psalms Scrolls*, 39.
4. Schuller, "Apocryphal Psalms," 2095.
5. Gurtner, "Psalms 151–155."
6. Charlesworth with Sanders, "More Psalms of David," 2:612.

151B (XXVIII, 14–15). The remainder of Psalm 151B in 11QPs[a] is lost.[7] The manuscript was copied between 30 and 50 CE.[8] Psalm 151 is known from the Greek Psalter preserved in several Greek codices (A B א). A Hebrew antecedent bearing the superscription "A Hallelujah of David the Son of Jesse" (הללויה לדויד בן־ישי, hllûyâ ldwîd bn-yšy) was found at Qumran (11QPs[a] XXVIII, 3]). In addition to Psalm 151 (11QPs[a] XXVIII, 4–13) this manuscript preserves a fragmentary narrative of David's encounter with Goliath (11QPs[a] XXVIII, 14–15; cf. 1 Sam. 16–17). The former (11QPs[a] XXVIII, 4–13) is typically designated Psalm 151A and the latter (11QPs[a] XXVIII, 14–15) Psalm 151B. Psalm 151B has its own superscript: "The beginning of David's po[w]er, after God's prophet had anointed him" (תחלת גב[ו]רה לדויד משמשחו נביא אלוהים, tḥlt gb[û]râ ldwîd mšmšḥû nbi᾽ ᾽lôhîm; 11QPs[a] XXVIII, 14). In the Greek version of Psalm 151, both these texts have been conflated and truncated. Psalm 151 was originally composed in Hebrew.[9] The origins of the Greek version are unknown, though from it versions in Ethiopic[10] and Old Latin are derived.[11] The Syriac of Psalm 151 derives from the Greek (Septuagint),[12] but the Syriac of Psalms 152–155 come directly from the Hebrew.[13] The Syriac manuscripts date from the sixth to the sixteenth century.[14] The presence of Psalm 151 in the Greek Psalter suggests a date prior to the second century BCE. F. M. Cross argues for a date no later than the third century BCE.[15] This means that it could not have originated with the sectarians at Qumran, whose community did not originate until the middle of the second century BCE.[16]

Psalms 152 and 153 are extant only in Syriac, which may have been translated from a Hebrew original,[17] though no evidence for them is extant in the Dead Sea Scrolls.[18] The Syriac of both psalms betrays cumbersome transliterations of some Hebrew words taken from the Hebrew Psalter. The Syriac

7. Flint, *Dead Sea Psalms Scrolls*, 40–41.
8. J. A. Sanders, *Psalms Scroll of Qumran Cave 11*, 6–9; J. A. Sanders, *Dead Sea Psalms Scroll*, 6; Cross, "David, Orpheus, and Psalm 151:3–4."
9. J. A. Sanders, "Qumran Psalms Scroll (11QPs[a]) Reviewed."
10. Strelcyn, "Le Psaume 151."
11. Weber, *Le Psautier romain*.
12. Charlesworth with Sanders, "More Psalms of David," 2:612.
13. See Strugnell, "Text and Transmission," 278.
14. Charlesworth with Sanders, "More Psalms of David," 2:609–10. They are Baghdad, Library of the Chaldean Patriarchate, MS 1113, fols. 118b–20b (ca. twelfth century); London, British Museum, Add. MS 14.568, fols. 49b–50a (sixth century); and JRL Syr 7, Manchester, John Rylands Library, Syriac Manuscript 7, folio 135a (sixteenth century). The latter contains only Psalm 151 of this collection.
15. Cross, "David, Orpheus, and Psalm 151:3–4," 70.
16. Charlesworth with Sanders, "More Psalms of David," 2:612.
17. Strugnell, "Text and Transmission," 259.
18. J. A. Sanders, *Dead Sea Psalms Scroll*, 141.

versions may originate as early as the second or third century BCE, though it is impossible to be certain.

Psalms 154 and 155 were originally composed in Hebrew, from which the extant Syriac is likely translated.[19] Nothing in either psalm suggests Davidic affiliation. Instead, the superscriptions identify them as prayers of Hezekiah, though nothing in the texts corresponds to known events from his reign. Since the Dead Sea manuscript in which both Psalm 154 and 155 are found (11QPs[a]) dates from the first century CE, some think that these two psalms originate in the second or third century BCE.[20]

Contents

Psalm 151A is a narrative of David, who recounts his upbringing as the youngest among brothers in a shepherding family (v. 1).[21] From there he launches into praise, first with his flute (v. 2), then from the hills, mountains, and flocks around him (v. 3). Here the Hebrew and Syriac diverge: the former narrates David's anointing by Samuel and being chosen by God to lead his people (vv. 4–7), whereas the Syriac (vv. 4–5) states that God's angel took David, rather than his brothers, from his father's sheep. Whereas the Hebrew of Psalm 151A found in 11QPs[a] finishes there, the Greek and Syriac continue by joining what in Hebrew is known as Psalm 151B. David confronts "the Philistine," who curses him (151B:1 = Greek 151:6), after which David slays Goliath and removes the shame from Israel (151B:2 = Greek 151:7).

Psalm 152 is superscripted "Spoken by David after Fighting against the Lion and the Wolf Which Took Sheep from His Flocks." In it the psalmist pleads for help from "killers," whom he depicts as a lion destroying his father's flocks (vv. 1–3). He asks for deliverance as God's "elect one" that he may praise God when he is saved from the mouths of beasts (vv. 4–5). Finally, he implores "Adonai" to come quickly to lift him from the gaping abyss (v. 6). Similarly, Psalm 153 is, according to its superscript, "Spoken by David after Receiving God's Grace When He Delivered Him from the Lion and Wolf and Those Two He Killed by His Hands." It begins with an exhortation for the nations to bless the Lord for his deliverance of his elect holy one from destruction (vv. 1–3). Prior to God's intervention the psalmist was nearly torn in two by beasts (v. 4), until God sent his angel to close their mouths (v. 5). The psalmist will therefore praise and exalt God for his graces (v. 6).

19. Gurtner, "Psalms 151–155."
20. Sanders, Charlesworth, and Rietz, "Non-Masoretic Psalms," 171.
21. Gurtner, "Psalms 151–155."

Though the first two lines of the Hebrew of Psalm 154 are absent, the Syriac begins with an exhortation to the multitude to extol God (vv. 1–2).[22] In both versions the psalm then exhorts people to associate with the righteous in order to make known God's power (vv. 3–4)—that is, to make known God's deeds among the community and beyond (vv. 5–9). Those who praise God are depicted as those who offer sacrifices (vv. 10–12). God's law is the subject of fixed attention by the righteous (vv. 13–14; in contrast to the wicked, v. 15), who receive God's compassion and care (vv. 16–17). God is blessed for his care for the righteous among Israel (vv. 18–20).

Psalm 155 resembles Psalms 22 and 51, and its confession of sin may be compared with the Prayer of Manasseh. The Hebrew is a "broken acrostic."[23] The psalmist cries out to God for deliverance (vv. 1–4) and protection from the wicked (vv. 5–6). He expresses trust in God as judge and appeals to him for forgiveness and instruction (vv. 7–18; the Hebrew is missing for vv. 19–21).[24]

Critical Issues

Some scholars estimate that Psalms 151–155 raise important questions about the development and composition of the Psalter of the Hebrew Bible.[25] Peter W. Flint[26] argues that 11QPs[a] is not a "secondary liturgical compilation" of psalms, as Shemaryahu Talmon says,[27] but rather a "true scriptural Psalter."[28] Though this may hold to some extent for the collections of the Psalter at Qumran,[29] it remains uncertain what shape the Psalter took elsewhere. Some have argued that the Psalter was already set as a canonical norm by the second century BCE[30] and that 11QPs[a] is a composite document that serves as a "Jewish prayerbook"[31] or a "library edition" of the "standard collection of 150 Psalms."[32] Regardless, together these psalms demonstrate that into the Second Temple period poetic traditions from the Hebrew Bible continued to influence later poetic compositions and that David continued to be celebrated as a poet

22. Gurtner, "Psalms 151–155."
23. Sanders, Charlesworth, and Rietz, "Non-Masoretic Psalms," 179.
24. Gurtner, "Psalms 151–155."
25. Gurtner, "Psalms 151–155."
26. Flint, *Dead Sea Psalms Scrolls*, 204–27.
27. Talmon, "Hebrew Apocryphal Psalms," subsequently translated into English as Talmon, "Extra-Canonical Psalms."
28. Flint, *Dead Sea Psalms Scrolls*, 204–5, 227.
29. Charlesworth with Sanders, "More Psalms of David," 2:610.
30. Goshen-Gottstein, "Psalms Scroll (11QPs[a])."
31. Talmon, "Extra-Canonical Psalms."
32. Skehan, "Apocryphal Psalm 151"; Skehan, "Liturgical Complex in 11QPs[a]."

and composer of psalms. Finally, they attest the preservation, transmission, and translation of texts found near Khirbet Qumran in the collection of text translations later collected in the Septuagint and adopted by Syriac-speaking Christianity.

Contribution and Context

Though attested at Qumran, the affiliation of Psalms 151A and 151B with the sectarian interests of the community (*yaḥad*) is uncertain. Their genre resonates with the Psalter of the Hebrew Bible as well as with works like the Prayer of Manasseh (esp. Pss. 154–155) and the Psalms of Solomon.[33] A rather different circumstance is found in Psalm 154, which is the one psalm among this group most closely aligned in thought with the Dead Sea Scrolls. Its discussion of the "many ones" (or "many"; 154:1) may correspond to the technical terminology that defines "the fully initiated members of the Qumran community" (e.g., 1QS VI, 8–VII, 25; cf. Isa. 53:11). Furthermore, the "assembly" to which one joins (Ps. 154:4) may correspond to the "community" (*yaḥad*) at Qumran (e.g., 1QH^a XI, 19–23; XIX, 10–14).[34] A final question pertains to the relation of the Hebrew of the psalms, especially Psalm 155 (11QPs^a XXIV, 3–17), to the extant Syriac, which is likely a *Vorlage* for the later skilled translator.[35]

---

33. Gurtner, "Psalms 151–155."
34. Charlesworth with Sanders, "More Psalms of David," 2:617–18.
35. Gurtner, "Psalms 151–155."

20

Psalms of Solomon

Introduction

A collection of eighteen pseudonymous hymns or poems, attributed to
Solomon, are known as the Psalms of Solomon. In general, they convey a
Jewish community's response to persecution and a foreign invasion,[1] likely
in reference to the Romans in the first century BCE.[2] The community responsible for the psalms regard themselves as "the pious" and "the righteous,"
and the psalms are distinct from the canonical psalms and Psalms 151–155
in their identification, to some degree, of the community's circumstances
and their appeal to God both for the punishment of wicked Israelites, who
are rightly judged for their iniquity, and for judgment on the gentile rulers,
who are the means of God's judgment on wicked Israelites. In this respect
God is appealed to throughout as the righteous judge who dispenses rewards and punishments for human actions.[3] At what point in its history
the work was attributed to Solomon is unclear, though it seems evident
that the reference to the "son of David" (Pss. Sol. 17:21) was the cause of
its Solomonic affiliation.[4]

1. Atkinson, "Psalms of Solomon," 1903.
2. R. Wright, "Psalms of Solomon," 2:639.
3. Nickelsburg, *Jewish Literature*, 239.
4. Atkinson, "Psalms of Solomon," 1903.

Language and Manuscripts

Though Psalms of Solomon is preserved today only in Greek[5] and Syriac[6] translations, most scholars believe it was composed in Hebrew.[7] Shortly afterward it was translated into Greek, and at some later date into Syriac.[8] However, no Hebrew manuscripts survive from antiquity, and the extant Greek texts are relatively late. Its Greek text exhibits clear indications of "Semitisms" and other features of translation from Hebrew. The Greek translation makes use of the Septuagint Psalter, and it is likely that the Psalms of Solomon translator sought to harmonize his Greek rendering with that of the Septuagint. The Greek text of the Psalms of Solomon is quoted in 1 Baruch, which requires that the Greek translation was available by the end of the first century CE.[9]

Provenance

The central concern of Jerusalem in the Psalms of Solomon suggests to most scholars that the work was written in that city or its nearby vicinity.[10] Jerusalem is explicitly addressed (Pss. Sol. 11) and even speaks (chap. 1). Furthermore, it is identified as the seat of the Sanhedrin (4:1), and some suggest that the vices described are particularly urban.[11]

Subject to considerable discussion is the identification of the three main groups that find a place in the Psalms of Solomon. These include the devout, the gentiles, and the sinners. The devout are the authors of the Psalms of Solomon, often identified as the Pharisees. Items consonant with this attribution include the claim of human responsibility for actions (9:4), belief in the resurrection (3:12), a concern for piety and a righteous life, and a distinction between the righteous and the sinner.[12] To these could

---

5. The Greek manuscripts date from the tenth to the sixteenth century. See Trafton, *Syriac Version*, 6–9; R. Wright, *Psalms of Solomon*, 13–26.

6. The Syriac manuscripts date from the seventh to the sixteenth century. See Trafton, *Syriac Version*, 5–6.

7. Atkinson, "Psalms of Solomon," 1903; R. Wright, "Psalms of Solomon," 2:640. But see, most recently, Joosten, "Reflections."

8. R. Wright, "Psalms of Solomon," 2:640. Trafton shows that the Syriac is based primarily, if not exclusively, on a Hebrew *Vorlage* (*Syriac Version*, 217–18). For the Syriac text, see Baars, "Psalms of Solomon."

9. R. Wright, "Psalms of Solomon," 2:640.

10. Trafton, "Solomon, Psalms of," 1:503; Atkinson, "Psalms of Solomon," 1903; R. Wright, "Psalms of Solomon," 2:641; Nickelsburg, *Jewish Literature*, 247.

11. R. Wright, "Psalms of Solomon," 2:641.

12. Nickelsburg, *Jewish Literature*, 246.

be added the notion of theocracy (2:30, 32; 5:18, 19; 17:1, 34, 46), the sanctity of the law (e.g., 4:8; 10:4), and divine providence (5:3–4).[13] There are, however, objections to Pharisaic authorship. These include the absence of other distinctive Pharisaic concerns, such as Sabbath observance and table fellowship.[14] Also, some of the characteristics typically attributed to the Pharisees apply just as well to the Essenes (e.g., a doctrine of retribution; 2:34, 35; 13:6; 15:12, 13; 17:8).[15] But it is widely recognized that so little is known about the Pharisees prior to 70 CE that identification of their distinctive beliefs to the extent of identifying them with a particular document remains tenuous. Others have argued for an Essene origin for the Psalms of Solomon,[16] but the characteristic dualism and sectarian nature of the Dead Sea Scrolls are not found here. Whatever the precise origin of the author and his community, it is clear that they understood themselves as the "congregation of the pious" (συνεδρίῳ ὁσίων, synedriō hosiōn, 4:1; συναγωγὰς ὁσίων, synagōgas hosiōn, 17:16; cf. Ps. 149:1).[17] This self-designation distinguishes them not only from their gentile oppressors but also from impious Israelites.

As we have seen above, the gentiles are best identified with the Romans under the leadership of Pompey.[18] There is no hope for gentiles, who are rejected by God and lawless by nature (Pss. Sol. 2:2, 19–25; 7:1–3; 8:23; 17:13–15); though they are the instrument of God's judgment on the sinners in Israel (chap. 8), they will ultimately be purged from Israel (chap. 17). It is (pious) Israel that is chosen "above all nations" (9:8–11) as the object of God's covenantal care and salvation.[19]

The sinners are Jewish opponents of the devout, sometimes associated with the Hasmonean Sadducees. Regardless of their identification, they have laid hold of the kingship by violence (17:5–8, 22), they are lax in their observance of ritual purity and ceremonial observances (1:8; 2:3, 5; 7:2; 8:12; 17:45), and they are scandalously compliant with foreign customs (8:22).[20] Though little is made of the law explicitly in the Psalms of Solomon (cf. 4:8; 14:1–3), it is undoubtedly the violations of God's law that underlie the psalmist's designation of these Israelites as sinners.

13. R. Wright, "Psalms of Solomon," 2:642.
14. Nickelsburg, *Jewish Literature*, 246.
15. R. Wright, "Psalms of Solomon," 2:642.
16. Dupont-Sommer, *Essene Writings from Qumran*, 296; see also Eissfeldt, "Psalms of Solomon."
17. Nickelsburg, *Jewish Literature*, 246–47.
18. So also R. Wright, "Psalms of Solomon," 2:642.
19. R. Wright, "Psalms of Solomon," 2:644.
20. R. Wright, "Psalms of Solomon," 2:642.

Date

There are some indications of a date for some, though not all, of the psalms. First, references to a foreign invader taking Jerusalem (e.g., Pss. Sol. 2:1–2; 8:18–22; 17:7–13)[21] are generally believed to refer to the invasion of the Roman general Pompey in 63 BCE.[22] Second, the mention of an assassination of the "dragon" in Egypt (2:26–27) is typically thought to refer to the assassination of Pompey in 48 BCE.[23] It seems likely that more than one author composed the psalms and their collection likely took a couple of decades.[24] And so most of the psalms are thought to date from around the time of—before or after—Pompey's death.[25] Some have proposed a date for select passages during the early years of Herod's reign (37–4 BCE), and so this would suggest clear parameters for the composition of the entirety of the Psalms of Solomon between 63 BCE and the turn of the era.[26]

Contents

Psalm 1 is superscripted "A Psalm of Solomon."[27] The psalmist recalls crying aloud to the Lord when he was troubled by sinners (1:1), when suddenly the clamor of war was heard before him (1:2a). He consoled himself that the Lord would hear him because he, the psalmist, is righteous (1:2b–3). But his enemies exalted in their wealth in arrogance (1:4–6), and their sins surpassed those of the gentiles and profaned the sanctuary of the Lord (1:7–8).

Psalm 2 is labeled "A Psalm of Solomon Concerning Jerusalem." It begins with a complaint that God did not interfere when a battering ram was at the walls of Jerusalem and gentile foreigners trampled the sanctuary (2:1–2). Also, the "sons of Jerusalem" defiled the sanctuary and so were removed by the Lord (2:3–4). God's glory was despised and his children were captured by gentiles (2:5–6). This was done because of Israel's sins (2:7–10). They performed depraved and defiling acts in broad daylight (2:11–13). The psalmist is troubled by all this but acknowledges that God is right in his judgments (2:14–19). Jerusalem has thrown off the glory given to it by God (2:20–21),

21. Atkinson, "Psalms of Solomon," 1903.
22. Josephus, *J.W.* 1.6.4–7.7 §§131–158; *Ant.* 14.3.2–4.5 §§41–79; Plutarch, *Pomp.* 39.3–41.2; Dio Cassius, *Hist. rom.* 37.14.2–20.2.
23. Caesar, *Bell. civ.* 3.103.2–104.3; Appian, *Syriaca* 2.84–86; Dio Cassius, *Hist. rom.* 42.3.1–5.7.
24. Trafton, "Solomon, Psalms of," 1:503.
25. Atkinson, "Psalms of Solomon," 1903.
26. R. Wright, "Psalms of Solomon," 2:640–41.
27. On the superscripts to the Psalms of Solomon, see R. Wright, *Psalms of Solomon*, 32–33.

and so the psalmist implores God to bring judgment on it by the hand of the "dragon" (Rome; 2:22–25; cf. Ezek. 29:3; 32:2; Jer. 51:34). God answers this with the murder of Jerusalem's assailant in Egypt (Pss. Sol. 2:26–31; Pompey, 48 BCE).[28] The psalmist calls on the officials of the earth to witness God's judgment and calls on those who fear the Lord to praise him (2:32–37).

The superscript for Psalm 3 reads, "A Psalm of Solomon Concerning the Righteous." It begins with the psalmist imploring his own soul to praise the Lord (3:1–2), reminding himself that the righteous remember the Lord and do not esteem his discipline lightly (3:3–8). But the sinner who curses his hardship does not acknowledge God's hand and multiplies his own sins (3:9–12).

Psalm 4 is called "A Conversation of Solomon with Those Trying to Impress People." It begins with a rebuke to the profaner who flatters others in word and appearance (4:1–2a) and whose judgments are hypocritical (4:2b–3). He is devious with women and deceptive in his words and conduct (4:4–5). The psalmist prays for his removal and exposure (4:6–7). The sinners will be driven out as they deceitfully quote the law and destroy wisdom with insatiable lawlessness (4:8–13). The psalmist implores God for their disgrace and ruin (4:14–24) but for mercy on those who love him (4:25).

Psalm 5 is simply "A Psalm of Solomon." Here the psalmist sings praises to God for his mercy and care for the poor (5:1–2a). He implores God to hear his cry in need (5:2b–4) and under persecution (5:5–6). But even if God does not restore him, he will still come to God, who cares for the wildlife and kings alike (5:7–11a). For God alone is the hope of the poor and needy (5:11b–14), and those who fear the Lord are content with moderation in his provision (5:15–19).

The superscript for Psalm 6 reads, "In Hope. Of Solomon." It pronounces blessed the one whose heart is ready to call on the Lord (6:1). His ways are directed by God, and so he is not fearful and trusts God (6:2–4). He prays for his household and trusts in the Lord's provision (6:5–6).

"Of Solomon. About Restoring" is the title of Psalm 7. The psalmist asks God not to depart from his community lest their enemies, whom God has rejected, overtake him (7:1–2). He asks God to discipline his community but not turn them over to gentiles, appealing to God's kindness not to destroy those among whom his name dwells (7:3–6). God is their protector and they are under his yoke forever, even in discipline (7:7–10).

The superscript for Psalm 8 is "Of Solomon. To Victory." This psalm begins with the sound of war and destruction in Jerusalem (8:1–4) and the psalmist's

28. Cf. Appian, *Historia romana* 2.84–86; Caesar, *Bell. civ.* 3.104; Dio Cassius, *Hist. rom.* 42.3–4; Plutarch, *Pomp.* 77–80. Atkinson, "Psalms of Solomon," 1906, 1922.

anxiety (8:5). But God's judgments against the sinners is just (8:6–7). God exposed their sins (8:8–9), adultery (8:10), theft from the sanctuary (8:11), and pollution of the sanctuary (8:12). Their sins were worse than that of gentiles, and so God brought judgment by bringing someone from the end of the earth to declare war against Jerusalem and its land (8:13–15). They came ready for war (8:16–20) and took away captives (8:21). But the sinners, just like their ancestors, persisted in their defilement of Jerusalem, and so God was proven right in his condemnation (8:22–23). The psalmist then declares God's praises and pleads for mercy (8:24–34).

Psalm 9 is called "Of Solomon. For Proof." It describes Israel being taken into exile for neglect of the Lord (9:1–2). People choose to do right or wrong and receive consequential life or destruction from the Lord (9:3–5). God will care for those who call on him and will forgive those who repent (9:6–7). Then the psalmist appeals to Israel's covenant with God as the basis for his appeal for mercy (9:8–11).

The superscript for Psalm 10 is "A Hymn of Solomon." The psalmist declares happy those who are protected from evil by the Lord's rebuke, even by a whip (10:1–2). They will be directed toward righteousness and be remembered by God in mercy (10:3–4). God is just and shall be praised in the synagogues of Israel (10:5–7). The psalm concludes with the author's plea for salvation on the house of Israel (10:8).

A superscription reading "Of Solomon. In Anticipation" precedes Psalm 11. The psalmist calls for the sounding of the trumpet from the sanctuary to indicate that God is watching over Israel (11:1–2). God has assembled them from afar and made level paths for their journey (11:3–5). Israel proceeds under God's supervision and Jerusalem is robed in splendor (11:6–7), and the psalmist pleads for God's mercy on Israel (11:8–9).

Psalm 12 is superscripted "Of Solomon. About the Tongue of Criminals." The psalmist pleads for the Lord to save his soul from the wicked, whose words are twisted and false (12:1–3). He also asks for God to remove the wicked, protect those who live peacefully, and grant an inheritance of the Lord's promises to the devout (12:4–6).

The title for Psalm 13 is "Of Solomon. A Psalm: Comfort for the Righteous." It begins with a declaration of God's mighty arm saving and preserving the psalmist from hardships and the fate of sinners (13:1–2). The Lord protected him from wild animals (13:3–4), while the godless and sinners faced a terrible destruction (13:5–6). The psalmist then outlines the difference between the discipline of the righteous for things done in ignorance and the destruction of sinners (13:7–12). The righteous are disciplined in secret as an expression of God's affection and to preserve their life (13:8–11a, 12), but the sinners are taken to destruction (13:11b).

Psalm 14 is called "A Hymn of Solomon." It begins by lauding the faithfulness of God to those who love him, endure discipline, and live by the law (14:1–2). These devout are called the Lord's "paradise" and "the trees of life" who are firmly planted forever (14:3–5). Sinners and criminals enjoy only brief pleasures, since God knows the secrets of the heart and will deliver them to their inheritance in Hades (14:6–9), whereas the devout will inherit "life in happiness" (14:10).

Psalm 15 is "A Psalm of Solomon with Song." Here the psalmist calls on the Lord's name when persecuted and is saved because God is a refuge and empowers those who confess his name (15:1–2). And so the psalmist praises God, knowing that the one who does so will never be disturbed by the unrighteous (15:3–5). God marks the righteous for salvation and delivers them from famine, which will overtake sinners who are marked for destruction (15:6–9). Their inheritance is destruction and darkness at the day of the Lord's judgment, when those who fear the Lord will find mercy (15:10–13).

Psalm 16 is headed "A Hymn of Solomon. For Help for the Devout." The psalmist recounts a time when he was far from the Lord and near the gates of Hades (16:1–3a). Only when God's mercy intervened, jabbing him like a goaded horse, was he rescued by his savior (16:3b–4). And so the psalmist gives thanks to God and pleads that he will be kept from the seduction of sin (16:5–8). He also asks God to direct his work, his steps, and his speech (16:9–11a) and asks to be disciplined if he sins (16:11b–14) and so receive mercy from the Lord (16:15).

Psalm 17 begins with a superscript reading, "A Psalm of Solomon, with Song, to the King." After acclaiming the kingship of God, the psalmist acknowledges a person's life is brief but God's strength and his kingdom are eternal (17:1–3). He then recalls God's promise of David's kingship to his descendants (17:4). But Israel's sins have caused "sinners" to rise up against it and establish a monarchy (Hasmoneans) while despoiling the throne of David in arrogance (17:5–6).[29] But God raised a man "alien to our race" (i.e., the Roman gentile Pompey) who hunted them all down to bring about judgment on them (17:7–10). This "lawless one" (Pompey entered the Holy of Holies; cf. Pss. Sol. 2:2; Josephus, *J.W.* 1.7.6 §152; *Ant.* 14.4.4 §72)[30] laid waste to the land and expelled its inhabitants (17:11–13), doing in Jerusalem

---

29. These are not gentiles but Hasmoneans. Atkinson, "Psalms of Solomon," 1918.
30. Atkinson, "Psalms of Solomon," 1918.

what gentiles do for their gods elsewhere (17:14). Even the Israelites living among the "gentile rabble" adopted these practices (17:15). The pious did not remain in Jerusalem but fled to the wilderness (17:16–17), while the wicked in Jerusalem continued to practice their iniquity, appointing commoners to leadership and criminals to rule (17:18–20). The psalmist then implores the Lord to raise up the king, the son of David, to rule over Israel, asking him to destroy unrighteous rulers and purge Jerusalem of gentiles (17:21–24). He will cause nations to flee and gather a holy people (17:25–26). He will not tolerate unrighteousness among them and will distribute them upon the land (17:27–28). He will judge the peoples and have the gentile nations serve him (17:29–30a). He will purge Jerusalem and make it holy, and nations will come from the ends of the earth to see its glory (17:30b–31). The Lord Messiah will be a righteous king, and his strength will come from hope in God (17:32–34a, 37–40a). He will be compassionate to the nations that revere him and bless the Lord's people (17:34b–35), while he himself will be free from sin in order to rule well and drive out sinners (17:36). He will shepherd the Lord's flock in holiness and discipline the house of Israel with pure words (17:40b–43). The psalmist concludes by pronouncing a blessing on those born in that day, asking God to deliver Israel from the pollution of profane enemies, and acknowledging the eternal kingship of the Lord (17:44–46).

For Psalm 18 the superscript reads, "A Psalm of Solomon about the Lord Messiah." It begins with an acclamation of the watchful and compassionate care of God for the descendants of Abraham (18:1–3). God's discipline cleanses Israel for the time when the messiah will reign (18:4–5), when the "Lord Messiah" will rule with the rod of discipline to direct people in the fear of God (18:6–9). God is great and glorious, and the fear of him governs the stars and the hours of the day (18:10–12).

Critical Issues

Form and Shape

This collection has a distinctive shape. Its eighteen psalms are provided a primary frame by the two short psalms that open and close it. Psalm 1 relates a crisis on a national level for the Jewish people in the throes of warfare (Pss. Sol. 1:2), whereas Psalm 18, the last psalm, affirms God's goodness to Israel (18:1) and looks forward to the eschatological reign of God's messiah (18:5). A second frame consists of the two longest psalms, Psalms 2 and 17. The former describes the destruction and defilement of

Jerusalem by gentile invaders, while the latter depicts the retributive justice of God at the hands of a messianic son of David, who will smash the
unrighteous rulers and reign over Israel. Within these frames the remaining
psalms deal with similar concerns of nationalistic (Pss. Sol. 4, 7, 8, 9, 11,
14, 15) or personal (Pss. Sol. 3, 5, 6, 10, 12, 13, 16) interests.[31]

Historical Events

The Psalms of Solomon are significant in their explicit identification of
known historical events and the psalmists' responses, which aid in locating
them historically and in understanding the mindset of at least some Jews in
Jerusalem during or shortly after the national tragedies they depict. They
recount the invasion of gentile rulers who laid waste to Jerusalem (e.g., 1:1–2;
2:1–2, 19–24; 8:18–21; 17:7–14) and, as Joseph L. Trafton observes, exhibit
four responses to this problem. First, they recognize that this disaster brought
on Israel was the direct result of God's righteous judgment on Jerusalem because of the iniquities of Jewish "sinners" (e.g., 1:4–8; 2:3–14; 8:8–15; 17:5–6).
Second, the instrument of God's judgment (the "dragon") was likewise the
recipient of divine judgment (2:25–31). Third, in the eschatological outlook
of the Psalms of Solomon, God will raise up a messiah to "make everything
right" (e.g., 17:21–46; 18:1–9). Fourth, the pious Jews are exhorted to trust
in God (cf. 2:33–37; 4:23–25; 5:1–2, 18–19) and the righteousness of his judgments (e.g., 2:15–18; 3:3; 4:8; 8:7, 26) while embracing their own hardships as
the Lord's discipline and direction toward the avoidance of sin (e.g., 3:4–8;
7; 10:1–3; 13:8–12; 14:1–5).[32]

Contribution and Context

Eschatology

The Psalms of Solomon's perception of the end of days and its relation
to the pious Jews in their crisis plays an important role in the text. This
crisis comes to bear in the text in two primary ways: first, it is in part the
just retribution of God himself and can only be resolved by divine intervention; second, it serves a role of purifying the faithful Israelites. The only
solution to the immediate crisis is God's intervention, which is depicted
as God's benevolent oversight of his covenant people (cf. Pss. Sol. 10:4;
11:6; 15:12). Even the present sufferings are intended to be redemptive,

---

31. Trafton, "Solomon, Psalms of," 1:501.
32. Trafton, "Solomon, Psalms of," 1:501–2.

purging the faithful of sin (10:1–3), which God justly reproves (3:3–10; cf. 13:8–10; 16:14; 18:4). This is to motivate the pious to seek atonement (3:7–8; 13:7) and respond with humble repentance (3:8; 9:6–7; 10:1; 13:10). These righteous will be honored and raised (2:31; 3:12), while the "sinners" are marked for destruction (2:31, 34; 15:12; cf. 3:9–12; 14:9–10).[33] Though some of the terminology is not thoroughly explained, it is clear that when God intervenes and establishes his kingly rule in the messiah, the pious will experience resurrection (2:31; 3:12) and the blessings of eternal life (13:11).

Messianism

Integral to God's benevolent intervention for the righteous is the depiction of the messiah. The Psalms of Solomon is widely regarded as one of the most important sources for a conception of the messiah in Second Temple Judaism.[34] John J. Collins remarks that clear messianic references are rare in the Jewish pseudepigrapha. The only passages dealing with a Davidic messiah among this literature that dates prior to the turn of the era come from the Psalms of Solomon 17–18.[35] The expectation of a Davidic messiah is rooted in key texts from the Hebrew Bible (e.g., 2 Sam. 7:12–16; Isa. 9:7) and attested in other Second Temple texts (e.g., 4Q252; 4Q285; 4Q174; 4 Ezra 12:32), including the New Testament (e.g., Matt. 1:1–17; Luke 1:32–33; Rom. 1:3; Rev. 5:5). It has piqued Christian interest because it contains (in Pss. Sol. 17:21–46) the "longest continuous extant description of the messiah prior to the coming of Jesus."[36] We have seen above in the summary of contents that this messiah will defeat enemies, rule and judge God's people, expel unrighteous rulers, cleanse Jerusalem, and distribute people on the land.[37] The messianism of the Psalms of Solomon is particular to the political occasion of the Hasmonean rule in the first century BCE. It is important to note that Psalm 17 in particular is devoted to the subject of kingship, with God himself as king utilizing human agents for his reign—namely, David and his descendants (17:1–4). In typical Deuteronomistic fashion, it is the sins of Israel that led to their downfall (17:5a). And, indeed, there were "sinners" who rose up against the legitimate rulers, those "to whom [God] did not make the promise" (17:5c),

33. R. Wright, "Psalms of Solomon," 2:644.
34. Atkinson, "Psalms of Solomon," 1903.
35. J. Collins, *Apocalyptic Imagination*, 176. See also Charlesworth, "Concept of the Messiah."
36. Trafton, "Solomon, Psalms of," 1:503.
37. See esp. Trafton, "What Would David Do?"

meaning those usurping the throne were Israelites, Hasmoneans in particular, but not of the legitimate line of David. Nevertheless, they "drove us out" and "took away from us by force" the rule of Israel (17:5b, d). God in turn overthrew these illegitimate Israelite rulers by raising up against them "a man alien to our race" (17:7c), who, as we have seen, is the gentile Roman general Pompey, who deposed Hasmonean rule when he sacked Jerusalem in 63 BCE. Even Simon Maccabee (r. 142–135; 1 Macc. 14:41, 47) and John Hyrcanus (r. 135/134–104 BCE; Josephus, *Ant.* 13.10.7 §300), though eminent Hasmoneans, did not make a claim to kingship. Instead, according to Josephus, the first Hasmonean to make this explicit claim was Alexander Jannaeus (r. 103–76 BCE).[38] And yet the psalmist, writing after the death of Pompey (48 BCE), recalls vividly the usurpation of the Davidic throne (cf. Pss. Sol. 1:4–8; 8:8–13).[39] And so the sacking of Jerusalem and the deposing of Hasmonean rule by Pompey, the "lawless one" (17:11) and "the dragon" (2:25),[40] were a righteous act of God's retributive justice. But Pompey's downfall, too, is celebrated (2:26–30), and in his messianic fervor the psalmist turns from the illegitimate Hasmoneans and the lawless gentile Romans to hope in a Davidic king. Herein lies the psalmist's messianic hope and prayer for God's intervention through the messiah (17:21–25; 18:6–8; cf. Isa. 11:2–4). Here the figure is undeniably a political and nationalistic figure establishing his messianic rule through violence while shepherding the people, or at least the pious, toward holiness (17:26). In summary, then, one finds in the Psalms of Solomon a messiah distinctly in the line of David, who will liberate Jerusalem, defeat and subjugate gentiles, and establish a reign marked by peace and by guiding the people in righteousness.[41]

Hebrew Bible

Robert B. Wright contends that the Psalms of Solomon is composed in "conscious imitation of the Davidic psalter"[42] but also contains echoes of other books from the Hebrew Bible. These include a depiction of adversaries who have trodden down the sanctuary (Pss. Sol. 1, 2; cf. Isa. 63:16–19), a presentation of Israel as the "shoot of my planting," which "shall possess the land forever" (Pss. Sol. 14:3–4; cf. Isa. 60:21), and cries to God in times of distress (Pss. Sol. 2:8; cf. Pss. 13:1; 22:24; Isa. 64:7; Ezek. 39:23–24). Other

---

38. J. Collins, *Scepter and the Star*, 54.
39. J. Collins, *Scepter and the Star*, 55.
40. On "dragon" mythology, see A. Collins, *Combat Myth*, 76–79.
41. J. Collins, *Scepter and the Star*, 59.
42. R. Wright, "Psalms of Solomon," 2:646.

influences from the Hebrew Bible in the Psalms of Solomon include the notion of a wreath of glory thrown to the ground (Pss. Sol. 2:21; cf. Lam. 2:1) and the comparisons between the fate of the righteous and that of the wicked (Pss. Sol. 3:9–12; cf. Prov. 24:16–22).[43]

Second Temple Judaism

The Psalms of Solomon belongs to the category of psalms and hymns attested in other texts, such as the Thanksgiving Hymns (1QH[a]) from Qumran or embedded hymns like those found in Tobit 13 and Judith 16 (cf. 1 Macc. 1:7–13; 3:3–9; 14:4–15). Wright considers a number of parallels between the Psalms of Solomon (11:2–5) and 1 Baruch (5:5–9), though whether one drew from the other or they shared a common source is undetermined.[44] They both implore Jerusalem to stand and look at her children (Pss. Sol. 11:2; 1 Bar. 5:5), indicate that God flattened high mountains into level ground (Pss. Sol. 11:4; 1 Bar. 5:7), and show God making fragrant trees grow and forests shade Israel (Pss. Sol. 11:5; 1 Bar. 5:8). Wright further observes points of correspondence between the Psalms of Solomon and the Dead Sea Scrolls, often noting that Isaiah 11 exerts "strong influence" on both (e.g., Isa. 11:2 [cf. Pss. Sol. 17:37–40; 1QSb V, 25]; Isa. 11:4 [cf. Pss. Sol. 17:23–24; 1QSb V, 24–25a]; Isa. 11:5 [cf. Pss. Sol. 17:22; 1QSb V, 26a]). But there are also similarities in their depictions of the flight of the righteous from Jerusalem (e.g., Pss. Sol. 17:15–17; CD-A IV, 15–18) and other concepts such as the "tree of life" (1QH[a] XVI, 5–6; Pss. Sol. 14:3), being "driven" or "fleeing" "from the nest" (1QH[a] XII, 8–9; Pss. Sol. 17:16), punishment for families (CD-A III, 1; Pss. Sol. 9:5), and lions breaking the bones of the strong (1QH[a] XIII, 7; Pss. Sol. 4:19; 13:3).[45] Within the context of Second Temple Judaism, it is important to recognize that the Psalms of Solomon exhibits a polemic not just against the gentile invaders but also against other Jews, the Hasmoneans. This kind of inner-Judaic conflict is found elsewhere, such as in the Animal Apocalypse (1 En. 85–90), the book of Jubilees, the sectarian documents in the Dead Sea Scrolls, and also in the New Testament (e.g., Matt. 21:12–13; 23; Mark 7:1–13; 11:15–17; Luke 13:10–17; 19:45–46; John 2:13–16; 8:54–55; 9:40–41). The Psalms of Solomon also shares with the New Testament some distinctive features, such as the notion of God's kingdom (e.g., Pss. Sol. 5:18; 17:3; cf. Mark 1:15; 4:11, 26, 30; and parr.), the language of justification (Pss. Sol. 2:15–18; cf. Rom. 2:13; 3:4, 20, 24, 28; 4:1; Gal. 2:16–17; etc.),

---

43. R. Wright, "Psalms of Solomon," 2:646–47.
44. R. Wright, "Psalms of Solomon," 2:647–48.
45. R. Wright, "Psalms of Solomon," 2:648–49.

and resurrection (Pss. Sol. 3:12; cf. Luke 14:14; John 11:24; 1 Cor. 15:50–53; 1 Thess. 4:13–17).[46]

Reception History[47]

The Psalms of Solomon was preserved in a few medieval Greek manuscripts of the Septuagint, with the fifth-century Codex Alexandrinus presenting it after the Old and New Testaments and the two letters of Clement. In other Greek manuscripts it is placed alongside other Wisdom literature, likely because of its attribution to Solomon.[48] In Syriac the Psalms of Solomon is presented immediately following the Odes of Solomon as a single book, with Psalms of Solomon 1 actually identified as the final chapter of the Odes (Ode 43). It is likely that in both Jewish contexts (perhaps synagogues; cf. Pss. Sol. 10:7) and Christian communities, the Psalms of Solomon was utilized in corporate liturgical recitations.[49]

46. Trafton, "Solomon, Psalms of," 1:502.
47. See further the detailed account in R. Wright, *Psalms of Solomon*, 1–7.
48. R. Wright, "Psalms of Solomon," 2:647.
49. Atkinson, "Psalms of Solomon," 1903; Trafton, "Solomon, Psalms of," 1:504.

21

Sentences of Pseudo-Phocylides

Introduction

The Sentences is a didactic wisdom poem of 230 verses attributed to Phocylides. It is written in Greek and expounds on a combination of ethical
commands from the Greek translation (Septuagint) of the Law alongside
non-Jewish Hellenistic writers of moral treatises.[1] In doing this the author
melds the Pentateuch with Wisdom literature into "moral precepts."[2]

Language and Manuscripts

The nature of the poetry ensures that Greek was the original language of the
Sentences. The work is preserved in more than 150 Greek manuscripts dating
from the tenth to the sixteenth century.[3] In one manuscript (ψ, *Psi*) the text
of the Sentences (lines 5–79) is inserted into the Sibylline Oracles (between
2:55 and 2:149). Here seventy-five lines of the Sentences occupy ninety-five
lines in the Oracles because this manuscript inserts twenty additional lines.

1. Van der Horst, "Pseudo-Phocylides, *Sentences*," 2353.
2. Kampen, "Wisdom Literature."
3. Van der Horst, "Pseudo-Phocylides, *Sentences*," 2353. The five most important date from
the tenth to the thirteenth century. These are M (Mutinensis; tenth century), B (Baroccianus;
tenth century), P (Parisinus; eleventh or twelfth century), L (Laurentianus; thirteenth century),
and V (Vindobonensis; thirteenth century). Wilson, *Sentences of Pseudo-Phocylides*, 40.

It is debated whether these twenty were original to Pseudo-Phocylides,[4] and some regard the insertion as a later Christian interpolation.[5]

Provenance

The work is attributed to a popular Greek poet, Phocylides, who lived in the sixth century BCE in Ionia (Miletus).[6] Though only a few of Phocylides's writings survive, he was famous in his day for composing maxims with useful advice for daily life.[7] Today most scholars recognize the Sentences was written by a much later Jewish author, though this was not realized until the end of the sixteenth century,[8] for the author concealed his Jewish identity by avoiding distinctively Jewish customs and enveloping his ethic in Greek (Ionic) hexametric poetry.[9] Sean A. Adams explains the complicated facets involved in the author's choice of adopting the persona of Phocylides.[10] First, the author may have wished to employ a style of writing for which Phocylides was famous and utilized his name as the preeminent giver of wisdom for daily life (cf. lines 1–2, 229). Second, the use of Phocylides, rather than a Jewish name such as Solomon, afforded the author the opportunity of blending Greek and Jewish cultures to reach a broad readership. Others suggest it was simply an opportunity to integrate Jewish and Greek culture.[11] Regardless of the reasons, other Jewish writings of the Hellenistic diaspora made use of well-known pagan authoritative names, such as the Sibyl and Orpheus.[12] And perhaps the author's intended readership encompassed Hellenized Jews, illustrating the compatibility of biblical and Greek ethics.[13]

A Jewish document written in Greek in a highly Hellenized form immediately conjures thoughts of Alexandria, Egypt. Indeed, Alexandria is generally held to be the city of origin, but for a very particular reason: a single line of the poem (line 102) condemns the practice of human dissection, and so far as is known, Alexandria is the only location in antiquity where study of

    4. Van der Horst, "Pseudo-Phocylides," 2:565.
    5. Wilson, *Sentences of Pseudo-Phocylides*, 40–41.
    6. J. Collins, *Jewish Wisdom*, 158.
    7. Van der Horst, "Pseudo-Phocylides," 2:565; J. Collins, *Jewish Wisdom*, 159; van der Horst, *Sentences of Pseudo-Phocylides*, 60–62.
    8. Van der Horst, "Pseudo-Phocylides," 2:565. For a history of research, see van der Horst, *Sentences of Pseudo-Phocylides*, 3–54.
    9. Van der Horst, "Pseudo-Phocylides," 2:565.
    10. Adams, "Pseudo-Phocylides."
    11. Van der Horst, "Pseudo-Phocylides, *Sentences*," 2353.
    12. J. Collins, *Jewish Wisdom*, 159.
    13. Van der Horst, "Pseudo-Phocylides, *Sentences*," 2353.

the human anatomy made use of that procedure. And so between the Hellenized character of the work and the reference to dissection, Alexandria is generally thought to be the likely place of origin for the Sentences.[14] But this is far from certain. Walter T. Wilson makes the case that the verse (line 102) in its context may not refer to dissection at all but rather to the disinterment and desecration of a corpse.[15] Even if it does refer to autopsies, the ancient references to autopsies are so sparse that one could by no means rule out the possibility that the practice was carried out elsewhere,[16] such as Syria.[17] John J. Collins looks to other evidence for Alexandria, suggesting that the appeal for foreigners to be held in equal honor among citizens (lines 39–41) suits the Jewish settlers in Alexandria struggling for civil rights under the Roman prefect Flaccus.[18] But this condition would be difficult to limit to Alexandria.[19] And so Alexandria may seem the most probable locale, but it cannot be determined with certainty.

Date

The lack of references to any political events or historical circumstances complicates the effort to date the Sentences, so scholars turn to linguistic features for help.[20] It has been suggested that some fifteen Greek words are found in the work that are not otherwise attested before the first century BCE.[21] The author's familiarity with the Septuagint of the Prophets and Wisdom literature (e.g., Jer. 9:23 in line 53; Prov. 6:6–8c in lines 164–74) also suggests a date not earlier than 100 BCE. Furthermore, the author's affinity with Stoic writers from the first century CE, such as Musonius Rufus, Hierocles, and Seneca, suggests a date of composition for the Sentences around the same time.[22] It is generally held that the Sentences dates from the first century BCE to the first century CE.[23] But if an Alexandrian provenance can be presumed, the lack of any antagonism between Jews and Greeks in the Sentences points to

14. Van der Horst, "Pseudo-Phocylides," 2:565; van der Horst, *Sentences of Pseudo-Phocylides*, 82–83; van der Horst, "Pseudo-Phocylides Revisited," 15.
15. Wilson, *Sentences of Pseudo-Phocylides*, 12, 143–45.
16. Wilson, *Sentences of Pseudo-Phocylides*, 12–13.
17. Derron, *Les sentences du Pseudo-Phocylide*, lxiii–lxv.
18. J. Collins, *Jewish Wisdom*, 164.
19. Wilson, *Sentences of Pseudo-Phocylides*, 13; Schürer, *History of the Jewish People*, 3.1:126–37; Trebilco, *Jewish Communities in Asia Minor*, 167–72.
20. Van der Horst, "Pseudo-Phocylides," 2:567.
21. Van der Horst, *Sentences of Pseudo-Phocylides*, 81.
22. Van der Horst, "Pseudo-Phocylides," 2:567.
23. J. Collins, *Jewish Wisdom*, 158–59.

a time of relative harmony during the reign of Augustus (30 BCE–14 CE) or Tiberius (14–37 CE).[24]

Contents

The work begins with a prologue attributing the sayings to Phocylides, the "wisest of men," and describing them as counsels of God (lines 1–2). There is a brief summary of the Ten Commandments (lines 3–8; cf. Exod. 20:2–17; Deut. 5:6–21). This is followed by an exhortation to dispense justice impartially in all affairs (lines 9–21) and an appeal to show mercy to the poor and needy (lines 22–41). The author warns about the love of money, which destroys life and divides families (lines 42–47). He then exhorts his readers to avoid duplicity, be sincere and modest, and exercise self-control (lines 48–58). Moderation, applicable in all spheres of life, is the subject of the next unit (lines 59–69). This is followed by an extensive elaboration on envy and other vices that the author regards as dangerous (lines 70–96). The author presents a collection of sayings advising the reader on how to deal with matters of death—one's own and that of others—and the afterlife (lines 97–115), since life can be unpredictable (lines 116–21). He then instructs on the wise use of speech (lines 122–31) and the wisdom of avoiding the companionship of the wicked (lines 132–36) in favor of self-restraint and virtue (lines 137–52). The virtues of hard work are lauded for the benefits of providing for oneself and not depending on the labors of others (lines 153–74). The author then turns to the virtues of marriage and propriety in sexual behavior (lines 175–206). In family life the reader is exhorted to be gentle with his children and guard them well (lines 207–17). Furthermore, he is to revere the elderly and treat slaves with justice (lines 218–27). The Sentences concludes with an epilogue (lines 228–30) that lauds the virtues of purity and righteous living.

Critical Issues

Genre

The Sentences of Pseudo-Phocylides belongs to a genre of Greek writings known as "gnomic poetry," which is the "closest Greek analogue to the proverbial wisdom found in Proverbs and Sirach."[25] Thus it employs "short sentences

---

24. Van der Horst, "Pseudo-Phocylides," 2:567.
25. J. Collins, *Jewish Wisdom*, 159.

giving a rule for conduct in daily life" (gnomes).[26] This tool, used by the likes of Aristotle (who defines it in *Rhetoric* 2.21), juxtaposes single-line sayings that lend themselves to citation elsewhere, typically dealing with moral issues and widely used in educational contexts for training in philosophy and rhetoric.[27]

Sources

In his melding of Jewish legal material with Hellenistic didactic poetry, the author of the Sentences has used literary sources from both kinds of writings. There is an "unquestionable" debt Pseudo-Phocylides has to biblical traditions, though explicit citations and direct usages are difficult to identify.[28] Nonetheless, numerous parallels can be identified to the LXX, especially to the Decalogue (Exod. 20 and Deut. 5) but also to Proverbs, Sirach (Ben Sira), Job, Ecclesiastes, and other texts. Notably among these are instances where the author interacts with a particular passage in the LXX source (e.g., lines 147–48a; cf. Exod. 22:30) and influential texts from the Pentateuch regarding covenant (Exod. 20–23), holiness (Lev. 18–20), and moral provisions (Deut. 5, 20–24, 27). All of these are influential for the author's summarizing in moral terms. It is likely that the author deliberately selected Septuagint passages that reflected commonly held ethical perspectives rather than anything identifiably Jewish.[29] The Greek sources used by the Sentences are evident not by citation or paraphrase but by the use of vocabulary derived from the likes of Homer and Hesiod and the treatment of subjects familiar from ancient Greek moral poets. This is important because it demonstrates how the author uses Greek poetic words to transfer the moral teachings of the Septuagint into gnomic poetry. So, for instance, the cluster of Homeric words in lines 220–22 are a way of "classicizing" Leviticus 19:32. Finally, there is evidence that Pseudo-Phocylides maintained his guise by imitating the work of Phocylides himself. Though the latter is praised by Dio Chrysostom as "one of the highly renowned poets" and Isocrates regards him among "the best advisors for human life,"[30] only fifteen or sixteen fragments of his work survive. Yet enough remains to conclude that the Sentences includes specific concepts and priorities consistent with Phocylides,[31] and the author likely wrote a unified poem like Phocylides did as well.[32]

26. Van der Horst, *Sentences of Pseudo-Phocylides*, 79.
27. J. Collins, *Jewish Wisdom*, 159. See also Derron, *Les sentences du Pseudo-Phocylide*, xxii; Wilson, *Mysteries of Righteousness*, 18–33; Wilson, *Sentences of Pseudo-Phocylides*, 7–12.
28. Wilson, *Sentences of Pseudo-Phocylides*, 17–22.
29. Adams, "Pseudo-Phocylides," 1:441.
30. Dio Chrysostom, *Borysthenitica* 36.10–15; Isocrates, *Discourse* 2.43 (*To Nicocles*).
31. Wilson, *Sentences of Pseudo-Phocylides*, 14–17.
32. West, "Phocylides," 164.

Structure

The Sentences, like other Wisdom literature, creates difficulty for those looking for a literary structure, and it has often been contended that it simply has none. Whereas previous scholarship saw a distinct structure utilizing certain literary and argumentative strategies found in similar Greek literature,[33] more recent work finds that the organization in the Sentences is topical. Topical paragraphs frequently pertain to matters such as the Decalogue (lines 3–8), justice (lines 9–21), mercy (lines 22–41), wealth (lines 42–47), moderation (lines 59–69), envy (lines 70–75), death and the afterlife (lines 97–115), fortune (lines 118–21), speech and wisdom (lines 122–31), and work (lines 153–74).[34] This first part Wilson has described as a catalogue of cardinal virtues.[35] The remainder (lines 175–227) pertains generally to maxims around household duties.[36] This is all framed by a prologue (lines 1–2) and an epilogue (lines 228–30).

Contribution and Context

Scripture

It is frequently noted that the Sentences is unique in its "studious avoidance of any specifically Jewish precepts."[37] Such features include dietary restrictions, Sabbath observance, circumcision, cultic rituals, or any such aspects of Jewish religion that distinguish it from others. Instead, emphasis lies squarely on moral precepts. Yet even here one observes the influence of Hellenistic moralists, presented as essentially in accord with the teachings of Torah. Related to this, the Sentences makes no effort at proselytizing or even prioritizing the teachings of Torah over against those of gentiles.

Theology

Elucidating the author's theological views is notoriously difficult with a work intent on furnishing moral exhortations. Some theological positions are evident but can in no way be removed from the author's intended ethical instructions. These include his view that God is rich in blessings (line 54), must be honored above all other things (line 8), and loans his image to

---

33. Wilson, *Mysteries of Righteousness*, 178. See also J. Collins, *Jewish Wisdom*, 160–61.
34. Wilson, *Sentences of Pseudo-Phocylides*, 23.
35. Wilson, *Mysteries of Righteousness*, 178.
36. Wilson, *Sentence of Pseudo-Phocylides*, 23.
37. Van der Horst, "Pseudo-Phocylides, *Sentences*," 2353.

human beings (line 106). Hating dishonesty and sharing with those in need (lines 17, 29) are attributes of God that he expects in people. God grants people the ability of speech, which is to be used wisely (lines 125–28). God is the judge of all humanity (line 11) and ruler of both the humble and the exalted (line 111). The Sentences gives some indications, though inconsistent, on matters pertaining to death and afterlife (lines 97–115). On the one hand, the souls of the dead remain with their bodies (line 105), but on the other, they go to an everlasting home (lines 111–12) or are released into the air (lines 107–8). And yet the author holds out hope for the resurrection of the dead (lines 103–14; cf. 2 Macc. 7; Sib. Or. 4) and insists the remains of the dead be treated with respect (line 102).[38] Regardless, he seems to hold that the spirit survives the body, which is also found in other Jewish writings (e.g., 1 En. 22; Jub. 23).[39]

Ethics and Virtues

Among the author's numerous moral exhortations, a few figure more prominently than others. Among the virtues espoused that would appeal to a Hellenized readership, many find resonance in the Hebrew Bible (e.g., Prov. 1:2–3). Considerable attention is given to justice (lines 9–21), which likewise reflects some biblical teachings regarding deposits (line 13; cf. Lev. 5:20–26; Exod. 22:6–12) and just measurements (Deut. 25:14–15; Lev. 19:35–36).[40] Notably, there is considerable attention to a wide variety of sexual sins (lines 177–94).[41] This is coupled with a clear affirmation of marital relations (lines 175–76). Hellenistic influences are found in the exhortations to moderation and temperance (line 42; cf. Sir. 8:2; 31:5, 12–31; 1 Tim. 6:10; Theognis 335),[42] which are regarded as Greek ideals (lines 69, 98, 136).[43] Likewise the notion of mercy (lines 9–41) is equally compatible in Greek and Jewish morality. Particularly noteworthy is the exhortation to the duties of charity (lines 22–41) and its affinities with Deuteronomy (e.g., Deut. 20:19–20; cf. 23:25).[44] Other teachings, such as the commonality of suffering, are notable features of Greek tragedies.[45]

38. Van der Horst, "Pseudo-Phocylides," 2:570–71.
39. J. Collins, *Jewish Wisdom*, 165. Cf. esp. Nickelsburg, *Resurrection*, 31–33, 134–37.
40. J. Collins, *Jewish Wisdom*, 162–63.
41. Van der Horst, "Pseudo-Phocylides," 2:571.
42. See van der Horst, *Sentences of Pseudo-Phocylides*, 142–46.
43. Van der Horst, "Pseudo-Phocylides," 2:571.
44. J. Collins, *Jewish Wisdom*, 164–65.
45. Cf. Pseudo-Isocrates, *Ad Demonicum* 29; Menander, *Monostichoi* 10; Euripides, *Supplices* 226; Plutarch, *Vita Numae* 14.5.

Context

In addition to the author's use of and affinities with the Hebrew Bible surveyed above, there are numerous affinities with other Second Temple Jewish
texts, particularly the writings of Philo (*Hypoth.* 7.1–9) and Josephus (*Ag.
Ap.* 2.190–219 §§22–30). All of these pertain to their respective summaries of
the Jewish law; some are paralleled only in Josephus and others only in Philo.
But among those shared with all three traditions are teachings on adultery and
homosexuality,[46] theft,[47] fair scales,[48] almsgiving,[49] the mother bird,[50] burying
the dead,[51] abortion,[52] rape,[53] and slaves.[54] Though it is likely that these three
writings share a common literary source rather than draw from one another,[55]
it is striking how many of the topics of concern the respective authors share.

Purpose

The purpose of the Sentences is not entirely clear, but three possibilities have
been suggested. First, the author simply wrote for his own personal enjoyment, perhaps as "a kind of exercise in versification."[56] Or perhaps, second,
the author simply wished to assert to his (fellow) Jewish readership that the
best of Greek ethics is largely in agreement with the ethical instructions of
the law, and so, seemingly by inference, the readers need not regard the ethics of their Jewish identity as substandard. Third, it is possible the work was
directed to a pagan readership to elicit gentile sympathy toward Judaism in
a Hellenistic context.[57] Of these options, the third is the most commonly
suggested, with the explanation that Jews sometimes intended to propagate
principles without intending to convert the reader to Judaism. Also, scholars
have noted similarities between the Sentences and passages found in Philo
of Alexandria (*Hypothetica*) and Josephus (*Against Apion*) to contend for
an apologetic and propagandistic function.[58] And yet the Sentences is void

46. Lines 3, 190–91; cf. Josephus, *Ag. Ap.* 2.199 §24, 215 §30; Philo, *Hypoth.* 7.1.
47. Lines 5–6; cf. Josephus, *Ag. Ap.* 2.208 §27, 216 §30; Philo, *Hypoth.* 7.2, 6.
48. Lines 14–15; cf. Josephus, *Ag. Ap.* 2.216 §30; Philo, *Hypoth.* 7.8.
49. Lines 22–23, 29; cf. Josephus, *Ag. Ap.* 2.211 §29; Philo, *Hypoth.* 7.6.
50. Lines 84–85; cf. Josephus, *Ag. Ap.* 2.213 §29; Philo, *Hypoth.* 7.9.
51. Line 99; cf. Josephus, *Ag. Ap.* 2.211 §29; Philo, *Hypoth.* 7.7.
52. Line 184; cf. Josephus, *Ag. Ap.* 2.202 §24; Philo, *Hypoth.* 7.7.
53. Line 198; cf. Josephus, *Ag. Ap.* 2.200 §24; Philo, *Hypoth.* 7.1.
54. Lines 223–27; cf. Josephus, *Ag. Ap.* 2.215 §30; Philo, *Hypoth.* 7.2.
55. Wilson, *Sentences of Pseudo-Phocylides*, 19–21.
56. Van der Horst, "Pseudo-Phocylides," 2:565.
57. Van der Horst, "Pseudo-Phocylides," 2:565–66; cf. Feldman, "Jewish 'Sympathizers.'"
58. Crouch, *Origin and Intention*, 89–94.

of any such interest, and so Pieter W. van der Horst instead favors a view in which the author wrote for other Jews, either to minimize the difference between Jewish and Greek ethics or to show the adaptability of the Jewish law to Greek hexametric poetry. Van der Horst goes further, suggesting that it was intended as a Jewish schoolbook like other such collections in Hellenistic contexts, yet he is duly cautious about the uncertainty this and any theory of purpose entails.[59] Collins regards the theory with more certainty, contending that gnomic writings like the Sentences were generally used for educational purposes in schoolrooms. He opines that the use of the name Phocylides afforded the work usage by pupils regardless of their adherence to Judaism, without any effort to put forward a view toward Jewish identity. The subject matter is morality rather than Judaism.[60]

Reception History

The vast number of manuscripts alone testifies to the popularity of the Sentences among Christians in the Middle Ages, though van der Horst notes that it was unknown in Jewish contexts.[61] It is clear that its popularity was due to the assumption that it was an authentic work of Phocylides.[62]

59. Van der Horst, "Pseudo-Phocylides," 2:566.
60. J. Collins, *Jewish Wisdom*, 176.
61. Van der Horst, "Pseudo-Phocylides, *Sentences*," 2353.
62. J. Collins, *Jewish Wisdom*, 158.

22

Additional Writings

*Hellenistic Synagogal Prayers, Prayer of
Joseph, and Prayer of Nabonidus (4Q242)*

As noted earlier, few Jewish prayers among the Pseudepigrapha from the
Second Temple period survive independent of other documents. The majority
are embedded within other texts. Some are preserved in Christian circles and
emended for the purposes of those communities. Inevitably these are heavily
"Christianized" through the course of their transmission and incorporation
into Christian liturgies, and so discerning the Jewish original is highly problematic. Such is the case of the so-called Hellenistic Synagogal Prayers as
well as the Prayer of Joseph, discussed below. Others are of a very different
nature, unquestionably Jewish and predating Christian texts; these are the
prayers found among the Dead Sea Scrolls. The problem here is not that they
are infused with Christian beliefs but rather that they are fragmentary and
incomplete. One such text, the Prayer of Nabonidus, is more complete than
most and is discussed below along with other features of Qumran prayers.

Hellenistic Synagogal Prayers

Introduction

One collection of texts that falls into this category but is nonetheless
worthy of brief consideration is the collection of six prayers known as the

Hellenistic Synagogal Prayers, preserved in the fourth-century Christian liturgical writings of the Apostolic Constitutions. These prayers were originally Jewish but were adapted by Christians for use in worship services. Typically, it is nearly impossible to excise Christian elements to recover the original Jewish prayers, but some identifications can be clearly, though not comprehensively, made,[1] and it is likely that their present form preserves enough of the original to warrant some consideration. This collection of prayers has been studied for some time in the context of the Apostolic Constitutions, and there has been some debate as to which of the prayers contained in that work may serve as witnesses to a form of Hellenistic Judaism.[2]

Contents

There remains considerable debate as to what constitutes the original substratum of the Jewish text and what does not.[3] So we will focus attention on those generally agreed to be primarily Jewish in their present form from the Apostolic Constitutions 7.33–38.[4] The first prayer is a prayer of praise to God as the savior of Abraham's race (Apos. Con. 7.33.2–7).[5] The second prayer meditates on God's creative power that comes upon sinful people in their redemption (7.34.1–8).[6] In the third prayer, the person praying joins all nature in praising God as the only great and merciful God (7.35.1–10).[7] In the fourth prayer, the person praying praises Israel's God for his redemptive deeds for the nation and for the institution of the sacred festivals and the Sabbath (7.36.1–7).[8] The fifth prayer calls on God, who always accepts the worship of his people, to accept the prayers of the present congregation as

1. See Stuckenbruck ("Apocrypha and Pseudepigrapha," 159), who regards Christian interpolations as easy to identify, noting, e.g., Hel. Syn. Pr. 5:4–8, 20–24; 7:4c.
2. The most important work sorting through the material is Fiensy, *Prayers Alleged to Be Jewish*. His conclusions are summarized in van der Horst and Newman, *Early Jewish Prayers in Greek*, 19–21.
3. For the present purposes we will follow the translation by Fiensy and Darnell ("Hellenistic Synagogal Prayers," 2:677–97), making use of their headings and omitting discussions of what they regard as Christian interpolations. Yet that publication includes works that are clearly Christian.
4. Similarly van der Horst, "Greek Synagogal Prayers," 2110.
5. This is presented second by Fiensy and Darnell, "Hellenistic Synagogal Prayers," 2:677–78. The prayer designated first by Fiensy and Darnell ("Hellenistic Synagogal Prayers," 2:677) is depicted as a prayer recited after the celebration of the Eucharist (Apos. Con. 7.26.1–3).
6. Presented third by Fiensy and Darnell, "Hellenistic Synagogal Prayers," 2:679.
7. Presented fourth by Fiensy and Darnell, "Hellenistic Synagogal Prayers," 2:680.
8. Presented fifth by Fiensy and Darnell, "Hellenistic Synagogal Prayers," 2:682.

well (7.37.1–5).[9] In the sixth prayer, the speaker gives thanks to God for his acts of redemption to Israel in the past and continued care in the present (7.38.1–8).[10]

Contribution

Among the contributions of the Hellenistic Synagogal Prayers is its testimony to the exercise of piety through prayer in a manner that is simultaneously Jewish and deeply influenced by Hellenistic thought.[11] Furthermore, the Prayers show that Christian communities, likely in Syria (see below), were amenable to the inclusion of Jewish prayers in their own liturgies and corporate worship, albeit often in a Christianized form. The Prayers speak to a number of theological points.[12] Foremost among these is the authors' presentation of God, who acted in creation (Hel. Syn. Pr. 1:4; 3:2–23; 4:16–21, 38; 5:1) and history (5:9–14; 6:4–12) on behalf of humanity. God is all powerful (1:7; 2:1–2; 4:23b–24) and desires his people to repent (2:3, 6–7; 4:2–3, 23a; 6:1b). Humanity is created rational (3:18; cf. 3:21) with an immortal soul and corruptible body (3:20–21). Finally, wisdom is presented in personal form as the creation of God (5:3; cf. 4:38) and the means by which God created the world (3:19; 4:7, 38).

Particular affinities with Jewish writings are found in the contexts of the diaspora writings of Philo of Alexandria and the Wisdom of Solomon. With the former the Hellenistic Synagogal Prayers share an exhortation of thanksgiving for God's creation of the world (Hel. Syn. Pr. 7:7–8; cf. Philo, *Spec. Laws* 1.38) and expositions on the significance of the number seven (Hel. Syn. Pr. 5:15; cf. Philo, *Alleg. Interp.* 1.4–6). With the Wisdom of Solomon the Prayers share an interest in the presence of Wisdom at creation as God's agent (Hel. Syn. Pr. 3:19; cf. Wis. 9:2, 9) and the immortality of humanity (Hel. Syn. Pr. 7:9; cf. Wis. 2:23).[13]

Text and Provenance

Since the Hellenistic Synagogal Prayers are preserved only in the Apostolic Constitutions, discussion of the text of prayers requires analysis of the text of the Constitutions. This collection of texts is preserved in

---

9. Presented sixth by Fiensy and Darnell, "Hellenistic Synagogal Prayers," 2:684.
10. Presented seventh by Fiensy and Darnell, "Hellenistic Synagogal Prayers," 2:685.
11. Van der Horst, "Greek Synagogal Prayers," 2111.
12. Fiensy, "Hellenistic Synagogal Prayers," 2:674. References in this section are based on Fiensy's numbering of prayers and verses.
13. Fiensy and Darnell, "Hellenistic Synagogal Prayers," 2:674–75.

twenty-three manuscripts, nine of which, dating from the tenth to the sixteenth century, contain an assortment of prayers.[14] Some suggest the Hellenistic Synagogal Prayers were composed originally in Greek,[15] whereas others argue for a Hebrew original translated into Greek for use in diaspora synagogues.[16]

The compilation of the Apostolic Constitutions in the 380s CE requires a date for the Prayers before then. Some have argued that after the mid-second century CE Jewish and Christian relations had soured to the point that Christians borrowed less from synagogue liturgy, suggesting a date no later than that time.[17] But this is by no means certain. The Prayers' familiarity with Aquila's Greek version of the Old Testament (ca. 135 CE) requires a date after that.[18] And so it is often conjectured, though with caution, that the Prayers date between 150 and 300 CE.

The questions of provenance for these prayers, as we have seen, are problematic and subject to considerable discussion. Since they are preserved in a Christian document and bear evidence of Christian interpolations, David A. Fiensy has devised a set of criteria for discerning what may be from its original Hellenistic Jewish context and what should be considered a later (Christian) addition. Material regarded as secondary includes (1) text with explicitly Christian features; (2) words, phrases, or themes that were evidently added by a secondary editor as seen by his favored use of them elsewhere; (3) recurring words, phrases, or themes that appear elsewhere only in the known Christian portions of the Apostolic Constitutions (books 7 and 8); (4) material that is incongruent with the surrounding text; (5) material that has strong affinities with the ideas of (Pseudo-)Ignatius; and (6) material with demonstrable affinities with other contemporary Christian liturgies. Anything that does not meet these criteria is presumed to be original.[19] Pieter W. van der Horst and Judith H. Newman show that part of the interest of the compiler of the Apostolic Constitutions in incorporating Jewish prayers into his work was to stress the continuity between ancient Israel and the church, though it is void of legal material outside the Decalogue.[20]

14. Van der Horst, "Greek Synagogal Prayers," 2111. For a detailed account of the texts, see van der Horst and Newman, Early Jewish Prayers in Greek, 7–9.

15. Fiensy and Darnell, "Hellenistic Synagogal Prayers," 2:671.

16. Van der Horst, "Greek Synagogal Prayers," 2110; van der Horst and Newman, Early Jewish Prayers in Greek, 21.

17. Goodenough, By Light, Light, 357.

18. Fiensy, "Hellenistic Synagogal Prayers," 2:673.

19. Fiensy, Prayers Alleged to Be Jewish, 165–67.

20. Van der Horst and Newman, Early Jewish Prayers in Greek, 22.

The fourth-century Christian compiler of the Constitutions was in Antioch, and most scholars regard the Hellenistic Synagogal Prayers as having originated somewhere in Syria.[21] In their present form the six primary prayers resemble the first six of the "Seven Benedictions" of rabbinic tradition (b. Ketub. 7b–8a), which are ancient blessings for the Sabbath.[22] But it is notoriously difficult to discern what is originally Jewish and what is a secondary Christian addition. Sometimes the Christian compiler may use distinct vocabulary that can cue scholars that the hand of a later editor is at work, but this is not always consistent. Furthermore, Christian copyists and those responsible for adapting the original Jewish Prayers for Christian liturgical purposes do not always utilize distinctively Christian words or phrases. It is true that in some of the prayers phrases such as "through Christ" appear from time to time, but it is not always certain that one can simply excise that phrase to arrive at a Jewish original. Finally, the lack of any non-Christian Jewish manuscripts or even fragments of the Prayers means that scholars are without the opportunity to "check" what could be potential additions. This requires scholars to derive methods of discerning what goes back to the original Prayers. In this regard van der Horst is typical.[23] First, he looks for verbal agreements between the Prayers and extant ancient Jewish writings written in Hebrew as evidence for its derivation from a Jewish source. Second, he looks for clauses or sentences that "are characteristically Jewish and do not betray the vocabulary of the Christian compiler" to indicate that a prayer should be taken as Jewish. Finally, elements that are distinctively Christian are naturally taken to be a later insertion. The difficulty with this method is determining what is "characteristically" Jewish or Christian in antiquity, when in fact there is considerable overlap in the early centuries of the Jesus movement. One may consider, for instance, that the messianism of the Psalms of Solomon, especially Psalm 17, resembles the notion of Davidic kingship of the Gospel of Matthew to the degree that the Jewish and Christian forms are at least congruous. Similarly, the New Testament Letter of James is notably void of "characteristically" Christian elements that one would find in the writings of Paul. The point here is that points of ambiguity between Judaism and Christianity problematize the efforts to discern the Jewish original of the Hellenistic Synagogal Prayers. While no further consideration will be given to the Hellenistic Synagogal Prayers here, readers are directed to the complete and technical commentary by van der Horst and Newman.[24]

Prayer of Joseph

Introduction

Like the Hellenistic Synagogal Prayers, the Prayer of Joseph is preserved exclusively in Christian contexts, here in the writings of Origen (185–254 CE).[25] Though known as the Prayer of Joseph (Προσευχὴ Ἰωσήφ, *Proseuchē Iōsēph*) the primary subject matter throughout is the patriarch Jacob and his rank and role in contrast with that of the angel Uriel. It seems likely that this curious work was attributed to Joseph and that the original text, of which only fragments survive, was an extended account developing Jacob's blessing of Joseph's sons (Gen. 48).[26]

Contents

The text is preserved in three fragments (A, B, and C). Fragment A begins with a first-person account of Jacob, who claims also to be Israel, an angel of God, and a ruling spirit (v. 1). He also claims to be the firstborn of every living thing, including Abraham and Isaac (vv. 2–3). He says that the angel Uriel was envious of him and wrestled with him, claiming that he, Uriel, should be above Jacob (vv. 4–5). Jacob tells Uriel he is merely eighth in rank (after Jacob) and exclaims a litany of titles and ranks by which he, Jacob, is known (vv. 6–9). Fragment B has only a single line, in which the speaker (who is unnamed) claims to have read in the heavenly tablets that everything shall befall an unnamed person and that person's sons. About Fragment C, Origen writes that Jacob was greater than mere human beings, and quotes Jacob's declaration "in the same book from which we quoted," referencing again the reading of heavenly tablets and claiming that Jacob was a chief captain of the power of the Lord, as in Fragment A.

Contribution

Several facets of the Prayer of Joseph are unique among Second Temple literature. Here Jacob is wrestling not with an unnamed angel, as in Genesis

---

24. Van der Horst and Newman, *Early Jewish Prayers in Greek*, 3–93.
25. Origen, *Comm. Jo.* 2:31; cf. *Philocalia* 23:15, 19. Joseph, "Joseph, Prayer of."
26. Smith, "Prayer of Joseph," *OTP* 2:699.

32:24, but with the angel Uriel. Furthermore, Jacob is presented as an angel in human form, extending angelic ancestry to Israel's descendants. Simon Joseph remarks that this is reminiscent of the Enochic Book of Parables, where Enoch himself is regarded as the "son of man" (1 En. 71:14). And Jacob himself is revered among later Jewish texts (e.g., Gen. Rab. 68:12), placing him among exalted figures like Enoch, Moses, and Melchizedek.[27] Indeed, the most striking feature of the Prayer of Joseph is the complexity of titles ascribed to Jacob:[28] he is an "angel of God" (ἄγγελος θεοῦ, angelos theou) and a "ruling spirit" (πνεῦμα ἀρχικόν, pneuma archikon). He is also described, like Michael, as the "archangel of the power of the Lord" (ἀρχάγγελος δυνάμεως κυρίου, archangelos dynameōs kyriou; cf. Dan. 12:1), the "chief captain" (ἀρχιχιλίαρχος, archichiliarchos; cf. Dan. 8:11 LXX; 2 En. 22:6; 33:10; 3 Bar. 11:1), and the "first minister before the face of God" (ὁ ἐν προσώπῳ θεοῦ λειτουργὸς πρῶτος, ho en prosōpō theou leitourgos prōtos). The Prayer of Joseph uses other titles reminiscent of still other literature, such as the designation of Jacob as the "firstborn of every living thing" to whom God gives life (πρωτογόνος παντὸς ζώου, prōtogonos pantos zōou; cf. Prov. 8 [Wisdom]; Philo, QG 2.62; Col. 1:15, 17).[29] All of these seem to expand from Jacob traditions[30] and may be inspired by the claim that he saw God (Gen. 32:30; cf. Hos. 12:4–6; Jub. 32), conflated with the firstborn status of Israel (Exod. 4:22; cf. Exod. Rab. 19:7).[31] In this respect Jacob becomes paradigmatic of the true or ideal Israelite,[32] bearing a paradigmatic function for subsequent Israelites to emulate.[33]

Text and Provenance

According to one tradition,[34] the Prayer of Joseph at one time contained as many as eleven hundred lines. Yet today it survives in only 164 words in three fragments. Fragment A comes from Origin's Commentary on John; Fragment B is found in the compilation of Origen by Gregory of Nazianzus and Basil the Great (the Philocalia) as well as in the work of Eusebius (Preparation of the Gospel) and Procopius of Gaza (Commentary on Genesis [in Latin]). Fragment C also comes from the Philocalia and paraphrases Fragment A and quotes Fragment B. The original language of the Prayer of Joseph is

---

27. Joseph, "Joseph, Prayer of."
28. Smith, "Prayer of Joseph," OTP 2:701–4.
29. Joseph, "Joseph, Prayer of."
30. Smith, "Prayer of Joseph," 43.
31. Joseph, "Joseph, Prayer of."
32. Smith, "Prayer of Joseph," 31, 59, 61; J. Collins, Between Athens and Jerusalem, 240.
33. Joseph, "Joseph, Prayer of."
34. The Stichometry of Nicophorus I of Constantinople (fl. 806–815).

uncertain. J. Z. Smith observes that the mere 164 words that survive from it (in quotation) are too few to afford scholars any certainty as to its original language. Accordingly, it is also debated whether it was composed by a Jew or a Christian. Even the scant linguistic and theological data is inconclusive, exhibiting at the same time parallels to Egyptian Greek texts, Coptic Jewish and Christian texts, and in some details Aramaic materials. Origen says that the Prayer of Joseph was an "apocrypha" used at his time "among the Hebrews."[35] This indicates 231 CE as the latest possible date. From parallels with other literature, Smith has argued that, while its geographical origin (Palestine or diaspora) is uncertain, it likely dates from a first-century-CE Jewish context. The incomplete nature of the work means no further attention will be given to it here. Readers are instead encouraged to consult the introduction and notes by Smith in the second volume of the *Old Testament Pseudepigrapha*.[36]

Prayer of Nabonidus (4Q242)

Introduction

The Prayer of Nabonidus (4Q242) reads as a statement of Nabonidus, the last king of Babylon (556–539 BCE). The text involves confession and praise but no actual prayer, which is inferred and thought to be among the lost portions of the text.[37]

Contents

The work is repetitive, but its fragmentary state renders it difficult to grasp the essence of its content or the course of events.[38] The text identifies itself as a prayer issued when the king was afflicted with illness by God for seven years (4Q242 1–3 1–3). When he prayed, God forgave him, and prompted by a Jew from among the exiles, he writes of how he was afflicted, though he prayed to man-made idols "because [I thoug]ht that t[hey were] gods [. . .]" (4Q242 1–3 8). The remainder (frag. 4) is fragmentary but includes the statement "I was healed" (4Q242 4 1). In essence it is a first-person account of God's punishment of Nabonidus, along with his repentance by turning from idolatry and worshiping the God of Israel[39] and his recovery from disease.[40]

35. Origen, *Comm. Jo.* 2.25.186–92.
36. Smith, "Prayer of Joseph," *OTP* 2:699–714.
37. J. Collins, "Prayer of Nabonidus," 1604; J. Collins, "4Q242."
38. Justnes, "Nabonidus, Prayer of."
39. J. Collins, "Prayer of Nabonidus," 1604.
40. Justnes, "Nabonidus, Prayer of."

Contribution

John J. Collins regards the account as a "court tale" analogous to the stories found in Daniel 1–6. It is sometimes regarded as a link between Babylonian traditions and the book of Daniel.[41] One scholar has argued that it was an earlier and even original version of Daniel,[42] though few embrace this view.[43]

The Prayer of Nabonidus is frustratingly incomplete. But it does raise the question of other prayers found among the Dead Sea Scrolls. While we have surveyed the various extant prayers at the outset of this section, it is worth outlining here the role of prayer at Qumran and briefly accounting for the differing forms and contexts in which prayers appear among the Dead Sea Scrolls. The Jews at Qumran were fastidious observers of the law—or, rather, their interpretation of it—who isolated themselves from the Jerusalem temple and its sacrifices, which the sect regarded as impure. Here is where prayer served as a substitute for sacrifice. Prayers are regarded as an "offering of the lips" that is a "sweet fragrance (offered by) the righteous" (1QS IX, 5).[44] Prayers at Qumran were often communal (1QS VI, 8; X, 14) and scheduled for particular times of day and of the year (1QS X, 1–8). Among the daily prayers (4Q503, 4Q408; cf. 1QS X, 10–14)[45] are those designated for the morning and evening blessings (4Q503), petitions for each day of the week with a hymn of praise for the Sabbath (4Q504, 4Q506), as well as a mystical collection of Sabbath songs (4Q400–407, 11Q17).[46] The festival prayers (1Q34, 4Q507–509; cf. 4Q409)[47] commemorate, among other things, the beginning of a new year and the Day of Atonement, typically beginning with an exhortation for the Lord to remember particular reminiscences associated with particular events of the festival, and concluding with a blessing.[48] Likewise there are designated prayers for Qumran rituals, such as purification (4Q284, 4Q414, 4Q512) and possibly marriage (4Q502). Also included here are a collection of blessings and curses (4Q286–290) and collections of exorcisms and prayers for warding off evil (4Q510, 4Q511, 4Q444, 4Q560, 11Q11).[49] Among the embedded prayers in the Scrolls is a prayer in the context of the annual covenant ritual (1QS I, 18–II, 18), which entails a confession of sins (1QS I, 16–II, 1) in addition

41. J. Collins, "Prayer of Nabonidus," 1604.
42. Fröhlich, *"Time and Times and Half a Time,"* 28–32.
43. Justnes, "Nabonidus, Prayer of."
44. Chazon, "Psalms, Hymns, and Prayers," 2:714.
45. Mizrahi, "Songs of the Sabbath Sacrifice."
46. Falk, "Hymns, Prayers, and Psalms."
47. Mizrahi, "Songs of the Sabbath Sacrifice."
48. Chazon, "Psalms, Hymns, and Prayers," 2:711.
49. Eshel, "Apotropaic Prayers"; Falk, "Hymns, Prayers, and Psalms."

to the designated times for communal daily and mealtime prayers (1QS VI, 2–8; cf. IX, 26–X, 5). Another prayer is found in the War Scroll, which depicts operations for an eschatological battle between the Sons of Light and the Sons of Darkness, before which there are designated prayers appealing for God to rout the enemies of his elect (1QM X, 8–XII, 18; XVIII, 5–XIX, 8). There is also a prayer of thanksgiving to be said upon the inevitable victory of the Sons of Light (1QM XIII, 1–XIV, 1; XIX, 9–12; cf. 1QM XIV, 2–XV, 2).[50] Finally, there is an extensive assortment of prayers of thanksgiving among the Dead Sea Scrolls, responding to any number of interventions from God. These tend to exhibit consistent patterns at their beginnings and endings,[51] sometimes beginning with a simple but explicit statement of thanks (e.g., 1QHᵃ IV, 29) or an abundance of examples simply blessing God and then giving a litany of reasons for doing so (e.g., 1QHᵃ VIII, 26; 1QS XI, 15; 1QM XIII, 2; XIV, 4).

Text and Provenance

The Prayer of Nabonidus was initially published as four fragments from Qumran in 1956.[52] An additional fragment was published in 1962[53] and collectively published as 4Q242 in 1996.[54] The manuscript consists of four fragments; of the four fragments (known as Fragments 1, 2a–b, 3, and 4), the largest is Fragment 1, which comes from the beginning of a scroll and preserves the top and right margins of the first column.[55] The manuscript dates from the second half of the first century BCE at the latest,[56] or from slightly earlier (75–50 BCE).[57] The original composition likely comes from the late second or early first century BCE.[58]

50. Chazon, "Psalms, Hymns, and Prayers," 2:711–12.
51. Schuller, "Some Observations."
52. Milik, "'Prière de Nabonide.'"
53. Meyer, Das Gebet des Nabonid.
54. J. Collins, "4Q242."
55. Justnes, "Nabonidus, Prayer of."
56. Milik, "'Prière de Nabonide,'" 407.
57. Cross, "Fragments of the Prayer of Nabonidus."
58. Justnes, "Nabonidus, Prayer of."

Conclusion

At the outset of the volume, we examined the meaning of the designation "pseudepigrapha" in an effort to dispel some of the negative connotations the term may imply. As we saw, the use of the name of an ancient worthy gave an ancient author or community a hearing to address a situation arising in their own time from the context of Israel's past. This allowed the readers to appreciate a sense of continuity with Israel's God and was a means of exhorting the readers to learn from lessons of the past. But it also became evident that not all works categorized as "pseudepigrapha" actually use the name of an ancient figure. Indeed, unlike with other writings, such as the Apocrypha, which comprises literature found in major Greek manuscripts of the Old Testament but not in the Hebrew Bible, it is difficult to determine what qualifies as a pseudepigraphon. Often by default the category is used to designate what a writing is not rather than what it is. So we have attempted here to cover texts that are *not* among the Apocrypha, which is so ably addressed in a volume by David A. deSilva.[1] But the literature this entails is incredibly diverse—Jewish and Christian, prior to the Common Era and long into it. So we have limited the scope of our discussions to a selection of literature that is Jewish and dates from the Second Temple period, the limits of which we set at the end of the Bar Kokhba revolt (135 CE). This has enabled us to consider a small subsection of the literature but by no means has eliminated our problems. For as readers will by this time observe, the date and provenance of many of these writings remain obscure and debated. So we have given primary attention to those for which the Jewish provenance and date from the Second Temple period are generally accepted by scholars, and secondary consideration to

1. DeSilva, *Introducing the Apocrypha.*

those whose date or provenance is less certain. The result, though certainly not comprehensive, has been a discussion of a very wide swath of literature illustrating the complexities of the kinds of literature preserved from the Second Temple era and the difficulties and circumstances related to the people who composed and preserved them. These we have surveyed very broadly according to literary genre.

Apocalypses are by far the most prevalent kind of writing discussed here, largely because of the place of the composite work known as 1 Enoch, but also, in no small part, because of the tremendous influence the book of Daniel (esp. chaps. 7–12) had on Judaism of the Second Temple period. We have seen that 1 Enoch is composed of a number of distinct works that may date as many as four centuries apart but were brought together by common interest in the biblical Enoch, the seventh from Adam (Gen. 5:21–24). Its importance is recognized by its popularity even today in the Ethiopic language, the only language in which the text survives in full. Yet its presence at Qumran in the Aramaic language, all portions of which are attested except the Similitudes, indicates its ancient importance as well, and it gives scholars a unique opportunity to compare the more recent Ethiopic texts, which date from the fifteenth century, with the original Aramaic texts, many of which date prior to the turn of the era. We saw first a work that describes righteous Enoch's reception of heavenly visions and gives an account of the rebellion of angels, or Watchers. Enoch ascends to heaven, where he is commissioned as a prophet of judgment before he travels throughout the earth and receives visions of judgment (Book of Watchers, 1 En. 1–36). We saw another account of Enoch's visions and angelic interpretation in which another figure appears, called the "Chosen One" and "Son of Man" (the Similitudes of Enoch, or Book of Parables, 1 En. 37–71). In the Astronomical Book (1 En. 72–82) we saw the importance of the role and structure of heavenly and earthly bodies as well as a deep concern for the solar calendar of 364 days. Two visions are found in the Book of Dreams (1 En. 83–90), the first is about the coming flood (1 En. 83–84) and the second (1 En. 85–90), also called the Animal Apocalypse, recounts human history, using animals to represent people and people to represent angels. The Epistle of Enoch (1 En. 91–108) is only partly an actual letter (Epistle of Enoch [92:1–5; 93:11–105:2]). It is first an exhortation (91:1–10, 18–19), followed by the Apocalypse of Weeks (1 En. 93:1–10; 91:11–17), which gives a visionary account of human history from the time of Enoch to the end of days. The Birth of Noah (106:1–107:3) provides a fictitious account of that biblical figure, and 1 Enoch ends with the Eschatological Admonition (108:1–15). The earliest of these texts could date from the third century BCE, with manuscripts dating as early as the second century BCE.

We also surveyed other apocalypses of a rather distinctive sort. Written in the wake of the destruction of Jerusalem and its temple in 70 CE, the books of 4 Ezra, 2 Baruch, and the Apocalypse of Abraham each in their own way responds to the crisis. Fourth Ezra is set thirty years after the destruction of Jerusalem by the Babylonians (ca. 557 BCE). The setting is appropriate for the real author, who though writing centuries later is forced to come to terms with the culpability not only of Israel's gentile oppressors but of Israel itself. The author also wrestles with the notion of God's justice in allowing these events to occur to Israel, with whom God himself made a covenant. That the main figure, Ezra, is generally regarded to have lived over one hundred years later misses the point: that he is probably utilized as the protagonist for his role in restoring instruction of Torah to Israel (4 Ezra 14). A very similar apocalypse to 4 Ezra is that of 2 Baruch. Baruch, the scribe of Jeremiah, is called from his role as companion and secretary to the prophet (Jer. 36:4–10, 26, 32) and placed as a nobleman (Jer. 21:12; 43:2–3; 51:59) to become himself the recipient of a prophetic revelation. Like 4 Ezra, this work was written after the destruction of the temple in 70 CE and is trying to process the inexplicable tragedy that befell the people of God. This trilogy of post-70 apocalypses is completed with the Apocalypse of Abraham. Unlike those other works, however, and more like the book of Daniel, this text constitutes a first-person narrative of the patriarch's youth and pilgrimage from the idolatry of his fathers (Apoc. Ab. 1–8) and an apocalypse proper in which God makes revelations to him (chaps. 9–32).

Then we left discussion of post-70 apocalypses for a work that utilizes the gentile Sibyl, a Greek prophetic female figure, for its own apocalyptic aims. This work, the Sibylline Oracles, contains several books, some of which are Christian and later, but a few of which (books 3–5, 11) are most likely Jewish and earlier. The Sibylline Oracles are analogous to the other apocalypses studied in that they are historical in nature, meaning that they reflect on the course of history. However, they are notably different in that they are written in the diaspora and do not contain reviews of history but do contain heavenly ascents of the visionary figure. The Sibyllines, however, are presented as oracles given not in a vision but through the inspired speech of the Sibyl—a woman in the ancient world who uttered oracles of future events while in a trance-like state, sometimes regarded as a strand of political prophecy. Sibylline Oracles 3 is the oldest of the Sibylline tradition. It is a collection of oracles that dates from the second century BCE through early in the first century CE and stems from various settings, but it generally deals with the struggle for kingship and sovereignty. Sibylline Oracles 4 is likewise political in nature and is a composite work from different times. It is addressed to Asia and Europe and mentions the destruction of Jerusalem in 70 CE (v. 116), the legend of Nero's (d. 68 CE) flight to the Parthians (vv. 119–24, 138–39), and the eruption of Mount Vesuvius in 79 CE (vv. 130–35). Book 5 of the Sibylline Oracles was written in Egypt. Its six oracles were compiled into their present form somewhere between 70 and 132 CE. Sibylline Oracles 5 reviews history from Alexander the Great to Hadrian (or Marcus Aurelius), mentioning successive emperors not by name but by numbers corresponding to their initials (gematria). The enthusiasm toward Ptolemaic (Egyptian) rule found in Sibylline Oracles 3 has turned to antagonism in Sibylline Oracles 5, where one finds hostility (vv. 82–85, 484–96) and evidence of persecution (vv. 68–69). And much of Sibylline Oracles 5 is devoted to oracles of retribution against Egypt and rebuke of Rome for its immorality, destruction of Jerusalem, and especially claims to divinity, with Nero himself the particular object of scorn. Sibylline Oracles 11 provides a narrative of historical events from the flood to the death of Cleopatra (30 BCE). As in book 5, historical figures are identified by numbers representing their names or initials (gematria). The author has made some notable adjustments to the sequence attested in the Hebrew Bible and other narratives. In contrast to other oracles, here one finds no depiction of eschatological judgment, interest in the temple, or polemic against sexual immorality and idolatry. Furthermore, the review of history carries no ethical or religious exhortation as one finds in books 4 and 5. And so Sibylline Oracles 11 is relatively thin on theological and historical contributions.

In addition to these apocalyptic writings, we gave brief consideration to a handful of apocalyptic writings that were either fragmentary or of disputed provenance. Second Enoch is a diaspora writing that narrates the life of Enoch to the onset of the flood, amplifying the narrative of Genesis 5:21–32. The main text (2 En. 1–68) describes Enoch's ascent to the seven heavens, where he encounters God enthroned, and then returns to earth to exhort his family and others with messages from God. The remainder of the book (2 En. 69–73) describes Enoch's successors and the miraculous birth of Melchizedek. Like 4 Ezra and 2 Baruch, 3 Baruch is an apocalypse dealing with the destruction of Jerusalem but cast in the setting of the first temple. For the readers, the destruction of the temple in 70 CE is fresh, and the mysteries of God "allay the original grief and fear."[2] The visionary ascends to the fifth heaven, is given a message from God, and returns to earth to relate the message to others. The Apocalypse of Zephaniah is unique in that it is attested only in brief fragments and a quotation from Clement of Alexandria (150–215 CE), with an estimated one-fourth of the original Apocalypse surviving from antiquity. Yet from what remains it is clear that at least part of it claims to be a vision

2. J. Collins, *Apocalyptic Imagination*, 313.

of Zephaniah, and it is likely that the original Apocalypse of Zephaniah presented the seer's heavenly journey, view of the final judgment, and descent into and vision of hell. Despite its name, the Testament of Abraham contains a narrative and an apocalypse combined into a single work that deals with the fear of death itself and one's attitudes about death's relationship to God's judgment. Furthermore, whereas most apocalypses discussed in this volume depict the first-person narrative of the named figure, the account here is in the third person. It survives from antiquity in two major recensions, and though it is often considered a Jewish work from the first century CE, both points are debated. Finally, though there is no single apocalypse preserved in its entirety among the Dead Sea Scrolls, apocalypticism in general permeates much of the thought world of Qumran and is evident in a number of texts. These include the so-called Vision of Daniel (4Q243–244; cf. 4Q245) and the Aramaic Apocalypse (4Q246). We also looked at the Apocryphon of Jeremiah (4Q383, 4Q384, 4Q385a, 4Q387, 4Q388a, 4Q389), the Apocryphon of Ezekiel (4Q385, 4Q385b, 4Q386, 4Q388), the Book of Giants (4Q203, 4Q530–532, 6Q8, 1Q23, 2Q26), the Messianic Apocalypse (4Q521), and the New Jerusalem text (4Q554–555, 5Q15, 11Q18, 1Q32, 2Q24), in addition to several others that illustrate the lively way in which apocalypses contributed to the thoughts of the Jewish sectarians at Qumran.

In the second section of this volume we looked at testaments and related texts. Here we drew on the biblical accounts of the last words of figures such as Jacob (Gen. 49) and Moses (Deut. 33–34) to show how these settings evolved into a specific category of literature. In general these testaments typically present the discourse of the main figure in the first person, followed by an account of his death in the third person. Testaments can also occur as segments of larger Jewish works that belong to another genre. First we looked at the Testament of Moses, a farewell exhortation given to Joshua by Moses before the transfer of leadership of the people of Israel. Though the ending of the book has been lost, it is generally assumed that Moses's death was narrated at some point in the earlier text. The narrative is almost entirely attributed to Moses and is in the form of a predication of Israel's people from their entrance into Canaan until the end of days. Similarly, the Testament of Job is an embellishment of the biblical book of Job, presenting Job imparting wisdom to his progeny prior to his impending death with particular emphasis on the virtue of patient endurance. Most of the work (T. Job 1:4–45:4) is Job's first-person account of the cause and consequences of his hardships, and it concludes with Job's death, the ascent of his soul, and his burial (T. Job 51–53).

We then turned to a lesser-known but very important text known as the Aramaic Levi Document. This is a testament-like narrative recounting the life story of the patriarch Levi but extending beyond his life and advice to his progeny, which one finds in a formal "testament." Instead, the work gives particular attention to Levi's establishment of the Levitical priesthood long before the time of Aaron and to the sacred laws for sacrifices that he received from his grandfather, Isaac. As Levi was the head of the priestly tribe, the exhortations in this document articulate the responsibilities and prerogatives of the priests. Thus the Aramaic Levi Document presents the ideal priest as a zealous warrior for God who is also a punctilious observer of ritual purity, an inspiring teacher, and a recipient of divine revelation through dreams and prophecy. The entire work is presented as a first-person narrative attributed to the biblical Levi and is the most extensive of a series of three works, including the Testament of Qahat (4Q542) and the Visions of Amram (4Q543–549), that contain distinct instructions for the Levitical priesthood, set in an autobiographical narrative. The Testament of Qahat was unknown until the discovery of the Dead Sea Scrolls, and the extant text (4Q542) is missing its beginning and end, so whether it contained a narrative and/or prophetic vision, like other testaments, is unknown. It contains Qahat's exhortations, sustained throughout, addressed to his sons and concentrating on priestly traditions and preserving the books that contain them. It is named for Qahat, or Kohath, who is the son of Levi (Gen. 46:11; Exod. 6:16; Num. 3:17) and father of Amram (Exod. 6:18; Num. 3:19, 27). Similarly, the Visions of Amram was found among the Dead Sea Scrolls (4Q543–549) and is likewise fragmentary in its present form. From the Hebrew Bible we know that Amram is the father of Moses, Aaron, and Miriam, though he is little known in the Old Testament, where he is only mentioned in genealogical lists as the son of Qahat (Exod. 6:18; Num. 3:19; 26:58; 1 Chron. 5:28; 6:3; 23:12); he married his father's sister Jochebed, with whom he fathered Aaron, Moses, and Miriam (Exod. 6:20; Num. 26:59), whose descendants were in the Levitical line (1 Chron. 5:29; 6:2–3, 18; 23:12–13; 24:20, 26:23). The Visions of Amram presents his words pertaining to a vision in the form of a book delivered to his sons on the day of his death.

In addition to the works above, we discussed several other testaments in the ancient world. Despite its name, the Testament of Solomon only loosely belongs to the genre of testament, since it lacks the deathbed scene and the imparting of wisdom to his progeny and seems primarily concerned with demonic lore. Furthermore, in its present form it is a Christian document from around the third century CE, which may be based in part on Jewish material from the first century CE. The Testaments of the Twelve Patriarchs is perhaps the most important of the testamentary literature, though we gave it only sparse attention here. The work is a collection of twelve distinct testaments woven into a single unit, modeled after Jacob's last words (Gen. 49; cf. Deut. 33). These testaments are perhaps the most important examples of the testament genre from the Second Temple period and early Christianity. They have received the most scholarly attention in part because they, uniquely, contain the word "testament" (διαθήκη, *diathēkē*) in their titles, and they contain deathbed speeches from each of the twelve sons of Jacob addressing ethical matters all framed, with the exception of Asher, within a narrative of the figure's life. They each conclude with predictions about Israel's future, utilizing the rubric of sin-exile-restoration, and instructions for the patriarch's burial, which are then followed at the end. And yet the Testaments of the Twelve Patriarchs is widely regarded as a work originally written in a Jewish context from the Second Temple period, but, in its present form, it has been thoroughly reworked by Christians so as to become a Christian text. Furthermore, there is considerable debate as to whether the later Christian interpolations can be recognized and excised so as to arrive at the earlier Jewish text.

A different work is the Testament of Naphtali (4Q215), which was copied no later than the end of the first century BCE and is unquestionably Jewish. Yet this fragmentary text preserves no moral exhortation or prophetic word to round out the features typical of a testament. Instead, it recounts the narrative of the birth of Naphtali (Gen. 30:7–8), the fifth son of Jacob, born to Jacob and Bilhah, one of two handmaidens, along with Zilpah, to Jacob's wives Rachel and Leah (Gen. 29–30). This work is one of several even more fragmentary testaments found at Qumran, including the Testament of Jacob (4Q537), Testament of Judah (3Q7, 4Q484, 4Q438), and the Testament of Joseph (4Q539). Though they received little attention here, their existence testifies to the importance and popularity of the genre. As a whole, our discussion showed that the genre of testament has a place in Jewish contexts while being adopted in and adapted to Christian settings as well.

From testaments we turned to narrative material of a different sort, broadly called "legends and expansions of biblical traditions." The nomenclature here is difficult to describe, with expressions like "rewritten scripture" and "parabiblical" attempting to convey the concept. Writings discussed in this section have sometimes used a narrative or setting from the Hebrew Bible to launch into a distinct narrative of their own. At other times the author has recast the same narrative while being both selective as to what is addressed and explanatory in dealing with difficult or problematic texts. It is important that there is no evidence that an author is attempting to replace or supersede the biblical text. Rather, these works presume the enduring voice of the text on which they build and in some instances could be regarded as lenses through which particular Jewish communities addressed concerns in their own contexts in relation to the biblical narrative.

One sees this at work in the book of Jubilees, which is largely a retelling of the biblical books of Genesis and early parts of Exodus (chaps. 1–24) and is sometimes regarded as the most important and influential book written by Jews prior to the turn of the era. It claims to have been dictated to Moses on Mount Sinai by the "Angel of the Presence" (Jub. 1:29; 2:1) alongside the law at his first ascent up the mountain (Exod. 24:12–18). The majority of the book constitutes the content of the revelation (Jub. 2–50), which answers questions about the biblical narrative that the original leaves unexplained. All of this is couched in an exhortation to the author's strict interpretation of the law, in which he typically recasts the narrative or makes additions to it in line with his own interests. The work's most distinctive characteristic is its chronological framework, including numbered months, 364-day years, seven-year periods ("weeks of years"), and units of seven seven-year periods (forty-nine years) called jubilees. The entire book of Jubilees traces biblical history from creation until the entry into the promised land as fifty jubilees (2,450 years). Though sometimes called "Little Genesis," the book of Jubilees is actually longer than the biblical text on which it is based.

The book of Biblical Antiquities was once thought to be written by Philo of Alexandria. However, it is now known that he was not the author, and so scholars refer to the person who composed the work as "Pseudo-Philo." Like the book of Jubilees, the Biblical Antiquities recasts biblical narratives, in this case from the time of Adam to King David, from the perspective of a setting prior to the building of Solomon's Temple (LAB 26:12). Sometimes the author omits or summarizes the biblical narrative, and at other times he inserts material, such as prayers, speeches, or narrative sections, not found in the Hebrew Bible. While recounting the sins of Israel and the eternal light of the law, the consistent burden of the text is that God will never abandon his people and will in the end grant to Israel salvation and victory.

The Genesis Apocryphon (1Q20 or 1QapGen) was entirely unknown until its discovery in Cave 1 at Qumran in 1947. It was copied no later than early in the first century CE. It narrates stories of Enoch, Lamech, Noah, and Abram related to accounts in Genesis 6–15. As a pseudepigraphon, it presents many of these accounts in the first person (Lamech, Enoch, and Noah). Yet as a "rewritten scripture" it contains considerable additions, omissions, and various amendments to the biblical account. The extant text contains an account of the miraculous birth of Noah (cols. 0–V), the life of Noah and an account of the flood (cols. V–XVIII), and a narrative about Abram, which is incomplete (cols. XIX–XXII?).

The Letter of Aristeas is widely regarded as a fictitious account of the origins of the Greek translation of the Torah from the Hebrew. It is presented as a letter from a certain Aristeas to his brother, claiming that the Egyptian king instructed his librarian to solicit the high priest in Jerusalem to furnish them with a delegation to translate the Jewish Scriptures to Greek for the collection of Alexandria's library. A delegation of seventy-two Jews come to Egypt to undertake the task with much pomp and ceremony. Though the Letter of Aristeas was really written by an unknown Alexandrian Jew and is of little historical value, it generated considerable apologetic interests for advocating the legitimacy of the Greek translation not only of the Torah but of the whole Hebrew Bible, which was used and further embellished by Christians. Joseph and Aseneth is likewise a narrative set in Egypt, but instead of an account of the origins of the Greek translation of the Torah, it furnishes readers with a fanciful tale of the patriarch Joseph and his Egyptian wife Aseneth, the daughter of Potiphera, priest of On (Gen. 41:45). Joseph and Aseneth expands on this material to create a narrative that describes Aseneth prior to her marriage to Joseph, how they met, and their subsequent marriage. It explains that Aseneth's repentance, which is displayed in her rejection of idols and prayer to God, indicates her conversion to Judaism and thus enables a devout Jew like Joseph, who otherwise could not marry the daughter of a gentile idolatrous priest since that is strictly forbidden in Scripture (Gen. 24:3–4, 37–38; 27:46; 28:1; cf. Jub. 20:4; 22:20; 30:7–16), to marry her.

Additional legends and expansions of biblical tradition received only brief attention, for various reasons. The Greek version of the Life of Adam and Eve is a creative expansion of Genesis 4–5, developing key elements of the biblical narrative pertaining to God's mercy on Adam and Eve, the inevitability of death because of their sin, and their expulsion from the garden of Eden. Fourth Baruch, attributed to Baruch the scribe, describes events at the time of the fall of Jerusalem to Nebuchadnezzar (587/586 BCE) but before the death of Jeremiah by stoning. It is generally agreed that the fall of Jerusalem to "Babylon" is a contextual recasting of the destruction of Jerusalem by the Romans in 70 CE. And so the work as a whole is set after the destruction of the Jerusalem temple in 70 CE and before the completion of the Bar Kokhba revolt (ca. 135 CE). A work known as the *Exagōgē*, meaning "exodus," is a Greek tragedy composed by a certain Ezekiel, a poet of tragedies. As a play it is modeled on the great classical tragedies of fifth-century-BCE Athens. Its extant 269 lines, which preserve only part of the work, recount the story of the exodus from Egypt (Exod. 1–15), presented as a Jewish form of Greek tragedy.

The next section on psalms, Wisdom literature, and prayers, described how the various expressions of religious piety among Second Temple Jews occasioned a large assortment of psalms, hymns, and prayers. These are often embedded in larger texts, rather than being, for example, prayers utilized in individual practice. The two sets of psalms discussed here represent a small cross section of what are widely regarded as psalms and hymns compiled during the Second Temple period both for corporate worship within the temple and for educational purposes. Wisdom literature is well attested in Second Temple Judaism, primarily in the Dead Sea Scrolls and the Apocrypha. One that belongs to the Pseudepigrapha is a text that was originally attributed to the ancient figure of Phocylides, which we discuss in some detail. Though prayer in ancient Judaism is very well attested as an act of communication with God with the purpose of getting some result from the interaction, there is little that is not embedded in larger narratives or that falls under the category of Jewish pseudepigrapha from the Second Temple period. So our treatment of that subject was necessarily limited.

In addition to the 150 psalms in the Hebrew Bible, the additional collection of Psalms 151–155 emerges during the Second Temple period and was discussed. These are part of a larger legend (11QPs^a = 11Q5) claiming that King David wrote an astonishing 4,050 works, including 3,600 psalms, 364 songs for daily offerings, 52 songs for the Sabbaths, 30 songs for the festivals, and 4 songs for "making music over the stricken" (11QPs^a XXVII, 2–11). All of these are said to be spoken by David through the prophetic influence of God (11QPs^a XXVII, 11). The Psalms of Solomon is one of a number of apocrypha and pseudepigrapha related in some degree to King Solomon. This group is a collection of eighteen pseudonymous hymns or poems that generally convey a Jewish community's response to persecution and foreign invasion, likely in reference to the Romans in the first century BCE. In this respect, God is appealed to throughout as the righteous judge who dispenses rewards and punishments for human actions. God's intervention is keenly expected, particularly through the intervention of a messianic figure in the form of the dramatic and violent advent of a kingly son of David.

The Sentences is a didactic wisdom poem of 230 verses attributed to Phocylides, a popular Greek poet who composed maxims with useful advice for daily life in the sixth century BCE. The Sentences were written much later by someone writing under the guise of Phocylides, and so the author is typically referred to as Pseudo-Phocylides. The writing expounds on a combination of ethical commands from the Greek translation (Septuagint) of the law alongside non-Jewish Hellenistic writers of moral treatises. In doing this the author melds the Pentateuch with Wisdom literature into "moral precepts."

Since most prayers in Second Temple Judaism are embedded in other documents, belong to another category of literature such as the Apocrypha, or come from an uncertain provenance, our discussion of prayers, as noted, was necessarily limited. We first looked at a collection of prayers preserved exclusively in a fourth-century Christian writing. This collection of prayers, called the Hellenistic Synagogal Prayers, was likely used in Jewish diaspora synagogues but adapted to service in Christian liturgies. So we sifted through what were most likely to be the Jewish originals behind a selection of these prayers while underscoring the ambiguities in undertaking such a task. Another kind of prayer is the Prayer of Joseph, which at face value has nothing to do with Joseph but rather Jacob. Moreover, like the Hellenistic Synagogal Prayers, the Prayer of Joseph is preserved exclusively in Christian contexts, but it is very fragmentary. Its primary subject matter is Jacob and his rank and role in contrast to that of the angel Uriel. It seems likely that the original of this curious work was much longer and contained an extended account developing Jacob's blessing of Joseph's sons (Gen. 48). Finally, we looked at the fragmentary and repetitive Prayer of Nabonidus (4Q242), which reads as a statement of Nabonidus, the last king of Babylon (556–539 BCE), and likely contained in its original form not only the extant confession and praise but also an actual prayer. This brought us to consider more broadly the nature of prayer among the Dead Sea Scrolls, which was both pious and regimented. Prayers emerged for a variety of occasions for this strict, sectarian group of Jews and were even thought to replace temple sacrifices, to which the group no longer had access.

It is clear from the texts preserved among the Pseudepigrapha from the Second Temple period alone that Judaism was a rather diverse religion. This assessment does not even account for the writings of the Apocrypha or most of the extensive corpus of literature among the Dead Sea Scrolls. The pseudepigraphic writings exhibit points of overlap, notably the profound influence of select portions of the Hebrew Bible. Yet even here they differ. Some attempt to recast the biblical narratives, carefully clarifying points of ambiguity. Others are clearly inspired by the biblical text but quite content to use the names and genres of non-Israelites to communicate their points. Still others make clear that some engagement with gentiles is acceptable, whereas others are fastidious in their regard for the special place of only the righteous among Israel. All this illustrates that identifying the beliefs of the Jews of the Second Temple period defies reductionism and requires careful study of the surviving writings from the period in their own contexts, a task toward which it is hoped the present volume has been of some assistance.

Bibliography

Adams, Sean A. "Pseudo-Phocylides." *ESTJ* 1:441–42.

Ahearne-Kroll, P. D. "Joseph and Aseneth and Jewish Identity in Greco-Roman Egypt." PhD diss., University of Chicago, 2005.

Albeck, Chanoch. *Das Buch der Jubiläen und die Halacha*. Sieben und vierziger Bericht der Hochschule für die Wissenschaft des Judentums in Berlin. Berlin: Siegfried Scholem, 1930.

Alexander, P. S. "From Son of Adam to Second God: Transformations of the Biblical Enoch." In Stone and Bergren, *Biblical Figures outside the Bible*, 87–122.

———. "Retelling the Old Testament." In *It Is Written: Scripture Citing Scripture; Essays in Honour of Barnabas Lindars, SSF*, edited by D. A. Carson and H. G. M. Williamson, 99–121. Cambridge: Cambridge University Press, 1988.

Allegro, J. M. "*Tanḥûmîm*." In *Qumrân Cave 4.I (4Q158–4Q186)*, 60–67. DJD 5. Oxford: Clarendon, 1968.

Allison, Dale C., Jr. *James*. International Critical Commentary. London: T&T Clark, 2013.

———. *Testament of Abraham*. CEJL. Berlin: de Gruyter, 2003.

Andersen, F. I. "2 (Slavonic Apocalypse of) Enoch." *OTP* 1:91–221.

Anderson, Gary A. "Life of Adam and Eve." *OTB*, 1331–58.

Angel, J. L. *Otherworldly and Eschatological Priesthood in the Dead Sea Scrolls*. STDJ 86. Leiden: Brill, 2010.

Antonissen, Hugo. "New Jerusalem Text." *ESTJ* 1:397–98.

———. "The Visionary Architecture of New Jerusalem in Qumran." In *Qumran und die Archäologie*, edited by J. Frey, C. Clausen, and N. Kessler, 439–80. WUNT 278. Tübingen: Mohr Siebeck, 2012.

Assefa, Daniel. *L'Apocalypse des animaux (1 Hen 85–90): une propaganda militaire? Approches narrative, historico-critique, perspectives théologiques.* JSJSup 120. Leiden: Brill, 2007.

Atkinson, Kenneth. "Moses, Assumption of." *ESTJ* 1:385–87.

———. "Psalms of Solomon." *OTB*, 1903–23.

———. "Taxo's Martyrdom and the Role of the *Nuntius* in the *Testament of Moses*: Implications for Understanding the Role of Other Intermediary Figures." *JBL* 125 (2006): 453–76.

Attridge, Harold W. "Melchizedek in Some Early Christian Texts and 2 Enoch." In Orlov and Boccaccini, *New Perspectives on 2 Enoch*, 387–410.

———. "Testament of Job." *OTB*, 1872–902.

Attridge, Harold W., John J. Collins, and Thomas H. Tobin, eds. *Of Scribes and Scrolls: Studies on the Hebrew Bible, Intertestamental Judaism, and Christian Origins Presented to John Strugnell on the Occasion of His Sixtieth Birthday.* Lanham, MD: University Press of America, 1990.

Aviam, Mordecai. "The Book of Enoch in the Galilean Archaeology and Landscape." In Bock and Charlesworth, *Parables of Enoch*, 159–70.

Avigad, Nahman. "The Paleography of the Dead Sea Scrolls and Related Documents." In Rabin and Yadin, *Aspects of the Dead Sea Scrolls*, 56–87.

Baars, W. "Psalms of Solomon." In *The Old Testament in Syriac according to the Peshiṭta Version*, 1–27. Part IV, Fascicle 6. Leiden: Brill, 1972.

Baillet, M. "Livre des Jubilés (i, ii)." In Baillet, Milik, and Vaux, *Les "Petites Grottes" de Qumrân*, 77–79.

———. "Remarques sur le manuscrit du Livre des Jubiles de la grotte 3 de Qumran." *RevQ* (1964–1966): 423–33.

———. "Une prophétie apocryphe." In Baillet, Milik, and Vaux, *Les "Petites Grottes" de Qumrân*, 96–98.

Baillet, M., J. T. Milik, and R. de Vaux. *Les "Petites Grottes" de Qumrân.* DJD 3. Oxford: Clarendon, 1962.

Barclay, John M. G. *Jews in the Mediterranean Diaspora from Alexander to Trajan (323 BCE–117 CE).* Edinburgh: T&T Clark, 1996.

Barthélemy, D., and J. T. Milik. "Testament de Lévi." In *Qumran Cave I*, edited by D. Barthélemy and J. T. Milik, 87–91 and plate xvii. DJD 1. Oxford: Clarendon, 1955.

Bartlett, John R. *Jews in the Hellenistic World: Josephus, Aristeas, the Sibylline Oracles, Eupolemus.* Cambridge: Cambridge University Press, 1985.

Bauckham, Richard J. "Apocalypses." In *Justification and Variegated Nomism*, Vol. 1, *The Complexities of Second Temple Judaism*, edited by D. A. Carson, P. T. O'Brien, and M. A. Seifrid, 135–87. WUNT 2.140. Tübingen: Mohr Siebeck, 2001.

———. "The Continuing Quest for the Provenance of the Old Testament Pseudepigrapha." In Oegema and Charlesworth, *Pseudepigrapha and Christian Origins*, 9–29.

———. *Jude, 2 Peter.* Word Biblical Commentary 50. Waco: Word, 1983.

Bauckham, Richard, and James R. Davila. "Introduction." In Bauckham, Davila, and Panayotov, *Old Testament Pseudepigrapha*, 1:xvii–xxxviii.

Bauckham, Richard, James R. Davila, and Alexander Panayotov, eds. *Old Testament Pseudepigrapha: More Noncanonical Scriptures.* Vol. 1. Grand Rapids: Eerdmans, 2013.

Bautch, Kelley Coblentz. *A Study of the Geography of 1 Enoch 17–19: "No One Has Seen What I Have Seen."* JSJSup 81. Leiden: Brill, 2003.

Baynes, Leslie. *The Heavenly Book Motif in Judeo-Christian Apocalypses 200 BCE–200 CE.* JSJSup 152. Leiden: Brill, 2012.

Becker, Michael. "Genesis Apocryphon." *ESTJ* 1:218–20.

———. "Messianic Apocalypse (4Q521)." *ESTJ* 1:368–70.

Beckwith, R. T. "The Earliest Enoch Literature and Its Calendar: Marks of Their Origin, Date and Motivation." *RevQ* 10 (1981): 365–403.

Beer, Bernhard. *Das Buch der Jubiläen und sein Verhältniss zu den Midraschim.* Leipzig: Wolfgang Gerhard, 1856.

———. "Noch ein Wort über das Buch der Jubilaen." *MGWJ* 6 (1857): 1–23.

Ben-Dov, Jonathan. *Head of All Years: Astronomy and Calendars at Qumran in Their Ancient Context.* STDJ 78. Leiden: Brill, 2008.

Bernstein, Moshe J. "Contours of Genesis Interpretation at Qumran: Contents, Contexts, and Nomenclature." In *Studies in Ancient Midrash*, edited by J. L. Kugel, 57–85. Cambridge, MA: Harvard University Center for Jewish Studies, 2001.

———. "Pseudepigraphy in the Qumran Scrolls: Categories and Functions." In Chazon, Stone, and Pinnick, *Pseudepigraphic Perspectives*, 1–26.

———. "'Rewritten Bible': A Generic Category Which Has Outlived Its Usefulness?" *Textus* 22 (2005): 169–96.

Black, Matthew. *The Scrolls and Christian Origins.* London: Nelson, 1961.

Bledsoe, Amanda Davis. "Daniel, Pseudo-Texts." *ESTJ* 1:153–55.

Boccaccini, Gabriele. *Beyond the Essene Hypothesis: The Parting of the Ways between Qumran and Enochic Judaism.* Grand Rapids: Eerdmans, 1998.

———, ed. *Enoch and the Messiah Son of Man: Revisiting the Book of Parables.* Grand Rapids: Eerdmans, 2007.

Boccaccini, Gabriele, and Giovanni Ibba, eds. *Enoch and the Mosaic Torah: The Evidence of Jubilees.* Grand Rapids: Eerdmans, 2009.

Bock, Darrell L., and James H. Charlesworth, eds. *Parables of Enoch: A Paradigm Shift.* JCT 11. London: T&T Clark, 2013.

Bogaert, P.-M. *Apocalypse de Baruch, introduction, tradition du Syriaque et commentaire*. 2 vols. SC 144–45. Paris: Cerf, 1969.

Bohak, Gideon. *Joseph and Aseneth and the Jewish Temple in Heliopolis*. EJL 10. Atlanta: Scholars Press, 1996.

———. "A New Geniza Fragment of the *Aramaic Levi Document*." *Tarbiz* 79 (2011): 373–83.

Böttrich, Christfried. *Das slavische Henochbuch*. JSHRZ V/7. Gütersloh: Gütersloher Verlagshaus, 1995.

———. "Enoch, Slavonic Apocalypse of (*2 Enoch*)." *EST J* 1:185–89.

———. *Weltweisheit, Menschheitsethik, Urkult: Studien zum slavischen Henochbuch*. WUNT 2.50. Tübingen: Mohr Siebeck, 1992.

Box, G. H. *The Apocalypse of Abraham*. London: SPCK, 1919.

———. "*4 Ezra*." APOT 2:542–624.

Brock, S. P. "A Fragment of Enoch (6:1–6) in Syriac." *JTS* 19 (1968): 626–31.

Brooke, George J. "Men and Women as Angels in Joseph and Aseneth." *JSP* 14, no. 2 (2005): 159–76.

———. "Rewritten Bible." *EDSS* 2:777–81.

———. "The Temple Scroll: A Law unto Itself?" In *Law and Religion: Essays on the Place of the Law in Israel and Early Christianity*, edited by B. Lindars, 34–43, 164–66. Cambridge: J. Clarke, 1988.

Brooke, G. J., J. Collins, T. Elgvin, P. Flint, J. Greenfield, E. Larson, C. Newsom et al., eds. *Qumran Cave 4, XVII: Parabiblical Texts, Part 3*. DJD 22. Oxford: Clarendon, 1996.

Buitenwerf, Rieuwerd. *Book III of the Sibylline Oracles and Its Social Setting: With an Introduction, Translation, and Commentary*. SVTP 17. Leiden: Brill, 2003.

———. "Sibylline Oracles 3." *EST J* 1:495–96.

Burchard, Christoph. "Joseph and Aseneth." *OTP* 2:177–247.

———. "Joseph und Aseneth: Eine jüdisch-hellenistische Erzahlung von Liebe, Bekehrung und vereitelter Entfuhrung." *Theologische Zeitschrift* 61 (2005): 65–77.

Burns, Joshua Ezra. "Midrash." *EST J* 2:499–500.

Candlish, J. S. "On the Moral Character of Pseudonymous Books." *Expositor* 4 (1891): 91–107, 262–79.

Casey, Maurice. *Son of Man: The Interpretation and Influence of Daniel 7*. London: SPCK, 1979.

———. "The Use of the Term 'Son of Man' in the Similitudes of Enoch." *JSJ* 7 (1976): 11–29.

Ceriani, A. M. "Fragmenta Parvae Genesis et Assumptionis Mosis ex Veteri Versione Latina." *Monumenta Sacra et Profana* 1, no. 1 (1861): 15–54.

Charles, R. H. *The Apocalypse of Baruch*. London: SPCK, 1929.

————, ed. *The Apocrypha and Pseudepigrapha of the Old Testament*. 2 vols. Oxford: Clarendon, 1913.

————. "Assumption of Moses." *APOT* 2:407–24.

————. *The Assumption of Moses*. London: Black, 1897.

————. *The Book of Enoch*. Oxford: Clarendon, 1893.

————. *The Book of Jubilees or the Little Genesis*. London: Black, 1902.

————. "1 Enoch." *APOT* 2:163–281.

————. *The Greek Versions of the Testaments of the Twelve Patriarchs*. Oxford: Clarendon, 1908.

————. "2 Baruch, or the Syriac Apocalypse of Baruch." *APOT* 2:470–526.

Charles, R. H., and W. R. Morfill, *Book of the Secrets of Enoch*. Oxford: Clarendon, 1896.

Charlesworth, James H. "The Books of Enoch: *Status Quaestionis*." In Bock and Charlesworth, *Parables of Enoch*, xiii–xvii.

————. "The Concept of the Messiah in the Pseudepigrapha." *ANRW* 19.1 (1979): 188–218.

————. "The Date and Provenience of the *Parables of Enoch*." In Bock and Charlesworth, *Parables of Enoch*, 37–57.

————. "Expansions of the 'Old Testament,'" *OTP* 2:5.

————. "Foreword: The Fundamental Importance of an Expansive Collection of 'Old Testament Pseudepigrapha.'" In Bauckham, Davila, and Panayotov, *Old Testament Pseudepigrapha*, 1:xi–xvi.

————, ed. *The Old Testament Pseudepigrapha*. 2 vols. Garden City, NY: Doubleday, 1983–85.

Charlesworth, James H., with J. A. Sanders. "More Psalms of David." *OTP* 2:612–24.

Chazon, Esther G., ed. *Liturgical Perspectives: Prayer and Poetry in Light of the Dead Sea Scrolls*. STDJ 48. Leiden: Brill, 2003.

———— "Psalms, Hymns, and Prayers." *EDSS* 2:710–15.

Chazon, Esther G., Michael E. Stone, and A. Pinnick, eds. *Pseudepigraphic Perspectives: The Apocrypha and Pseudepigrapha in Light of the Dead Sea Scrolls*. STDJ 31. Leiden: Brill, 1997.

Chesnutt, R. D. "The Dead Sea Scrolls and the Meal Formula in *Joseph and Aseneth*: From Qumran Fever to Qumran Light." In *The Bible and the Dead Sea Scrolls*, edited by C. D. Elledge, 401–10. Archaeology and Biblical Studies 14. Leiden: Brill, 2005.

————. *From Death to Life: Conversion in Joseph and Aseneth*. JSPSup 16. Sheffield: Sheffield Academic, 1995.

————. "*Oxyrhynchus Papyrus* 2069 and the Compositional History of *1 Enoch*." *JBL* 129 (2010): 485–505.

————. "Revelatory Experiences Attributed to Biblical Women in Early Jewish Literature." In "*Women Like This*": *New Perspectives on Women in the Greco-Roman World*, edited by A.-J. Levine, 107–25. Atlanta: Scholars Press, 1991.

————. "The Social Setting and Purpose of Joseph and Aseneth." *JSP* 2 (1988): 21–48.

Cioată, Maria. "Job, Testament of." *EST J* 1:281–83.

Cioată (Haralambakis), Maria. *The Testament of Job: Text, Narrative and Reception History*. LSTS 80. London: T&T Clark, 2012.

Clarke, Kent D. "The Problem of Pseudonymity in Biblical Literature and Its Implications for Canon Formation." In *The Canon Debate*, edited by Lee Martin McDonald and James A. Sanders, 440–68. Peabody, MA: Hendrickson, 2002.

Cohn, Leopold. "An Apocryphal Work Ascribed to Philo of Alexandria." *JQR* (1898): 277–332.

Collins, Adela Yarbro. *The Combat Myth in the Book of Revelation*. Havard Dissertations in Religion 9. Missoula, MT: Scholars Press, 1976.

————. "Composition and Redaction of the Testament of Moses 10." *HTR* 69 (1976): 179–86.

————. "Introduction: Early Christian Apocalypticism." *Semeia* 36 (1986): 1–11.

————. "The Theology of Early Enoch Literature." *Hen* 24 (2002): 107–12.

Collins, Adela Yarbro, and John J. Collins. *King and Messiah as Son of God: Divine, Human, and Angelic Messianic Figures in Biblical and Related Literature*. Grand Rapids: Eerdmans, 2008.

Collins, John J., ed. *Apocalypse: The Morphology of a Genre*. Semeia 14. Missoula, MT: Scholars Press, 1979.

————. *The Apocalyptic Imagination: An Introduction to Jewish Apocalyptic Literature*. 3rd ed. Grand Rapids: Eerdmans, 2016.

————. "The Apocalyptic Technique: Setting and Function in the Book of the Watchers." *CBQ* 44 (1982): 91–111.

————. *Apocalypticism and the Dead Sea Scrolls*. London: Routledge, 1997.

————. "Apocrypha and Pseudepigrapha." *EDSS* 1:35–39.

————. "The Background of the 'Son of God' Text." *Bulletin for Biblical Research* 7 (1997): 51–62.

————. *Between Athens and Jerusalem: Jewish Identity in the Hellenistic Diaspora*. 2nd ed. Grand Rapids: Eerdmans, 2000.

————. "Daniel, Book of: Pseudo-Daniel." *EDSS* 1:176–78.

————. "The Date and Provenance of the Testament of Moses." In Nickelsburg, *Studies on the Testament of Moses*, 15–37.

————. "The Development of the Sibylline Tradition." *ANRW* 20 (1987): 421–59.

————. "4Q242: Prayer of Nabodius ar." In Brooke et al., *Qumran Cave 4, XVII*, 83–93.

———. "The Genre of the Book of *Jubilees*." In *A Teacher for All Generations: Essays in Honor of James C. VanderKam*, edited by Eric F. Mason, Kelley Coblentz Bautch, Angela Kim Harkins, and Daniel A. Machiela, 737–55. 2 vols. JSJSup 153/I–II. Leiden: Brill, 2012.

———. "The Heavenly Representative: The 'Son of Man' in the Similitudes of Enoch." In *Ideal Figures in Ancient Judaism: Profiles and Paradigms*, edited by G. W. E. Nickelsburg and J. J. Collins, 111–33. SCS 12. Missoula, MT: Scholars Press, 1980.

———. "Introduction: Towards the Morphology of a Genre." *Semeia* 14 (1979): 1–20.

———. "The Jewish Adaptation of Sibylline Oracles." In *Seers, Sibyls, and Sages in Hellenistic-Roman Judaism*, 181–98. Leiden: Brill, 1997.

———. "The Jewish Apocalypses." *Semeia* 14 (1979): 21–59.

———. *Jewish Wisdom in the Hellenistic Age*. Edinburgh: T&T Clark, 1997.

———. "*Joseph and Aseneth*: Jewish or Christian?" *JSP* 14, no. 2 (2005): 97–112.

———. "Prayer of Nabonidus." *OTB*, 1604–6.

———. *The Scepter and the Star: Messianism in Light of the Dead Sea Scrolls*. 2nd ed. Grand Rapids: Eerdmans, 2010.

———. "Sibylline Discourse." In Tigchelaar, *Old Testament Pseudepigrapha*, 195–210.

———. "Sibylline Oracles." *AYBD* 6:2–6.

———. "Sibylline Oracles." *OTP* 1:317–472.

———. *The Sibylline Oracles of Egyptian Judaism*. SBLDS 13. Missoula, MT: Scholars Press, 1974.

———. "Some Remaining Traditio-Historical Problems in the Testament of Moses." In Nickelsburg, *Studies on the Testament of Moses*, 38–43.

———. "The Son of Man in First Century Judaism." *NTS* 38 (1992): 448–66.

———. "Structure and Meaning in the Testament of Job." *SBLSP* 1 (1974): 35–52.

———. "The Testamentary Literature in Recent Scholarship." In Kraft and Nickelsburg, *Early Judaism and Its Modern Interpreters*, 268–85.

———. "Testaments." In *Jewish Literature of the Second Temple Period*, edited by Michael E. Stone, 325–56. Assen: Van Gorcum; Philadelphia: Fortress, 1984.

Collins, John J., and P. W. Flint. "4Q243–245: Pseudo-Daniel." In Brooke et al., *Qumran Cave 4, XVII*, 95–164.

Collins, John J., and Daniel C. Harlow, eds. *The Eerdmans Dictionary of Early Judaism*. Grand Rapids: Eerdmans, 2010.

Collins, Nina. *The Library in Alexandria and the Bible in Greek*. VTSup 82. Leiden: Brill, 2000.

Conybeare, F. C. "Testament of Solomon." *JQR* 11, no. 1 (1898): 1–45.

Cook, Edward M. "Remarks on the Testament of Kohath from Qumran Cave 4." *JJS* 44, no. 2 (1993): 205–19.

Cox, Claude E. "Job." In *T&T Clark Companion to the Septuagint*, edited by James K. Aitken, 385–410. London: T&T Clark, 2015.

Crawford, Sidnie White. *Rewriting Scripture in Second Temple Times*. Grand Rapids: Eerdmans, 2008.

———. "The 'Rewritten' Bible at Qumran: A Look at Three Texts." *Eretz-Israel* 26 (1999): 1*–8*.

Cross, F. M. "David, Orpheus, and Psalm 151:3–4." *Bulletin of the American Schools of Oriental Research* 231 (1978): 69–71.

———. "The Development of the Jewish Scripts." In *The Bible and the Ancient Near East: Essays in Honor of William Foxwell Albright*, edited by G. Ernest Wright, 133–202. Garden City, NY: Doubleday, 1961.

———. "Fragments of the Prayer of Nabonidus." *Israel Exploration Journal* 34 (1984): 260–64.

Crouch, J. E. *The Origin and Intention of the Colossian Haustafel*. Forschungen zur Religion und Literatur des Alten und Neuen Testaments 109. Göttingen: Vandenhoeck & Ruprecht, 1972.

Davenport, G. L. *The Eschatology of the Book of Jubilees*. StPB 20. Leiden: Brill, 1971.

Davies, P. R. "The Social World of Apocalyptic Writings." In *The World of Ancient Israel*, edited by R. E. Clements, 251–71. Cambridge: Cambridge University Press, 1989.

Davila, James R. "Aramaic Levi: A New Translation and Introduction." In Bauckham, Davila, and Panaytov, *Old Testament Pseudepigrapha*, 1:121–42.

———. *Liturgical Works*. ECDSS 6. Grand Rapids: Eerdmans, 2000.

———. *The Provenance of the Pseudepigrapha: Jewish, Christian, or Other?* JSJSup 105. Leiden: Brill, 2005.

———. "Pseudepigrapha, Old Testament." *EDEJ*, 1110–14.

Davis, C. J. Patrick. "Torah-Performance and History in the *Golah*: Rewritten Bible or 'Re-Presentational' Authority in the *Apocryphon of Jeremiah C*." In Flint, Duhaime, and Baek, *Celebrating the Dead Sea Scrolls*, 467–95.

Davis, Kipp. *The Cave 4 Apocryphon of Jeremiah and the Qumran Jeremianic Traditions: Prophetic Persona and the Construction of Community Identity*. STDJ 111. Leiden: Brill, 2014.

———. "Jeremiah, Apocryphon of." *ESTJ* 1:271–72.

Delcor, M. "Le Testament de Job, la prière de Nabonide et les traditions targoumiques." In *Bibel und Qumran: Beiträge zur Erforschung der Beziehungen zwischen Bibel- und Qumranwissenschaft*, edited by S. Wagner, 57–74. Berlin: Evangelische Haupt-Bibelgesellschaft, 1968.

Derron, P. *Les sentences du Pseudo-Phocylide: Texte, traduction, commentaire*. Paris: Les Belles Lettres, 1986.

deSilva, David A. *Introducing the Apocrypha: Message, Context, and Significance.* 2nd ed. Grand Rapids: Baker Academic, 2018.

―――. *The Jewish Teachers of Jesus, James, and Jude: What Earliest Christianity Learned from the Apocrypha and Pseudepigrapha.* New York: Oxford University Press, 2012.

―――. "The Testaments of the Twelve Patriarchs as Witnesses to Pre-Christian Judaism: A Re-assessment." *JSP* 23 (2012): 21–68.

Diebner, B. J. "Zephanjas Apokalypse." *JSHRZ* V/9. Gütersloh: Gütersloher Verlagshaus, 2003.

Dillmann, August. "Das Buch der Jubiläen oder die kleine Genesis." *Jahrbücher der Biblischen Wissenschaft* 3 (1851): 1–96.

Dimant, Devorah. "The Qumran Aramaic Texts and the Qumran Community." In *History, Ideology and Bible Interpretation in the Dead Sea Scrolls: Collected Studies*, edited by D. Dimant, 185–94. FAT 90. Tübingen: Mohr Siebeck, 2014.

―――. *Qumran Cave 4, XXI: Parabiblical Texts, Part 4: Pseudo-prophetic Texts.* DJD 30. Oxford: Clarendon, 2001.

―――. "The Sons of Heaven—the Teaching about the Angels in the Book of Jubilees in Light of the Writings of the Qumran Community." In *A Tribute to Sarah: Studies in Jewish Philosophy and Kabbalah*, edited by Moshe Idel, Devorah Dimant, and Shalom Rosenberg, 97–118. Jerusalem: Magnes, 1994.

―――. "Two 'Scientific Fictions': The So-Called Book of Noah and the Alleged Quotation of Jubilees in CD 16:3–4." In *Studies in the Hebrew Bible, Qumran, and the Septuagint Presented to Eugene Ulrich*, edited by Peter Flint, James VanderKam, and Emanuel Tov, 230–49. VTSup 101. Leiden: Brill, 2006.

DiTommaso, Lorenzo. "Dating the Eagle Vision of *4 Ezra*: A New Look at an Old Theory." *JSP* 20 (1999): 3–38.

―――. *The Dead Sea New Jerusalem Text.* TSAJ 110. Tübingen: Mohr Siebeck, 2005.

―――. "The Development of Apocalyptic Historiography in Light of the Dead Sea Scrolls." In Flint, Duhaime, and Baek, *Celebrating the Dead Sea Scrolls*, 497–522.

―――. "Pseudepigrapha Research and Christian Origins after the OTP." In Oegema and Charlesworth, *Pseudepigrapha and Christian Origins*, 30–47.

Docherty, Susan. *The Jewish Pseudepigrapha: An Introduction to the Literature of the Second Temple Period.* London: SPCK, 2014.

Dochhorn, Jan. *Die Apokalypse des Mose: Text, Übersetzung, Kommentar.* Tübingen: Mohr Siebeck, 2005.

Doering, Lutz. *Ancient Jewish Letters and the Beginnings of Christian Epistolography.* WUNT 1.298. Tübingen: Mohr Siebeck, 2012.

Donaldson, Terence L. *Judaism and the Gentiles: Jewish Patterns of Universalism (to 135 CE).* Waco: Baylor University Press, 2007.

Drawnel, Henryk. "Amram, Visions of." *EDEJ* 326–27.

―――. *The "Aramaic Astronomical Book" (4Q208–4Q211) from Qumran.* Oxford: Oxford University Press, 2011.

―――. "Aramaic Levi Document." *ESTJ* 1:106–9.

―――. *An Aramaic Wisdom Text from Qumran: A New Interpretation of the Levi Document.* JSJSup 86. Leiden: Brill, 2004.

―――. "The Literary Form and Didactic Content of the Admonitions (Testament) of Qahat." In *From 4QMMT to Resurrection: Melanges qumraniens en hommage á Émile Puech*, edited by F. Garcia Martinez, A. Steudel, and E. J. Tigchelaar, 55–73. Leiden: Brill, 2006.

―――. "The Mesopotamian Background of the Enochic Giants and Evil Spirits." *DSD* 21 (2014): 14–38.

―――. "Moon Computation in the *Aramaic Astronomical Book.*" *RevQ* 23 (2007): 3–41.

―――. "Priestly Education in the *Aramaic Levi Document (Visions of Levi)* and *Aramaic Astronomical Book* (4Q208–211)." *RevQ* 22 (2006): 547–74.

―――. "Qahat, Admonitions (Testament) of." *EDEJ*, 1124–25.

Duke, Robert R. "Amram, Visions of." *ESTJ* 1:104–6.

―――. *The Social Location of the Visions of Amram (4Q543–547).* Studies in Biblical Literature 135. New York: Peter Lang, 2010.

Duling, D. C. "Testament of Solomon." *OTP* 1:935–87.

Dunn, James D. G. "The Son of Man in Mark." In Bock and Charlesworth, *Parables of Enoch*, 18–34.

Dupont-Sommer, A. *The Essene Writings from Qumran.* Translated by G. Vermes. Gloucester: Peter Smith, 1973.

―――. *Les Ecrits esseniens decouverts pres de la mer Morte.* Bibliotheque historique. Paris: Payot, 1959.

Eissfeldt, O. "The Psalms of Solomon." In *The Old Testament: An Introduction*, translated by P. R. Ackroyd, 610–13. Oxford: Blackwell, 1965.

Endres, John C. *Biblical Interpretation in the Book of Jubilees.* CBQMS 18. Washington, DC: Catholic Biblical Association of America, 1987.

Erho, Ted. "The Ahistorical Nature of *1 Enoch* 56:5–8 and Its Ramifications upon the *Opinio Communis* on the Dating of the *Similitudes of Enoch.*" *JSJ* 40 (2009): 23–54.

Eshel, E. "Apotropaic Prayers in the Second Temple Period." In Chazon, *Liturgical Perspectives*, 69–88.

Evans, Craig A. "The Genesis Apocryphon and the Rewritten Bible." *RevQ* 13 (1988): 153–65.

Falk, Daniel K. *Daily, Sabbath, and Festival Prayers in the Dead Sea Scrolls.* STDJ 27. Leiden: Brill, 1998.

―――. "Hymns, Prayers, and Psalms." *ESTJ* 2:347–45.

———. *The Parabiblical Texts: Strategies for Extending the Scriptures among the Dead Sea Scrolls*. LSTS 63. Companion to the Qumran Scrolls 8. London: T&T Clark, 2007.

Felder, Stephen. "What Is the Fifth Sibylline Oracle?" *JSJ* 33, no. 4 (2002): 363–85.

Feldman, L. H. "Jewish 'Sympathizers' in Classical Literature and Inscriptions." *Transactions and Proceedings of the American Philological Association* 81 (1950): 200–208.

Feldman, L. H., James L. Kugel, and Lawrence H. Schiffman, eds. *Outside the Bible: Ancient Jewish Writings Related to Scripture*. Lincoln: University of Nebraska, 2013.

Fiensy, David A. "Hellenistic Synagogal Prayers." *OTP* 2:671–98.

———. *Prayers Alleged to Be Jewish: An Examination of the Constitutions Apostolorum*. Brown Judaic Studies 65. Chico, CA: Scholars Press, 1985.

———. "Prayers, Hellenistic Synagogal." *ABD* 5:450–51.

Fiensy, David A., and D. R. Darnell. "Hellenistic Synagogal Prayers." *OTP* 2:671–98.

Fink, U. B. *Joseph und Aseneth: Revision des griechischen Textes und Edition der zweiten lateinischen Übersetzung*. Fontes et Subsidia ad Bibliam Pertinentes 5. Berlin: de Gruyter, 2008.

Finkelstein, L. "Pre-Maccabean Documents in the Passover Haggadah." *HTR* 36 (1943): 19–24.

Fishbane, Michael. *Biblical Interpretation in Ancient Israel*. Oxford: Clarendon, 1985.

———. "Inner Biblical Exegesis: Types and Strategies of Interpretation in Ancient Israel." In *Midrash and Literature*, edited by Geoffrey H. Hartman and Sanford Budick, 19–37. New Haven: Yale University Press, 1986.

Fisk, Bruce Norman. *Do You Not Remember? Scripture, Story and Exegesis in the Rewritten Bible of Pseudo-Philo*. JSPSup 37. Sheffield: Sheffield Academic, 2001.

Fitzmyer, J. A. *The Genesis Apocryphon of Qumran Cave 1 (1Q20). A Commentary*. Biblica et Orientalia 18/B. 2nd ed. Rome: Pontifical Biblical Institute, 2004.

Fleming, J. *Das Buch Henoch: Äthiopischer Text*. Leipzig: J. C. Hinrichs, 1902.

Fletcher-Louis, C. H. T. *All the Glory of Adam: Liturgical Anthropology in the Dead Sea Scrolls*. STDJ 42. Leiden: Brill, 2002.

Flint, Peter W. *The Dead Sea Psalms Scrolls and the Book of Psalms*. STDJ 17. Leiden: Brill, 1997.

Flint, P. W., J. Duhaime, and K. S. Baek, eds. *Celebrating the Dead Sea Scrolls: A Canadian Collection*. EJL 30. Atlanta: Society of Biblical Literature, 2011.

Flusser, D. "The Four Empires in the Fourth Sibyl and in the Book of Daniel." *Israel Oriental Studies* 2 (1972): 148–75.

———. "Psalms, Hymns and Prayers." In Stone, *Jewish Writings*, 551–77.

Frankel, Z. "Das Buch der Jubilaen." *MGWJ* 5 (1856): 311–16, 380–400.

Franklin, S. "A Note on a Pseudepigraphical Allusion in Oxyrhynchus Papyrus No. 4365." *VT* 48 (1998): 95–96.

Freyne, S. *Galilee from Alexander the Great to Hadrian 323 BCE to 135 BCE: A Study of Second Temple Judaism.* Edinburgh: T&T Clark, 1980.

Fröhlich, I. *"Time and Times and Half a Time": Historical Consciousness in the Jewish Literature of the Hellenistic and Persian Periods.* JSPSup 19. Sheffield: Sheffield Academic, 1996.

García Martínez, Florentino. "The Eschatological Figure of 4Q246." In García Martínez, *Qumran and Apocalyptic,* 162–79.

———. "4Q Amram B I,14: Melki-Resha O Melki-Sedeq?" *RevQ* 45 (1985): 111–14.

———. "The Heavenly Tablets in the Book of Jubilees." In *Studies in the Book of Jubilees,* edited by Matthias Albani, Jörg Frey, and Armin Lange, 243–60. TSAJ 65. Tübingen: Mohr Siebeck, 1997.

———. *Qumran and Apocalyptic: Studies on the Aramaic Texts from Qumran.* STDJ 9. Leiden: Brill, 1992.

Garrett, S. R. "The 'Weaker Sex' in the Testament of Job." *JBL* 112 (1993): 55–70.

Gaylord, H. E. "The Slavonic Version of III Baruch." PhD diss., Hebrew University of Jerusalem, 1983.

———. *The Slavonic Version of III Baruch.* Studia Judaeoslavica. Leiden: Brill, 2012.

———. "3 (Greek Apocalypse of) Baruch." *OTP* 1:653–79.

Geller, F. Badalanova. "Heavenly Writings: Celestial Cosmography in *The Book of the Secrets of Enoch.*" *Starob'lgarska literatura* 45–46 (2010): 197–244.

Gilders, William. "The Concept of Covenant in Jubilees." In Boccaccini and Ibba, *Enoch and the Mosaic Torah,* 178–92.

Gillingham, S. E. "The Levites and the Editorial Composition of the Psalms." In *The Oxford Handbook of the Psalms,* edited by William P. Brown, 201–13. Oxford: Oxford University Press, 2014.

Goff, M. J. *4QInstruction.* Wisdom Literature from the Ancient World 2. Atlanta: Society of Biblical Literature, 2013.

Goldstein, Jonathan A. "The Date of the Book of Jubilees." *Proceedings of the American Academy of Jewish Research* 50 (1983): 69–72.

———. "The Message of *Aristeas to Philokrates*: In the Second Century B.C.E., Obey the Torah, Venerate the Temple of Jerusalem, but Speak Greek, and Put Your Hopes in the Ptolemaic Dynasty." In *Eretz Israel, Israel and the Jewish Diaspora: Mutual Relations,* edited by Menachem Mor, 1–23. Studies in Jewish Civilization 1. Lanham, MD: University Press of America, 1991.

Goodenough, E. R. *By Light, Light: The Mystic Gospel of Hellenistic Judaism.* New Haven: Philo Press, 1935.

Gooding, D. W. "Aristeas and Septuagint Origins: A Review of Recent Studies." *VT* 13 (1963): 357–64.

Goshen-Gottstein, M. H. "The Psalms Scroll (11QPsᵃ): A Problem of Canon and Text." *Textus* 5 (1966): 22–33.

Grabbe, L. L. "Chronography in 4 Ezra and 2 Baruch." *SBLSP* (1981): 49–63.

———. "The Social Setting of Early Jewish Apocalypticism." *JSP* 4 (1989): 27–47.

Grant, R. M. *Heresy and Criticism: The Search for Authenticity in Early Christian Literature.* Louisville: Westminster John Knox, 1993.

Greenfield, Jonas C. "*The Words of Levi Son of Jacob* in Damascus Document 4.15–19." *RevQ* 13 (1988): 319–22.

Greenfield, Jonas C., and Michael E. Stone, "The Enochic Pentateuch and the Date of the Similitudes." *HTR* 70 (1977): 51–65.

———. "Remarks on the Aramaic Testament of Levi from the Geniza." *RB* 85 (1979): 214–30.

Greenfield, Jonas C., Michael E. Stone, and Esther Eshel. *The Aramaic Levi Document: Edition, Translation, Commentary.* SVTP 19. Leiden: Brill, 2004.

Grelot, P. "La Géographie mythique d'Hénoch et ses sources." *RB* 65 (1958): 33–69.

Gross, Andrew D. "Testament of Kohath." *OTB*, 1869–71.

Gruen, Erich S. *Heritage and Hellenism: The Reinvention of Jewish Tradition.* Berkeley: University of California Press, 1998.

Gruen, W. "Seeking a Context for the Testament of Job." *JSP* 18 (2009): 163–79.

Gurtner, Daniel M. "Danielic Influence at the Intersection of Matthew and the Dead Sea Scrolls." In *Matthew within Judaism: Israel and the Nations in the First Gospel*, edited by Anders Runesson and Daniel M. Gurtner, 309–28. Early Christianity and Its Literature 27. Atlanta: SBL Press, 2020.

———. "The Eschatological Rewards for the Righteous in *2 Baruch*." In *Interpreting "4 Ezra" and "2 Baruch": International Studies*, edited by G. Boccaccini and J. M. Zurawski, 107–15. LSTS 87. London: T&T Clark, 2014.

———. "The Historical and Political Contexts of Second Temple Judaism." *ESTJ* 1:21–89.

———. "Introduction: Apocrypha, Pseudepigrapha, Philo and Josephus." In *A Comparative Handbook to the Gospel of Mark: Comparisons with Pseudepigrapha, the Qumran Schrolls, and Rabbinic Literature*, edited by Bruce Chilton, Darrell Bock, Daniel M. Gurtner, Jacob Neusner, Lawrence H. Schiffman, and Daniel Oden, 1–6. New Testament Gospels in Their Judaic Contexts 1. Leiden: Brill, 2009.

———. "Noncanonical Jewish Writings." In *The World of the New Testament: Cultural, Social, and Historical Contexts*, edited by Joel B. Green and Lee Martin McDonald, 291–309. Grand Rapids: Baker Academic, 2013.

———. "On the Other Side of Disaster: Soteriology in 2 Baruch." In Gurtner, *This World and the World to Come*, 114–26.

———. "Psalms 151–155." *ESTJ* 1:450–53.

———. *Second Baruch: A Critical Edition of the Syriac Text. With Greek and Latin Fragments, English Translation, Introduction, and Concordances*. JCT 5. London: T&T Clark, 2009.

———, ed. *This World and the World to Come: Soteriology in Second Temple Judaism*. LSTS 74. London: T&T Clark, 2011.

———. "The 'Twenty-Fifth Year of Jeconiah' and the Date of *2 Baruch*." *JSP* 18, no. 1 (2008): 23–32.

Gurtner, Daniel M., and Loren T. Stuckenbruck, eds. *The T&T Clark Encyclopedia of Second Temple Judaism*. 2 vols. London: T&T Clark, 2020.

Hadas, Moses. *Aristeas to Philocrates (Letter of Aristeas)*. New York: Harper & Brothers, 1951.

Hagen, Joost L. "No Longer 'Slavonic' Only: 2 Enoch Attested in Coptic from Nubia." In Orlov and Boccaccini, *New Perspectives on 2 Enoch*, 7–34.

Halpern-Amaru, Betsy. "Flavius Josephus and the *Book of Jubilees*: A Question of Source." *HUCA* 72 (2001): 15–44.

Hanneken, Todd. "Angels and Demons in the Book of Jubilees and Contemporary Apocalypses." *Hen* 28 (2006): 11–25.

Hanson, P. D. "Rebellion in Heaven, Azazel, and Euhermeristic Heroes in *1 Enoch* 6–11." *JBL* 96 (1977): 195–233.

Harkins, Angela Kim, Kelley Coblentz Bautch, and John C. Endres, eds. *The Watchers in Jewish and Christian Traditions*. Minneapolis: Fortress, 2014.

Harlow, Daniel C. *The Greek Apocalypse of Baruch (3 Baruch) in Hellenistic Judaism and Early Christianity*. SVTP 12. Leiden: Brill, 1996.

Harrington, Daniel J. "The Bible Rewritten (Narratives)." In Kraft and Nickelsburg, *Early Judaism and Its Modern Interpreters*, 239–47.

———. "The Biblical Text of Pseudo-Philo's *Liber Antiquitatum Biblicarum*." *CBQ* 33 (1971): 1–17.

———. "Interpreting Israel's History: The Testament of Moses as a Rewriting of Deut. 31–34." In Nickelsburg, *Studies on the Testament of Moses*, 59–68.

———. "The Original Language of Pseudo-Philo's *Liber Antiquitatum Biblicarum*." *HTR* 63 (1970): 503–14.

———. "Pseudo-Philo." *OTP* 2:297–377.

Harrington, Daniel J., J. Cazeaux, C. Perrot, and P.-M. Bogaert, *Pseudo-Philon, Les Antiquités Bibliques*. 2 vols. SC 229–30. Paris: Cerf, 1976.

Hayward, C. T. R. "Genesis and Its Reception in *Jubilees*." In *The Book of Genesis: Composition, Reception, and Interpretation*, edited by Craig A. Evans, Joel N. Lohr, and David L. Petersen, 375–404. VTSup 152. Leiden: Brill, 2012.

———. "Philo, Pseudo- (LAB)." *ESTJ* 1:435–39.

Helyer, Larry R. "Gematria." *ESTJ* 2:284–85.

Henze, Matthias. "4 Ezra and 2 Baruch: Literary Composition and Oral Performance in First-Century Apocalyptic Literature." *JBL* 131, no. 1 (2012): 181–200.

———. *Jewish Apocalypticism in Late First Century Israel*. TSAJ 142. Tübingen: Mohr Siebeck, 2011.

Herzer, Jens. *4 Baruch (Paraleipomena Jeremiou): Translated with an Introduction and Commentary*. WGRW 22. Atlanta: Society of Biblical Literature, 2005.

Hicks-Keeton, Jill. "Joseph and Aseneth." *ESTJ* 1:294–96.

Hill, D. "Dikaioi as a Quasi-Technical Term." *NTS* 11 (1965): 296–302.

Hillel, Vered. "Demonstrable Instances of the Use of Sources in the Pseudepigrapha." In *Dead Sea Scrolls: Texts and Context*, edited by C. Hempel, 325–38. STDJ 90. Leiden: Brill, 2010.

———. "Patriarchs, Testaments of the Twelve." *ESTJ* 1:411–15.

———. "Testaments." *ESTJ* 2:787–89.

Himmelfarb, Martha. *Ascent to Heaven in Jewish and Christian Apocalypses*. Oxford: Oxford University Press, 1993.

———. "The Book of the Watchers and the Priests of Jerusalem." *Hen* 24 (2002): 131–35.

———. "Earthly Sacrifice and Heavenly Incense: The Law of the Priesthood in *Aramaic Levi* and *Jubilees*." In *Heavenly Realms and Earthly Realities in Late Antique Religions*, edited by Ra'anan S. Boustan and Annette Yoshiko Reed, 103–22. Cambridge: Cambridge University Press, 2004.

———. "Revelation and Rapture: The Transformation of the Visionary in the Ascent Apocalypses." In *Mysteries and Revelations: Apocalyptic Studies since the Uppsala Colloquium*, edited by John J. Collins and James H. Charlesworth, 79–90. JSPSup 9. Sheffield: JSOT Press, 1991.

———. *Tours of Hell*. Philadelphia: University of Pennsylvania, 1983.

Hody, Humphrey. *Contra Historiam LXX Interpretum Aristeae nominae inscriptam Dissertatio*, Oxford, 1684.

Hogan, Karina Martin. "Ezra, Fourth Book of." *EDEJ*, 623–26.

———. "The Meaning of *tôrâ* in 4 Ezra." *JSJ* 38 (2007): 530–52.

———. *Theologies in Conflict in 4 Ezra: Wisdom Debate and Apocalyptic Solution*. JSJSup 130. Leiden: Brill, 2008.

Holladay, Carl R. *Historians*. Vol. 1 of *Fragments from Hellenistic Jewish Authors*. Society of Biblical Literature Texts and Translations, Pseudepigrapha Series 10. Chico, CA: Scholars Press, 1983.

Hollander, H. W., and Marinus de Jonge. *The Testaments of the Twelve Patriarchs: A Commentary*. SVTP 8. Leiden: Brill, 1985.

Honigman, Sylvie. *The Septuagint and Homeric Scholarship in Alexandria*. London: Routledge, 2003.

Howard, George. "The *Letter of Aristeas* and Diaspora Judaism." *JTS* 22 (1971): 337–48.

Humphrey, Edith M. *Joseph and Aseneth*. GAP. Sheffield: Sheffield Academic, 2000.

———. *The Ladies and the Cities: Transformation and Apocalyptic Identity in Joseph and Aseneth, 4 Ezra, the Apocalypse and the Shepherd*. JSPSup 17. Sheffield: Sheffield Academic, 1995.

Hunt, A. S., ed. "2069. Apocalyptic Fragment." In *The Oxyrhynchus Papyri, Part 17*, 6–8. London: Egypt Exploration Society, 1927.

Isaac, E. "The Ethiopic History of Joseph: Translation with Introduction and Notes." *JSP* 6 (1990): 3–125.

———. "1 (Ethiopic Apocalypse of) Enoch." *OTP* 1:5–89.

Jacobson, Howard. "Biblical Quotation and Editorial Function in Pseudo-Philo's *Liber Antiquitatum Biblicarum*." *JSP* 5 (1989): 47–64.

———. *A Commentary on Pseudo-Philo's "Liber Antiquitatum Biblicum."* 2 vols. Leiden: Brill, 1996.

———. *The Exagoge of Ezekiel*. Cambridge: Cambridge University Press, 1983.

———. "Ezekiel, the Tragedian." *OTB*, 730–42.

———. "Marginalia to Pseudo-Philo *Liber Antiquitatum Biblicarum* and to the *Chronicles of Jerahmeel*." *Revue des études juives* 142 (1983): 455–59.

———. "Pseudo-Philo, Book of Biblical Antiquities." *OTB*, 470–613.

Jellinek, A. *Bet ha-Midrasch*. 7 vols. Leipzig: F. Nies, 1853–57.

Johnson, M. D. "Life of Adam and Eve." *OTP* 2:249–96.

Johnson, Sara Raup. *Historical Fictions and Hellenistic Jewish Identity: Third Maccabees in Its Cultural Context*. Berkeley: University of California Press, 2005.

Jones, F. Stanley. *An Ancient Jewish Christian Source on the History of Christianity: Pseudo-Clementine Recognitions 1.27–71*. Society of Biblical Literature Texts and Translations 37. Christian Apocrypha Series 2. Atlanta: Scholars Press, 1995.

Jonge, Marinus de. *Pseudepigrapha of the Old Testament as Part of Christian Literature: The Case of the Testaments of the Twelve Patriarchs and the Greek Life of Adam and Eve*. SVTP 18. Leiden: Brill, 2003.

———, ed. *Studies on the Testaments of the Twelve Patriarchs: Text and Interpretation*. SVTP 3. Leiden: Brill, 1975.

———. *The Testaments of the Twelve Patriarchs: A Study of Their Text, Composition, and Origin*. 2nd ed. Assen: Van Gorcem, 1975.

———. "Two Messiahs in the Testaments of the Twelve Patriarchs?" In *Jewish Eschatology, Early Christian Christology, and the Testaments of the Twelve Patriarchs*, edited by Marinus de Jonge, 191–203. Leiden: Brill, 1991.

Jonge, Marinus de, H. W. Hollander, H. J. de Jonge, and Th. Korteweg. *The Testaments of the Twelve Patriarchs: A Critical Edition of the Greek Text*. PVTG 1.2. Leiden: Brill, 1978.

Jonge, Marinus de, and Johannes Tromp. *The Life of Adam and Eve and Related Literature*. GAP. Sheffield: Sheffield Academic, 1997.

Joosten, Jan. "Reflections on the Original Language of the Psalms of Solomon." In *The Psalms of Solomon: Language, History, Theology*, edited by E. Bons and P. Pouchelle, 31–47. EJL 40. Atlanta: SBL Press, 2015.

Joseph, Simon. "Joseph, Prayer of." *ESTJ* 1:297–99.

Jull, A. J. Timothy, Douglas J. Donahue, Magen Broshi, and Emanuel Tov. "Radio-carbon Dating of Scrolls and Linen Fragments from the Judean Desert." *Atiqot* 28 (1996): 85–91.

Justnes, Årstein. "Nabonidus, Prayer of (4Q242/4QPrNab)." *ESTJ* 1:388–89.

Kahle, Paul. *The Cairo Geniza*. 2nd ed. Oxford: Blackwell, 1959.

Kampen, John I. *Wisdom Literature*. ECDSS. Grand Rapids: Eerdmans, 2011.

———. "Wisdom Literature." *ESTJ* 2:822–24.

Kautzsch, Emil, ed. *Die Apokryphen und Pseudepigraphen des Alten Testaments*. 2 vols. Tübingen: Mohr Siebeck, 1900.

Kee, H. C. "'The Man' in Fourth Ezra: Growth of a Tradition." *SBLSP* 20 (1981): 199–208.

———. "Satan, Magic and Salvation in the Testament of Job." *SBLSP* 1 (1974): 53–76.

———. "The Testaments of the Twelve Patriarchs." *OTP* 1:775–828.

Kister, Menahem. "Newly-Identified Fragments of the Book of Jubilees: Jub. 23:21–23, 30–31." *RevQ* 12 (1987): 529–36.

Klijn, A. F. J. "2 (Syriac Apocalypse of) Baruch." *OTP* 1:615–52.

Klutz, Todd E. *Rewriting the Testament of Solomon: Tradition, Conflict, and Identity in a Late Antique Pseudepigraphon*. LSTS 53. London: T&T Clark, 2005.

Knibb, Michael A. "Apocalyptic and Wisdom in 4 Ezra." *JSJ* 13 (1982): 56–74.

———. "The Date of the Parables of Enoch: A Critical Review." *NTS* 25 (1979): 345–59.

———. "Enoch, Similitudes of (1 Enoch 37–71)." *EDEJ*, 585–87.

———. *The Ethiopic Book of Enoch: A New Edition in the Light of the Aramaic Dead Sea Fragments*. 2 vols. Oxford: Clarendon, 1978.

Knibb, Michael A., and P. W. van der Horst, eds. *Studies on the Testament of Job*. SNTSMS 66. Cambridge: Cambridge University Press, 1989.

Kobelski, P. J. *Melchizedek and Mechiresha*. CBQMS 10. Washington, DC: Catholic Biblical Association of America, 1981.

Kohler, K. "The Origin and Composition of the Eighteen Benedictions with a Transla-tion of the Corresponding Essene Prayers in the Apostolic Constitutions." *HUCA* 1 (1924): 387–425.

———. "The Testament of Job, an Essene Midrash on the Book of Job." In *Semitic Studies in Memory of Rev. Dr. Alexander Kohut*, edited by G. A. Kohut, 264–338. Berlin: S. Galvary, 1897.

Kolenkow, Anitra Bingham. "The Genre Testament and the Testament of Abraham." In Nickelsburg, *Studies on the Testament of Abraham*, 139–52.

———. "The Literary Genre 'Testament.'" In Kraft and Nickelsburg, *Early Judaism and Its Modern Interpreters*, 259–67.

Korteweg, Th. "The Meaning of Naphtali's Visions." In Jonge, *Studies on the Testaments of the Twelve Patriarchs*, 261–90.

Kraemer, Ross S. "Recycling Aseneth." In *Recycling Biblical Figures: Papers Read at a NOSTER Colloquium in Amsterdam, 12–13 May 1997*, edited by A. Brenner and J. W. van Henten, 234–65. Studies in Theology and Religion 1. Leiden: Deo, 1999.

———. *When Aseneth Met Joseph: A Late Antique Tale of the Biblical Patriarch and His Egyptian Wife, Reconsidered*. Oxford: Oxford University Press, 1998.

Kraft, Robert A. "Baruch, Fourth Book of." *ESTJ* 1:127–28.

———. "'Ezra' Materials in Judaism and Christianity." *ANRW* 19, no. 1 (1979): 119–36.

———. "The Pseudepigrapha and Christianity, Revisited: Setting the Stage and Framing Some Central Questions." In *Exploring the Scripturesque: Jewish Texts and Their Christian Contexts*, edited by Robert A. Kraft, 35–60. JSJSup 137. Leiden: Brill, 2009.

———. "The Pseudepigrapha in Christianity." In *Tracing the Threads: Studies in the Vitality of Jewish Pseudepigrapha*, edited by John C. Reeves, 55–86. Atlanta: Scholars Press, 1994.

Kraft, Robert A., and George W. E. Nickelsburg. *Early Judaism and Its Modern Interpreters*. Atlanta: Scholars Press, 1986.

Kugel, James L. "Book of Jubilees." *OTB*, 272–465.

———. *The Ladder of Jacob: Ancient Interpretations of the Biblical Story of Jacob and His Children*. Princeton: Princeton University Press, 2006.

———. "Levi's Elevation to the Priesthood in Second Temple Writings." *HTR* 86 (1993): 1–64.

———. "Some Translation and Copying Mistakes from the Original Hebrew of the Testaments of the Twelve Patriarchs." In *The Dead Sea Scrolls, Transmission of Traditions and Production of Texts*, edited by S. Metso, H. Najman, and E. Schuller, 45–56. STDJ 92. Leiden: Brill, 2010.

———. "Testaments of the Twelve Patriarchs." *OTB*, 1697–1700.

———. *A Walk through "Jubilees": Studies in the "Book of Jubilees" and the World of Its Creation*. JSJSup 156. Leiden: Brill, 2012.

Kugler, Robert A. *From Patriarch to Priest: The Levi-Priestly Tradition from "Aramaic Levi" to "Testament of Levi."* EJL 9. Atlanta: Scholars Press, 1996.

———. "Naphtali, Testament of." *EDSS* 2:602–3.

———. "Testaments." *EDSS* 2:933–36.

———. *The Testaments of the Twelve Patriarchs*. GAP. Sheffield: Sheffield Academic, 2001.

Kugler, Robert A., and Richard L. Rohrbaugh. "On Women and Honor in the Testament of Job." *JSP* 14, no. 1 (2004): 43–62.

Kulik, Alexander. "Apocalypse of Abraham." *EST J* 1:93–94.

———. "Baruch, Third Book of." *EST J* 1:125–27.

———. *Retroverting Slavonic Pseudepigrapha: Toward the Original of the Apocalypse of Abraham*. Atlanta: Society of Biblical Literature, 2004.

———. *3 Baruch: Greek-Slavonic Apocalypse of Baruch*. CEJL. Berlin: de Gruyter, 2010.

Kurfess, A.-M. *Sibyllinische Weissagungen*. Berlin: Heimeran, 1951.

Kutscher, E. Y. "The Language of the 'Genesis Apocryphon': A Preliminary Study." In Rabin and Yadin, *Aspects of the Dead Sea Scrolls*, 1–35.

Lanfranchi, Pierluigi. "Ezekiel the Tragedian." *EST J* 1:204–5.

———. *L'Exagoge d'Ezéchiel le tragique*. SVTP 21. Leiden: Brill, 2006.

Lattey, C. J. "The Messianic Expectation in 'The Assumption of Moses.'" *CBQ* 4 (1942): 9–21.

Lester, Olivia Stewart. "Sibylline Oracles 4–5." *EST J* 1:496–98.

Levinson, Bernard M. *Deuteronomy and the Hermeneutics of Legal Innovation*. New York: Oxford University Press, 1997.

Levison, John R. "Adam and Eve in Romans 1.18–25 and the Greek *Life of Adam and Eve*." *NTS* 50 (2004): 519–34.

———. "Adam and Eve, Life of." *EST J* 1:96–100.

———. *Texts in Transition: The Greek "Life of Adam and Eve."* EJL 16. Atlanta: Society of Biblical Literature, 2000.

Licht, J. "Taxo, or the Apocalyptic Doctrine of Vengeance." *JJS* 12 (1961): 95–103.

Lied, Liv Ingeborg. "Die Syrische Baruchapokalypse und die 'Schriften': Die Syrische Baruchapokalypse als 'Schrift.'" In Tigchelaar, *Old Testament Pseudepigrapha*, 327–49.

———. "*Nachleben* and Textual Identity: Variants and Variance in the Reception History of *2 Baruch*." In *Fourth Ezra and Second Baruch: Reconstruction after the Fall*, edited by M. Henze, G. Boccaccini, and J. M. Zurawski, 403–28. Leiden: Brill, 2013.

———. *The Other Lands of Israel: Imaginations of the Land in "2 Baruch."* JSJSup 129. Leiden: Brill, 2008.

———. "2 Baruch and the Codex Ambrosianus: Studying Old Testament Pseudepigrapha in Their Manuscript Context." *JSP* 26, no. 2 (2016): 67–107.

Lightfoot, J. L. *The Sibylline Oracles: With Introduction, Translation, and Commentary on the First and Second Books*. Oxford: Oxford University Press, 2007.

Lim, Timothy H., and John J. Collins, eds. *The Oxford Handbook of the Dead Sea Scrolls*. Oxford: Oxford University Press, 2010.

Longenecker, Bruce W. *2 Esdras*. GAP. Sheffield: Sheffield Academic, 1995.

Ludlow, Jared W. *Abraham Meets Death: Narrative Humor in the "Testament of Abraham."* JSPSup 41. Sheffield: Sheffield Academic, 2002.

———. "Abraham, Testament of." *ESTJ* 1:95–96.

Macaskill, Grant. "Personal Salvation and Rigorous Obedience: The Soteriology of 2 Enoch." In Gurtner, *This World and the World to Come*, 127–42.

———. *Revealed Wisdom and Inaugurated Eschatology in Ancient Judaism and Early Christianity*. JSJSup 115. Leiden: Brill, 2007.

———. "2 Enoch: Manuscripts, Recensions, and Original Language." In Orlov and Boccaccini, *New Perspectives on 2 Enoch*, 83–101.

———. *The Slavonic Texts of 2 Enoch*. Studia Judaeoslavica 6. Leiden: Brill, 2013.

Mach, M. *Entwicklungsstadien des judischen Engelglaubens in vorrabbinischer Zeit*. TSAJ 34. Tübingen: Mohr Siebeck, 1992.

Machiela, Daniel A. *The Dead Sea Genesis Apocryphon: A New Text and Translation with Introduction and Special Treatment of Columns 13–17*. STDJ 79. Leiden: Brill, 2009.

Malina, B. J. "What Is Prayer?" *The Bible Today* 18 (1980): 214–20.

Matlock, M. D. *Discovering the Traditions of Prose Prayers in Early Jewish Literature*. LSTS 81. London: T&T Clark, 2012.

McCown, C. C. *The Testament of Solomon*. Leipzig: J. C. Hinrichs'sche Buchhandlung, 1922.

Mearns, C. L. "Dating the Similitudes of Enoch." *NTS* 25 (1979): 360–69.

Meecham, Henry G. *The Letter of Aristeas: A Linguistic Study with Special Reference to the Greek Bible*. Manchester: Manchester University Press, 1935.

Mendels, Doron. *The Land of Israel as a Political Concept in Hasmonean Literature*. TSAJ 15. Tübingen: Mohr Siebeck, 1987.

Mertens, Alfred. *Das Buch Daniel im Lichte der Texte vom Toten Meer*. Stuttgarter biblische Monographien 12. Würzburg: Echter, 1971.

Metzger, Bruce M. "The Fourth Book of Ezra." *OTP* 1:517–59.

———. *An Introduction to the Apocrypha*. New York: Oxford University Press, 1957.

Meyer, Rudolf. *Das Gebet des Nabonid: Eine in den Qumran-Handschriften wiederentdeckte Weisheitserzählung*. Berlin: Akademie-Verlag, 1962.

Milik, J. T. *The Books of Enoch: Aramaic Fragments from Qumran Cave 4*. Oxford: Clarendon, 1976.

———. "Écrits préesséniens de Qumrân; d'Hénoch à 'Amram." In *Qumrân: Sa piété, sa théologie et son milieu*, edited by M. Delcor, 91–106. BETL 46. Paris and Gembloux: Leuven University Press, 1978.

———. "4QVisions d'Amram et une citation d'Origène." *RB* 79 (1972): 77–97.

———. "Fragments grecs du livre d'Hénoch (P.Oxy. xvii 2069)." *Chronique d'Égypte* 46 (1971): 321–43.

———. "Livre des Jubilés." In *Qumran Cave 1*, edited by D. Barthélemy and J. T. Milik, 82–84. DJD 1. Oxford: Clarendon, 1955.

———. "Milkî-sedeq et Milkî-resha' dans les anciens écrits juifs et chrétiens." *JJS* 23, no. 1 (1972): 95–144.

———. "'Prière de Nabonide' et autres écrits d'un cycle de Daniel." *RB* 63 (1956): 407–15.

———. "Problemes de la litterature henochique a la lumiere des fragments arameens de Qumran." *HTR* 64 (1971): 333–78.

Mizrahi, Noam. "Songs of the Sabbath Sacrifice." *ESTJ* 1:512–16.

Moore, Stewart. *Jewish Ethnic Identity and Relations in Hellenistic Egypt: With Walls of Iron?* JSJSup 171. Leiden: Brill, 2015.

Morgenstern, Matthew J., and Michael Segal. "Genesis Apocryphon." *OTB*, 237–62.

Mowinckel, S. "The Hebrew Equivalent of Taxo in Ass. Mos. IX." In *Congress Volume: Copenhagen 1953*, edited by G. W. Anderson, 88–96. VTSup 1. Leiden: Brill, 1953.

———. *He That Cometh*. Nashville: Abingdon, 1955.

Müller, U. B. *Messiahs un Menschensohn in jüdischen Apokalypsen und in der Offenbarung des Johannes*. Gütersloh: Mohn, 1972.

Murphy, Frederick J. "Divine Plan, Human Plan: A Structuring Theme in Pseudo-Philo." *JQR* 77 (1986): 5–14.

———. "The Eternal Covenant in Pseudo-Philo." *JSP* 3 (1988): 43–57.

———. *Pseudo-Philo: Rewriting the Bible*. Oxford: Oxford University Press, 1993.

———. "Retelling the Bible: Idolatry in Pseudo-Philo." *JBL* 107. no. 2 (1988): 275–87.

———. *The Structure and Meaning of Second Baruch*. SBLDS 78. Atlanta: Scholars Press, 1985.

Najman, Hindy. "Ezra, Fourth Book of." *ESTJ* 1:207–11.

———. *Seconding Sinai: The Development of Mosaic Discourse in Second Temple Judaism*. JSJSup 77. Leiden: Brill, 2003.

Navtanovich, Liudmila. "The Provenance of 2 Enoch: A Philological Perspective." In Orlov and Boccaccini, *New Perspectives on 2 Enoch*, 69–82.

Neugebauer, Otto. *Ethiopic Astronomy and Computus*. Vienna: Österreichische Akademie der Wissenschaften, 1979.

Newman, Judith H. *Praying by the Book: The Scripturalization of Prayer in Second Temple Judaism*. EJL 14. Atlanta: Scholars Press, 1999.

Nickelsburg, George W. E. "Apocalyptic and Myth in *i Enoch* 6–11." *JBL* 96 (1977): 383–405.

———. "Apocalyptic Texts." *EDSS* 1:29–35.

———. "The Assumption of Moses as a Testament." In Nickelsburg, *Studies on the Testament of Moses*, 71–77.

———. "The Bible Rewritten and Expanded." In Stone, *Jewish Writings*, 89–156.

———. "Enoch, Levi, and Peter: Recipients of Revelation in Upper Galilee." *JBL* 100 (1981): 575–600.

———. "Enochic Wisdom: An Alternative to the Mosaic Torah?" In *Hesed Ve-Emet: Studies in Honor of Ernest S. Frerichs*, edited by Jodi Magness and Seymour Gitin, 123–32. Atlanta: Scholars Press, 1998.

———. "Eschatology in the Testament of Abraham: A Study of the Judgment Scenes in the Two Recensions." In Nickelsburg, *Studies on the Testament of Abraham*, 23–64.

———. *1 Enoch 1*. Hermeneia. Minneapolis: Fortress, 2001.

———. *Jewish Literature between the Bible and the Mishnah: A Historical and Literary Introduction*. 2nd ed. Minneapolis: Fortress, 2005.

———. "Patriarchs Who Worry about Their Wives: A Haggadic Tendency in the Genesis Apocryphon." In *Biblical Perspectives: Early Use and Interpretation of the Bible in Light of the Dead Sea Scrolls; Proceedings of the First International Symposium of the Orion Center for the Study of the Dead Sea Scrolls and Associated Literature, 12–14 May, 1996*, edited by Michael E. Stone and Esther G. Chazon, 177–99. STDJ 28. Leiden: Brill, 1998.

———. *Resurrection, Immortality, and Eternal Life in Intertestamental Judaism and Early Christianity*. Expanded ed. Cambridge, MA: Harvard University Press, 2006.

———. "Seeking the Origins of the Two-Ways Tradition in Jewish and Christian Ethical Texts." In *A Multiform Heritage: Studies on Early Judaism and Christianity in Honor of Robert A. Kraft*, edited by Benjamin G. Wright, 95–108. Scholars Press Homage Series 24. Atlanta: Scholars Press, 1999.

———. "Stories of Biblical and Early Post-Biblical Times." In Stone, *Jewish Writings*, 33–87.

———. "Structure and Message in the Testament of Abraham." In Nickelsburg, *Studies on the Testament of Abraham*, 85–93.

———, ed. *Studies on the Testament of Abraham*. SCS 6. Missoula, MT: Scholars Press, 1976.

———, ed. *Studies on the Testament of Moses*. SCS 4. Missoula, MT: Scholars Press, 1973.

———. "Two Enochic Manuscripts: Unstudied Evidence for Egyptian Christianity." In Attridge, Collins, and Tobin, *Of Scribes and Scrolls*, 251–60.

Nickelsburg, G. W. E., and James C. VanderKam. *1 Enoch. The Hermeneia Transla-*
tion. Minneapolis: Fortress, 2012.

———. *1 Enoch 2: A Commentary on the Book of 1 Enoch, Chapters 37–82.* Hermeneia. Minneapolis: Fortress Press, 2012.

Nicklas, T. "Food of Angels (Wis 16:20)." In *Studies in the Book of Wisdom,* edited
by G. G. Xeravits and J. Zsengeller, 83–100. JSJSup 142. Leiden: Brill, 2010.

Nir, Rivka. *The Destruction of Jerusalem and the Idea of Redemption in the Syriac
Apocalypse of Baruch.* EJL 20. Atlanta: Society of Biblical Literature, 2003.

———. *Joseph and Aseneth: A Christian Book.* Hebrew Bible Monographs 42. Sheffield: Sheffield Phoenix, 2012.

Nitzan, Bilhah. *Qumran Prayer and Religious Poetry.* STDJ 12. Leiden: Brill, 1994.

Norelli, Enrico. *Ascensio Isaiae.* Vol. 1, *Comentarius.* Turnhout: Brepols, 1995.

Oegema, Gerbern S. *Early Judaism and Modern Culture: Literature and Theology.*
Grand Rapids: Eerdmans, 2011.

Oegema, Gerbern S., and James H. Charlesworth, eds. *The Pseudepigrapha and Christian Origins: Essays from the Studiorum Novi Testamenti Societas.* London: T&T
Clark, 2008.

Olson, Daniel C. *A New Reading of the Animal Apocalypse of 1 Enoch: "All Nations
Shall Be Blessed."* SVTP 24. Leiden: Brill, 2013.

Orlov, Andrei A. "The Sacerdotal Traditions of 2 Enoch and the Date of the Text."
In Orlov and Boccaccini, *New Perspectives on 2 Enoch,* 103–16.

———. *2 Enoch: A Commentary.* Hermeneia. Minneapolis: Fortress, forthcoming.

Orlov, Andrei A., and Gabriele Boccaccini, eds. *New Perspectives on 2 Enoch: No
Longer Slavonic Only.* Studia Judaeoslavica 4. Leiden: Brill, 2012.

Overman, J. A. *Matthew's Gospel and Formative Judaism: The Social World of the
Matthean Community.* Minneapolis: Fortress, 1990.

Parke, H. W. *Sibyls and Sibylline Prophecy in Classical Antiquity.* Edited by B. C.
McGing. London: Routledge, 1988.

Paul, Shalom M. "Heavenly Tablets and the Book of Life." *Ancient Near Eastern
Society Journal* 5–6 (1973–74): 345–53.

Pelletier, A. *Lettre d'Aristée a Philocrate.* SC 89. Paris: Les Éditions du Cerf, 1962.

Penn, M. P. "Identity Transformation and Authorial Identification in Joseph and
Aseneth." *JSP* 13, no. 2 (2002): 171–83.

———. *Kissing Christians: Ritual and Community in the Late Ancient Church.* Philadelphia: University of Pennsylvania Press, 2005.

Penner, Ken M. "Qahat, Testament of." *ESTJ* 1:462–63.

Perrin, A. *The Dynamics of Dream-Vision Revelation in the Aramaic Dead Sea Scrolls.*
Journal of Ancient Judaism Supplements 19. Göttingen: Vandenhoeck & Ruprecht,
2015.

Pervo, R. I. "Joseph and Asenath and the Greek Novel." *SBLSP* 10 (1976): 171–81.

Philonenko, Marc. *Joseph et Aséneth: Introduction, texte critique, traduction et notes*. StPB 13. Leiden: Brill, 1968.

———. "Le Testament de Job et les Therapeutes." *Semitica* 8 (1958): 41–53.

Picard, J.-C. *Apocalypsis Baruchi Graece*. PVTG 2. Leiden: Brill, 1967.

Piotrkowski, Meron M. *Priests in Exile: The History of the Temple of Onias and Its Community in the Hellenistic Period*. Studia Judaica 106. Rethinking Diaspora 4. Berlin: de Gruyter, 2019.

Price, R. M. "Implied Reader Response and the Evolution of Genres: Transitional Stages between the Ancient Novels and the Apocryphal Acts." *Hervormde teologiese studies* 53 (1997): 931–35.

Priest, J. "Testament of Moses." *OTP* 1:919–934

Puech, Émile. "534–536. 4QNaissance de Noé^{a–c} ar: Introduction." In Puech, *Qumrân Grotte 4, XXII*, 117–27.

———. "554–554a–555. 4QJérusalem Nouvelle^{a–c} ar." In Puech, *Qumrân Grotte 4, XXVII*, 91–152.

———. "4QApocryphe de Daniel ar." In Brooke et al., *Qumran Cave 4, XVII*, 165–84.

———. "4Q543–4Q549. 4QVisions de 'Amram^{a–g} ar." In Puech, *Qumrân Grotte 4, XXII*, 283–405.

———. "Fragment d'une apocalypse en araméen (4Q246 = pseudo-Dand) et le 'Royaume de Dieu." *RB* 99 (1992): 98–131.

———. "Fragments d'un apocryphe de Lévi et le personnage eschatologique. 4QTestLévi^{c–d}(?) et 4QAJa." In *The Madrid Congress: Proceedings of the International Congress on the Dead Sea Scrolls, Madrid, 18–21 March, 1991*, edited by Julio Trebolle Barrera and Luis Vegas Montaner, 2:449–501. 2 vols. STDJ 11. Leiden: Brill, 1992.

———, ed. *Qumrân Grotte 4, XVIII: Textes Hébreux (4Q521–4Q528, 4Q576–4Q579)*. DJD 25. Oxford: Clarendon, 1998.

———, ed. *Qumrân Grotte 4, XXII: Textes Araméens, premiere partie (4Q529–549)*. DJD 31. Oxford: Clarendon, 2001.

———, ed. *Qumrân Grotte 4, XXVII: Textes arameens, deuxieme partie (4Q550–4Q575a, 4Q580–4Q587)*. DJD 37. Oxford: Oxford University Press, 2009.

———. "Testament de Qahat." In Puech, *Qumrân Grotte 4, XXII*, 262–64.

Rabin, Chaim, and Yigael Yadin, eds. *Aspects of the Dead Sea Scrolls*. Scripta Hierosolymitana 4. Jerusalem: Magnes, 1958.

Rahnenführer, D. "Das Testament des Hiob in seinem Verhältnis zum Neuen Testament." PhD diss., Martin-Luther-Universität Halle-Wittenberg, 1967.

———. "Das Testament Hiob und das Neue Testament." *Zeitschrift für die neutestamentliche Wissenschaft und die Kunde der älteren Kirche* 62 (1971): 68–93.

Rajak, Tessa. *Translation and Survival: The Greek Bible of the Ancient Jewish Diaspora*. Oxford: Oxford University Press, 2009.

Ravid, Liora. "The Special Terminology of the Heavenly Tablets in the Book of Jubilees." *Tarbiz* 68 (1999): 463–71.

Reed, Annette Yoshiko. "The Construction and Subversion of Patriarchal Perfection: Abraham and Exemplarity in Philo, Josephus, and the *Testament of Abraham*." *JSJ* 40, no. 2 (2009): 205–12.

———. "The Modern Invention of 'Old Testament Pseudepigrapha.'" *JTS* 60, no. 2 (2009): 403–36.

———. "Retelling Biblical Retellings: Epiphanius, the Pseudo-Clementines, and the Reception History of *Jubilees*." In *Tradition, Transmission, and Transformation, from Second Temple Literature through Judaism and Christianity in Late Antiquity*, edited by Menahem Kister, Hillel Newman, Michael Segal, and Ruth Clements, 304–21. STDJ 113. Leiden: Brill, 2015.

Reynolds, Benjamin E., ed. *The Son of Man: Critical Readings*. London: Bloomsbury, 2018.

Reynolds, Bennie H. *Between Symbolism and Realism: The Use of Symbolic and Non-Symbolic Language in Ancient Jewish Apocalypses 333–63 BCE*. Journal of Ancient Judaism Supplements 8. Göttingen: Vandenhoeck & Ruprecht, 2011.

Riessler, Paul. *Altjudisches Schrifttum auserhalb der Bibel*. Augsburg: Filser, 1928.

Robertson, R. G. "Ezekiel the Tragedian." OTP 2:803–20.

Robinson, S. E. "4 Baruch." OTP 2:413–26.

Rönsch, Hermann. *Das Buch der Jubiläen oder die Kleine Genesis*. Leipzig: Fue, 1874.

Rowley, H. H. "Notes on the Aramaic of the *Genesis Apocryphon*." In *Hebrew and Semitic Studies Presented to Godfrey Rolles Driver*, edited by D. Winton Thomas and W. D. McHardy, 116–29. Oxford: Clarendon, 1963.

Rubenstein, A. "Hebraisms in the 'Apocalypse of Abraham.'" *JJS* 5 (1954): 132–35.

———. "Hebraisms in the Slavonic 'Apocalypse of Abraham.'" *JJS* 4 (1953): 108–15.

———. "A Problematic Passage in the Apocalypse of Abraham." *JJS* 8 (1957): 45–50.

Rubinkiewicz, R. "Apocalypse of Abraham." OTP 1:681–705.

Russell, D. H. *The Method and Message of Jewish Apocalyptic*. Philadelphia: Westminster, 1964.

Sacchi, Paulo. "The 2005 Camaldoli Seminar on the Parables of Enoch: Summary and Prospectus for Future Research." In Boccaccini, *Enoch and the Messiah Son of Man*, 499–512.

Sanders, E. P. "Testament of Abraham." OTP 1:871–902.

Sanders, J. A. *The Dead Sea Psalms Scroll*. Ithaca, NY: Cornell University Press, 1967.

———. *The Psalms Scroll of Qumran Cave 11 (11QPsᵃ)*. DJD 4. Oxford: Oxford University Press, 1965.

————. "The Qumran Psalms Scroll (11QPsª) Reviewed." In *On Language, Culture, and Religion: In Honor of Eugene A. Nida*, edited by M. Black and W. A. Smalley, 79–99. The Hague: Mouton, 1974.

Sanders, J. A., J. H. Charlesworth, and H. W. L. Rietz. "Non-Masoretic Psalms." In *The Dead Sea Scrolls: Hebrew, Aramaic, and Greek Texts with English Translations*. Vol. 4A, *Pseudepigraphic and Non-Masoretic Psalms and Prayers*, edited by J. H. Charlesworth, H. W. L. Rietz, P. W. Flint, D. T. Olson, J. A. Sanders, E. M. Schuller, and R. E. Whitaker, 155–215. Princeton Theological Seminary Dead Sea Scrolls Project. Tübingen: Mohr Siebeck; Louisville: Westminster John Knox, 1997.

Satran, David. *Biblical Prophets in Byzantine Palestine: Reassessing the "Lives of the Prophets."* Leiden: Brill, 1995.

Sayler, G. B. *Have the Promises Failed? A Literary Analysis of 2 Baruch.* SBLDS 72. Chico: SBL, 1984.

Schaller, B. "Zur Komposition und Konzeption." In Knibb and van der Horst, *Studies on the Testament of Job*, 46–92.

Schiffman, Lawrence. "Sacrificial Halakhah in the Fragments of the *Aramaic Levi Document* from Qumran, the Cairo Geniza, and Mt. Athos Monastery." In *Reworking the Bible: Apocryphal and Related Texts at Qumran*, edited by Esther G. Chazon, Devorah Dimant, and Ruth Clements, 177–202. STDJ 58. Leiden: Brill, 2005.

Schiffman, Lawrence H., and James C. VanderKam, eds. *Encyclopedia of the Dead Sea Scrolls*. Oxford: Oxford University Press, 2000.

Schmidt, F. *Le Testament grec d'Abraham: Introduction, édition critique des deux recensions grecques, traduction.* TSAJ 11. Tübingen: Mohr Siebeck, 1986.

Schuller, E. M. "Apocryphal Psalms." *OTB*, 2095–105.

————. "Barki Nafshi (4Q434–438)." *ESTJ* 1:119–20.

————. "Prayers and Psalms from the Pre-Maccabean Period." *DSD* 13, no. 3 (2006): 306–18.

————. "Some Observations on Blessings of God in Texts from Qumran." In Attridge, Collins, and Tobin, *Of Scribes and Scrolls*, 133–43.

Schürer, Emil. *The History of the Jewish People in the Age of Jesus Christ 175 BC–AD 135*. Revised and edited by G. Vermes, F. G. Millar, and M. Goodman. 3 vols. Edinburgh: T&T Clark, 1975–87.

Schwartz, Daniel R. "Tribes of As. Mos. 4:7–9." *JBL* 99 (1980): 217–23.

Scott, James. *On Earth as in Heaven: The Restoration of Sacred Time and Sacred Space in the Book of Jubilees.* JSJSup 91. Leiden: Brill, 2005.

Segal, Michael. "Between Bible and Rewritten Bible." In *Biblical Interpretation at Qumran*, edited by M. Henze, 10–29. Studies in the Dead Sea Scrolls and Related Literature. Grand Rapids: Eerdmans, 2005.

————. *The Book of Jubilees: Rewritten Bible, Redaction, Ideology and Theology.* JSJSup 117. Leiden: Brill, 2007.

————. "Who Is the 'Son of God' in 4Q246? An Overlooked Example of Biblical Interpretation." *DSD* 21 (2014): 289–312.

Segal, Moshe. *The Complete Book of Ben Sira.* Jerusalem: Keter, 1972.

Shutt, R. J. H. "Letter of Aristeas." *OTP* 2:7–34.

Skehan, P. W. "The Apocryphal Psalm 151." *CBQ* 25 (1963): 407–9.

————. "A Liturgical Complex in 11QPsᵃ." *CBQ* 35 (1973): 195–205.

Slater, Thomas B. "One Like a Son of Man in First-Century CE Judaism." *NTS* 41 (1995): 183–98.

Slingerland, H. D. *The Testaments of the Twelve Patriarchs: A Critical History of Research.* Society of Biblical Literature Monograph Series 21. Missoula, MT: Scholars Press, 1977.

Smith, J. Z. "The Prayer of Joseph." In *Map Is Not Territory: Studies in the History of Religions,* 24–66. SJLA 23. Leiden: Brill, 1978.

————. "Prayer of Joseph." *OTP* 2:699–714.

Sommer, Michael. "Zephaniah, Apocalypse of." *ESTJ* 1:551–54.

Sparks, H. F. D., ed. *The Apocryphal Old Testament.* Oxford: Clarendon, 1984.

Spitta, F. "Das Testament Hiobs und das Neuen Testament." In *Zur Geschichte und Literatur des Urchristentums,* vol. 3, pt. 2, 139–206. Göttingen: Vandenhoeck & Ruprecht, 1907.

Spittler, R. P. "Testament of Job." *OTP* 1:829–68.

Stackert, Jeffrey. *Rewriting the Torah: Literary Revision in Deuteronomy and the Holiness Legislation.* FAT 52. Tübingen: Mohr Siebeck, 2007.

Standhartinger, Angela. *Das Frauenbild im Judentum der hellenistischen Zeit: Ein Beitrag anhand von "Joseph und Aseneth."* Arbeiten zur Geschichte des antiken Judentums und des Urchristentums 26. Leiden: Brill, 1995.

————. "Recent Scholarship on *Joseph and Aseneth* (1988–2013)." *Currents in Biblical Research* 12, no. 3 (2014): 353–406.

————. Review of *When Aseneth Met Joseph: A Late Antique Tale of the Biblical Patriarch and His Egyptian Wife,* by R. S. Kraemer. *Journal of the American Oriental Society* 120, no. 3 (2000): 488–89.

Stokes, Ryan E. "The Throne Visions of Daniel 7, *1 Enoch* 14, and the Qumran Book of Giants (4Q530): An Analysis of Their Literary Relationship." *DSD* 15 (2008): 340–58.

————. "Watchers, Book of the (1 Enoch 1–36)." *EDEJ,* 1332–34.

Stökl, Jonathan. "A List of the Extant Hebrew Text of the Book of Jubilees, Their Relation to the Hebrew Bible and Some Preliminary Comments." *Hen* 28 (2006): 97–124.

Stone, Michael E. "The Book(s) Attributed to Noah." *DSD* 13, no. 1 (2006): 4–23.

———. "The Dead Sea Scrolls and the Pseudepigrapha." *DSD* 3 (1996): 270–96.

———. *Fourth Ezra: A Commentary on the Book of Fourth Ezra.* Hermeneia. Philadelphia: Fortress, 1990.

———. "4Q215." In Brooke et al., *Qumran Cave 4, XVII,* 73–82.

———. "The Genealogy of Bilhah." *DSD* 3, no. 1 (1996): 20–36.

———, ed. *Jewish Writings of the Second Temple Period: Apocrypha, Pseudepigrapha, Qumran Sectarian Writings, Philo, Josephus.* Compendia Rerum Iudaicarum ad Novum Testamentum 2/II. Assen: Van Gorcum; Philadelphia: Fortress, 1984.

———. "Levi, Aramaic." *EDSS* 1:486–88.

———. "Naphtali, Testament of (4Q215)." *ESTJ* 1:393–94.

———. "Pseudepigraphy Reconsidered." *Review of Rabbinic Judaism* 9 (2006): 1–15.

———. *The Testament of Levi: A First Study of the Armenian Manuscripts of the Testaments of the XII Patriarchs in the Convent of St. James, Jerusalem, with Text, Critical Apparatus, Notes and Translation.* Jerusalem: St. James, 1969.

———. "Why Naphtali? An Internet Discussion." In *Apocrypha, Pseudepigrapha and Armenian Studies: Collected Papers,* 1:261–64. Leuven: Peeters, 2006.

Stone, Michael E., and Theodore A. Bergen, eds. *Biblical Figures outside the Bible.* Harrisburg, PA: Trinity Press International, 1998.

Stone, Michael E., and J. C. Greenfield. "Aramaic Levi Document." In Brooke et al., *Qumran Cave 4, XVII,* pp. 1–72 and plates i–iv.

Stone, Michael E., and Matthias Henze. *4 Ezra and 2 Baruch: Translations, Introductions, and Notes.* Minneapolis: Fortress, 2013.

Strelcyn, S. "Le Psaume 151 dans la tradition éthiopienne." *JSS* 23 (1978): 316–29.

Strugnell, John. "Notes on the Text and Transmission of the Apocryphal Psalms 151, 154 (= Syr. II), and 155 (= Syr. III)." *HTR* 59 (1966): 257–81.

Strugnell, John, and Devorah Dimant. "4Q Second Ezekiel." *RevQ* 13 (1988): 45–56.

Stuckenbruck, Loren T. *Angel Veneration and Christology.* WUNT 70. Tübingen: Mohr Siebeck, 1995.

———. "Apocrypha and Pseudepigrapha." *EDEJ,* 143–62.

———. "The *Book of Enoch*: Its Reception in Second Temple Jewish and in Christian Tradition." *Early Christianity* 4 (2013): 7–40.

———. "The Building Blocks for Enoch as the Son of Man in the Early Enoch Tradition." In Bock and Charlesworth, *Parables of Enoch,* 315–28.

———. "Daniel and Early Enoch Traditions in the Dead Sea Scrolls." In *The Book of Daniel: Composition and Reception,* edited by J. J. Collins and P. W. Flint, 368–86. VTSup 133. Formation and Interpretation of Old Testament Literature 2. 2 vols. Leiden: Brill, 2001.

———. *1 Enoch 91–108.* Berlin: de Gruyter, 2007.

———. "1 Enoch or Ethiopic Enoch in Outline." Condensed outline. Academia.edu. Updated 2014. https://www.academia.edu/7820262/Condensed_Outline_and_Intro duction_to_1_Enoch_or_Ethiopic_Enoch_2014.

———. "4QEnochª." In Qumran Cave 4, XXVI: Cryptic Texts and Miscellanea, Part 1, edited by Stephen J. Pfann and Philip Alexander et al., 3–94. DJD 36. Oxford: Clarendon, 2000.

———. "Genesis 6:1–4 as Basis for Divergent Readings during the Second Temple Period." Hen 24 (2002): 99–106.

———. "Messianic Ideas in the Apocalyptic and Related Literature of Early Judaism." In The Messiah in the Old and New Testaments, edited by Stanley E. Porter, 90–116. Grand Rapids: Eerdmans, 2007.

———. The Myth of the Rebellious Angels: Studies in Second Temple Judaism and New Testament Texts. Grand Rapids: Eerdmans, 2017.

———. "To What Extent Did Philo's Treatment of Enoch and the Giants Presuppose a Knowledge of the Enochic and Other Sources Preserved in the Dead Sea Scrolls?" Studia Philonica Annual 19 (2007): 131–42.

Stuckenbruck, Loren T., and Gabriele Boccaccini, eds. Enoch and the Synoptic Gospels: Reminiscences, Allusions, Intertextuality. EJL 44. Atlanta: SBL Press, 2016.

Suter, D. W. "Fallen Angel, Fallen Priest: The Problem of Family Purity in 1 Enoch 6–16." HUCA 50 (1979): 115–35.

———. "Masai in the Similitudes of Enoch." JBL 100 (1981): 193–212.

———. "Revisiting 'Fallen Angel, Fallen Priest.'" Hen 24 (2002): 137–42.

Tabor, J. D., and M. O. Wise. "4Q521 'On Resurrection' and the Synoptic Gospel Tradition: A Preliminary Study." JSP 10 (1992): 149–62.

Talmon, Shemaryahu. "Extra-Canonical Psalms from Qumran—Psalm 151." In The World of Qumran from Within: Collected Studies, 244–72. Leiden: Brill, 1990.

———. "Hebrew Apocryphal Psalms from Qumran." Tarbiz 35 (1966): 214–34.

Tcherikover, V. "The Ideology of the Letter of Aristeas." HTR 51, no. 2 (1958): 59–85.

Testuz, M. Les idées religieuses du livre des Jubilés. Geneva: Droz; Paris: Minard, 1960.

Thackeray, H. St. J., ed. "Appendix: The Letter of Aristeas." In An Introduction to the Old Testament in Greek, edited by H. B. Swete, 501–18. 2nd ed. Cambridge: Cambridge University Press, 1902.

Tigchelaar, Eibert, ed. Old Testament Pseudepigrapha and the Scriptures. BETL 270. Leuven: Peeters, 2014.

Tigchelaar, Eibert, and A. S. van der Woude. "11QJubilees." In Qumran Cave 4, XXIII: Unidentified Fragments, edited by D. M. Pike and A. Skinner, 207–20. DJD 23. Oxford: Clarendon, 2001.

Tiller, P. A. A Commentary on the Animal Apocalypse of 1 Enoch. EJL 4. Atlanta: Scholars Press, 1993.

Tisserant, Eugène. "Fragments syriaques due Livre des Jubilés." *RB* 30 (1921): 55–86, 206–32.

Torijano, Pablo. "4 *Baruch*." *OTB*, 2662–80.

Tov, Emanuel. "Further Evidence for the Existence of a Qumran Scribal School." In *The Dead Sea Scrolls Fifty Years after Their Discovery: Proceedings of the Jerusalem Congress, July 20–25, 1997*, edited by L. H. Schiffman, E. Tov, and J. C. VanderKam, 199–216. Jerusalem: Israel Exploration Society in cooperation with the Shrine of the Book, Israel Museum, 2000.

———. "Rewritten Bible Compositions and Biblical Manuscripts, with Special Attention to the Samaritan Pentateuch." *DSD* 5 (1998): 334–54.

Trafton, Joseph L. "Solomon, Psalms of." *ESTJ* 1:501–4.

———. *The Syriac Version of the Psalms of Solomon: A Critical Evaluation.* SCS 11. Atlanta: Scholars Press, 1985.

———. "What Would David Do? Messianic Expectation and Surprise in Ps. Sol. 17." In *The Psalms of Solomon: Language, History, Theology*, edited by E. Bons and P. Pouchelle, 155–74. EJL 40. Atlanta: SBL Press, 2015.

Trebilco, Paul. *Jewish Communities in Asia Minor.* SNTSMS 69. Cambridge: Cambridge University Press, 1991.

Tromp, Johannes. *The Assumption of Moses: A Critical Edition with Commentary.* SVTP 10. Leiden: Brill, 1992.

———. *Life of Adam and Eve in Greek: A Critical Edition.* SVTP 6. Leiden: Brill, 2004.

———. "Two References to a Levi Document in an Epistle of Ammonas." *NovT* 39 (1997): 235–47.

Uhlig, Siegbert. *Das athiopische Henochbuch.* JSHRZ V/6. Gütersloh: Mohn, 1984.

Ulrich, Eugene. *The Dead Sea Scrolls and the Origins of the Bible.* Studies in the Dead Sea Scrolls and Related Literature. Grand Rapids: Eerdmans, 1999.

Uusimäki, Elisa. "Instruction (4QInstruction)." *ESTJ* 1:247–49.

Vaillant, A. *Le livre des secrets d'Hénoch: Texte slave et traduction française.* 2nd ed. Textes publiés par l'Institut d'Études slaves IV. Paris: Institut d'Études slaves, 1976.

van der Horst, Pieter W. "Greek Synagogal Prayers." *OTB*, 2110–37.

———. "The Images of Women in the Testament of Job." In Knibb and van der Horst, *Studies on the Testament of Job*, 93–116.

———. "Pseudo-Phocylides." *OTP* 2:565–606.

———. "Pseudo-Phocylides, *Sentences*." *OTB*, 2353–61.

———. "Pseudo-Phocylides Revisited." *JSP* 3 (1988): 3–30.

———. *The Sentences of Pseudo-Phocylides.* Leiden: Brill, 1978.

van der Horst, Pieter W., and Judith H. Newman. *Early Jewish Prayers in Greek.* CEJL. Berlin: de Gruyter, 2008.

VanderKam, James C. "The *Angel of the Presence* in the Book of Jubilees." *DSD* 7 (2000): 378–93.

———. *The Book of Jubilees.* GAP. Sheffield: Sheffield Academic, 2001.

———. *The Book of Jubilees: A Critical Text.* 2 vols. Corpus Scriptorum Christianorum Orientalium 510–11. Scriptores Aethiopici 87–88. Louvain: Peeters, 1989.

———. "The Book of Parables within the Enochic Tradition." In Boccaccini, *Enoch and the Messiah Son of Man*, 91–98.

———. *Calendars in the Dead Sea Scrolls: Measuring Time.* Literature of the Dead Sea Scrolls. London: Routledge, 1998.

———. "The Demons in the Book of Jubilees." In *Demons: The Demonology of the Israelite-Jewish and Early Christian Literature in Context of Their Environment*, edited by Armin Lange, Hermann Lichtenberger, and K. F. Diethard Romheld, 339–62. Tübingen: Mohr Siebeck, 2003.

———. "Enoch Traditions in Jubilees and Other Second-Century Sources." *SBLSP* 1 (1978): 1:229–51. Reprinted in *From Revelation to Canon: Studies in the Hebrew Bible and Second Temple Literature*, edited by J. C. VanderKam. JSJSup 62. Leiden: Brill, 2000.

———. *Enoch and the Growth of an Apocalyptic Tradition.* CBQMS 16. Washington: Catholic Biblical Association, 1984.

———. *From Joshua to Caiaphas: High Priests after the Exile.* Minneapolis: Fortress, 2004.

———. *An Introduction to Early Judaism.* Grand Rapids: Eerdmans, 2001.

———. *Jubilees: A Commentary.* 2 vols. Hermeneia. Minneapolis: Fortress, 2018.

———. "The Manuscript Tradition of Jubilees." In Boccaccini and Ibba, *Enoch and the Mosaic Torah*, 3–21.

———. "Mastema in the Qumran Literature and the Book of Jubilees." In *Sibyls, Scriptures, and Scrolls: John Collins at Seventy*, 1346–60. 2 vols. JSJSup 175. Leiden: Brill, 2017.

———. "Moses Trumping Moses: Making the Book of Jubilees." In *The Dead Sea Scrolls: Transmission of Tradition and Publication of Texts*, edited by Sarianna Metso, Hindy Najman, and Eileen Schuller, 25–44. STDJ 92. Leiden: Brill, 2010.

———. "Righteous One, Messiah, Chosen One, and Son of Man in 1 Enoch 37–71." In *The Messiah: Developments in Earliest Judaism and Christianity*, edited by J. H. Charlesworth, 169–91. Minneapolis: Fortress, 1992.

———. "Scripture in the Astronomical Book of Enoch." In *Things Revealed: Studies in Early Jewish and Christian Literature in Honor of Michael E. Stone*, edited by E. G. Chazon, D. Satran, and R. Clements, 89–103. JSJSup 89. Leiden: Brill, 2004.

———. "The Textual Affinities of the Biblical Citations in the Genesis Apocryphon." *JBL* 97 (1978): 45–55.

———. *Textual and Historical Studies in the Book of Jubilees*. Harvard Semitic Monographs 14. Missoula, MT: Scholars Press, 1977.

———. "The Textual Base for the Ethiopic Translation of 1 Enoch." In *Working with No Data: Studies in Semitic and Egyptian Presented to Thomas O. Lambdin*, edited by D. Golomb, 247–62. Winona Lake, IN: Eisenbrauns, 1987.

VanderKam, James C., and J. T. Milik. "Jubilees." In *Qumran Cave 4, VIII: Parabiblical Texts, Part 1*, edited by H. Attridge, T. Elgvin, J. T. Milik, S. Olyan, J. Strugnell, E. Tov, J. VanderKam, and S. White, 1–186. DJD 13. Oxford: Clarendon, 1994.

van Henten, Jan Willem. "*Nero Redivivus* Demolished: The Coherence of the Nero Traditions in the *Sibylline Oracles.*" *JSP* 21 (2000): 3–17.

van Koningsveld, P. S. "An Arabic Manuscript of the Apocalypse of Baruch." *JSS* 6 (1975): 205–7.

van Ruiten, Jacque T. A. G. M. "Abraham, Job and the Book of *Jubilees*: The Intertextual Relationship of Genesis 22:1–19, Job 1:1–2:13 and *Jubilees* 17:15–18:19." In *The Sacrifice of Isaac: The Aqedah (Genesis 22) and Its Interpretations*, edited by Ed Noort and Eibert Tigchelaar, 58–85. Themes in Biblical Narrative 4. Leiden: Brill, 2002.

———. "Angels and Demons in the Book of Jubilees." In *Angels: The Concept of Celestial Beings; Origins, Development and Reception*, edited by Friedrich V. Reiterer, Tobias Nicklas, and Karin Schopflin, 585–609. Deuterocanonical and Cognate Literature Yearbook 2007. Berlin: de Gruyter, 2007.

———. "Jubilees, Book of." *EST J* 1:307–12.

Vaux, R. de. Review of *The Genesis Apocryphon of Qumran I: A Commentary*, by Joseph A. Fitzmyer. *RB* 74 (1967): 100–105.

Vermes, Geza. *Scripture and Tradition in Judaism: Haggadic Studies*. 2nd ed. StPB 4. Leiden: Brill, 1973.

Violet, Bruno. *Die Apokalypsen des Esra und des Baruch in deutscher Gestalt*. Die griechischen christlichen Schriftsteller der ersten Jahrhunderte 32. Leipzig: Hinrichs, 1924.

———. *Die Esra-Apokalypse*. Leipzig: Hinrichs, 1910.

Walck, Leslie W. *The Son of Man in the Parables of Enoch and in Matthew*. JCT 9. London: T&T Clark, 2011.

Wassmuth, Olaf. "Sibylline Oracles 1–2." *EST J* 1:493–95.

———. *Sibyllinische Orakel 1–2: Studien und Kommentar*. Ancient Judaism and Early Christianity 76. Leiden: Brill 2011.

Watley, G. L. "Sibylline Identities: The Jewish and Christian Editions of Sibylline Oracles 1–2." PhD diss., University of Virginia, 2010.

Weber, R., ed. *Le Psautier romain et les autres anciens psautiers latins*. Collectanea Biblica Latina 10. Rome: Abbaye Saint-Jérôme, 1953.

Werline, R. A. "Reflections on Penitential Prayer: Definition and Form." In *Seeking the Favor of God*, edited by M. J. Boda, D. K. Falk, and R. A. Werline, 209–25. EJL 22. Leiden: Brill; Atlanta: Society of Biblical Literature, 2007.

Werman, Cana. "The Attitude towards Gentiles in the Book of Jubilees and Qumran Literature Compared with the Early Tannaic Halakha and Contemporary Pseudepigrapha." PhD diss., Hebrew University of Jerusalem, 1995.

———. *The Book of Jubilees: Introduction, Translation, and Interpretation*. Between Bible and Mishnah. Jerusalem: Yad Izhak Ben-Zvi Publications, 2015.

West, M. L. "Phocylides." *Journal of Hellenic Studies* 98 (1978): 164–67.

White, L. Michael, and G. Anthony Keddie. *Jewish Fictional Letters from Hellenistic Egypt: The Epistle of Aristeas and Related Literature*. WGRW 37. Atlanta: SBL Press, 2018.

Whitters, Mark. *Epistle of Second Baruch: A Study in Form and Message*. LSTS 42. London: T&T Clark, 2003.

Willett, T. W. *Eschatology in the Theodicies of 2 Baruch and 4 Ezra*. JSPSup 4. Sheffield: JSOT Press, 1989.

Wills, Lawrence M. *The Jewish Novel in the Ancient World*. Ithaca, NY: Cornell University Press, 1995.

———. "Novels." *ESTJ* 2:547–47.

———. "The *Testament of Abraham* as a Satirical Novel." In Wills, *The Jewish Novel in the Ancient World*, 245–56.

Wilson, Walter T. *The Mysteries of Righteousness: The Literary Composition and Genre of the Sentences of Pseudo-Phocylides*. Tübingen: Mohr Siebeck, 1994.

———. *The Sentences of Pseudo-Phocylides*. CEJL. Berlin: de Gruyter, 2005.

Winter, P. "Note on Salem-Jerusalem." *NovT* 2 (1957–58): 151–52.

Wintermute, O. S. "Apocalypse of Zephaniah." *OTP* 1:497–515.

———. "Jubilees." *OTP* 2:35–142.

Wise, Michael O., Martin G. Abegg Jr., and Edward M. Cook. *The Dead Sea Scrolls: A New Translation*. New York: HarperOne, 2005.

Wright, Benjamin G., III. "Aristeas, Letter of." *ESTJ* 1:109–11.

———. *The Letter of Aristeas: "Aristeas to Philocrates" or "On the Translation of the Law of the Jews."* CEJL. Berlin: de Gruyter, 2015.

———. "The *Letter of Aristeas* and the Reception History of the Septuagint." *Bulletin of the International Organization for Septuagint and Cognate Studies* 39 (2006): 47–67.

———. "Pseudonymous Authorship and Structures of Authority in the *Letter of Aristeas*." In *Scriptural Authority in Early Judaism and Ancient Christianity*, edited by Geza G. Xeravits, Tobias Nicklas, and Isaac Kalimi, 43–62. Deuterocanonical and Cognate Literature Studies 16. Berlin: de Gruyter, 2013.

————. "Transcribing, Translating, and Interpreting in the *Letter of Aristeas*: On the Nature of the Septuagint." In *Scripture in Transition: Essays on Septuagint, Hebrew Bible and Dead Sea Scrolls in Honour of Raija Sollamo*, edited by Anssi Voitila and Jutta Jokiranta, 147–61. JSJSup 126. Leiden: Brill, 2008.

————. "Translation as Scripture: The Septuagint in *Aristeas* and Philo." In *Septuagint Research: Issues and Challenges in the Study of the Greek Jewish Scriptures*, edited by Wolfgang Kraus and R. Glenn Wooden, 47–61. SCS 53. Atlanta: Society of Biblical Literature, 2006.

Wright, J. E. "Baruch: His Evolution from Scribe to Apocalyptic Seer." In Stone and Bergren, *Biblical Figures outside the Bible*, 264–89.

————. "The Social Setting of the Syriac Apocalypse of Baruch." *JSP* 16 (1997): 81–96.

Wright, Robert B. "Psalms of Solomon." *OTP* 2:639–70.

————. *The Psalms of Solomon: A Critical Edition of the Greek Text*. Jewish and Christian Texts in Context 1. London: T&T Clark, 2007.

Wyrick, Jed. *The Ascension of Authorship: Attribution and Canon Formation in Jewish, Hellenistic, and Christian Traditions*. Cambridge, MA: Harvard University Press, 2004.

————. "Pseudepigraphy." *EDEJ*, 1114–17.

Yardeni, Ada. "4QDamascus Document." In *Qumran Cave 4.XIII: The Damascus Document (4Q266-273)*, edited by Joseph M. Baumgarten, 23–94. DJD 18. Oxford: Clarendon, 1996.

Zahn, Molly M. "Rewritten Scripture." In Lim and Collins, *Oxford Handbook of the Dead Sea Scrolls*, 323–36.

Zeitlin, S. "The Dead Sea Scrolls: 1. The Lamech Scroll: A Medieval Midrash: 2. The Copper Scrolls: 3. Was Kando the Owner of the Scrolls?" *JQR* 47, no. 3 (1957): 245–68.

Zimmerman, F. "Textual Observations on the Apocalypse of Baruch." *JTS* 40 (1939): 151–56.

Author Index

Scripture Index

Judges

1–3 269
1:13 264, 269
3:5–6 264
3:7–14 269
3:9–11 264
4 264
4:4 125
5 30, 264
6 265
7 264
7–8 265
9 265
9:28–41 264
10 265
10:3–6 265
11 265
11:30–31 265
11:32–38 265
11:39–40 265
12:11–13 265
12:13–15 265
13:1 265
14–15 266
16 266
17 266
19 266
19:27–20:6 266
20 266
20:1 269
20:18 269

Ruth

2:12 112n23

1 Samuel

1:2–13 267
1:14–17 267
1:18 267
1:20–26 267
2:1–11 267
2:11–16 267
2:22 267
2:23–25 267
3:1–11 267
3:15–18 267
4:1–11 267
4:14–21 267
5:2–6:19 267
6:4 267
6:12 269

7:17 267
8:4–9 267
9:1–10:9 267
12 165n1, 267
15 267
15:12 269
15:21 269
15:33 269
16 268
16–17 336
16:1–3 267
16:4 269
16:4–7 268
16:11–13 268
17:15 268
17:16–36 268
17:34–37 268
17:49–51 268
17:55–58 268
18:3 268
19:18–23 268
20:3–8 268
20:23 268
20:41–42 268
22:9–21 268
28:3 268
28:3–7 268
28:11 268
28:12–25 268
31:1–4 268

2 Samuel

1:7–10 268
7:12–13 264
7:12–16 349
24:17 66

1 Kings

2:1–9 165n1
4:29–34 207
6–7 207
10 207
11 207
16:13 112n23
16:26 112n23
22:17 66

2 Kings

17:15 112n23
17:24–41 325

20 31
21:3 55
21:10–15 121
22:14–20 125
23:4–12 55
24:8 109
24:12 109
25:1–20 61
25:27 109

1 Chronicles

3:17 92, 109
5:28 199, 378
5:29 199, 378
6:2–3 199, 378
6:3 199, 378
6:16–18 194
6:18 199, 378
10 258
16:35–36 333
21:17 66
23:12 199, 378
23:12–13 199, 378
24:20 199, 378
26:23 199, 378
28–29 165n1

2 Chronicles

18:16 66
36:17–20 61
36:21 83

Ezra

1:8–10 62
5:2 62
5:14–16 62
7:6 28
7:11 28
7:12 188
9 333
9–10 326
10:2 250n105
10:10 250n105
10:17–18 250n105
10:44 250n105

Nehemiah

1:5–11 333
8:1 28

9 333
10:2 325
12:1 325
12:12 325
12:34 325
13:23–27 326
13:27 250n105

Job

1–2 182, 240, 249
1:1 LXX 180
1:12 182
2:6 182
2:9 182
9:33 174
29–31 LXX 182
31:26–28 55
38:3 181
42:7–17 LXX 182
42:17 LXX 179, 182

Psalms

2:2 38, 43
22 338
44:11 66
44:22 66
49:14 66
51 338
74:1 66
78:52 66
79:13 66
95:7 66
100:3 66
101 335
118:22 206, 207
119 73
119:176 66
149:1 342
150 335

Proverbs

1:2–3 359
1:15–16 73
2:12–13 73
2:18–19 73
4:10 73
4:14–19 73
5:56 73
6:6–8 355
7:27 73

Ancient Writings Index

Made in the USA
Las Vegas, NV
05 January 2024

83848692R00281